NOT FREE TO DESIST

Naomi W. Cohen

NOT FREE
TO DESIST

The American Jewish Committee
1906-1966

Introduction by Salo W. Baron

Philadelphia 5732–1972
The Jewish Publication Society of America

The day is short and the work is great. . . .
It is not thy duty to complete the work,
but neither art thou free to desist from it.

—Sayings of the Fathers

Contents

Preface

This study traces the activities of the American Jewish Committee, the oldest Jewish defense organization in the United States, during the first sixty years of its existence. It views those activities against a background of twentieth-century trends in American and world Jewish history. Many of the issues treated here could have been developed separately in lengthy monographs, but I have on occasion sacrificed all-inclusiveness in the interest of clarity and overall balance.

I have not carried the history of the Committee beyond 1966. Since then some policies have been modified or amplified, and new ventures have been initiated. Leadership, too, has changed. After a quarter century of service, John Slawson retired as executive vice-president and was succeeded by Bertram H. Gold. Morris B. Abram, president of the Committee from 1964 to 1968, was followed by Arthur J. Goldberg, who held the post for one year. His successor and the current president is Philip E. Hoffman.

Although the American Jewish Committee commissioned this study as part of the observance of its sixtieth anniversary, its direction ended there. I was given complete and unlimited access to all archives and records. Staff members responded to my queries freely and critically. I formed my own opinions, and I alone am responsible for the interpretation of the materials. "They'll never believe you," Dr. Slawson warned me. That may be, but I would like to keep the record straight.

The staffs of the Committee's library and records department were especially helpful in the course of my research. I am also grateful to the many others at the Committee who answered questions and located papers. Their interest and courtesies were unfailing. Nor do I minimize their cooperation when I single out a few—Harry J. Alderman, Lucy S. Dawidowicz, Rose Grundstein, Phyllis Sherman, John Slawson—whose encouragement and technical aid far transcended any call of duty. Sonya Kaufer and Martha Jelenko of the AJC contributed their editorial skills. From the inception of the study to its completion, Milton Himmelfarb, the Committee's director of information and research services, was both wise counselor and loyal friend.

I am indebted to Admiral Lewis L. Strauss, Mr. Richard C. Rothschild, Mr. Alan M. Stroock, Mr. Harry Schneiderman, Mr. Sidney Wallach, and the late Mr. Arthur D. Morse for sharing reminiscences and private papers with me. The late Judge Joseph M. Proskauer graciously permitted me to consult his *Reminiscences* on file at the Oral History Research Office of Columbia University. My thanks go also to Rabbi Victor Mirelman for assisting me in the research for chapter 21 and to *Jewish Social Studies* for permitting me to republish the bulk of my earlier article on the abrogation of the Russo-American treaty of 1832. Special archival material was made available to me by the National Archives, the Franklin D. Roosevelt Library, and the American Jewish Archives. Dr. Chaim Potok, editor of the Jewish Publication Society, reacted to the manuscript with his usual sharp insight and valuable suggestions. Mrs. Kay Powell of the JPS handled innumerable editorial details with meticulous care.

As always, my chief sources of emotional support throughout the writing of this book were my husband and my children.

N. W. C.

Hunter College of the City University of New York
Fall 1971

Introduction

A comprehensive, well-documented history of the American Jewish Committee has long been overdue. The Committee, a leading Jewish defense organization, has not only deeply influenced the American Jewish community and world Jewry, but it has also contributed much to American public life as a whole. Its vicissitudes during the sixty-five years of its existence have necessarily reflected also the tremendous changes in the twentieth-century world, changes which have catapulted the United States into a position of world leadership and transformed American Jewry into the most populous, affluent, and culturally diversified group of the entire Jewish people.

At the outset the Committee merely intended to help "prevent infringement of the civil and religious rights of Jews and to alleviate the consequences of persecution." It emphasized above all the defense of Jewish rights abroad. Yet its greatest accomplishments in the early years consisted in its helping keep the doors of the United States open to East European immigration and in persuading American public opinion and the American government to abrogate, on January 1, 1913, an eighty-year-old commercial treaty with Russia, because the czarist regime was refusing to grant visas to American citizens of the Jewish persuasion. This action became a landmark in international relations and gave a new humanitarian meaning to the long controversial interpretation of "reciprocity" in international law. Since that time the Committee has carefully watched developments on the American and world scene and stood guard over the rights of Jews against the onslaughts of anti-Semitism, which reached its climax during the Nazi era.

Ultimately, it also turned inward and began to fulfill the other function suggested by some of its founders, namely, "to promote the cause of Judaism." It did so in recent years particularly by helping segments of its distraught youth in their quest for Jewish identity.

As usual, the Committee had its ups and downs. The most critical period in the two-thirds of a century of its existence occurred in the early years of the Great Depression, which coincided with the passing of its distinguished leader Louis Marshall. Time and again it was also criticized for being a self-appointed, undemocratic group. These critics overlooked, however, the fundamental fact that what many American voluntary organizations had been suffering from was not so much the lack of eager candidates in democratic elections as the paucity of truly qualified leaders willing to take on the often arduous tasks of fund raising and of guiding their fellow citizens through a maze of both highly complicated decisions and boring daily routines. On the whole, Americans have been a "nation of joiners"; Will Rogers once declared that "two Americans can't meet on the street without one banging the gavel and calling the other to order." But while willing to join organizations, they are not always prepared to lead. As a rule, unspoken approval by a constituency much larger than its actual membership has given the Committee the right to appear as a major spokesman for the mass of American Jews.

For this reason we are grateful to Professor Cohen and the sponsors of this project for placing before the reader a well-balanced, lucid, and interesting description of the Committee's diversified activities over its first six decades. We are assured by the author that the Committee leadership has exercised unusual restraint in offering suggestions for the evaluation of the vast amount of documentary material it freely placed at the researcher's disposal. If in her general analysis Professor Cohen proves to be quite sympathetic to the Committee's outlook and functions, she is actually less partial to it than are most biographers (of the nondebunking school) describing the lives and works of individuals long dead. Certainly the literature of American Jewish history has been greatly enriched by the present volume, and the general public will, it is to be hoped, derive from its perusal many valuable insights into the workings of a dintinguished communal organization.

Salo W. Baron

Columbia University
New York City
December 1971

Part One

Part One

1

Organization Was in the Air

On Saturday evening, February 3, 1906, thirty-four American Jews assembled in New York City to consider the formation of a national Jewish defense organization. From different walks of life, but each prominent in his field, they shared a common concern for the fate of world Jewry, a concern intensified by developments in czarist Russia. There the corrupt and reactionary regime of Czar Nicholas II had embarked on a series of pogroms as a major strategy in the effort to choke the growth of liberal and revolutionary forces. The government-instigated atrocities perpetrated in Kishinev in 1903 shocked the Western world and evoked public protests. Yet Kishinev was only the best known of many such ravaged communities. In October 1905, when the revolutionaries forced the czar to recognize the basic civic rights of his subjects, a wave of pogroms spearheaded by the Black Hundreds rolled across western Russia. Over seven hundred communities fell victim; the number killed, injured, and rendered homeless or propertyless exceeded two hundred thousand.

These events elicited an urgent response from American Jewry. Funds were raised, petitions circulated, protest meetings held. The leaders of the community enlisted the sympathy of President Theodore Roosevelt, who added his authority to the condemnation of the czarist policies. In August 1905 a Jewish delegation met with the Russian diplomat Count Sergius Witte to bargain for the rights of their Russian coreligionists. Such ad hoc action, however, could not satisfy the aroused American Jewish community, particularly as its numbers were being steadily and significantly augmented by refugees fleeing the czarist terror. Suggestions for a permanent organization and for united action cropped up in various quarters. It also was becoming increasingly obvious that communal problems other than Russian relief had emerged. Who, for instance, would assume the leadership of the newly aroused community? And what directions should any new organization follow?

It was against this background that the February 3 meeting was convoked—a step leading ultimately to the formation of the American Jewish Committee (AJC).

I

The United States, as foreign observers since Tocqueville have noted, abounds in organizations. Yet despite the national penchant, in its antecedents the American Jewish Committee derived more from Jewish than from American sources. Previously, no ethnic or religious group in the United States had organized for the sole purpose of defending its rights and those of its brethren outside America.* The National Association for the Advancement of Colored People, to give but one example, was still in the future, and its foremost sponsors would come from the ranks of white liberals rather than from the Negro community. The founders of AJC emulated the Jewries of Europe. The Alliance Israélite Universelle, universalist in theory but in reality limited to French Jewish concerns, the Anglo-Jewish Association and

*The National German-American Alliance, a federation of German-American organizations established in 1901, stood for the preservation of the German cultural heritage, besides defense against nativist prejudice.

Board of Deputies of British Jews, and the Hilfsverein der deut-schen Juden offered paradigms of how other Western Jews guarded the interests of native and foreign Jews. Before 1906 no single group had succeeded in uniting or mobilizing the Ameri-can Jewish community. The Board of Delegates of American Israelites, created in 1859 in the wake of the Mortara case,* soon became a mere adjunct of the Union of American Hebrew Con-gregations (UAHC), the congregational arm of Reform Judaism. B'nai B'rith, though concerning itself with issues of broader Jew-ish interest, remained a basically fraternal organization. And Alli-ance Israélite Universelle efforts to set up active branches in the United States failed.

The lack of a national organization whose leadership would be recognized by the community did not mean, however, that American Jews had remained indifferent to the immediate needs of their coreligionists. Singly or in small groups, from the 1880s on they had quietly but persistently pressured the government in behalf of Russian and Rumanian Jews. The famous note to Ru-mania signed by Secretary of State John Hay in 1902 and the transmission to Russia of the Kishinev petition in 1903 were but highlights of a long history of extraorganizational lobbying. Those episodes also indicated the growing initiative of American Jews, after a century of West European Jewish leadership. In-deed, in 1891 when Baron Maurice de Hirsch, one of the world's great Jewish philanthropists, established in the United States a trust fund fashioned according to the suggestions of some Ameri-can Jews, he thereby acknowledged that the New World commu-nity was no longer a junior partner in efforts to deal with international Jewish problems.

The early responses to crises, usually of East European ori-gin, followed the *Hofjude* or shtadlan approach—intercession with the authorities by a Jew who enjoyed government favor or

*Edgar Mortara, a Jewish child living in Bologna, was abducted by papal guards after having been secretly baptized. Despite a wave of international pro-test, papal authorities refused to release him to his parents.

had the ear of the powerful. When necessary, the mediator would approach leaders and molders of public opinion and, if required, would seek to galvanize the Jewish community into action. Thus in 1891 a small number of Jews arranged with George Jones, owner of the *New York Times,* to finance reporter Harold Frederic's mission to Russia for a firsthand account of the miseries endured under czarist rule. In 1902 Jacob H. Schiff, head of Kuhn, Loeb & Company, Oscar S. Straus, a former minister to Turkey, and Congressman Lucius N. Littauer used their connections to convince President Theodore Roosevelt and Secretary Hay to protest anti-Jewish discrimination in Rumania. In 1905 three Jews heading the National Committee for the Relief of Sufferers by Russian Massacres directed the American Jewish community in a mammoth relief drive which within a month netted over one million dollars. Committed to the ideal of noblesse oblige, the intercessors did not shrink from using their social or economic positions to help less fortunate Jews.

In an individualistic America, where the idea of stewardship had always flourished as a cardinal tenet of philanthropy, this pattern found reinforcement. Inevitably, however, the surging democratic thrust inherent in the country's development clashed with the notion of self-appointed leaders, even those who sought no private gain. In the case of American Jewry the situation was further compounded by cultural tensions, notably the cleavage between the German and East European Jews, which divided the community at the turn of the century. The East Europeans, the newcomers, often resented the patronization of the more affluent and acculturated Germans, and challenged both the latter's assumption of leadership and the values according to which they sought to shape American Jewry. Through their own philanthropies and social agencies, newspapers, and occasional spokesmen, the East Europeans leveled charges against the *Hofjude* (literally, court Jew) and his behind-the-scenes methods. Thus in 1905, when, as noted, a delegation of American Jews conferred on the situation of Russian Jewry with Count Serge Witte, the ranking

Russian envoy at the signing of the Russo-Japanese peace treaty in Portsmouth, New Hampshire, the action was loudly decried. Many were aghast at the idea of Jews sitting down with a hench-man of the czar, as well as at the self-appointed nature of the representation. That same year, too, veiled charges of misuse of funds were spread about the National Committee for Relief; this despite the fact that its treasurer, Schiff, forwarded to Europe sums out of his own pocket before they had even been collected.

The experience of the National Committee for Relief provided one stimulus in the movement toward a permanent organization. Not only did their critics' charges rankle, but the leaders of that endeavor—Schiff, Oscar Straus, Cyrus L. Sulzberger—saw no immediate respite to their labors. They were well aware that anti-Semitism had become a czarist government tool for economic, social, and counterrevolutionary purposes, and that it was unlikely to disappear, short of radical upheavals. The perilous situation demanded a commensurate response.

American diplomatic action was a vital, but uncertain, element. The Roosevelt administration, cooperative in the past, had begun to show signs of growing annoyance. The president had prodded Witte in 1905, but a few months later he called a halt to any further protests to Russia. He would not threaten aimlessly, he declared in true Roosevelt fashion, without troops or ships to back up his words. Perhaps, the Jewish leaders must have reasoned, an organization which could appear significant in terms of votes might reawaken government interest.

Planning constructively for the emancipation of East European Jewry posed even more challenging tasks. American Jews, the stewards decided, had to be ready with the machinery to ascertain the facts, appeal when necessary for government support, disburse relief funds, and cooperate with European organizations. Indeed, as early as 1903 Oscar Straus had written to Lord Nathaniel Rothschild in London on the potential benefits of a committee in the United States which could work with a similar group in England. An organized body might even tap new sources of leadership.

The conservative Jewish leaders traditionally had shied away from popular organizations, which they associated with demagogic rabble-rousing. Not only were such tactics futile in attaining desired goals, they insisted, but an organized and brash minority could evoke the antagonism and enmity of the public at large. Popular organizations, they felt, would unquestionably hinder, if not nullify, the efforts of individual intercessors employing the tried methods of backstairs diplomacy. As the prominent New York attorney Louis Marshall wrote, organization was in the air; and if the conservative leaders remained quiescent, control of the community would slip through their fingers, to be assumed, perhaps, by upstart extremist bodies with radical programs, such as—unthinkable prospect—the California-based International Jewish League or the Jewish Self-Defense Association, created by Rabbi Judah L. Magnes to finance Jewish resistance in Eastern Europe. In order to channel and moderate such efforts, which drew support from the ever-increasing numbers of immigrants, the Jewish stewards perforce overcame their distaste for a permanent organization and began to lay their plans.

In December 1905 the Wanderers, a group of prominent New York Jews who met monthly for social and discussion purposes, considered the subject of a permanent Jewish committee. Louis Marshall reported that "although we all felt the danger of such a movement," the consensus was that someone would doubtless form an organization and that "in order to avoid mischief it was desirable that we should take the initiative." A committee consisting of Cyrus L. Sulzberger, Samuel Greenbaum, Nathan Bijur, Joseph Jacobs, and Marshall was therefore appointed to form some plan for an organization.

Spurred on by these deliberations, one of the Wanderers, Dr. Cyrus Adler, broached the idea publicly in a letter to the *American Hebrew* in January 1906. Urging the desirability of a representative authoritative body—one voice to speak for American Jewry on national and international affairs—Adler dismissed the existing American organizations as unrepresentative and proposed a national committee comprised of delegates (the number to be fixed according to population) from committees to be set up in every state and territory.

Three days later a letter signed by Marshall's committee went out to fifty-nine leading Jews, inviting them to the February meeting in New York City. Taking care to include those men who had pushed the idea of organization—Magnes, Rabbi Jacob Voorsanger of San Francisco, Reverend H. Pereira Mendes of New York—the committee cited the need for continuing aid to oppressed Jewries but also cautioned that if "such a Committee be organized, it shall be on such lines as shall not only meet with the approval of the general public, but shall be free from all objectionable tendencies."

II

The call for a meeting struck a responsive chord. While only thirty-four of the fifty-nine invited persons attended, fourteen sent letters of regret (and one of these sent a substitute). Only eleven did not reply, but of these, two appeared at the next preliminary conference held in May. If it is borne in mind that there were delegates from as far away as San Francisco, Milwaukee, New Orleans, and four from Chicago, the showing must be regarded as impressive. Though the sponsors had paid close attention to geographic considerations in extending their invitations, it was inevitable that New York City, with 450,000 of the 1,400,000 American Jews, would dominate the meeting.

The delegates constituted a young group: over half were under fifty. Predominantly lawyers, rabbis, and businessmen, most had achieved fame in Jewish philanthropic endeavors. An interesting sidelight, foreshadowing much of the American Jewish Committee's future history, was the proportionately large number of judges; present at the 1906 meeting were jurists Mayer Sulzberger, Julian W. Mack, and Samuel Greenbaum. Other delegates included Simon Wolf, former president of the Independent Order of B'nai B'rith (IOBB), and Oscar Straus, who had served in the diplomatic corps and who within a few months would be appointed secretary of commerce and labor, the first cabinet member of Jewish faith.

Over one-third of the delegates were American-born and most had been educated in the United States. Those of immigrant origin in most cases had come from Western Europe, preceding the immigration of the 1880s which largely drew from Russia and Poland. Only among the New York delegates were there men who could be said to represent the new stratum of East European Jews: Nicholas Aleinikoff, active in Yiddish intellectual and socialist circles; Jacob Saphirstein, publisher of the influential Yiddish-language *Jewish Morning Journal;* and Abraham Schomer, son of a Yiddish playwright. For the rest, Western traditions and Reform affiliation set the dominant tone. Indeed, four of those present, Emil G. Hirsch, David Philipson, Judah Magnes, and H. G. Enelow, were Reform rabbis of national stature.

III

The first question confronting the delegates was whether or not a new national organization was indeed desirable. The Wanderers had privately reached a favorable conclusion, but not all their guests concurred. Judge Mack asserted that religious and charitable issues were best handled by groups already in existence and, seconded by Nathan Bijur and Rabbi Isaac Leucht of New Orleans, voiced the opinion that emergencies could be met by special ad hoc committees. Adolf Kraus, president of the IOBB and jealous for the prestige of his organization, saw no reason for a national body, but said he would go along with a small "clearing" committee which could occasionally call a conference for the purpose of united action in behalf of Russian Jewry. Simon Wolf, similarly defensive of his record in B'nai B'rith and as the spokesman of the Board of Delegates, would only agree not to oppose a new organization. At the other extreme stood Abraham Schomer, whose pet project was an international rather than a national group, a "Congress of All-Israel" to be made up of elected representatives from all countries.

The general consensus, however, favored the establishment of an American committee whose primary function would be safeguarding Jewish rights abroad. Such a committee could serve to coordinate appeals to the government, unite Jews of different sections of the country, and prevent immoderate free-lance activities. By way of illustrating the last point, O. J. Wise revealed that in his city, San Francisco, three thousand Jews were advocating armed intervention against Russia.

A far knottier problem involved the makeup of the new committee. The Wanderers had devised no plan to submit to the delegates, knowing full well that the issue would evoke heated debate. In his letter to the *American Hebrew*, Adler had asked for a "representative" body, without further defining the term. Did it mean representative of numbers, of money, of geographic section, or of existing Jewish organizations? Also, how would the members be chosen? Would they be co-opted from the top or elected by American Jews at large? The latter alternative seemed especially dangerous to the delegates, who regarded a *congress* of Jews as "un-American"; its echoes of a "state within a state," they feared, would raise charges of political disloyalty. A congress, Rabbi Hirsch warned, might even revive the spirit of Know-Nothingism. The conservative delegates also expressed distrust of a democratically elected body, arguing that it would be unwieldy and indiscreet. Among the supporters of the congress idea were two Reform rabbis, Judah Magnes and Max Heller. Significantly, unlike the majority of their colleagues, they were Zionists.

Indeed, Jewish nationalism of any variety was anathema to

the majority of the assembled delegates, offensive to both their American and Jewish sensibilities. In line with the popular view that immigrants to America must speedily assimilate to the prevailing norms, they believed that the only link which united American Jewry—and which could serve as the base for a national organization—was religion. Louis Marshall, who at this time aimed for a true democratic body, thought the solution lay in having individual congregations across the land send representatives to a national convention, at which an executive committee would be chosen. This procedure, he felt, was not only democratic but also within the American pattern, since Protestant denominations were organized along such lines. Marshall outlined his suggestions at the Sunday session of the conference, but he was countered by Oscar Straus, who proposed that the conference choose an executive committee of fifteen, with power to increase its numbers, which would work to secure civil and religious rights for Jews. Consistently conservative on Jewish affairs, Straus argued for ability rather than democracy. Tension had obviously reached critical proportions, and a committee of five was appointed to report that same day on the various suggestions.

The committee announced shortly that it had reached no conclusion on the advisability of creating a permanent organization. If such a body were formed, however, the committee recommended the Straus plan both as to composition and purpose. Marshall quickly objected. Since the conference had no mandate to appoint a representative body, he insisted that body would be rejected by American Jews. Once more he defended his plan, noting that its religious base would increase solidarity among Jews and stressing its provisions for the popular elections that were so desired by the community.

At this point Nicholas Aleinikoff challenged the definition of Judaism assumed by Marshall and his coterie. What of representation for those who were not affiliated with congregations but still claimed Jewish identity? Though the implications of his question were bypassed, both Cyrus Sulzberger and Emil Hirsch agreed that Marshall's plan ignored the importance of noncongregational communal workers, "the experts in this age of experts," as Rabbi Hirsch called them. Joining these critics, Straus explained that two systems of representation existed in the United States, the democratic and "gravitational," and that only the latter could work because it recognized the weight and authority of individuals.

Siding with Marshall were Samuel Greenbaum and Jacob H. Schiff. Perhaps more farsighted than his colleagues, Schiff saw the need for broadening the base of Jewish leadership. A new Jewry had come into existence in the United States since 1881, he said, and its confidence, so vital for the success of a general representative body, could not be secured by a self-appointed committee.

When the matter was finally put to a vote, the decision was to establish a general Jewish organization. The Straus plan was carried sixteen to thirteen, but the delegates, realizing that the closeness of the vote boded ill for chances of united action, again referred the plans to a subcommittee. The conference would reconvene upon completion of that group's deliberations.

IV

After several weeks of meetings and study the new committee reverted to a modified version of Marshall's original plan. Its report called for an organization "whose purpose shall be to promote the cause of Judaism and to aid in securing the civil and religious rights of the Jews in all countries where such rights are denied or endangered." It proposed that every five years all incorporated congregations which paid a small fee would elect a convention of 150 delegates. Ballots would be distributed in proportion to their membership; unaffiliated Jews could participate by submitting independent ballots. The convention would in turn elect an executive committee of 23 (an echo of the ancient smaller Sanhedrin).

As planned, the original delegates were invited to reconvene in New York on May 19 to discuss the report. It was clear from the outset that the chances for unity had diminished. Only twenty-two of the original fifty-nine delegates came. Seven who refused to attend sent a lengthy statement of opposition to the chairman, Mayer Sulzberger. Basically, they rejected the need for a new organization which, they charged, aimed to supplant, or at least ignore, existing agencies, expecially the UAHC and B'nai B'rith. They also charged that the committee's plan would establish a congress, a course of action which was condemned at the February meeting and one which probably would lead to a transfer of leadership from "conservative elements" to "radical theorists." Signed by three Reform rabbis and four members of B'nai B'rith's executive board, the statement underscored the partisan jealousy of existing organizations and, more important, their keen distrust of the masses of new immigrants.

As it turned out, the fears of those who dreaded democratic control were allayed. The delegates to the meeting first raised objections to the phrase "to promote the cause of Judaism" because of its religious connotations. The bulk of the debate, however, centered on the makeup of the new organization. Marshall delivered an impassioned defense of the committee's report, but he stood virtually alone. Magnes, the outspoken democrat, was absent and so was Schiff, whose respected position and strong influence might have silenced the critics. Again Straus led the opposition to Marshall, maintaining that a national body for a religious purpose would split the community and that a democratic body would result only in disorganization. The bickering continued, punctuated by motions to adjourn. Straus almost wrecked the conference by moving that a central representative body was both unnecessary and unwise. When Adler reminded the delegates that they had adopted a contrary resolution in February, Straus moved the reconsideration of the February vote. His motion passed eleven to seven; thus the conference undid all that had been accomplished.

Cyrus Adler finally broke the deadlock. Recognizing that Marshall's plan could never muster sufficient support, he proposed an executive committee of fifteen, with power to increase its number to fifty, to cooperate with different national organizations. Adler's move pacified the Straus group and helped renew relations with B'nai B'rith and the UAHC. Marshall's motion to substitute his plan lost four to eight; Adler's resolution passed ten to three. Chairman Sulzberger, who, with five others, was authorized to appoint the committee of fifteen, ended the deliberations with an eloquent plea for harmony within the Jewish community:

> The need of a better feeling between the native and foreign elements of American Jewry is recognized, and I deplore the license of speech that has grown among us. The suggestion that mere numbers can give rise to statesmanlike advice in matters affecting the Jewish people is unthinkable. The know-nothing element among the native American Jewish people ought to be crushed, and the unrestrained license of speech and arrogant assumption of the so-called East Siders that mere numbers give wisdom ought to be treated as nil. There is more to American Jewry than what is comprised within the Ghettos; there is a Jewry in the South and in the West, whose opinions and whose interests are as important as the sometimes extravagant desires of those who live in the congested quarters. Both elements, both influences, the assumed superiority of the native Americans, and the belief of the unnaturalized that numbers should rule, ought to be nullified.

V

The executive committee of fifteen, whose names were announced by Sulzberger on June 17, then chose thirty-five additional members. They divided the country into districts and apportioned the number of delegates in accordance with the Jewish population in each. They not only had to select able men from different sections of the country, but also had to win the support of influential opponents. They could not afford to lose the rabbis or the UAHC; they aimed to conciliate the IOBB despite its initial antagonism; they could ignore neither the weak but aggressive Federation of American Zionists nor the spokesmen of the immigrants. With these guidelines in mind, the makeup of the original body of fifty followed most logically.

On November 11, 1906, the American Jewish Committee held its first meeting in New York's Hotel Savoy. Increasing its number to sixty, the Committee agreed to a constitution providing for five-year terms for members to be elected by district advisory councils, with one-fifth of the members to leave office each year. The general committee was to meet annually and elect an executive committee of thirteen. While ultimate control rested in a few hands (five of the executive committee constituted a quorum; the executive could report to the members at its discretion), the provision for advisory councils was a serious attempt to broaden the base of leadership. Chosen by Committee members of a district and consisting of those members plus ten times their number, advisory councils were to elect the general committee and fulfill tasks assigned them by the executive or general committee. Although they could not initiate action, they could make recommendations and, it was envisaged, investigate and supervise purely local issues. To the sincere regret of many on the executive, the advisory councils never developed to the stage of functioning actively, and leadership remained the unchallenged prerogative of a small group.

The creation of advisory councils, which could in no sense be considered popularly controlled, again elicited debate on the merits of a democratic body. Adolf Kraus continued his fulminations against a popular organization, denying that the Committee need represent the "riffraff," and Judah Magnes continued to support the masses. It remained for a new voice, that of Louis Dembitz of Kentucky, to utter advice ultimately vindicated by history. There is no need to fear control by the poor or ignorant immigrants, he said, no matter how numerous they are, for the same men will always be at the top, be it as an elected or as a self-appointed committee. In explaining what social scientists would later describe as a minority's choice of "leaders from the periphery," Dembitz supported popularly chosen leaders, for he believed that they could exercise greater power.

Despite the mood of the day, however, which preached democracy as the panacea for most social ills, the founders of the Committee created an organization which would derive its strength not from numbers but from the quality and status of its handpicked membership. These founders had read the signs of the times; they had admitted others to their exclusive circle—but by invitation and not by gate-crashing. Recognizing the difference between conservatism and futile stagnation, they adapted sufficiently to the new directions so that they too could keep their place in a century of rapid change.

The Committee plotted its course around the extension of popular liberties. Its constitution formulated the purpose of the organization in matter-of-fact terms: "to prevent infringement of the civil and religious rights of Jews, and to alleviate the consequences of persecution." Yet the founders aimed for more. They determined not only to guard rights already given but to strive for liberties not yet bestowed. Born in a decade characterized by a pervasive optimism, a belief in the basic rationality of man, and a faith in progress and humanitarian reforms, the Committee would predicate its activities on the conviction that the universal recognition of human rights was an attainable goal. Confidence in rational progress was bolstered by personal experiences. The Jewish leaders had found security in the United States, security sufficient to overcome doubts about helping alien Jews and absorbing strange immigrants. Unlike their European counterparts, they did not face a national tradition of political anti-Semitism associated with counterrevolutionary or reactionary movements. The United States offered as an additional advantage the tradition of humanitarian diplomacy—a policy of sympathetic aid motivated by humanitarian instincts—which fitted nicely the purposes of an organization seeking intercession in behalf of oppressed groups abroad. Thus when the Committee inscribed on its first seal the Hebrew words *ḥazaq wenitḥazzeqah be'ad 'ammenu* (1 Chronicles 19:13)—"Be of good courage and let us prove strong for our people"—it affirmed a tradition of communal responsibility, a zeal for justice, and a faith in its American destiny.

2

Patricians at Work

Louis Marshall, the second president of the American Jewish Committee, died in 1929. For the Committee, as for the country at large, that year marked the end of the era of rugged individualism. During Marshall's tenure, the Committee firmly rooted itself in American soil as he and his fellow stewards devotedly built a small, aristocratic organization. For the first twenty-five years of its existence, the Committee's functions were limited, its scope narrow. Yet its founders endowed it with independence, purpose, and resilience. In 1929, bereft of its foremost leader and faced with threats on the national and international scenes, the Committee could rally and face the future.

I

The founders of the American Jewish Committee planned for no more than a skeleton organization, which could be expanded in times of emergencies, to be run by a small group of handpicked leaders. Very often the meetings of its thirteen-man executive committee (later enlarged to twenty-five) mustered only half a dozen participants. The geographically apportioned general committee of sixty met annually to place an official stamp of approval on the executive report and on a predetermined slate of officers. In theory the sixty represented district constituencies of six hundred, i.e., advisory councils, but, as the Committee itself reported: "In most districts the Councils were never completed, and the scheme gradually became inoperative altogether."

Suggestions for broadening the Committee's base came periodically from both within and without the organization's ranks. Later the general committee was enlarged, as provisions were made for the selection of members-at-large in addition to district representatives (1909), for the affiliation of a group of national organizations (1911), and for the representation of each state in the union (1912). In 1916 district membership rose to one hundred when a new plan providing for three categories of membership was adopted: (a) district members to be apportioned according to the population (only cities with a Jewish population of twenty thousand or more were included); (b) delegates from national organizations; and (c) members-at-large. The general committee, except for the second category, remained in existence until 1921, when sustaining members (those who contributed five dollars or more annually) were given the right to elect the district representatives.

As new estimates of the Jewish population were made, district membership grew proportionately, and in 1931 (the Committee's quarter century mark) it reached 300 when 198 communities were granted representation. The community representatives were chosen by sustaining members and the local federations which contributed to the Committee. The organization had grown to 357 (300 plus 27 organizational representatives plus 30 members-at-large), seven times its original number.

In an era of rampant individualism, when wealth and privilege were still the trappings of leadership, the American Jewish Committee made no pretense of being, nor did it aspire to become, a democratic organization. It was fashionable to talk about democracy in 1906, Marshall recalled twenty-three years later, and for a while some Committee leaders genuinely aimed for the evolution of a representative, if not democratic, body. Hence the invitations to other organizations to affiliate with the Committee, the creation of advisory councils, and the encouragement of the kehillah movement.* But when democratic methods proved unwieldy, or when the Committee's definition of democracy did not coincide with that of its critics, it readily gave up its democratic pretense. Marshall, for instance, in the decades following his unsuccessful bid to create a democratic body, didn't mind in the least the characterization of the Committee as an "an autocratic institution without any democratic feeling or quality . . . worthy of notice." That, he declared, "just suited us. We felt that it would be very much better if our work was done quietly . . . , but that whatever would be done would indicate the result of mature thought."

The Committee genuinely prized dedication above numbers. It sought no publicity and it cared little if its name was unknown in non-Jewish circles. Cyrus Adler, for example, could not see "what possible advantage can come from making the Christian clergymen and the Christian religious press acquainted with the organization of our Committee." Some members also reasoned that too large a membership might evoke an anti-Semitic reaction.

Financial necessity, which might have forced the Committee to change from a restricted club into a popular organization, was not a question. The organization's quarters in New York City were modest—first located in the Hebrew Charities Building, then at 31 Union Square West, and then at 171 Madison Avenue. The post of executive secretary, filled by Herbert Friedenwald from 1906 to 1913, and Herman Bernstein from 1913 to 1914, stayed empty for fourteen years until the appointment of Morris D. Waldman in 1928. Harry Schneiderman, assistant secretary

*See below, pp. 23–24.

from 1908 to 1949 and the only paid executive, ran the office with the help of three or four low-salaried clerks. The Committee, under the watchful eyes of its wealthy directors, did not believe in wasting money on expensive staffs.

In those early years the American Jewish Committee depended on voluntary contributions to meet its expenses. At the beginning, quotas were imposed upon the districts, and in some cases that was sufficient. When District XII (New York City) was assessed $5,000 in 1909, four pledges, including $1,000 each from Schiff, Adolph Lewisohn, and Daniel Guggenheim, accounted for over two-thirds of the total. But not all districts were so affluent or so committed, and it was not until World War I that the Committee raised over $10,000.

In time the Committee sought contributions from nonmembers. After concerted efforts by small groups of prominent Jews, its annual receipts jumped from less than $25,000 in 1926 to over $60,000 in 1929. Still, it was never forced to engage in massive fund-raising drives, for individual subscriptions were supplemented by contributions from organizations interested in special projects (e.g., the Jewish Welfare Board for a compilation of war statistics, the New York Foundation for creating a statistical bureau) and, increasingly, from community welfare funds. American Jewish Committee supporters occasionally left bequests to the organization, and individuals made contributions for specific tasks (Felix Fuld for an examination of the czarist archives, Felix Warburg for a survey of anti-Semitism in Europe in 1926). Jacob Schiff could always be counted on in time of emergency: he was ready to spend $25,000 for the campaign to abrogate the Russian treaty, and he donated $12,500 for the relief of Palestinian Jewry at the outbreak of World War I. Finally, $190,000, amassed by the Committee for the Relief of Sufferers by Russian Massacres, was placed in the organization's custody and aptly dubbed the Pogrom Endowment Fund by Cyrus Sulzberger.

That the Committee was not completely soured on democracy was indicated by its support of the kehillah experiment. Here, too, it was motivated by the realization that a refusal to go along with the democratic forces might seriously jeopardize its leadership. The story began in the fall of 1908 when, in the wake of Police Commissioner Theodore Bingham's charge that the Jews of New York City were responsible for 50 percent of the city's crimes, the Jewish Lower East Side erupted in anger. Denunciations of Bingham were coupled with sharp criticisms of the Committee for its seeming inaction in the face of slanderous attack. Although Marshall and Schiff were the key figures in compelling an apology from Bingham, those who considered the Committee too restricted to represent the local interests of the ever-increasing East European element seized the opportunity to push through plans for an all-inclusive Jewish kehillah of New York. *Yiddishes Tageblat* wrote: "There is not a single Jew on the East Side who does not recognize the importance to American Jewry of a Jacob Schiff and a Louis Marshall. . . . But we wish self-recognition, as well. . . . We wish to give our famous Jews their honored place in an American Jewish organization in the measure that they earned it. But we wish them to work with us and not over us." Rabbi Judah Magnes, first chairman of the kehillah, considered that body an achievement of the democratic representation he had championed at the founding meetings of the Committee.

As the kehillah set out to unite delegates from synagogues, federations, fraternal lodges, and Jewish professional societies, the leaders of the downtown Jews and the uptown magnates of the Committee came to recognize their mutual interdependence. The East-Siders could not hope to succeed without the financial and prestigious backing of the stewards; the Committee, if it remained aloof, could be threatened by a "democratic golem." Planners of the kehillah met with the New York members of the Committee and arrived at a modus vivendi. The kehillah would deal solely with local matters and leave all national and international issues to the jurisdiction of the Committee; the twenty-five-

man executive body (for which American citizenship was mandatory) would be the representatives of the Committee's New York
City district. At the annual meeting of the Committee in November 1908, Jacob H. Schiff argued pragmatically, and with an appeal to patrician responsibility, when he urged endorsement of
the kehillah:

> Here is a desire . . . on the part of the tremendous body
> of the Jews of New York . . . and these gentlemen who have
> started this movement come to us and they say "Here we are;
> we do not want to do anything in excess of good judgment,
> we do not want to have it thrown in our mouths that we are
> agitators for power; we want to have the guidance of intelli-
> gent men, and we want you to cooperate with us." . . . Shall
> we repel these men and say . . . we do not want any of them?
> . . . It is a mighty stream which we have an opportunity to
> keep in these waters, and the boats are swimming on it, and
> it is a good opportunity to start them right.

As it turned out, the Committee's approval was a wise step,
if for no other reason than self-enhancement. The New York Jews
applauded its action and elected ten Committee members to the
kehillah's first executive committee. The self-same critics of the
Committee freely chose the aristocratic uptowners to lead their
democratic organization.

The enthusiasm for the kehillah plan spread to Philadelphia,
where a relationship paralleling that of New York was worked out
with the Committee. However, those who might have envisaged
the Committee as eventually representing a string of kehilloth
were disappointed. The New York kehillah declined rapidly after
1917, and the entire idea was abandoned.

II

The creation of the American Jewish Committee did not significantly alter the *Hofjude* pattern of Jewish defense which the founders had traditionally pursued. Discreet pressure and backstairs diplomacy remained the trademark of the organization. Bureaucracy was as repugnant as direct democracy. The Committee men wrote their own letters, planned their own strategies, and did their own lobbying. Their devotion to the organization was unimpeachable. True, up until the 1930s they encountered fewer complications than in the years to follow; but, as one observer noted, the Committee leaders gave of their means and prestige without thought of using the organization to advance their own positions.

Policy and strategy were mapped out by the executive committee. The agenda of executive meetings included all sorts of issues—from the thorny ramifications of immigration restriction to the specific question of Jewish representation on the boards of public museums. The members as a group formulated answers to letters which the agency or they singly had received from individuals and organizations. They deliberated over items appearing in the press, and they pooled their knowledge of developments in government policy. Their discussions were informal and unstructured. Decisions were usually arrived at by consensus rather than vote-taking, in an easy and almost automatic fashion which reflected the basic affinity among members in values and perspectives. When necessary, ad hoc committees of two or three researched points of interest, and special assignments of executing policy were delegated to the president or secretary.

As the first president of the American Jewish Committee Judge Mayer Sulzberger wrote his numerous directives to the New York office from his home in Philadelphia. Among the older men in the founding group—Sulzberger was sixty-three at the time of his election—he was known not only for his judicial attainments, but also for his deep interest in Jewish books and scholarship. Harry Schneiderman described him as follows:

> He was of medium height with broad shoulders somewhat rounded by sedentary living. His impressive head was covered with white hair; under his shaggy eyebrows, blue eyes normally twinkled with fun, but would on occasion flash with indignation or anger. He was inclined to be impatient with more slowly witted people and would make satirical remarks at their expense. But he was so highly esteemed that he was readily forgiven.

Sulzberger followed cautious and conservative policies. He was especially concerned not to undertake partisan activities which might cast doubts on the neutrality of his judicial office. In charting Committee action he sought the agreement of his colleagues on the executive committee, willingly sharing his leadership with them.

Since Sulzberger rarely came to New York, direction of the New York office routine fell largely to Cyrus Adler. A Semitics scholar who was associated with the Smithsonian Institution until his appointment to head the Dropsie College for Hebrew and Cognate Learning in Philadelphia, Adler (a young relative of Sulzberger's) worked closely with Secretary Friedenwald. Under Adler the Committee set up its first Washington office, principally as a listening post for Capitol Hill gossip which might bear upon the Committee's interests. That office was later headed by Fulton Brylawski, a lawyer who functioned as a bearer of messages, as a legal research worker, and as a reporter of the shifts in government policy. It was Brylawski who approached the solicitor of the Post Office Department about the possibility of barring Populist Tom Watson's scurrilous newspaper, the *Jeffersonian,* from the mails and who tried to find out what instructions were given to the ambassadors to Russia.

The closest associates of Judge Sulzberger and Adler in guiding the Committee's activity were Cyrus L. Sulzberger, Louis

Marshall, and Jacob H. Schiff. Cyrus Sulzberger, a successful businessman prominent in numerous civic organizations, was the Committee's expert on the social ramifications of immigration. Marshall, already recognized as one of New York's foremost legal minds, drew up briefs, formulated statements for presentation to congressional committees, and worked to advance the cause of legislation prohibiting discrimination against minorities. The dominant personality in the triumvirate, however, was Jacob Schiff. A German-born banker whose firm ranked among the most influential in financial and railroad circles, he was acknowledged as the representative American Jew by uptowners and downtowners alike. Medium in build and fastidiously groomed, Schiff, with his vandyke beard, walking stick, and fresh flower in his lapel, was a colorful figure. He was exuberant in mannerisms and speech, quick to lose his temper but equally quick to calm down and forgive. Only a Jacob Schiff in the heat of anger could have disdained a presidential handshake and left the White House with a curt bow, as occurred on one occasion.

An unspoken division of labor existed among the Committee's leaders. Proud, forceful, strong-willed individualists, and outwardly most formal—it was only "Mr. Schiff," "Judge Sulzberger," "Dr. Adler"—they respected and knew how to utilize the individual talents and resources of their associates. Schiff, a veritable elder statesman on all issues, was particularly important for his contacts with Jewish organizations and individuals abroad. Adler's forte was the domestic political scene; Oscar Straus advised the Committee on how to present its case to the administration; Max J. Kohler served as the expert on immigration law and Jewish rights at international congresses; Judah Magnes was the Committee's liaison with the Lower East Side, and Harry Friedenwald, its contact with the Federation of American Zionists. Other members dealt with purely local problems: A. Leo Weil of Pittsburgh reported on the correlation of Jews and organized prostitution in his city; Felix Fuld of Newark investigated an alleged Polish boycott of Jews in New Brunswick. The Committee disapproved of wildcat action by its members which might undermine fixed policy and expected members who broke with the organization to refrain from airing their grievances in the press.

The oligarchic nature of the Committee in some ways retarded its growth; scant attention was paid to seeking out new leadership. A man usually reached the rarefied heights of the executive only if he was known to others and had basically the same outlook. Thus when Cyrus Adler suggested the recruitment of Louis Brandeis, the "people's attorney" was passed over without comment; his talents notwithstanding, Brandeis's actions had displeased too many Committee members. Since the executive conducted its sessions in secrecy and was usually quite chary about how much to reveal to the general membership, some members grew restless and others bored.

This state of affairs became more pronounced in the years between World War I and the stock market crash of 1929. The quips in the 1920s about how American Jewry was ruled by Louis XIX or lived under "Marshall law" were well founded. Louis Marshall had taken over the presidency in 1912 and in the declining years of Schiff and Mayer Sulzberger had emerged as the Committee's guiding force. He was a short, stocky man of stern appearance, always confident in his opinions and impatient with those who differed with him, whose forthrightness permitted no public display of humor or sentiment. However, none could gainsay his abilities. A forceful and convincing speaker who courageously fought for his beliefs regardless of their popularity, he earned the respect of the community and the tremendous esteem of his colleagues. In 1923 the prominent socialist Yiddish-language *Forward* had to admit:

> Louis Marshall maintains reactionary views in most problems and is naturally also reactionary in his methods. In spite of that, Marshall still . . . in his way serves profoundly in a spirit of self-sacrifice.

Yet the strength of his personality, while effective in chalking up victories for the causes he espoused, weakened the Committee as an organization. With Marshall to answer anti-Semitic charges, fight for stranded immigrants, or rush to Washington "to indoctrinate the secretaries of state with the truth," his colleagues increasingly relaxed their activities. The executive met to hear Marshall report on what he had done between meetings; and to the public at large he and the American Jewish Committee became one and the same.

III

A loosely knit organization led by a small group of activists, the Committee nevertheless set certain ground rules to govern its behavior. In keeping with its original purpose, it confined itself to matters touching American Jewry as a group or involving foreign Jewish communities. To be sure, the Committee appealed for funds in behalf of all the victims of an Italian earthquake and filed a brief as amicus curiae in the Oregon parochial-school case. But until the 1930s participation in non-Jewish affairs was limited and unplanned. Especially interesting in light of later developments was the Committee's refusal to fight Negro segregation in government service during the Wilson administration. The Committee also skirted issues affecting individuals or limited numbers of Jews; in some cases it sought to divest the issue of any Jewish label. Accordingly, though Louis Marshall served as counsel for Leo Frank,* the Committee refused to act officially *as an organization,* insisting upon treating the case as a travesty of justice, of concern to all Americans irrespective of religion.

Another of the Committee's cardinal principles was strict

---

*In 1913, Frank, a factory superintendent in Atlanta, was accused of the murder of a fourteen-year-old girl employee. Popular anti-Semitism played an important part in his conviction and subsequent lynching.

neutrality regarding the American political scene. In line with the regnant creed of the founders that the Jews differed from their fellow Americans in religion only, it followed axiomatically that there was no distinctively Jewish political behavior. Jews became affiliated with political parties and voted on issues or for candidates, just as Presbyterians, Episcopalians, or Unitarians did; Jews were bankers, workers, low-tariff advocates, or farmers before they were Jews.

When Israel Zangwill touched on the advantages of a Jewish vote during a speech in the United States in 1923, Louis Marshall was quick to respond:

> I disagree totally with Mr. Zangwill's intimation that the Jews of this country should unite for political action, or that there should be such a thing as a Jewish vote in the United States. The thought cannot be tolerated that the citizens of this country shall form racial or religious groups in the exercise of their civic and political functions. The citizens of the United States constitute one people, and there can be no divergent interests among them so far as government is concerned. For years the leaders of Jewish thought in this country have with emphasis decried the intimation, emanating from those who do not understand the genius of American institutions, that recognition should be given to an Irish, a German, a Jewish, or a British vote. In like manner, the idea that there should be a Jewish Republican or a Jewish Democratic, or an Irish Republican or an Irish Democratic, political club has been justly deprecated. It is the glory of our country that before the law all men are equal, that every member of the state owes unqualified loyalty to it, that its laws must be free from discrimination, and apply equally to all citizens. . . . It is therefore inconceivable that a government of laws and not of men, such as ours is, can exist if the electorate is divided and subdivided into a multitude of segments or blocks, each considering merely its own interests. I am confident that there is no part of the population of this country which would with such determination oppose such an idea of political segregation as the Jews. For centuries their ancestors in foreign lands suffered from the conse-

quences of an enforced segregation of this character, and they would not be so fatuous as to create voluntarily a condition which in effect would establish an American ghetto. Our fellow-citizens need not fear that Mr. Zangwill's views on this subject are shared by any appreciable number of Jews of the United States.

In large measure this policy proved a source of strength. Since the Committee was politically neutral, it never evoked partisan attacks from non-Jews; it could also appeal for support to every Jew regardless of party affiliation—Republican and Farmer-Laborite, Democrat and Prohibitionist. It never hoped to be wooed by politicians, as was Samuel Gompers's American Federation of Labor, but at the same time it sidestepped the hazards of internal factionalism.

That the Committee determined to vote *American*, without any other labels, was a logical choice in light of the existing political structure. No major party in the United States had ever represented an exclusionist or anti-Semitic philosophy. Under the twin impulses of democracy and capitalism, unimpeded by a feudal heritage, American parties had room for all groups within the demos, and Jews, unlike their European counterparts, were not limited to left-of-center movements. As long as the parties remained open and differed from each other no more than—in the words of William A. White—Tweedledum and Tweedledee, American Jews had no reason to act in unison on political issues. In fact, it was a safer course to keep Jewish affiliation diffuse, thereby reinforcing the broad base of the major parties.

To say that American Jews had no fixed or separate political stance was one thing; to deny that Jews could express a common unity on a given issue in an election was quite another. Certainly in the calculations of non-Jewish politicians, bloc voting among Jews did exist. Senator James Clarke of Arkansas, who had done the Committee a few favors, expected its support when he stood for reelection. In 1920 a Democratic campaign manager outraged Louis Marshall when he crudely reminded American Jews that Wilson had elevated one of their own to the Supreme Court. Congressman William Sulzer of New York, the author of the resolution which led to the abrogation of the Russo-American treaty of 1832, dramatically related to his Jewish audiences, on his campaign tours in 1912, how he had humbled the czar. Although the Committee preferred to deny publicly the existence of a Jewish vote, even on specific questions, it used that vote as a weapon when bargaining with political leaders. For pragmatic purposes it realized that the strength of a minority in a democracy rested on the ballot. As early as 1908 Mayer Sulzberger directed Marshall to "have careful statistics prepared of all the Jewish wards in greater New York with comparative tables of votes for previous years."

Fortunately for the American Jewish Committee, its major concerns before 1930 which touched upon governmental policy —immigration and czarist Russia—crossed party lines. Thus the organization could maintain its political neutrality. At the same time, though, it submitted sympathetic planks (carefully varying the wording for each party) to party leaders for incorporation in their platforms, and cultivated influential contacts within both parties. When top administration action appeared particularly desirable, the Committee usually found somebody with direct access to the chief executive—Oscar Straus to Presidents Roosevelt and Taft, Lewis Strauss to President Hoover.

In line with its attitudes, the Committee never saw cause to back Jewish candidates for office. In the thick of the fight on immigration restriction, Representative William Bennet informed the Committee that as more Jews were elected to Congress, talk in the legislature about the undesirability of Jews diminished. The Committee ignored the implication and continued to refuse to back Jewish candidates. It did on occasion seek the help of Jews, Senators Simon Guggenheim of Colorado and Isador Rayner of Maryland, and Congressman Adolph Sabath of Illinois, but at least as often it turned to its non-Jewish liaisons, notably Congressmen Bennet and Francis B. Harrison of New York, Senators Clarke of Arkansas and Boies Penrose of Pennsylvania. Consistently rejecting the practice of Jewish lobbying through Jewish officeholders, the Committee also preferred to avoid situations in which a Jewish congressman, posing as the champion of his people, might attempt to direct policy independently of the Jewish stewards.

The notable exception to the Committee's self-imposed neutrality occurred in connection with abrogation of the treaty with Russia. When, before the 1908 election, President Taft publicly promised his support, Sulzberger, Marshall, and Straus boomed the Republican candidate in Jewish circles. Four years later Jacob Schiff and Louis Marshall openly endorsed William Sulzer's New York gubernatorial bid in gratitude for his role in effecting abrogation. In that campaign Sulzer ran against a Committee man, Progressive candidate Oscar S. Straus. While Sulzer sought to capitalize on the Jewish vote, Straus, following Committee policy to his own disadvantage, asked Jews *not* to vote for him just because he was Jewish.

IV

The American Jewish Committee strongly stressed "enlightenment" as its proper function as a defense agency. Seeing scientific inquiry as a tool for social planning, it assumed many of the tasks of a research bureau. At the first level was self-edification. Since it was axiomatic that the Committee leaders should know the situation of Jews abroad, they invited reports from officials of other Jewish organizations, gave financial assistance to the Jewish Telegraphic Agency, and employed a staff to read and translate foreign periodicals. They initiated research on the general subject of race classifications and ferreted out legal precedents for abrogating a treaty or for using American consulates as refuges for pogrom victims. They wanted to know the number of Jewish congregations and the number of Jewish criminals, how American Jewish farmers lived, and how Prohibition would affect Jewish religious practices. Inquiries were not be be "purely pathological," Cyrus Adler maintained, but rather were to be employed with merit for all aspects of Jewish life.

The Committee set up a Bureau of Jewish Statistics, which later was amalgamated into the Bureau of Jewish Social Research and Statistics. It also assumed responsibility for the publication of the *American Jewish Year Book,* a Jewish almanac full of facts and figures, on whose articles the executive expended a great deal of thought. The Committee's statistical machinery permitted it to cooperate with the government in the periodic censuses of religious bodies and, more important, to disseminate significant information to the general public.

Obviously, all this activity was not purely disinterested. The distribution of articles on czarist Russia, the exposure of the *Protocols of the Elders of Zion,* and the analysis of the economic effects of immigration were all directed to mobilize mass sympathy for immediate and concrete problems. Studies like *Jewish Disabilities in the Balkan States* and *Jews in the Eastern War Zone* were circulated among government officials as a prelude to Committee requests for diplomatic intercession. The Committee even had ready a scholarly rebuttal when criticisms of the ritual method of animal slaughter arose. Less immediate but more ambitious was Joseph Jacobs's study *Jewish Contributions to Civilization,* answering the "higher anti-Semitism" propagated by Werner Sombart, Houston Stewart Chamberlain, and their ilk.

V

Immediately upon its establishment, the Committee informed both national and foreign Jewish organizations of its existence. Through personal friendships and business connections of its members, it cemented close working relationships with leaders of the British Joint Foreign Committee, the German Hilfsverein, and the French Alliance Isráelite Universelle. It even worked out a code for its international correspondence. Although the Committee was made privy to all current information on European Jewish affairs and to efforts involving international diplomacy, it consistently turned down periodic invitations from abroad to attend international Jewish meetings, conferences, or missions. (It did, however, participate in a conference of organizations held in Brussels in 1912 for the purpose of coordinating relief activities for Jewish sufferers in the Balkan Wars.) The Committee was well aware that European alignments precluded the effective cooperation of foreign Jewish groups, and it believed that the uncertainties of the world situation increased the hazards of concerted action. Besides, the Committee preferred not to disclose to its European counterparts too much of what it knew about official American policy.

Relations between the Committee and the leading American Jewish organizations, where competition for communal power aggravated ideological differences, were less cordial. In 1907 committees of the United American Hebrew Congregations, B'nai B'rith, and the American Jewish Committee made futile efforts to define the spheres of activity of the three organizations. To be sure, they undertook joint action on aspects of the immigration and abrogation issues, but here too the older organizations, resentful of the powerful upstart, proved difficult partners. Simon Wolf and Adolf Kraus, who had been appointed to the original committee of fifty, resigned from the American Jewish Committee in 1907. The Zionists were even less tractable, for they had profound ideological differences with the Committee. In 1915 it was communal responsibility, not friendship, that moved the Committee to alert the Federation of American Zionists about confidential reports from Turkey which it had received from Ambassador Henry Morgenthau.

Undaunted by its rivals and critics, the Committee played a lone hand, where necessary. (Only the *American Hebrew* among the Anglo-Jewish periodicals was a loyal supporter; the Yiddish press, except for occasional kind remarks by the conservative *Jewish Morning Journal,* was consistently hostile.) Other than the short-lived kehillah episode, the Committee made no effort to mold a cohesive community or even to bridge the gap between the old and new immigrants. Nor did it ever seriously consider how it might shape the thinking of the American Jewish community. It remained aloof, ever the beneficent patrician—a guardian, yet a spectator—until the world-shaking events of the 1930s launched it upon new paths.

3

In Defense of the Immigrant

On Friday afternoon, February 14, 1913, Herbert Friedenwald wired Cyrus Adler: "PRESIDENT VETOED IMMIGRATION BILL THIS AFTERNOON GOOD SHABBOS." This news undoubtedly cheered Adler's Sabbath, but after six years of uninterrupted campaigning he was too scarred a veteran to regard Taft's veto as a lasting victory. More likely he spent at least part of his Sabbath planning the Committee's next steps in its continuing campaign to keep the doors of America open to the oppressed.

What held true for Adler applied equally to other members of the executive. Indeed, if any one example had to be singled out as evidence of the organization's altruism and humanitarianism, it was its activity in behalf of unrestricted immigration. The Committee's case was simple: as long as Jews suffered disabilities in other countries, the opportunity to start their lives afresh in a land of freedom must be preserved. Not that the first generation of Committee leaders shared the habits or Weltanschauung of the would-be immigrants from Eastern Europe. The East European Jews, with their shtetl ways, were as alien to the American Jewish Committee patricians as were the exotic Falashas of Africa. In fact, it would have been far easier for these stewards to favor curbs on immigration. As firmly established members of their community they bore the responsibility of ministering to the physical and educational needs of the new arrivals, and they stood to lose a great deal were public disapproval of the Eastern Jews to rub off on them. Nor were they guaranteed any loyalty or gratitude from those they helped; as likely as not, within a few years of their arrival the immigrants would cast aspersions upon the "silk-stocking" Jews and their pretensions to power. The men of the Committee could have fallen back on the same dichotomy employed by many restrictionists: the emancipated Jew from Western Europe was welcome but not the ghetto Jew, who would only be an alien presence. Nineteenth-century American Jews had not always supported free immigration, and thus there would be no need to explain any sharp break in tradition. Yet the fact that the Committee consistently stuck its neck out, thereby incurring more ill will than praise, testifies not only to its faith in the assimilatory power of a free environment but also, more important, to its unshakable commitment to the ideal of stewardship. True, before World I the Committee's concern encompassed merely the Jew, but it would be only a short step to the realization that the struggle for freedom in America is indivisible, that it could not be won within the confines of a single ethnic group.

I

The American Jewish Committee was born in a decade which witnessed an unprecedented increase in immigration. For the first time in American history, immigration in 1905 topped one million persons; in 1906 the total rose an additional 75,000. More significantly, the type of immigrant had changed. The overwhelming majority represented the "new immigration," a term used to describe the arrivals from southern and Eastern Europe, as distinct from the "old immigration" from northwest Europe. For the years 1891–1900, the "new" immigrants accounted for 51.9 percent of the total; in the next decade their percentage

jumped to 70.8. In actual numbers, out of a total immigration of
8,800,000 between 1901 and 1910, over 2 million persons came
from Austria-Hungary, 2 million from Italy, and 1.5 million from
Russia. Many Anglo-Saxon Protestant Americans read ominous
signs into the numbers: these aliens, it was feared—Latin and
Slavic in stock, Catholic and Jewish in religion, concentrating in
the congested urban areas of the East Coast—would change the
face of the United States. Forgetting that native Americans were
also flocking to the cities in search for a better life, critics sought
to explain urban ills—slums, crime, political corruption—not as
the result of a rapidly industrializing society but rather as the
work of the foreign elements.

Officially, the immigrant was still welcome. Federal restrictive laws, except those concerning the Chinese, had been of a
piecemeal nature. Since the 1880s the government had excluded
contract laborers, labeled certain foreigners inadmissible for
health and moral reasons, forbidden the entry of anarchists, provided for a deportation procedure, and imposed head taxes on
all immigrants. But these restrictions did not apply to the masses.
However, when nativist feeling revived in the decade following
1905, fed largely by the sectional prejudices of the South and the
West Coast, restrictionist demands increased, with much accom-
panying talk by intellectuals of "superior races," "race improvement," and "race suicide." As used by the New England
Brahmins, who equated the decline in their status with moral
degradation and national ruin, science taught the dangers of
crossbreeding with "inferior stock," that is, the new immigrants.
New York socialite Madison Grant, in his popular book *The Passing of the Great Race,* fulminated:

> These immigrants adopt the language of the native
> American, they wear his clothes, they steal his name and they
> are beginning to take his women, but they seldom adopt his
> religion or understand his ideals and while he is being el-
> bowed out of his own home the American looks calmly

abroad and urges on others the suicidal ethics which are exterminating his own race.

According to Grant, the product of a racial mixture reverted to the lower type: "The cross between any of the three European races and a Jew is a Jew."

In an age when American industry eagerly welcomed additions to the labor market and Americans still regarded the national mission as giving asylum to the oppressed, restrictionists, for all their zeal, could not dare to dream of legislation suspending immigration. The best they could hope to achieve was to increase the categories of inadmissibles. In the past they had tried to deter immigration by such devices as quarantine regulations or by tightening naturalization procedures. Now the weapon was the literacy test. As expounded by economist Edward Bemis in 1887, the idea that would-be immigrants must prove that they could read and write their own language became a major plank of the Immigration Restriction League, the organization of the New England Brahmins. The league believed that a literacy test would keep out the worst of the "racially unfit," and organized labor, for its own reasons, concurred. Samuel Gompers, the immigrant president of the American Federation of Labor, was, of course, concerned with the threat of cheap labor, but he too couched his arguments in the popular jargon of the day.

II

A bill embodying the requirements of a literacy test for immigrants was introduced in Congress in 1906. Opposed by big business and by the increasingly vocal immigrant groups themselves, the Dillingham bill quickly became a matter of concern for the American Jewish Committee, but it handled the matter through its individual members rather than as a group. Fearful lest they give the appearance of a political lobby, the executive committee resolved in January 1907 that members turn as private citizens to their congressmen in an effort to avert the bill's passage. This meant a continuation of the procedures begun before the Committee came into existence, when Jewish leaders had quietly campaigned against the bill in individual conferences with legislators and members of the administration. In the past they had argued with the secretary of state on grounds of international amity and had pointed out potential losses in Italian and Jewish votes to Republican politicians. They had even induced the liberal Catholic prelate James Cardinal Gibbons to protest to the Roosevelt administration in behalf of the would-be arrivals from Hungary and Italy.

The Committee's executive body, operating behind the scenes, now mounted a more intensive campaign. Documents, statistics, and government publications on the question of restriction were collected and studied, as were articles in the popular periodicals. The archrestrictionist groups—the Immigration Restriction League and its anti-Semitic leader, Prescott Hall; the American Federation of Labor; and the Pennsylvania nativist group, Junior Order United American Mechanics—were kept under special scrutiny. American Jewish Committee members sought out and cultivated contacts with congressional leaders, particularly the New York and Pennsylvania delegations, and with the all-important House Committee on Rules and its powerful chairman, Speaker Joe Cannon. President Roosevelt, whose stand on immigration was the subject of conjecture and conflicting reports, was watched anxiously. Especially active in sifting the Washington gossip for nuggets of fact were Committee members Cyrus Adler, then assistant secretary of the Smithsonian Institution, attorney Nathan Bijur, and Isadore Sobel, former president of the Pennsylvania League of Republican Clubs. Secretary of Commerce and Labor Oscar Straus, who had resigned officially from the Committee but daily walked to his office with Adler, was an invaluable source of information.

While keeping a daily scorecard of the alignments in Congress as the bill proceeded through both houses and then to a conference committee, the Jewish leaders formulated their own answers to the restrictionists. In line with Bijur's suggestion that an educational campaign be conducted, the Committee prepared replies to the stock charges that immigrants lowered the standard of citizenship, threatened the livelihood of American workers, carried contagious diseases, and spread the blight of poverty. Though they shunned the racist issue, the counterarguments, replete with statistics, enumerated the services of the immigrants to the country and their beneficent effect on its economy. Committee president Mayer Sulzberger publicly challenged restrictionism in an interview with the *North American Review,* the respectable journal of the New England patricians, and Bijur joined in with an open letter to the *New York Tribune.*

The Committee's tactics called for a moderate campaign, gauging the proper moment to apply pressure and restraining individual Jews from making incorrect or intemperate statements. It frowned upon indiscriminate agitation which not only "wasted powder and shot" but stimulated activity among opponents. Although the Committee reluctantly cooperated with the National Liberal Immigration League, under the direction of Edward Lauterbach and Nissim Behar, it disapproved of that organization's penchant for mass meetings. Congressman William Bennet of New York, a Committee partisan, found the organization far too circumspect, and only when he demanded wires and letters from the public to strengthen his hand in the conference committee did Sulzberger relent and go along with a more public drive. At Bennet's insistence, the Committee also tried to weaken the influence of Senator Henry Cabot Lodge, the political leader of the Brahmins and a key sponsor of the literacy measure. The Committee alerted Lee Friedman of Boston to exert pressure the senator, and it asked A. Leo Weil and Isadore Sobel to keep Pennsylvania's senators from supporting Lodge.

Although the stewards of the Committee calculated that Jews

stood to lose less by the impending legislation than other immigrant groups, they persisted in opposing restrictionism; indeed, theirs was the major role. In this they were impelled by their concern for East European Jewry. Fortunately, their cause coincided with the views of Speaker Cannon, who saw no reason why immigrants could not become loyal Republican voters, and when the Dillingham bill became law in 1907 the literacy test was dropped.

Though the new act tightened administrative procedure for immigration and deportation, increased the head tax, and broadened the categories of those morally and physically unfit to enter, the Committee regarded its passage as a victory. As Secretary Friedenwald commented to Cyrus Adler: "In most respects I think it an admirable measure. . . . We can breathe freely once more." They were aware, however, that they had achieved only a respite, not a final decision. The 1907 act had forged no new policy but had referred the matter for study to a special Immigration Commission. Pending that body's final report, restrictionist clamor would be partially silenced, but the anti-immigration forces, the Committee knew, would not give up.

III

Forced into a posture of constant alert, the Committee first attempted to secure an appointment on the Immigration Commission (which consisted of three senators, three congressmen, and three public representatives chosen by the president) for one of its members or friends. When that failed—Roosevelt refused to appoint anyone with a pronounced viewpoint—the executive appealed directly to the chairman of the Immigration Commission, Senator William P. Dillingham. Opening with a brief description of the plight of Russian Jews, they took their stand in favor of regulative, as opposed to either restrictive or completely free, immigration:

We are keenly alive to the right and duty of every government to protect its people against the incursion of criminals, paupers, lunatics, and other persons who would be public charges, but we deprecate most sincerely any nerveless or unmanly timidity about evils which may be coolly and sanely guarded against, without violating our national traditions and the dictates of common humanity, or depriving our country of a natural and healthy means of increasing its population and prosperity.

Having thus made the point that theirs was the traditional American position, the Committee spokesmen continued in a more daring vein:

It is a matter of common knowledge that in many European countries political parties are organized, whose platform contains a plank inculcating hatred of Jews as such. That prejudices so promulgated color the minds of many well-meaning persons in such environment is inevitable, and that these prejudices tend to be reflected in testimony that may be offered before you is highly probable.

Therefore, the Committee concluded, it asked if the senator would hear its factual and unprejudiced testimony.

Dillingham's group did not take up the offer for over two years, and until then the Committee worked principally to prevent any chipping away of the status quo. The prime requisite was for capable informants who, as Mayer Sulzberger explained, would "enable us to bring intelligent and concentrated effort to the defeat of hostile schemes or at all events to insist on their modification." Through its Washington office and its liaisons in Congress, the Committee kept a watchful eye on the restrictionists.

At the same time, the Committee worked to mend the immigrant fences and so nullify the restrictionists' charges. When certain congressmen pointed to the support of Jewish aliens by public institutions, the Committee began an inquiry into the number and nature of such cases with a view to transferring the needy to the care of relatives or Jewish charities. Of greater significance were the efforts by Committee members to relieve the congested immigrant settlements, the special target of their opponents who lashed out against the "unassimilable" masses of the ghetto. President Roosevelt, never a rabid restrictionist, had told Jacob Schiff privately that "he viewed the large immigration settling to so great an extent in a few cities with the greatest alarm, as he felt sure that upon the appearance of hard times the distress would be very severe, and there might be even worse things than distress."

Roosevelt's successor, William Howard Taft, also saw the problem as one of immigrant distribution rather than restriction. Accordingly, in 1907 Schiff pushed the Galveston Plan, which aimed to divert the immigrants from the eastern seaboard to the southern ports of Galveston and New Orleans. Upon arrival, the immigrants were sent to more sparsely settled regions where labor was needed. Cyrus L. Sulzberger, for years the chairman of the Industrial Removal Office, worked in a similar direction. In testimony before the House Committee on Immigration and Naturalization in 1910, Sulzberger, then speaking for the Committee, denied Prescott Hall's charge that distribution was "a bluff of the Jews and steamship companies to throw dust in the eyes of the ignorant and prevent proper legislation." He summarized the work of his Industrial Removal Office as follows:

> According to the latest report of this office, there have been sent from New York 45,711 persons, of whom 24,123 were breadwinners, the remainder being wives and children. These 24,123 persons represented 221 occupations, and were sent to 1,278 cities and towns, and the 3,500 distributed in 1909 were sent to 298 cities and towns. These persons have been distributed to all parts of the United States, towns and villages as well as cities, and, according to the records of the office, 85 per cent of the breadwinners are engaged in gainful occupations at the places to which they

were sent. These persons are distributed through the co-operation of friendly committees in the receiving places, excepting where the receiving places are small. Where we send a larger number, we have a reception committee to whom we send these people, not in response to immediate requisition, but from a general knowledge of the conditions as to what kind of workingmen they can use, and we send such classes of workingmen. . . . These reception committees consist of public-spirited citizens of the Jewish community in the locality, who are interested in the work. They know perfectly well that they are able to place them; otherwise they would not ask us to send them.

The champions of distribution pressured for government appropriations to erect immigration stations on the Gulf Coast, and they turned even further afield in their constant search for havens for the persecuted Russian Jews. It was no coincidence that the same men who were active in the American Jewish Committee also organized, in 1906, an American branch of the Jewish Territorial Organization.*

The Committee realized that even without legislation the fortunes of the immigrants could be affected by the prejudices and powers of the administrative officials. Since immigration was the province of the Department of Commerce and Labor, the Committee found some comfort during the secretaryship of Oscar Straus, who echoed its sympathetic and latitudinarian approach. Straus held his ground steadfastly despite Prescott Hall's vicious charges of marked Jewish bias; but the restrictionists found their own allies in succeeding years. When the assistant secretary of commerce and labor under Taft sought to wreck the Galveston project by ordering the deportation of many immigrants, or when Commissioner William Williams, an out-and-out restrictionist who was in charge of the port of New York, fixed stringent financial requirements which increased the number of

---

*Organized in opposition to the Zionists, who looked exclusively to Palestine and who rejected a 1905 British offer to settle Jews in Kenya, this body sought any available territory on which to build an autonomous Jewish settlement.

deported, the Committee swung into action. Legal briefs were filed in Washington, habeas corpus proceedings for several of those ordered deported were initiated, and the Taft administration was frankly threatened with the loss of Jewish goodwill— efforts which for the most part proved successful. At the same time, the Committee lobbied against any bill which sought to restrict naturalization to white persons or non-Asiatics. Although the Committee as yet made no attempts to further the cause of other minority groups (the Japanese were the principal target at the time), it was well aware that the purpose of all such legislation was to curb immigration generally. More specifically, legal ambiguities could conceivably place Jews in the categories of Asiatics or non-Caucasians. Finally, such measures reinforced the racist temper, always a potential danger to Jewish interests.

While the Bureau of Naturalization, the Bureau of the Census, and individual congressmen were busily setting up racial categories and classifications—they could not always agree on where the Jews fitted in—the Committee took the position that the Jews as a race did not exist. The Committee men successfully influenced the Bureau of the Census to delete the item of racial background from its questionnaire, and they objected to the classification "Hebrew" used in the reports of the Immigration Bureau. Ironically, other Jewish groups sided against the Committee on this issue. When Judge Julian W. Mack denied the existence of a Jewish race in his testimony before the Dillingham Commission, in 1909, his statement raised a storm of protest by Zionist lodges and societies.

To avoid more serious communal rifts, the Committee wisely decided to cooperate with other Jewish organizations on the immigration problem. Though it rejected invitations to national or international conferences on the subject, on the grounds that the public could easily misunderstand and misrepresent such projects, it joined in common briefs and testified before congressional committees with other groups, notably the Board of Delegates and B'nai B'rith. While cooperation inevitably brought about personality clashes—Simon Wolf's egotism especially irritated the Committee—it did result in stronger pressure and increased resources. Most important, by recognizing and endorsing activities of other interested groups, the Committee could achieve a "safe" Jewish policy. Thus, wary of Nissim Behar's unpredictable actions, it prevailed upon the president of the National Liberal Immigration League to agree that his group would take no action without consulting with Committee members. Again, when the Yiddish press began to agitate against Commissioner Williams's proceedings, the Committee feared that this might stir new restrictionist sentiments and endanger Jewish efforts in other fields. In order to curb the more excitable elements in the community, as well as to gain a forum for its point of view, the Committee participated in small conferences on immigration where representatives of interested organizations aired their opinions. Meantime, the Immigration Commission invited the views of the Jewish agencies on immigration legislation, and in November 1910 the Committee, Board of Delegates, and B'nai B'rith sent the commission a lengthy memorandum in which the three organizations declared their opposition to more stringent restrictive devices, argued for due process of law for the immigrants, and reaffirmed their faith in the assimilability of the Jewish aliens.

IV

When the Immigration Commission finally released its report in 1911, the friends of immigration saw that they had lost. To be sure, the commission did not resort to the racist argument, but the American Jewish Committee concluded that

> the reports . . . evidence but slight desire to adhere to the time-honored tradition that has made this country a refuge for the oppressed of all lands. It was contended that on

economic grounds the increase of our population by immigration was too rapid, and that some method of restriction should be adopted. The Commission favored a reading and writing test as likely to effect most equitably the desired end. In reaching this determination, the object seems to be to decrease the immigration from Southern and Eastern Europe, which forms the bulk of our immigration. . . . The restrictionists now affect to deplore the paucity of German and Irish immigrants, and hope to stimulate their coming by excluding as many as possible of other immigrants. The real situation is that there have always been persons hostile to immigration. As times change, these shift their arguments, but do not change their position.

The restrictionists swiftly pressed their advantage and in 1912 presented their demands in the Senate in the Dillingham bill and in the House in the Burnett bill. Both embodied the literacy test; but the Dillingham bill, which required certificates of character and incorporated the Root amendment to deport any alien conspiring for the violent overthrow of a foreign government, seemed especially harsh.

The Committee's task now became more difficult. The majority of the congressmen were uninformed or apathetic on the immigration issue. Although the Committee had the ear of Senators Penrose of Pennsylvania and James O'Gorman of New York and of the two Jewish senators, Rayner and Guggenheim, no one in the Senate took "an active interest in opposition to the bill, at all comparable to Lodge's persistence in pushing it through." As for the public at large, only the Jewish segment was aroused—the Catholic Church was unwilling to speak out—and even at that, many Jews did not oppose restrictionism as strongly as they could have.

Undaunted by these odds, the Committee continued its resistance to restrictionism generally and to the literacy test in particular. It testified before the House Committee on Immigration and Naturalization, circulated antirestrictionist literature—notably a chapter from a book by Dr. I. Hourwich on the economic benefits of immigration—and, in a shift from its usual policy, endorsed mass protest meetings. Other minority groups joined in at these meetings, as the following account by Cyrus Adler illustrates:

> A mass meeting was held last night with results which I admit surprised me. Although we did not start in until Sunday afternoon there were nearly a thousand people present, representing all classes of the community, Germans, Italians, Jews, Scotchmen, everything. The Irish seemed to hold aloof. Dr. C. J. Hexamer . . . president of the German American Alliance, presided and made an excellent address. Other addresses were made by Chevalier Baldi who is known in Philadelphia as the Mayor of the Italian section, Mr. Louis E. Levy, Dr. S. Solis-Cohen. We adopted resolutions . . . [which] were sent off last night to the Speaker of the House and the President of the Senate. . . . We can count upon the hearty cooperation of the Germans and the Italians. The Catholic Church was practically not represented in any way.

There was also cooperation from the National Liberal Immigration League and the socialists, whose indignation over the Root amendment drew them to the side of the Jewish patricians.

Simultaneously, but more quietly, the Committee fought the bill introduced in 1912 to create a separate Department of Labor which would have jurisdiction over immigration affairs. Although a labor man traditionally filled the post of commissioner-general of immigration, labor's bias could be more easily blunted if final administrative authority rested in the hands of a sympathetic or simply business-minded secretary of commerce. The Committee spoke earnestly and persistently to various congressmen, but labor's power, especially in an election year, outweighed other pressures.

A more daring move by the Committee was its attempt to exploit the presidential elections for its purposes. Contacts were established with the state and national political committees, and pressure was applied to keep the political platforms free of restrictionist planks. A terse directive reached Secretary Friedenwald, who went to Baltimore for the Democratic convention: "Gompers will want anti-injunction as well as restriction. Play one against the other." The AFL got its anti-injunction plank but lost out on restrictionism.

The American Jewish Committee's executive also appointed three special committees to elicit the views of the Republican, Democratic, and Progressive candidates on the literacy test. Taking care not to inject the Jewish vote directly into politics and avoiding alignment with any one party, they prepared, nevertheless, to present the information to the community and let the voters take it from there. President Taft, the Republican nominee, responded favorably:

> I have an abiding faith in the influence of our institutions upon all who come here, no matter how lacking in education they may be, if they have the sturdy enterprise to leave home and to come to this country to seek their fortunes. . . . The second generation of a sturdy but uneducated peasantry, brought to this country and raised in an atmosphere of thrift and hard work, and forced by their parents into school and to obtain an instrument for self-elevation, has always contributed to the strength of our people, and will continue to do so.

Democrat nominee Woodrow Wilson, governor of New Jersey, who for political reasons alone had to repudiate anti-immigration statements he had made in the past, wrote:

> I am in substantial agreement with you about the immigration policy which the country ought to observe. I think that this country can afford to use and ought to give the opportunity to every man and woman of sound morals, sound mind and sound body who comes in good faith to spend his or her energies in our life, and I should certainly be inclined . . . to scrutinize very jealously any restrictions that would limit that principle in practice.

The election came and went, and despite their new chief's stand, the Democratic House of Representatives (a lame duck Congress) passed the Burnett bill 202–62. According to Representative Albert Burleson, later Wilson's postmaster general, "the labor men had terrorized the members of the House so that they did not dare to vote against Burnett's bill." Although one clause of the bill exempted from the literacy test those who had fled religious persecution, the conference committee in Congress restored the original Dillingham measure, long since passed by the Senate. Because of Committee agitation, however, the provision requiring certificates of character had been omitted. Now the Committee could only call for a presidential veto, and it joined other friends of immigration who pleaded with Taft in a personal interview to veto the bill. Taft did: "I cannot make up my mind to sign a bill which in its chief provision violates a principle that ought, in my opinion, to be upheld in dealing with our immigration. I refer to the literacy test." However, since the veto was sustained by only four votes, it was clear that a restrictionist victory was only a matter of time. Acting on this assumption, Cyrus Adler wrote in February 1913:

> A list ought to be made up of all the new Senators and Representatives who will be members of the 63rd Congress and a systematic effort ought to be made to reach them by literature and through the constituents . . . to have them made favorable to our views. This ought to be done in time for the extra session of Congress. While [incoming] President Wilson is not likely to recommend legislation on this subject at this session, with such determined men as Burnett in the House and Lodge in the Senate, the matter may nevertheless come up.

Indeed, the restrictionists kept right on stubbornly reviving the literacy bill. Louis Marshall suggested a counter bill embodying the liberal viewpoint, to be introduced by Congressman Sabath and Senator O'Gorman, but the attempt was futile. The

Committee stood by its policy of opposing the literacy test, but at the same time, in interviews with congressmen and the president, it sought to overcome the effects of that contingency by pushing for a clause exempting victims of persecution. The clause prepared by Marshall was defeated, but its defeat confirmed President Wilson in his opposition to the measure. Wilson granted the immigrants and organizations like the Committee a stay with his veto of the bill in 1915. Finally, in 1917, reinforced by the surge of wartime nationalism, Congress pushed through a literacy test over the president's second veto. By then, however, the Committee was not unduly upset. It had secured exemptions to the law which modified the more objectionable features. Besides, the war in Europe had curtailed immigration, and with the collapse of the czarist regime the American Jews looked for an end to Russian emigration. As the momentous year 1917 came to a close, the Committee could look back with pride on its record. Not only had it been instrumental in keeping the gates of America open for Europe's persecuted masses, but it had served faithfully and unswervingly to remind the American government and people of their humanitarian traditions.

4

The Abrogation Campaign

The American Jewish Committee has always regarded its key role in the fight to bring about abrogation of the Russo-American treaty of 1832 as one of the organization's major achievements. This occurred in 1911, when the Committee, only a handful in number but fired by strong passion, succeeded in arousing American public opinion and in forcing the hand of an antagonistic administration.

The mounting distress of East European Jewry had been a prime factor in the Committee's establishment and in its campaign for unrestricted immigration. It also underlay the Committee's fight for abrogation, which in essence sought to end persecution before there were victims. The gravity of the situation and the high stakes encouraged the Committee to let down its usual conservative guard and use more daring tactics. Not only did it discard backstairs diplomacy in favor of a public campaign, but it also cultivated cooperation with non-Jews and threw its weight into the political arena. The story of the abrogation fight is one of a successful campaign by a minority group, and its happy outcome greatly enhanced the Committee's stature. Yet ultimately the victory proved neither complete nor lasting. The underlying aim of the Committee was never realized, and in later emergencies public sympathy was no longer so easily aroused. Finally, the Committee itself did not learn all it might have from the episode.

I

Article 1 of the treaty of commerce and navigation between the United States and Russia, signed in 1832, provided that

> there shall be between the territories of the high contracting parties a reciprocal liberty of commerce and navigation. The inhabitants of their respective states shall mutually have liberty to enter the ports, places and rivers of the territories of each party, wherever foreign commerce is permitted. They shall be at liberty to sojourn and reside in all parts whatsoever of said territories, in order to attend to their affairs, and they shall enjoy, to that effect, the same security and protection as natives of the country wherein they reside, on condition of their submitting to the laws and ordinances there prevailing, and particularly to the regulations in force concerning commerce.

In the last quarter of the nineteenth century, as the czarist government plotted its anti-Jewish course, American Jews who happened to be on Russian soil found themselves subjected to various economic and residential restrictions. Russia disclaimed any violation of the treaty by this discrimination, for did not Article 1 stipulate "on condition of their submitting to the laws and ordinances there prevailing"? Despite the fact that at the time the treaty was negotiated there was no intention of including Russian domestic anti-Jewish restrictions, and despite a counter interpretation in American circles that Article 1 sanctioned no distinctions among citizens of the United States, Russia went one step further and embarked in the 1890s on a policy of refusing to visa the passports of American Jews.

A brief against the czarist regime began to take shape: (1) Russia violated the intent, at the very least, of the 1832 treaty by limiting the rights of a certain group of Americans, native-born as well as former Russian subjects; (2) Russia conducted a "religious inquisition" repugnant to American institutions by inquiring into the beliefs of those applying for visas; (3) Russia insulted the United States by not honoring American passports; (4) Russian attacked a sacred principle in the American code of liberties, namely, freedom of religion. To be sure, there were sporadic protests from the State Department and American diplomatic agents in St. Petersburg, and in individual cases Russia yielded. Congress, too, took note of the situation in several resolutions objecting to treaties curtailing the rights of American citizens. Russia, however, never regarded the protests significant enough to warrant a retreat in principle.

Obviously the most interested in the question were those most directly affected: American Jews. True, very few of the then two million Jews in America planned to visit or take up residence in Russia, and since Russia made exceptions on grounds of wealth and commercial position, even fewer Jews who sought entry were denied visas. For the leaders of the Jewish community the Russian discrimination meant no personal inconvenience. It did, however, place them in the intolerable category of second-class citizens. As long as the United States effected no change in the czarist attitude, the American government was acquiescing, however unwillingly, in Russian-made distinctions; why, they argued, did the United States condone anti-Jewish discrimination when it would not have condoned any other? As Louis Marshall stated in his famous address on the passport question:

> If Russia should declare that no citizens of the United States residing west of the Mississippi or south of the Ohio should receive the benefits of this treaty, not only the South and the West, but our entire country would stand aghast at the dishonor inflicted on the entire nation. If Russia should

announce that it would not honor the passport of the United States when held by an Episcopalian or a Presbyterian, a Methodist, or a Roman Catholic, our country would not look upon this breach of treaty obligation as a mere insult to the Episcopalians or the Presbyterians, the Methodists or the Roman Catholics of this country, but would justly treat it as a blow inflicted upon every man who holds dear the title of American citizen.

Until the spring of 1908 American Jews made no mention of abrogation, trusting that diplomatic intercession might rectify the matter. After the Kishinev pogrom of 1903 had exposed Russian brutality, Jewish leaders succeeded in getting both Republicans and Democrats to adopt resolutions in their party platforms of 1904 pledging equal protection under treaties to all citizens. Theodore Roosevelt, perhaps at the reminder of Jacob H. Schiff that the one hundred thousand votes of New York's Jewish East Side might be decisive in the forthcoming election, discussed the problem in his acceptance speech as presidential nominee. Again in 1905, chiefly under the influence of Oscar S. Straus, Roosevelt wrote Count Sergius Witte that Russo-American friendship might benefit if Russia granted visas to American Jews.

The turning point in American Jewish thinking on how to solve the passport question came in 1907, when the State Department officially announced that

> Jews, whether they were formerly Russian subjects or not, are not admitted to Russia unless they obtain special permission in advance from the Russian Government, and this Department will not issue passports to former Russian subjects or to Jews who intend going to Russian territory, unless it has the assurance that the Russian Government will consent to their admission.

The Committee protested in shocked terms to Secretary of State Elihu Root that the United States was reversing its traditional stand and "seeks to . . . apply an unconstitutional religious test to upwards of a million of our own citizens, . . . thus practically justifying Russia in her violation of her treaty obligations and condoning her contemptuous disregard of the American passport." Though the State Department revoked the objectionable directive and even invited the Committee's views on a new draft, the Jews summed up Root's attitude as too pro-Russian to defend their interests, much less to force the czar's government to stop the discriminatory policy. A few months later, in May 1908, the Committee submitted a lengthy memorandum to President Roosevelt reviewing Russia's violation of the 1832 treaty and suggesting that the government terminate the existing treaties with Russia and negotiate no new ones without assurance of Russia's compliance. (The only other Russo-American treaty in existence was the unpopular extradition agreement of 1887.)

The 1907 circular was the catalyst in crystallizing the change in demand from diplomatic protest to outright abrogation, but there were additional factors. The executive branch had grown weary of the numerous Jewish demands for verbal admonitions to Russia. Theodore Roosevelt, who saw no point in empty scoldings, said to Cyrus Adler: "Do you want me to go to war with Russia?" Even if Root continued the policy of his more sympathetic predecessors, that policy was at best defensive and unlikely, after twenty-five years, to effect any sudden change in Russia's attitude. Besides, with the increasing volume of trade between Russia and the United States, greater attention and importance were being given to the commerce treaty; the threat of abrogation, it was felt, might impel the Russians either to accept the American interpretation of the old treaty or to agree to a new one embodying explicit assurances of equality. Finally, and perhaps most important in the minds of leading American Jews, the situation of Russian Jewry was growing steadily more intolerable. Abrogation, it was hoped, would achieve at least the partial emancipation of Russian Jewry.

The logic was quite simple. Given the Russian premise that

foreign Jews could not be treated any differently from native Jews, it followed that if foreign Jews were permitted commercial privileges equal to those granted other foreigners (and by treaty terms equal to those enjoyed by Russians), Russia would be forced eventually to grant the same privileges to the native Jews. As the condition of Russian Jewry continued to deteriorate, therefore, it became all the more imperative to gain free entry for foreign Jews. Abrogation seemed to be the quickest way to compel Russia to grant equal rights to American Jews; this would cause other nations to demand similar rights for their Jewish citizens, which in turn would serve to unshackle Russian Jews.

It should be noted that the connection between equal rights for foreign and Russian Jews was not a private insight of the Committee's. That connection had been explored in 1879 by the editor of the *American Israelite* and in 1881 by Secretary of State James Blaine. Schiff, who reiterated this position throughout the campaign for abrogation, had stated, even before the establishment of the American Jewish Committee: "When foreign Jews are equally entitled to cross the Russian border with other foreigners, then the Russian Government will not long be able to insist on maintaining the scandalous restrictive laws against her own Jews." The Committee pursued this line of reasoning. In its first letter broaching abrogation to Roosevelt, it called attention to the unhappy plight of Russian Jewry, pointing out that it was this situation which had produced the mass Russian Jewish immigration to the United States. Abrogation, the Committee continued, might induce Russia to revise its domestic Jewish policy.

Indeed, Russia too had worked out the obvious syllogism from the premise of similar treatment of foreign and native Jews. But if the choice was either rights for both or disabilities for both, it could only be the latter, for Russia remained obdurately committed to a policy of anti-Semitism, which served its assorted economic, nationalistic, religious, and counterrevolutionary purposes.

II

Neither President Roosevelt nor the State Department revealed their opinion on the Committee's memorandum of May 1908, but with a presidential election a few months away the Jewish leaders now sought to obtain more positive commitments on the passport question. The party platforms restated their pledges of 1904, and when accepting the nomination, William Howard Taft promised that "the Republican party and administration will continue to make every proper endeavor to secure the abolition of such distinctions, which in our eyes are both needless and opprobrious." A more important achievement was the stand taken by the *Cincinnati Times-Star,* a paper owned by Taft's brother. As a result of a briefing by Secretary of Commerce and Labor Straus, the editors published an article by Marshall on the passport question and ran an editorial suggesting that Russia's discriminatory practices might be stopped if the United States denounced the treaties of 1832 and 1887. According to Marshall, that was the "strongest expression which has ever emanated from any non-Jewish source in America, on the subject of the American passport and the course which should be pursued by our Government." The quid pro quo was obvious: the Jewish leaders would try to deliver the Jewish vote to Taft, and accordingly, Marshall sent copies of the *Times-Star* clippings to the Anglo-Jewish and Yiddish press for reproduction.

Another seemingly positive gain came in a letter of October 19, 1908, from Secretary Root to Schiff, which said: "We have now communicated to Russia an expression of the desire of this Government for a complete revision and amendment of the Treaty of 1832. . . . We have expressed our views that such a course would be preferable to the complete termination of the treaty." However, the Roosevelt administration finished out its term without effecting any change.

Since Taft had lashed out in campaign speeches and in his inaugural address at foreign discrimination against American passport holders, and since he privately promised that W.W. Rockhill, the new ambassador to St. Petersburg, would do everything possible to settle the question, the Committee at first refrained from any pressure on the new administration. But by February 1910 watchful waiting seemed futile, and a majority of the Committee's executive could not see letting matters drift any longer. "We have been fed on similar promises and assurances for many years," Schiff remonstrated, and "four years more will pass and nothing will have been accomplished. . . . We were simply licking the hands of the President. We do not respect ourselves sufficiently to come out boldly and demand our rights." Schiff was the most outspoken, but others suggested bringing the matter to Congress and enlisting the aid of non-Jews. Finally they agreed to ask the president for an interview, which would give him a last chance to act before the Committee undertook to stir up the Congress.

Later events bolstered the Committee's determination to press for "the ruder method of denunciation" in place of "the mere platitudes of negotiation." A presidential proclamation extended the benefits of minimum tariff rates to Russia, even though the Tariff Board recommended that prior assurances be obtained on equal treatment for American Jewish travelers. When Russia expelled the Jews from the city of Kiev shortly thereafter, Ambassador Rockhill still insisted that Premier Piotr Stolypin and most Russian officials were "distinctly friendly" to the Jews. He strongly advised against American interference in what he called an internal Russian matter. In a special survey of the Jewish question which he filed with the State Department, the ambassador revealed his sympathy with the reigning party and the "objective" reasons for the existence of anti-Semitism.

Interestingly enough, that same spring President Taft asked Sulzberger and Schiff to suggest a successor to Rockhill, who was expected to resign. The Jewish leaders sidestepped the offer. To imply that Taft's choice had failed might further antagonize the administration, and to choose a successor could bind them to the

status quo of innocuous and ultimately futile diplomatic inter-
changes.

In May 1910 Rockhill was in Washington at a conference
including the president, Secretary of State Philander C. Knox,
and Committee members Sulzberger, Schiff, and Adler. In contrast to previous meetings, where Jewish demands elicited sympathetic assurances, the administration now opposed the
petitioners. Drawing on Rockhill's survey, the State Department
had prepared a memorandum depicting the situation of Russian
Jewry as one of relative calm and cited the desires of the government to relax restrictions. Rockhill added a specific warning to
American Jews that if foreign Jews received rights to travel
throughout Russia, native Jews would have to enjoy similar privileges, and the result would be massacres by a hostile people.

The Committee, challenging the State Department's information, was willing to risk the chance of massacres. Sulzberger
presented the Committee's plan: (1) the State Department
should transfer the seat of negotiations to Washington, since
nothing had been achieved in St. Petersburg; (2) the United
States should intimate that it might be necessary to denounce the
extradition treaty, which meant much to Russia but little to
America; (3) if Russia persisted in her discrimination, the United
States should terminate the 1832 agreement; exports to Russia
amounted to no more than $17 million, and, it was argued, while
Russia would not suffer any heavy economic losses, she would
prefer to keep American friendship. Though it was left unsaid at
the meeting, the first proposal stemmed from the belief that the
American ambassador was being unduly influenced by court circles in St. Petersburg and kept in ignorance of true conditions,
as his report showed. Further, with negotiations in Washington
under the direct supervision of the president, it would be easier
to hold Taft responsible for their outcome.

The president agreed to further study of the subject, but the
months passed with no answer from the White House. The Committee considered taking its demands to the public, even though

a public campaign was a gamble fraught with many dangers. It would mean open conflict with the administration and a possible loss of future bargaining power. Also, it would require a thorough campaign of public education, since even congressmen were uninformed on the problem. Even if the Committee spent the money and effort for education, there was no guarantee of public support. And if the Committee lost after a public fight, its prestige with both the Jewish and general public would shrink considerably.

At the end of 1910, with the aid of Colonel Isaac N. Ullman, a powerful Connecticut Republican and associate of the president, the Committee submitted to the White House a letter urging abrogation. Representative Herbert Parsons of New York also reviewed the passport matter in a letter to President Taft, advising him to endorse the abrogation before it was effected by a Democratic Congress. These efforts were made in the hope that Taft would bring up the subject in his annual message, but he ignored the passport question completely. Shortly thereafter the State Department sent to the president its long-awaited memorandum spelling out its case against abrogation: America's commercial interests, her plans in the Far East, her negotiations with Japan involving immigration, and her desire to pursue the suggestion for a new treaty of commerce with Russia would all be adversely affected by championing abrogation. According to Secretary Knox, more could be accomplished by "quiet and persistent endeavor."

The Committee soon learned of Knox's general conclusions, and a public airing of the question now seemed all the more desirable. If the president was not yet committed to the State Department's position, public opinion might jolt him into support of abrogation. If he chose to side with Knox, a public campaign aimed at congressional rather than executive action was the only way left to achieve abrogation. The opportunity came when the Union of American Hebrew Congregations invited Marshall to address its convention on the passport matter. When Charles

D. Norton, Taft's secretary, advised that a public address might help Taft in any action he might take, Marshall consented, resolving to discuss the matter as one affecting the American people as a whole. On January 19 he officially opened the public campaign for abrogation.

III

Marshall's address set the pattern, both in content and tone, for the entire campaign. He opened with an appeal to American pride, defining Russian discrimination against American Jews as an insult to the entire nation. The Jew, he told his audience, "is now more than a Jew—he is also an American citizen, and the hand that smites him inflicts a stain on his citizenship. It is not the Jew who is insulted; it is the American people. And the finding of a proper remedy against this degradation is not a Jewish, but an American question."

Marshall now proceeded to legal arguments. He cited judicial opinions affirming that treaties were to be interpreted in a broad and liberal spirit, and that neither party could construe a treaty to justify exceptions that both signatories had not agreed on. By making exceptions to Article 1 of the 1832 treaty, Russia violated the compact; the United States faithfully lived up to its treaty obligations, but Russia inquired into the religion of American passport holders and refused to honor the passports of Jews. Since diplomatic methods had failed to remedy the evil, America's only recourse was to terminate the treaty. Both the treaties of 1832 and 1887 included provisions for termination, but even if they did not, international law provided that a treaty could be abrogated under analogous conditions.

Even commercial considerations, Marshall continued, could not gainsay the need for abrogation, for Americans would not sacrifice ideals for dollars. As for the possibility of American capital investment in Russia, the czarist government had shown by its untrustworthiness that such investments would be most risky. Neither could the claim of Russia's historic friendship for the United States warrant continuance of treaty relations. If Russia had done anything to benefit America in the past, it had been motivated solely by political expediency; America owed no favors to the czarist regime.

Marshall's presentation, for all its eloquence and tight reasoning, omitted one crucial consideration: the alleviation of Russian Jewry's misery. But obviously he would not spell out from a public platform this basic aim which underlay the Committee's efforts. He ignored other aspects of the problem as well. Would threats of coercion effect a change in Russia's discriminatory policy? Would abrogation act adversely on Russian or American Jewry? Could abrogation fit into the United States' larger diplomatic pattern? Furthermore, even those areas which Marshall did cover had their other side.

The counterarguments were best expressed in various memorandums formulated by the State Department largely from Ambassador Rockhill's dispatches. In the first place, the State Department regarded the passport matter as a strictly Jewish issue and abrogation as serving, in Knox's words, "the interests of the Jewish population of the United States." Second, to coerce Russia, so sensitive on the question of Jewish policy, "would be an act of unprecedented disdain towards a friendly nation, which could scarcely fail to arouse antagonism and challenge retaliation." Not only would Russia remain unmoved in its treatment of foreign Jews and refuse to consider the proposal made in 1908 for a new treaty, but resultant ill feeling would bring about more hardships for both Russian and American Jews: the czarist government would no longer make exceptions for prominent Jews wishing to enter the country, and American Jews of Russian origin would lose their right of inheritance in Russia as guaranteed by Article 10 of the 1832 treaty. Besides, why should the United States bear the brunt of Russian displeasure at a time when European nations with large Jewish populations did nothing, especially in light of Russian cynicism, which interpreted the government's altruistic attitude toward Jews merely as a means of buying votes?

More important, it was argued, abrogation would harm vital American interests. Rockhill estimated Russia's annual consumption of American goods as close to $150 million and American capital investments in Russia as more than $225 million. Abrogation would remove the United States from a most-favored-nation position, and American companies in Russia would become subject to arbitrary administrative justice. Further capital concessions, now in the offing and sure to enhance American influence and prestige, would be out of the question.

As for the configuration of power politics in the Far East, Russia loomed increasingly important as a counterpoise to Japanese expansion. Abrogation would turn Russia against American policies in China, and the European powers would interpret America's anti-Russian action as an identification with the Central Powers against the Triple Entente. American interests in the Middle East, and even matters before the Hague Court, might suffer. All this, according to Rockhill, boded only ill for the United States. And the clinching argument was the question of whether national interests were to be subservient to a small group of individuals. After all, only twenty-eight American Jews resided in Russia, and the State Department knew of only four cases in five years where American Jews were denied admission into Russia.

Legal principles did not counterweigh diplomatic or commercial considerations for, according to the State Department, Russia had not violated the treaty. The qualifying clause in Article 1 adequately covered the restriction on the entry of Jews. Once in Russia, a foreign Jew was subject to regulations governing Russian Jews, for these were part of the "national treatment" extended by the treaty. Furthermore, it was contended, how could the United States in all good faith gainsay Russia's right to regulate immigration while a similar American exclusionist policy, directed toward the Chinese and Japanese, was in practice? And just as the United States, in an attempt to protect American workers, emphasized its sovereign right to exclude certain aliens, so Russia sought to exclude Jews for economic reasons. Abrogation would only embarrass the government on all scores; in any event, if left alone the problem would, in all likelihood, ultimately be settled to everyone's satisfaction by Russian ministerial action.

In the course of the public campaign the proabrogation forces stepped up their arguments. To hammer home the thesis that theirs was an *American* cause, the Committee leaders recounted over and over how Russia also refused visas to Catholic priests and Protestant missionaries. Without a treaty Russia could refuse to recognize an American passport, but she had done that even with a treaty. Legally, Article 1 might be construed literally in Russia's favor, but there was no question that Russian practices on granting visas violated American traditions safeguarding liberty of conscience. Nor was the exclusion of Orientals a proper analogy, for that referred to immigration and not temporary sojourn under a treaty; besides, Chinese exclusion conformed with diplomatic arrangements between the two countries. Finally, the Committee put no stock in hopes for ministerial action, for Russia held out vague promises only to forestall definitive progress.

The Committee, one of whose chief concerns was to avoid arousing popular ill feeling against Jews, was ready to gamble on the possible adverse effect of abrogation on the Jewish community. Both Taft and ex-President Roosevelt warned that a public campaign might stir up anti-Semitism in the United States, to which Marshall gave a forceful reply:

> If insistence upon rights of citizenship and of protection and equality with every other citizen can be productive of such a consequence, then we must bear it. We will have at least acted the part of men, and will have at least indicated

that we no longer possess the cringing Ghetto spirit. No man who is not already an anti-Semite will become one, merely because his Jewish fellow-citizens are seeking the same rights which he possesses and which are assured to them under the Constitution, to which both have sworn fealty. We cannot get rid of anti-Semitism merely by speaking with bated breath, or by attempting to shield ourselves against the possible consequences of asserting our rights in a dignified manner.

The Committee never publicly discussed American diplomatic goals in the Far East, but it could not dismiss the commercial argument as superficially as Marshall had. It contended during its campaign that even if Russia refused to negotiate a new treaty, abrogation would not harm those interests which sought economic concessions in Russia. Commerce did not depend on a treaty, and if Russia or America had anything to sell, abrogation would not keep the other from buying. Once an American entered Russia, violation of his rights constituted grounds for intervention by his government, and that too was dependent on treaty relations. As for industrial plants, they functioned under Russian charters; abrogation would not interfere with their operations. Neither would capital investments suffer, since the same motives which prompted Russia to grant concessions to Americans would insure their protection.

The Committee's case for abrogation wasn't completely airtight, but the very fact that its campaign was conducted in public covered up any shortcomings in the arguments. (Conversely, the administration's opposing views were weakened precisely because they were not made public. Secretary Knox did not mention American interests in the Far East even when he discussed abrogation with the chairman of the Senate Committee on Foreign Relations!) When the issue was put before the public in idealistic terms as a stain on America's honor and an affront to a citizen's sense of justice, other considerations became only matters of legal pedantry or crass materialism. Besides its emotional appeal as a crusade against the forces of despotism, the issue was a "safe" one. Comparatively few Americans knew what was involved, and even fewer had conflicting interests. Politicians, too, could latch on to abrogation, since it was easy to arouse public sympathy where it cost nothing. Fortunately for the campaigners, they operated when the ideal of international morality was widely acclaimed. Most people were outraged at the Russian discrimination, and those who were not were loath to pit themselves publicly against the popular currents.

IV

Marshall's public appeal did not convince Taft, for the State Department, with the help of Rockhill, was building up its case simultaneously. When, in February 1911, the president met with representatives from the American Jewish Committee, the Union of American Hebrew Congregations, and B'nai B'rith, his mind was made up. He reviewed the arguments against abrogation, and he showed them Rockhill's reports on which he relied. Incensed by those prejudicial statements and disappointed by Taft's unyielding position, the Jews left the White House in anger. (It was on that occasion that Schiff refused to shake the president's hand.) They now knew that abrogation would come about only if they could stir up enough pressure in Congress and in the country to force the president's hand. Taft, too, remained adamant, reasserting privately: "I am president of the whole United States, and the vote of the Jews, important as it is, cannot frighten me in this matter."

With an antagonistic president and State Department, the Committee was more than pleased when Representative Parsons introduced a resolution for abrogation early in February. The Jewish leaders gratefully accepted the support given their cause by Parsons and Representative Francis B. Harrison of New York and roundly criticized their own coreligionist, Representative

Henry M. Goldfogle, for equivocating before the Committee on Foreign Affairs on the need for abrogation. Parsons's resolution died in committee—a demise attributed to Secretary Knox's influence—and the Committee leaders looked to the next session of Congress and the more difficult task of seeing such a resolution through the Senate.

Meanwhile, the publicity campaign was getting under way. The first step was the distribution of Marshall's address, and thirty-two thousand copies in all were sent to members of Congress, state legislators, newspapers and magazines, politicians, educators, clergy, lawyers and judges, and even fraternal organizations. Schiff brought a copy of the address to a dinner of the executive of the Friends of Russian Freedom, which cooperated by establishing a bureau of information to furnish the press with news of political developments in Russia. By the end of February Dr. Herbert Friedenwald could report that, as a result of the distribution of Marshall's address, resolutions had been introduced and would undoubtedly pass in the legislatures of New Jersey, New York, Wisconsin, and Arkansas. The Committee then distributed Parsons's proabrogation speech of February 22 in the House, a speech which had the added advantage of non-Jewish authorship.

More extensive publicity was planned in the succeeding months. Envisioning a campaign that would last over a year, the Committee decided that "the matter should be given such publicity that resulting agitation would be so active by the next presidential campaign that one of the parties would pledge itself to bring about the abrogation of the treaty with Russia." The Committee provided the material for popular articles and proabrogation statements which appeared in the *New York Evening Mail, The Outlook*, and the *New York Times.* Articles as well as a special feature on the passport question written for the *American Jewish Year Book* were distributed to the press in both larger cities and in outlying districts. When editorials or statements appeared which might have affected the cause adversely, the Committee prepared public rebuttals. It also publicized the experiences of two of its members, Oscar Straus and Harry Cutler (a Rhode Island assemblyman), who were affected by Russian discrimination even though they were American officeholders.

Besides newspapers and magazines, the Committee utilized other channels to arouse the public. It continued to push for resolutions by state legislatures, and drew up proabrogation planks for the various state party platforms. It disseminated unsolicited material which it received, e.g., speeches by prominent men and resolutions in favor of abrogation passed by various organizations. Since Russia also refused entry to Roman Catholic priests and Protestant missionaries, the Committee appointed a special subcommittee to seek the cooperation of the clerical bodies concerned, and additional material was circulated specifically among religious groups. Toward the end of the campaign the Committee also encouraged proabrogation rallies in various cities. The most notable of these, held in New York under the auspices of the National Citizens Committee, included in its roster of distinguished speakers Woodrow Wilson, Andrew D. White, William Randolph Hearst, and Champ Clark. Public sympathy mounted rapidly, and the number of proabrogation petitions which reached Congress in 1911 testified to the success of the Committee's labors.

The Committee widened its base of operations for the campaign. It invited the active cooperation of B'nai B'rith, particularly because of that body's popular strength in the West, as well as of the Board of Delegates of the UAHC. Petty disagreements cropped up during the year, but officially the three groups ran the campaign jointly. Besides gaining additional resources, the Committee avoided any major challenge from within the Jewish community to its handling of the passport question. Also, with the major organizations allied, attempts by individuals to conduct independent lobbying could be more easily discouraged. When a Chicago lawyer sought to appear before the House Committee on Foreign Affairs, Marshall stopped him in no uncertain terms:

"It would be better to allow that part of our work to be conducted by the regular organizations which have the matter in charge and by those who have studied this subject, not only recently, but for years. The members of our committees are personally acquainted with many of the men whose action will be controlling, and we have no illusions on this subject." In the final analysis, however, major strategy, financing, and overall direction remained in the hands of the American Jewish Committee.

V

While the publicity campaign moved into high gear, the Committee skillfully pushed developments in Congress. The plan was to force the hand of the chief executive by having Congress pass a joint resolution for abrogation, and the Committee armed itself with precedents of treaties repealed by Congress and Supreme Court opinion on the subject. When Congress convened, five resolutions for abrogation were introduced. Of the five, the Committee favored that of William Sulzer (new chairman of the Committee on Foreign Affairs) which phrased the question as an American rather than a Jewish one. It immediately contacted him, sending him relevant material and documents, and requesting permission to testify in the event that his committee considered the resolution. However, when the Committee later learned that the resolution would not be reported out until December, it surmised that Representative Oscar Underwood, virtual ruler of the House, was not interested in bringing up abrogation, and it made a special note to publicize abrogation in Underwood's district in Alabama.

In the Senate, the Committee expected some opposition from the Committee on Foreign Relations, but Senator Simon Guggenheim, another of its liaisons, was sure that if abrogation passed the House, nine or ten of the fifteen committee members would support it. Once the resolution reached the Senate floor, the Committee felt confident that public sentiment would force the senators to pass it. At the beginning of the special session, Senator Charles Culberson of Texas introduced a resolution for abrogation, but Chairman Shelby Cullom of the Committee on Foreign Relations, convinced by Knox of the folly of abrogation, tried to postpone action on it, at least until the next congressional session in December. This would give the State Department time to effect a change in Russia's policy, for Knox had convinced Cullom of the real possibility of amelioration by Russian executive action. To help offset Knox's influence over the Senate group, the Committee established contact with Culberson, as it had with Sulzer. Appearing at the end of July before the Committee on Foreign Relations, Culberson rejected the chairman's suggestion for postponement and queried Secretary Knox directly on the chances of securing the right of passport. His efforts proved futile. The State Department deemed it inadvisable to divulge the progress of negotiations, and Congress adjourned before Cullom's committee acted on the resolution. However, Culberson managed to salvage something. He informed the American Jewish Committee of questions raised by certain senators about abrogation, and, more important, he secured Cullom's permission for a representative of the Committee to testify when the resolution was considered in December.

The Committee had its standard-bearers in both houses of Congress, but it knew it had to muster additional support for any definitive action. The State Department had impressed its views on the Committee on Foreign Relations; the president still believed that Russia was becoming more tolerant and would modify its policy; and Ambassador Rockhill was openly voicing his hostility to abrogation. Nor was any change in policy expected when the president appointed Curtis Guild to succeed Rockhill. Guild rejected the idea of abrogation and resented the efforts of Committee members and friends to influence his opinion.

Even before Guild arrived at his post, the press reported (falsely, as it later proved) that the czarist government had removed restrictions on American Jews seeking to enter Russia for business purposes. Taft received numerous laudatory telegrams from Jews on the success of his diplomacy, and the Committee was especially upset that American Jews were so quick to congratulate the president. As Marshall wrote: "They are always ready to be patted on the back, to crawl on their bellies, to be undignified, and to seek an excuse for communicating with the powers that be, even though as a result of it they gain nothing but the contempt which they deserve."

Marshall's bitterness reflected certain internal divisions over the Committee's uncompromising stand. The publisher of the *New York Times,* Adolph S. Ochs, described as having no definite stand on any Jewish subject, equivocated on abrogation. Though he was too influential to quarrel with, the *Times* could not be counted on. Simon Wolf of B'nai B'rith and the UAHC played both sides; officially in agreement with the Committee, he nevertheless urged that pressure for abrogation be let up so that Taft would have more time to pursue his own tactics. Since the president regarded him as an ally, he thus weakened Committee efforts. A later rift in the Committee's solidarity occurred when Theodore Roosevelt entered the abrogation picture with an editorial in *The Outlook* proposing arbitration to solve the impasse with Russia. In this instance Oscar S. Straus argued with Marshall for Roosevelt's position, which in fact was Straus's idea originally.

VI

Throughout its campaign the Committee avoided any appeal in Congress to partisan politics. Had it sought a party label for abrogation, logic would have dictated Democratic affiliation. But although the Republican administration had failed the Jews, the Committee thought it safer to seek strength in both major parties. The top leaders of the Committee were loyal Republicans, and partisanship would weaken the Committee's attempt to present the issue as a moral one. Also, as Marshall explained:

> We cannot afford to antagonize the Republican party, which controls the Senate, and which numbers many who under normal conditions will vote with us, but who might resent the issuance of a document which reflects upon the leader of the party. Taft is a very obstinate man, and will be more apt to become actively hostile, if he feels that we are attacking him. . . . We need all the friends we can get; until the Republican party acts against us, we cannot afford to become adjunct of the Democratic party, or make the A.J.C. a cog in the campaign of that party.

Accordingly, they brought their case before most prominent political figures; special efforts were made to get the backing of Senator Robert La Follette, leader of the Progressive forces, and Governor Woodrow Wilson, whose influence was growing among Democrats. There was no attempt, however, to define the issue as "progressive" or "liberal"; the Committee's foremost political allies were all "regulars." Of course, the Committee could not shut its eyes to the fact that, morally convinced or not, the Democrats would seize on abrogation as an antiadministration weapon. Schiff bluntly advised Republican leader Herbert Parsons that if the Republicans did not assume responsibility for "positive remedial action," the Democrats would. True, Schiff equivocated, a Jewish vote should not and did not exist, but if the Jews became convinced that the Republican promises had been only campaign gestures, it would cost that party 150,000 votes in New York City alone.

In the fall the Committee stepped up the personal suasion side of their campaign. A delegation of leading Philadelphia Jews reviewed the passport situation in a conference with Senator Boies Penrose of Pennsylvania and received his promise of active aid in denouncing the treaty. He further suggested that Jewish societies throughout the country publicly petition their senators.

Thereupon the Committee urged its members to arrange meetings similar to that held in Philadelphia and to publicize such meetings. A count was kept of the standing of the pivotal legislators; letters went to and from the Committee's office on progress in securing positive commitments on abrogation. Cyrus Adler toured the South and established contact with Charles Jacobson of Little Rock, who promised to deliver the votes of seven southern states. By the end of November, Schiff, noting Congressman Underwood's pledge to support Sulzer's resolution, predicted easy passage: "It almost looks as if it was becoming fashionable to be on our side."

By mid-November the administration admitted the seriousness of the pressure for abrogation. Ambassador Guild's idea for a general arbitration treaty was shelved, and Washington notified the embassy in St. Petersburg that abrogation was certain to pass during the coming congressional session. When a delegation of Jews unofficially conferred with Taft and Knox about Taft's treatment of the problem in his annual message, the president agreed that, while he would not urge it, he would approve abrogation by congressional resolution. The secretary of state was more accommodating, too, promising to impress the Russian ambassador with the need for immediate action and, if that failed, to confer again with the Jewish leaders.

Suspicious of Taft's change of heart, the Committee watched for new moves by the administration to block its plans. But Knox no longer tried to save the treaty. Realistically appraising the tide of public opinion in favor of abrogation, the secretary of state now hoped to reach a joint agreement with Russia on terminating the treaty and on planning for a new one within the year between notice of termination and final lapsing. With the approval of the Russian ambassador, in his annual message on December 7 Taft announced the progress of negotiations with Russia on the passport question and the possibility of concrete gains by the time Congress reconvened after the Christmas recess.

Knox's plan to forestall congressional action did not succeed. The American Jewish Committee was not deterred by the more amenable attitude of the executive branch, and in the final weeks before Congress convened it concentrated on applying pressure on key senators. Congress, too, moved ahead despite the president's message. On December 4 Chairman Sulzer of the House Committee on Foreign Affairs reintroduced his resolution, and hearings were held a week later. Seventeen witnesses spoke for abrogation, with the Committee represented by Mayer Sulzberger, Louis Marshall, Oscar S. Straus, Harry Cutler, and Jacob H. Schiff. Buttressing their case with numerous references from diplomatic history, international law, and Russian history, they presented a stirring and convincing plea to a most sympathetic group of congressmen.

Two days later the House of Representatives discussed the resolution. The *Congressional Record* on the debate reads as if most members could not wait to express their horror of Russian barbaric practices, their eulogies of the Jewish people and of American Jews in particular, and their insistence upon the inviolability of the rights of American citizens. The vote was never in doubt; 301 to 1, the House resolved that

> the people of the United States assert as a fundamental principle that the rights of its citizens shall not be impaired at home or abroad because of race or religion; that the Government of the United States will not be a party to any treaty which discriminates, or which by one of the parties thereto is so construed as to discriminate, between American citizens on the ground of race or religion; that the Government of Russia has violated the treaty between the United States and Russia, concluded at Saint Petersburg December eighteenth, eighteen hundred and thirty-two, refusing to honor American passports duly issued to American citizens, on account of race and religion; that in the judgment of the Congress the said treaty, for the reasons aforesaid, ought to be terminated at the earliest possible time; that for the aforesaid reasons the said treaty is hereby declared to be terminated and of no further force and effect from the expiration of one year after

the date of notification to the Government of Russia of the terms of this resolution, and that to this end the President is hereby charged with the duty of communicating such notice to the Government of Russia.

Sulzer's resolution went to the Senate on December 14 and was referred to the Committee on Foreign Relations. At this point Knox stepped in. He was certain of favorable action by the Senate and aware that a presidential veto would only stir up further agitation without changing the outcome; yet he hoped to ward off the insult to Russia inherent in the House resolution. He wired Guild on December 15 to relay to the Russian Foreign Office a notice of termination couched in terms stressing the friendly relations between the two countries. Knox also hoped that Russia would agree to his making a public announcement to the effect that both countries considered the treaty imperfect and that they would endeavor to negotiate a new one before January 1, 1913. This conciliatory move was also too late, for the Russian minister of foreign affairs, Sergei Sazonov, indignantly interpreted the notice as an unprovoked affront to Russia's self-respect, and therefore would not even entertain the thought of consenting to a public announcement. Knox managed to halt action on the House resolution, and on December 19 the Senate unanimously endorsed the executive notice of termination in a resolution more soft-spoken than Sulzer's. The House agreed to these amendments the following day, and on January 1, 1913, the treaty of commerce and navigation between the United States and Russia no longer existed.

VII

As the months passed, the earlier predictions of the executive branch seemed to come true: a bitter and unfriendly Russia, a decline in trade, anti-Semitic and anti-American reprisals in

Russia. Foreign countries did not follow America's action but sought rather to reap the benefits of her rift with Russia. In the United States abrogation brought adverse reaction for American Jews in some quarters. A year after abrogation Taft laughed privately at the joke on the Jews; from their pulpits rabbis were declaiming that the United States had scored a victory against bigotry and intolerance, but America and the Jews, not Russia, had lost out. Although it became popular in the State Department to blame the undesired results on those Jews who had instigated the campaign for abrogation, they alone could not have achieved that end. The receptivity of the American public to a moralistic crusade, the refusal of the State Department to prod Russia discreetly, and the silence of the commercial interests during the congressional hearings were significant components of the Committee's victory.

The American Jewish leaders, flushed with victory, rejoiced in their achievement. Schiff reacted with the most fervor:

> We have just passed through an episode which, in my opinion, is of greater importance than anything that has happened, since civil rights were granted Jews under the first Napoleon, or since English Jews were admitted to Parliament. . . . For the first time, Russia, that great Colossus, has received a slap in the face from a great nation, which act, I cannot help thinking, must be of the greatest consequence in the history of civilization.

The Committee doubted whether there would be a popular reaction to their principle of no discriminatory treaties; but ever cautious, it prepared to keep watch on any negotiations for a new treaty with Russia. Through the party platforms of 1912 and 1916 and in communications to American diplomats, it consistently reaffirmed its demands for the guarantee of equal rights. Whether Russia eventually would have yielded to terms satisfactory to the Committee remains conjectural, for the czarist government collapsed before a new treaty was negotiated.

The Committee's victory in the abrogation fight was largely vitiated by its inability to spark protest movements against Russia in other European countries. Since England and France were not allied with Russia in the Triple Entente, American Jews could now count on Jews in those lands to join in the struggle. Therefore, despite the expectations of American Jews, abrogation never did start the chain of events which was to turn world opinion against Russia and lead to the emancipation of Russian Jewry.

True, the Committee had proved that American Jews would not accept the status of second-class citizenship. But that accomplishment, too, did not remain a fixed principle in the twentieth century. In 1944 John Slawson, then executive vice-president of the American Jewish Committee, reminded the State Department of the abrogation episode when he inquired whether American Jews were affected by the British White Paper of 1939, suspending Jewish immigration into Palestine. The department admitted that American Jews were being barred, but hastened to add that in any case transport could not be had for such persons in time of war!

Insofar as Committee policy was concerned, abrogation set no precedents; it was a single, self-contained episode. The Committee might have learned that the government did not grant favors to polite requests alone; it might have transferred its customary reliance upon the executive branch to Congress. Yet after successfully completing an open campaign where issues were aired, popular cooperation solicited, and political noses counted, the American Jewish Committee retreated into its shell of caution. Never again did it publicly show the same degree of self-confidence.

5

Wartime Alliances

In the decade before the outbreak of World War I, American Jews, like so many others of their countrymen, flocked to the ranks of the organized peace movement. Jacob Schiff, Oscar Straus, Daniel Guggenheim, and Adolph Lewisohn were some of the outstanding American Jewish Committee leaders who figured prominently in the activities of the New York Peace Society. The peace movement, reflecting the general optimism of the age and the fixed belief in the basic rationality of man, appealed to all segments of society, and the public officials, businessmen, and corporation lawyers who joined testified to the respectability of the cause. When war broke out in August 1914 the American peace workers regrouped their forces and looked to preparations for the millennium: a postwar world in which war would be unknown. For leaders of the Jewish community another goal emerged: to secure in that world the emancipation of the East European masses.

I

The immediate plight of the Jews in war-torn Europe, as well as the campaign to achieve permanent political reform, had been dealt with by the American Jewish Committee on a lesser scale during the Balkan Wars of 1912–1913. As the small Balkan states nibbled away at the Ottoman Empire, vying with each other for territorial gains, the condition of the Jews living in what had formerly been Ottoman territory took a turn for the worse. Victims of the fighting and of disease, uprooted and made destitute in the wake of the contending forces, the Jews of Eastern Europe found relief only through the great sums amassed by West European and American Jews. Working closely with the Hilfsverein der deutschen Juden and other European Jewish organizations, AJC raised over thirty thousand dollars in war relief funds.

The Committee's overriding concern, however, soon focused on the large numbers of Jews that were now transferred from Ottoman jurisdiction to the Christian states of Greece, Serbia, Bulgaria, and Rumania. There was just cause for apprehension. Anti-Semitism was more rife in these Greek Orthodox countries than under Islam, and it was feared that increased misery for the Jews would result in forced migrations. The Committee thus pressed for guarantees for the security of Balkan Jewry.

Before the powers assembled to redraw the boundaries of Eastern Europe, an appeal was addressed to President Taft in January 1913 to make known to the delegates

> the satisfaction with which the United States would regard the insertion in any such treaty of peace of a clause which will effectively secure to all people of every race and religion whatsoever, now domiciled in the conquered territory, ample protection for their lives, their liberty and their property, equality of citizenship and the right to worship God according to the dictates of their conscience.

The Committee rested its case on the precedents of American intervention for reasons of humanitarianism and on the oft-used argument that persecution would result in an influx of impoverished refugees to the United States. Marshall met with Taft a few days later and suggested that Oscar S. Straus, three-time American representative to the Turkish government, be appointed special commissioner to the international conference to call the attention of the authorities to the Jewish question. Despite the president's sympathetic response, Secretary of State Knox, no doubt recalling the Committee's obstinacy in the passport affair, turned down the entire proposal.

Two months later Adler and Friedenwald approached President Wilson, who, after more prodding, informed the American ambassador in London that the United States would welcome a treaty proviso guaranteeing full civil and religious liberties to all inhabitants of the Balkans. Similar instructions were forwarded to the American ministers in the various Balkan states. The American views reached the peace delegates then meeting in Bucharest, but the conference refused to act on the Jewish question, and the Committee had to content itself with the paper guarantees of the Bulgarian and Serbian constitutions and the public assurances of Rumania's foreign minister.

Though Rumania made glib promises, it was no secret that, under a consistent policy of discriminatory legislation since 1878, she denied civil and religious equality to her 270,000 Jewish subjects. Indeed, since its inception the Committee had anxiously watched that country, gleaning what facts it could from Rumanian Jews and from European Jewish organizations, and transmitting the information to the American ministers in Bucharest. When AJC learned that the United States contemplated an extradition treaty with Rumania, it hoped to tack the Jewish question onto the official negotiations. Simultaneously, the Committee supported the strong press campaign against Rumanian anti-Semitism and saw to it that resolutions of sympathy for the Jewish victims were passed in Congress and in state legislatures.

While it seemed clear that Rumania could be forced by the signatory powers of the treaty of Berlin to recognize Jewish citizenship and equality, international apathy permitted her to flout her obligations openly. During the Balkan Wars she had promised full rights to fifteen thousand Jews mobilized for military service, but that promise too was broken. In 1914 the Committee considered an ambitious plan advanced by the Joint Foreign Committee in London to effect emancipation in Rumania, but the issue lost significance when the World War brought graver concerns.

II

Perhaps it was symbolic that World War I, which brought untold misery to countless numbers, officially began on the ninth day of the Hebrew month of Ab, which according to Jewish tradition also marked the destruction of the First and Second Temples and the expulsion of the Jews from Spain. Indeed, East European Jewry found ample reason to relate the Great War, as it was called, to the other historic disasters which had befallen the Jewish people. For over and beyond the hardships which patriotic Jewish soldiers and civilians shared with their countrymen, the Jews were singled out for more miseries.

Concentrated principally in the Russian Pale of Settlement (made up of Russian Poland and fifteen western Russian provinces) and in Galicia, the frontier province of Austria-Hungary, East European Jewry stood directly in the path of the contending armies. As territories shifted back and forth, Jews were accused by defender and invader alike of assisting the enemy. The czarist government ordered the evacuation of Jews from the border areas, thereby increasing the number of homeless. The Russian armies, long subject to anti-Semitic indoctrination by government and church, attacked both Russian and non-Russian Jews. The Poles, irrespective of the fortunes of war, added physical abuse to the economic boycott of the Jews they had instituted before the war.

The first call for relief came, however, from the Jews of Palestine. Since the war brought a halt to charity from abroad, on which they almost totally depended, the bulk of the Palestinian Jews were left destitute. The agricultural settlements had to find new markets for their crops and absorb the Jewish laborers thrown out of work. At the end of August 1914 the ambassador to Turkey, Henry Morgenthau, cabled the American Jewish Committee for a minimum sum of fifty thousand dollars to ease the crisis. Jacob Schiff personally pledged a quarter of the amount, provided the Committee contributed half and the Federation of American Zionists the other quarter. The Committee and the Zionists responded quickly, and subsequently an additional fifty-two thousand dollars was transmitted to Morgenthau.

Appeals from Europe followed in rapid succession, and relief drives, variously sponsored by the Zionists, B'nai B'rith, religious groups, and labor circles, sprang into action. The Committee realized the need for united action, both for reasons of efficiency and for its own organizational interests. It could not hope to raise the needed sums by itself, and rather than compete publicly with existing organizations, it favored a neutral cooperative agency. On October 9, 1914, Marshall urgently invited representatives of thirty-nine national Jewish organizations to a conference to plan united action. At this meeting, held at Temple Emanu-El in New York City two weeks later, the American Jewish Relief Committee (AJRC), consisting of one hundred representatives from various organizations, was created. However, not until the Orthodox and labor elements joined the AJRC in what later became the Joint Distribution Committee (JDC) were notable results achieved. The American Jewish Committee maintained no control over the AJRC, but it was inevitable that the relief group's representatives on JDC were among the most prominent of the Committee's executive.

Even after the AJRC had come into existence, two members of the Committee expressed doubts over the wisdom of Jewish collections earmarked for Jewish victims. Julius Rosenwald and Jacob Hollander warned that the effort might boomerang; other agencies would withhold aid from Jews, and the exclusion of non-Jewish recipients might result in popular riots abroad. Sulzberger, Adler, Marshall, and Schiff made short shrift of these criticisms—Schiff stated that "a Jew would rather cut his hand off than apply for relief from non-Jewish sources"—and the Committee resolved to contribute one hundred thousand dollars from its emergency trust fund as a nucleus for the AJRC's drive.

A year after the war began, the Committee distributed twenty-five thousand copies of a book entitled *The Jews in the Eastern War Zone*. The purpose was twofold: to disseminate accurate information on the conditions abroad to counteract anti-Jewish charges, and to alert the public to the need for postwar reforms. At the end of 1915, after receiving clearance from the administration, the Committee sent a copy of the book to the Vatican with a plea that Pope Benedict XV persuade European Catholics to refrain from anti-Jewish persecution. Though Poland was not mentioned by name, the meaning was clear enough: "In some of the lands where [Jews] have long resided their very neighbors are bent upon their annihilation, practising against them the most refined cruelty, and in many instances by means of an economic boycott condemning them to literal starvation." The Committee had vainly attempted since 1913 to fight the Polish boycott with the help of the American Catholic hierarchy. Now the Vatican responded in positive terms, and various Polish bishops took steps to allay anti-Jewish prejudice. The Committee was invited to follow up the matter when a group of leading Poles and Jews planned to confer privately in Switzerland but, warned by an official in the British Foreign Office to stay out of European politics, it disavowed further interest in the issue.

The Committee turned to international diplomacy again in 1917, to relieve the plight of Palestinian Jewry. When Turkey declared war in the fall of 1914, Russian Jews in Palestine who were not Turkish citizens became enemy aliens and were subject to deportation. As the war progressed, the Ottoman military regime stepped up its harassment of Jews, and in the spring of

1917 word came of plans for the wholesale massacre of Palestinian Jewry. The Committee's informants, Drs. A. S. Yahuda and Max Nordau, had already appealed for Spanish intervention. They asked American Jews likewise to turn to King Alfonso of Spain, as well as to their own government. Since the United States was now a belligerent, however, the American government could only act indirectly by soliciting intervention from neutral states. Marshall, Oscar Straus, and Henry Morgenthau presented the case to the State Department with the request that the neutrals also be asked to extend protection to Jews through their consular officials. The government directed its minister to Sweden to obtain the cooperation of that country, and, although it refused to do more, it permitted the Committee directly to approach the Dutch and Spanish ministers in the United States. Apparently these moves convinced Turkey to halt its anti-Semitic program.

III

When, in 1914, President Wilson urged Americans to remain neutral, the Jews, along with the vast majority of the people, agreed that the United States should stay out of the European conflict. It was more difficult to heed the presidential call for neutrality in thought, however, and both sets of European belligerents enjoyed American sympathies. This division was reflected in the American Jewish Committee executive, where Jacob Schiff (at least at the onset of the war) represented strong pro-German sentiments, and Oscar Straus publicly espoused the cause of the Triple Entente. Nevertheless, as a group the Committee resolved that specifically Jewish needs dictated a policy of strict neutrality.

In the first place, there were Jews fighting on both sides, and for American Jewry to align itself openly with the Allies or the Central Powers might only reinforce the doubts already spreading among European governments regarding the loyalty of their

Jewish subjects. Second, as long as the outcome of the war was uncertain, it would be the height of folly to alienate any European power which might play a significant role at the peace conference, which, it was hoped, would consider full emancipation; rights for European Jewry could not be sacrificed for partisanship. The Committee also followed the president's thinking on neutral rights. Wilson aspired to a mediated peace at which he, the spokesman of a neutral nation, would press for the sanctity of neutral rights. Perhaps, the Committee thought, the president might join the case for the Jews with the rights of neutrals.

In the United States, too, neutrality seemed the safest course. Wartime tensions had heightened the feelings of nationalism among ethnic groups, and the Committee looked to resist any move which might set Jews apart from the general populace, as was happening to German-Americans and Irish-Americans. To take sides publicly while the government remained officially neutral might well antagonize the administration. Also, when men like Thomas Edison and David Starr Jordan blamed Jewish businessmen in Germany for starting the war, or when the British ambassador, Cecil Spring-Rice, fumed about ties between the American Jewish bankers and the kaiser's government, neutrality alone could blunt the charges. The Committee also knew that only a restrained attitude could offset the anti-Russian clamor of the Yiddish press. The East European immigrants' hatred of czarist Russia was understandable, but if there was the slightest chance that England and France might force Russia to enfranchise her Jews before the end of the war, it was not politic for American Jews to vent their anti-Russian feelings openly. AJC leaders failed to persuade the Jewish community to their views, but the Committee itself followed a course of neutrality successful enough to evoke open attacks by the London *Jewish Chronicle* as well as the German Jewish press.

Beset by criticism from both sides, AJC nevertheless pushed for immediate enfranchisement of Russian Jewry. A few days after the war broke out Oscar Straus spoke to Sir Edward Grey, the British foreign secretary, on how the Allies might improve their public image if Russia granted civil rights to Jews. Since Straus, a former diplomat and cabinet official, had blamed Germany for the war in newspaper interviews geared to American consumption, British officials saw no reason to dissuade him from pressing the issue of Russian Jewry. Straus did so privately, with the Russian ambassador to Great Britain, and publicly, at a second press conference in London. Unfortunately, the timidity of leading British Jews prevented the full exploitation of the initial sympathetic response in England.

In the United States other opportunities, not nearly as good, were seized. The Committee arranged for several of its members to confer with the American ambassador to Russia; it distributed a translation of a speech delivered in the Duma against the persecution of Jews; Louis Marshall approached Lord Reading, the British chief justice, when the latter arrived on an official mission to the United States.

Nor did the Committee ignore the possibility of financial pressure. When the press reported that Russia was seeking a loan from American banking interests, Marshall confronted the president and the secretary of the treasury with the argument that American participation would violate the spirit underlying the abrogation of the 1832 treaty. The United States had made it clear then, Marshall pointed out, that it disapproved of commercial intercourse with a country which discriminated against a certain group of American citizens. Since the government did not forbid the extension of credits to belligerents, however, no action could be taken. A year later, when he was invited to subscribe to a $50 million loan to Russia, Marshall chided the banking syndicate directly for its disregard of American honor.

In a letter to a Russian agent in 1915 Marshall spelled out the Committee's terms for financial support:

> The leading Jews of the United States, including Mr. Schiff, have no hesitation in giving the assurance that ar-

rangements can be made to secure for Russia a loan of one, or even two, hundred million dollars, if the money be expended for such purchases as shall hereafter be made by Russia in the United States, but solely on the following conditions, which are to be complied with before any money is forthcoming:

First: The Duma, with the approval of the Council of the Empire and the sanction of the Czar, shall enact and put into operation by appropriate proclamation, permanent laws, which shall for all time abolish the pale of Settlement and confer upon all Jews the same freedom of habitation and sojourn in any part of the Russian Empire as shall be possessed by any other of its subjects, and which shall repeal all laws and regulations restricting them in respect to education, business pursuits, occupations and professions, or hampering them in their civil and religious liberties.

Second: A new treaty of commerce and navigation shall be entered into with the United States, in which is to be mutually recognized the right of expatriation and the equality of all Russian and American citizens, respectively, in the enjoyment of all rights, privileges and advantages conferred by such treaty, regardless of race, religion or previous allegiance.

I am convinced that a glorious day will dawn for Russia were such a program effectuated. She would thereby gain the undying friendship, as well as the admiration, of every true American, and the grateful prayers of every Jew.

Schiff had formulated these conditions several years earlier, when attempting to close the American money market to the czarist government. In light of these activities it is no wonder that the American Jews took offense when English Jews accused them of exploiting the war for profit.

IV

American Jews of all shades of opinion endorsed the aim of a postwar Europe in which Jews would live in freedom. They agreed, too, that the peace conference gave Jews the opportunity to present their demands. There consensus stopped. The questions of who would speak for the Jews and what specific requests would be made sharply divided American Jewry from 1914 to 1917.

The American Jewish Committee, which began its consideration of a Jewish brief for the peace conference as early as August 1914, saw no reason to abandon its customary tactics. The first step would be to gather information on the specific conditions and needs of Jews in the countries in question and then to apply discreet pressure in the right places to further emancipation. The underlying assumption that the Committee would direct the diplomatic negotiations, at least for the American side, rested on the premise that public discussions on these delicate matters were futile and foolhardy. Though at the beginning the formula of rights was not broached, it was understood that the demands would include civil and religious equality for Jews in Europe and some sort of recognition of Jewish interests in Palestine.

Other organizations and individuals, however, did not wait for the Committee to plan the moves. To the discomfiture of the conservative Jewish stewards, those elements mapped out their own policies and presented them for public approval. The idea of an American Jewish congress, that is, a democratically elected body of representatives which would formulate and submit the Jewish demands to the peace conference, quickly captured the imagination of many. A congress had been spoken of years before the war, but taken up by the American Zionists, in August 1914, it soon became the paramount issue for the nationalist-minded East Europeans. Spearheaded by the nationalists and the Yiddish press, a Jewish Congress Organization Committee was organized in March 1915. The American Jewish Committee was immediately involved. In a pattern set by Joseph Barondess, a Committee member who was also the chief mover behind the congress idea, public attacks on Committee leadership as "undemocratic" and "*hofjüdisch*" were coupled with appeals for support of a congress. The New York kehillah, too, requested its parent organization to consider calling such a congress. The Committee yielded under this pressure, but attempted to deflect the agitation for a congress by calling for a *conference* of two representatives from all national Jewish organizations to discuss postwar procedure.

This concession did not suffice, for the Committee never grasped the appeal of the congress movement. True, the Zionists exploited the matter for their own partisan motives, and critics of the Committee found in the issue a suitable cover for mudslinging. But a congress filled deep needs as well: (1) through a congress American Jews as individuals could identify more closely with the fight for Jewish freedom; (2) since Jewish soldiers fought like everyone else, pride and dignity dictated that Jewish demands be voiced openly and fearlessly; (3) a *democratic* congress, particularly in an America which was then adopting new political devices to augment the power of the common man, had become, as Louis Brandeis put it, a moral issue.

The majority of the Committee united in opposition to the notion of a congress, and resentment, bitterness, even near-hysteria colored their responses. A "calamity," Cyrus L. Sulzberger expostulated; the "darkest day" for Jewry, Jacob Schiff predicted. How could mass meetings handle delicate diplomatic questions? The Committee shuddered at the serious repercussions to the Jewish cause which would inevitably follow hot-tempered speeches at a congress. A congress would no doubt evoke anti-Russian statements, and the Jews would lose the advantages of neutrality. American Jews could gain recognition at a peace conference only through the United States government, and a congress could well destroy any Jewish influence with the government. Besides—and here even Julian Mack, a prominent Zionist, agreed—a congress could not be truly representative of American Jewry.

The Committee was concerned more with the idea of a congress, its democratic character and procedure, than with the type of demands it would formulate. Certain members of the AJC executive, notably Schiff and Straus, especially feared that a con-

gress would stamp American Jews as a "nation within a nation."
In Schiff's words:

> This proposition for a Jewish congress goes much
> deeper and further than appears on the surface. It is the old
> standing contention against which I have raised my voice
> year in year out. The question is now to be decided, and I
> am afraid to be decided in the affirmative as to whether the
> Jews are a nation within a nation. The holding of a Jewish
> Congress means nothing less than a decision in the affirma-
> tive, that we are Jews first, and Americans second. If we are
> not Jews first, if we are Americans of the Jewish faith, or
> Jewish people only, we have absolutely no right to hold such
> a Congress. The Congress means the establishment of a new
> government, a government for the Jews by which the Jews
> are to be bound. This is something new in Jewry since the
> dissolution of the Jewish nation two thousand years ago.
> . . . We will become a people by ourselves. We will become
> a compact mass of Jewish Americans, and not of American
> Jews.

Formation of a congress could only result, he concluded, in jeopardizing the security of the Jews in the United States.

Realizing, too, that the congress movement constituted an
open challenge to its leadership, AJC was forced on the defensive. It had several alternatives. (1) It could publicly repudiate the
congress (a course of action recommended by Cyrus L. Sulzberger), which would admittedly expose the discord within the
community and alienate adherents, but would keep the Committee free of responsibility with its principles uncompromised were
the congress to fail. (2) It could bow to the popular demand,
accept a congress on Zionist terms, and thus, recognizing representation of numbers rather than of wealth and position, relinquish its claim to leadership. (3) It could bargain with the
congress leaders, seek to consolidate its position within the community by moderate concessions, and thereby exercise a restraining influence in negotiations affecting world Jewry.

Members of the Committee actually did consider the second

alternative, but none would say that the American Jewish Committee had outlived its usefulness. The third path was chosen, and the Committee, with scant regard for the democratic sensibilities of the kehillah, induced that body to change its original demand in favor of a conference of representatives from Jewish organizations. Differing from the Committee only in the recommendation that these representatives be *elected,* the kehillah recognized the Committee's leadership in calling the conference. Four weeks later a specially convened session of the entire Committee membership adopted the following resolutions:

> *Resolved,* that a Conference be held of delegates from Jewish national societies throughout the country, for the sole purpose of considering the Jewish question as it affects our brethren in belligerent lands. . . .
>
> That a special committee of seven be appointed to designate the organizations to be invited to participate in the Conference, and to work out a basis of representation for the various organizations to be invited;
>
> That the Conference shall take place at Washington, D.C., as nearly possible to October 24, 1915. . . .
>
> That the Executive Committee be empowered to defer the convening of the Conference if circumstances shall arise to render such action advisable.

The strategy seemed to work. The Committee resumed the initiative; it set an early date for its conference, thereby effectively undercutting the popular success of a congress, and it was free to abandon the conference if it deemed that international conditions so warranted.

While the Committee proceeded to draw up its list of invitees to the conference, other Jewish organizations endorsed the plans of the Jewish Congress Organization Committee. An attempt to bring the two sides together was made in July 1915 when Cyrus Adler, chairman of the AJC executive committee, met with Louis D. Brandeis, the prestigious leader of the Provisional Zionist Committee. Since the Zionists condemned as undemocratic the procedure of the Committee in unilaterally defining the membership of the conference and the scope of its deliberations, Brandeis suggested a preliminary conference at which one or two dozen organizations would discuss these questions. When the executive of the Committee stood by its original plan, agreeing only to ask eight other organizations to cosign the invitations, Brandeis called a halt to further meetings. In a polite exchange of letters with Adler he suggested that the Committee reopen the question of convening a representative body before a meeting of its entire membership, but no progress was made.

In the meantime the Committee was subjected to increasing vilification, which Cyrus Adler interpreted as "a determined effort on the part of the Zionist Organization, who have joined with the Socialist agitators for the purpose of capturing the American Jewish Committee." Adler's colleagues agreed that their enemies were out to destroy AJC, and indeed this was no empty charge, for the Zionists began to couple their attacks with attempts to force Zionist members of the Committee to resign.

These tactics created bitter feelings throughout the community. Dr. Harry Friedenwald, president of the Federation of American Zionists, left the Committee after a public rupture on the congress issue, and so did Professor Felix Frankfurter. Rabbi Judah Magnes quit the Provisional Zionist Committee, and Professor Israel Friedlaender washed his hands of both groups. The climax was reached in May 1916 when Schiff, the favorite target of the nationalists (followed closely by Louis Marshall and Cyrus Adler), threatened to sever his connections entirely with organized Jewish activities.

The non-Jewish public joined in commenting on the congress question. The Zionists received endorsements from various prominent individuals: the *New York Evening Post* favored the idea of a democratic congress but questioned the Jewish assumption of quasi-national status; President Charles Eliot of Harvard asked

Schiff if it was true, as the Zionists charged, that the Committee operated solely in secret sessions. As charges mounted, some Committee members even began to regret those steps toward united action which their body had taken. In a defensive mood the Committee published, in 1915, its first history, to correct the misrepresentations of its character and activities. Schiff adopted a more aggressive tone, reasoning that American Jewry had the right to expect some organization to labor in behalf of the emancipation of the Russian Jews. If the Committee did not discharge this responsibility, he said, then those who danced around the "golden calf" of the congress could rightly exclaim: "This man Moses [i.e., the American Jewish Committee] is dead, these are your gods, O Israel!"

Aware of its loss of prestige, the Committee acceded to further negotiations. When B'nai B'rith turned mediator and called a conference of the presidents of national Jewish organizations in October 1915, the Committee agreed to the resolution that "at the appointed time the Jews of this country should, through concerted action," present their demands for Jewish rights. The Committee also conferred with the labor elements, organized in the National Workmen's Committee for Jewish Rights, with a view toward communal unity. That move led to a major concession by the Committee: at its annual meeting in November 1915 it resolved:

> That the American Jewish Committee join with other national Jewish organizations in the calling of a Conference for the purpose of considering the rights of Jews in belligerent lands and in Roumania, and that it take steps to call a Congress on a democratic basis after the termination of hostilities and at such place and in such manner as it may seem best for the securing of these rights.

In officially joining the congress movement, the Committee yielded at the crucial juncture to the pressure of public opinion, as it had at its very inception and in the formation of the kehillah.

Again the Committee's strategy was to bow to the communal will, at the same time tempering the more radical elements. At this point the Committee placed greater importance on deferring the congress until after the war than on avoiding a democratically elected congress.

A subcommittee began meetings with representatives of the National Workmen's Committee and the Congress Organization Committee, but negotiations were suspended when, at Schiff's insistence, AJC resolved to hold another meeting of its general membership. Meanwhile, the Congress Organization Committee summoned a preliminary conference in March 1916 to arrange for a congress, but since it had no assurance that its stipulation on a postwar date would be met, the Committee refused to participate. The labor group also boycotted that conference, but, undaunted, congress advocates fashioned their plans for a congress to be held before the end of 1916.

At a special meeting in May 1916, the Committee resolved to convene a conference of national organizations (its original plan for a conference in October 1915 had been abandoned pending the interorganizational negotiations) to consider "suitable measures" for securing full rights for Jewry. Twenty-seven organizations sent representatives to New York's Hotel Astor on July 16, and reports were heard on what various organizations had already accomplished for that cause. Although the Zionists did not officially participate, a delegation of guests headed by Brandeis, newly appointed justice of the Supreme Court, presented the Zionist case and invited the assembled delegates to join the congress movement. Magnes and Straus criticized aspects of the nationalist brief, but later accounts, purporting to reveal how the Committee had arranged the conference in order to attack Brandeis for using his new position to benefit the Zionists, are totally unfounded. Mayer Sulzberger meant his own colleagues as well as the Zionists when he exclaimed, before stalking from the room: "I did not come here to make fancy speeches. I did not come here thinking you would get anything but fancy speeches. Five million of our brethren are bleeding to death and they want action, not speeches."

The session ended with agreement on a congress as the means of achieving united action. After minor disagreements were ironed out, both sides arrived at a common platform. The Committee yielded on the timing of the congress, but it managed to salvage the points that the congress would not be permanent and that 25 percent of the representation would be distributed among organizations.

As it turned out, the Committee lost less than it appeared to. The rift within the community was healed, and now that the Committee was in the congress movement, American Jews could turn again to the tried leadership of the stewards. Circumstances helped too; America's entry into the war deferred the opening date of the congress until December 1918. More important, as will be seen, the congress's program of formulating and presenting the case for Jewish rights was largely the work of the American Jewish Committee. If the Committee miscalculated, as Julian Mack told Cyrus Adler as early as September 1915, it was in refusing to admit that a democratic congress was inevitable.

V

Hardly had the congress issue been resolved when the Russian Revolution of March 1917 jolted Jewish thinking on postwar rights. The fall of the Romanov dynasty, long the symbol for Jews of medieval barbarity in a modern world, was jubilantly hailed throughout the Western world. Jews, said Louis Marshall, owed "gratitude to the Almighty for the wonderful manifestation of His power," for the "hour of liberation" was at hand. When the new constitutional government abolished the anti-Jewish restrictive laws, the Committee cabled its congratulations to Professor Paul Miliukov of the provisional government:

Every Jew hails free Russia's advent with prayer, thanksgiving and pledges for co-operation. The ideal of human
rights now proclaimed by you and your associates with the
voice of liberty has caused the horrible spectre of absolutism
to vanish forever and the true Russia long hidden from the
world to rise triumphant.

The Committee realized almost immediately, however, that
the problem of Russian anti-Semitism had not disappeared. In
the first flush of joy, American Jews had offered their cooperation
to the new regime in the form of a large loan, but Ambassador
David R. Francis in St. Petersburg sent a sobering warning that
popular opinion in Russia might react adversely to a government
which dealt too closely with Jews. When President Wilson appointed a goodwill mission to Russia in response to suggestions
from numerous quarters, the Committee strove to secure a place
on the commission for a Jew. A Jewish member, the Committee
believed, would fire the wartime morale of Russian Jewry and
improve the Jewish image in Russia. The Committee communicated its desires to Wilson, but the president, convinced that
Russian authorities disapproved of "overplaying the Jewish element," turned down the request.

When rumors spread that Russia would negotiate a separate
peace with Germany, the Committee feared a return to autocracy
and further anti-Jewish manifestations. Miliukov sought to allay
this anxiety, but the growing demand for peace within Russia
contributed to the success of the Bolshevik revolution a few
months later. Under Bolshevik leadership the Russians withdrew
from the war and accepted the harsh terms of the Treaty of
Brest-Litovsk. For Western Jewish leaders the separate peace
meant that Russia would not be a party to the general peace
conference and that the rights of Russian Jewry could not be
guaranteed by international rescript. More important ultimately,
the entrenchment of the Bolsheviks brought additional concern
for the traditionally middle-class Jews, who were opposed by the

Communist government on both economic and religious grounds. And the fact that some Russian Jews joined the Bolsheviks raised fears of radical Jewish conspiracies in other lands.

VI

The Committee's postwar planning was slowed temporarily when the United States officially entered the war in April 1917, and for the duration the Committee placed its emphasis on proving the complete patriotism of American Jewry. At its eleventh annual meeting AJC adopted a resolution of loyalty which it sent to the president, and in public reports it proudly called attention to the war activities of many of its members. Not only did it lavish praise on Jews serving in the armed forces, but it also initiated an ambitious project, involving much time and money, of gathering statistics on all Jewish servicemen. The Committee executive, as individuals, had little patience with the pacifist stand taken by Judah Magnes, and they criticized Jewish Socialists, who followed their party's antiwar policy. Cyrus Adler suggested that Jewish Socialist groups be denied representation on the Committee, and in the mayoralty campaign of 1917 Oscar Straus attacked the Socialist candidate, Morris Hillquit, in speeches before Jewish audiences in the Bronx.

The stress on Americanism reflected the Committee's unspoken awareness of in-group/out-group tensions in time of crisis. When Germans became "hunjabbers" and "liberty cabbage" replaced sauerkraut, it seemed more imperative than ever that the Jewish minority conform entirely to the majority pattern. If a Jew had to be different, let it be only in terms of greater sacrifice or more conspicuous valor. What is perhaps most interesting is that during this era of heightened nationalism the Committee never once reflected that perhaps such behavior in itself proved that Jews were not quite assimilated.

The other side of the coin was the Committee's increased

sensitivity to anti-Semitic manifestations. Statements and articles containing derogatory remarks about Jews were systematically tracked down and answered. Government agencies were scrutinized with particular care, and a notice from the United States Shipping Board or War Department or Liberty Loan Committee advertising for Christian workers or an army manual commenting on the tendency of Jews to malinger was swiftly countered. The compilation of war statistics, it was expected, would provide useful ammunition for answering criticism or attacks. The Committee hoped, too, that the Jewish Welfare Board,* which was established with its active participation, would help reduce friction between Jew and non-Jew, at least in the armed forces. But even here the greater responsibility for proper behavior was the Jews': "There is no doubt that the Board and its cooperating agencies have done much to help the Jew in the ranks of our Army and Navy to render his full measure of service."

Patriotism dictated certain brakes on specifically Jewish undertakings. When the government in 1917 frowned on a loan to the new Russian government because this would siphon off funds from American bond drives, the American Jews notified their Russian coreligionists that their best security lay in the American war effort. The Committee also rejected suggestions from Jewish organizations abroad for a Jewish commission to visit Russia and for an international conference on Jewish rights, because it seemed more politic merely to follow American guidelines and refrain from independent diplomatic activity. In this area pragmatic reasoning converged with patriotism, and the Committee bided its time, investing in American official goodwill for the cause of Jewish rights at the peace conference to come.

*The JWB was formed in April 1917 for the purpose of promoting the social and religious welfare of Jews who served in the American armed forces.

6

―――――

"The Greatest Charter of Liberties"

The plan to introduce the Jewish question at the peace deliberations in Versailles was not without precedent. International parleys throughout the nineteenth century had dealt with problems affecting the Jews. In the last instance, at Algeciras in 1906, American representative Henry White had called the attention of the powers to anti-Jewish discrimination in Morocco.

The effort to establish a congress of American Jews revolved around the issue of who would represent American Jewry at the peace conference. Officially the Committee relinquished the initiative when it agreed to affiliate with the newly formed American Jewish Congress. Yet the Committee emerged as the prime shaper of American Jewish diplomacy at Paris. The sponsors of a congress had theorized about a democratically elected body which would, in open sessions, formulate the demands and choose the delegates to the peace conference. In turn, those delegates working in concert with foreign Jewish representatives (also to be democratically elected, it was hoped) would present the Jewish demands to the peacemakers. As it turned out, however, in another of history's ironies, the achievement of minority rights for Jews in 1919 was largely the work of the practitioners of backstairs diplomacy, the shtadlanim of the American Jewish

Committee. The democratically elected American Jewish Congress met in December 1918 and proceeded to pick its delegates to Paris. But the bill of rights it adopted had for the most part been formulated before the Congress met by Louis Marshall and his colleagues, for use in their private bargaining with Polish leaders. In fact, a copy had already reached the hands of President Wilson. At Paris the congress delegation, headed by Marshall and Julian Mack, emerged as the buffers between the East and West European Jewish representatives. While the Jewish delegations devoted most of their time to hammering out a list of demands for submission to the Supreme Council, the real work of diplomacy was done by Mack, Marshall, and Cyrus Adler (who was not even a member of the American Jewish Congress group). They functioned not by proclamation or petition, but by personal contacts and private interviews with high officials. Those efforts, rather than the memorial presented by the Committee of Jewish Delegations—which in fact was filed *after* the minority clauses had been drawn up—were largely responsible for the Jewish successes at Versailles, most particularly the achievement of minority rights for the Jews of Eastern Europe.*

When the Balfour Declaration, calling for the establishment of a Jewish homeland, was issued on November 2, 1917, the American Jewish Committee for the first time felt called upon to express publicly its views on Zionism. The Committee, however, both as a body and in statements of individual members, had long

---

*At President Wilson's request, the convoking of the American Jewish Congress was postponed until after the war. Yet until 1919, as it had done since 1914, the American Jewish Committee prepared for its ultimate role at the peace conference by researching and cataloguing Jewish postwar needs. By 1915 AJC had arrived at a simple formula for its postwar program: "Full rights for the Jews in all lands, and the abrogation of all laws discriminating against them." In 1916 Louis Marshall drafted planks for the platforms of the two major parties which endorsed the goal of equal rights to inhabitants of foreign lands. The Committee's labors were strengthened by outside factors: the issuance of the Balfour Declaration in 1917; the obstinacy of the anti-Semitic Polish nationalist leaders; and a sympathetic American president who preached national self-determination as a sine qua non for international readjustment.

grappled with various facets of the Zionist issue. The reaction to Zionism was based on opposition to the theory of the Herzlian program and the Zionist Organization in the United States, and doubt as to the practicability of the movement's goals.

Political Zionism, as formulated by the 1897 Zionist Congress in Basle, was anathema to most of the Committee leadership. True, men like Harry Friedenwald, Julian W. Mack, and Judah Magnes gave strong support to the Zionist cause, but the majority of the AJC leaders flatly rejected the aspiration of Jewish statehood, subscribing to the anti-Zionist position enunciated by Reform Judaism: "America is our Palestine, Washington our Jerusalem." The AJC leaders agreed that Palestine differed from all other lands in its historic significance for Jewry, but felt that to affirm a separate Jewish nationality would endanger the rights secured by Jews throughout the emancipated world. The secular cast of Zionism troubled them, too: if Judaism primarily meant, as it did for most of them, a belief in the God of Israel and His Law—interpreted variously according to Reform, Conservative, or Orthodox teaching—then how could one identify with a movement which substituted nationhood for God and a state for the kingdom of heaven? Despite their opposition, the Committee leaders as a group refrained from public debates with the Zionists or criticisms of them. To be sure, David Philipson, a prominent Reform rabbi, seized every opportunity to denounce Zionism, but he was an exception. Caution dictated a policy of silence, for to voice anti-Zionist sentiment too openly would only supply ammunition for the anti-Semites.

It proved more difficult, however, for the Committee to remain silent in its dealings with American Zionists. While the Committee conceded that Zionist aspirations might have some legitimacy where Jews were unenfranchised, it felt that *American* Zionists could offer no such justification to their fellow American Jews. Further, the AJC leaders, even those sympathetic to Zionism, considered the Federation of American Zionists (FAZ) highly unpalatable. Weak in numbers and funds, the FAZ nonetheless attracted orators and journalists who took particular delight in sneering at the Committee for its undemocratic organization, discreet methods, and lack of "Jewish heart." Frequently an Adler or Sulzberger would turn to the Committee's Zionists to call off their taunting friends. The Committee interpreted the Zionist methods of mass appeal, geared particularly to the new immigrants, as a means of capturing the leadership of the American Jewish community. Indeed, in 1912 the FAZ refused the Committee's invitation to affiliate unless its stipulation not to be bound by any Committee policy was met.

Ideology and personalities aside, the Committee took seriously the practical potential of the Zionist movement. If Palestine could be developed as another refuge for the persecuted East Europeans, then Zionism had its merits. But why alienate the Turks with an audacious demand for autonomy or put the Western world on its guard with chimerical programs and proclamations? The sensible approach, the Committee reasoned, would be to build up the resources of Palestine and capitalize on Jewish yearning for the Holy Land by making the land physically attractive to the East Europeans. Without fanfare or flags, Jews could settle there in moderate numbers, enjoy the traditional tolerance of a Muslim government, and provide another ray of hope to Jews in Russia and Rumania. By advancing such goals, as Cyrus Adler explained, the AJC leaders were better friends of the Zionist cause than the Zionists themselves, whose agitation only frightened the Turks and jeopardized the security of the Palestinian settlers.

The American Jewish Committee judged Herzl's program to be totally unrealistic. Oscar Straus, who met the Zionist leader in 1900, recorded his impressions of a man untrained in diplomacy, whose attempts to secure international support were doomed from the start. Since for them only the refuge aspect of Zionism carried weight, the American Jewish stewards saw greater opportunities in supporting general territorialist schemes than in joining the campaign to regain an arid land—one, moreover, claimed by Christians and Muslims as well as Jews. Consequently, when Israel Zangwill broke with the Zionists over the issue of Palestino-centrism, the two Sulzbergers, Oscar Straus, and Daniel Guggenheim organized an American branch of the Jewish Territorial Organization. Of all the lands proposed for Jewish settlement, Mesopotamia most intrigued the Americans. Strategically located between Africa and Asia, historically the birthplace of Abraham, Mesopotamia was repeatedly noted as a desirable alternative to Palestine: in a letter from the Americans to Herzl, in a dispatch from Minister Straus to the State Department, in Jacob Schiff's interest in the Berlin-to-Baghdad railway. In 1909 several of the AJC's executive met with Straus on the eve of his departure for Constantinople, where he was to take up duties as American ambassador, once more to plan a Mesopotamian settlement. By then, however, realities militated against success. The nationalistic policies of the newly established young Turks precluded any encouragement of alien elements, and the Turkish government increasingly clamped down on Jewish immigration to the Ottoman Empire.

The Jewish settlement in Palestine had engaged the Committee's attention on several occasions before the outbreak of the war. When the Turks required foreign Jews to surrender their passports upon entering Palestine and issued them a receipt—the so-called red ticket practice, which aimed at limiting sojourners to three months—the Committee complained to the State Department in behalf of American Jews so affected. The Committee also showed concern over the abuses of the philanthropy system on which so many Palestinian Jews seemed to be permanently dependent; many AJC members actively supported a variety of enterprises designed to promote the Palestinian economy. But in addition to all these activities, which involved a commitment no different from that felt for Jews in any foreign land, the non-Zionists of the American Jewish Committee could not deny a special bond with Palestine. Louis Marshall eloquently expressed this in a letter to Nathan Straus, a leading Zionist:

As you know, I am not a Zionist, certainly not a Nationalist. I am a Jew from conviction and sentiment, one who takes a pride in the literature, the history, the traditions, and the spiritual and intellectual contributions which Judaism has made to the world, and as I grow older, the feelings of love and reverence for the cradle of our race increase in intensity.

Marshall went on to extol the Jewish colonization work and reclamation projects in Palestine, which regenerated the "Maccabean spirit" among the Jews, and added:

[It] becomes the bounden duty of those of our people who have been blessed by Providence with worldly possessions, and who are at the same time imbued with the sentiments of love and loyalty for Judaism and its institutions, to concentrate their efforts toward the development of that land, which, after all, should rouse the most tender feelings in the heart of every Jew.

The Committee leaders appreciated the religious tug of Palestine upon some Jews and planned for an "untrammeled" existence for Jews in Palestine after the war. In June 1915, before the American Jewish Congress or World Zionist Organization had even formulated their requests, Cyrus Adler, a confirmed antinationalist, broached the Jewish aspirations to Charles Jacobson, his contact with Senator Clarke. The most urgent need, he said, was to insure the right of Russian and Rumanian Jewry to live as "human beings"; on the matter of Palestine, he added, Jews had some claim to a favorable treatment, if only for religious reasons.

The British government went further than most had dared hope when it issued the Balfour Declaration. Despite ambiguities in phraseology which would plague Zionists and non-Zionists alike for years to come, the document at once changed the Basle program from that of vague fantasy into a political reality. No matter what England's more devious motives were or the conflicting promises simultaneously made to Arab leaders, Theodor Herzl had been vindicated.

AJC privately reacted to the Balfour Declaration with mixed feelings. Grateful that England and France sanctioned Jewish settlement in Palestine, it remained wary of the phrases "a national home" and "Jewish people." To reinforce its fear, Professor Albert Bushnell Hart of Harvard University, following issuance of the declaration, categorically announced that American Jews had to choose between Zionist and American citizenship, for the two were incompatible. Several members advised the Committee to refrain from taking a public stand on the Balfour Declaration, since, they felt, it lay outside AJC's sphere and also might tear the organization apart.

But the other side mustered weightier arguments: the Committee was the major American Jewish organization to whom the community looked for leadership; to keep silent would mean that AJC had abdicated on the issue in favor of the Zionists. While political questions about Palestine were within the province of the Zionists, they had no monopoly. Also, it seemed only proper to respond favorably to a position adopted by America's allies, especially as the Wilson administration grew increasingly sympathetic to the Zionist cause. Finally, it was stressed, here was the opportunity to deny that the Balfour Declaration created a Jewish sovereignty and conferred dual citizenship upon the Jews. Palestine would never be *the* home of the Jewish people; a Jewish settlement under British authority could never command the political allegiance of the masses of emancipated Jewry. The chances of creating an autonomous Jewish state had no foundation in reality for a generation at least, and the non-Zionist leaders of the American Jewish Committee preferred not to quibble over phrases when the matter doubtless would remain academic.

The AJC statement on the Balfour Declaration was formulated by Marshall and approved at a special membership meeting in April 1918. The fact that it mustered an almost unanimous endorsement from the members and from the American Jewish press attests to its dignified and honest approach, as well as to its essentially middle-of-the-road position:

The American Jewish Committee was organized
primarily to obtain for the Jews in every part of the world
civil and religious rights, to protect them against unfavorable
discrimination, and to secure for them equality of economic,
social and educational opportunity. These will continue to
be its objects.

The Committee regards it as axiomatic that the Jews of
the United States have here established a permanent home
for themselves and their children, have acquired the rights
and assumed the correlative duties of American citizenship,
and recognize their unqualified allegiance to this country,
which they love and cherish and of whose people they constitute an integral part.

This Committee, however, is not unmindful that there
are Jews everywhere who, moved by traditional sentiment,
yearn for a home in the Holy Land for the Jewish people.
This hope, nurtured for centuries, has our whole-hearted
sympathy.

We recognize, however, that but a part of the Jewish
people would take up their domicile in Palestine. The
greater number will continue to live in the lands of whose
citizenship they now form a component part, where they
enjoy full civil and religious liberty, and where, as loyal and
patriotic citizens, they will maintain and develop the principles and institutions of Judaism.

When, therefore, the British Government recently made
the declaration, now supported by the French Government,
that "they view with favor the establishment in Palestine of
a national home for the Jewish people, and will use their best
endeavors to facilitate the achievement of this object," the
announcement was received by this Committee with profound appreciation. The conditions annexed to this declaration are regarded as of essential importance, stipulating as
they do that "nothing shall be done which may prejudice the
civil and religious rights of existing non-Jewish communities
in Palestine, or the rights and political status enjoyed by Jews
in any other country." These conditions correspond fully
with the general purposes for which this Committee has
striven and with the ideals of the Jews in America.

The opportunity will be welcomed by this Committee to
aid in the realization of the British declaration, under such

protectorate or suzerainty as the Peace Congress may determine, and, to that end, to co-operate with those who, attracted by religious or historic associations, shall seek to
establish in Palestine a center for Judaism, for the stimulation of our faith, for the pursuit and development of literature, science and art in a Jewish environment, and for the
rehabilitation of the land.

The Committee stood by its statement and, until peace was concluded, frowned upon militant anti-Zionist projects initiated by
a handful of American Jews.

II

In line with the policy of maintaining cordial relations with the
administration and seeking to elicit, if possible, official expressions of sympathy and endorsement, the American Jewish Committee cleared its Palestine statement with Secretary of State
Robert Lansing. It also kept the administration apprised
throughout the war on the shifting conditions and emerging
needs of the Jews of Eastern Europe. A few days before hostilities
ended, the Committee had a report of substance to relay to
President Wilson, an accounting of its negotiations with the leaders of the National Polish Committee: Roman Dmowski, Ignace
Paderewski, and John Smulski.

Discussions had begun in the spring of 1918, when the Poles
asked the American Jewish leaders to endorse the aspirations
(both verbally and with capital investment) of a free and independent Poland, in the name of both American and Polish Jewry. The
Americans, who knew that the anti-Semitic proclivities of Paderewski and Dmowski were spreading among the 4 million Poles
in the United States, first demanded an unqualified end to the
boycott which had been instituted in 1912 to effect the economic
strangulation of Polish Jews. The Poles, however denied that the
boycott still existed and even denied that pogroms had ever

occurred in their country; and they were far too confident to take seriously the demands of the American Jews. Armed with Allied promises of freedom, they took no pains to hide their anti-Semitism; Dmowski even boasted that he had invented the boycott. The National Polish Committee announced its commitment to a democratic constitution under which all Polish citizens would be equal before the law, but AJC's negotiators turned down the statement as inadequate, adhering to their stand that the following specific guarantees be incorporated in the new Polish constitution:

(1) All inhabitants of the territory of the Polish State shall for all purposes be citizens thereof, provided, however, that such as have heretofore been subjects of other states, who desire to retain their allegiance to such states or assume allegiance to their successor states, to the exclusion of Polish citizenship, may do so by a formal declaration to be made within a specified period.

(2) All Polish citizens, without distinction as to origin, race or creed, shall enjoy equal civil, political and religious rights, and no law shall be made or enforced which shall abridge the privileges or immunities of, or impose upon any citizen any discrimination whatsoever, on account of race or religion, or deny to any person the equal protection of the laws.

(3) At no election for members of any legislative, administrative or judicial body, whether national, district, municipal or local, at which the electors are to choose more than two members of any such body, shall any elector vote for more than two-thirds of the members thereof to be voted for at the election.

(4) Polish shall be the official language, but no law shall be passed restricting the use of any other language, and all existing laws declaring such prohibition are repealed.

(5) The Jews shall be accorded autonomous management of their own religious, educational, charitable and other cultural institutions.

(6) Those who observe the seventh day as their Sabbath shall not
be prohibited from pursuing their secular affairs on any other
day of the week so long as they shall not disturb the religious
worship of others.

One copy of these provisions was left with the Poles and
another was sent to Senator Henry Cabot Lodge of the Foreign
Relations Committee. A third copy went to President Wilson with
the request that he indicate to the Poles that putting a stop to
anti-Semitism was in their national interest. Wilson refused to
make such a pronouncement, but promised to use his influence
at the peace conference.

The rights outlined by the Committee received new impetus
at the American Jewish Congress,* which finally convened in
Philadelphia in December 1918. Although nine members of the
Committee's executive had been chosen as representatives to the
congress, and the congress proceeded to elect Louis Marshall
and Harry Cutler as two of its vice-presidents and Jacob Schiff as
its treasurer, the spirit of the gathering was most un-Committee-
like. The sessions consisted largely of speeches, as delegate after
delegate rose to express the historical significance of the occasion
or to praise the Jewish people, the administration, and the cause
of freedom. The lengthy discourses were in Hebrew as well as in
English and Yiddish, and the remarks were liberally sprinkled
with quotations from the Bible.

If the AJC representatives winced at the oratory, they did not
permit this to interfere with their participation in the congress.
Marshall was conspicuous as chairman of the committee on rights
for East European Jewry, and he and Cutler were included in the
nine-man commission appointed to the peace conference. That
commission was instructed to cooperate with representatives of
other Jewish organizations to gain recognition for a Jewish homeland in Palestine under British trusteeship and to work for the

---

*The American Jewish Congress referred to here was a temporary body
which adjourned officially in 1920. The permanent organization of the same
name currently in existence was established in 1922.

implementation of a bill of rights for the new states of Eastern Europe. The bill of rights, with only very slight changes in wording, was a copy of the demands sent by the American Jewish Committee to the Poles and to President Wilson. The phrase *national rights* appeared in the new document, but as Marshall explained:

> The word "national" as used by those of Eastern Europe has an entirely different significance from that term as used in this country and has merely a racial and ethnical connotation. . . . All that it can mean will be that if in any country those of any particular race shall be accorded national rights, then the Jews should have the same privilege to claim such national rights. . . . It is contended by some . . . groups . . . that the welfare of the State and the happiness of its people will be best promoted by the stimulation of the several racial cultures. It is not for us in the United States to determine the wisdom of that conception.

Before the delegation of the American Jewish Congress left for Paris, three of its members, Mack, Marshall, and Stephen S. Wise, met with President Wilson to present him with memorials on the Jewish position on Palestine and on Eastern Europe. Wise was a close friend of the president's, and Wilson received the delegates cordially. He had recently returned from Paris, but his awareness of the conflicting pressures at the peace conference had not lessened his determination to support the cause of minorities:

> America, through me, is the only disinterested friend that the smaller nations or States have. I am concerned about the question which you raise, not only because of my own personal conviction, but because there has been no more fruitful source of war than just this question which you submit.

The president said he originally had hoped to secure the same ends by inserting a clause against religious discrimination into the covenant of the League of Nations. But when Japan, to the delight of Poland, demanded the outlawing of racial discrimination, the proposition stirred fears of unlimited Asiatic immigration, and the entire matter was dropped.

Wilson continued:

> I may confidentially tell you what my program is. Every one of the groups and peoples that is intolerant of the Jews is an applicant to us for something, for some help and favor at our hands. In every one of the arrangements to be entered into with these new countries . . . I mean to insist that the thing we are discussing shall be written into the new covenant that is to be made with every one of them.

When Judge Mack raised the specific question of group rights in Poland, Wilson answered unhesitatingly: "Racial minorities must be taken care of everywhere, not only Poland. There will be hell to pay if they are not."

Mack, an experienced shtadlan, asked Wilson where his delegation might best bring pressure, and the world's most prominent advocate of open diplomacy replied: "Do not seek out the counsel of any one particular group. Distribute your conversations and convince all the groups." Wilson's confidential talk bolstered the delegates' determination, and Marshall promised the Committee he would not return from Paris without "a verdict or a fight."

The Committee designated Cyrus Adler as its special representative at the peace conference, and it formulated its official stand as follows: "[The Committee] does not claim for the Jews any rights in any land other than those which are possessed by or conferred upon the citizens of the lands in which they dwell; but it does claim these rights in their entirety." While the Committee thus held aloof from the fixed demand of the congress for national rights, it was prepared to go along with the nationalist-minded thinking in cases of countries where other groups as well as the Jews received distinct national status. More pragmatic than antinationalist, it was willing to accept the dichotomy between Eastern and Western Jewry and to recognize that the former, under certain conditions, would constitute a separate national group.

Elements within the American Jewish community found reasons to attack the Committee's delegates even before they arrived in Paris. Some tried to link Marshall and Adler with Congressman Julius Kahn of California, who was preparing to present the extreme anti-Zionist position to the peace conferees. The *Jewish Morning Journal* editorially questioned Marshall's right to represent the American Jewish Congress, since he was so prominent a spokesman of the *Yahudim*, the wealthy, uptown German Jews. Yet it was precisely because Marshall wore the hat of the American Jewish Committee as well as that of the American Jewish Congress that he was able to achieve so much at Paris.

III

Marshall and Adler arrived in Paris on March 27 and found themselves immediately with a crisis on their hands. The delegations from Central and Eastern Europe had clashed with their antinationalist coreligionists from England and France, who then proceeded to file separate memorandums for Jewish rights. Judge Mack, head of the American Jewish Congress delegation, termed the Western action a "breach of faith" and allied the Americans with the Eastern Europeans in what was called the Comité des Délégations Juives auprès de la Conférence de la Paix (Committee of Jewish Delegations). The West Europeans were further alienated by Mack's "truculence"; Lucien Wolf of England's Joint Foreign Committee would only cooperate with Marshall in his capacity as president of the American Jewish Committee.

Decrying any agreement which ignored the British and French Jews, Marshall set out to achieve unity among the delegates. He and Adler capitalized on the close ties which they and the Committee as a whole had always maintained with the West European leaders, and convinced them to resume efforts to iron out the misunderstandings.

To provide a more neutral setting Marshall moved the meetings of the Jews from Zionist headquarters to the Great Synagogue in the Rue de la Victoire. The deliberations were long and arduous. Marshall's eloquent appeal for rapprochement was ably seconded by Adler, the erstwhile antinationalist who had dissociated himself from the American Jewish Congress even after the Committee had joined, but who now stood ready to support the request for national rights. Adler's about-face was prompted by listening to the experiences of the Eastern Jews as well as in the interest of unity; but the French refused to budge. As Baron Edmond de Rothschild later explained to the Americans, French Jewry had to cope with a consistently hostile Roman Catholic Church. Also, for protection of their own interests the French could never support any nationalist aspirations. Marshall's efforts at formal unity failed, but he did secure the cooperation of his Western colleagues at the crucial instances when the Jewish demands were up for consideration.

The Americans were shocked too, by the inept flounderings of the Committee of Jewish Delegations. Unorganized, lacking funds and an adequate clerical staff, the Jewish representatives "would have drunk their tea and engaged in . . . dialectics until the end of time," Cyrus Adler caustically wrote. Only when Marshall and Mack took matters into their hands did the talk end and concrete action begin.

Marshall and Mack presented their brief in an interview with American peace commissioners Robert Lansing, General Tasker Bliss, and Henry White, who heard their case with the appropriate "great interest." Adler followed up this meeting with one of several personal visits to Henry White, who promised to relay the message to Wilson. Individuals close to the president were approached—Colonel House, Herbert Hoover, Ray Stannard Baker. A substantial asset lay in Mack's and Marshall's friendship with David Hunter Miller, legal adviser to the American peace commission. Miller and his assistant, Manley O. Hudson, worked closely with the Jewish lawyers and helped draft the Jewish bill of rights for presentation to the peacemakers.

The brief was transmitted to Colonel House at the end of April for submission to the Big Four; the next step was to muster support for its passage. While attempting to keep the Western Jews from undercutting the minority clauses, Mack, Marshall, and Adler restrained the American anti-Zionists, Henry Morgenthau and Congressman Kahn, from similar attacks. More direct cooperation was elicited from Henry White and Oscar Straus, then representing the League to Enforce Peace. When a Committee on New States was set up to deal with the question of minority rights, the American Jews, together with some of their Eastern colleagues, applied new pressure on its various members. Mack and Marshall resisted attempts to water down Jewish claims, and new appeals went to Bernard Baruch and even to the president.

By May 26, when Marshall and Adler finally saw President Wilson, Mack had left Paris and Marshall had become the head of the Committee of Jewish Delegations. The first treaty embodying minority rights had already been submitted to Poland for ratification (that treaty was to be the model for all others drafted for the East European states), but continued Jewish pressure was necessary to offset the opposition of Poland and others who were like-minded. The Jewish case was—unfortunately—strengthened as a result of the pogroms in Eastern Europe in April and May; Marshall and Adler brought Wilson a cable reporting a mass demonstration by Jews and Christians in New York against those outbreaks. Wilson agreed that guaranteed rights would prevent future pogroms, but, as he put it, he meant only "racial, religious and linguistic rights. . . . [He] feared that the demands for separate national rights would defeat the object of those who requested it; that it would mark these minority groups off as a separate corporate body and would thereby render them liable to jealousy and attacks."

It was pointed out to the president that without national recognition the Jews of Eastern Europe would be unable to appeal to the League of Nations if their rights were infringed upon; but Wilson believed that American and British Jews, as guardians of their coreligionists' interests, could bring such infractions to the league's attention through their respective governments.

Last-minute tensions arose when the small powers, led by Poland and Rumania, opened their campaign against minority rights. The Jews received assurances, however, that no substantial changes would result. Premier of France Georges Clemenceau was reported to have said: "The Poles may have been able to fool us, but about these Rumanian gentlemen we know something." After minor readjustments, the Poles signed the treaty incorporating minority rights on June 28, the first of several to be drawn up for Eastern Europe. The Jews did not gain recognition as a separate national group, but they secured full political and civil rights and, along with other "racial, religious or linguistic" minorities, received the privilege of controlling their own educational and social institutions.

The leaders of the American Jewish Committee could look back on this achievement with satisfaction. For nearly four months they had labored steadily. Though they had lost out on the issue of national rights, they had won, through quiet and persistent pressure, many long-sought guarantees for their less favored coreligionists. (The Committee of Jewish Delegations finally filed its brief on June 9, making it a purely academic document.) Although the American Jewish stewards had subscribed to and loyally served the basic views of the East European Jews, their campaign in essence combined two elements: a bill of rights derived from Committee activities of 1918, and a program of active behind-the-scenes diplomacy. Marshall may have been immodest but not inaccurate when he wrote that it was "given" to him to bring about the minority treaties, and that "I am perhaps more responsible for the Minority Treaties than any other man."

IV

Just as the principle of national self-determination had spurred the Jews of Eastern and Central Europe to seek minority rights, so other nationalities—Czechoslovakians, Poles, Lithuanians—were encouraged in their drives for independence. In those cases, however, heightened nationalism was accompanied by an intensification of xenophobic feeling, directed primarily at the traditional target, the Jew, and expressed through the traditional means: anti-Jewish outbreaks. The Committee delegates attending the peace conference, though they had not been instructed to become involved in anything other than peacemaking affairs, again demonstrated the individualistic emphasis of AJC by working without reservations to combat the pogroms.

Four days after Marshall and Adler arrived in Paris, they dined at the apartment of Oscar Straus, along with Mack, Felix Frankfurter, Aaron Aaronsohn (a Palestinian agricultural expert), Lucien Wolf, Lewis Strauss, and George Selden of the *New York Times*. The topic of conversation was Czechoslovakia. Young Strauss, then secretary to Herbert Hoover and in Paris to direct the program of food relief abroad, had learned from two American relief administrators of the press campaign against the Jews in Czechoslovakia. At a previous dinner Oscar Straus had bluntly warned Eduard Beneš, foreign minister of the new Czech republic, that anti-Jewish eruptions would alienate American sympathy and result in discontinuing the food shipments. Beneš had responded favorably, but Straus's guests were briefed once again on the unsatisfactory conditions in Czechoslovakia. The presence of a newspaper reporter was a calculated gesture, aimed at arousing public support should private pressure fail.

In postwar Poland the Jews were hungry, homeless, politically divided, and subject to periodic eruptions of popular fury. Reporters, military personnel, Red Cross workers, and JDC officials kept the AJC leaders informed of Polish Jewry's plight. When, in mid-April, thirty-seven Jews were reported shot in Pinsk, Hoover suggested an investigation to Paderewski and implicitly threatened to curtail food shipments. Heartened by intimations of Hoover's support, Adler sounded him out directly in an interview arranged by Strauss. Hoover promised assistance to JDC relief work, but warned most forcefully against separate political action by Polish Jewry, including agitation for national rights. Meetings on Poland multiplied; alternatives were discussed with Zionists, non-Zionists, and even a high official of the Catholic Church. In an upsetting development, reports circulated in the name of the American minister to Poland, Hugh Gibson, blaming the Jews for unrest in that country.

President Wilson received Marshall's report of the New York demonstrations against those pogroms which Paderewski denied had taken place. Since the Polish leader also supported an impartial investigation, Colonel House asked Marshall to suggest Americans most qualified to undertake the mission. Aware of his government's partiality toward a new Poland and desiring to offset Minister Gibson's intimations, Marshall agreed with House that no Jew or American of Polish origin should participate. Notwithstanding the pressure brought by Marshall, Adler, and Frankfurter, as well as by Jewish leaders in the United States, the president asked Henry Morgenthau to head the investigative body.

The Jewish stewards briefed Morgenthau; they conferred directly with Gibson, who convinced them that he was truly sympathetic to the plight of the Jews; they alerted Boris Bogen, director of the JDC relief work in Poland, to help keep Gibson's eyes open to the true conditions; and they arranged for an account of Jewish sufferings to appear in the *New York Times*. As good politicians, they congratulated Poland on achieving independence; and although Marshall and Zionist leader Nahum Sokolow deplored the pogroms in an interview with Paderewski, the AJC leaders formally called upon the Jews of Poland to cooperate loyally in the building of the reconstituted state. However, they knew that the only real chance for the future of Polish Jewry lay in the enforcement of the minority treaties.

A knottier problem arose in connection with a major pogrom in Lithuania in May. Marshall suggested to General Bliss and Secretary Lansing that the dispatch of an American military mission to Lithuania might deter further anti-Semitic outbreaks. He also pleaded with Wilson to insist that any new states carved out of the former Russian Empire be forced to recognize Jewish rights and to assume responsibility for anti-Jewish attacks by their peoples. Lithuania, however, could not be really separated from the general problem of bolshevism, for the Russian Jews were then caught between the battling "White" and "Red" armies. Warned by Russians in Paris that if bolshevism collapsed, the Jews, because of their affiliation with the movement, would reap severe popular punishment, the AJC leaders considered what policy toward Russia would be safest.

Every course of action seemed fraught with danger. To support the "White" armies of Kolchak and Denikin, as suggested by the Russian Jews in Paris, would mean recognition of the anti-Semitic old regime and would assuredly alienate the East European masses in the United States. To side with the Bolsheviks was unthinkable from all points of view. Yet to issue from Paris an "international Jewish statement" against bolshevism, an action which was considered, might further jeopardize the Jewish situation in Russia, furnishing "evidence" to those who believed in an international Jewish conspiracy. Having decided on no positive course, the American Jews put the Russian problem aside to await the conclusion of peace negotiations.

V

Their job in Paris completed, Marshall and Adler returned to the
United States in July 1919. (The Jewish demands on Palestine
had been formulated in February, before the Committee leaders
arrived, and would not be acted upon until a separate treaty with
Turkey was drawn up.) The Senate, under the leadership of
Henry Cabot Lodge, had begun its emasculation of Wilson's
League of Nations, and within a few months the United States
would officially reject all that had been wrought at Paris. To be
sure, AJC alone could not have stemmed the anti-Wilson tide, but
its inaction at this juncture appears inexcusable. Louis Marshall
is the best case in point. A good Republican who ridiculed the
concept of a League of Nations until he went to Paris, he came
to recognize the need for an international organization to prevent future wars. As a Jewish representative who worked up to
eighteen hours daily in Paris to secure the rights of East European Jewry ("the greatest charter of liberties that has ever been
written in any official documents . . . anywhere"), he realized that
only an effective League of Nations could enforce the paper
guarantees. And yet he made no effort to put the American Jewish Committee on record in support of the league, much less to
galvanize the local communities to a proleague stand. True,
Cyrus Adler wrote to Mayer Sulzberger that efforts in favor of the
league should be made through Pennsylvania's senators, and
years later, when it was too late, the Committee did publicly
support American affiliation with the World Court. But by its
silence and its often exaggerated aloofness from political issues,
the Committee retreated when the battle was only half won. The
United States was not ready for a League of Nations, and the
American Jewish Committee was unprepared to guide public
opinion to new directions.

7

America Loses Confidence

"It is sad for those of us who have hitherto been proud of our fine [American] traditions," wrote Louis Marshall, "to note what a change has occurred since the armistice." Indeed, in the decade following the war, America repudiated her traditional mission. The exemplar of democracy, the haven of the oppressed, the nation which interlaced diplomacy with humanitarianism turned disillusioned and cynical. The seeming futility of the crusade abroad and the "100-percent Americanism" generated by the war effort created a mood of fervent nationalism which erupted first in the Red scare of 1919–20 and found expression also in a revitalized Ku Klux Klan, the restriction of immigration, and heightened racism.

The "Anglo-Saxon decade" was not a good time for minorities, who found themselves beset by double tensions. As Americans they shared the frustrations of a society whose ideals had soured; as not-quite-acceptable Americans their feeling of security in that society was shaken. American Jewry was severely jolted when, for the first time in the country's history, anti-Semitism assumed significant social proportions. No longer was it merely a matter of insulting hotel signs which read "JEWS AND CONSUMPTIVES NOT WANTED"; now it was Henry Ford and his hate literature, the Klan, quotas in universities, studied exclusion from professions and industry.

The new challenges confronting the American Jewish community, added to the continuing crises in Europe, increased the tasks of the American Jewish Committee. At the same time, new conditions were developing—the growing homogeneity of the American Jewish community and an infectious anti-Semitism capable of crossing national boundaries—which would ultimately bring about radical changes in the Committee's makeup and philosophy and increase the advantage of alliances with general liberal forces.

I

The Bolshevik Revolution haunted "proper" Americans. Originally interpreted as a German-fomented movement to paralyze the Allied war effort, it soon became synonymous with treason. Bolshevik eruptions outside Russia and the creation of the Communist International intensified fears of an evil plot to destroy Western democratic life. Immigrants and strikers were the obvious radicals to Americans who sought to weed out the "Red" from the "true blue."

In February 1919 a subcommittee of the Senate Judiciary Committee conducted hearings on Bolshevik propaganda. The Reverend George A. Simons, a Methodist minister who had served in Russia, expressed a popular concept that was becoming increasingly widespread: that of the Jew/Bolshevik. Not only were Russian Jews leaders of the Bolsheviks, according to Simons, but their fellow agitators largely were transplanted Jews from New York's Lower East Side. Simons twice stated in the name of non-Bolshevik Russians that the new regime was German and Hebrew and not Russian at all. As for Bolshevik propagandists in the United States, whose literature included "some of the most seditious stuff I have ever found against our own Government," Simons estimated that nineteen out of twenty were Jews. "I have no doubt in my mind that the predominant element in this Bolsheviki movement in America is, you may call it, the Yiddish of the East Side," he concluded. Clearly impressed, the senators conducting the inquiry repeatedly referred to the "Yiddish elements" in the Bolshevik conspiracy.

Simon's allegations drew heated rejoinders from Herman Bernstein, a journalist who also testified before the committee, and from Louis Marshall. In a letter to Senator Lee Overman of North Carolina, Marshall defended the unjustly maligned:

> The residents of the East Side of New York are, as a whole, as reputable, honorable and patriotic a body of people as are to be found in any other part of the country. They are industrious, law-abiding and intellectual; they perform the duties of citizenship; they pay their taxes; they participate in elections; they have ideals; they educate their children; they understand the spirit of America, and are in every way entitled to fair treatment. There are but few illiterates among them, no paupers, and no intemperance. They are ambitious and are unwilling to be exploited. The records of our public libraries show that they read more books, and better books, than are read in any other part of the city, and, I may add, in the country. I have attended meetings of push-cart peddlers where they listened with interest and understanding to lectures on philosophy and the high mathematics. I have visited classes of boys and girls who worked hard for a livelihood, who were engaged in studying Aristotle's ethics and politics. . . . It has become fashionable for newspaper men who desire copy, to treat the East Side as a bugaboo. By this time the average citizen of other States imagines that the East Side is . . . the dwelling place wherein evils of every kind lurk. Consequently, . . . Bolshevism, with gnashing teeth and scraggly beard and dripping dagger, is pictured as stalking through noisome alleys in the imaginary East Side. The actual picture of the East Side . . . would lead [a visitor] to wonder how it is possible in these days and generation, to permit prejudice and ignorance to malign an entire community which possesses qualities which will even-

tually be recognized as constituting one of the most valuable assets in American life. . . . A sense of sadness possesses me when I consider the injustice which has been inflicted for as long, and which seems never to end, upon these people.

This letter was jointed with a statement, also released by the *New York Times,* which asserted the incompatibility of Judaism and communism:

> Everything that real Bolshevism stands for is to the Jew detestable. His traditions wed him to law and order, make of him a legalist. The Bolshevists are the enemies of law and order. The Jew makes the very center of his life and of his existence the home and the family. The Bolshevists decry marriage and condemn morality. The Jew is justly noted for being thrifty and economical, and with recognizing as necessary the institution of property. The great mass of the Jews are faithful to their ancient religion, and are ever ready to help their brethren in distress. The club of the Bolshevist knows no brother and he despises religion.

Yet, as the Committee well knew, the Jew/Bolshevik specter could not be so easily dismissed. As early as July 1918, A. J. Sack, director of the Russian Information Service, an agency of the Kerensky government, had warned the Jewish leaders of a new threat. Although the masses of Russian Jews were openly anti-Bolshevik, the fact that a large number of Bolsheviks were of Jewish origin made it possible for reactionary elements to present the entire movement as Jewish. A representative of the Hebrew Sheltering and Immigrant Aid Society (HIAS) reported that influential anti-Bolshevik Russians had voiced similar charges to foreign visitors and reporters. It was feared that anti-Bolshevik sentiment in Russia would find release in pogroms. In the fall of 1918 the American Jewish Committee formulated a statement disavowing any connection between Jews and Bolsheviks, in a move to appease the Russian masses and protect Russian Jewry.

The Committee not only had to weigh its words in defense

of Russian Jews, but it also had to consider its image in the United States. At the end of September, Rabbi Judah Magnes, captivated by the ideal of a Communist experiment, resigned from the executive in protest over the Committee's anti-Bolshevik stand. Several Jewish journalists used the incident to attack the Committee, especially after a distorted story appeared in the *New York Tribune* about some Committee leaders criticizing fellow Jews who sympathized with the Russian Revolution. While the Committee had applauded those Jewish revolutionaries who had fought to overthrow the czarist regime, it made no attempt to analyze why Jews might side with the Bolsheviks. The Communist ideology with respect to property and religion repelled the Jewish stewards. They also feared hostile reaction from the non-Jewish community to a too-close identification of Jews and Bolsheviks.

The Jew/Bolshevik image as seized upon by the public confirmed the Committee's fears. In Philadelphia prominent citizens warned Adler that agitation against radical movements would assume an anti-Jewish cast; in Brooklyn, anti-Semites set up the *Anti-Bolshevist,* "A Monthly Magazine Devoted to the Defense of American Institutions against the Jewish Bolshevist Doctrine of Morris Hillquit and Leon Trotsky"; the Committee of American Citizens of Polish Birth and Descent accused the Jews of subverting both Poland and the United States; *McClure's* printed an article by an American Red Cross official defining bolshevism as the method of Jewish control over economic life; speakers for the Greater Iowa Association, a conservative businessmen's organization, depicted the "Jewish Bolshevik" to Rotary Club meetings.

The Red scare reached a crescendo toward the end of 1919 and then faded rapidly. Anti-Semitism, however, was kept alive in the United States with the appearance of the *Protocols of the Elders of Zion* and its adaptation to American nativist currents. Purportedly revealing the machinations of international Jewish leaders in their diabolical schemes to secure world domination, the *Protocols* had been concocted and disseminated in Russia by czarist agents before the outbreak of the World War. They were brought into the United States during the war by Lieutenant Boris Brasol, a leader of the Romanov restoration movement who had helped prosecute Mendel Beilis in the notorious ritual-murder case of 1913. Brasol found a sympathetic audience in Dr. Harris A. Houghton, director of the New York section of the army military intelligence service, whom journalist Norman Hapgood described as a "sincere and energetic Jew-hater" whose hobby was to investigate prominent Jews. Houghton had the *Protocols* translated in 1918 by Natalie de Bogory, a member of his staff and an ally of Brasol. In typescript the *Protocols* made its way around Washington government and social circles. According to its sponsors, it proved conclusively that bolshevism was an integral part of the Jewish international conspiracy.

The American Jewish Committee knew of the existence of *Protocols* in the United States almost as soon as it had been translated. Charles Evans Hughes received a copy and showed it to Marshall. Utterly astounded by the preposterous account, Marshall nevertheless decided against any public action at the Paris peace conference that might lend credence to the international Jewish conspiracy charge. Thus he rejected a plan for a joint statement denouncing bolshevism to be signed by leading Jews of Russia, France, England, and the United States. In the summer of 1919 a blackmailer threatened to publish *Protocols* unless the Committee bought the documents from him for fifty thousand dollars. The Committee turned him down, and shortly thereafter Marshall acquired a free copy. (Henry Ford later reported that he had purchased his copy for ten thousand dollars.)

Unbelievable as it was to the Committee, the *Protocols* received serious attention at home and abroad. It was published in London in February 1920, and two American versions, one prepared by Brasol and one by Houghton, soon followed. Marshall did not believe that any reputable publishing house would handle the *Protocols,* but George Haven Putnam, a publisher who was "an unregenerate anti-Semite" according to Marshall, used a small firm as his front for the Houghton edition.

The Committee also heard that Houghton was giving parlor readings from the *Protocols,* that the National Civic Federation was amassing a dossier on the Jewish question, and that President Wilson, after reading the *Protocols,* exclaimed excitedly: "Brandeis has betrayed me." Adler, on information from a reputable source, summarized the nature of the alleged "Jewish conspiracy" in America: "Mr. Marshall was supposed to be the head of it; [the Protocols alleged] that his principal lieutenants were Brandeis and Frankfurter; that the Warburgs managed the international and banking end; that the department stores had a combined system whereby they controlled credits; that [Horace] Kallen was the head of our secret service and that I [Adler] was the propagandist among the intellectuals."

II

The organizations which propagated "100-percent Americanism"—the National Security League, the American Defense Society, the National Civic Federation—played up the Jewish specter. But the individual most responsible for indoctrinating the American public with anti-Semitic teachings was Henry Ford. Brasol and a fellow czarist agent had met Ford personally, and as a result of these connections the auto king used the *Protocols* as the basis for his campaign in the *Dearborn Independent* against "the international Jew."

Beginning in May 1920 and continuing long after the *Protocols* had been exposed as an utter fraud, the paper expounded the theme of Jewish control of business, finance, and the public information media. Economic domination, the *Dearborn Independent* informed its readers, went hand in hand with Jewish international schemes for seizing political power; and as part of their nefarious design the degenerate Jews undermined traditional morality.

The paper also blasted individual Jews: Schiff, Warburg, Marshall, Baruch. Rothschild, of course, was the archetype; the very name was translated "Redshield," which, it was stated, explained why radicals were known as "Reds." Unconcerned with logic, the paper fused bolshevism and capitalism in defining Jewish traits. Non-Jews, particularly liberals who were friendly with Jews, were castigated as tools of the Jewish conspiracy.

Ford's campaign found receptive ears. In a decade when rural, fundamentalist America unsuccessfully fought to stem control by urban forces, what better target for nonurban America than the Jew—the prototype of the alien hordes who filled the cities, the unproductive financier exploiting the farmer, the atheist preaching evolution, the gin-swilling city slicker flouting the moral code? While populism may not have been deliberately anti-Semitic, the image of the conniving urban Jewish money man had deep roots in rural populist regions. Ford, the farm boy and mechanical genius who made good without allowing Wall Street to get its claws on his auto empire, was the folk hero who could best tap the anti-Semitic vein. Capitalizing on the popular repudiation of Wilsonian idealism and internationalism, Ford invoked the ancient myth of Jewish international designs to ruin Christendom.

Jacob Schiff had counseled in August 1918 that "it is better all around to take preventative measures than to have later on, when the threatened mischief has been done, to endeavor to take curative action." But when confronted by the manifestations of anti-Semitism that emerged after the war, the Committee took no action, aside from Marshall's statement to the Senate subcommittee and his rebuttal of an anti-Semitic article in a New Jersey newspaper. Unfortunately, Marshall's dignified and reasoned denial of link between Judaism and bolshevism was insufficient to counter the charges of the hatemongers. After two issues of the *Dearborn Independent* had appeared, Marshall wired Ford:

The statements which they contain are palpable fabrications and the insinuations with which they abound are the emanations of hatred and prejudice. They consitute a libel upon an entire people who had hoped that at least in America they might be spared the insult the humiliation and the obloquy which these articles are scattering throughout the land and which are echoes from the dark middle ages. . . . On behalf of my brethren I ask you from whom we had believed that justice might be expected whether these offensive articles have your sanction whether further publications of this nature are to be continued and whether you shall remain silent when your failure to disavow them will be regarded by the general public as an endorsement of them. Three million of deeply wounded Americans are awaiting your answer.

An insulting reply arrived from the Dearborn Publishing Co.:

Your rhetoric is that of a Bolshevik orator. . . . Incidentally you cruelly overwork your most useful term which is "antizamitism" [*sic*]. These articles shall continue and we hope you will continue to read them and when you have attained a more tolerable state of mind we shall be glad to discuss them with you.

At this point the Committee floundered. Marshall, whipped up to a fighting mood, pressed for an open campaign. He dismissed the idea that the matter was one best handled by the Detroit Jewish community or by individual American Jews. It was a national, even a world issue, he maintained, and therefore properly within the Committee's jurisdiction. Nevertheless, largely at the advice of Schiff, the Committee bided its time. In one of the last letters written before his death Schiff said:

If we get into a controversy we shall light a fire, which no one can foretell how it will become extinguished, and I would strongly advise therefore that no notice be taken of these articles and the attack will soon be forgotten.

Adler, who also feared that the press might exaggerate the issue, seemed to place the blame for the attacks on the Jews themselves:

> We have made a noise in the world of recent years . . . far out of proportion to our numbers. We have demonstrated and shouted and paraded and congressed and waved flags to an extent which was bound to focus upon the Jew the attention of the world and having got this attention, we could hardly expect that it would all be favorable.

The AJC executive committee decided not to respond directly but agreed that all relevant material should be collected. As copies of the *Protocols* and of Ford's articles flooded the country, the Committee listened to various suggestions, including a boycott against Ford Motor Company, and submission of the charges to an independent panel or a congressional committee for investigation. A subcommittee consisting of Marshall, Adler, and Straus considered the strategy of seeking out allies and the possibilities of refuting the charges. The Committee carefully avoided, however, injecting the "Jewish issue" into the election campaign. Finally, the subcommittee agreed only to issue a public statement denouncing the *Protocols* and repudiating the Jew/Bolshevik image, for which the endorsement of the entire membership was to be obtained.

On November 14, 1920, representatives of B'nai B'rith, the Central Conference of American Rabbis (CCAR), the United Synagogue, and the American Jewish Congress attended the annual meeting of the Committee, where the problem of anti-Semitic propaganda was discussed in executive session. The atmosphere was generally one of aggrieved bewilderment. As Rabbi Samuel Schulman of the CCAR observed, he never would have thought twenty-five years before that, as an American, he would be faced with such charges. Yet the mood generated action rather than despair. Aware of the extensive circulation of the libels and the devious tactics on the part of the Ford organization, the group agreed that this most serious problem ever to confront American Jewry must not go on unanswered. In the overwhelming opinion of the assembly, this called for a widely publicized fight against Ford, for which Christian cooperation was needed. Stressing the need for Jewish unity, the delegates also decided to issue the statement of the executive and to invite other organizations to sign it. Some even envisaged a long-range campaign and talked of a special body or bureau to direct the Jewish response. Ultimately, however, they rested their hope for success on their faith in enlightened American opinion. Marshall summed it up succinctly: "If we have lived in this country as long as we have, have attained the rights that we have in this country, have worked for this country as we have, and our assurance as men is not to receive consideration, then adieu, good-bye, for our future."

The Committee's course of action—which basically followed Marshall's urging to present a sanely drawn, well-documented Jewish case and let the truth win out in the marketplace of ideas —was rather simplistic. It did not examine the reasons for the popularity of the *Protocols* or the eagerness with which certain groups received the Ford propaganda. Only rarely did it refer to the political or financial motives of the anti-Jewish agitators. More typical was its dismissal of Henry Ford as an illiterate and mentally unbalanced fanatic who, Marshall thought, had been influenced by the anti-Semitism of David Starr Jordan. The American public, it believed, was not anti-Semitic, merely misled.

The Committee did not attack Ford publicly or try to reach his supporters. It was too late to begin a program of education geared to the rural elements; nor was the Committee equipped to handle such a task. The Committee's course of action, and the only one with any chance to succeed, was to inform and galvanize enlightened, liberal, and as yet uninfected public opinion against the anti-Semitic onslaught. Following this strategy, on December 1, 1920, the Committee published a statement cosigned by eight other Jewish organizations, exposing the spurious character of the *Protocols* and contesting the Jew/Bolshevik image. Referring to Ford as a dupe, the statement charged the fomenters of anti-Semitism with "seeking a scapegoat for their own sins, so that they may be enabled under the cover of a false issue to deceive the public." What those anti-Semites hoped to achieve, the Committee did not reveal.

The statement was widely distributed, and it was followed shortly by the Committee-sponsored book by Herman Bernstein, *The History of a Lie,* which analyzed the layers of untruthful accretions that culminated in the Russian *Protocols.* Still believing in the efficacy of apologetics, the Committee also distributed thousands of copies of a volume by John Spargo, *The Jew and American Ideals,* as well as Joseph Jacobs's *Jewish Contributions to Civilization.* AJC refused to dignify with an answer any specific charge which appeared in the *Dearborn Independent,* but Cyrus Adler believed that studies should be made, and the results publicized, of the extent of Jewish control over the finances and press of the country. When Ford's paper blamed the Jews for Benedict Arnold's treason, Adler also suggested that A. S. W. Rosenbach prepare a response.

Holding fast to a position of dignified indignation and reasoned rejoinder, the Committee refused to sanction any rash attack on Ford. It advised against a boycott, against attempts to ban the *Dearborn Independent* from libraries, against investigative commissions, and against individual libel suits. The Committee, however, did not reflect the sentiment of the enire Jewish community, and others proceeded with suits against Ford and resolutions calling for a congressional investigation. AJC reached its target, however. The educated public was quick to denounce Ford, and the criticisms of the reputable press and the Protestant clergy were eminently gratifying to the Committee. The high point of the non-Jewish response came in a statement, "The Peril of Racial Prejudice," written by John Spargo and signed by Wilson, Taft, and a hundred other leading Americans.

The furor over the *Protocols* had largely died down by the end of 1921. Ford's campaign lasted five years longer and did not seem to have been significantly altered by Marshall's attempts to enlist the aid of Presidents Harding and Coolidge. Finally, in the summer of 1927 representatives of Ford approached Marshall with offers of peace. As Marshall reported:

> They told me that they thought that Ford would be willing to do whatever I thought was right for the purpose of putting an end to existing conditions, that he had found that Cameron, the editor of the *Dearborn Independent,* had been deceiving him, and that he had no idea of the real character of the publications which appeared in the *Dearborn Independent.* . . . I told them I was interested merely in protecting the good name of the Jews and in procuring from Ford a document which would be acceptable by the Jews and which would so far as it was possible make amends for the harm that he had tried to do them. . . . They left saying they would confer with Ford and see me later. About a week or ten days thereafter they called on me again and said that my terms were acceptable to Ford and that if I would prepare such a statement as I deemed necessary they would present it to him. . . . Accordingly I prepared the paper . . . and . . . Ford . . . agreed to make the statement just as it had been prepared.

Marshall said that he aimed to explode the Ford myth and to expose him as "an ass" and "a liar" in all "his intellectual nakedness." Indeed, if he were Ford, Marshall said, he would not have signed so humiliating a statement. Marshall added a further gibe when he assured Ford that he took his apology seriously:

> So far as my influence can further that end, it will be exerted, simply because there flows in my veins the blood of ancestors who were inured to suffering and nevertheless remained steadfast in their trust in God. Referring to the teachings of the Sermon on the Mount, Israel Zangwill once said that we Jews are after all the only Christians. He might

have added that it is because essentially the spirit of forgiveness is a Jewish trait.

III

Ford's anti-Jewish campaign coincided with the rabble-rousing activities of the Ku Klux Klan, which in its crusade to keep American "pure" directed its hatred at Jews as well as at Negroes and Catholics. Capitalizing particularly on rural fears of the immoral city, the Klan grew in membership until public indignation and internal scandals caused a temporary disintegration. Since the Jews were not the sole targets of the Klan, the American Jewish Committee consistently claimed that the problem was one for all Americans rather than for Jews alone. A directive to that effect went out to AJC members, other organizations and the Jewish press urging that since the Klan pretended to represent Protestants, the matter be left to the Protestant churches. Non-Jewish leaders agreed with this reasoning, for, as Marshall explained: "The moment that the Jews take the lead in fighting the Klan you may rest assured that the immediate effect will be to increase the numbers of the Klan, because many of our enemies who otherwise would never think of joining the Klan would permit their animosity to the Jews to lead them into that organization." When invited by the *New York World* to comment on Klan policy, Marshall branded the society as un-American and again called for its repudiation by the American people, and particularly by the Protestant churches.

In true Committee fashion, quiet pressure exerted in the right places was considered the proper procedure; thus, when the Committee learned that an active Klan group in Idaho was openly threatening Jews and Catholics, both Marshall and Lewis Strauss informed the Union Pacific Railroad that the ringleaders were in its employ. Being opposed to open agitation, the Committee urged Jews not to work for anti-Klan planks in the 1924 platforms of the political parties. Marshall publicly repudiated the Hebrew-American League of New Jersey, which campaigned against Coolidge for not having condemned the Klan, though Marshall himself wrote the president urging an unqualified pronouncement on the subject.

Logic perhaps dictated that the Committee join with other victims of Klan agitation for mutual defense. But fear obstructed cooperation. The Committee remembered the Presbyterian minister in Philadelphia who accused Jews and Catholics of conspiring to do away with Sunday laws and with Bible-reading in the schools. Yet there was a realization that discrimination directed against one group threatened all groups. Marshall (who became a director of the NAACP in 1923) filed a brief for the Committee as amicus curiae in the case contesting the Klan-inspired law prohibiting parochial schools in Oregon. Officially, he intervened on behalf of Jewish parents and teachers who maintained Jewish schools, but his plea rested on the broad grounds of freedom of thought. "If private, parochial and denominational schools are . . . to be deprived of the right to educate the children and the parents are forbidden to send the children to such schools," Marshall argued, "then we shall be in precisely the same situation as that which now exists in Russia."

IV

Neither Henry Ford nor the Ku Klux Klan could muster sustained political support. Of far greater significance in putting the Anglo-Saxon stamp on American society was the immigration legislation of the 1920s. The isolationism sweeping the country in the wake of the war fed the general demand for restriction of immigration. It seemed, too, that Americans had lost faith in the efficacy of the "melting pot." In a far-ranging analysis of the immigration question Cyrus Adler noted:

A great many people . . . still cherished the idea of America as an asylum for the persecuted and oppressed and had also conceived the notion that through our public school system, the immigrants . . . were being surely molded into the American body politic. When the draft law was passed and our Army was assembled, this theory . . . was rudely overthrown. It was found that we had tens of thousands of citizens who did not know enough English to get the word of command; that even in a state like Massachusetts there were two entire regiments of which this was true. One of Roosevelt's last phrases was that it appeared that we had not developed a nation, but a polyglot boarding house.

Adler continued:

The forces that are operating toward . . . restriction are too numerous and powerful to be overcome. The American Federation of Labor, in spite of its fine phrases, is one of the most potent of these influences. Right here in Philadelphia, all of the publications controlled by Mr. Curtis, himself a New England man, are militantly restrictionist.

Adler also took note of the racist teachings in respectable scientific articles which promoted the restrictionist sentiment:

Our scientific men, especially the biologists and anthropologists, have taken up the subject of the mixed race which they declare is being produced here and have issued all kinds of warnings against it as tending to degeneracy. Professor Henry Fairfield Osborne of Columbia, probably the most distinguished man in the biological sciences in America, is taking this ground and Professor Conklin of Princeton, a very eminent zoologist is following the same line.

These views, you will see, therefore, are being spread not only among the masses through a five-cent paper like the *Saturday Evening Post,* but in college and university circles by leading professors. . . . The people who are promulgating these ideas are sincere in their conviction that the American people, the American spirit, and the English language are seriously threatened.

Unrestricted immigration was, of course, a cornerstone of American Jewish Committee policy. In opposing restriction, however, the Committee was motivated by more than tradition. Neither the war nor the minority treaties had solved the Jewish problem in Eastern Europe, and the need for refuge remained as great as ever. In addition, though restriction would affect all minorities, it manifested a particularly anti-Semitic strain. Burton Hendrick, whose study *The Jews in America* was serialized by the popular *World's Work,* proclaimed the Jews of Eastern Europe to be racially inferior and called for barring their entry. Kenneth Roberts, in the *Saturday Evening Post,* and Gino Speranza, also in the *World's Work,* pursued a similar line. Even more disquieting was the consular report submitted to the House Committee on Immigration and Naturalization: written by Wilbur J. Carr, an anti-Semite of long standing, it abounded in derogatory evaluations of Jewish immigrants.

Feelings favoring restrictions on immigration ran high, and in 1921 Congress passed the act which inaugurated the system of immigration quotas. Based on the number of foreign-born from each country of origin in the United States in 1910, the law restricted annual immigration to 3 percent of each national total. It was soon discovered that the 1910 base allowed far too many immigrants from southeastern Europe to please the advocates of Anglo-Saxon superiority, and a new act was passed in 1924, cutting the percentage to two and changing the base year to 1890. The new law also provided for the eventual computation of quotas according to the national origins of the population, thus pitting ethnic groups against each other in formal legislation.

The American Jewish Committee realized that restrictionism was really aimed at prohibiting immigration altogether, and Marshall, who to all intents and purposes was the Committee in those years, kept up an incessant barrage, writing to congressmen, testifying at hearings, pleading for presidential vetoes, and challenging racist-minded journalists. At the same time, the Committee had to resist the pressures of foreign Jews, particularly the English, who sought to keep the gates of America open to needy Jews. "Hands off," Marshall warned them, pointing out that their efforts would only arouse more concerted restrictionist drives. He also demanded to know how they dared mount such a campaign when they had meekly acquiesced in their own country's restrictionist policy.

A more serious problem was posed by those within the American Jewish community who approved of restrictionism; like Speranza, who had whistled a different tune when he served with Marshall on the New York Immigration Committee in 1908, these Jews abandoned principles for conformity. There was also the problem of the Consular Service, which was quick to spread anti-Semitic slurs, determined to exclude Jews from its ranks, and not averse to capitalizing on the misfortune of foreigners who applied for visas.

Under Marshall's leadership the Committee raised various objections to restrictionist legislation. It charged that the laws were arbitrary, undemocratic, divisive in effect, and contrary to America's historic position. Immigrants, it noted, had contributed to all aspects of American progress, and their sacrifices for the country, as proved by the lists of war casualties, could not be disputed. The mechanics of computing quotas and national origins, it argued, were cumbersome and would lead to inaccuracies. What of the Jews in particular—were they to be counted as a separate nationality? There was no reason to fear inundation by immigrants, the Committee argued, and the immigration law of 1917 was sufficient to exclude the physically and morally undesirable. Before succumbing to racist teachings, the Committee advised, Congress would do well to set up an immigration commission, similar to that of 1907, to study the question exhaustively. Finally, it was politically unwise for a Republican Congress to antagonize the growing numbers of immigrant voters in the urban areas. Marshall, a loyal Republican, pointed out to Senator David Reed, a leader of the restrictionists, the folly of insulting the new Americans:

> The Honorable Alfred E. Smith, thrice Governor of the State of New York, naturally a Republican State, understands that, because he takes pains to familiarize himself with all of his constituents and their needs. He laughs with them and weeps with them, not as an actor, but as a genuine human being. . . . He is a friend of the people 365 days in the year, and not merely during a political campaign.

Although there were eight Jews in the House of Representatives and urban progressivism was developing, the city voters in or out of ethnic blocs could not counteract the restrictionist forces. "Our gates are closed," Marshall wrote, "except to Mexican peons and mythical Nordics."

Despite its seemingly futile campaign, the Committee did achieve some results. Marshall claimed that its opposition frustrated the original attempt by the House of Representatives to suspend immigration entirely. Once the immigration laws were passed, the Committee dug in to resist more drastic legislation, particularly on registration and deportation of aliens. The specter of government surveillance and bureaucratic despotism was effectively raised by men like Marshall and Max J. Kohler, and those schemes, despite presidential endorsement, did not succeed. The Committee also worked for lenient interpretation of naturalization laws, even for non-Jewish applicants, appealing on the basis of America's time-honored recognition of the right of expatriation.

The Committee sympathized particularly with those immigrants whose chances of bringing their families to the United States were substantially reduced by the new quotas, and those would-be immigrants who held American visas but learned en route to the United States, or when they were about to disembark, that their national quota was filled.

To discuss ways to helping these stranded immigrants, denied entry into the United States and repatriation to their former countries, the Committee joined with the American Jewish Congress, the Hebrew Sheltering and Immigrant Aid Society, the National Council of Jewish Women, and the three leading Jewish labor organizations in calling a meeting of national Jewish societies. Over forty organizations sent representatives to the Conference on Jewish Refugees, held in June 1924, which led to the establishment of an emergency committee under Marshall's presidency. This committee determined to raise five hundred thousand dollars to be used for the following purposes:

(1) to alleviate the plight of the stranded refugees;
(2) to make possible the repatriation of those who wish to return to the countries of their origin;
(3) to investigate immigration conditions in Palestine and in other countries; and
(4) to help, insofar as the funds will permit, the settlement of the refugees in countries which are found to possess opportunities for such settlement.

The Committee made financial contributions to those Jews who ultimately found refuge in Canada and Cuba, and it surveyed the possibility of more extensive settlement in Mexico. For the immediate relief of the five to six thousand refugees stranded at ports of embarkation, it joined in a cooperative venture with the Jewish Colonization Association and the Emigdirect*; the new organization, called the United Evacuation Committee, had disposed of over four thousand cases by November 1926. This united action was severely restricted by the fact that most countries shut their doors to aliens.

*An agency created in the 1920s to direct emigration of Jews from Eastern Europe.

V

The same respectable Americans who denounced the anti-Semitism of the *Dearborn Independent* and the Klan often helped other forms of anti-Semitism to become entrenched. Thus the president of Harvard, A. Lawrence Lowell, advocated a numerus clausus for Jews in American universities. The American Jewish Committee officially took no part in opposing the college quota system, but individual members, particularly Marshall and Judge Mack, a member of Harvard's Board of Overseers, quietly applied whatever pressure they could on the faculty committee studying the admissions policy. The suggestions for official discrimination were rejected, but Lowell achieved the same ends by instituting complicated admission procedures. Columbia and New York University had already cut their percentage of Jewish students; unofficial quotas were common, particularly in centers with large Jewish populations. Even the Jewish student who passed the hurdle of admission usually encountered prejudice on the campus. If he wanted to go on to a career in medicine or college teaching, he faced even greater obstacles. His only chance in the academic world, the story went, was to have Felix Warburg endow a chair for him.

The same pattern of discrimination pervaded the business world. Reputable firms openly advertised for Christian office help; in the order of preference Jews ranked below Italians and foreigners. The *New York Times,* which refused to print discriminatory advertisements, was charged with being an "organ of Jewish propaganda." As corporate growth and consolidation enhanced the power of the managerial class in industry, Jews as a group were excluded from national firms, with few distinctions, if any, being made between individual Jews or between the old and new elements in the Jewish community.

The American Jewish Committee developed no positive program to combat the creeping discrimination. (B'nai B'rith's Anti-Defamation League, Cyrus Adler snorted, was ridiculous both in name and in fact.) Marshall spent a great deal of time writing long letters to individual anti-Semites and the Committee toyed with the idea of sponsoring an anthropological survey to examine the validity of racist premises, but it formulated no guidelines for the behavior of the community. A loss of confidence was inevitable. In 1929 Cyrus L. Sulzberger, a Committee leader since its founding, soberly reflected that there was "a good deal to make one ponder how long it will be before antisemitism becomes virulent in the United States. . . . I do not wish to 'paint the devil on the wall' [but] almost any day we may find conditions here much worse than they have been in the past."

VI

Though beset by problems at home, the Committee could not cast aside its responsibilities to the European Jews, who, in the new postwar states of Eastern and Central Europe, found little respite from their woes. Heightened nationalism, the drive for economic autarchy, and the advance of popular education brought the exclusion of Jews from trade, the professions, and the civil service. The boycott, an effective prewar weapon in Poland, spread to other regions and was rendered more effective by the creation of state monopolies. Cultivated by the press and fostered by the government, anti-Semitism also found outlets in physical violence, political restrictions, the numerus clausus in educational institutions, and special discriminatory taxes. The universities in particular were hotbeds of hatred, and student riots against Jews were common. The rights guaranteed to minorities by the peace treaties were openly flouted as the newly constructed states proved the accuracy of Jacob Schiff's quip: "Chambermaids when they marry make the most tyrannical mistresses." In the Soviet Union, the Bolshevik reordering of the economy and hostility to religion created a new set of problems; nor was popular anti-Semitism in Russia laid to rest.

The Jews in these lands had few alternatives. Their genuine desire to prove their patriotism was rebuffed by government and citizenry alike, and they lacked the political strength to effect official changes. Complaints over the infraction of minority rights could be heard by the League of Nations; but in most cases a member state had to file the complaint, and there was no one to speak for the Jews. Even emigration, the solution of desperation, became more difficult as Western nations shut their doors to refugees.

The American Jewish Committee, in attempting to cope with the ramifications of postwar European discrimination, could not resort to its time-honored practices. Letters still went to the State Department and to American diplomats reporting on physical violence suffered by Jews, but it became increasingly clear that an isolationist government would not resuscitate its prewar policy of humanitarian diplomacy. In fact, the government finally announced that it could make no representations to a foreign state on issues in which no American citizens were involved and no American interests at stake. Moreover, since the United States was a member of neither the League of Nations nor the World Court, it was pointless to seek her defense of the minority clauses. Given the chauvinistic sentiment in the country at large, it was even more unrealistic to try to activate the government through popular or congressional pressure.

Thrown more and more upon its own resources, the Committee reversed its prewar policy of open hostility toward anti-Semitic countries. It now set out to cultivate the goodwill of the governments in question, particularly Rumania and Poland, and it sought out friendly contacts with foreign emissaries and tried to convince them that the East European Jews were sincerely patriotic and would prove themselves assets to their respective homelands. Since the Committee believed that reforms could only be effected by the new states themselves, it tried to control the more vocal critics in the Jewish community. Thus it stopped individual congressmen from pushing unfriendly resolutions, re-

jected suggestions for investigative commissions which would
kindle the resentment of the newly independent states, and in
1928 advised Jews not to block Rumania's negotiations for a $60
million loan.

The Committee's new policy of cooperation with governments traditionally hostile to Jews was dictated also by its new
theory on the causes of anti-Semitism. Although it usually shied
away from the theoretical and applied itself only to the practical,
the Committee came to believe that anti-Semitism was the product of abnormal economic conditions which, if set right, would
in turn reduce or eliminate anti-Jewish persecution. The wise
course, therefore, was to encourage such states as Poland and
Rumania in solving their economic problems.

The Committee was perhaps too optimistic in its evaluation
of the situation, but it did see a marked improvement over the
prewar years. To be sure, the League of Nations was weak; but
the minority treaties still held great promise. In fact, the Committee had only harsh words for Turkish Jewry for renouncing the
guarantees of the Treaty of Lausanne. Whenever mass emigration from Eastern Europe was mentioned, Marshall argued that
it was unnecessary, undesirable, and unfeasible. When others
suggested self-defense units for Eastern Jewry, the Committee
shut its ears. Nor did the Committee deem the situation serious
enough to warrant long-range planning with other organizations.
It bitterly opposed the establishment of a permanent American
Jewish Congress and proposals for an international conference
on Jewish rights. It preferred the non-Zionist Alliance Israélite
Universelle and Joint Foreign Committee, but when Marshall met
with representatives of the European organizations in 1928 the
Committee bound itself only to an exchange of information.

VII

In the 1920s anti-Semitic agitation in Germany appeared no different from that in other countries. Max Warburg described it as "alarming," and the Committee contributed five thousand dollars in 1922 to counteract the trend. However, in its annual report for that year the Committee did not show particular concern:

> Here too [in Germany] the iron hand of the militaristic agitators and of its dethroned aristocrats is manifest. It would be a confession of the bankruptcy of civilization if these manifestations of barbarism and stupidity were to prevail for any length of time. Good sense and the plainest dictates of humanity and decency are certain to triumph.

Although Marshall brought the question of Nazi threats against Jews to the attention of Secretary of State Charles Evans Hughes, he himself could not believe the accuracy of the reports. In 1924 he wrote reassuringly about the Hitler movement, which he dubbed the "German Ku Klux Klan":

> From all that I have been able to learn, the utterances of that unspeakable group are nothing more than sound and fury. They are irritating and humiliating, but at the same time, like rattlesnakes, they give notice of their purposes so that it is easier to deal with them than would be possible were they to operate in the dark and in silence. There is not the slightest likelihood that their plan will ever be carried out to the slightest extent.

When the leading German Jewish defense organization, the Centralverein deutscher Staatsbürger jüdischen Glaubens, appealed for help from the Committee, Marshall believed their plea exaggerated. American Jews had successfully fought Ford and the *Protocols* with ridicule and contempt; German Jews might do the same with the Nazis. Marshall pointed out that anti-Semitism was nothing new in German history, implying that an accommodation could be worked out without serious threat to the continuing survival of German Jewry. Not all Committee men shared Marshall's confidence; Adler, Felix Warburg, and Morris Waldman (appointed secretary in 1928) listened more attentively to the reports from German sources. However, Marshall's determination of Committee policy was unquestioned, and in this episode his judgment reflected that of most individuals steeped in the liberal traditions of the nineteenth century.

With anti-Semitism taking a virulent form in so many countries, rumors spread of international cooperation among the various hate organizations. Felix Warburg's brother reported in 1920 that Belgrade was the headquarters for an anti-Semitic organization operating throughout the world. The Committee was also informed that anti-Semitic projects in Germany were financed largely by Henry Ford and the American Ku Klux Klan. The same story, according to an article in the *New York Times*, was current in Berlin. That Ford's hatemongering campaign, including the translation of *The International Jew* into different languages, had its repercussions in Europe was a fact. Marshall publicly referred to Ford as the "inspirer" of the racist diatribes of Hitler and General Ludendorff, and he made it a condition of accepting Ford's retraction that Ford agree to halt publication and dissemination of his articles abroad. However, when a German organization asked the Committee privately if there was any evidence of Ford's giving financial aid to European anti-Semitic groups, the answer was no. The implication remained, however, that if anti-Semitism could be strengthened in Europe by American developments, the opposite was also true.

In 1926 Jacob Landau, director of the Jewish Telegraphic Agency, who had long been convinced of the existence of an international bureau which disseminated anti-Semitic propaganda, undertook a survey of anti-Semitism for the Committee. His lengthy report emphasized, in particular, the strength of anti-Jewish movements in Poland and Germany. He recounted the activities of the international anti-Semitic conferences of 1925 and 1926, at which representatives from the Western democracies and Central Europe planned a program "to free the enslaved people of the world from the domination of International Jewry." Noting the parallels in arguments and propaganda in all countries and the connections among anti-Semitic circles, he convincingly demonstrated the organized character of international Jew-hatred. The Committee feared the effect of publicizing Landau's study and agreed to give only the relevant sections to responsible Jewish leaders in the countries concerned.

In 1928 a confidential memorandum from Berlin which gave further details of international anti-Semitic activities reached the Committee. It related that the Budapest Congress of 1925 resolved to work to have Jews stripped of their civil rights and eventually deported from Christian states. The conferees also decided to press for a numerus clausus in universities throughout the world, a decision which according to the report, had had a marked effect in Rumania, Hungary, and Germany. The memo, probably written by the Centralverein, cited those facts to gain the cooperation of American Jews in a joint fight against anti-Semitism. Such a move would not be charity, the Germans emphasized, for if left unchallenged, anti-Semitism would spread inexorably to the United States.

VIII

In marked contrast to the Committee's typical defense activities was its work in connection with Palestine. Technically the Committee as a group had nothing to do with Palestine after its participation in the peace conference of the American Jewish Congress. However, the leaders of the Committee as individuals were sought out by the Zionists in the postwar years to cooperate in the physical rehabilitation of Palestine. Thus while the Committee officially adhered to its cautious 1918 pronouncement on

Zionism, stronger bonds were forged between American Zionists and non-Zionists.

There were several reasons why men like Marshall, Adler, Oscar Straus, Felix Warburg, and Irving Lehman became more receptive to Zionist activities. First, many Zionist leaders played down the ideology of Jewish nationalism and stressed practical projects to meet the challenge of transforming deserts and swamps into an economically sound country. The knowledge that Palestine remained the one land of refuge open to victims of persecution only intensified that challenge. Marshall and his colleagues could never support the Zionist notion which denied any possibility of meaningful Jewish survival in the Diaspora, nor would they ever encourage American Jewish emigration to Palestine; but the non-Zionists of AJC recognized in Palestine a haven for East European Jewry. Finally, not only had the Allies incorporated the substance of the Balfour Declaration into the terms of the British Mandate over Palestine, but the United States had also officially approved the establishment of a Jewish homeland. The world powers now waited for Jews to seize that opportunity, and every Jew was morally bound to respond in a positive way. Marshall warned the non-Zionists that "indifference . . . can do us a thousand times more harm than all the Ku Klux Klans and Henry Fords." The non-Zionists on the American Jewish Committee had never admitted that the question of Palestine was the exclusive preserve of the Zionists, and they reaffirmed that view in their determination to aid in the development of the land.

Non-Zionists channeled their money to Palestine through business, scientific, and cultural projects. To insure their continued financial assistance, the World Zionist Organization resolved to enlarge the Jewish Agency by inviting the participation of non-Zionists of all countries. By the terms of the British Mandate, the Zionist Organization was originally recognized as the Jewish Agency for Palestine, but provision was made "to secure the cooperation of all Jews who are willing to assist in the establishment of the Jewish National Home." Negotiations directed toward the Americans were led by Dr. Chaim Weizmann, president of the World Zionist Organization, who approached Louis Marshall and Felix Warburg in 1923. (Weizmann's choices were obvious: Marshall was the dominant leader of the American Jewish community and not merely of the Committee; Warburg, chairman of the Joint Distribution Committee, symbolized American Jewish wealth.) A call for a national conference of Jews not affiliated with the Zionist Organization went out above the names of Marshall, Adler, Horace Stern, and Herbert Lehman. At that conference, in February 1924, American non-Zionists reached two decisions: to establish a new investment corporation (eventually the Palestine Economic Corporation) for the upbuilding of Palestine and to formulate an appropriate plan for American participation in an enlarged Jewish Agency.

Negotiations on non-Zionist affiliation continued for five more years, and two additional conferences were held. Initial Zionist opposition to Weizmann's plan finally disappeared when the non-Zionists accepted the term *Jewish National Home* in the preamble of the Jewish Agency's constitution. In 1928 a committee of seven non-Zionists (five of them from AJC) was appointed to name forty-four American members for the enlarged agency. Several months later the agreement was officially concluded in Zurich. Weizmann was chosen president and Marshall chairman of the agency's council, in which Zionist and non-Zionist held 112 seats each. Although the agency did not realize its sponsors' hopes, it did attract additional funds despite the onset of the world depression. For AJC, the identification of its prominent members with the agency meant deeper involvement in Palestinian affairs.

Neither Marshall nor Adler, who had attended the Zurich meeting, could long enjoy its achievement. The day after the conclusion of the agency agreement Marshall became gravely ill. Meantime Adler, aboard ship returning to the United States at the end of August, heard the news of the anti-Jewish Arab riots in Palestine. He immediately radioed Waldman, who asked the

State Department to urge England to take the necessary steps to prevent the spread of anti-Jewish excesses to neighboring Arab countries. Unaware of the seriousness of Marshall's condition, Adler and Waldman believed that he had begun some sort of action in Switzerland. Committee members in New York held an emergency meeting to formulate policy. They did not join public protests against the riots in the United States, although the Committee, like many other informed parties, also held the British administration responsible. Indeed, Waldman had intimated as much in his wire to the State Department, but, as he noted in his report, he exercised caution:

> My communications to the Department of State were more diplomatic than forceful but at that time we hadn't quite realized the culpability of the British officials in Palestine and I was careful to avoid what might appear as sensationally condemnatory utterances. I felt that our Department of State should realize that, though profoundly horrified as we were, not all the Jews of the United States had lost their heads.

Upon his return home Adler advised urging President Hoover to send a warship to Haifa, as a gesture of American interest. The Zionist office in London similarly pressed for American intervention, and Judge Abram I. Elkus, a member of the Committee and former Ambassador to Turkey, argued that Muslims would be impressed only with a show of force. However, Felix Warburg, who headed the deputation from the Jewish Agency to British Prime Minister Ramsay MacDonald, radioed otherwise: "TELL ADLER RECEIVED . . . REASSURING [MESSAGE] FROM WEIZMANN AFTER HIS TALK PASSFIELD. FEEL WE MUST SHOW WE RELY AND BELIEVE ABILITY AND INTEREST GREAT BRITAIN TO DO ALL IN POWER AND MUST NOT SHOW DISTRUST FOR TIME BEING."

When President Hoover, for his own reasons, privately told Lewis Strauss that he opposed direct American action, the Committee dropped the matter. It agreed with Warburg that if England failed to preserve order in Palestine, recourse could be had to the League of Nations; if the league failed, it would be time to approach the United States.

Marshall's death in Zurich on September 11, 1929, was the worst blow the Committee ever sustained. He had been the vital force in all its affairs, as he had been the prime mover in the American Jewish community at large. Indeed, some Jewish papers even suggested that with Marshall gone the Committee should terminate its existence as an independent organization. Since Marshall would have been the first to laugh such advice out of court, the Committee determinedly set about to regroup and strengthen its forces. The decade of the twenties had raised new issues as yet unresolved, and in the fall of 1929 none could confidently say that the signs for the thirties looked any more promising.

8

The Nazi Fury

At a dinner given by Herbert Bayard Swope in 1943, one of the guests observed that the American Jewish Committee had proved itself useless by its failure to prevent the rise and entrenchment of nazism. Aside from the highly questionable assumption that the Committee could have done something had its eyes been open, the charge completely ignored the essence of the Nazi movement. True, the Committee neither toppled Hitler nor held back the destruction of European Jewry; but its failure was that of all Western forces grounded in the teachings of the Age of Reason. The primitivism of the Nazi fury, which contradicted the accepted canons of statesmanship, was unfathomable. For the Jews, whose very emancipation was bound up with the Enlightenment, the liberal tradition evoked an emotional as well as a rational commitment. Even if they had grasped the meaning of nazism, an equally irrational response would have meant spiritual bankruptcy.

At the annual meeting of the American Jewish Committee in 1933, the following statement was read:

> Despite the frenzied chauvinism in Germany and elsewhere throughout the world, we will not, indeed we dare not,

admit that the elemental rights to life and liberty have been permanently laid low. The civilized world, which is overwhelmed at this time by an unprecedented depression, which has produced political issues of the gravest kind, may not be in the position to defend or even assert these principles in a formal way. But we Jews must not accept the situation in Germany as a permanent disaster, or believe that the civilized world will be willing to accept that situation as normal and unchangeable. . . . To accept the defeat as permanent would be a repudiation of the ideals of peace and justice proclaimed by our prophets, for which the Jews have suffered for twenty or more centuries.

Thus AJC prepared to meet its most serious challenge. Almost overnight, its professional staff and budget grew to unforeseen size; new committees and departments were formed, new tactics of research and public education were developed, meetings were held incessantly.

No single pattern marked AJC's actions between 1933 and 1939. Any idea holding out the slightest hope of relieving the plight of German Jewry was seized upon, provided it would not boomerang or endanger the American Jewish community. The Committee for the most part used its traditional methods of backstairs diplomacy, and many instances of behind-the-scenes intervention will never be known, for its documents often purposely omitted stories of personal suasion. Often the Committee floundered, admitting that it could not guarantee the soundness of its conclusions. It sought advice from Jews and non-Jews throughout the Western countries, and their opinions frequently reflected that same uncertainty. People who predicted certain amelioration one month reverted to despair the next. Some wildly imagined total economic ruin or forced emigration for Germany Jewry, but no one, even privately, confessed to fantasies of extermination.

I

At the close of the 1920s it was evident that the growing Nazi movement could no longer be dismissed as a German version of the Ku Klux Klan. Its anti-Semitic ideology, which in the early years of the movement expressed itself through crude propaganda and acts of vandalism, was now beginning to find economic and political outlets. In small towns where local officials allied themselves with Hitler's forces, Jews were subject to boycott as well as to physical violence; in Thuringia the government added an anti-Semitic passage to the official state prayer; in Bavaria ritual slaughter of animals was prohibited. The 1930 elections catapulted the Nazis into national prominence, increasing their seats in the Reichstag from 12 to 107 and foreboding the end of the Weimar Republic. Their political successes multiplied, and in January 1933 President Hindenburg appointed Adolf Hitler chancellor of Germany.

The Centralverein deutscher Staatsbürger jüdischen Glaubens, while not minimizing the threat, saw no reason to despair. "We are thoroughly able to hold our own and to fight successfully against the attacks made by Mr. Hitler and his followers," it declared. The Centralverein, a defense organization which represented over sixty thousand of Germany's six hundred thousand Jews, limited its fight to the anti-Semitic aspects of nazism. Through the press, its own numerous publications, and court action, it mounted a defensive campaign based on the traditional techniques of rational argument, discreet pressure, and enlightened persuasion, all in keeping with the liberal, middle-class outlook of German Jewry. The tactics were, however, ill suited to meet the Nazi onslaught.

The Centralverein had established regular contact with the American Jewish Committee in 1928, when it asked for a grant to help its publicity campaign, particularly among the lower classes. It sought no advice and wanted no pressure brought to bear by Jewish groups abroad. It did suggest, however, that its foreign friends look to their own safety, for anti-Semitism could cross boundaries and penetrate tariff walls.

Louis Marshall at first turned a cold shoulder to the Centralverein's request for financial aid. Even if the situation was as serious as reported, why couldn't the wealthy German Jewish community handle it alone, Marshall wanted to know. Besides, he did not think the Centralverein's publications particularly effective. However, he apparently recognized the gravity of the situation when he met with Centralverein representatives in Zurich in 1929, shortly before his death. The contacts were continued by Cyrus Adler who, although more apprehensive about the situation than Marshall had been, was not certain at first if the entire affair lay within AJC's jurisdiction. At the urging of the Warburgs (Felix's brother Max in Germany was a strong protagonist of the Centralverein's cause), the Committee became more cooperative, but could hardly meet the Centralverein's request for $175,-000 annually. AJC had been trying to increase its own financial resources since 1927, and the 1929 stock market crash had paralyzed its fund-raising efforts. At the beginning of 1930, the Committee turned over to the Centralverein $7,500, of which some $2,000 was the final balance of the Emergency Trust Fund, originally created to aid the unemancipated Jews of Eastern Europe.

As the information from the Centralverein and from friends and relatives in Germany fell into place, the Committee watched the German developments with growing alarm. Morris Waldman spent three months in Europe in 1930 as an observer for AJC, and his reports underscored the dangers posed by Nazi gains. Finally, in November 1930, shortly after the Nazi success at the polls, the Committee invited a small group of prominent American Jews, most of whom had not been identified with Jewish activities, to a special meeting on the German situation. If Adler, Warburg, and Waldman could convince them of the gravity of the situation, financial aid might be enlisted for German Jewry. However, the meeting was dominated by those men who refused to

take alarm. Jewish history, they pointed out, was a saga of persecution down through the ages; Hitler was just one more adversary who, with the help of the Almighty and improved economic
conditions, would also fade away.

It would have been surprising had they reacted differently.
Theirs was a generation schooled in Graetz's *Leiden und Lernen*
philosophy, men who had witnessed the czarist persecutions in
Russia and the Dreyfus affair in France. Children of the Enlightenment, they could not, at this early stage, fathom the irrational
frenzy in the Nazi movement. To be sure, they sympathized with
the German Jews and politely discussed the value of the German
suggestion for an anthropological study to refute the charge
of racial inferiority. But only one person, the rabbi of a German-
speaking congregation, advocated organized action. Adler could
only repeat his warnings of the ominousness of the situation, but
he and Warburg lacked the force of a Schiff or a Marshall.

Despite its failure to arouse American Jews to the Nazi
threat, and its own increasing financial difficulties, AJC gave limited cooperation to German Jewry during 1931 and 1932. It took
its cues from German Jewish leaders, however, for the German
Jews were cultured Westerners who did not fit the guardian-ward
pattern which the Committee had adopted in its dealing in behalf
of East European Jewry. And since Hitler was not yet in power,
it was feared that imprudent actions abroad might strengthen
pro-Nazi sentiment in Germany.

All the advice the Committee garnered stressed caution
above all—which meant no Jewish protests or demonstrations,
lest they feed charges of an international Jewish alliance. Instead,
the Committee was urged to work for a sympathetic anti-Nazi
press in the United States, enlist the cooperation of non-Jewish
liberals, and try to halt the spread of Nazi teachings in America.
Not all the German Jewish leaders agreed with the "noiseless"
approach of concealing Jewish activity behind a non-Jewish
façade. Some, particularly the Zionists, advocated the mobilization of Jewish efforts throughout the world. However, the Com-

mittee's own tradition inclined toward the quieter position, which was endorsed by leaders of the Centralverein and the Hilfsverein, and by Dr. Bernhard Kahn, head of the JDC's European office, who was the Committee's respected adviser on European affairs. The Committee worked to secure anti-Nazi statements from such groups as the National Conference of Jews and Christians and the Federal Council of Churches of Christ. It also cooperated actively with a new organization, American Friends of German Jews, to get favorable publicity in the German-American press, which in turn might have beneficial reverberations in Germany itself. Individual Committee members cultivated non-Jewish friends prominent in intellectual, religious, and political life, and Jacob Landau of the Jewish Telegraphic Agency, working closely with the Committee, led the movement to organize liberal anti-Nazi sentiment through a League for Human Rights.

In March 1932 both the Committee and the American Jewish Congress were asked by German Jews to secure public declarations against Hitlerism from President Herbert Hoover and Senator William E. Borah, chairman of the Foreign Relations Committee. Borah offered to go with Adler and Congress president Stephen S. Wise to see Hoover, but Adler, unwilling to embarrass the president, refused. At the same time, Adler did give the Scripps-Howard papers a brief on the anti-Semitism of the Nazi movement. Although he asked them not to mention Jewish organizations in their accounts, the papers disclosed that German Jews had appealed to the United States for help and that Adler was in touch with congressional leaders. Adler denied the report, but he got the undesired publicity without any official sympathy.

The Committee may have appeared irresolute and timid in its approach to nazism—so timid, Waldman said, that it was afraid to whisper Hitler's name; but no one else had surer ideas of how to respond to the crisis. Early in 1932, representatives of the Committee and the American Jewish Congress discussed the

German situation, but they could only admit they were groping. On and on the discussion went: Should Jewish groups intervene? The German government in power had done nothing to justify intervention. And if the Nazis came to power, the responsibility of office might prove sobering and their anti-Semitic program might not be carried out.

As developments in 1932 unfolded, the Committee strengthened its ties with foreign Jewish organizations. That spring it sent Roger Straus to meet with the Alliance Israélite Universelle and the Joint Foreign Committee of England. European leaders discussed the possibility of having to arrange for the migration of a hundred thousand German Jews, should the Nazis gain political control. On March 5, 1933, the Nazi victory at the polls turned the premise into reality.

II

For most German Jews, the Nazi anti-Semitic policy was marked by three distinct phases. From March 1933 until September 1935 Jews were subjected to numerous restrictive measures which, in rapid succession, barred them from public service and the professions. Except for a short period of disorders following the 1933 elections, they suffered no physical mistreatment. At this time German apologists explained the Nazi tactics as an attempt to balance the occupational distribution of the Jews, who were overrepresented in the professions and in administration. Indeed, some German Jews (the Warburgs, for example) admitted that there was some truth to this and were sympathetic to the idea of removing Jews from public prominence.

The Nuremberg laws of 1935, however, struck a qualitatively different note. These "sacral" measures, as Léon Poliakov called them, translated the Nazi myth of Aryan racial superiority into law. By 1938 Hermann Göring announced that the German economy—indeed, Germany itself—would have to be free of

Jews. In November of that year the infamous *Kristallnacht,* when synagogues throughout Germany were attacked and destroyed, inaugurated the third phase, marked by government-sanctioned brutality and destruction, a phase which easily led to the adoption of the "Final Solution" some two years later.

Only during the first phase did AJC have any hope of stopping Hitler's anti-Semitism. Would it have been realistic for the Committee to aim at crushing the Nazi regime itself? Morris Waldman, who often fretted at the Committee's predilection for moderate action, thought so. On August 8, 1933, he wrote:

> The only hope, it seems to me, is to destroy the Hitler regime. Whatever power and influence we Jews have should be directed to that end. . . . Do we know what is the financial and commercial condition of Germany? Shouldn't we know? Why shouldn't we engage a Keynes to study that situation and tell us? Is Germany getting credits or likely to get credits? Do the bankers, including the Jewish bankers, prefer Hitlerism to Communism? What bankers are friendly to Germany? What pressure can be brought on them? . . . *We must undermine Germany's economy, bring her to the point of starvation as in 1918.**

Judge Joseph M. Proskauer, a forceful figure who was rapidly assuming prominence on the Committee's executive, called Waldman's letter a "counsel of perfection." Yet nothing of what Waldman outlined was attempted. Even had the Committee set aside its fears of the negative impact of concerted international Jewish action, there was little chance of success. True, Germany's economy was in a precarious state and to cut off her foreign trade would have spelled economic strangulation. But such sanctions could be effective only if applied universally, and that course, which would have been extremely difficult to achieve in normal

---

* The same bankers, Waldman thought, could financially accommodate the countries of Eastern Europe so as to free them from Germany's sphere of influence.

times, became virtually impossible during the Great Depression, when economic recovery depended on expansion rather than contraction of trade.

Jewish influence in banking circles notwithstanding (and the degree of that influence was often overrated), the Western world would not isolate Germany economically. George Messersmith, a State Department official who served in Germany and Austria in the 1930s, could not convince the American government to suspend the shipment of raw materials to Germany, despite his assurances that the Nazi regime would thereupon collapse. More typical of the times was Cordell Hull's statement: "The friendly and willing cooperation of Germany is necessary to the program of world recovery."

Nor was the threat to cut off capital exports particularly menacing, for the volume of such exports, like the volume of international trade, had already shrunk drastically. In 1929 the net outflow of direct private loans from the United States was over $600 million; in 1933 the inflow exceeded the outflow by $32 million. Bankers were hard pressed to find a market for German securities in any case, and it was the Great Depression and not nazism that had shut off the flow of capital. Despite the contraction in trade and loans, Germany ultimately managed to build up her economy. And in truth there was little world Jewry, and American Jews in particular, could do directly to affect matters in Germany. Rabbi Morris Lazaron of Baltimore went to Berlin to see if he could find ways to reason with the authorities; ignored by all, he only jeopardized his own life. In May 1933 a few leading American Jews, including Committee members Proskauer, Irving Lehman, and Roger Straus, met privately in New York with Dr. Hjalmar Schacht, the German financial wizard, and received a promise that he would try to intercede with the Nazi regime in German Jewry's behalf. The promise was quickly forgotten upon his return home.

Equally futile was the boycott of German goods which was undertaken in various countries, though it did provide Jews with

a way to express their feelings. In the United States the movement was sparked by the Jewish War Veterans, whose DON'T BUY
GERMAN GOODS stickers became a common sight. Samuel Untermyer, a prominent lawyer, organized the American League for
the Defense of Jewish Rights as a vehicle to further the boycott.
By the summer of 1933 Stephen Wise and the American Jewish
Congress fell into line, leaving the Committee and B'nai B'rith
as the principal opponents. Differences between the "pros" and
"antis" engendered public squabbling which did not help the
cause of Jewish unity. The general press, too, became involved,
with the *New York Post* supporting and the *Herald-Tribune* and
World-Telegram opposing the boycott.

Its stand against the boycott lost the Committee considerable prestige in the community. Although the boycotters could
not pretend to be hurting Germany significantly, their activity
was sufficiently annoying to evoke complaints by German officials
to the State Department. Many aroused American Jews taunted
the Committee for its do-nothing policy. But the Committee
regarded the boycott as dangerous: a Jewish boycott only served
to define nazism as a Jewish problem and the Committee insisted
that nazism had to be fought as a threat to world freedom. Besides, the German Jews themselves were opposed to boycotts and
public demonstrations, since they could expect to bear the brunt
if the German government should decide to seek revenge. Further, it was argued, a boycott would harm the German Jewish
merchants too, and, as George N. Shuster wrote in *Commonweal*,
would no doubt alienate Germans not yet committed to anti-
Semitic policies. It would move Catholic businessmen to ally
themselves with the militants of the Nazi regime.

A further consideration was the threat of increasing anti-
Semitism at home. An effective boycott meant publicity, and publicity meant noise. A public Jewish outcry could help no one,
warned prominent (even sympathetic) non-Jews in England,
France, and the United States. It would only evoke public antagonism, arouse popular prejudice, and squelch any discreet

negotiations in progress. Morris Waldman pointed out that the boycott had indeed antagonized the influential German population in the United States, which originally had been sympathetic to the Jewish cause, and had led to a counter boycott against American Jews by such groups as the German-American Protective Alliance. By the spring of 1934 even Untermyer was ready to ease up on the boycott in the face of growing American anti-Semitism.

AJC, allied with B'nai B'rith, counseled that "prejudice must not be fought merely with appeals to passion and resentment, however justified passion and resentment may be." It said:

> Dismayed as we are that no evidence has as yet been given by the authorities of Germany of their intention to undo the incalculable injury inflicted upon an innocent part of their citizenry, and fully understanding and appreciating the natural desire of human beings to express sorrow and indignation, we nevertheless consider such forms of agitation as boycotts, parades, mass-meetings and other similar demonstrations as futile. They serve only as an ineffectual channel for the release of emotion. They furnish the persecutors with a pretext to justify the wrongs they perpetuate and, on the other hand, distract those who desire to help with more constructive efforts.

When an international meeting to foster the boycott was called in Amsterdam in the summer of 1933, the Committee notified the State Department that it was in no way connected with Untermyer or his organization.

It should be pointed out, however, that the Committee objected to the *public* aspect of the boycott rather than to the boycott itself. It tended to agree with the South African leader Jan Christiaan Smuts and Czech premier Eduard Beneš, who in effect advised: Boycott, but keep your mouths shut. To bark without biting would only convince the Nazis still further of Jewish impo-

tence. An AJC office memorandum of May 1933 suggested how
the boycott might privately be put to good use:

> Private business men, firms, corporations, and trade or-
> ganizations should be influenced to address communica-
> tions to persons and firms with which they have business
> dealings in Germany, informing . . . [them] that such a boy-
> cott movement exists in the United States in spite of the fact
> that it has not the official sanction of any important Jewish
> or other organization; that this boycott is practised not only
> by Jews, but also by non-Jews; that it is not at the present
> time a reaction to the reports of physical outrages, (although
> it may have been initiated by indignation at such reports),
> but to failure to mitigate official measures against Jews; and
> that it would be well for the German people to know these
> facts. These letters should close with a suggestion that the
> recipients call the matter to the attention of the German
> authorities, as the boycott movement in the United States is
> a serious handicap to international trade.

The heart of the Committee's strategy lay in finding non-
Jewish allies for the fight against nazism. But in May 1934, when
the chairman of the executive committee, Sol M. Stroock, and
Waldman visited Louis D. Brandeis in the company of Stephen
Wise and Horace Kallen (the liberal Supreme Court justice was
now the respected elder statesman of all Jewish factions), Stroock
admitted that they had failed to obtain Christian support. He did
not, however, blame the boycott for this. "When asked by L.D.B.
whether he favored abandoning the Jewish boycott," Waldman
reported, "he answered in the negative, but advised that it be
carried on under distinct limitations." Indeed, when Proskauer
later denounced the boycott and impugned the patriotism of its
proponents in an interview with the New York *World-Telegram*, the
executive committee agreed that its members must consult each
other before issuing statements that might reflect upon the organization.

To the Committee the practical value of the boycott lay in its

bargaining possibilities. AJC supported the National Civic Federation in its efforts to mediate between the Nazis and the American
Jews, and Adler agreed that renunciation of the boycott would be
a fair exchange for Nazi agreement to halt the anti-Semitic drive.
When the National Civic Federation directed an appeal for a
truce simultaneously to the Nazi party in Munich and to the
American Jewish Congress, prominent German-Americans like
the Ridders, Herman Metz, and George Sylvester Viereck privately assured the German authorities that American Jews would
cease their propaganda.

Despite Germany's refusal to call off her own Jewish boycott,
planned for April 1, the National Civic Federation persisted in its
campaign. At the beginning of May 1933 it called a meeting of
leading German-Americans and representatives of the Committee, the American Jewish Congress, and B'nai B'rith. Resolutions
calling for mutual cooperation in the interest of economic recovery were unanimously passed and subsequently formulated into
a memorandum for submission to Hjalmar Schacht—who turned
a totally deaf ear to the entreaty. Blaming the provisions of the
Treaty of Versailles for developments in Germany, Schacht maintained that Americans did not understand the German situation.
As for anti-Jewish discrimination, he maintained, that was the
natural result of the disproportionately important role the Jews
had captured in German economic and political life. Especially
culpable were the East European Jews who had immigrated to
Germany since the war, profiteered during the inflation, and
caused the impoverishment of Germany's middle class.

III

The Committee's cooperation with the National Civic Federation
was in line with the drive to mobilize Christian support against
nazism—although the federation, which had taken up the Jew/
Bolshevist line of the 1920s, was not the most savory of allies. In

1933 the federation assured the State Department that it had refused to join American Jewish groups in seeking government intervention in behalf of persecuted Jews abroad and that, should resolutions be introduced in Congress calling for such action, it was prepared to have them amended to include the persecution of Catholics in Mexico, Spain, and Russia. Nevertheless, Committee members Proskauer and Max Kohler used the opportunity provided by the meetings with the federation to stress the seriousness of the situation in Germany and to counter the argument that nazism was principally an anti-Communist movement.

Nor did political ideology deter the Committee in its drive for allies. Just as it sought to impress the British Labour Prime Minister, Ramsay MacDonald, with the urgency of the situation, so it also approached Benito Mussolini. Shortly after Hitler's appointment as chancellor, Cyrus Adler and Horace Stern met with John Di Silvestro, a Philadelphia lawyer and president of the Sons of Italy order. Convinced of his sincerity and desire to help, they briefed him for a mission to Rome. When Di Silvestro asked for evidence that not only Jews but American Catholics as well were disturbed over the Nazi developments, Adler obtained a letter to that effect from the Catholic Alfred E. Smith, which Di Silvestro was authorized to show Mussolini. Di Silvestro met with Mussolini three times and duly reported back to the Committee that Il Duce, besides calling the Nazis "amateurs and butchers," promised to protest through the Italian embassy. Di Silvestro also alerted the Committee to attempts by German and Austrian "tourists" to foment anti-Semitic propaganda in Italy, and to the creation of an anti-Semitic organization in Switzerland.

A more formidable ally would have been the Vatican. Although the records of the Committee are silent on any direct approach to Pope Pius XI during the early days of the Nazi regime, feelers, if not actual appeals, must have been extended. In February 1933 the Catholic publisher Victor Ridder suggested that the pope be reached by asking Alfred E. Smith to approach the American cardinals. Two months later, at a special AJC membership meeting on the German situation, chairman Irving Lehman was queried directly as to whether the pope had been asked for a statement. Lehman replied vaguely:

> [It] is perfectly evident that they [the Catholic hierarchy] are not willing at the present time to take any action which might jeopardize what they feel of the greatest importance for the future. I think they may work with us indirectly, but a statement from them at the present time would be out of the question.

Despite the Committee's close relations with prominent Catholic laymen, such as Smith and Carleton Hayes, the Vatican remained silent. In 1934 Adler revealed that several Catholic contacts of the Committee would transmit to the pope the request that he condemn the ritual-murder accusation, as had six of his predecessors. But Pius XI did not respond. Scattered references suggest that the Catholics were not ready to help until the Jews took up the fight against Catholic persecution in Mexico. In 1935 James McDonald, then the League of Nations high commissioner on refugees, approached Cardinal Pacelli (soon to become Pius XII) with an official request that the church use its good offices to facilitate the immigration of Jewish refugees to South American countries. When McDonald reported back to American Jewish leaders with a plan for a Jewish-Catholic alliance specifically geared to the Mexican situation, the Jews interpreted this as Pacelli's demand for a quid pro quo.

The Committee discussed the proposition but decided that the precarious situation of the twelve thousand Jews in Mexico prevented such an association. And apparently Jewish initiative in a call for religious freedom in Russia, to be signed by a representative of each of the three major faiths, and the AJC's blanket condemnation of persecution in the Old and New Worlds were not enough to satisfy the Catholics. Puzzled by the fact that the infinitely more powerful church desired their assistance, the Jews avoided futile commitments.

IV

If the church had its reasons to keep silent between 1933 and 1935, so did the American government. The breakdown of the Versailles treaty, the rise of European dictatorships, and the problems of the Great Depression at home swelled isolationist ranks. Popular opinion began to interpret America's entry into World War I not simply as an error but rather as a step engineered by profit-hungry manufacturers and bankers. Senator Gerald P. Nye's investigation emphasized that view, as did such Book-of-the-Month Club selections as *Merchants of Death* and *The Road to War*. For the fourth and last time the United States refused to join the World Court, and Congress determinedly set out to legislate a course of neutrality. Against this background the newly elected president, Franklin Delano Roosevelt, who as a vice-presidential candidate in 1920 had run on a pro-League of Nations platform, now concentrated on the New Deal at the expense of internationalism.

As the world learned of the Nazi horrors, the State Department began to receive numerous messages from shocked Americans—and from fraternal lodges, women's clubs, and business associations. But these soon tapered off, and Washington saw no need to issue a formal protest. The "good old days" of humanitarian diplomacy, on which AJC had so often relied, were clearly over. When Max J. Kohler submitted a lengthy memorandum reminding the State Department of numerous instances of American intervention on humanitarian grounds, the department responded that those precedents did not "make out a convincing case for representations." Nazi persecution was on internal German matter which did not permit American interference.

In the 1930s the Committee neither contested the underlying premise of American isolationism nor argued an anti-Nazi policy on the basis of America's self-interest. The notion of a pluralistic society was not yet firmly enough entrenched for such behavior on the part of minorities, who tended either to dissociate themselves from the Establishment (joining third parties, for example), to threaten the Establishment with votes (as in the case of the AFL), or to come to the Establishment as supplicants. The minority represented by the Committee, whose self-confidence was significantly shaken by events in Germany, did not dream of arguing that its objectives better served the national interest. True, it was pointed out to the State Department that the Nazi terror sowed discord throughout the world and that the effects of persecution threatened the international economy and world peace. But fundamentally the Jews saw the Nazi menace as a *moral* challenge to the free nations. As AJC and other Jewish organizations wrote to the State Department: "It is inconceivable that the American Government should stand passively by and neglect to lift its voice against these assaults upon humanity, or to utter its condemnation of the violation of the fundamental principle of human rights."

The Committee did not relax its pressure on the administration. Several AJC members—Samuel Rosenman, Irving Lehman, Herbert Lehman, Joseph Proskauer, Sol Stroock—were influential in Democratic circles, and they believed that President Roosevelt was truly sympathetic to their cause. It was the State Department, they felt, that sought to soft-pedal the matter. Nevertheless, they knew that the president refused to take a public stand. Beset by the internal problems of the London economic conference and the disarmament conference, he preferred that they work through Secretary of State Cordell Hull. More important, he would take no step until he was certain that a large section of the public approved of America's speaking against the Nazi treatment of Jews.

Members of the Committee had spoken privately to Roosevelt when he was president-elect about his choice of an ambassador to Germany, and the president did instruct his appointee, William Dodd, a professor of history, to do what he could through unofficial and personal channels to moderate the Nazi anti-Jewish excesses. Roosevelt himself may have been confused about what the Jews really wanted him to do. A story then circulating told how some individuals privately advised the president to keep hands off. The Jewish leaders were quite certain, however, that Roosevelt expressed his disapproval of Nazi anti-Semitism in private talks with Dr. Schacht and Dr. Hans Luther, the German ambassador to the United States.

Ambassador Dodd and Consul General George Messersmith were sympathetic, too, and the Committee privately communicated its position to Dodd before he left for Berlin as well as during his subsequent visits home. Secretary Hull, however, remained the focus for the protests. Periodically a delegation, usually consisting of representatives of the Committee, the American Jewish Congress, and B'nai B'rith, would go to his office to present the latest information on the German Jewish crisis. The secretary would listen patiently to requests for intercession or relief for refugees. Although he promised little, he kept fully informed of conditions in Germany through frequent reports from his representatives in Berlin. At the end of March he cabled the American chargé d'affaires:

> We are under heavy pressure to make representations [in behalf of German Jews] to the German Government. I am of the opinion that outside intercession has rarely produced the results desired and has frequently aggravated the situation. Nevertheless, if you perceive any way in which this Government could usefully be of assistance, I should appreciate your frank and confidential advice.

When Hull received word that the situation had improved and that the United States was being attacked in the German press for its anti-German "campaign of calumny," intercession appeared even less desirable. A week later, however, Germany prepared for the national boycott against Jews, and at this point Hull found legal justification for a protest by the American Embassy to the German Foreign Office:

You should make it clear that it is not the purpose of this Government to interfere in any way in matters which are essentially the domestic concern of Germany. The situation which is now developing, however, . . . has assumed an international aspect. I am informed that a retaliatory boycott is even now under serious consideration in certain American cities. More important, however, the German Government should appreciate that the human element involved in the situation is such that the friendship of the people of the two countries might not remain unaffected.

Secretary Hull tried an eleventh-hour move to avert the boycott. If Germany would call it off, Hull promised, he would issue a public statement playing down the atrocity stories and deploring the rise of anti-German sentiment in the United States. In both Washington and Berlin, German official complaints about American public opinion were countered by references to the seriousness of the Jewish situation. Resolutions of condemnation introduced on the floor of Congress were, as Americans pointed out to the Germans, strictly the domain of the legislative branch. When Hermann Göring said to George Messersmith: "We don't make a fuss in Germany every time a gangster shoots down innocent people in the streets of Chicago," Messersmith replied that he was sure the *Reichsminister* did not wish his SA men to be compared to gangsters.

Secretary Hull recorded the notes of one conversation with Luther which prove that, at least within the framework of diplomatic exchange, he had tried to ameliorate the situation. After Hull had repeated in forceful terms his desire for a halt to discrimination, Luther assured him "that the worst has been over for some time, . . . that there is no purpose to expel the Jews as a race from Germany . . . , and that it will only be a question of a reasonable time when normal conditions and relationships will, to a measurable extent, be brought about."

Given the isolationist trend of the time and the perceptible rise of an anti-Semitic current in the United States, American

Jewish leaders feared that rash debates in Congress might evoke pro-Hitler statements. The other Jewish organizations shared this view, although all had welcomed the outspoken condemnations of the Nazis in the British House of Commons and the French Chamber of Deputies. Hull encouraged the idea of a debate but did not look favorably on resolutions which might demand action by the executive branch. The Jewish members of Congress met daily to discuss what steps they could take, and the Committee deemed it wise to keep them informed of what it considered a suitable course. Largely as a result of Proskauer's briefing, on June 10, 1933, Senators Joseph T. Robinson and Jesse H. Metcalf made stirring speeches in the Senate on the plight of German Jewry. Resolutions were introduced in both houses; AJC endorsed those offered by Representative Hamilton Fish and Senator Millard Tydings, but neither was released from committee.

V

The American Jewish Committee, in those early days of Nazi ascendancy, also looked to the League of Nations for a measure of redress, even though the league's inability to halt Japanese aggression in the Far East demonstrated its decline in power. Franz Bernheim, a German Jew living in Upper Silesia, filed a complaint with the league, maintaining that the Nazi anti-Semitic ordinances constituted a violation of the minority rights granted the Jews of that region, and the league formally reminded Germany of her obligations in this matter. To be sure, the Jews of Germany neither enjoyed nor desired "minority rights"; they regarded themselves, in fact as well as in law, as full-fledged citizens of the land where they had lived for so long. Nevertheless, even though Germany ignored the league's reprimand, people like Cyrus Adler believed the Bernheim episode could lead to the restoration of Jewish rights in Germany. After all, it was the league's business to maintain international security, and any threat to it might properly be brought to its attention.

Another opportunity for League of Nations action appeared in the form of a petition for the creation of a High Commission on Refugees (Jewish and non-Jewish) from Germany. The Committee eagerly seized upon the idea and, under the guidance of Max J. Kohler and James N. Rosenberg and with the help of international lawyers, prepared a statement for presentation at Geneva in the fall of 1933. The value of the petition, its sponsors knew, transcended any actual help that might be given the refugees. First, it was a good occasion for anti-Nazi statements by ranking diplomats of various countries. Second, a League of Nations High Commission could conceivably negotiate directly with the Nazis in behalf of the Jews. As Adler put it, the best way to help refugees was to prevent them from becoming refugees.

The first aim was realized. The Committee, with the backing of the American Jewish Congress and B'nai B'rith, worked closely with members of England's Joint Foreign Committee and, after much discreet lobbying, persuaded the Dutch representative to bring the petition officially before the League of Nations. In the ensuing debates delegate after delegate agreed that the humanitarian aspect of the situation outweighed the argument that the treatment of the German Jews was an internal German concern. A refugee commission was authorized, to be supported by private funds, and James G. McDonald, the former president of the Foreign Policy Association, was chosen as high commissioner.

In actuality, McDonald's agency coordinated the relief activities of the different Jewish communities and undertook to negotiate with various governments about opening their doors to refugees. It also sought to map out schemes for large-scale migrations and settlement. Although it was planned as a service to all German refugees, Christian groups failed to assume a share of the responsibility, and the commission depended for its existence on Jewish subsidies. The second aim—that of enabling an international officer to deal with the Nazis—failed. McDonald received little attention, much less cooperation, in Berlin, especially when he proposed that refugees be permitted to take their property with them. And even those governments which made financial contributions showed no desire to admit the refugees. The high commissioner privately summed up the situation: "I would say that the world has become disagreeably conscious of the Jews; they are considered a drug on the market."

VI

Side by side with its efforts to bring pressure on the German government through diplomatic channels, the American Jewish Committee worked to arouse public opinion against the Nazi policies. For the same reasons which determined its opposition to a Jewish boycott of Germany, it resolved that its own role should be that of catalyst rather than public agitator. In April 1933 Judge Proskauer, stressing the need for a broad-based attack, suggested that AJC stimulate the organizing of non-Jewish liberals to lead the opposition to nazism. The recently created League for Human Rights was still ineffectual, and AJC contacted Dr. Nicholas Murray Butler as the most likely candidate to head the drive. Butler agreed that the Nazi question was more than a strictly Jewish concern. He refused, however, to lead a Christian movement, explaining to Stroock and Proskauer that he could be more of an asset as president of the Carnegie Peace Foundation, through which he promised to use his influence. (Butler no doubt was unwilling to compromise his chances of being appointed as Roosevelt's ambassador to Berlin.) Confident that liberal opinion in Germany would reassert itself, Butler advised against any provocation of the Nazi government, lest that lead to total suppression of the German moderates.

Undeterred, the Committee continued to look for Christian allies. It welcomed resolutions of protest from diverse groups— Baptists, Methodists, musicians, lawyers, and doctors—who condemned the persecution of their German Jewish colleagues, particularly since these protests were unsolicited. Arturo Toscanini's refusal to appear in Bayreuth, for instance, and letters from the Mayo brothers denouncing the Nazi terror were especially gratifying. The Committee published its own "white book," *The Jews in Nazi Germany,* and distributed *The Voice of Religion,* a collection of anti-Nazi statements by Christian leaders in English-language periodicals. It contributed to the publication of anti-Nazi works by Christian writers—*Swastika,* by Professor W. Brown; *The Strange Case of Mr. Hitler,* by Everett Clinchy; *Hitler's Reich,* by Hamilton Fish Armstrong—and unobtrusively suggested ideas for (and on occasion even wrote) features for periodicals. It monitored the press for misleading reports. When a translation of *Mein Kampf* was published in the United States, the Committee made sure that Hitler's original criticisms of all liberal institutions were made known. On occasions such as the arrival of Ambassador Luther from Germany, AJC stimulated a wave of editorial criticism of the Nazi regime. It also elicited protests from non-Jews against holding the 1936 Olympic Games in Berlin because Germany discriminated against its Jewish athletes.

As the months passed, the Committee also shifted its tactics from apologetics to a historical-scientific attack on nazism. More meaningful than accounts of Jewish accomplishments, AJC president Adler insisted, was the refutation of "racial science." This could be done by creating "a public opinion in this country against Hitler and his party absolutely without reference to the Jews at all. . . . I am of the opinion that we cannot be constantly thrusting ourselves before the public without danger to ourselves. They will get tired of us. What I want them to do is to get tired of Hitler." Accordingly, the Committee helped subsidize the work of Columbia University's famous anthropologist, Franz Boas, and other social scientists in refuting the Aryan myth.

VII

From 1933 to 1935 Jews clung to the hope that the situation in Germany might somehow improve. In September 1935, however, with the passage of the Nuremberg laws eliminating the Jews from national life, it became impossible to entertain such illusions. Moreover, the economic collapse of Germany, which had appeared so imminent, was no longer a serious possibility; nor was there any likelihood of internal dissension wrecking the Nazi party. Only a handful of liberals outside Germany had spoken out against the anti-Jewish assaults; governments everywhere followed political considerations of self-interest; the Catholic Church remained silent.

The Committee debated its course of action at this critical moment. Rejected out of hand was the idea, suggested by some, that it bore from within the Nazi ranks to effect a change in the anti-Semitic policies. Neither would it consider the possibility of encouraging armed resistance. This left only the tried weapon of public opinion. AJC also redoubled its drive to evacuate Jews from Germany and at the same time, concentrated on immunizing Germany's neighbors against the Nazi teachings.

To further these goals the Committee expanded its activities abroad. Roger Straus conferred with foreign Jewish organizations in 1932, and Lewis Strauss and Morris Waldman participated in a similar conference in 1933, principally on the matter of refugees and relief. The establishment of the Jewish Central Information Office in Amsterdam and a bureau in Paris made possible greater coordination. Supported by the Committee and European groups (principally Alliance Israélite Universelle, Joint Foreign Committee, and Jewish Colonization Association), these bodies served as clearinghouses, supplying their members as well as foreign journalists with on-the-spot reports of developments in Germany and other countries. They gathered dossiers of anti-Semitic writings current in Europe to help the Jewish organizations prepare counter propaganda for dissemination through pamphlets, periodicals, and radio broadcasts. The Amsterdam and Paris bureaus also carried out the political and diplomatic moves decided on by the Jewish leaders of various countries.

Morris Waldman, who pressed the idea of a Jewish brain trust, despite fears of feeding the myth of an international Jewish conspiracy, sought out additional foreign contacts for the Committee. The officers of the Joint Distribution Committee were among the Committee's chief advisers. A particularly close relationship was maintained with leaders of the Joint Foreign Committee: Sir Osmond d'Avigdor-Goldsmid and Neville Laski. Jacob Landau, director of the Jewish Telegraphic Agency, often represented Waldman in international dealings. Special informants reported directly to Waldman: journalist Edward Kleinlerer; Leo Simon, a former German industrialist; and Joseph Wirth, an ex-chancellor of the Weimar Republic.

Waldman supplemented a voluminous, though often veiled, correspondence with these men by periodic trips which he and his assistant, Sidney Wallach, made to the continent. He regarded Wirth's help as especially valuable, for Wirth, a Catholic, seemed the most logical person to approach the Vatican and the clergy in Eastern Europe. Indeed, Waldman later credited him with convincing Pius XI to issue the famous encyclical *Mit brennender Sorge* (With Burning Sorrow), an eloquent condemnation of the Nazi horrors. Though employed by the Committee, Wirth was instructed "not to give the faintest impression that he had any special Jewish interest. . . . His interest was purely that of a Catholic and a Democrat, . . . [and] his efforts to enlist the sympathy of influential individuals and bodies must be purely on the basis of Catholicism and Democracy." Wirth not only was to impress on the Vatican that anti-Semitism discredited the church, he also was urged to point out that it led to the weakening of Christian loyalties.

The American Jewish Committee followed with growing alarm developments in Central and Eastern Europe. Hitler was a menace to Austria and Danzig; the plight of the Jews in Poland and Rumania grew steadily more intolerable. AJC hoped that Austria might be kept from Germany's clutches, and on the advice of high American officials it initiated a last-ditch drive to bolster Austria's trade so as to strengthen her ability to resist Nazi advances. Searching desperately for a way to stop the Nazis, the Committee even considered briefly supporting a Hapsburg restoration, an idea which still had some currency in Vienna. To bring a measure of reassurance to the apprehensive Jews of Danzig, AJC and its European allies contributed funds for counter propaganda. Similar contributions were made to the nonsectarian Commission for the Defense of the Rights of Jews in Eastern Europe.

In Rumania and Poland domestic anti-Semitism threatened to cause incalculable suffering even before their capitulation to Germany. The growth of discrimination in those countries during the 1920s was now abetted by the racist teachings of the Nazis. Returning from a trip to Europe in 1935, Waldman reported on increasing restrictions on Jews in schools, in the professions, in political life, and in industry. After Poland signed a nonaggression pact with Germany, the Poles began to talk openly (with echoes from Rumania) about how they could end anti-Semitism by the forced emigration of large numbers of Jews.

The Jewish organizations were at a loss as to how to stem this tide. It was futile to invoke the peace treaties, for not only had Poland repudiated the minority-rights agreements in 1934, but the League of Nations had become no more than a faint shadow of Woodrow Wilson's grand design. Approaches to the American government and to Polish envoys helped little; events in Germany had revealed Jewish impotence, and East European leaders no longer responded as seriously as they once had to expressions of disapproval by foreign Jews. Besides, Polish Jews asked would-be intercessors not to protest to their government, because they feared that such action would impugn their own avowals of patriotism.

Jewish diplomatic action, however, alerted France to the spread of German propaganda in Rumania, and France, jealous of her traditional influence in that country, supported the anti-Nazi drive. Two Committee representatives also conferred with Cardinal Pacelli, who visited the United States in 1937, and the cardinal promised the reissuance of Benedict XV's 1916 declaration dissociating the church from the persecution of Jews in Poland.

For a time consideration was given to easing the pressures on the Jewish middle class by helping Poland build up her economy. Following Louis Marshall's precedent, in 1937 Felix Warburg discussed with Polish leaders the possibility of large financial loans. The Committee refused to be blackmailed into financing emigration from Poland, however, and in the face of the continuing crisis it decided on a different course of action. Money from the Jewish organizations was channeled to Poland and Rumania for a variety of projects, including political and propaganda activities, aid to Jewish financial institutions, and relief. AJC, which bore one-third to one-half the total cost, now thought that "educational" work in previous years might have averted the crises.

How local Jews should disburse the sums, whether Jews should back the Socialists and risk inciting the church, the assignment of European and American Jews to particular labors—all these issues raised serious problems. But the American Jewish Committee persisted in trying to save as many European Jews as possible, learning through bitter experience that long-term educational projects yielded better results than last-minute relief drives.

VIII

In Erfurt, Germany, the Nazis established an international headquarters for assorted anti-Semitic groups throughout the world and published *World Service,* an organ of anti-Semitic propaganda that appeared in numerous languages and was distributed throughout the world. The Erfurt headquarters also directed the so-called shirt organizations set up by the Nazis in different countries (Silver Shirts in the United States, Black Shirts in England, Gold Shirts in Mexico, Grey Shirts in South Africa), and the city was the scene of an international anti-Semitic conference in 1937. Among the favorite items of Nazi propaganda were the *Protocols of the Elders of Zion* and Henry Ford's *The International Jew.* At the request of the Jewish Central Information Office, the Committee resurrected Ford's repudiation of *The International Jew,* but efforts to secure a new disavowal from Ford (who was decorated by the Nazis in 1938) failed.

The Committee, together with other Jewish organizations, also aided the plaintiffs in a court trial in Berne, Switzerland, in 1934 and 1935, which challenged the authenticity of the *Protocols.* Although Colonel Ulrich Fleischhauer, director of *World Service,* testified that "all presidents of the United States and President Wilson in particular were under Jewish influence" and insisted that the League of Nations and the Kellogg-Briand Pact of 1928 were "Jewish creations," the court upheld the plaintiffs. At the same time, AJC, still interested in a scientific airing of the myth of Aryan supremacy, helped organize an international conference on race, securing the participation of Professor Franz Boas as an American delegate.

A final effort to convict Germany at the bar of public opinion came in connection with James McDonald's resignation as high commissioner for refugees. Special consultants from AJC worked with him to prepare a document which the Committee widely publicized and distributed. McDonald's agency had resettled approximately sixty-five thousand refugees during its two years of existence, but the high commissioner, hampered by the fact that his committee was never an integral part of the League of Nations machinery, had been rebuffed by nations and individuals alike in his search for new homes for the persecuted. At best, his job was remedial rather than curative, for he never was permitted to enter into direct diplomatic negotiations with the Nazis. When the Nuremberg laws were passed, McDonald felt that international political action was called for:

> [In] the new circumstances it will not be enough to continue the activities on behalf of those who flee from the Reich. Efforts must be made to remove or mitigate the causes which create German refugees. . . . It is a political function, which properly belongs to the League itself. . . . The moral authority of the League of Nations and of States Members of the League must be directed towards a determined appeal to the German Government in the name of humanity and of the principles of the public law of Europe. They must ask for a modification of policies which constitute a source of unrest and perplexity in the world, a challenge to the conscience of mankind, and a menace to the legitimate interests of the States affected by the immigration of German refugees. . . . The problem must be tackled at its source if disaster is to be avoided.

Commenting upon the high commissioner's resignation, the *San Francisco Chronicle* wrote: "Perhaps it is nobody's legal business. . . . But when a nation which once stood among the leaders of the world's civilization descends to this uncivilized course, is it not the moral business of civilization?" Despite the urgent tone of McDonald's letter, League of Nations action (little as that was worth in 1936) was not forthcoming. AJC tried to press the matter and asked two scholars, Oscar Janowsky and Melvin Fagen, to draft a petition citing legal justification and historical precedents for international intervention. James N. Rosenberg, a member of the Committee with special interest in the rights of individuals under law, largely underwrote the cost of the project. The Committee's friends in England cooperated, although they doubted the value of the petition since they knew that Britain, eager to bring Germany back to the league (from which it had resigned in 1933), would have nothing to do with such a document.

After months of preparation, the petition and its voluminous supporting material were ready. Signed by ten organizations, most of them non-Jewish, the document was to have been officially introduced by one of the member states in the League of Nations Assembly, where, it was hoped, it would lead to open debate. However, heightened tensions arising from the civil war in Spain forced abandonment of the plan, and the petition's sponsors had no alternative but to present it privately to the assembly's president. Although its immediate goal was not achieved, AJC made wide use of the petition in the United States. Sol M. Stroock, chairman of the executive committee, discussed the document and the desperate situation inside Germany in a special radio address. Endorsements were gathered from prominent clerical, political, and civic figures, and the petition itself was widely distributed in book form.

IX

Even if an aroused world opinion could have achieved censure of Germany by the League of Nations, what force would it have had in light of the league's performance with regard to Manchuria, Ethiopia, and the invasion of the Rhineland? With the Western nations clinging to isolationism and appeasement of Germany, should Jews have challenged the prevailing mood and fought more vigorously for collective security?

For a while AJC considered support for the Defence of Freedom and Peace movement, an English group headed by journalist Wickham Steed (its most impressive member was Winston Churchill), which sought to educate the British government to the realities of the Nazi totalitarian threat. The Committee considered bringing Churchill to the United States to stimulate the creation of an American counterpart to the movement, but ultimately discarded the plan for fear of antagonizing American public opinion. Anglophobes might interpret Churchill's visit as an effort to involve America in a European problem, it was argued. According to a 1937 Gallup poll, 64 percent of the American people still believed that America's entry into World War I was a mistake, and there was fear that any known connection between Churchill and the Jews would bring charges of warmongering from anti-Semites. The U.S. ambassador to the Court of St. James's, Joseph P. Kennedy, warned a prominent British Jew that "there were still people of sense who at the back of their minds had the idea that the Jews would like Germany to be punished by defeat in a war." He added: "I tell you on the authority of no less a person than Franklin Delano Roosevelt that if the United States is dragged into war with Germany there might even be a pogrom in the U.S.A. itself."

The Committee compromised and brought Steed rather than Churchill to the United States. Arriving October 5, 1937, the day of Roosevelt's "quarantine" speech, the British journalist met with individuals and small groups from the Council of Foreign Relations, Harvard University, and circles in Washington. Although the reaction to Roosevelt's speech revealed that Americans still saw no reason to abandon isolationism, the Committee believed Steed's visit had some salutary effect on American and British policy.

X

As conditions in Germany worsened, Jews left in increasing numbers. The American Jewish Committee, alerted since 1933 to expect a flow of refugees from Nazi persecution, sometimes discussed the need to evacuate the German Jews; but it did not advocate emigration as the solution, or even a partial solution, until after the passage of the Nuremberg laws. Even then many German Jews did not wish to leave their homeland, and others were ready to leave but were unwilling to do so before specific havens were found for them.

The Committee never dealt with concrete problems of immigrant aid, though many of its members worked with the JDC and various other service organizations set up for the purpose. However, it was fully within the Committee's tradition to agitate for the admission of immigrants to the United States.

In 1935, shortly before he resigned as high commissioner for refugees, James McDonald urgently recommended that American Jewish leaders help plan for the evacuation of two hundred thousand young Germans over a ten-year period. He still hoped that negotiations with Schacht would result in permission to transfer Jewish capital out of Germany, and he proposed the admission of ten thousand German Jews annually to Palestine and five thousand to the United States. U.S. immigration laws allotted an annual quota of over twenty-five thousand to German immigrants, but since only a fraction of that number was admitted, McDonald's request required a deliberate shift in consular policy.

Governor Herbert H. Lehman of New York, one of AJC's strongest contacts with the White House, wrote a moving letter to President Roosevelt, pointing to the high caliber of earlier German Jewish immigrants and asking him to ease America's admission policy. Roosevelt repeated his assurances that U.S. consuls abroad had been instructed to treat refugee applicants "with consideration"; but there was no significant change in the restrictionist mood, and America's vigorous enforcement of the quota laws was another sign to Hitler that the democracies were not much concerned about his anti-Semitic policies.

With the onset of the Great Depression in 1930, anti-immigration sentiment rose sharply. While extreme restrictionists sought in the next decade to cut quotas by as much as 90 percent, liberals tried to avoid permanent legal measures by arguing that the same results could be achieved by administrative action. Indeed, when the State Department announced in September 1930 that the "l.p.c." provision—which barred immigrants "likely to become a public charge"—would be interpreted to exclude all but the most prosperous, the quotas were in reality reduced by 90 percent. Unremitting activity by the Committee, usually in conjunction with other groups, Jewish and non-Jewish, kept the problem of German refugees before the government. Time and time again Cyrus Adler, Max J. Kohler, Joseph Proskauer, and Julian Mack pleaded the cause of the German Jews before the Labor and State Departments. Secretary of Labor Frances Perkins and Commissioner of Immigration Daniel MacCormack tried to help, but the administration would not rescind its 1930 directive, especially when William Green, president of the American Federation of Labor, warned the president against relaxation of immigration procedure "in the name of the 11,000,000 unemployed." The most that American Jews achieved was greater leniency toward applicants unable to submit all the required documents from their governments, and a ruling that bond might be posted in the United States for an applicant who might otherwise be excluded under the l.p.c. clause.

Warned by Washington officials that relaxing the immigration requirements might increase anti-Semitism in the United States, the Committee deliberately advised its friends in Congress against proposals for open hearings. However, under the leadership of Max J. Kohler, AJC continued to present briefs against bills for reducing quotas or increasing deportations. The Committee supplied background material to humanitarian organizations like the National Committee on the Cause and Cure of War, headed by Mrs. Carrie Chapman Catt, the peace leader who espoused the refugee cause. AJC also endorsed plans for the temporary adoption of several hundred German children. But all this was merely a holding operation. Not until the spring of 1938, when Roosevelt called for an international conference on refugees to be held at Evian, France, was there evidence of real American concern for refugees. Even then it was clear that the quota system remained sacrosanct.

XI

In 1938 earlier vague premonitions turned into grim realities. Anschluss, Munich, the occupation of the Sudetenland, the *Kristallnacht,* Italy's adoption of a racist policy—all testified to the Nazi triumph and the plight of the Jews in Central Europe. Morris Waldman, who was in Europe in the fall of 1938, described the general mood of despair at the Jewish meetings he attended:

> We all feel that it is futile at the present moment to come to any decision with respect to future activities. . . . The situation has changed in such revolutionary fashion as to vitiate any plans for overseas work. . . . Our friends . . . seem to feel as if the situation in all of Europe is hopeless, that our enemies have surrounded us completely, and that we are at their mercy. . . . They . . . seem to see no hope for Democracy and the Jews.

The portents were unmistakable: unless the free world took action, not only the Jews but liberty itself was doomed. Jewish survival depended on those who would stand up and be counted as the defenders of democracy.

The horrors of the *Kristallnacht,* in November 1938, evoked a chorus of protests across the Atlantic. At a press conference President Roosevelt condemned the outrages in outspoken terms, and American Jews showered him with grateful messages. Roosevelt's sympathy was now fully aroused. In a letter to Ambassador William Phillips in Italy he wrote: "It gives [the Jews] little comfort to remind them that they have been 'on the run' for about four thousand years." Yet Roosevelt made no constructive move, aside from the gesture of recalling Ambassador Hugh Wilson from Berlin. It was in response to public and congressional pressure in behalf of the Jewish refugees that the president called for the Evian Conference—and in so doing, he followed State Department reasoning that executive action would avert moves to liberalize the immigration laws.

Getting Jews out of Germany became the prime goal of the Jewish organizations after 1938. Contrary to expectations, the Evian Conference accomplished little more than to create an ineffectual Inter-Governmental Committee on Refugees, based in London. The various schemes of the AJC leaders, individually or with other groups, to save Jews on the eve of the war will never be completely known. The records do show that Sol Stroock was involved in drives to raise "astronomical" sums, that Cyrus Adler badgered the State Department for the admission of individual European rabbis, and that in 1940 James Rosenberg won agreement from the Dominican Republic to colonize a group of Jews. Lewis Strauss has written movingly of his experiences with the Coordinating Foundation, a corporation created in 1939, during negotiations between German officials and the Inter-Governmental Committee on Refugees for the purpose of "buying" the right of emigration for German Jews: "I might have done so much more than I did. I risked only what I thought I could afford. That was not the test which should have been applied, and it is my eternal regret."

XII

History ultimately vindicated those Zionists who had urged mass Jewish immigration to Palestine from the very first days of Hitler's rise to power. While the Committee knew that Palestine was absorbing the greatest number of German Jews, it could not agree that it was the sole haven, lest that be construed as arguing that only in a Jewish homeland was Jewish survival possible. (Cyrus Adler commented in 1933 that Hitler would be pleased no end if all the Jews of Germany left for Palestine.)

The Committee's effort to maintain a distinction between Zionism and the need for a Jewish haven in Palestine was difficult for many people to understand, particularly during those troubled years. But this distinction guided AJC's reaction to events in 1937–39.

During the 1920s, when the Committee leaders joined the Zionists in projects for developing Palestine, none believed that Jewish statehood was imminent. Rooted in an Emancipationist philosophy, they always resented the charges of dual allegiance and separatism which Zionism had brought down upon world Jewry. But when England recommended partition of Palestine into Jewish and Arab states in the wake of the 1936 Arab riots, AJC opposed the plan*—not for anti-Zionist, but for pragmatic reasons. With the Nazi threat paramount, all of Palestine had to be kept open to the European refugees, with no obstacle save its physical capacity to absorb them. This was the promise, the Committee maintained, of the Balfour Declaration and the British mandate.

Since the Arab riots, which precipitated the partition decision, had been Nazi-inspired, the Committee argued, Britain should not be permitted to yield. Her presence as the mandatary power was necessary to insure the security of the Jews, at least in that corner of the world, and her fulfillment of the mandate's provisions was an international obligation which civilized nations could not violate. Moreover, the specific Jewish state envisaged by the royal commission was unacceptable on political and economic grounds; even the non-Zionists would not accept a permanent minority status. The myriad problems of creating and maintaining an independent state would only cause further

---

*This was a departure from customary procedure, for with the enlargement of the Jewish Agency in 1929 the Committee had preferred to leave all political questions affecting Palestine to that body. Only in cases of emergency —the riots of 1929, the discriminatory recommendations of the Passfield White Paper of 1930—had the Committee taken separate action. By 1937, however, the situation had changed. The Jewish Agency, in fact run by Zionists, never turned out to be, as planned, representative of both Zionists and non-Zionists. AJC members like Adler and Felix Warburg, who filled high posts in the Jewish Agency, determined that the non-Zionist position as worked out by the Committee would be made to bear on the agency's deliberations regarding partition.

disunity within Jewish ranks and drain off resources needed to fight the Nazis. It was not the Committee's task to discuss the merits of a Jewish state, Sol Stroock insisted to the organization's membership. AJC closed ranks on the issue and, together with all shades of Jewish leadership, both Zionist and anti-Zionist, opposed the British partition stand.

In July 1937 Felix Warburg met with Adler, Stroock, Irving Lehman, and Maurice Karpf to plan strategy. There is no record of the discussion, but apparently the ideological question of Jewish statehood was not paramount. A memorandum by Adler reveals that his quarrel was with those preaching Diaspora nationalism. He did not believe that a state would create grave problems for Jewish citizens of democratic nations—provided, of course, that the Jewish Agency and World Zionist Organization ceased to exist as political bodies. It might have been better, he added, had the peace conference established a Jewish state in 1919. Instead, the Jews were stuck with the phrase *national home*, which could be variously interpreted, and which to Adler sounded like a "a big orphan asylum."

Warburg traveled to Europe twice that year in connection with the partition question and succeeded in having the Jewish Agency go on record in favor of Jewish-Arab conferences, while reserving the right to pass on any concrete proposal for partition. Thus the non-Zionists not only increased their strength in the Jewish Agency, but the idea of conferences as a means of promoting Arab-Jewish amity, on which they insisted, was later taken up by the British.

In the summer of 1937, Lewis L. Strauss, George Backer, and Morris Waldman, who were more acceptable to the Arabs than the Zionist spokesmen, met quietly with three Arab leaders in an attempt to find an Arab-Jewish solution to the Palestine problem. If the Arab and Jewish views on immigration and land settlement could be reconciled, the two groups could appeal jointly to England for a settlement in an undivided Palestine.

American Zionist leaders supported these exploratory talks, for they too opposed partition.

The Committee's strategy here seems to have been prompted more by a desire to establish its primacy in the Jewish community than by antinationalist feeling. Convinced that the Zionists were exploiting the European situation for their own organizational benefit, the AJC leaders strove for control when the situation impinged on the larger goal of saving European Jewry. They hoped to deal directly with the Arabs and set down ground rules for Jewish settlement in Palestine. If and when the Jews ever constituted a majority there, a revitalized non-Zionist group in the Jewish Agency (that is, leaders of the Committee) could decide if the time was ripe for statehood.

The aim of a broader Jewish Agency did not materialize; and Felix Warburg, who had privately financed non-Zionist activities, died at the end of 1937. Nevertheless, early in 1939, when the British gave up the idea of partition and called for conferences, Committee leaders talked of sending a representative. They knew that Prime Minister Neville Chamberlain, resentful that the Jewish question weakened his policy of appeasement, did not look favorably upon their claims. Meanwhile, Nazi policies were instituted in Austria and Czechoslovakia, and the need for refuge grew more urgent. No American non-Zionist delegate attended the parleys, but together with Solomon Goldman of the Zionist Organization of America and Justice Brandeis (and, through Brandeis, with Roosevelt and Chamberlain), they worked to keep immigration open.

American Jewry waited apprehensively. "This present crisis . . . has turned some of the most ardent non-Zionists and possibly anti-Zionists around just the other way," wrote Cyrus Adler. The American Jewish Committee and other groups sent new official appeals against curtailing immigration to both the British government and the State Department. But no favorable solution emerged from the conferences in London. In May the British government issued a white paper which limited Jewish immigration to seventy-five thousand annually for a period of five years, and empowered the high commissioner to restrict land sales which might impair the Arab position. Aware that this restriction would have serious consequences for European Jewry, Zionists and non-Zionists, Jews and Christians, all joined in shocked protest to the British government. The situation seemed more helpless than ever.

9

Bigotry and Defense, American Style

Had it not been for the Nazi threat of the 1930s, the American Jewish Committee might have faded into insignificance or even ceased to exist. The death of Louis Marshall, AJC's mainstay and moving force, was a serious blow; but the Committee's future looked bleak for other reasons as well. The very structure of AJC worked to its disadvantage. After the crash of 1929, elitism, particularly that based on money, was suspect in the public mind. Also, the affluent German Jews on whom AJC relied so heavily for leadership and support in its first decades lost much of their influence as new groups gained prominence in the American Jewish community during the 1920s.

The German Jews of AJC were third- or fourth-generation Americans who reflected the deep inroads of assimilation, as well as the widespread American antipathy to organizations smacking of ethnic separatism. Nor could the Committee find much support among the masses who, long resentful of AJC's aloofness, turned to organizations like B'nai B'rith, with its network of lodges, or the American Jewish Congress and its chapters. Thus the Committee was now reduced to a handful of men on the East Coast, none outstanding for leadership qualities.

Marshall's domination had lulled AJC into inertia and indifference; restless members who complained of knowing too little of Committee activities were politely ignored. To be sure, the Committee could still boast of more illustrious names than the other organizations, but the necessary spark was missing. Even Cyrus Adler, a dedicated and conscientious worker, was only a pale reflection of his famous predecessors.

The most famous of them was, of course, Louis Marshall, who tangled with Henry Ford and fought anti-Jewish discrimination on campuses and in employment. If few Jews associated these activities with AJC it did not really matter, since the Committee shunned publicity and ignored the public as long as it was financially independent. After the 1929 crash, however, contributions fell off drastically, and the development of community welfare funds and federations also worked against independent fund raising. The carefree days when Jacob Schiff would pick up the tab were over.

In the decade preceding World War II, the American Jewish Committee faced two major challenges: to meet the Nazi crisis despite the organization's weakened condition and to lay the foundations for a more solid, permanent structure.

I

On February 20, 1929, a German journalist, Kurt G. W. Luedecke, appeared at Louis Marshall's office with several letters signed by Adolf Hitler indicating that Luedecke represented the Nazi movement in the United States, Hungary, and Italy. Luedecke described to Marshall his experiences as a devoted Nazi and as Hitler's personal friend, and gave his prognosis of the effect of the rise of nazism on Europe. Claiming to be disillusioned and no longer hopeful about the ultimate success of the movement, he offered to work for the Jews within the Nazi party ranks. AJC rejected the proposition, but that was not the last time Luedecke was heard from. A frequent visitor to America after

World War I and married to an American citizen, Luedecke had been a volunteer propagandist for the Nazis since 1924. After the Nazi victory in the 1930 election, he became one of the first paid propagandists for national socialism in the United States. A press representative for all Nazi newspapers, he gained access to many government circles in Washington and became known as Hitler's unofficial ambassador.

Luedecke's approaches to Marshall were not the only indication of the organized effort to disseminate Nazi doctrines. In 1931 and 1932 AJC learned of Teutonia, a National Socialist federation headed by a Walter Kappe, and of local Nazi activities, particularly in New York and Chicago. Nazi anti-Semitism was spread also by means of the German-language monthly *Vorposten* (to which both Kappe and Luedecke contributed) and the Boston *American Guard*. These facts reinforced warnings to the Committee from friends in Germany that it had better look to its own defenses. With the Great Depression in full swing and prominent intellectuals debating the bankruptcy of democratic capitalism and the need to turn definitely "right" or "left," Nazi hate propaganda was clearly a far more serious matter than anti-Jewish discrimination by a hotel or an employment agency.

The Committee's first countermeasure was to create, in 1931, a German department to scrutinize German-sponsored anti-Semitic propaganda in the United States. Two years later, at the urging of Judge Proskauer and James Rosenberg, attorney Wolfgang Schwabacher volunteered to investigate the work of the anti-Semitic organizations. Schwabacher's unit, known as the Information and Service Associates, operated out of his own office and was financed by a handful of men outside the Committee. Although Schwabacher had complete control of his operation, he often consulted with the Committee on policy, and Sidney Wallach, Waldman's assistant, worked with the Schwabacher unit.

The Information and Service Associates' dual task was to expose organizations and agitators in the United States and "im-

munize the American people against the virus of anti-Semitism."
Aiming at a non-Jewish audience, the unit sought to interpret
nazism as a menace to the democratic way of life, not to Jews
alone. This approach was supported by the findings of a small
survey conducted in 1933—the first of its kind undertaken by the
Committee—which revealed that public opinion was still un-
formed on the Nazi issue, particularly as it affected the Jews.
Those interviewed expressed both a distaste for Hitler's methods
and an antipathy toward "undesirable" Jews. Most were not convinced of the soundness of the Nazi approach, but, on the other
hand, they did not believe the reports about Nazi atrocities.

Schwabacher's unit embarked on a program of education
through the press, radio, and lectures. Special emphasis was
given to reaching German-Americans, as well as to cooperation
with Christian organizations. A secondary goal of the program
was to insure the respectability of anti-Nazi propaganda.

The Information and Service Associates lasted little more
than a year. Schwabacher feared that the contributors would not
renew their support; also, he had to neglect his law practice.
Morris Waldman, who complained that Schwabacher merely
"nibbled" at his task, transferred the unit back to his own jurisdiction. Against the mounting agitation, he continued to push for
an expansion of counter propaganda. A warning from Max Warburg on the inadequacy of American Jewish defense resources
brought support from a group on the AJC executive committee.
Lewis Strauss spearheaded a campaign to collect funds and enroll
interested laymen. Within a short time six hundred thousand
dollars was raised, enough to insure an intensive program of two
to three years. In October 1936 the direction of that program was
entrusted to the Survey Committee.

The members of the Survey Committee—so named because
of their earlier assignment to investigate the agency's educational
enterprises—came from AJC ranks or were co-opted from the
larger Jewish community. Some had never participated actively in
a Jewish organization before; many served on the committee

without joining AJC itself. Never larger than thirty members, the Survey Committee was a young group, mostly men in their forties. The requirements for membership were a sense of commitment and duty, a willingness to give up all other philanthropic activities, availability for innumerable meetings, and "grueling" assignments. A member might be asked to assume the chairmanship, which rotated every three months; at other times, he might be named to head a specific project or department. He would report on his progress at the meetings. Wallach, working in an administrative capacity with the Survey Committee, recalled the "selfless" and competent men who devoted countless hours to their self-imposed tasks. Edward Greenbaum, perhaps the most highly respected member of the group, summed it up more matter-of-factly to Cyrus Adler: "I am scarcely practicing law these days."

Under the Survey Committee, AJC's lay leadership reached its peak of importance. Teamwork substituted for the individual action of the prewar days, and, unlike the pattern set by Marshall, no one man was permitted to dominate. In making and executing policy the laymen as a group became the professionals.

Though officially subject to AJC policy, the Survey Committee was in reality an autonomous organization. It had its own budget and raised and disbursed funds at its own discretion. At the end of 1938, when the Wertheim campaign was launched to replenish the Survey Committee's funds, AJC suspended its own fund-raising efforts. Contributions to AJC fell off, but by the beginning of 1940 the Survey Committee had raised over $1.25 million. At the height of the Survey Committee's operations, in 1938 and 1939, there were, in fact, two American Jewish Committees—the Survey Committee, which ran the domestic program, and the central office under Waldman, which concentrated on the foreign scene. To some it appeared as if the Survey Committee outstripped its parent in importance, and Waldman tried repeatedly, and often unsuccessfully, to keep the offspring in line. But any long-term worries on that score were unjustified. The Survey

Committee was a direct response to the immediate crisis: American Jews mobilized against the Nazi propaganda attacks which they interpreted as directly threatening to them. When that crisis ended they felt they had completed their task.

Beginning with an annual budget of two hundred thousand dollars—seven times larger than the entire AJC budget in 1932 —the Survey Committee undertook an intensive educational and investigative program.* In 1937 George Backer's publications division disbursed fifty thousand dollars for the writing and distribution of leaflets and pamphlets, sponsorship of books, and subventions to anti-Nazi papers. Judge Samuel Rosenman, in charge of the schools division, handled the endowment of a chair in human relations at Newark University, arranged with Professor Allan Nevins of Columbia to direct investigations of anti-immigration sentiment contained in history textbooks, and kept watch over German exchange students and professors who spread Nazi teachings. Arthur Goldsmith directed the speakers' bureau; Benjamin Buttenweiser formulated ideas for radio programs; and Roger W. Straus, a cochairman of the National Council of Jews and Christians, kept an eye on religious textbooks and interfaith projects. Matters relating to legislation affecting civil liberties, Nazi organizations, and refugees were coordinated by Carl Austrian, while Edward Greenbaum handled relations with Jewish and non-Jewish organizations. Samuel Leidesdorf was responsible for the physical plant and the creation of regional offices, and Lewis Strauss collected the money.

Special projects were handled by others: David O. Selznick, for example, served as liaison with the film industry; Judge Phillip Forman evaluated a plan for a "League of Democracy." The Survey Committee as a whole planned the general policy, and all members used their personal political and social contacts to obtain help for the various projects.

The Survey Committee's design was to activate others—

*The latter is treated separately on pp. 200–202.

individuals and groups—and to step out of the picture once a project was launched. It contributed funds to Christian and non-sectarian organizations working to reach major groups in the country—Catholics and Protestants, labor, women, colleges and universities. Constantly evaluating its own activities and methods, it kept a critical eye on those it endowed. Guided by public-opinion polls, counsel from public relations experts, and criticisms solicited from the community, it would cancel or renew operations according to changing needs and results achieved.

II

The charter members of the Survey Committee interpreted their task in broad humanistic terms:

> Our program is based upon the belief that the civil and religious rights of the Jews in the United States are dependent upon the maintenance of our democratic form of government and that we can best help maintain these rights by fortifying adherence to the fundamental principles of democracy, and that specific action relative to educating the public must be integrated with the major task of maintaining peaceful relations between the various groups composing our population. . . . We wish to appeal to the spirit of democracy and with it the spirit of fair play in this country.

The goal—considerably broader than that of the Central-verein—was admittedly admirable, but the early techniques lacked sufficient direction. How possible was it to "sell" the abstract value of democracy? All Americans, even those having specific prejudices, insisted upon their allegiance to the democratic creed. Would support of democracy in the abstract lessen the virulence of the Nazi-inspired hatred? The promotion of courses in human relations and revision of history books were obviously investments in the distant future. But did the distribution of books and pamphlets or the subvention of organizations reach vital nerve centers of opinion or did they merely touch the insignificant periphery? Were those methods strong enough to challenge traditional anti-Semitism or combat the kind of anti-Semitism which seemed to coincide with upheavals in the economy? Opinion polls conducted during the late 1930s revealed that the common charges leveled at the Jews—inordinate economic power, unscrupulous conduct, communism, unpatriotic behavior, warmongering—reflected prejudices in existence long before Hitler. What, then, was the most efficacious way to stem the acute anti-Semitism before it reached tidal proportions?

Aware of the need for a more distinct course—especially as polls continued to register increased anti-Semitism—the Survey Committee welcomed the advice offered in 1938 by a new member, Richard Rothschild. An expert in advertising and public relations techniques, as well as a teacher of philosophy, Rothschild began with what he called the "principle of adequacy": a job had to be more than well done to be effective—it had to be adequate to its purpose. He charted a six-point plan predicated on the practical assumption that the Committee would deal neither with the traditional anti-Semitism nor the prejudices exacerbated by business cycles, but would concentrate on "propagandized" anti-Semitism emanating from Nazi ideologues. Rothschild's objectives were to (1) correct the misconceptions about Jews brought to light by the polls; (2) expose the Nazi system in all its brutality; (3) test the efficacy of a direct attack on anti-Semitism in one city; (4) investigate and take appropriate measures against violent anti-Semitic groups; (5) instruct the Jewish community in the use of constructive techniques in fighting anti-Semitism; and (6) create a "Jewish civil service" which would carry out the plan as a whole.

Of the six points, the first and second were the crux of the educational program aimed at the general public. (The third point was never implemented; the fourth was left to the legal and investigative staff to carry out.) Rothschild emphasized a positive approach: build a public image of the Jew against which the misconceptions would be dismissed as ludicrous; teach the public that Hitlerism was not only a personal threat to the Jews but also a depraved ideology attacking religion, morality, and basic human dignity; refuse to answer Nazis charges directly, but show how they worked to undermine the democratic way of life; avoid fighting anti-Semitism head on, but undercut it by attacking its chief sponsor.

Rothschild also worked with allies, a technique successfully used by the Committee for many years. Since the Committee's message was one of essential decency, most people would support it. On that premise the Survey Committee approached public-spirited men who reached large audiences—writers, newspaper editors and publishers, group leaders, radio program directors—the majority of whom made use of material supplied by the Committee.

Illustrative of the Survey Committee's methods was the refugee campaign initiated in 1938. Particularly after the passage of the Nuremberg laws, an increasing number of persons appealed to AJC for visas and jobs. Actively cooperating with nonsectarian agencies, the Survey Committee dealt with the special problems of the refugee doctor, the refugee student, relations between the newly hired refugee and his employer. Particular attention, however, centered on efforts to gain public acceptance for the refugee. This meant breaking down many popular misconceptions, which grossly exaggerated the number of refugees, equated refugees with radicals, and blamed them for displacing American workers.

An educational program was launched, enlisting prominent non-Jewish individuals and groups: the Quakers agreed to issue a pamphlet on the refugees; Walter Winchell explained in one of his broadcasts how refugees helped the American economy; gentile physicians signed a statement refuting the charge that refugees were overcrowding the medical profession; a religious news syndicate distributed stories showing that the problem of refugees concerned non-Jews as well as Jews. The Survey Committee staff prepared the background data, sometimes even writing the material; but throughout, the Committee itself remained behind the scenes. Within a few months its material reached millions of Americans. Though opinion polls continued to register popular fear and alarm over the influx of foreigners, it seems clear that the Survey Committee's efforts did help prevent the emergence of even more intense prejudice.

Rothschild had barely begun implementing his six-point plan when war broke out in Europe in September 1939. The onrush of events shifted the focus and emphasis of the Survey Committee's work; but its basic strategy was set, and determined that of AJC in the difficult years to come.

III

Another dimension of the Committee's educational program was the focus upon the Jewish community itself. Preaching brotherhood was not enough. As long as Jewish behavior could lend substance to age-old myths, it would be impossible to "immunize" the public against anti-Semitism. Leaders of the American Jewish Committee had long bemoaned the economic distribution of the Jews, with which the Jew-baiters of the 1920s and the Nazi apologists justified their anti-Semitism. In the 1930s this particular plaint grew more common. A survey drawn up for Felix Warburg in 1934 emphasized the dangers of the Jewish economic situation in the United States. Out of a Jewish population of 4.5 to 5 million, with 2 million normally employed, the "nonproductive" element (tradesmen, real estate brokers, financiers, professionals, civil servants, white-collar workers, middlemen) outnumbered the "productive" by three to one. (The proportion in the general population was slightly over one to one.)

More significant for shaping AJC policy was a memorandum on anti-Semitism prepared by Professor Alvin Johnson in 1937 for the Survey Committee. Like other comments from sympathetic Gentiles, it indicated that cultural pluralism had made little headway. Johnson estimated that four hundred thousand Americans had been swayed by Hitler's propaganda, particularly identification of Jews with Communists and the baneful influence of Jews on the arts and professions. Since Jews would always bear the onus of minority status—which meant, Johnson said, that in the public mind Brandeis was not a Jewish judge, but Leopold and Loeb were Jewish criminals—it was the responsibility of Jewish leaders to raise the standards of behavior among Jews, specifically by developing organizations to influence the public conduct of young people. Jewish youth should be encouraged to look to a Brandeis and a Lehman as exemplars and not to political or social revolutionaries. Johnson added a list of proscriptions for the entire Jewish community: not to form secret or seemingly antigentile organizations, not to preach Zionism or any sort of Jewish nationalism, not to become allied with other oppressed groups such as Negroes or Orientals, and, above all, to avoid notoriety or overconspicuousness.

If these were the carefully considered opinions of a liberal non-Jew, there is little wonder that the Survey Committee took fright. Johnson's report reinforced their own code and proclivities, but it also saddled them with enormous responsibilities. At Johnson's suggestion the Survey Committee agreed that "it would be well to have different Jewish groups meet together to formulate common programs of action, through the leavening influence of the presence of non-Jews."

> Mr. Backer and Mr. [Maurice] Wertheim have met with Dr. Johnson and have started the ball rolling. The idea is that they obtain names from our group and from the American Jewish Congress . . . and submit them to Dr. Johnson. He will select certain of these men to be invited to a conference. The selection of non-Jews will be done in the same manner, Dr. Johnson this time furnishing the names to us.

Thus with the aid of rabbinical groups there began quiet, unpublicized efforts to insure that American Jewish behavior would provide no ammunition for anti-Semites. The difficulties were compounded by the lack of interorganizational unity and by varying reactions to anti-Semitic manifestations on the part of the different socioeconomic groups in the Jewish community. Even if all Jews were saints, some asked, would anti-Semitism disappear?

The American Jewish Committee labored to inform local communities of its concern about internal Jewish behavior. It hoped, too, that by establishing links with the outlying areas it could build up its own image. Not that the Committee wished to become a mass organization. Its diplomatic maneuvering against nazism and the performance of the Survey Committee vindicated AJC's preference for elitist control. Besides, the Committee leaders still abhorred all that went with mass support—large meetings and demonstrations, "the tactics and the methods of the Wises and the Untermyers." But their policy of discretion was criticized by friends and rivals alike, and there were even charges that the "plutocratic" Committee refused to come out against the Nazis in order to protect the interests of German Jewish bankers who contributed to the Nazi cause! To overcome community criticism, the AJC executive committee at first planned to have its members meet with small groups of influential Jews in different communities, but it soon realized that it would need a professional field staff to teach American Jews its defense techniques and to neutralize anti-Committee propaganda.

At first AJC experimented with regional branch offices but found these unsatisfactory. It also considered organizing local committees. But until the end of the 1930s it preferred to work through corporate members, who usually held prominent positions on the all-inclusive Jewish community councils. Also, 350 "vigilance members" throughout the country kept the New York office informed about local events related to its educational and investigative programs. Increasingly, the Committee was asked for advice in defense matters, and in 1939 a Community Service Department was set up, as a non-fund-raising adjunct of the Survey Committee. Its function was to supply materials to AJC members as well as to councils, defense committees, and public relations committees in different localities. Where no such councils or committees existed, the Community Service Department would organize them. The Committee also inaugurated the *Contemporary Jewish Record,* a bimonthly journal devoted to serious analyses of issues affecting Jews.

Rothschild's program called for the creation of a "Jewish civil service," and AJC's work with Jewish professionals throughout the country contributed to that goal. Defense work, the Committee emphasized, had need of the technical expert rather than of what one staff member called "the Jewish comforter"—the leader who understood and sympathized with Jews. The "needs of the Jewish community," as interpreted by AJC, took precedence over the *Jewish* needs of the community.

IV

The American Jewish Committee's domestic program was largely aimed at immunizing the American public against Nazi anti-Semitism, and at countering the organized and militant home-grown anti-Semitism intensified by the Great Depression. In no small measure the defensive tactics of organizations like AJC kept anti-Jewish prejudice from taking deeper root in American soil.

Anti-Semitic organizations multiplied during the 1930s; by 1939, according to AJC estimates, there were over five hundred such groups. Encouraged by Nazi success in Germany and by German agents and funds, these groups attracted mostly urban, middle-class Americans of average education. Until the heyday of Father Charles E. Coughlin, a Catholic, membership was predominantly Protestant and, aside from the German-American Bund, of old American stock. The chief centers were the Middle

Atlantic States and the Pacific Coast. Besides the openly anti-Semitic groups—William Dudley Pelley's Silver Shirts, Reverend Gerald B. Winrod's Defenders of the Christian Faith, the James True Associates—there were organizations like the Paul Reveres which, cloaked in patriotism, attracted prominent and affluent people who would have been embarrassed to support crass Jew-baiting. And the Nazi propaganda machine, operating out of the German consulates, provided vital backing for the hate groups. Besides working with the German-American community, German consular officials sought out and cultivated American sympathizers. Winrod, for example, was invited to Germany at Nazi expense in 1935, to be lavishly entertained and apparently also to have his funds replenished.

The teachings of the anti-Semites, disseminated through pamphlets, leaflets, and public meetings, again made popular the *Protocols of the Elders of Zion.* The aging Henry Ford, despite his public apology in 1927, continued to mutter darkly about Jewish plots. Rallying to the familiar charge of a Jewish conspiracy for world domination, the hatemongers repeated the stock warnings of a Jew/Communist menace and of Jewish economic power and immorality. The charges were updated to incorporate contemporary events. Franklin Delano Roosevelt was said to be of Jewish extraction and was denounced as a puppet controlled by Frankfurter, Brandeis, and Baruch. The rise of the Congress of Industrial Organizations was pointed to as a sign of a Jewish-inspired revolt; a medically inspired antisyphilis campaign, it was charged, aimed "for the wholesale inoculation of Gentiles with vaccine syphilitic germs." There were even echoes of the ritual-murder charge in the Nazi propagandists' interpretations of the Lindbergh kidnapping case.

Their inflammatory nature aside, the very crudity of the more blatant anti-Semitic accusations made their refutation relatively simple. The fears and suspicions of the uncommitted public had to be allayed, but the rabid Jew-haters did not warrant a response. With the clear-cut aim of putting anti-Semitic organizations out of business, Jewish defense lay in gathering information on the different groups and their leaders, screening reports for possible infractions of the law, turning pertinent information over to the authorities, and publicizing the facts in newspapers and magazines. Wolfgang Schwabacher had initiated this approach in 1933, and it became more refined with the work of the Survey Committee.

Technically part of Carl Austrian's legal division, the surveillance of anti-Semitic individuals and groups was conducted by a staff headed by George Mintzer, a former U.S. district attorney. Although Cyrus Adler and Morris Waldman had serious reservations about the propriety of undercover work, Mintzer's staff gathered material on anti-Semitism and un-American activities in the United States. Jewish and non-Jewish private detectives attended numerous rallies and meetings, infiltrated hate organizations, and set up connections with known Nazi operatives. In some cases the agents worked directly within the organizations to sow dissension. The agents' voluminous reports, supplemented by newspaper research and volunteer tips, were indexed and tabulated. Often they contained documented evidence of anti-American subversion. In five years the staff amassed a card index of fifty thousand names, copies of which were filed with the FBI and the army and naval intelligence units. Government agents were frequent visitors at Mintzer's law office—purposely distinct from the Committee—where the files were housed.

One of the most dramatic coups by the investigative department was the exposure of a German agent's plot to build a united Nazi front in the United States. A member of Mintzer's staff recounted the story:

> Word came to us that somewhere in New York City a Nazi agent had set up sumptuous quarters, where he was entertaining many Americans. Acting on this information, we scoured the better sections of the city, and finally discovered that a Baron George von Stein, tenant of a Park Avenue

apartment for several years, had fled, and in his hasty departure for the Fatherland, left behind a large cabinet. This cabinet came into our possession. It contained a mass of important correspondence, and plans and specifications for the construction of a submarine, and a listening device prepared by Krupp's in Germany. Way down on the bottom was the Baron's own diary for 1933. We turned the plans over to United States Naval Intelligence at once. From the diary and correspondence, we were able to piece together the entire story, which also went to our Government, of course.

The Baron had been sent here by Herr Goebbels himself, to work among us independently of the German Embassy or Consulates. You remember that the Nazi plan was to organize subversive work under a native leader or leaders who would function through familiar local channels. The Baron's diary established conclusively that it was his job to create American organizations that would follow the Nazi line—and to find a native leader.

Among Baron von Stein's intimate friends was one Royal Scott Gulden. Stein had got him to organize a native American group called "The Order of '76," with a ritual full of patriotic verbiage and oaths of allegiance to Gulden's leadership. Every member received a membership card, the back of which bore the legend: "In case of pogrom, please pass bearer through police lines."

Another frequent guest of the Baron's was William Dudley Pelley, self-styled Fuehrer, and organizer of the Silver Shirts. Pelley, who always spoke of himself in the third person as "The Chief," usually wore a grey version of Hitler's favorite uniform. His Silver Shirts adopted the swastika as their emblem, along with the Fuehrer principle.

Both Pelley and Gulden were intimates of James True, who issued a vicious "newsletter" from Washington, Robert Edmondson, a prolific writer of anti-Semitic canards and—most important of all—George Deatherage.

George Deatherage founded The Knights of the White Camellia, explaining that he took the title from an elite group within the original Klan of the 1860's. He had one burning ambition: to bring about a coalition of all of the bigot elements under the leadership of one man. What more could the Nazis ask?

The diary tells us that after many conferences—and some took place in Wall Street, and one or two at a certain well-known club in New York City—Baron von Stein effected an alignment of the following pseudo-patriotic groups: The Order of '76, the American Nationalist Party, The Silver Shirts, and The Knights of the White Camellia. This took care of one important phase of the Nazi plan for America.

By a not-so-strange coincidence, the first openly anti-Semitic speech in Congress came soon after Hitler's accession to power. Congressman Louis T. McFadden of Pennsylvania delivered an address entitled, "In the United States Today, the Gentiles Have Slips of Paper, While the Jews Have the Gold and Lawful Money." This legislative bigot, under the guise of attacking a bill for the revaluation of the gold standard, quoted at length from the fraudulent "Protocols of the Elders of Zion," and charged that the proposed legislation was part of a world Jewish conspiracy. . . . The Baron's diary shows that shortly before Congressman McFadden made that vicious speech, he visited the Nazi Baron in the Park Avenue Headquarters. The Congressman conferred there with the Baron, William Dudley Pelley, Gulden and Colonel Emerson. Then he went back to Washington to serve the Nazis instead of his constituency. . . . McFadden established the precedent of inserting anti-Semitic matter into the Congressional Record. He used his Congressional frank to deliver Nazi propaganda throughout the country at Government expense. This vicious procedure was followed by many other legislators later on.

While the Committee was quick to share with the government any significant information about Nazi agitators, it preferred that legislative bodies refrain from punitive action. Outraged citizens pressed for criminal-libel laws to forbid dissemination of racist materials, but the Committee along with various civil liberties groups discouraged this tactic. While the Committee was sensitive to the curtailment of American freedoms, it also knew that prosecuting bigots would increase their notoriety without necessarily disproving their propaganda. Thus in 1936, when a grand jury indicted Jew-baiter Robert Edmondson for libeling certain individuals, as well as the Jewish religion, AJC's special lawyers' advisory committee thought the indictment unfortunate and preferred that the case not come to trial. AJC publicly upheld Edmondson's rights to speak as he chose, and joined the American Civil Liberties Union and other organizations in pleading for the dismissal of the indictment. "It [is] better to suffer the activities of a bigot than to deprive him of the right of freedom of speech and of the press," the Committee declared.

Nor did the Committee see any need for congressional investigations of Nazi, Fascist, or Communist activities—lumped together under the term "un-American." Here, too, the crude publicity and animosities stirred up by the hearings outweighed the gains of exposing a few more subversives. As the *Herald-Tribune* warned, witch-hunting could result in a Goebbels-type department of propaganda in the United States. The McCormack-Dickstein congressional investigating committee of 1934 did a good job, but its recommendations for legislation were not heeded. On that ground, the Committee strongly opposed Representative Samuel Dickstein's 1937 proposal for a new investigation. When Congress set up the Dies Committee on Un-American Activities in 1938, AJC kept close watch on its activities and those of its chairman. It learned that Martin Dies privately predicted the growth of American anti-Semitism, warned of Fascist leanings among certain industrialists and patriotic societies, and promised to hunt Fascists as zealously as Communists. The congressman considered himself a guardian of tolerance and claimed to understand the problem of anti-Semitism; nevertheless, he clearly believed there was a strong Jewish identification with the Communist party. Aware of all this and of the growing liberal opposition to Dies, the American Jewish Committee maintained a cautious attitude toward his operation. It supplied the House Committee on Un-American Activities (HUAC) with material on Nazi subversives, but it refused to aid Dies in his political campaign and publicly reasserted its abhorrence of totalitarian assaults, from both the Left and the Right.

V

For American Jews, the 1936 elections were a test of strength of organized anti-Semitism. The American Jewish Committee kept watch over the anti-New Deal groups, for nearly all anti-Semites were opposed to Roosevelt. The prominence of Jews among the presidential advisers gave rise to increasing slurs against President "Rosenfeld" and his "Jew Deal." In the campaign Brandeis, Cardozo, Morgenthau, Lehman, Frankfurter, and Dubinsky were cited as "evidence" of Jewish domination of the president; and since Jews were linked to Moscow, clearly Roosevelt was scheming to capture the country for Bolshevik rule. The *American Gentile* (a semimonthly for the "Defense of Gentile Culture and Civilization") in its September 1936 issue urged its readers to "Vote Gentile—Defeat Roosevelt." The paper ran a cartoon showing Stalin and members of his secret police holding a Russian flag which sported a Star of David and laughing at corpses and skulls strewn about a landscape marked "Jewish Dictatorship." To one side, also laughing, was Roosevelt, with "Hot Dog" (Justice Frankfurter) perched on his shoulder. With the poor showing at the polls of both the Communists and Father Coughlin's Union party, however, political anti-Semitism disappeared, and some of the leading anti-Semitic agitators were temporarily silenced.

Morris Waldman looked to the elections for another result: "The negligible vote polled by the Communist Party will, I hope, so attenuate the fears of some of our . . . unduly disturbed Jews, that they will not be so ready as they were recently, to throw themselves into the arms of both church and lay anti-Communistic groups." Indeed, to some Jews that seemed the surest way to refute the Jew/Communist charge. AJC itself had been under strong pressure to issue an anti-Communist statement. In 1934, in the wake of American recognition of the Soviet Union and the information uncovered by the McCormack-Dickstein congressional investigating committee, a hysterical Red-hunt, fed in large measure by William Randolph Hearst, began. The Committee's apprehension grew when it learned that the Hearst papers planned a series of articles on Jews and communism. At the same time, the notorious Red-baiter Elizabeth Dilling wrote to a Committee staff member advising that Jews take action against communism. Even former ambassador to Germany James Gerard warned publicly "that if the American nation ever gets the idea that the Jewish race and communism are synonymous there is a possibility of a pogrom in the United States that will make those of the Czar's era in Russia look like a small parade." Responsible American Jews, Gerard continued, had to keep the public from entertaining that idea "by discouraging members of the race from embracing communism."

Clearly, the American Jewish Committee held no brief for communism. Particularly disturbed at Soviet religious persecution, it had quietly sought to obtain for Russian Jewry the right to set up its own schools and to practice its religion freely. In 1933, when the Roosevelt-Litvinov talks laid the basis for American recognition of the Soviet Union, AJC sent a petition to Washington, cosigned by Cyrus Adler and a Catholic and a Protestant leader, calling for freedom of religion in Russia. However, public renunciation of Jewish affiliations with the Communist movement, the Committee believed, raised other difficulties. Since communism was an excuse for, rather than the cause of, anti-Semitism, a response would only add weight to the anti-Semitic charge. As true Americans, Jews were obligated to uphold freedom of political belief for everyone. Also, if they assumed the posture of militant anti-Communists, like the superpatriotic and reactionary groups, they stood to lose the sympathy of the liberal elements. Finally, a condemnation of communism might harm Jews in the Soviet Union and in other countries which might fall under Communist rule.

The Committee was moved to action, however, by the passage of the Nuremberg laws in 1935, which the Germans explained as necessary to counteract the Jewish/Communist menace. Joined by B'nai B'rith and the Jewish Labor Committee, AJC drew up a public statement stressing that both German and Russian Jews were against communism. It underscored the loyalty of Jews to their particular homelands, and the affinity between Jewish and American ideals. When Hitler reiterated the Jewish/Communist stereotype in an interview with the president of United Press, the latter invited AJC to issue a reply. This was done by Cyrus Adler, who coupled his refutation with an attack on the Nazi racial theories. A year later, also in answer to Nazi propaganda, a second anti-Communist statement, signed by Adler and Stroock, was circulated by the Committee through the press and radio.

AJC actions brought some unfavorable comment. Stephen Wise, president of the American Jewish Congress, refused to sign the statement, maintaining that German Jews were being persecuted because they were Jews, not for their political views. The Yiddish-language paper *The Day* defended the right of Jews to their own political opinions and questioned the propriety of the Committee, B'nai B'rith, and the Jewish Labor Committee in speaking for all American Jews. Congressman Maury Maverick of Texas joined in the discussion:

> [It] seems to me that when the Jews themselves distinguish between the various good or bad philosophies of Jews . . . they are . . . doing the Jews injustice. In my opinion, a Jew has as much right to advocate communism as a German, or a Chinaman, or an American. . . . Why is it necessary for the Jewish people to continuously apologize and explain that they are not Communists? . . . [The] Jews should take the attitude that they are free-born human beings . . . and that they have as much right to be communists, pacifists, fascists, Democrats, Republicans, or anything else that they please.

Meantime, the Committee tried to estimate how many American Jews were in the Communist party and how many Jewish Communists were deported. Anti-Communist pressure rose during the election campaign of 1936, when the Roman Catholic Church said communism was its chief adversary. Pope Pius XI called on Catholics all over the world to organize in the Pro Deo movement to fight communism; Cardinal Pacelli's visit to the United States allegedly was connected with this effort. As a symbol of the movement the Catholics, in cooperation with the other faiths, sought to erect a gigantic statue of Jesus in Washington, D.C. The project caused the Committee no little concern; to withhold cooperation meant alienating the church, perhaps lending credence to Jewish/Communist charges. On the other hand, the Pro Deo movement suggested an alignment of the church with Fascist forces. Not only was the Committee disturbed by the church's relation to the rulers of Italy, Germany, Austria, and the rebel forces in Spain, but it also noted the American church hierarchy's strong stand against communism while playing down the totalitarianism of the Fascist states. How then, for all its aversion to communism, could AJC join in a movement which seemed to underscore Hitler's own anti-Communist crusade? Furthermore, could AJC risk joining a Catholic-controlled movement? How would the American Jewish community react to its cooperation with the Pro Deo forces?

In the tense weeks before the elections, one reassuring fact emerged. The large body of Protestant opinion in the United States, particularly the Federal Council of the Churches of Christ, was unswayed, and was even irritated, by the Catholic move. Thus if AJC rejected an invitation from the Catholics, the Jews would be in good company. The Committee planned its moves cautiously. Lewis Strauss and Joseph Proskauer had an appointment with Cardinal Pacelli (arranged before the Pro Deo development to discuss possible church action to counter ritual-murder charges, the *Protocols of the Elders of Zion,* and anti-Semitism in the Catholic countries of Central and Eastern

Europe.) Should the cardinal suggest Jewish participation in the anti-Communist drive, it was decided, Strauss and Proskauer would offer the names of *individuals* (but not organizations) who might be willing to join a broad *religious* movement to fight atheism. Years later Lewis Strauss did not recall the Pro Deo movement as a topic of discussion with Cardinal Pacelli. AJC involvement in the church campaign ended after that interview, but the Survey Committee continued to watch for anti-Semitic trends in Catholic drives against communism.

VI

Tirades linking Jews with a Communist conspiracy did not cease with the 1936 elections. Anti-Semites received a tremendous boost in 1938, when Father Charles E. Coughlin openly converted his National Union for Social Justice into an anti-Semitic organization. The Canadian-born priest of Royal Oak, Michigan, who reached millions through his weekly broadcasts and his newspaper, *Social Justice,* had long broken with the New Deal and strongly supported fascism. Coughlin's prejudice was revealed in earlier attacks on Jewish bankers and labor leaders and in his advocacy of silver as the "gentile metal," but for a long time he disclaimed any anti-Semitic beliefs. When individual Jews criticized him for certain remarks, he indignantly lodged a complaint with the Anti-Defamation League.

AJC had watched Coughlin's activities since 1934 and had advised Jews neither to support nor to challenge him. However, after *Social Justice* reprinted the *Protocols of the Elders of Zion* in 1938, Father Coughlin could no longer be ignored. But Jews could do little about him, for he seemed virtually invulnerable. His popularity grew despite the criticism of prominent Catholic clergy and laymen. Joseph Wirth, AJC's closest contact with the Vatican, added his condemnation, but to no avail. Even the Dies Committee steered clear of Coughlin, reasoning that to question him would only increase his publicity. The American Jewish Committee collected extensive files on Coughlin and called attention to his penchant for misquoting facts and lifting material straight out of Nazi speeches. Much of this information was published in 1939 by the General Jewish Council, a clearinghouse for the activities of American Jewish defense organizations. Neither the Survey Committee nor the local communities it polled felt that an open national debate with the priest would be fruitful. However, because of Coughlin's propaganda and the charges then being voiced before the Dies Committee, AJC felt constrained once again to clarify its position on communism. In June 1939 it adopted a statement made by Governor Herbert H. Lehman at the Russell Sage College commencement exercises as its official position:

> The vast majority of the people of our country sincerely abhor Nazism, Fascism and Communism. And yet many of our loyal and devoted citizens appear to feel that they are compelled to make a choice between them—that there is no alternative. Nothing could be more untrue—nothing could be more dangerous. There is no choice between the different forms of totalitarian governments. Their objectives are substantially identical. . . . All stand for dictatorship of an individual or of a ruthless small group . . . for the breaking down of religious influence . . . for the arraying of class against class . . . for the arousing of hatreds and for the regimentation of the individual to the end that he becomes merely a cog in the great machine of the State.
> We gain nothing if in our fight against Communism we invoke Fascism. We gain nothing if in our fight against Fascism we invoke Communism. Both Fascism and Communism can successfully be fought only by invoking an uncomprising devotion to democracy.

Coughlin broadened the base of organized American anti-Semitism by activating the Irish Catholic and other urban lower-income elements. He also injected a militant note by calling for the creation of shock troops to form a "Christian Front." A more violent development was the organization of the Christian Mobilizers and American Destiny party, led by Joe McWilliams, which allied itself directly with the German-American Bund. These hatemongers concentrated on street meetings which preached violence against Jews. George Mintzer estimated that just before World War II broke out, some eighty such meetings were held weekly in New York City alone. The Committee's legal department described them:

> Many . . . were held in thickly populated, as well as heavily trafficked sections. The speakers used threatening, insulting, offensive and abusive language. Many of their remarks were extremely vicious and highly provocative. . . . Various pieces of literature, insulting and abusive, were distributed. . . . As a result many disorders took place. There were fights, street brawls, assaults and on several occasions the situation approached the riot stage. A number of arrests were made, and in some instances convictions followed and short prison terms were imposed.
>
> In several instances the police permitted these anti-Semitic groups to start meetings in sections inhabited predominantly by Jews. In some instances innocent bystanders were arrested for protesting against the provocative remarks of the speakers. On many occasions people in the audience requested the police officer in charge to make an arrest or to assist a citizen who desired to make an arrest. In the majority of instances these requests were refused.

With a substantial portion of the city's police enrolled in the Christian Front, it was difficult to get police protection. James Wechsler, writing on "The Coughlin Terror" in *The Nation*, claimed that the press ignored the frequent street incidents provoked by the Coughlin group for fear of treading on Catholic toes.

In cooperation with the other defense organizations, Mintzer set up a tightly knit system to expose as many agitators as possible:

We were able to obtain each day a list of all the street meetings and when and where they were to be held. To each meeting we sent several intelligent observers as well as a skilled stenographer who took down the speeches verbatim. We organized a panel of about a hundred lawyers [all volunteers] who were available on call each night, and . . . a central clearing station through which the witnesses could immediately communicate with the lawyers. . . . We had several conferences with high officials in the Police Department who issued instructions to the officers at the meetings to cooperate with us. Whenever a speaker said something that appeared to be in violation of the law our representative would notify a police officer and demand his arrest. We had agreed that the speaker would be allowed to finish his speech so as to prevent disorders. At the conclusion of the speech the offender would be arrested; our witnesses would accompany them to the police station; and one of our lawyers . . . would hurry down to present the case. As a result . . . there were during a six months' period when the agitation was at its height one hundred and twelve convictions.

America's entry into World War II finally silenced Coughlin and his cohorts. Meanwhile, the American Jewish Committee played an important role in preventing the Nazi plan for a union of American anti-Semites. In 1939 the various hate groups agreed upon a leader: Major General George Van Horn Mosely, a distinguished World War I soldier and a rabid Jew-hater. In a private home on Long Island fifty leading anti-Semites, including Fritz Kuhn of the German-American Bund, met secretly to hear Mosely's plans for a national organization. Although Bund storm troopers screened carefully all guests, one AJC man was present. He heard Mosely's schemes for establishing a military dictatorship in the United States and relegating American Jews to second-class citizenship. AJC turned his report over to the government, and Mosely was called before the Dies Committee, where he and his associates were publicly discredited.

VII

Since the American Jewish Congress and B'nai B'rith also fought anti-Semitism, logic dictated some sort of cooperation or division of labor among the three major Jewish defense agencies. The duplication of effort in educational campaigns and in tracking down anti-Semites annoyed many Jews, who rightfully fretted over the waste of time and money. Combined fund raising through community and welfare drives grew more popular, and the directors of those organizations saw little justification for separate subventions for the same purposes. However, cooperative ventures had little success. Partisan jealousies and mutual distrust, stemming from and reinforcing different tactics and philosophies, kept the groups apart.

When the Joint Consultative Council was set up in the spring of 1933 to discuss the Nazi challenge (with two representatives each from AJC, the American Jewish Congress, and B'nai B'rith), the Committee expected no major accomplishments. It recalled that in the past B'nai B'rith had rarely followed through on cooperative ventures; and as for the American Jewish Congress— which had reconstituted itself in 1922 as a permanent successor to the temporary American Jewish Congress of World War I—it still had the stigma of illegitimacy for AJC leaders who remembered the acrimony of the 1914–16 years. Despite a weak modus vivendi worked out between the two organizations shortly before Louis Marshall's death, the mutual suspicions and the constant sniping had not ceased. The Committee thought it unrealistic to expect the publicity-seeking American Jewish Congress to submerge itself willingly in joint projects. Jealous and resentful of the growing popularity of the American Jewish Congress and its methods, even among its own members, AJC looked upon their activities as designed to achieve national and even international domination. Thwarting the American Jewish Congress was a weighty reason for the Committee to agree to joint consultations.

But the paper unity worked out in 1933 did not guarantee

a truce, much less a rapprochement. Morris Waldman correctly styled the Joint Consultative Council a "sham" and a "delusion," for though it lasted several years, each organization went its own way. Joint action on anti-Semitism in the United States was more of a dream than a reality, even though the council endorsed Schwabacher's department in principle; the petition to the League of Nations for a refugee commission, which began as a Joint Council project, was abandoned in midstream by the American Jewish Congress.

The Committee was irritated by B'nai B'rith's vacillating behavior. But it fumed at the American Jewish Congress's habit of not living up to the agreement to inform the other two organizations before taking action—its adoption of a proboycott stand, for example, and its call for mass meetings. Nor was the lack of harmony concealed from the public. The Committee was repeatedly and openly attacked by American Jewish Congress leaders on the familiar grounds of autocracy, cowardice, appeasement of Germany, and intent to wreck the efforts of the American Jewish Congress. Stephen Wise even charged that Roosevelt was kept from taking action against Germany in 1933 by a group of "thrice-damned" German Jews and American Jews who thought of Germany first and their Jewish honor second. Most often Waldman and Adler were the special targets of the American Jewish Congress, which explains the depth of Adler's feeling on the subject of Stephen Wise. Too proud to answer in kind, the AJC president fulminated in private about the "blackguard" and his dishonest practices.

This partisan mudslinging underscored a wide ideological rift between the American Jewish Committee and the American Jewish Congress. The new American Jewish Congress, like its predecessor, preached Jewish national consciousness and ethnocentricism. Don't hide your Jewish interests, it admonished the rank and file. "I have been an American all my life," declared Stephen Wise, "but I've been a Jew for 4,000 years." This stance, apart from its psychological attraction for those who felt impelled by nazism to stand up and be counted as Jews, was also very much in keeping with the principles of cultural pluralism then becoming popular. However, this philosophy was still alien to the AJC leaders, who defined Judaism as primarily a spiritual legacy and shuddered at any intimation of dual loyalties.

According to the Committee, too, the American Jewish Congress compounded its basic error by inflaming the masses with melodramatic moves. In May 1937 a report of the Committee on Cooperation, consisting of representatives from various organizations and different regions of the United States, advocated intergroup cooperation as the most effective means of fighting anti-Semitism. Prominent AJC members—Edward Greenbaum, Carl Austrian, Lewis Strauss—signed the report, but by then another issue, the projected formation of a World Jewish Congress, had further split the Jewish organizations.

The idea of a worldwide Jewish organization stemmed from the Comité des Délégations Juives, which had officially represented the Jewish interests at Versailles. Instead of disbanding entirely in 1920, many delegates maintained a loose organization to watch over the newly won minority rights. In 1927 it reorganized as the Council for the Rights of Jewish Minorities, which campaigned for a central international organization. In the face of the rising Nazi menace, the American Jewish Congress took up the idea and called a meeting of representatives of world Jewry for August 1932 to plan a World Jewish Congress.

As in 1915, the American Jewish Committee labored futilely to convince American Jewish Congress adherents of the project's inadvisability. Again, more immediate concerns than the underlying issue of Jewish nationalism alarmed Committee members. Most important was the fact, known to the American Jewish Congress as well, that the Jews of Germany, Rumania, and Poland did not want intervention in their behalf, particularly by public petition. And despite the gravity of the problems a World Jewish Congress would discuss, what could such a speech-making assembly—especially one opposed by the leading Jewish organizations of Western Europe—accomplish? Doubtless the anti-Semites, particularly in Germany, would seize upon the gathering as a proof of an international Jewish conspiracy, and no possible gains could offset the certain tragic consequences. These arguments, however, evoked the charge that the Committee was obviously "assimilationist" and "dictatorial."

The 1932 conference, which drew ninety-six representatives from eighteen countries, favored the establishment of a permanent World Jewish Congress, "based upon the concept of the Jewish people as a unified national organism . . . to deal with all questions affecting Jewish life, and to represent the Jewish people to the outside world, in its struggle for its civil and national rights." Shocked as AJC was at that resolution, it was even more horrified by a later call for democratic elections for the World Jewish Congress in 1935. The Committee's fears were realized when the American press described the planned organization as "Jewish parliament" and "super-government." Despite its reluctance to expose rifts in the Jewish community and despite the taunts of cowardice its statement called forth, the Committee publicly dissociated itself from the movement. It marshaled the support of the anti-World Jewish Congress organizations in Europe and also launched a campaign of public education against the project.

In a militant mood, at the end of 1934 AJC prepared to fight the exponents of Jewish political nationalism. A showdown between the Committee and its opponents could no longer be averted. Judge Proskauer, who like James Rosenberg and Cyrus Adler was strongly convinced that in this case preserving appearances of unity was secondary, put the issue in forceful terms:

> The vice of the proposal is that it converts the Jewish community into a quasi-political entity. It converts us into a minority, politically isolated. The greatest danger we face is the accentuation of the Hitler idea that Jews may live in a country for generations and centuries, but that they never

cease to be Jews first, and always remain merely guests of the countries in which they live. We must not think for a moment that the Hitler idea has not already penetrated American thought. We are already regarded in many quarters as a sort of international people. . . . If we let the notion back of the world Congress idea go without protest, we will be giving our enemies the best alibi for anti-Semitism they have ever had. We must fight. We cannot afford to let it pass by in silence. Our objective should be so to undermine the movement as, if possible, to smash it entirely. If we cannot succeed in doing this, we should try so to reduce the number of voters as to make the number negligible, and to make any claim that the resulting organization is representative of the Jews in America ridiculous. It should be the function of the Committee to lead this fight—to lead, to inform, to educate Jewish opinion. We should be ready to cooperate with all others who share our views, but *we* must lead.

AJC was confident that it could mobilize the widespread, but so far unorganized, opposition to the idea of a World Jewish Congress; the Jewish labor movement, B'nai B'rith, important periodicals, and even some Zionists were potential allies. When the American Jewish Congress took steps to iron out the differences, the Committee stood firm, refusing to countenance any sort of international body. Its annual meeting in January 1935 unanimously adopted a statement repeating warnings of the futility and dangers of a World Jewish Congress. The statement closed with an expression of faith axiomatic to the Committee since 1906:

> The American Jewish Committee holds it to be self-evident that the Jews of the United States have here established a permanent home for themselves and their children, have acquired the rights and assumed the correlative duties of American citizenship, and recognize their unqualified allegiance to this country. . . . The Committee believes that as American citizens, Jews have the right, individually or associated in groups, to approach the government of the

United States and solicit its good offices in behalf of the betterment of the lot of oppressed Jews in other lands. The Committee does not believe, however, that it is consistent with these principles for them to associate themselves with the citizens of other countries in creating an international body which will assume or attempt to speak for the Jews of this country.

The fight was now in the open, and AJC and others continued their opposition throughout 1935 and 1936. Although they could not prevent the convening of the World Jewish Congress in the summer of 1936, their arguments had some moderating effect. Not only did Stephen Wise categorically reject the concept of a Jewish parliament, but at the request of the American delegates the World Jewish Congress also resolved not to interfere in the internal matters affecting Jews in various countries.

The Committee had attacked the American Jewish Congress proposal as "a plan to supplant tried agencies . . . and to take their direction out of the capable hands in which they are," but it sought to avoid appearing as an opponent of unity in the United States. When the Joint Consultative Council collapsed at the end of 1936, the Jewish defense agencies worked together for a short time in a new consultative body, the Committee on Cooperation. The latter accomplished little toward unified programing, but it kept the organizational strife out of the public eye.

In May 1938, however, the American Jewish Congress broke the tenuous truce by announcing an election to establish a united democratic front to protect Jewish rights. All American Jews over eighteen who paid a fee of ten cents would be allowed to vote for delegates to a special conference. They would also indicate on their ballots whether they wanted a single defense agency for the American Jewish community. The Committee, B'nai B'rith, and the Jewish Labor Committee raised their voices in shocked protest. AJC pointed out that the American Jewish Congress scheme allowed anyone to purchase as many ballots as he desired. It also argued against a single Jewish voice. American Jews differed in background, ideals, and interests; to impose consolidation by fiat was not only unrealistic but also totalitarian. In the long run, the Committee insisted, Jewish security depended on the goodwill of the community, and an all-inclusive agency would be seized upon by anti-Semites as proof of an exaggerated ethnic solidarity.

Had the Committee formally stated its objectives at the very beginning and without the help of public relations experts, Waldman later remarked, it might have dealt the American Jewish Congress a crushing blow. Its statement finally appeared at the beginning of June and was, as both Waldman and Adler admitted, unsatisfactory. Describing itself as an organization of "Americans who are Jews," the Committee dissociated itself from the elections, the referendum, and any attempt to set apart "Americans who are Jews" as a distinct political unit. That self-conscious phrase, which appeared five times in a two hundred-word release, accomplished no more than to provide grist for *Time* magazine's mill.

Edgar Kaufman, a Jewish communal leader in Pittsburgh, invited the four major groups to work out plans for restoring unity. The drawing card was the tacit understanding that the American Jewish Congress would abandon its referendum. The Committee swallowed its pride and joined what mild-mannered Sol Stroock called the "unholy alliance." After a preliminary agreement, the General Jewish Council was officially organized in August 1938. Proscribed from encroaching on the "religious, racial, national or economic philosophies" of the separate organizations, the council could, within that limitation, set policy and coordinate the defense activities of its members. It functioned rather smoothly for a year, and while its plans for links with local communities failed, its committee on public relations did achieve positive results.

The 1938 agreement did not provide for common funds, and the Committee's large-scale and successful financial campaign of 1938–39 made the American Jewish Congress and B'nai B'rith increasingly resentful. Supported by the welfare and federated agencies, they pressed for joint fund raising. A few days after war broke out Stephen Wise called on his partners to merge their organizations in a joint effort to meet the new problems. The Committee replied that cooperation rather than consolidation was the most effective response. It seemed clear, however, that the Committee was primarily concerned with the choice of partners. The Survey Committee had begun working more and more closely with the Anti-Defamation League, even outside the purview of the General Jewish Council, and while Wise's proposal and later variations were under discussion by the council, the Committee and the B'nai B'rith's Anti-Defamation League were negotiating a Joint Defense Appeal. Although Maurice Wertheim of the Committee formulated a plan for a different type of defense union, AJC never really wanted to be bound to the nationalist-minded American Jewish Congress. Closer in philosophy and method to B'nai B'rith, AJC had never competed with that organization for leadership of the American Jewish community nor had there been serious personality clashes between the two leaderships.

But while the Committee's actions may have been valid and practical, the American Jewish Congress attacked the bilateral negotiations for destroying the General Jewish Council. When the American Jewish Committee and the Anti-Defamation League announced the organization of their Joint Defense Appeal at the beginning of 1941, the American Jewish Congress officially resigned from the General Jewish Council. The episode reflected the institutional loyalties which shaped the organizations' behavior more decisively than counter pressures from the community. It also showed that, by the end of the 1930s, the American Jewish Committee had recouped sufficient strength and self-confidence to seize the initiative on the domestic front from its major rivals.

10

The Years of the Holocaust

The outbreak of hostilities called a temporary halt to the Committee's operations with respect to European Jewry. AJC had been at war with nazism since 1933; now its repeated warning that Hitler's Germany was a threat to democracy was finally recognized by the Western powers. With the Jewish cause subsumed, indeed eclipsed, by the war effort, there were no longer any possibilities for independent maneuvering or rescue operations. Even when news of Hitler's "Final Solution" leaked out to the Western world, American Jewish organizations could only appeal to their government and hope that the Allied military campaign would include measures to save the doomed Jewish population of Europe.

The Committee's activities on other fronts compensated for its enforced idleness on the European scene. Beginning with attempts to find countries of refuge for Jews who were able to flee Europe, AJC initiated what later became a broad Latin American program. In anticipation of postwar reconstruction, it invested heavily in a research institute which studied Jewish and communal needs. Within the American community it stepped up the fight against anti-Semitism.

The tension of the crisis-ridden years brought a major

change within the Committee. Faced with the annihilation of European Jewry and an undercurrent of American Jewish self-assertiveness, AJC was forced to grapple with basic questions of purpose and philosophy. Was there room for an independent agency, or did contemporary problems dictate organizational unity? Did separate existence call for substituting a mass base for elitist control? Did the fate of European Jewry prove the fallaciousness of Emancipationist philosophy and validity of political Zionism? If Diaspora Jewry survived, what were the responsibilities of an American Jewish organization to its own community?

AJC would have preferred not to answer these questions. From its inception it had stressed its pragmatic approach, its nonideological base, its ability to speak for all strata of Jews. But having no ideological commitment it found itself, in the 1940s, without a raison d'être. Other organizations, too, had defense programs, peace planning, contacts with Latin America, and outspoken views for or against Zionism. For the first time the Committee had to articulate a credo and compete for the ideological support of American Jewry. Its choice of principles ultimately recast its traditional structure and steered it along new paths.

I

When the Nazis invaded Poland the American Jewish Committee was seized by confusion, fear, and uncertainty as to its role in a nation still neutral. Obviously, its European projects could no longer be continued; but some AJC leaders thought that the organization's domestic program was also blocked. That notion, however, quickly dissipated as it became clear that despite the surge of anti-Nazi feeling the self-styled native führers still ranted on; nor had popular anti-Semitism disappeared. In fact, prominent anti-Nazis sometimes were strongly prejudiced against Jews.

The Survey Committee carefully analyzed its task in light of the new conditions. Before 1939 it had concentrated on discrediting the Nazi ideology. With the outbreak of war, however, two factors prompted a change of emphasis: the growing popular revulsion against nazism eliminated the need for more propaganda; and there was fear that continued anti-Nazi campaign might aggravate the charge that Jews were warmongers, seeking to destroy America's neutrality. The Committee substituted a "prodemocracy" campaign, which contrasted democratic institutions with their totalitarian counterparts.

Again, anti-Semitism was deliberately treated as an auxiliary issue: the enemies of democracy, it was emphasized, used group animosities, including anti-Semitism, to weaken the nation. This was strikingly borne out in the spring of 1940 when the invasion of Norway and the Low Countries revealed Nazi reliance on a fifth column.

By defining anti-Semitism as part of a general threat to the United States, the Committee allayed the fears of those members who saw a danger in fighting the battles of minorities in a period of heightened national tension. The tactic also reflected the Committee's determination, inherent in Richard Rothschild's six-point plan, to rid itself of the traditional apologetic response to anti-Semitism. Instead of marshaling answers to individual charges against the Jews—which never convinced the anti-Semite but only publicized his argument more widely—the Committee took the offensive by setting out to prove that anti-Semitic prejudices endangered the security of the American way of life. Rothschild, who directed the Survey Committee and its successor, the Public Relations Committee, described the new approach in a 1940 article titled "Are American Jews Falling into the Nazi Trap?":

> Anti-Semites claim that the issue in the world today is between non-Jews and Jews—Christian civilization versus Jewish communism, orderly capitalism versus Jewish "international bankers," peace versus Jewish war-mongers. And every defense of Jews as such is only too likely to accentuate

this false issue which the rabble-rousers are trying to put over. But it *is* a false issue. And what must be done is to present to the world the *real* issue, namely, the defense of civilization against totalitarianism, democracy against dictatorship. It is only natural that we Jews should be burning up with justifiable resentment and feel impelled to cry out against the libellous attacks of our enemies. But the situation is far too critical for any such self-indulgent, weak-kneed, defensive policy. What is required is a policy of attacking the enemy on a battleground chosen by right-thinking men rather than where the enemy himself wishes to fight.

These strictures, further popularized by Dr. Solomon Andhil Fineberg of the AJC's Community Service Department, in his book *Overcoming Anti-Semitism,* were the heart of the Committee's message to the local Jewish communities.

The "prodemocracy" theme apparently was intended, at the very least, to stimulate general sympathy for the countries fighting nazism. If Nazi designs imperiled democracy everywhere in the world, it followed that (1) the war was not merely an imperialistic contest, as many on the left contended; (2) England was America's first line of defense and therefore deserved military aid; and (3) war preparedness was necessary to safeguard American democracy against a probable Nazi challenge. However, the Committee could not openly call for American intervention in the European conflict. The charges of warmongering had been hurled against the Jews long before 1939—from Henry Ford's canard that the Jews had caused World War I to scholarly references to the house of Rothschild as the symbol of predatory financiers who engineered armed conflicts for profit. And they were heard more and more often after hostilities began. Ever since 1933, when Jews as a group fought nazism, they were suspect in the eyes of American isolationists, who stressed the classic Washingtonian and Jeffersonian injunctions to stay clear of foreign entanglements. American Jewry must not do anything, AJC decided, to turn isolationists into anti-Semites.

It would be wrong to regard all isolationists of the years 1939 to 1941 as anti-Semitic or Nazi. It is true, however, that hate-mongers pressed their advantage through isolationist fronts. When, after the fall of France, the "great debate" over foreign policy erupted and catapulted the America First Committee into national prominence, John Roy Carlson was but one of many public figures who regarded the America Firsters as "the spearhead of an American fascist movement."

A private investigation conducted by AJC came to a more moderate conclusion. It found that no pronouncements by the America First Committee or its official speakers contained anti-Semitic references—although some remarks could be judged anti-Semitic by implication and were so regarded by certain audiences. Some America First leaders attempted to disavow Nazi and anti-Semitic support, but the anti-Semitic groups and publications (such as Coughlin's *Social Justice* and Pelley's *Roll Call*) stood by their endorsement of America First. Despite the findings of AJC, which were ultimately borne out in a history of the America First Committee, the organization became increasingly linked with anti-Semitism in the public mind, particularly when Charles Lindbergh, one of its most prominent members, announced in September 1941: "The three most important groups who have been pressing this country to war are the British, the Jewish and the Roosevelt administration." His speech evoked wide comment and condemnation, and those who had argued all along that the isolationists were purposefully, rather than fortuitously, anti-Semitic pointed to it as proof. On the other hand, Jews could take comfort in the fact that Lindbergh's statements dealt a severe blow to the America First Committee. Nevertheless, there was no mass Jewish support for interventionism. In the South, the most interventionist section of the country, Jews constituted a very small minority; in New York, where Jewish numbers might have made difference, sentiment was about evenly divided between isolationism and interventionism.

II

The attack on Pearl Harbor brought the demise of the America First Committee and ended the careers of some active anti-Semites. But anti-Semitism was still a problem, and AJC prepared to deal with Nazi-inspired charges of draft-dodging, profiteering, and other canards traditionally leveled against Jews in time of war.

From 1941 to 1945, the Committee counteracted such propaganda with accounts of Jewish heroism in battle, but it did not attempt to answer each charge that was made. The major thrust of the Committee's efforts was to expose the Nazi tactic of "divide and conquer"—to show how the enemy sought to weaken national unity by setting group against group, race against race, religion against religion, and by getting Americans to fight each other instead of their common enemy. A month after Pearl Harbor, President Roosevelt warned against that danger in his State of the Union address:

> We must guard against divisions among ourselves and among all the other United Nations. We must be particularly vigilant against racial discrimination in any of its ugly forms. Hitler will try again to breed mistrust and suspicion between one individual and another, one group and another, one race and another, one Government and another.

In this campaign, the Committee worked closely with writers and editors, advertisers, radio networks, clubs, and labor unions, all of whom helped develop suitable materials emphasizing unity. In 1944 Judge Joseph Proskauer, then president of AJC, proposed a four-point pledge of American unity emphasizing brotherhood, mutual respect, and intergroup cooperation:

1. I will spread no rumor and no slander against any sect.
2. I will never try to indict a whole people by reason of the delinquency of any member.

3. I will daily deal with every man in business, in social and in political relations, only on the basis of his true individual worth.

4. In my daily conduct I will consecrate myself, hour by hour, to the achievement of the highest ideal of the dignity of mankind, human equality, human fellowship and human brotherhood.

Endorsed by religious and lay leaders of different faiths and walks of life, the pledge was circulated in the United States and abroad.

The program of the Committee's Public Relations Committee was aimed at influencing the vast majority of Americans who were neither hard-core anti-Semites nor philo-Semites. To do so more effectively, special attention was given to various subgroups. Because foreign-language elements and organized labor were viewed as primary targets of totalitarian propaganda, the Committee enlisted the cooperation of the CIO and AFL to spread its message of intergroup harmony through the labor press, in speeches and posters, and by special study groups for union members. AJC also advocated the passage of state and federal fair-employment laws and pressed both labor and management to support such measures.

AJC also worked with other special-interest groups—women, farmers, youths, veterans, Negroes, clergy, businessmen—and continued to do so in peacetime. Nondiscriminatory labor practices, for example, were important not merely in wartime; programs designed for veterans helped combat anti-Semitism when peace returned. And the Committee's continuing cooperation with non-Jewish groups in these efforts did much to break down anti-Semitic barriers.

With this approach the Committee took a major step toward a commitment to cultural pluralism. In 1943 the Public Relations Committee defined its long-range goal as follows: "To increase public appreciation of the fact that Americanism means diversity rather than goose-step uniformity—the idea that the very strength of America lies in the variety of its people, the richness of its heritage, rather than in any stereotyped homogeneity." Still not ready to emphasize that Jews were a distinct group, AJC nonetheless acknowledged that only in a pluralistic society could the traditional anti-Jewish feelings, on which active hate movements fed, be successfully challenged.

In an evaluation of the Committee Morris Waldman asserted in 1943 that the domestic program had not gone far enough. He found AJC too present-minded, too unaware of anti-Semitism in its historical perspective, and too apt to concentrate on radical eruptions rather than on underlying causes. But AJC had, in fact, undertaken a number of long-range projects to correct traditional misconceptions about Jews. It supported programs of intercultural education in the public schools to teach children the meaning and values of racial and ethnic pluralism, and it encouraged the reexamination and revision of Protestant religious textbooks to eliminate anti-Semitic references in accounts of the crucifixion and in other New Testament stories. It remained for Waldman's successor, John Slawson, to direct the Committee toward the scientific analysis of prejudice and anti-Semitism.

In May 1944 the Committee sponsored a conference of social scientists to discuss the nature of anti-Semitism and measures to combat it. In a two-day exchange of knowledge and ideas, the scholars examined the psychological dimensions of prejudice and laid the foundation for an in-depth interdisciplinary investigation of the problem, which was ultimately summarized in the five-volume Committee-sponsored *Studies in Prejudice* series—a major contribution to the understanding of bigotry and its root causes. In line with the Committee's new approaches, Slawson announced the appointment of Dr. Max Horkheimer, a sociologist and director of the Institute of Social Research at Columbia University, as research consultant for its domestic programs. And as the research progressed, AJC prepared to supplement its earlier efforts with newer and more effective programs.

III

While the Public Relations Committee was the core of AJC's defense structure, three other units now came into prominence: the Library of Jewish Information, the Community Service Department (CSD), and the Legal and Investigative Committee.

A far cry from the early years when Cyrus Adler and Harry Schneiderman clipped articles and ordered occasional books, the Library of Jewish Information developed into an impressive, functioning department. Its vast collection of materials on contemporary Jewish problems—including an assortment of Nazi anti-Semitica unsurpassed elsewhere—was intended principally as a resource for the Committee's staff. Specialized research workers worked side by side with policy-makers to provide necessary facts for domestic and foreign projects. The library was also used by scholars and government agencies—the Office of War Information (OWI), the United Nations Information Center, the Federal Bureau of Investigation, and many others. During the war, researchers prepared material on the battle of the Warsaw ghetto for the OWI, supplied information to the Department of Labor on the position of Jews in Eastern Europe, and furnished government agencies, church groups, and public-opinion molders with information about Nazi atrocities.

The Community Service Department concentrated on giving service to the community, rather than on "selling" AJC. It collaborated effectively with local community relations agencies, which existed in eighteen of the country's largest cities and serviced individuals in unorganized communities, members of the armed forces, and non-Jewish organizations which requested the Committee's educational material. It distributed pamphlets and articles, made suggestions for local educational projects, and held training seminars for directors of community relations activities. George Hexter and Solomon Andhil Fineberg, directors of the department, periodically visited outlying areas to consult with professionals and laymen. In addition to its more immediate wartime concerns, CSD also initiated long-range programs of postwar planning and intercultural education.

The Community Service Department favored broadly based local agencies representing diverse elements within the Jewish community and, encouraging local autonomy, took care to counsel rather than command. Although AJC had united with the Anti-Defamation League of B'nai B'rith in a Joint Defense Appeal, competition between the two agencies for local dominance continued. By encouraging community freedom and initiative, the Committee ultimately succeeded in establishing firm community bases. Through its CSD, the Committee learned from the experiences and needs of different localities and relayed this information to other communities and to the strategy formulators of AJC's Public Relations Committee. Inevitably, the Committee's image in the communities was enhanced. A year after the Community Service Department began its work, Hexter estimated that allocations to AJC from welfare funds in cities it serviced had risen by 19 percent. More secure in its growing strength in the local communities, the Committee joined the National Community Relations Advisory Council (NCRAC), a cooperative venture of the four national Jewish agencies and representatives of local organizations in policy-making for Jewish defense.

The work of the Community Service Department dovetailed with that of the Legal and Investigative Committee. Local directors of Jewish organizations kept the CSD informed about Nazi activities in their area: a James True bulletin being circulated in Richmond; fifth-column proclivities of the National Workers' League in Detroit; automobile stickers in Delaware reading WALTHAM (We Are Loyal To Hitler And Mussolini). Special note was made of pro-Nazi politicians—those already in office and those aspiring to office.

After Pearl Harbor cooperation between the Committee's investigative staff and the government increased. When President Roosevelt wanted a memorandum on the subversive press in the United States, the Committee furnished one with photos. "Now when [Attorney General Francis] Biddle comes in to argue with me about this I can confront him with the facts," Roosevelt commented. Shortly afterward, the Post Office Department instituted proceedings against *Social Justice,* and a more energetic policy toward seditionists was announced by the Justice Department. The Committee supplied evidence against the thirty defendants indicted in the sedition trial of the war years; largely on the basis of AJC documentation, Lawrence Dennis, often called "the leading intellectual Fascist of America," and Joe McWilliams, organizer of the Christian Mobilizers and American Destiny party, were brought to court by the Justice Department. But the sedition case ended in a mistrial, and many of the anti-Semites immediately renewed their hatemongering.

AJC efforts proved more successful in the exposure and conviction of enemy agents who ran a secret Nazi camp in New Jersey. The Committee's work also cleaned up a dangerous situation on Ellis Island:

> We received reports from our investigators that enemy aliens, Nazi and Fascists who were being interned on Ellis Island as dangerous enemy aliens were allowed to go off the Island with guards, under the pretext of visiting a dentist or doctor or for shopping purposes, but when they came off the Island they were permitted to go about unguarded. An appointment to meet the guard at a later hour was made to return to the Island. This gave the Nazis an opportunity to carry on their subversive activities although they were supposed to be interned as dangerous aliens. We also received reports of anti-Semitic demonstrations on Ellis Island by these Nazis. When the six saboteurs were executed they held memorial services. Anti-Semitic literature and pictures were posted on the walls and bulletin board. At the suggestion and with the cooperation of the Immigration section of the Department of Justice we made a survey of conditions on the Island and made numerous recommendations to the Commissioner General. These recommendations were adopted

and the situation was cleaned up. We received a letter from the Commissioner General expressing his appreciation for our cooperation.

IV

The expansion of the American Jewish Committee's program required more personnel, and the professional staff played an increasing role in formulating policy and carrying out programs. True, such lay leaders as Alan Stroock actively concerned themselves with the local communities, but the work of the Community Service Department carried the discernible imprint of Hexter and Fineberg; and although Victor Riesenfeld or Harold Guinzberg served as chairmen of the Public Relations Committee, its basic approach reflected the principles outlined by Richard Rothschild. Lay policy-making, which was characteristic of the Committee's early days—the days of Sulzberger, Schiff, and Marshall—gave way to institutional policy, worked out by trained professionals.

AJC's organizational structure also changed. During the 1930s and 1940s the executive committee was expanded. To achieve unity in time of crisis, representatives from affiliated organizations were included; and, for the first time, women sat on the executive committee. Since the larger group was unwieldy, the executives organized a smaller administrative committee in 1940 and a still smaller steering committee in 1944. Policy-making, for the most part, rested with the small bodies, but even here the tendency was to abide by the recommendations of various standing committees (Overseas, later Foreign Affairs, Committee; Public Relations Committee; etc.). Those committees were staffed by laymen, but to a large degree the professionals assigned to work with them determined policy and strategy. Inevitably, lay leaders and the professional staff had differences, and there was confusion over their respective roles—a problem which arises from time to time even today. But in an age of complex and difficult problems—and one of specialization—a trained professional staff had become a sine qua non.

The passing of the individualist era was also reflected in the influence wielded by the Committee's presidents, all of whom expended much energy on the office. After Adler's death in 1940, Sol M. Stroock held the office until he died a year later. A tireless spokesman for AJC in the 1930s, Stroock had neither sufficient time in office nor the aggressive personality to gain wider recognition as an influential American Jewish leader. Maurice Wertheim, the son-in-law of Ambassador Henry Morgenthau, served until 1943; his presidency coincided with a divisive period of the Committee's history, when the issue of Zionism seriously threatened to disrupt the organization. Wertheim, who incurred the enmity of the anti-Zionist groups, was much relieved when his duties on the War Production Board gave him a good reason to resign. He was succeeded by Joseph M. Proskauer, a prominent Democrat active in Governor Al Smith's circle whose involvement with the Committee dated from the rise of Hitler. By far the most colorful of the Committee's wartime presidents, Proskauer's dynamic approach to all issues and his sense of self-importance ("I have a client—and my client is the Jewish community") assured him widespread recognition, if not consistent acclaim, among American Jews. Yet even a Proskauer could not personally supervise all the Committee's projects, which often proceeded under their own momentum, irrespective of changes in administration.

The Committee also experienced a managerial revolution, and the office of executive vice-president emerged as the locus of policy-making and administration. Morris Waldman served in that capacity from the time the new post was created until his resignation in 1943. His successor, John Slawson, prominent in Jewish social work, seconded Waldman's determination to make the Committee a vibrant, socially relevant institution, and the "Slawson era" (1943–1967) saw the Committee venture forth in a number of new directions.

V

On June 30, 1942, the British press and the Jewish Telegraphic Agency carried reports of the mass murder of Jewish civilian populations by the Nazis. Over a million Jews, they noted, had already been put to death. Soon thereafter confirmation of the horrors reached the United States, England, the Soviet Union, and the Vatican from several governments-in-exile. Generally, the stories were dismissed as incredible; but the American Jewish community had received reliable information about the mass murders and began to take action, though its traditional tactics were ill suited to this qualitatively different crisis.

The Jewish Labor Committee circulated a mass petition addressed to President Roosevelt; the Synagogue Council of America planned special religious services for Tisha b'Av; and the American Jewish Congress called for a mass meeting in Madison Square Garden. The American Jewish Committee remained aloof from these projects, angered that the Jewish Labor Committee had not cleared its petition through the General Jewish Council and that the American Jewish Congress planned to combine its protest against Nazi massacres with the demand that Jews in Palestine be permitted to form their own army. Instead of cooperating in the mass meeting, AJC president Maurice Wertheim merely sent a telegram to the gathering. The Yiddish daily *Jewish Morning Journal* editorialized critically on the Committee's absence: "The American Jewish Committee certainly owes an explanation as to what kind of 'Jewish' politics it is carrying on which holds it back from crying out at such a time when the Nazi massacres are more horrible than all massacres of Jews in the past."

In the fall of 1942 the reports of the Nazi atrocities were confirmed by the State Department. The Committee joined an ad hoc body called together by Stephen Wise, which prepared a memorandum to be delivered by hand to the White House. On December 8 a delegation composed of Wise, Wertheim, and the presidents of B'nai B'rith, the Jewish Labor Committee, and the

Union of Orthodox Rabbis pleaded with Roosevelt for action by the United States, in concert with other countries at war with the Axis,* to save what remained of European Jewry. The delegation also urged the appointment of an American commission "to receive and examine all evidence of Nazi barbarity against civilian populations and to submit this evidence to the bar of public opinion and the conscience of the world." In one memorandum the Jews appealed directly to Roosevelt, calling him "the symbol of humanity's will to fight for freedom . . . the prophetic voice of Democracy and human decency." A second memorandum detailed the gruesome facts of the exterminations.

By the time of the interview two million Jews had perished.

Roosevelt assured the delegates that the criminals would be held strictly accountable; that the United States, in conjunction with the United Nations, would make every effort to save those who could be saved; and that consideration would be given to the appointment of a joint United States–United Nations commission to deal with the issue.

To arouse public opinion against the atrocities, another mass meeting was arranged for March 1, 1943. A few days later a hastily dispatched message was received from Warsaw: "Liquidation of Warsaw remnants planned. . . . Alarm the world. . . . We suffer terribly. The remaining few hundred thousand Jews threatened with immediate annihilation. Only you can rescue us."

Almost immediately the Joint Emergency Committee on European Jewish Affairs, consisting of a dozen of the most prominent American Jewish organizations, was established. Determined to secure action by the Allied governments, the group undertook to inform the American public of the horrors and encouraged the organization of mass meetings throughout the country. But even in that desperate hour Proskauer, a cochairman of the Joint Emergency Committee, had to explain privately

---

*After 1942 the anti-Axis countries were known as the United Nations.

to many of the AJC leaders why the Committee found it necessary to work with the Zionists and to reverse its position on public demonstrations.

In a number of unpublicized moves Proskauer and Stephen Wise worked together harmoniously, and both repeatedly argued before government officials on the urgency of rescue operations. The Joint Emergency Committee's major task was the preparation of a detailed memorandum outlining a program of action, which was to be brought before the Bermuda Conference on refugees held in April 1943. It proposed that:

> The United Nations should approach the German Government, and the governments of the states it now partly dominates or controls, through neutral governments like Switzerland, Spain, Sweden, Turkey or Argentine, with a view to securing their agreement to the release of their Jewish victims and to the emigration of such Jews to such havens of refuge* as may be provided.
>
> The United Nations should, therefore, without delay, take steps to designate and establish a number of Sanctuaries in Allied and neutral countries to accommodate substantial numbers of Hitler's victims and to serve as havens of refuge for those Jews whose release from captivity may be arranged for, or who may find their way to freedom through efforts of their own.
>
> The procedure that now prevails in the administration of the existing immigration law in the United States, which acts as a deterrent and retardation of legal immigration under the established quotas, should be revised and adjusted to war conditions in order that refugees from Nazi-occupied territories, within such quotas, may find Sanctuary here.
>
> Subject to provisions for its national security, England should be asked to provide for receiving a reasonable number of victims escaping from Nazi-occupied territories and to provide for their accommodation for the duration.
>
> The possibilities in several British territories, both in

---

*"Havens of refuge" later developed into the "free ports" plan of the United States.

Africa and in the Caribbean, should be explored without delay . . . , if not for permanent settlement, at least for the duration.

The United Nations should urge the Republics of Latin America to modify such administrative regulations as now make immigration under the law extremely difficult, and to endeavor to find temporary havens of refuge for a substantial number of refugees.

Overriding pre-war political considerations, England should be persuaded to open the doors of Palestine for Jewish immigration and the offer of hospitality made by the Jewish community of Palestine should be accepted.

The United Nations should provide financial guarantees to all such neutral states as have given temporary refuge to Jews coming from Nazi-occupied territories and to provide for their feeding and maintenance and eventual evacuation. The neutral states should be guaranteed that the refugees will not become a public charge and that they will be transferred to permanent Sanctuaries as soon as possible.

In view of the fact that mass starvation is the design of the Nazi regime, the United Nations should take appropriate steps without delay to organize a system for the feeding of the victims of Nazi oppression who are unable to leave the jurisdiction and control of the Axis.

The United Nations are urged to establish an appropriate inter-governmental agency, to which full authority and power should be given to implement the program of rescue here outlined.

In order to do away with the lack of identity which many stateless refugees present, and to give them sponsorship and protection, an arrangement similar to that which existed under the League of Nations should be established and the stateless refugees should be given identification credentials analogous to the "Nansen" passports.*

It is submitted that the United Nations undertake to provide the financial guarantees that may be required for the execution of the program of rescue here outlined.

*Identification cards issued to displaced persons by the League of Nations; named for the Norwegian explorer and statesman Fridtjof Nansen.

Proskauer and Wise submitted the memorandum to Myron Taylor, chairman of the Inter-Governmental Commission of Refugees, and carried their case to British Foreign Secretary Anthony Eden and Undersecretary of State Sumner Welles as well. The Jewish leaders were concerned that the scope of the Bermuda deliberations was too narrow, and Proskauer asked Welles if he placed any hopes in the conference. Welles voiced only moderate optimism and rejected the idea of sending a Joint Emergency Committee delegation to Bermuda. Asked about an American appeal to Germany, Welles said that only the president could reverse the unfavorable official attitude toward that demand.

Bermuda proved to be the last major opportunity for concerted rescue operations. If the conference had adopted the basic points of the memorandum, vast numbers of lives might have been saved. As Proskauer explained to George Backer, who was spokesman for several organizations at the conference: "You, of course, recognize the difference between an attempt to save hundreds and an attempt to save hundreds of thousands—and that difference is enormous. . . . You know that I am not personally of the emotional type, but on this matter I see eye to eye with those who are much more emotional than I am."

But there is no indication that the Joint Emergency Committee's proposals were ever seriously considered. American delegates, instructed on what not to do, would not agree to negotiations with the Nazis, even when the rescue of human beings from extermination camps was at stake. In tangible results Bermuda was as much of a failure as the 1938 Evian Conference had been. Myron Taylor privately remonstrated with Secretary of State Hull about the inadequacy of the decisions and called essentially for a revitalization of the Inter-Governmental Commission of Refugees.

The Joint Emergency Committee, understandably bitter, sent a last desperate plea to Welles:

It was our hope that the official report would disclose that effective action was taken at that [Bermuda] Conference to save a substantial number of Jews within Nazi-occupied Europe from the extermination which awaits them.

The debate in the British Parliament and the official communiqué of our Government have sadly disappointed that hope. We would be failing in our duty to our Government, to the Jews of this country, and to our kinsmen abroad if we did not convey to you our deepest distress and apprehension, which is shared by large sections of democratic public opinion in our own country and abroad.

It now appears that less than 50,000 persons of all faiths, and only those who have already escaped from Nazi-occupied lands, will be helped in any way by the United Nations, at a time when several million Jews, unlike any other group, face imminent total destruction. . . .

To relegate the rescue of the Jews of Europe, the only people marked for total extermination, to the day of victory is . . . virtually to doom them to the fate which Hitler has marked out for them.

Prior to the meeting of the Bermuda Conference, we submitted a twelve point program for its consideration which we believed . . . represented practical possibilities for the immediate saving of some sections of European Jewry . . . predicated on the premise that what was suggested would not interfere with the successful prosecution of the war.

While appreciating that there are political and military considerations which impose limitations in dealing with the fundamental aspects of the problem involving the exit of Jews from Nazi-occupied lands and the feeding of those destined to remain, we respectfully point out that there are still large areas which, if fully explored, offer at least a partial solution. No implementation appears to have been given, for example, to Point D of the March 3rd communiqué of the State Department, which called upon the Bermuda Conference "to explore the possibilities for the temporary asylum of refugees with a view to their repatriation upon the termination of hostilities in countries other than neutral and their dependencies," and also to investigate "the question of the availability of shipping to effect the movement from Europe."

Meanwhile, . . . despite the heroic defense of the Jews of Poland in a last stand against destruction, the mighty Jewish community of the Warsaw Ghetto appears to have been annihilated. In all sections of Nazi-occupied Europe the program of extermination has received new momentum.

It is our firm conviction that without retarding the military operations of the United Nations, the United States and Great Britain are still in a position to take some action which will succeed in saving at least a substantial remnant of European Jewry. Accordingly, we urge upon our Government that such action be taken without further delay.

The leaders of American Jewry should probably not have expected much more. Having linked themselves solidly with the Allied cause, Jews had little bargaining power in top-level negotiations. To count on the conscience of Christianity, or of the State Department, proved most unrealistic. The patriarchlike appearance of the Orthodox rabbi who haunted Hull's waiting room might make the secretary from the Bible Belt unbend enough to grant a limited favor, but that was the unusual. The Jews had no allies. Pleas that the Allies bomb the death camps and suggestions, which AJC and Agudath Israel later made, that the inmates of the camps be considered prisoners of war went unheeded. Nor—as Secretary of the Treasury Henry Morgenthau discovered when he looked into the State Department's handling of rescue plans—was either the United States or England willing to listen to schemes for ransoming even sixty thousand Jews. Great Britain believed, Anthony Eden made clear, that the problems of transporting the Jews and absorbing them elsewhere were insurmountable. Both countries exaggerated the number of Jewish immigrants they had admitted and raised the specter of German agents who might infiltrate the refugees and undermine Allied security. A 1943 study summed up the situation: "The rescue effort was failing. Within the State Department there was disinclination to undertake large-scale action; within the Foreign Office there was fear of large-scale success; and within Axis Europe fewer and fewer Jews remained."

In January 1944, in response to growing public pressure and Morgenthau's forceful brief against the State Department's ineptitude, Roosevelt set up the War Refugee Board (WRB) "to take all measures within its power to rescue the victims of enemy oppression who are in immediate danger of death, and otherwise to afford such victims all possible relief and assistance consistent with the successful prosecution of the war." The WRB was composed of the secretaries of state, the treasury, and war, and was under direction of John W. Pehle of the Treasury Department. It could draw upon the expert knowledge of private persons and organizations in its attempt to carry out its work. Germany and her satellites were still not convinced that the United States was really concerned about the Jews, Pehle confided to two AJC representatives, but he hoped the War Refugee Board would change that situation. When Pehle asked AJC for its suggestions, the Committee again referred to the memorandum prepared for the Bermuda Conference and suggested that, in light of the Allied military successes, stronger pressure be put on the Nazi satellites to provide asylum for Jewish victims.

The War Refugee Board worked with the Committee and other Jewish organizations in efforts to save close to one million Jews after the Nazi occupation of Hungary. Pehle and leading American Jews pleaded with the Vatican for sustained intervention, and the pope personally asked Admiral Horthy, the regent of Hungary, to resist the Nazi plans for mass deportation of Jews. The Committee also appealed to Secretary Hull and the British ambassador, Viscount Halifax; and both President Roosevelt and Foreign Secretary Anthony Eden warned that perpetrators of "inhuman" crimes against civilians faced strict retribution. At the suggestion of a representative of the War Refugee Board, the Committee secured the signatures of seventy-four illustrious non-Jews on a statement condemning Hungary's compliance with Nazi demands; Archbishop Francis Spellman broadcast an appeal to the Catholics in Hungary. The WRB also planned to drop leaflets from a plane flying over Hungary, for which the Committee prepared the text.

Meanwhile, Pehle and his associates met with Dr. Eugene Hevesi, the Committee's consultant on East European affairs, who made various suggestions to the WRB—from enlisting the aid of Christian relief agencies to organizing an underground railroad to smuggle Jews out of the country. When, in response to protests from the United States, Britain, Sweden, and the Vatican, Horthy called a halt to the deportations and offered to release Jews holding foreign visas, it was essential to use every avenue for evacuating them. The American Jewish Committee, along with the other major Jewish organizations, pressed the WRB with suggestions for airlifts of children, exchange or ransom of Jewish prisoners, and the bombing of extermination facilities, but in most cases Pehle had to admit that his hands were tied by military policies.

Obtaining visas did not seem as difficult at this point as providing transportation. The Committee pleaded with the State Department to announce its readiness to provide transportation and shelter for the evacuees, arguing that, humanitarian aspects aside, the Jewish cause was the rallying point for the anti-Nazi and pro-Allied forces in Hungary. A few days later the United States and Britain made a joint announcement to that effect. Pehle doubted whether any Jews would, in fact, be permitted to leave Hungary; but he had an agent in Istanbul who was prepared to cooperate with representatives of the Jewish Agency, the JDC, and HICEM* to implement Horthy's promise. By this time, however, all Hungarian Jews except for those in Budapest had been killed. Horthy's government was soon overthrown, and new anti-Jewish measures were instituted. The surviving remnant did

---

*An acronym for the umbrella organization joining HIAS, the Jewish Colonization Association, and Emigdirect, formed from the initials of these three agencies. Emigdirect later withdrew from HICEM.

owe its escape, at least in part, to the War Refugee
Board.

The American Jewish Committee also consulted with the
War Refugee Board on other projects—supplying money to the
underground in Poland, providing interned Jews with foreign
passports (purchased, if necessary, from Latin American officials), arranging repatriation of refugees who escaped to neutral
countries, initiating warnings from Eisenhower's headquarters to
the German people on atrocities, bringing pressure on the State
Department to include Jews with foreign passports in exchanges
with the Germans. The records do not reveal the reaction to the
Committee's suggestions, or the results achieved. There is no
doubt, however, that the failure to halt the mass extermination
reinforced the Committee's determination to assure the safety
and well-being of the surviving remnant of European Jewry.

VI

That AJC should join with the Zionists in efforts to save Jews
surprised no one. But when the Zionists suggested cooperation
in a less urgent matter—the formulation of a joint program for
war and peace—there were innumerable stumbling blocks. True,
joint action would strengthen Jewish efforts in dealing with the
ruling powers, and any organization rejecting joint action in time
of crisis was certain to incur the hostility of an aroused Jewish
community. Also, the suffering of European Jewry had converted
the majority of American Jews to the Zionist philosophy and
program. Even the non-Zionists could not deny Palestine's attraction for the survivors. During the war years, however, an
anti-Zionist posture replaced the traditional non-Zionist position
among the Committee leaders.

The most important AJC body after 1938 was the Survey
Committee (p. 196 ff.). More assimilated than their predecessors
of the Sulzberg-Marshall era, its members saw themselves meet-

ing a challenge to their security as American citizens, rather than as protectors of the Jewish heritage. While they would not go so far as to blame Jewish nationalists for the Nazi disaster, they generally agreed that the noisy Zionists who continually harped on Jewish cohesiveness and ethnic loyalties did not help matters.

Although the Public Relations Committee began to talk of a pluralistic society, Jewish distinctiveness was never really envisaged in terms other than religious. AJC leaders resented the Zionists who presumed to speak in the name of Jewish masses, and saw this as a grave threat both to their own leadership and to their defense program. Some were attracted to AJC as a way of affirming their Jewish ties solely on a religious basis and repudiated Jewish nationalism in no uncertain terms. Judge Proskauer was outspokenly anti-Zionist. "Let the chips fall where they may and let those Zionists or national affiliates of the American Jewish Committee who disagree with it get out." When the World Jewish Congress called for joint efforts for a peace program in 1940, the anti-Zionists in the Committee were strong enough to reject the suggestion out of hand.

Morris Waldman did not go along with the anti-Zionists. He distinguished between nationalism, which marked Jews all over the world as a distinct nationality, and Zionism, which stood for some sort of a Jewish territorial entity in Palestine. While the former was anathema, the latter, he argued, was implied in AJC's earlier approval of the Balfour Declaration and the British Mandate. Unless the Committee repudiated that action, he noted, it was on record as not opposing—even if not actively favoring—a Jewish state. Waldman resented the attempts of some of the newer members to label the Committee as anti-Zionist; he preferred to maintain the organization's traditional broad base and to encompass Jews of every point of view.

Sol Stroock agreed that the Committee's position did not axiomatically preclude cooperation with the Zionists, and he concurred in Dr. Chaim Weizmann's suggestion, in 1941, that a small group of Zionists and non-Zionists explore areas of agreement. Carefully avoiding an open split in the Committee, Stroock designated several men to act, not as AJC representatives, but in a private capacity. The meetings with the Zionists (in which other organizations also participated) were confidential and not binding on either side; no minutes were kept or votes taken. After Stroock's death Maurice Wertheim continued the negotiations. He appointed a special subcommittee to meet separately with the Zionists and to formulate a policy for constructive joint action. Stressing the need for unity, Wertheim argued that a non-Zionist position no longer had validity or meaning:

> Actually, in my opinion there are only Zionists and anti-Zionists. I say this because up to twenty years ago with very small numbers of Jews in Palestine, we could all sympathetically regard the settlement there as a possible cultural and religious center, but now with almost 600,000 Jews residing there and a strong political party working day in and day out for the establishment of a self-governing community there, I think the possibility of a spiritual center is nothing but a comfortable delusion. It just will never be that, and the Jews in Palestine will perforce take things in their own hands, whether we extend support to them or not. Of course, they may not be successful, but the choice no longer lies between a cultural and a nationalist center, but between successful and unsuccessful nationalist aspirations. In other words . . . it is entirely illogical for anyone to be pro-Palestine and anti an eventual self-governing community there. To help bring people to Palestine, to establish economic corporations for their assistance and to assist colonization with money, etc. etc., only tends to strengthen the political position and aspirations of the Jews in Palestine. . . . To my mind, therefore, it is entirely inconsistent for us on the one hand to back a united Palestine appeal or even have a United Jewish Appeal at all, and on the other to withhold support from the objective of the Jews of Palestine.

The two sides finally arrived at a basic agreement. If the American Jewish Committee accepted the Zionist program for a Jewish state, the Zionist would in turn renounce the concept of Diaspora nationalism. In actuality that meant the dissolution of the World Jewish Congress. It also implied separate spheres of influence—Zionists to be paramount in matters affecting Palestine; the Committee, in foreign affairs outside of Palestine. Both sides, however, would support a general program to secure Jewish rights throughout the world, and in Palestine in particular.

At a special meeting at Wertheim's home in Cos Cob, Connecticut, the "Cos Cob formula" was adopted by the subcommittee in June 1942. The section on Palestine included the following:

> To aid in securing the fulfillment of the original purposes of the Balfour Declaration, whereby through unrestricted Jewish immigration and large-scale colonization under a regime designed for this purpose, Jews, upon constituting a majority in Palestine will establish an autonomous commonwealth, it being clearly understood that
>
> (a) In such a commonwealth, all the inhabitants, without regard to race or religion, shall enjoy complete equality of rights;
>
> (b) The establishment of this commonwealth will in no way affect the political or civil status and allegiance of Jews who are citizens of any other country;
>
> (c) Only such Jews who are inhabitants of Palestine may be eligible to become citizens thereof.

The original plans called for keeping the formula secret until its presentation at the Committee's meeting, but its contents soon leaked out. The anti-Zionists—notably James Rosenberg, Lewis Strauss, Joseph Proskauer, and Joseph Willen—swung into action. Some had opposed the negotiations from the start; Proskauer summed up the entire project as "a tragedy of American Jewry." The critics found added incentive when, in May of that year, at a meeting at the Hotel Biltmore in New York, the Zionists cast aside the moderate line they had followed since 1920 and resolved "that Palestine be established as a Jewish Commonwealth." A bitter controversy raged within the Committee as both sides continued to debate the issues of Jewish statehood, Arab-Jewish relations, and Diaspora Jewry.

Although Waldman prodded Wertheim to assert his leadership, the latter backed down. Negotiations with the Zionists were suspended, and a new committee was appointed to draft a statement on AJC views. Proskauer spoke for the anti-Zionists in sessions which revealed serious ideological and personality differences within the Committee. Since Wertheim refused to stand for reelection, political maneuvering for a successor soured dispositions still more. In order to restore unity it was agreed not to nominate a president until after the statement was formulated. When that task was completed, the Waldman-Wertheim faction could not prevent the presidency from going to Proskauer. The more moderate candidates they preferred—men like Governor Herbert Lehman and Judge Samuel Rosenman—declined. Besides, Proskauer's personal following in the Committee was far too strong to be overridden.

When the AJC Statement of Views was discussed at the annual meeting of January 1943, no one could find serious fault with the first seven paragraphs:

> At this time when our country is engaged in an epoch-making war, we, who are united with our brethren of all faiths in the common bond of American citizenship, pledge every effort and every sacrifice to the winning of the war, the achievement for the whole world of the Four Freedoms and the blessings of the Atlantic Charter and the establishment of a just and enduring peace.
>
> We reaffirm our devotion to our religion and pledge ourselves to maintain and perpetuate the vitality of the Jewish religious community, confident that its teachings have constituted and will continue to constitute a basic contribution to the development of civilization and of democracy.

We join with our brethren of all creeds in the continued fight against those who through bigotry and prejudice endeavor in any way to imperil the rights of any group of American Citizens and thus to divide our country and undermine the foundations of American liberty.

We urge upon the United Nations and upon those who shall frame the terms of peace the relief from the havoc and ruin inflicted by Axis barbarism on millions of unoffending human beings, especially Jews, their repatriation, rehabilitation and the complete restoration and safeguarding of their equal civil and religious rights.

To the extent that economic conditions in the war torn lands shall make emigration therefrom of their nationals necessary, we ask the implementation by those who shall frame the terms of peace of a program which shall under international supervision facilitate voluntary settlement elsewhere under the most favorable conditions.

We ask of the United Nations and those who shall frame the terms of peace, reaffirmation of the fundamental principle that Jewish citizens of every land, fulfilling their obligation of complete loyalty to their respective countries, shall be guaranteed the correlative right of complete equality. We applaud the recent statement of the Secretary of State, that we must have a world in which Jews like all others "are free to abide in peace and in honor."

Thus, while associating ourselves fully with all the purposes of human freedom and betterment proclaimed by the President of the United States, we have special concern with the two objectives, salvation of these suffering people and the preservation of the Jewish community as a spiritual force.

The following five paragraphs, which dealt with Zionism, did not muster the same support:

We recognize that there are now more than half a million Jews in Palestine who have built up a sound and flourishing economic life and a satisfying spiritual and cultural life, and who now constitute substantially one-third of the population, and that while this Palestinian immigration has been a blessed amelioration of the condition of this large number of Jews, and has helped to bring about a great development of the country itself, settlement in Palestine although an important factor, cannot alone furnish and should not be expected to furnish the solution of the problem of post-war Jewish rehabilitation.

We affirm our deep sympathy with and our desire to cooperate with those Jews who wish to settle in Palestine.

With respect to the government of Palestine, we recognize wide divergence of opinion and that under existing conditions there should be no preconceived formula at this time as to the permanent political structure which shall obtain there. Since we hold that in the United States as in all other countries Jews, like all others of their citizens are nationals of those nations and of no other, there can be no political identification of Jews outside of Palestine with whatever government may there be instituted.

We endorse the policy of friendship and cooperation between Jews and Arabs in Palestine and urge that every possible avenue be followed to establish good will and active collaboration between them.

We approve for Palestine an international trusteeship responsible to the United Nations for the following purposes:

(a) To safeguard the Jewish settlement in and Jewish immigration into Palestine and to guarantee adequate scope for future growth and development to the full extent of the economic absorptive capacity of the country.

(b) To safeguard and protect the fundamental rights of all inhabitants.

(c) To safeguard and protect the holy places of all faiths.

(d) To prepare the country to become, within a reasonable period of years, a self-governing Commonwealth under a Constitution and a bill of rights that will safeguard and protect these purposes and basic rights for all.

Judge Louis Levinthal of Philadelphia, president of the Zionist Organization of America, tried hard to keep partisan bias out of his criticism of the statement. Carefully avoiding any mention of statehood, he deplored the studied omission of the Jewish Agency in connection with the development of Palestine, the lack of sufficient force in the clause on immigration, and the inconsistency of holding to "no preconceived formula," yet advocating a trusteeship. Although Levinthal's suggestions were moderate, Proskauer argued strongly against changing the document. It was so constructed, he maintained, as to satisfy neither his own nor the pro-Zionist position, which was the only possible way to achieve a working unity. He had discussed the complete statement with Weizmann, who found it basically fair; it had also received a favorable nod from official circles in Washington. Proskauer made ratification of the document a prerequisite for his acceptance of the presidency. The statement was adopted without dissent, Judge Levinthal abstaining.

Other Zionists were less circumspect in their criticism. To them, the statement and the choice of president proved that the Committee had retreated from the Marshall-Adler position and had yielded completely to the anti-Zionists.

VII

Although the Committee referred to the statement as a compromise and Waldman sought privately to convince Weizmann that AJC was still open to discussion, the Zionists' criticism remained firm. Even before the Committee publicized its views, plans had been laid for a meeting of all the national Jewish organizations to discuss the postwar Jewish situation and the upbuilding of Palestine. If that conference declared itself in favor of the Biltmore resolution, the Zionists hoped, the Committee would be pressured into taking a position different from one adopted in small secret sessions; but if the Committee should remain intransigent, its isolationist stance would be clear for all to see. AJC declined the first invitation to the conference, sent out by Harry Monsky of B'nai B'rith. Labeling the conference "untimely" and "inadvisable," it criticized Monsky for having failed to clear the idea privately with the remaining member organizations of the virtually moribund General Jewish Council. Nevertheless, the conference was held in Pittsburgh early in 1943. It took no specific action on the Palestine issue, but resolved to convene an elected American Jewish Assembly to recommend action on the rights of the Jews in the postwar world.

When the invitation to participate in the American Jewish Assembly reached the Committee, Morris Waldman urged Proskauer to stand by his original refusal. Waldman was not opposed to a Jewish state in Palestine, but he resented Zionist encroachment on the diplomatic areas which he considered the Committee's domain. It was all a Zionist trick, he insisted, a "gang-up" on the Committee to promote the "overall" American Jewish Congress for which the Zionists had yearned since 1933. Monsky, Waldman declared, was the Zionist "stooge," delegated to bring the Committee into the Zionist-controlled American Jewish Assembly, where its representatives would be permanently outnumbered thirty to one. The Committee, he warned, would become "a tail to their kite."

To preserve AJC independence and leadership, Waldman suggested that the Committee warn Chaim Weizmann that the non-Zionists would quit the Jewish Agency if the scheme went through. Since it was only as a spokesman of the Jewish Agency that Weizmann could command a hearing by the great powers, the support of the non-Zionist faction was essential.

In AJC's view, the proposed American Jewish Assembly also included other unpalatable features, such as the political concept inherent in an elected body and the failure to provide recognition to locally organized or unaffiliated Jews. Nevertheless, the Committee bowed to public pressure for unity and began negotiations with the American Jewish Assembly. It is possible, too, that the presidency served to modify Proskauer's extreme partisanship. He had once said that it was the task of the president of the American Jewish Committee to "lead us out of Egypt" on the international scene. The Zionists, he agreed, should be allowed to demand a state at the peace conference; the Committee's function would be "to serve as a bridge between conflicting ideas and interests." After weeks of negotiation a solution was reached which satisfied the Committee's conditions for joining the assembly: (1) the name would be changed to American Jewish Conference (to avoid the connotation of Jewish political identity and the pitfall of binding votes); (2) each participating organization would retain the freedom to dissent from majority decisions; and (3) local as well as national groups would be entitled to representation. Waldman would have liked to bind the conference to defer any action on Palestine until the Zionist–non-Zionist deliberations were resolved, but even his own colleagues disagreed.

What followed was hardly calculated to please the Committee. The elections for the conference heightened tension within AJC; bloc representation was arranged, giving disproportionate strength to the Zionists; and the Zionist delegates pledged themselves to the passage of a pro-Jewish state resolution. The Committee watched these developments apprehensively as the conference date—the end of August—approached, at the same time looking for reactions from Washington.

In July, Committee member George Backer conferred with Sumner Welles, who told him of a Roosevelt-Churchill talk about a proposal to the Arabs. The president had advised that Ibn Saud be assured by the United States and Britain that they would pour huge sums of money into the development of Saudi Arabia if he would agree to a Jewish Palestine. Some Zionists were anxious to defer the conference pending further developments, but six weeks later, when the Committee urged leaders at the conference to withdraw their resolution (citing Washington's disapproval), only four delegates (including the three Committee representatives) opposed the endorsement of the full Zionist program.

If the Zionists had indeed planned to crush the Committee by sheer numbers at the conference, their victory was short-lived. When the conference leaders prepared to present their resolutions to Secretary Hull, Proskauer refused to participate. To keep silent would imply Committee acquiescence; to voice opposition would be, in Proskauer's words, a "blow below the belt." The question whether AJC should quit the conference was brought to a head. At a special meeting of the executive committee in October, the three AJC representatives to the conference—Proskauer, Jacob Blaustein, the chairman of the executive committee, and Fred Lazarus—all urged withdrawal. The Committee had proved itself cooperative, eager for unity, and sensitive to the factors inherent in wartime diplomacy. The conference had proved itself a rubber-stamp assembly for the political ambitions of Zionists rather than a bona fide forum for communal consultations. The Committee did accomplish certain things by joining the conference, Blaustein pointed out. It thwarted efforts to set up a permanent superorganization, and it demonstrated to the general public that a substantial organization opposed the Palestine resolution. Now, when its prestige was high, was the time to get out. The resolution to leave the conference passed by a vote of 52 to 13.

The Committee's stand evoked torrents of denunciation. A "new and disruptive line" from a "self-constituted . . . body representative of no one . . . and responsible to no one," said the American Zionist Emergency Council. By its "morally indefensible" action, the American Jewish Conference charged, "the Committee has introduced divisiveness in the councils of American Jewry, which is calculated to impair the effectiveness of the efforts on behalf of the Jewish people in the hour of its greatest need." Forty-two members (10 percent of the AJC membership) resigned from the Committee in protest during the next three months; various affiliated organizations and contributing agencies similarly dissociated themselves. Numerous meetings were held on how to justify the Committee's actions to the public. True, AJC received more publicity within a few days than it had had over many years; but its image was tarnished. Though deeply upset by the episode, Proskauer had faith in the Committee's future: "The American Jewish Committee stands for certain ideals, and they will survive over and above all the attacks that have been made on us. . . . Indeed, it is my belief that out of this turmoil will come the rebirth of the American Jewish Committee as an agency for good."

VIII

The credo by the Committee adopted in January 1943 now became the touchstone of its plans for revitalization. In a statement on its withdrawal from the conference, AJC pledged continuing efforts to keep the doors of Palestine open to immigration and declared:

> But much more than Palestine must occupy the attention of any responsible body which is vitally concerned with the total welfare of Jewry. Through the marshaling of public opinion, through representations to our government and through proper diplomatic channels, we shall continue to seek to achieve the quickest possible rescue of the Jews persecuted in Europe today and to attain for the millions who will be there tomorrow a normal life on a basis of equality with their fellow-citizens. We insist upon the right of Jews to live as equal citizens in Europe or anywhere.
>
> We shall continue assiduously our efforts to deal with anti-Semitism in this country and to expose its true character as a miserable anti-democratic and anti-American manifestation. By a broad educational program, by collaboration with all groups in America who recognize the divisive and demoralizing nature of anti-Semitism, we shall seek to bring about such a community of understanding between all religious and racial groups that bigotry and discrimination will be destroyed. By continuing to cooperate with those many vital Jewish institutions and movements in this country—religious, cultural, philanthropic—we hope to help nourish and enrich Jewish life in America. In all this we shall be moved by a conviction, shared, we believe, by an overwhelming number of American Jews, that the problems of world Jewry cannot be solved by any single political panacea, but by

concentrated activity toward the attainment of a secure place for Jews in all countries of the globe.

Only by emphasizing a positive plan of action could the Committee hope to hold on to, let alone increase, its popular support. On the day the executive committee voted to leave the conference, it authorized the administrative committee to formulate such changes in the agency's bylaws to be submitted to the next annual meeting, "as would render it a more effective instrument for the implementation of the Statement of Views."

The excitement of the 1944 annual meeting was heightened by a heated debate on a motion to reenter the conference. Name-calling, charges of undemocratic behavior, and sarcastic barbs flew between chairman Proskauer and the critics of his policy on the conference. However, the far-reaching significance of the meeting lay in the revision of the bylaws, which marked a new path for the American Jewish Committee. The new bylaws provided for the formation of local AJC chapters in areas with a significant number of Jews and for chapter representation on the national policy-making executive levels. Additional staff and a vigorous campaign to publicize the organization were bound to follow. Reluctant to depart from its "long and honorable tradition of modesty" regarding its achievements, the Committee resolved to publicize itself only in "a dignified manner." But its days as a tight-lipped organization controlled by a New York elite had officially ended.

Although there had been frequent talk ever since the 1930s about "selling" the Committee in various regions of the country, the conference experience gave the decisive push to the chapter proposal. Not only did the Committee need new sources of financial support to overcome losses from individual and group resignations, but it needed to explain the events of the conference. Morris Waldman, who met with small groups of Jews in different parts of the country during 1943, reported serious and widespread misconceptions about the Committee. It was vital for AJC to clear its reputation; if it remained silent, it would lend credence to the charge that it was nothing but a wing of the rabidly anti-Zionist American Council for Judaism. Also, the Committee now had a positive set of beliefs to propagate, and it felt certain that large numbers of sympathetic adherents could be found if the effort were but made. Clearly, if AJC were able to enroll a sizable membership it would refute the Zionist charge that the aristocratic German Jews, the *Yahudim,* had arbitrarily flouted public opinion. Perhaps, too, since Zionists respected strength based on numbers, they would be more willing to cooperate with a broad-based independent organization than with one tied to the conference.

The chapter plan could not hope to succeed if it were approached merely as a way of holding the line against the Zionists. Neither would the traditional program of the Committee—defense against anti-Semitism at home and support of persecuted Jews abroad—suffice to insure its future. A new orientation was required, a program which would provide meaningful justification for a continued Jewish existence in American society. A memo prepared for Committee leaders underscored the new educational aim: "A basic objective of our chapter plan is to bring about widespread understanding, not only among members, but within the community as a whole, of the concept of Jewish life for which we stand; it is the concept which is to be promulgated through projects and programs sponsored by the chapters."

The seeds of this new approach were planted by John Slawson at the annual meeting in 1944. In a short address at the very end of the sessions, Slawson expressed ideas differing sharply from traditional Committee philosophy. He posited as axiomatic the need for the Committee to collaborate with the Jewish community: "One cannot do things *for* the Jewish people; one must do it [*sic*] *with* the Jewish people." A far cry from the stewardship approach of the pre-World War I and Marshall eras and from Proskauer's "my client is the Jewish community," Slawson's approach called for the acceptance of the fact that the American

Jewish community was no longer a teeming mass of Yiddish-speaking immigrants. The New Deal, which had nurtured the recognition of the common man, had stimulated increasing egalitarian pressures within the society. The guardian-ward pattern was obsolete.

Slawson went further. To achieve proper collaboration with the Jewish community AJC had to strengthen the spiritual and cultural resources of American Jewry. Through research activities and publications, study courses, and chapter projects, "we would develop a Jewry in America whose views on life . . . would be based on knowledge, on understanding, on seasoned judgment. . . . We would have an informed constituency who would lead others . . . until ways of adjustment as American citizens of the Jewish religio-cultural identity would be achieved and whose conceptions with regard to the age-old Jewish problem would be global, . . . global in having the conception that the most wholesome approach for the Jews is an integration into the culture of the country where he lives and global as regards the defense of Jewish rights." Though he did not cast away the Committee's Emancipationist philosophy, Slawson rejected the melting pot theory entirely, on the grounds that it led to complete assimilation. It was particularly important, he concluded, to forge instruments for Jewish survival in the United States, for the fate of the Jews everywhere now rested largely in the hands of the American community.

In 1945 the Committee launched *Commentary*, a monthly journal of "significant thought and opinion on Jewish affairs and contemporary issues." The journal, which enjoyed complete editorial freedom, was seen as a reflection of the Committee's "new look." Under the editorship of Elliot Cohen and his successor, Norman Podhoretz, *Commentary* quickly established itself as one of America's foremost intellectual magazines and a leading voice of liberal American opinion. Uncompromisingly rigorous in its standards, it succeeded in fulfilling its charge "to enlighten and clarify public opinion." *Commentary* came to attract Jewish intellectuals, who had completely divorced themselves from Jewish commitments during the depression years, and provided them with a means of expression within a Jewish framework.

Not all active members of the Committee in 1944 were happy about the changes in structure or the Slawson educational approach. Trebling the membership did not automatically multiply the efficiency or quality of the organization. A mass following meant a greater bureaucracy, less susceptible to lay control. Nobody disagreed with the *need* to make the Committee a popular organization; but some could not find their place in such an agency. Others were more disturbed about the proliferation of Committee activities and questioned whether the many new interests legitimately belonged within the Committee's purview. Those who preferred a small Committee, or one devoted solely to defense work, either resigned or gave up their positions of influence. Some had planned to leave anyway when the war ended, believing that with the fall of Germany their job was done. But the steps taken by the American Jewish Committee from 1943 to 1945 foretold a future of never-ending responsibilities and attendant tasks.

11

To Guard the Remnant

An American military officer wrote to John Slawson in the summer of 1945: "As I write, I have before me your letterhead and a memorial roll from a concentration camp and the names of your Committee members can be duplicated on the memorial roll. Waldman, Lehman, Kaplan, Lazarus, Stern—are all names of persons in this concentration camp. It could have been they if their parents or grandparents hadn't moved to the U.S."

The American Jewish Committee needed no reminders of its responsibilities to the survivors of the holocaust. Indeed, it had concerned itself with problems of postwar reconstruction since 1940, when a special commission on peace studies was set up under Professor Morris Raphael Cohen. The Research Institute on Peace and Post-War Problems was designed to investigate and publish data pertaining to the rehabilitation of European Jewry. Created as an independent venture after the Committee rejected the World Jewish Congress suggestion for a joint enterprise, the institute brought together prominent Jewish scholars and experts in international law and the social sciences. Its goal was to inform the makers of policy about the condition of the Jews in twentieth-century Europe and their specific needs. As its director, Dr. Max Gottschalk, pointed out, the very creation of the institute was an "act of faith" predicated on belief in the ultimate destruction of the Nazi forces. In cooperation with prominent government and private peace-planning groups, the institute issued a stream of memoranda, pamphlets, and monographs on the protection of human rights, the abolition of discriminatory legislation, migration and repatriation, statelessness, war crimes, the Palestine issue, restitution, and indemnification.

The Committee's underwriting of the Research Institute's program reflected its revised views about Jewish survival. The Emancipationist philosophy, founded upon the optimism of rationalist thought, had been tempered by twentieth-century realities. The Committee believed more firmly than ever that Jewish survival depended on the triumph of democracy; but the years since 1919 had proved that paper rights afforded scant protection, that so-called democratic governments could tolerate blatant discrimination and look the other way while the most inhuman acts were being perpetrated. Furthermore, while European governments usually spoke up in behalf of their own nationals when they were imprisoned or deported by the Nazis, there was no one to represent the Jews of Germany and the satellite powers, the stateless Jews, the Jews who would not return to their former lands. As the fighting came to a close, Jews needed more than a general blueprint for a brave new world. The formal victories of democracy notwithstanding, Jewish efforts in behalf of Jews dared not abate. "We have to think in terms of the future [rather] than be guided by the conditions of the past. But we should take nothing for granted."

The AJC's postwar guidelines with respect to the survivors of the holocaust were clear—to insure the future of a shattered European Jewry; to call Jewish needs to the attention of statesmen and international councils; and above all to make certain that the destruction which befell the Jewish people would never be forgotten.

I

As the Allied armies began on the liberation of Europe, the American Jewish Committee set in motion a variety of projects to involve the free world in the plight of European Jewry. It requested the United States and the governments-in-exile to assure equal food rations for Jews; it suggested that the newly liberated states appoint special advisers on Jewish affairs; it brought pressure upon the United Nations Relief and Rehabilitation Administration (UNRRA) to aid enemy nationals who had been victims of the Nazis. In consultation with prominent European Jews and non-Jews and American and European officials, AJC deliberated on problems of repatriation and emigration. Both as an educational measure and as a precaution against prejudice by the military, it prepared material on Jews for the American army of occupation. And to bring to light the atrocities perpetrated by the Nazis it pressed the various European governments to establish commissions on war crimes.

Throughout the war there was evidence of apathy, ignorance, even occasional malevolence toward Jews on the part of the democracies. A bare two weeks after American invasion forces landed in North Africa in 1942, Adolph Berle of the State Department informed Jacob Landau, acting for the Committee, that steps to annul the anti-Jewish restrictions imposed by the Vichy government in North Africa were "on the agenda." At Berle's and Landau's suggestion, the president spoke out in favor of the annulment at a press conference. The Committee was particularly eager for the restoration of the Crémieux decree of 1870, which granted French citizenship to Algerian Jewry. When the State Department decided that the matter rested not with the American army but with the French authorities, AJC waited apprehensively for French action. After months of public prodding from both the United States and Britain, French High Commissioner General Henri Giraud did nullify the Vichy legislation; but he withheld restoration of the Crémieux Law, on the grounds that the French wished to equalize the legal status of the Muslim and Jewish inhabitants. One hundred thousand Jews remained without citizenship and the right to participate in civic activities.

The incident proved that a Nazi defeat did not, in and of itself, suffice to end anti-Jewish discrimination. Many individuals and organizations remonstrated with the State Department, and Felix Frankfurter, Baron Edouard de Rothschild, Joseph Proskauer, and George Backer contacted Sumner Welles directly. Welles, Secretary of State Hull, and the president favored the restoration of Jewish rights, but reactionary French circles were behind Giraud's blatantly anti-Semitic act. By giving the Jews and Muslims equal status, they hoped to discourage the Muslims from seeking mass naturalization.

Judge Proskauer pointed out that it was a perverse equality which stripped one group of its citizenship because another did not have it. George Backer added a pointed warning to Welles, which was particularly significant in view of mounting public criticism of American association with Admiral Darlan, vice-premier of the Vichy regime. Without a democratic policy in foreign affairs, Backer said, the United States would lose the support of the American foreign-language groups and the European masses.

The issue was considered crucial because North Africa was regarded as the testing ground for countries which would be liberated in the future. AJC spokesmen argued that Giraud's action violated the principles set down in the Atlantic Charter by the United Nations. The Committee submitted a brief to the State Department, which included significant press comments, and also sought public support for its position. Finally, instructions went out through the War and the State Departments for American representatives in Algeria to work toward a solution. In October 1943 the French Committee on Liberation under General Charles de Gaulle announced the reinstatement of the Crémieux decree.

II

The American Jewish Committee defended the special status conferred upon the Jews by the Crémieux decree because without it Jews were deprived of the rights they had enjoyed for seventy years. In general, however, AJC rejected the idea of group privileges, emphasizing instead the principle of an internationally recognized code of human rights. It had witnessed the failure of the minority rights approach to prevent oppression during the 1930s. Tied to an ineffectual League of Nations, the minority rights provisions had only succeeded in arousing intense nationalist feeling against the minorities they were designed to protect. From the very beginning of World War II, therefore, the Committee rejected the old Wilson formula of national self-determination and, along with other educational, religious, and peace groups, spoke out repeatedly in favor of an international bill of rights.

In 1942 the American Jewish Committee commissioned a study by Professor Hersh Lauterpacht of Cambridge University on the implications of an international bill of rights supported by effective enforcement machinery. To be sure, that remedy offered no guarantee of success. Its effectiveness would depend on widespread acceptance of the principle that persecutions within a country transcended the bounds of domestic jurisdiction. The Committee's position ultimately rested on faith—faith in the "establishment of an international system in which national sovereignty will be curbed" and faith that "extreme nationalism, the bane of our generation, will . . . be repressed and relegated to the background." But there was some reason to be hopeful. The Atlantic Charter underscored individual rights in a postwar world; and the United States committed itself, through the Fulbright-Connally resolution of 1943, to participation in a world organization.

Although aware that a bill of rights would tread on sensitive toes (e.g., in regard to the race question in the United States and freedom of expression in the Soviet Union), the Committee still continued to press for this concept. After representatives of the Big Four drafted a charter for an international organization at Dumbarton Oaks, the State Department invited suggestions on the draft from American groups studying the problems of peace. In a memorandum to Secretary of State Edward Stettinius, the Committee applauded the phrase in the Dumbarton Oaks proposal calling for respect of human rights and urged that the United States take the lead in the campaign for an international bill of rights. Early in 1945 the Committee summarized its postwar goals in a public statement, *To the Counsellors of Peace.* The section on human rights, largely the work of Hans Kohn, J. Salwyn Schapiro, and Arthur Kuhn, refrained from detailing specific rights in order to avoid controversy. Instead, it suggested that "a permanent commission should be set up at the earliest possible time by the United Nations Conference to fomulate an International Bill of Rights embodying the principles of human rights, fundamental freedoms, religious liberty, and racial equality, and a course of procedure for the implementation and enforcement of the Bill." Joseph Proskauer and Jacob Blaustein also discussed the issue of human rights with President Roosevelt shortly before his death.

Along with forty-one other labor, educational, and religious groups, AJC was designated as a consultant organization to the American delegation at the San Francisco conference, scheduled for the end of April 1945. Gratified both at the prospect of conferring directly with the policy-makers as well as by the fact that the American Jewish Conference was the only other Jewish group given similar recognition, the Committee concentrated its efforts on a proposal for a human rights commission. Indeed, credit for reversing the big powers' original reluctance to enlarge the Dumbarton Oaks provisions on human rights belongs to Joseph Proskauer and Jacob Blaustein. As the deadline for submitting amendments to the draft charter approached, the two AJC leaders mobilized the other consultants behind the Committee's proposal. Dr. O. Frederick Nolde of the Federal Council of the Churches of Christ read the consultants' statement at a meeting with Secretary Stettinius. Judge Proskauer followed with an impassioned plea:

> It isn't enough for the charter to speak for universal respect for and observance of human rights. If there is to be freedom in this world, and peace, human rights must be safeguarded and there must be machinery within the United Nations to promote such freedom, to make fundamental human rights a living reality.

When Proskauer sat down, Stettinius said: "Joe, I'm sold. I will go up and try and sell it to the delegation." Stettinius did what he promised, and the Big Four agreed to support the creation of a Commission on Human Rights. They also included among the aims of the United Nations Charter the "promotion and encouragement of respect for human rights and for fundamental freedoms for all without distinction as to race, language, religion or sex."

The Committee's representatives truly earned the tributes paid them by many observers at San Francisco; yet the scope of their achievement was limited. For as long as the UN Charter gave the international body no authority to implement and enforce basic freedoms, even in matters within the domestic jurisdiction of the member states, these freedoms were really no more secure than they had been under the 1919 minorities treaties. The Committee hoped that over the years the United Nations' role as the guardian of human rights might be gradually extended, though it realized that the champions of national sovereignty were unwilling to accept interference by a supranational agency.

While continuing to campaign for an international bill of rights, the Committee sought to make certain that the peace treaties with the former enemy states would insure the freedoms and human rights of their citizens. "We may hope that the successful working of such . . . detailed protection in the former enemy countries may serve as an example to all nations, and that the present members of the United Nations may eventually see fit to accept voluntarily measures which today they would regard as violations of their sovereignty."

III

The real drama of shaping a postwar world took place at the Yalta and Potsdam summit conferences. By comparison, the Paris Peace Conference of 1946 was strictly an anticlimax, for by the time that conference opened in July, the optimism generated by the Allied military victories had evaporated and Winston Churchill had delivered his "Iron Curtain" speech at Fulton, Missouri. Since the East-West split paralyzed any real progress toward world peace, a treaty with Germany was not even on the agenda when the delegates assembled to draw up treaties with Hungary, Rumania, Bulgaria, and Italy.

If the Paris of 1946 held out less promise to the world than did the Paris of 1919, the Jews had even less reason to be hopeful. In 1919 the future had seemed bright—there was the fall of czarist Russia, the Balfour Declaration, the recognition of minority rights. In 1946 everyone was keenly aware of the loss of European Jewry and of apprehension about the fate of Palestine.

The great powers preferred to ignore the Jewish cause. Some statesmen tried to avoid the issue of Zionism or Jewish nationalism; liberal spokesmen wanted to be sure that the Jews were treated no differently from anyone else; the Communist bloc would accept no directives on the treatment of its minorities. For one reason or another, nobody cared to discuss the Nazi program to exterminate a whole people. And even if interest or conscience could be awakened, how could the Jewish demands be dealt with? Unlike 1919, there was no sympathetic Wilson, nor was there any procedure for nongovernmental agencies to be heard. And in the face of the East-West split, the Jews could seek no sponsor among the major powers.

Despite the obstacles, Jewish leadership could not evade the challenge of the peace conference. The armistice agreements with Nazi satellite nations abolished some aspects of discrimination, but popular anti-Semitism remained, and so did the need for international safeguard of Jewish rights.

In the spring of 1946 the American Jewish Committee submitted to the State Department its recommendations for the future peace treaties—proposals advocating the customary guarantees of individual freedoms, as well as the rights of the Jews to nationality and citizenship, emigration, and restitution. AJC omitted the concept of group rights, although it did ask for the right of citizens to use their own language and to establish and maintain educational and cultural institutions. Like the briefs of other organizations, the Committee's proposals received scant attention, and Jewish leaders were sorely disappointed by the draft treaties presented to the Paris Peace Conference. The only recourse was to formulate amendments to the texts and press for their adoption in behind-the-scenes lobbying.

Since the Committee was convinced that its success at San Francisco resulted from its status as a consultant, it asked the State Department for similar recognition at Paris. The request was turned down; San Francisco's experiment in democratic policy-making was called "unique." Ultimately, the Committee joined forces with eight other Jewish organizations represented at the peace conference, and sent to Paris a delegation headed by Jacob Blaustein.

The decision to unite rested on the precedent set after World War I and on the need to satisfy the community's clamor for joint action. However, interorganizational rivalry (especially keen since the affair of the American Jewish Conference and strengthened anew at San Francisco) resulted in wrangling and delays. When Secretary of State James Byrnes and British Foreign Secretary Ernest Bevin refused to recognize a united Jewish delegation, the cooperative venture proved even more frustrating. Not only were Committee representatives certain that they could have accomplished more by independent lobbying, but, as Morris Waldman pointed out, the pitiful showing at Paris constituted a public spectacle of Jewish weakness and ineptitude. It is doubtful, however, that independent Committee action could have accomplished more. The East European Jews feared Jewish spokesmen from the West who might arouse the suspicions of the Soviets. They also were less interested than the Westerners in pushing for formal guarantees of their rights, which might arouse their governments' resentment. Finally, Secretary Byrnes was noticeably cool, even toward American citizens.

When the nine organizations completed their list of suggested amendments to the draft treaties—which included individual rights, restitution, and recognition of the religious and cultural rights of the Jewish "collectivity"—they searched in vain for a sponsor. Committee spokesmen and their colleagues conferred with Western, Eastern, oriental, and African delegates, but no country would back the list of over fifty proposals. The Jews then formulated their demands in single propositions, concentrating on human rights and restitution, and won United States and United Kingdom backing for amendments dealing with those subjects. The original treaty drafts had made only general provisions concerning human rights and had provided for restitution to Allied citizens and enemies of the satellites; but the new clauses put emphasis on the abolition of discriminatory legislation and practices (for the treaties with Hungary, Rumania, and Bulgaria) and the restoration of the property and interests of persons who had been persecuted on religious and racial grounds (for the treaties with Hungary and Rumania).

Although the peace conference adopted the proposed clauses, their inclusion in the treaties was not assured unless Russian UN delegate Molotov gave his approval at the Council of Foreign Ministers. The Jewish organizations approached the

Big Four during their fall meeting in New York and received assurances that the United States, Great Britain, and France would stand by the Paris clauses. Through personal contacts a meeting was arranged with Andrei Gromyko, the Russian ambassador to the U.S., and a letter was sent off to Stalin requesting Soviet support. Despite Communist charges that the Jewish organizations had served as tools of the Anglo-American bloc at Paris, Russia finally agreed, and the foreign ministers approved the pertinent clauses with only minor changes. Even though only a fraction of their original requests were granted, the Jews achieved all that was possible in the existing international climate.

IV

Even before the end of the war Jewish organizations talked about restitution and indemnification. In its 1945 report, *To the Counsellors of Peace*, the Committee advocated the following points:

> 1. In so far as the property of Jewish individuals, institutions or communities has been seized, damaged or destroyed in Axis countries or countries under their domination, the owners of such property or their heirs should be entitled in satisfaction of their claims to at least the same treatment as may be adopted for the benefit of other individuals, institutions or communities whose property has been similarly seized, damaged or destroyed.
> 2. In so far as the property of Jewish individuals, institutions or communities has been "Aryanized," such property should be restored to its original owners.
> 3. . . . In action taken by any of the United Nations with respect to compensation for damages arising out of acts of the Nazis or their satellites, no distinction should be made between stateless persons and persons of foreign nationality.
> 4. The proceeds of property formerly belonging to Jewish individuals of institutions, and escheating to the state for

> want of proper claimants, should in so far as necessary be assigned to the local Jewish communities for the reconstruction of religious, welfare, educational and cultural institutions, and for the relief and economic rehabilitation of Jewish victims of Nazi persecution.

The struggle for restitution lasted over twenty years and involved governments, communal organizations, and private industrial firms in several countries. In cooperation with other agencies the American Jewish Committee, and particularly Jacob Blaustein, later president of AJC, made outstanding contributions to its ultimate success.

There was nothing new about a victor's exacting reparations from a defeated nation; but Jewish claims against Germany did not fit the usual pattern. The Jews had not legally been at war with the Nazis; many of the victims were originally nationals of Germany and the satellite states; and in some cases, Jews had "voluntarily" transferred their property to the Nazis. Who was empowered to present the claims of the Jewish victims? Was it fair that the property of those who died heirless should revert to the state—in this instance, Germany?

In the long run, the principles adopted by the Committee proved successful: Jews, even nationals of enemy states, were entitled to indemnification; the Allies launched the program of restitution under *their* authority; and most important of all, an organization representing the Jewish community was recognized as the recipient of heirless Jewish property. Indeed, the success of the entire campaign in behalf of the Jewish victims depended on that last principle. To sustain the survivors rather than avenge the dead, the community would use the assets from unclaimed property for the monumental task of rehabilitation. Professor Herman Gray, a member of the Committee and its adviser on postwar relief problems, wrote in 1945: "[If that principle is secured,] we shall be able to put through a rehabilitation and resettlement program that will fire the imagination." The en-

dorsement of the collectivist principle by Jews and non-Jews alike
also indicated an unquestioned acceptance of the Jewish people
as an entity, a concept which a century and a half of emancipation
had not eradicated.

The Committee approached the issue of restitution quite
pragmatically. It was not prepared to permit Germany to buy
back her innocence, but neither would it refuse to negotiate with
Germany on the grounds that the country which gave rise to
nazism must forever be kept outside the family of nations. The
practical problem of what to do for the refugees, the ruined
families, and the wrecked communities staggered the imagination. Justice demanded that those responsible help shoulder the
burden. "We knew," said Blaustein, "that all the wealth the earth
contained could not atone for the Nazi murders and tortures. But
we also knew that the victims of nazism were in desperate need,
and that the German nation could and *should* take the first steps
to help ameliorate their terrible plight and, in some measure to
indicate, in a tangible way, the profound sorrow and poignant
sense of shame at the hideous and unspeakable crimes that were
committed against humanity in their name."

The first phase of restitution concerned identifiable property
in the occupied zones of Germany. Representatives of five organizations—the Committee, the Joint Distribution Committee, the
Jewish Agency, the World Jewish Congress, and the American
Jewish Congress—met regularly with officials of the State Department and the American military command in Germany to push
for restitution laws. The United States favored prompt handling
of the matter, but Great Britain, France, and Russia delayed.
Since speed was more important than united action, the Committee encouraged the American government to act unilaterally, a
course which the State Department finally agreed to follow.

Successive drafts of a claims law proved unsatisfactory to the
Jewish organizations until the project gained the backing of General Lucius D. Clay, the U.S. military governor of Germany. Clay
showed consistent sympathy toward Jewish needs and was im-

pressed by the arguments that Proskauer and Blaustein presented to him in private. When the general met with a delegation of the five organizations in November 1946 it was decided that (1) the military government (rather than the Germans) would designate a Jewish successor organization to inherit the heirless and unclaimed properties; (2) American officials would review the decisions of German restitution courts; and (3) the law would not preclude further claims against Germany for nonidentifiable property. On this basis the claims law for the American zone was promulgated in November 1947. With the appointment of the Jewish Restitution Successor Organization, Jewish victims were recognized as a collective legal party entitled to redress. (The same arrangements had already been written into the peace treaties with Rumania and Hungary.) The American legislation was followed shortly by similar enactments in the French and British zones. The Russians, however, refused to relinquish their share of the German spoils. During the next several years Blaustein, through his contacts with the Truman administration, helped strengthen the position of the Jewish Restitution Successor Organization in Germany and reinforce the claims of the Jewish survivors in that country.

The second phase of the restitution program involved the newly created State of Israel and the government of West Germany. Early in 1951 Israel addressed a note to the Allied powers asking for indemnification for individual victims of nazism and for payments by Germany of over one billion dollars in goods to meet the cost of resettling some five hundred thousand refugees from Nazi countries. Since only one of the belligerent states could place assessments upon the defeated enemy, the Allies replied that they had no power to exact reparations for Israel. Israel, they indicated, would have to deal with Germany directly.

Behind the scenes, meanwhile, the Committee had been involved in consultations on three fronts: with Israel, on how to phrase its demands; with the American government, on the justice of those demands; and with German authorities, on the need to meet the claims for indemnification. The Committee was the first to suggest to Washington that West Germany be permitted back into the family of nations if it agreed to reparations and indemnification. Two representatives of the Committee who spoke with prominent Germans pointed out that restitution would be one indication that an effective democratic government had been established in Germany. Clearly the key bargaining point with the Germans was official American sympathy with the plan of indemnification. (Years later, Blaustein recalled, West German Chancellor Konrad Adenauer explained that "he could never have come to the United States had he not made the declaration of restitution and followed it up with compensation.") On September 21, 1951, Adenauer officially accepted Germany's responsibility toward the Jewish victims of the Nazis. In a statement, which was first discussed with the Committee, he said: "Unspeakable crimes were perpetrated in the name of the German people, which imposes upon them the obligation to make moral and material amends, both as regards the individual damage the Jews have suffered and as regards Jewish property for which there are no longer individual claimants."

A month later representatives of twenty-two major Jewish organizations assembled in New York and organized the Conference on Jewish Material Claims against Germany. Actual administration was left to its three senior officers: Nahum Goldmann of the Jewish Agency and the World Jewish Congress, president; Jacob Blaustein, senior vice-president; and Moses Leavitt of the JDC, treasurer. Representatives of the conference and of Israel began negotiations with the German government in March 1952. Meeting in a secret location outside The Hague (to avoid disruption and interference by possible opponents of the Germans or the Jews), they labored for six months.

Pending the negotiations, it was imperative that the United States maintain its support of indemnification. A negative, or even a neutral, stand would have been seized upon by German opponents to Adenauer's policy and by extremists of both Left and Right for their own political advantage. To insure the success of the restitution demands and to gain the support of the democratic elements in Germany, the Committee worked to overcome opposition to indemnification in American government circles.

Some officials questioned particularly the economic implications of such a step. They feared that, as was the case after World War I, the United States would have to keep pouring money into Germany to enable her to pay reparations. Again, AJC president Jacob Blaustein made representations to the top policy-makers, communicating personally and in writing with President Truman and Secretary of State Dean Acheson. He also discussed the financial and technical aspects of indemnification with Henry Byroade, head of the German desk at the State Department, and succeeded in converting him into an influential supporter of German-Jewish settlements. When negotiations at The Hague reached a temporary impasse in June 1952, Blaustein turned directly to Truman. At a White House conference the president reiterated his desire for an honorable and satisfactory outcome. John J. McCloy, the U.S. high commissioner for Germany, repeated this sentiment to Adenauer, and the State Department gave the same message to the Israeli ambassador and representatives of other Jewish claimants. Throughout, the Committee's task was facilitated by the invaluable support of McCloy, for whom indemnification was a symbol of a new democratic Germany.

American support ultimately brought the bargaining at The Hague to a successful conclusion. In September 1952, in Luxembourg, Germany signed an agreement with Israel promising to pay $715 million in goods over a period of twelve to fourteen years and to extend the benefits of compensation laws to Israeli citizens. A separate settlement with the Claims Conference provided for payment of an additional $107 million to victims outside Israel and also stipulated that Germany would supplement and amend existing statutes in behalf of individual victims. Aside from the vast sums involved, the Luxembourg agreements were doubly significant: not only had a government voluntarily agreed to pay damages for injuries inflicted by its predecessor, but it had also signed a pact with a voluntary organization speaking in the name of individuals scattered throughout the world.

Later developments in the restitution program, some still in operation, included indemnification from Austria, reparations from German industrial firms (Krupp, I.G. Farben, and others) for the use of refugees who had been conscripted for slave labor, and benefits to Nazi victims who escaped from Iron Curtain countries after the signing of the Luxembourg agreements. The question of restitution for enemy nationals' property confiscated during the war was not resolved until 1962, but this too was finally negotiated. As long as additional resources could be tapped, the Committee continued to plead the cause of the surviving remnant of European Jewry. The successful negotiations for restitution made possible hundreds of projects for relief and rehabilitation, affecting over two dozen countries. On the sixtieth anniversary of the American Jewish Committee, Jacob Blaustein could speak with justifiable pride about the work of the Claims Conference and the American Jewish Committee in implementing a "Jewish Marshall Plan."

V

Unlike restitution, punishment of Nazi war criminals offered no tangible benefits to the victims. Still, from the war years until the present Jewish organizations have regarded it as their responsibility to help bring the guilty to justice. When the full horror of the holocaust was first revealed, retribution was regarded as a deterrent to further atrocities. The delegation of American Jews which called on Roosevelt in December 1942 urged the establishment of a war crimes commission that would ultimately bring the criminals to account. In 1944 the War Refugee Board, desperately seeking ways to save lives, broadcast to the enemy several warnings as to the punishment awaiting the perpetrators of war crimes. In biblical style the Moscow Declaration intoned the fate in store for those who assisted the murderers: "Let those who have hitherto not imbrued their hands with innocent blood beware lest they join the ranks of the guilty, for most assuredly the three Allied Powers will pursue them to the uttermost ends of the earth and will deliver them to their accusers in order that justice may be done."

However, when the war in Europe ended and threats of punishment were no longer a deterrent, opinions on the prosecution of war criminals were divided. Senator Robert Taft, for example, felt that he could not in good conscience favor punishment in the name of international law when that law had no provision for such proceedings. But the deep impulse to prove that the world was not prepared to shrug off the atrocities remained. The American Jewish Committee argued further in a brief prepared for the peacemakers:

> Punishment of these crimes is a necessity. If the perpetrators of crimes unprecedented in number and horror are allowed to go unpunished, no durable peace will be possible. The resentment and passions of the martyred peoples will introduce the reign of lynch law on the widest scale; there will be little discrimination between the guilty and the innocent, and respect for all law will be undermined. Responsible punishment of war criminals will be needed to establish law, as well as faith in the democracies, which have promised punishment. It will be necessary to prove that in international affairs, as in other realms of civilized life, "crime does not pay," and to serve a warning to those who would otherwise plan new wars and murders. Just punishment, imposed after just trials, will help to deter any inclination . . . to dismiss the Nazi record of torment and massacre as unfounded atrocity stories, invented to stir up a warlike spirit among the Allied peoples during the war, and devoid of merit as true history . . . Indeed, trial and punishment of the guilty should be welcomed by the peoples of the Axis nations

themselves as an opportunity to disassociate the relatively guiltless mass from the actual criminals.

The Committee pointed to various statements issued by the Allies and the governments-in-exile which spoke of vengeance against the guilty, and especially to a February 1945 statement by Acting Secretary of State Joseph Grew, calling for "the punishment of German leaders and their associates for their responsibility for the whole broad criminal enterprise, devised and executed with ruthless disregard of the very foundation of law and morality." In December 1945, after providing documentary material to the Office of Strategic Services, the Committee submitted a brief to the International Military Tribunal entitled "Crimes against Humanity," which recounted the criminal acts of seventeen individuals as well as of various groups.

Non-Jewish concern about "crimes against humanity" diminished after the dramatic trial of the top Nazis at Nuremberg, and early in 1951 High Commissioner McCloy and General Thomas Handy, commander in chief of the European Command, commuted the sentences of 89 of the 101 convicted criminals. The Committee, together with other Jewish organizations, protested to the State Department, arguing that McCloy's action weakened the morale of the democratic elements in Germany and vitiated the deterrent to potential aggressors. The government was sensitive enough to Jewish criticism to arrange for a private meeting at which officials concerned with the problem presented their case.

Although the American officials justified McCloy's action on legal and humane grounds, it was clear that the high commissioner had been under great pressure to commute the sentences. Appeals from the Vatican and other religious sources, pacifist organizations, and elements within Germany had forced a review of the convictions. Concomitantly, cold-war developments dictated the need to rearm Germany in the defense of Western Europe against communism and the need to gain German goodwill. Both McCloy and the State Department asserted that reducing the sentences would make Germans more amenable to accepting the whole concept of war criminals and give them an understanding of the original Nuremberg trials. The Jewish organizations, however, were not convinced, despite McCloy's invaluable cooperation in the restitution program.

Twenty years after the war, years in which it undertook many positive programs in regard to Germany, the American Jewish Committee still refused to withdraw its moral indictment of the Nazi criminals. At the end of 1964 the German government adopted a statute of limitations on the initiation of proceedings against Nazi criminals. The proposed cutoff date was May 8, 1965, the twentieth anniversary of V-E Day. Morris B. Abram, president of AJC, who served with the prosecution at the Nuremberg trials, met with German Minister of Justice Ewald Bucher in Bonn. On legal as well as moral grounds he argued that Germany's new statute was "indefensible." "The crimes involved are of such an unusual character as to be subject to law without a statute of limitations," he maintained. Besides, the right of West Germany to try criminals did not begin until the country regained sovereignty in 1955; hence a twenty-year statute of limitations should set the cutoff date at 1975. Bucher agreed that the time period could be extended, and two months later, after Abram's memorandum on the subject had been widely circulated in the United States and abroad, Germany changed the terminal date to December 31, 1969. The Committee called the decision an "unfortunate compromise," and a delegation headed by Abram brought up the issue again at a meeting with German chancellor Ludwig Erhard. If Germany would not agree to remove the statute of limitations completely, it should at least extend the cutoff to 1975; until then, Abram urged, all efforts should be made to bring known war criminals to justice. Two years later it appeared that the Committee had won its case; the new minister of justice, Gustav Heinemann, announced that he would seek to remove all time limitations on the prosecution of war criminals.

VI

For the tens of thousands of Jews living in DP (displaced persons) camps at the end of the war, protracted negotiations on indemnity payments or war crimes had little immediate relevance. Their all-absorbing problem was to live as normally as possible until permanent refuge could be found. To determine their day-to-day needs, the American Jewish Committee sent a team of observers to the camps. Jacob Blaustein, on his way home from the Paris Peace Conference, also visited the camps. The most important source of information of DP needs was the office of adviser on Jewish affairs, created in the summer of 1945 at the initiative of AJC and attached to the American military command in Germany. The adviser was to serve as buffer between the Jewish DPs and the military. Requests and complaints from both sides were routed through him. The American government valued the office because the adviser also kept the American Jewish organizations informed on military policy and received all their questions and recommendations.

The five major Jewish organizations (the Committee, the World Congress, the American Congress, the Jewish Agency, and the JDC) were promptly informed about trouble spots in the camps and could act quickly on this information. For example, when notified that the American authorities were considering closing their zone to DPs fleeing renewed persecution in Poland, the American Jewish groups quickly made their opposition known to the State Department and succeeded in preventing that blockade. On-the-spot reports also helped the organizations inform the world of the plight of the DPs, as the Committee did in its recommendations to UNRRA and its memorandum to the UN Special Commission on Refugees and Displaced Persons. The Jewish DPs benefited, too. The adviser not only worried about their needs—economic, cultural, and psychological—but he also served as their defender against unfriendly critics. When Lieutenant General Sir Frederick E. Morgan, chief of UNRRA operations in Germany, deplored the infiltration of "well-dressed and well-fed" refugees from Poland, Judge Simon Rifkind, a respected member of the Committee who served as the first Jewish adviser, quickly challenged that image. He had spoken in their own language to hundreds of those refugees fleeing hostility and violence in Poland, Rifkind told the press, and they were desperately searching for "freedom from fear."

Concern for the DPs also brought into the open the persistence of anti-Semitism in Germany. Time and again, the Jewish advisers reported anti-Jewish incidents, from which even the DPs were not immune. Anti-Semitism among American enlisted men (resulting in part from their fraternization with German girls), was another problem. The gravity of the situation, as well as the pressing need for the rapid evacuation of the DP camps, led the Jewish organizations to reconsider the possibilities for a reconstitution of Jewish life in Germany. Outside the DP camps the Jewish population numbered some nineteen thousand, over half of them from Eastern Europe. Was it realistic to pour funds into helping a community composed largely of aliens to take root in an antagonistic society? Was it not more practical to encourage all Jews to quit Germany? The Jewish Agency and the Central Committee for Liberated Jews, convinced that the latter course was correct, refused to aid the German Jewish communities. The American Jewish Committee, however, while generally agreeing that non-German Jews had no future in Germany, refused to abdicate its responsibilities to those who preferred to stay.

VII

Besides maintaining the camps as a permanent institution—an alternative no one really considered—there were three possibilities for solving the DP problem. The first was forced repatriation to the refugees' original homes. While this was the position of the Soviet Union, the American government agreed with AJC that no person should be compelled to return to the country from which he had been displaced. A second alternative was to integrate the DPs into the German and Austrian communities—an impossibility in light of the emotional factors involved and the postwar poverty in both lands. The only practical solution therefore was the emigration of the DPs to new and permanent homes. At the end of 1946 there were an estimated 850,000 nonrepatriables, of whom 200,000 were Jews. Had the nations of the world jointly extended hospitality to these unfortunates, the numbers seeking haven would not have loomed so large.

The Committee's humanitarian approach to the DP problem was summarized in a memorandum to the UN Special Committee on Refugees and Displaced Persons. It set forth demands for fair treatment of the stateless, the liberalization of immigration and naturalization laws, and the specific right of the Jewish DP to choose whether he wished to return to his country of origin, to emigrate, or to acquire citizenship in the country where he currently lived. The Committee's memorandum, however, failed to deal with realities. The UN could only make recommendations on immigration. European countries, faced with the task of rebuilding their economies, could not absorb refugees. The Soviet Union's westward advances further increased the numbers seeking asylum. The British White Paper of 1939 still governed immigration to Palestine. Countries which could take in the DPs—the United States, Canada, Latin America, Australia—did not want them. The Committee labored on several fronts at once to find homes for the DPs in the United States, in Palestine, and in countries loosely labeled "other than" the United States and Palestine (i.e., Latin America, Australia).

Aware of the persistent restrictionist sentiment in the United States, in 1945 the Committee pressed the White House and the State Department for modest favors—the reopening of consulates in Germany to expedite the processing of visas and the full utilization of the current available quotas. (As Jacob Blaustein pointed out to Secretary of State Byrnes, only 6 percent of the quotas for the European area had been filled between June 1944 and June 1945.) President Truman, whose sympathy toward the DPs was heightened by a report on the camps from his special emissary, Earl G. Harrison, issued a directive in December 1945 giving DPs preferential treatment within the quota system. When that step proved inadequate—only five thousand DPs entered the country by October 1946 (twenty-four hundred of them Jews)—the president announced he would ask Congress for special legislation. That signaled the mobilization of forces on both sides. The restrictionists grouped their forces to defend quotas based on national origins; the liberals were determined to forge an immigration policy more consonant with American international responsibilities.

Two days before Truman's announcement, Alan Stroock reported to the AJC administrative committee on the grave difficulties facing the Jewish DPs. He emphasized several key points: (1) in the face of Polish persecution, the number of Jewish DPs would rise to over two hundred thousand by the end of the year; (2) the outlook for opening the doors of Palestine had grown dimmer; (3) unless the United States acted first, little could be expected from other countries; and (4) any significant remedial action would have to come from a change in the quota laws.

The administrative committee resolved to campaign for liberalization of the immigration laws. Since the problem really concerned Americans of all faiths, it was decided to seek the support of other groups and to supplement the humanitarian appeal with an appeal to American self-interest. At its annual meeting three months later, the American Jewish Committee urged, in a formal resolution, "the prompt adoption by the Congress of the United States of temporary legislation which . . . would . . . admit to this country as its fair share of the total, approximately 400,000 displaced persons."

For a year and a half the Committee, together with other Jewish and non-Jewish organizations, worked toward that goal. Since a strictly Jewish campaign would clearly have reduced any chance of success, AJC actively cooperated in the formation of the Citizens Committee on Displaced Persons, an organization of prominent liberals of all faiths and professions. Helped in large measure by advice and funds from American Jews, the Citizens Committee succeeded in pleading the DP cause before the public. Irving M. Engel, who coordinated AJC's role in the campaign, believed that if it had not been for the Citizens Committee, the anti-immigration forces might even have renewed their fight for drastic cuts in the quotas. The Committee's own contributions lay in mustering the support of politicians, Catholic dignitaries, and labor leaders. Its chapters set up committees on DP legislation and distributed educational materials for local use. The Committee also prepared and distributed a widely discussed cartoon pamphlet, *The Face at the Window,* which, in simple drawings and text, explained the plight of the DPs and America's obligation to take them in. AJC members throughout the country were urged to express their views on the subject to their congressmen.

The proponents of special enabling legislation for the DPs centered their hopes on a bill introduced by Representative William Stratton, calling for the annual admission of one hundred thousand nonquota DPs for a period of four years. Simpler than the alternatives of filling unused quotas or scrambling national quotas, the bill was endorsed by the Citizens Committee, religious and humanitarian organizations, the AFL and the CIO, and cabinet members George Marshall, Robert Patterson, and Thomas Clark. Committee leader Herbert H. Lehman testified in favor of the measure on behalf of the Jewish organizations represented in the National Community Relations Advisory Council. The advocates of the bill did more than plead the cause of the DPs; they emphasized the obligation of America, as leader of the free world. *Life* magazine editorialized in a similar vein:

> If we are to remain the leading nation of One World, we also have a deep moral obligation not to be too exclusive. No other nation represents so many blood strains or has amal-

gamated so many viewpoints; that is an asset in our foreign relations which, if we really believe in it, gives us a special claim to leadership and a special duty to "set an example." The constitution of the United Nations proclaims the universality of human rights and freedoms, a clause the U.S. has often invoked and argued for. How then can we be so complacent about our immigration policy? Above all, in God's name can we go on doing nothing about those DPs?

Despite this formidable array of support for the DPs, the restrictionists, sparked by veterans' organizations, patriotic societies, and the southern Democrats, proved even stronger. Arguing against the admission of DPs on the grounds of American domestic needs and security, they delayed legislation until 1948. More seriously, the Displaced Persons Act, which was finally passed in June, hardened prejudice into law. The measure, which granted entry to two hundred thousand DPs (at the expense of future quotas), stipulated that 40 percent were to come from the Baltic states or Russian-annexed Poland, that 30 percent were to be experienced farmers, that all applicants had to have entered the Western zones of Germany before 1946, and that each had to possess a security clearance as well as assurances of a job and housing upon arrival. The discrimination against Jews was obvious. President Truman's stinging critique of the bill stressed that point:

> The bad points of the bill are numerous. Together they form a pattern of discrimination and intolerance wholly inconsistent with the American sense of justice.
> The bill discriminates in callous fashion against displaced persons of the Jewish faith. This brutal fact cannot be obscured by the maze of technicalities in the bill or by the protestations of some of its sponsors.
> The primary device used to discriminate against Jewish displaced persons is the provision restricting eligibility to those displaced persons who entered Germany, Austria, or

Italy on or before December 22, 1945. Most of the Jewish displaced persons who had entered Germany, Austria, or Italy by that time have already left; and most of the Jewish displaced persons now in those areas arrived there after December 22, 1945, and hence are denied a chance to come to the United States under this bill. By this device more than 90 per cent of the remaining Jewish displaced persons are definitely excluded. Even the eligible 10 per cent are beset by numerous additional restrictions written into the bill.

For all practical purposes, it must be frankly recognized, therefore, that this bill excludes Jewish displaced persons, rather than accepting a fair proportion of them along with other faiths.

The Jewish organizations were justifiably bitter, and some suggested that President Truman be pressed to veto the measure. The Committee opposed that idea, pointing out that if Jews alone made such a demand they would be charged with spitefully sacrificing all DPs. Also, the Committee anticipated that, in light of the unfriendly stance of Congress and particularly of the Senate leaders, moves to alter the general immigration law might well follow. If that happened, Jews could not afford to isolate themselves from other groups.

The Jewish organizations immediately appealed to Congress to correct the abuses in the DP law. They also outlined their objections to President Truman and Governor Thomas E. Dewey, the presidential contenders in 1948. They took issue with the provisions already noted, as well as with the section of the law which reserved 50 percent of the German and Austrian quotas to persons of German ethnic origin but not of German nationality. Not only did that clause substitute the concept of blood (a Nazi doctrine) for the concept of nationality (the traditional American policy), but it enabled those volksdeutsche who had spearheaded Nazi propaganda drives throughout Europe to bring their Nazi baggage to the United States. President Truman also pressed for a revision of the DP Act; but not until June 1950 did Congress amend its most objectionable features. By then, however, the urgency had subsided, for the State of Israel had come into being and any Jew who so desired was welcome to immigrate there.

12

"The State of Israel . . . Is Here to Stay"

I

The desperate need to resettle the victims of nazism ultimately convinced the American Jewish Committee to support the creation of a Jewish state in Palestine. Until 1946, however, it kept the issues of statehood and immigration separate, convinced that agitation for the first harmed the prospects for the second. In line with the position adopted in 1939, AJC spoke out against the British White Paper of 1939, which limited Jewish immigration into Palestine. Also, in accordance with its 1943 Statement of Views, the organization endorsed an international trusteeship for Palestine to safeguard the rights of Jewish immigration and settlement predicated upon the country's economic absorptive capacity. Trusteeship would be only a temporary status which would lead "within a reasonable period of years [to] a self-governing Commonwealth." AJC, ever pragmatic, did not define the vague term *commonwealth*. It hoped that a period of disinterested international control would remove Palestine from the arena of power politics, while simultaneously effecting a rapprochement between the Arab and Jewish communities; only then would it be realistic to resolve the future of Palestine. Aside from intrinsic merit, trusteeship as a transitional status had the value of being a stalling device. To raise the question of Palestine's ultimate destiny would only frighten the Arabs, disturb the military strategists, upset the politicians, and expose the disunity within the ranks of Western Jewry. The primary objective was to rescue as many Jews as possible from Europe and permit them to enter Palestine.

The Committee never regretted its decision to leave the American Jewish Conference. Freedom of action meant that AJC could augment Zionist expostulations against the White Paper with its own protest, which it did in a formal statement to Britain's Lord Halifax and the Foreign Affairs Committee of the House of Representatives, calling on England to abide by the obligations imposed by the mandate and to permit Jewish immigration and land purchases in Palestine. On the other hand, AJC openly criticized the agitation for immediate statehood, which it felt to be tactically inexpedient in wartime. Moreover, statehood as a political goal had never been explicitly specified in any international document, unlike the "homeland" promise of the Balfour Declaration. Eschewing the extremes of both the statists and the anti-Zionist American Council for Judaism, the Committee grew increasingly convinced of the practical value of its non-Zionist course. It initiated an appeal to Chaim Weizmann for non-Zionist representation in a reconstituted Jewish Agency. Since the Jewish Agency was the recognized Jewish spokesman in dealings with the mandatary power, the Committee hoped to use its influence in that body to moderate the Zionist views. Weizmann did little to further the request, but he was far too clever a diplomat to alienate the AJC leaders by rejecting their suggestion outright.

An important factor in the Committee's calculations was the belief that independent status meant more favorable attention in Washington. "The State Department hailed our dissent and withdrawal from the Conference with the deepest satisfaction," Waldman noted, adding: "Even though the Committee's position is not as anti-Zionist as the Department would like it to be, our separation from the Zionists . . . gives us a preferred position in the Department." Sumner Welles also praised AJC's Palestine formula, in which, he said, he concurred.

Meanwhile, the Zionists suffered a setback in 1944 when they failed in their attempts to get Congress to pass a resolution in favor of a Jewish state; opposition from General George Marshall, Secretary of War Henry Stimson, and the State Department was strong enough, even in an election year, to shelve the measure. Secretary of State Stettinius warned Jacob Landau that "noisy manifestations" at this time were tactically wrong. Even Roosevelt, who publicly endorsed Jewish statehood, privately remarked to Proskauer and Blaustein shortly before his death in 1945 that Zionist agitation was ill advised. Proskauer reported that

> he [Roosevelt] had informed one of the Zionist leaders, Dr. Wise, that he gravely feared a continuance of the agitation for a Jewish state at this time was provocative of a situation that might cause a third world war and also might cause grave disturbances in Palestine which would be most harmful to the Jewish settlement there; that when this Zionist leader replied to him that Churchill was a Zionist, he told him this anecdote: that Churchill had once said to him that he was a Zionist and that the President had replied inquiring what his plan was for Palestine; that Mr. Churchill replied that he had no plan, and that the President's comment to him was that what he really meant was that he could not have a plan for a Jewish state in Palestine that was consistent with the safety of the British Empire, and thereupon Mr. Churchill has expressed acquiescence in that view.
>
> The President then stated to us his belief that the project of a Jewish state in Palestine was, under present conditions, impossible of accomplishment and that the proper Jewish objective was to secure liberal immigration into Palestine and to secure, through a world organization, assurance of the rights of the Jewish people in every country.
>
> When we commented that this view was somewhat at

variance with his public utterances, the President turned to us and said that he had learned a great deal at Yalta;* that he was gravely concerned about the matter, and that he urged us . . . to do our best to moderate the sharpness of the propaganda of the extreme Zionists.

As a result of this conversation, Proskauer, an Al Smith Democrat who in 1940 had stumped for Wendell Willkie, the Republican candidate running against Roosevelt, added his voice to those who praised Roosevelt as "the best friend the Jews had."

The Committee took pains to explain how it differed from the Zionists, but its own "preferred" position made no significant impact on the Roosevelt administration or on British immigration policy. The State Department stood by its decision that the United States had no juridical right to intervene in the Palestine situation; and the American officials dealing with the Middle East —Wallace Murray, Harold Hoskins, Patrick Hurley—remained partial to the Arabs. One State Department official even commented that it was easier to deal with the Zionists than with the Committee people, for one always knew where they stood; the Committee was "always straddling the fence," and it was "impossible to tell what their position is on any problem." The Committee's course had no apparent success in counteracting the biases existing in the State Department.

AJC's independent position, as has been noted, gained it a separate invitation to serve as a consultant organization to the American delegation at the San Francisco founding conference of the UN. Despite the ongoing competition between AJC and the American Jewish Conference for favorable publicity, the two

---

* The minutes of the Yalta Conference do not record any discussion of Palestine or the Middle East. Perhaps the president was referring to his meeting with Ibn Saud shortly after the conference. When he returned home, Roosevelt commented in his speech to Congress on how much he had learned about the Arab and the Jewish problems in five minutes with Ibn Saud. At that meeting, and again several weeks later, Roosevelt promised the Arab king that he would not assist the Jews against the Arabs.

organizations jointly appealed to Stettinius for the creation of a trusteeship that would in no way imperil Jewish interests in Palestine. Meanwhile, Joseph Proskauer continued his correspondence with Lord Halifax, seeking to impress upon him the importance to Zionists and non-Zionists alike of keeping Palestine open to Jewish immigration. "The greatest difficulty I find in trying to hold my fellow-Jews to a rational and sensible course," the judge wrote from San Francisco, "is the appeal to the emotions that Jews are dying in Europe and cannot get into Palestine. Aside from the fact that it is right in my judgment for Great Britain to do this, I am satisfied and strongly believe that it is expedient." The Committee leaders requested both Halifax and Truman to bring up the subject of immigration to Palestine at the Potsdam Conference.

Neither the end of the war in Europe nor the victory at the polls of the British Labour party, which in 1944 had supported a Jewish state, brought any change in the Palestine situation. AJC was now receiving more detailed information on the desperate condition of Jewish survivors in Europe, and it urged the Truman administration to secure the one hundred thousand emergency visas to Palestine which the president had suggested. The prime concern was the DPs, but the Committee also worried that British intransigence might impel the Zionists to seek support from the Soviet Union. When an Anglo-American Committee of Inquiry was appointed to study the Palestine question, Proskauer presented the Committee's views on the White Paper of 1939 and on trusteeship in formal testimony. The recommendations of the Committee of Inquiry, hailed by by AJC, included immediate resumption of Jewish immigration to Palestine. England, however, would not yield. Prime Minister Clement Attlee announced in May 1946 that the resolution of Palestine's final status would have to precede any action on immigration. (The British were said to estimate that they would need two American divisions to carry out the recommended admission of one hundred thousand immigrants; and it was rumored that when Secretary Byrnes asked Eisenhower's opinion, the general said the estimate was too low.)

Nevertheless, AJC continued to support the recommendations of the Committee of Inquiry in discussions with American officials and in appeals to the general public. Although it condemned the actions of the Jewish terrorist groups in Palestine, the Committee made it clear in Washington that the delay in implementing the Anglo-American committee's recommendations was largely responsible for the unrest. AJC also called on the American government to support Weizmann's plea that England take the initiative in effecting an understanding between Jews and Arabs in Palestine. Meanwhile, the Allied military command in Germany was ready to transport large numbers of Jews to Palestine, but the possibility of immigration grew dimmer.

In the summer of 1946 a new Anglo-American commission proposed (in the so-called Morrison-Grady Plan) that Palestine be made into a federal state of one Arab, one Jewish, and two British zones, with immigration to remain in British control. The plan was opposed by Arabs, Zionists, and non-Zionists alike. At this point AJC was willing to alter its views for the sake of averting a stalemate. Federalization of Palestine was clearly not trusteeship, but the needs of the DPs came first. Accordingly, the Committee gave serious thought to the Morrison-Grady Plan, suggesting changes in the immigration and land settlement recommendations that might make the plan more workable. An opportunity for action came when Proskauer was called to Washington to see if he could reconcile the views of the first Anglo-American committee and the Morrison-Grady proposals. Although the assignment proved hopeless, Proskauer ultimately played an important role in the negotiations which led to the partition of Palestine in November 1947.

The creation of two separate states, Arab and Jewish, had been broached in 1937. The idea was revived in 1943 and periodically came to the fore, along with other suggested solutions. In 1946, when Britain determined to use the unsatisfactory Morrison-Grady Plan as the basis for conferences with Arabs and Jews on Palestine, the Jewish Agency decided to back partition as a better alternative. Nahum Goldmann, on behalf of the Zionists, called on Proskauer in Washington to seek his support. Earlier, Proskauer had explicitly rejected partition in his appearance before the Committee of Inquiry, but seven months of inaction made him more tractable.

Goldmann presented his case in persuasive fashion: (1) partition represented an obvious sacrifice in terms of land area for a Jewish state and was agreed to only reluctantly by the Jewish Agency; (2) partition offered a way of relieving the situation of the DPs and at the same time satisfying the Arabs; (3) in light of the growing gulf between the Jews of Palestine and the mandatary power, prolonged British rule, even trusteeship, would eventually prove unworkable; (4) separate Jewish and Arab states, side by side, could in time work out regional developments and some form of federal association; (5) a Jewish state would be Jewish only in that Jews would constitute a majority of the population; the rights of all groups would be protected; American Jews would in no way be politically involved; the word *Jewish* would not even be included in the name of the state; (6) a Jewish state would agree to safeguard British military requirements in the area; and (7) the creation of a state would, once and for all, remove Zionism from American domestic politics.

Proskauer told Goldmann that his answer would depend on the attitude of the American government. Secretary of War Robert Patterson gave his personal endorsement to partition. Acting Secretary of State Dean Acheson went even further, informing Proskauer "that partition was the only feasible course" and suggesting that Proskauer, "as the representative of a great Jewish organization which had not committed itself to the ideology of statehood, could render a great service by supporting the partition plan." The strategy now called for pressure on the British from Jews and from the United States government. Vindicated on the importance of non-Zionist leadership, Proskauer remained in

NOT FREE TO DESIST **300**

the United States to help direct the discussions on Palestine, instead of heading the Committee's delegation to the Paris Peace Conference. The man who helped wreck Wertheim's negotiations for unity with the Zionists in 1942 became the Jewish Agency's trusted partner.

An exchange of letters and cables between Proskauer and Goldmann, after the latter left for Europe, revealed the working harmony which the two men had established, as well as Proskauer's personal commitment to the agency plan.

Goldmann to Proskauer (letter, August 11, 1946):

> First I want to thank you again. It was a great thing you have done, not for me nor for yourself, but for the Jewish people. And it has helped me no end.
> On Friday I saw Dean [Acheson] again, who discussed with me their reply to the British. I hope it went as he told me. It is perfect. I also saw the British Ambassador for the second time. He will do his utmost. Everything depends on the British now.

Proskauer to Goldmann (cable): "ADVISE ME WHEN AND IF YOU CARE TO HAVE ME SEEK AUTHORITY TO GIVE FORMAL ENDORSEMENT FOR MY COMMITTEE TO AGENCY PLAN."

Goldmann to Proskauer (cable, August 15, 1946):"HAVE SEEN BEVIN COLONIAL SECRETARY HALL AM HOPEFUL STOP IMPORTANT YOUR COMMITTEE ENDORSES SOONEST YOUR SUPPORT OUR PROGRAM STOP . . . WILL SEE BLAUSTEIN STOP WEIZMAN [*sic*] ASKS ME CONVEY YOU HIS THANKS APPRECIATION YOUR SUPPORT."

Proskauer to Blaustein (letter, August 16, 1946):

> I am unequivocally for any plan which can be sold to the Agency, the Arabs and the British. That is the view of our Government. That is why they are trying to put through this plan. This is no time to split up on ideology. Too many human lives are at stake. . . . I very much hope that you will see eye to eye with me on Palestine. There never was a time when undivided leadership was more vital.

Proskauer kept Goldmann informed of the State Department's advice to employ moderation and counseled the Zionist leader not to issue statements to the press which might evoke controversy. At Goldmann's request, he himself released a message which praised the Jewish Agency and pledged his support. A grateful Goldmann promised to heed Acheson's advice and try to silence the Zionist extremists opposed to partition. He also planned to include AJC should a Jewish delegation be invited to confer with the British. Negotiations proceeded, and, encouraged by the support of some Arab leaders, the Jewish Agency refused to participate in a conference unless partition was on the agenda. Proskauer sharply criticized that decision and spoke more guardedly about partition at a meeting of the executive committee on September 15. At the moment, he explained, partition offered the quickest way to save hundreds of thousands of lives; but he did not want the Committee to endorse that proposal yet. Furthermore, the Committee had to insist on freedom of action if it was invited to the conference. If no invitation was forthcoming or no solution was reached, the Committee would consider the problem anew.

A major factor in Proskauer's hedging, no doubt, was the awareness that his colleagues would receive the idea of partition less enthusiastically than he had. Jacob Blaustein and the others in Paris had discussed the scheme at length with Goldmann, Chaim Weizmann, and David Ben-Gurion, but Blaustein refused to join in Proskauer's initial endorsement until the Committee acted formally. He cabled from Paris that a Committee statement should make clear that the organization was not a "a tail to the Zionist kite." The consensus of the executive committee, too, favored greater caution. In the discussion at the executive board meeting, several members questioned the wisdom of accepting an invitation from the Jewish Agency and reiterated their antipathy to Jewish nationalism or a Jewish state. The majority, however, finally agreed, though reluctantly, to Proskauer's moderate stand. Without mentioning partition, they resolved to attend the conference but to retain full freedom of action to achieve "the maximum Jewish immigration into Palestine at the earliest possible moment." Proskauer privately interpreted his authority more broadly: "If we come, Goldmann must understand we would act initially in spirit of my statement of August 20th, but if the Agency plan fails we are not committed to partition and are free to urge what we think best as the situation develops."

The anticipated conference with the British did not materialize, but developments in August did have lasting results. The American Jewish Committee continued to plan its strategy in cooperation with the Zionist-controlled Jewish Agency, with an eye to partition as a possible solution. "I have no 'position' on Palestine in the sense of a fixed ideological plan," Proskauer wrote to Bartley Crum, one of President Truman's appointees to the Anglo-American Committee of Inquiry. "The one great overwhelming objective is to get immediate and substantial immigration into Palestine and within limits, of course, I don't care very much how I get it."

On Thanksgiving Day, Proskauer met with the British Foreign Secretary Ernest Bevin. In frank but friendly terms, he criticized the White Paper of 1939 and Britain's inhumane policy of interning illegal immigrants on Cyprus.* He also informed the secretary that a solution like the Jewish Agency's partition plan, while not ideal, seemed the most practical course. In December an AJC subcommittee on Palestine studied the alternatives and resolved that trusteeship, federalization, and partition afforded the only viable solutions to the problem. However, at its annual meeting in January, the Committee backed none of the three plans, and again called on Britain to fulfill her obligations regarding immigration and land settlement, and on the United States to cooperate in the attainment of those goals. Condemning Jew-

---

*After the war thousands of Jewish DPs attempted to enter Palestine without official British authorization. The number apprehended and placed in detention camps on Cyprus reached well over thirty thousand by the time the mandate expired.

ish terrorism in Palestine, the resolution also asked that a way be found to bring all groups concerned to the negotiating table.

Throughout these discussions a small but important group within the Committee remained firmly convinced that a settlement had to be grounded in a substantive peace between the Arabs and the Jews in Palestine. Some backed projects of economic or political union, as formulated in Dr. Judah Magnes's plan for a binational state. Believing that partition could not be a permanent solution, since it would inevitably promote irredentism on both sides, this group hoped to effect a reconciliation within the existing boundaries of one Palestine. But as long as their program did not point the way to a speedy and satisfactory solution to the immigration problem, it could not muster the support of the majority.

Against the background of DPs in Europe awaiting resettlement and growing turmoil in Palestine, negotiations with the British broke down. At one point the Jewish Agency proposed that if Britain would permit one hundred thousand immigrants to enter Palestine over a period of two years, the agency would withdraw its demand for the immediate creation of a Jewish state. This move was applauded by the Committee, but it did not sway the British, who, blaming the United States and American Jews for wrecking chances for a compromise settlement, tossed the matter into the hands of the United Nations early in 1947.

AJC requested permission to testify before the UN Special Committee on Palestine (UNSCOP), and adopted a resolution declaring that if the UN contemplated no final settlement on statehood, then Britain should be urged to execute faithfully her obligations under the mandate, by the immediate admission of one hundred thousand Jews to Palestine. It was resolved

A. That any Mandate the UN may continue or trusteeship it may establish adopt as valid and as of continuing effect the principles of the Balfour Declaration and of the League of

Nations Mandate, particularly with reference to the facilitation of immigration of Jews into Palestine and also the close settlement of Jews upon and the unrestricted right of Jews to purchase land;

B. That a UN Trusteeship be created or, in the alternative, as the officers may determine, that the present Mandate be continued under conditions that will effectuate the provisions of [the above] paragraph A;

C. That there should be immediate and general placement of Jews and Arabs in positions of political and economic responsibility to the end that subject always to the fulfillment of the purpose of the Balfour Declaration and the League of Nations Mandate complete self-government with full equality for all citizens will ultimately eventuate;

D. That the General Assembly of the UN pending full consideration of the report of its Committee of Inquiry should urgently recommend to the Mandatory Government the immediate admission of one hundred thousand Jews to Palestine.

However, if the UN decided that a permanent political status for Palestine ought to be created, the Committee maintained, then "there should be partition of the country in a manner which would give scope for further adequate Jewish immigration and would provide equality to all its citizens in any of the divisions that may be created."

The American Jewish Committee thus officially endorsed partition, not as an ideal course but as one which promised amelioration for homeless European Jews and also had the backing of the United States government. Proskauer's influence undoubtedly was a major factor in the passage of the resolution, for he warned that without such authority, he would dissociate himself from the issue. The Committee's statement, as it was presented to UNSCOP, added a further comment on the validity of partition: "If the final political constitution of Palestine must be immediately determined, partition along the lines urged last summer by members of the Jewish Agency is the only solution, because it is the only one that does not turn over Palestine completely to undeserved Arab domination."

Events moved rapidly in the fall of 1947. UNSCOP reported in favor of partition, and the United Nations General Assembly upheld the UNSCOP recommendations. Britain scheduled the termination of the mandate for May 1948. That decision evoked mixed feelings on the part of Jews and hostility among the Arabs, and the British were bitter over the turn of events—all of which led President Truman to comment: "I surely wish God Almighty would give the Children of Israel an Isaiah, the Christians a St. Paul, and the Sons of Ishmael a peep at the Golden Rule."

The American Jewish Committee now turned to the problems which would inevitably arise from the creation of a Jewish state. Aided by reports from its chapters and by polls and opinion surveys, the professional staff pondered such issues as the structure and orientation of the state-to-be, its relationship to the East-West struggle, the impact of a Jewish state on non-Jews, the extent of American-Jewish involvement in the state, and the new state's effect on the Committee's program. While some of these issues were of long-range concern, others called for an immediate response. For example, rumors were circulating that American soldiers would have to die in the attempt to enforce partition. It was also suggested that the existence of a Jewish state open to refugees would turn public sentiment in America against the admission of DPs to the United States. Thus even before Israel was officially in existence, the Committee set about organizing an educational campaign to gain public sympathy for the new state.

The most immediate problem involved that perennial bogey, the charge of dual loyalties. A letter by Proskauer to the *Herald-Tribune*, January 1948, sought to set the record straight:

> We are told by the anti-Semite, through malice, and by some small sections of American Jewry, through confusion, that this partition has created a problem of possible inconsistency between our obligations as Americans and as Jews.

There is no such problem. Five years ago our committee stated: "There can be no political identification of Jews outside of Palestine with whatever government may there be instituted." These words state an axiom and remain true today. The Jews of America suffer from no political schizophrenia. Politically we are not split personalities, and in faith and in conduct we shall continue to demonstrate what the death rolls of our army on many a battlefield have attested: that we are bone of the bone and flesh of the flesh of America.

At the same time, the Committee discussed the political aspects of partition with Jewish Agency representatives, as well as with the Truman administration. Committee spokesmen pointed out that it was not enough for the United States to vote to adopt the UNSCOP report when the matter came before the UN General Assembly. The General Assembly's action would leave implementation of partition to the Security Council, and, as Proskauer and Blaustein noted, such implementation could not be accomplished without the use of force. AJC therefore called on the United States also to plan for appropriate UN action to make the partition decision stick.

After the General Assembly vote for partition on November 29, 1947, the situation grew more tense. The Arabs vowed to resist forcibly, and violence broke out in Palestine. The British refused to admit the UN into the country before they evacuated their military; nor would they permit a Jewish militia to repel Arab attacks. The Jewish Agency, echoing Proskauer's view, called for a UN police force. American Jews appealed to the State Department to lift the arms embargo against Palestine. The appeals went unheeded.

State and War Department officials who had opposed a Jewish state were only hardened in their attitudes by the developments that followed the partition vote. They argued that partition could not be achieved without force and that the use of force against the Arabs would imperil American security. The United

States, they contended, needed Middle East oil and could not afford to antagonize the Arabs. Furthermore, to fill the power vacuum occasioned by the British withdrawal, the United States had to predicate its Middle East policy on friendly relations with the Arabs, or the area would be lost to the Soviet Union. An international police force in Palestine which included Russian troops would give the Soviet Union a toehold and dislodgment would be difficult. And finally, the critics argued, from the point of view of domestic politics it would be folly to send American troops to fight in the Middle East.

Proskauer, who was in almost daily contact with the State Department, tried to rebut these arguments. He insisted that the General Assembly resolution could not be flouted, that the Security Council was empowered by the UN Charter to take measures against threats to world peace, and that any attempt to prevent implementation of partition in Palestine clearly constituted such a threat. He, too, called for lifting the arms embargo against Palestine and for the United States to indicate its readiness to participate directly in UN action to repel Arab force. "The hesitancy to use American troops is understandable," he declared, "but that eventuality was considered before the Assembly vote was taken. It was clearly envisaged as a possible consequence of the American position. We are aiding, by military assistance, Greece and other countries. Why not Palestine to maintain consistency in our position and to save the United Nations from destruction?"

President Truman, however, would not consider the use of force. He insisted later that he never shared the views of the pro-Arabs officials and that his overriding concern was to avert warfare. On March 19, 1948, the American delegate to the UN, Warren Austin, recommended to the Security Council that partition be suspended and that the UN set up a trusteeship for Palestine. Truman's statement, a few days later, that the United States still backed partition but was abandoning the plan temporarily until peace was achieved, did little to still the many protests which greeted Austin's announcement. As the *New York Times* observed, the need for force was obvious when the United States originally backed partition. Moreover, how could the government promise to use force to back trusteeship if it would not use force for partition?

America's about-face put the American Jewish Committee in a difficult position. Although some had suggested even before Austin's speech that partition might have to be jettisoned, the new American policy came as a shock. Indeed, the fact that the State Department did not notify Proskauer of its plans, though he was in constant touch with Washington, was regarded as a personal affront. Given the aroused temper of the Jewish community, acquiescence by the Committee in the new policy would be seen as appeasement. Moreover, AJC was aware that, upon the advice of the military, Truman had excised all references to immigration in his trusteeship proposal. On the other hand, it seemed foolhardy to condemn the administration's action—especially if it was dictated by national security—and thereby sever contact with the State Department.

The official switch increased the clamor of both the antinationalists and the binationalists in the Committee who hoped to push it into repudiating its stand on partition. On the other side, the faction supporting statehood was ably represented by Governor Lehman, who vehemently expressed his impatience with "any course of action based on timidity rather than on the moral principles of our faith." Declared Lehman:

> With immigration to Palestine apparently the only hope for solving the problem of Jewish DPs, our moral obligation to them must transcend our fears for ourselves. Moreover . . . we must not forget that the Jews are fighting to implement the decision of the United Nations, whereas the Arabs are fighting to flout it. For the American Jewish Committee to take any action which would disassociate it both from the efforts of Palestinian Jewry and from the decision of the United Nations, would be . . . inconceivable.

The Committee stood by its position favoring partition and, under Proskauer's leadership, cooperated in Security Council efforts to establish a truce in Palestine and work out details for the internationalization of Jerusalem. On May 14, 1948, however, Palestine Jews took matters into their own hands and proclaimed the independent State of Israel. Within minutes the United States extended de facto recognition to the new nation. This did not prevent the bloodshed, nor did it solve the many political problems; nevertheless, it was possible for Jacob Blaustein to declare with assurance, six months later: "The State of Israel is solidly established and is here to stay."

The Committee's activities leading up to the establishment of the State of Israel set a pattern for future AJC policy. From 1948 to the present day, the organization has responded quickly and constructively to the recurrent crises that have beset Israel. At the same time, it has striven to demonstrate the compatibility of support for Israel with a concern for American affairs. The consummation of the Zionist dream did not immediately obliterate the differences between Zionists and non-Zionists in AJC. The Committee, to be sure, recognized the positive impact of a Jewish state on Diaspora Jewry, and over the course of the years it has made many important contributions to Israel's welfare. Still, AJC has held firmly to its belief in the viability of a Jewish community outside a Jewish state.

II

In the postwar years the American Jewish Committee's international responsibilities, like those of the United States itself, multiplied. The Committee was particularly concerned with Israel—apart from any emotional ties—because it had played an important midwife role in the nation's birth. The Committee was eager to encourage Israel's development along Western democratic lines, and took upon itself the task of interpreting Israel's needs and rights to the American government and the American people. In return for a steady stream of aid and counsel, the Committee wanted from Israel only purposeful noninterference in American Jewish affairs.

When the executive committee met for the first time after the State of Israel had come into being, it deliberated at great length on the need to keep clear the political boundaries between Israel and Diaspora Jewry. Three months later the Committee revised its 1943 Statement of Views accordingly:

> We hold the establishment of the State of Israel to be an event of historic significance. We applaud its recognition by our own and other governments. We look forward to Israel's assumption of its full place among the family of nations as a government guaranteeing complete equality to all its inhabitants, without regard to race, creed or national origin, and as an advocate of liberty and peace in the Near East and throughout the world. Citizens of the United States are Americans and citizens of Israel are Israelis; this we affirm with all its implications; and just as our own government speaks for its citizens, so Israel speaks only for its citizens. Within the framework of American interests, we shall aid in the upbuilding of Israel as a vital spiritual and cultural center and in the development of its capacity to provide a free and dignified life for those who desire to make it their home.

Even before Israel was established, the Committee had sought and received assurance from the Jewish Agency that the Jewish state would refrain from interfering in American Jewish internal affairs. Israeli officials repeated those promises after May 1948. The Committee, however, continued to weigh all Israeli statements which might be construed as negating the possibility of a full Jewish life in the Diaspora. When an AJC delegation visited Israel in the spring of 1949 at Premier Ben-Gurion's invitation, they received further assurances that the Israeli government would confine its activities to its own Jews.

The officers of AJC were severely jolted a few months later by reports that Ben-Gurion had called for large-scale immigration to Israel by American Jewish youth. The Committee protested at once to Israel's ambassador to Washington, Eliahu Elath, and to Abba Eban, head of Israel's delegation to the UN. Jacob Blaustein wrote directly to Ben-Gurion, but disagreed with Judge Proskauer, who urged a clear-cut ultimatum threatening dissociation from the state. No doubt Elath and Eban forcefully conveyed the earnestness of the Committee's mood, for shortly thereafter conciliatory cables arrived from Ben-Gurion, asserting that he had been "misquoted." The American Zionists, too, were sufficiently impressed after a closed meeting with Committee representatives to adopt Ben-Gurion's explanation for themselves: they said they were not seeking to stimulate mass Jewish immigration from the United States but only to encourage those with technological skills to go there. The Zionists clearly were afraid of losing the Committee to the American Council for Judaism, which viewed any friendly gesture toward Israel by an American Jew as evidence of divided political loyalties. The Committee, on its part, strongly objected to the council's anti-Israel propaganda, which was put to good use by anti-Semites in the United States. Despite a strong defense of the council by AJC executive committee member Lessing Rosenwald (who was also a moving force in the council), the Committee formally voiced its disapproval of council methods in October 1949.

Concerned for its own principles and apprehensive about the council's activities, AJC sought to work out with Israeli representatives a more forceful expression of "noninterference" and a clarification of policy on immigration. The occasion arose in the summer of 1950 when Jacob Blaustein was again the guest of the Israeli government. After many hours of negotiating with top officials, alternately cajoling and threatening, he secured his basic objectives. The actual "entente" was in the form of a statement read at a luncheon by Prime Minister Ben-Gurion and a response by Blaustein. Ben-Gurion admitted, though in veiled language, that American Jews were not in exile (thereby implying that the ingathering of exiles did not apply to them) and that their internal affairs were not of concern to the State of Israel. Ben-Gurion continued:

> The Jews of the United States, as a community and as individuals, have only one political attachment and that is to the United States of America. They owe no political allegiance to Israel. In the first statement which the representative of Israel made before the United Nations after her admission to that international organization, he clearly stated, without any reservation, that the State of Israel represents and speaks only on behalf of its own citizens and in no way presumes to represent or speak in the name of the Jews who are citizens of any other country. We, the people of Israel, have no desire and no intention to interfere in any way with the internal affairs of Jewish communities abroad. The Government and the people of Israel fully respect the right and integrity of the Jewish communities in other countries to develop their own mode of life and their indigenous social, economic and cultural institutions in accordance with their own needs and aspirations. Any weakening of American Jewry, any disruption of its communal life, any lowering of its sense of security, any diminution of its status, is a definite loss to Jews everywhere and to Israel in particular.

Admitting that Israel's success depended in large measure on a strong Jewish community in the United States, Ben-Gurion continued:

> We, therefore, are anxious that nothing should be said or done which could in the slightest degree undermine the sense of security and stability of American Jewry.
> In this connection let me say a word about immigration.

We should like to see American Jews come and take part in our effort. We need their technical knowledge, their un-rivalled experience, their spirit of enterprise, their bold vi-sion, their "know-how." We need engineers, chemists, builders, work managers and technicians. The tasks which face us in this country are eminently such as would appeal to the American genius for technical development and social progress. But the decision as to whether they wish to come —permanently or temporarily—rests with the free discretion of each American Jew himself.

Blaustein, in his response, underscored the point on exile:

To American Jews, America is home. There, exist their thriving roots; there, is the country which they have helped to build; and there, they share its fruits and its destiny. They believe in the future of a democratic society in the United States under which all citizens, irrespective of creed and race, can live on terms of equality. They further believe that, if democracy should fail in America, there would be no fu-ture for democracy anywhere in the world, and that the very existence of an independent State of Israel would be prob-lematic. Further, they feel that a world in which it would be possible for Jews to be driven by persecution from America would not be a world safe for Israel either; indeed it is hard to conceive how it would be a world safe for any human being.

For the next ten years, whenever Israelis appealed to Dias-pora nationalism or implied that non-Israeli Jews had dual loyal-ties, the Committee could justify its protest with reference to the Blaustein–Ben-Gurion agreement. Prime Minister Ben-Gurion himself reaffirmed that agreement on several occasions. Blau-stein, who built up a cordial personal relationship with Ben-Gurion, in all candor told the prime minister in 1960:

Your August 1950 Statement did more than anything else to win the good-will of American Jews toward Israel, to free them in the minds of other Americans from the serious charge of dual-nationality, to thwart what otherwise would have been a far more effective thrust against your country by the Council for Judaism and like-minded people, and to make possible the climate for the successful UJA campaigns in this country and the sale of Israel bonds.

But, Blaustein continued, violations of that statement in recent months made necessary a reaffirmation of the "entente." He pointed to Israel's notes to the United States, England, and other countries, protesting the epidemic of swastika-daubings then plaguing Europe and America. This kind of diplomatic action, Blaustein insisted, infringed on the autonomy of the Jewish communities concerned. He also charged General Moshe Dayan and then Foreign Minister Golda Meir with making loose statements on the right of Israel to speak for non-Israeli Jews. These incidents, Blaustein declared, helped reactivate the American Council for Judaism and other enemies of Israel, alarmed various governments, and would adversely affect public fund raising and private investment in Israel.

In the Committee's view Ben-Gurion added a crowning insult to those violations when he announced, in an address before the twenty-fifth Zionist Congress in December 1960, that Jews living outside Israel were violating the precepts of Judaism and that in the free and prosperous lands Judaism "faces the kiss of death, a slow and imperceptible decline into the abyss of assimilation." Like other American Jewish organizations, the Committee expressed shock at these pronouncements. Herbert Ehrmann, the new Committee president, apprised Ben-Gurion of AJC's grave concern. He used the occasion to complain about Israel's nationality law, automatically granting citizenship to all Jews who came with immigrant visas. (The procedure led the State Department to issue a distinct warning to American Jews applying for visas.)

Ben-Gurion explained Israel's views to Ehrmann and, in private, to Blaustein. Though on some points Ben-Gurion considered the Americans' annoyance unjustified, he promised to respect their sensibilities. There was no doubt, he told Ehrmann, that Jewish survival depended on positive and friendly relations between Israel and American Jewry.

In April 1961 a joint statement by Blaustein and Ben-Gurion reaffirmed the "entente" of 1950, stipulating that Israel would in no way interfere in the internal affairs of American Jews, and defining immigration to Israel as a voluntary act based on individual choice. This statement went further than the original agreement: Ben-Gurion promised to see that it was respected by members of his government.

Ben-Gurion's 1950 action was privately criticized in certain Israeli quarters; his 1961 statement gave rise to numerous attacks. He was reprimanded for not leaving such negotiations to the World Zionist Organization and for joining with an individual from an "isolationist group" not representative of the American Jewish community. Despite a cabinet motion to censure him, Ben-Gurion stood his ground. It made no difference that Blaustein was not a Zionist, Ben-Gurion declared; American Zionists were not true Zionists (i.e., those who study Hebrew and settle in Israel) either.

Jacob Blaustein wrote a final footnote to his agreement with Ben-Gurion after the latter's retirement. In 1963 Blaustein reminded Ben-Gurion and his successor, Levi Eshkol, of the importance of continuing to abide by the agreement. He received assurances that the change in administration would in no way weaken the earlier pledges. Ben-Gurion added a warm and friendly plea to his personal friend: "Dear Yaacov—don't be afraid of dual loyalty. Every human being must have many loyalties."

NOT FREE TO DESIST **316**

III

While the Committee held well-defined views on the limits to Israeli interference in Diaspora affairs, the obverse posed knottier problems. True, in 1950 Blaustein had pledged: "Jewish communities, particularly American Jewry . . . , can offer advice, cooperation and help, but should not attempt to speak in the name of other communities, or in any way interfere in their internal affairs." But it wasn't so simple. Israel's growth, its very existence, depended in large measure on the support and influence of American Jewry; and Israel's behavior reflected on American Jewry.

It was clear that fellow Americans respected American Jews more because of Israel's military successes and its fortitude. How far could American Jews pressure Israel to insure the continuance of that favorable image? Was it legitimate for an American Jewish organization whose members made significant contributions to Israel to insist that Israel follow particular policies on such questions as communism or religious Orthodoxy, in order not to jeopardize the Jewish position in the United States? And since the Committee's support of Israel was marked out according to American national interests, was it within the Committee's province to press Israel to hold to a pro-American foreign policy? Finally, there was the question of American Jewish emotional identification with Israel. Should the Committee encourage cultural ties and interchange between the two communities and help build bridges between them? Bridges are two-way affairs which inevitably lead to increased involvement.

Communism was never a real threat in Israel. Irving M. Engel, then chairman of the executive committee, maintained in 1949 that two conditions in that country—a strong framework of civil liberties and an absence of extreme wealth or poverty—were sure guarantees against communism. Later, when the Soviet Union aided in the military buildup of Israel's enemies, distaste for communism became even more pronounced. On that issue, therefore, the Committee had no need to pressure Israel. AJC did arrange for publication in Israel of *The Jews in the Soviet Union,* a documented exposé of Russian anti-Semitism, but that could scarcely be construed as active interference in the country's internal policies.

The control of religious affairs by the Orthodox, particularly since they were a minority, irritated AJC more consistently than anything else in Israel. The absence of separation of church and state offended AJC's American sensibilities and tarnished Israel's image as a Western democracy, which it strove to maintain. In addition, it endangered the position of Jews elsewhere; for example, if the Committee pleaded for free exercise of religion for Soviet Jewry, the answer might be that not even the government of Israel abided by that principle. Not until 1964, however, did the Committee openly challenge Israel's religious pattern. Even then its "meddling" was indirect, since it was responding to a move by American Orthodox Jews. The latter, alarmed by Christian missionary work among new immigrants to Israel, appealed to Prime Minister Eshkol for legislation banning this activity. In a move to offset the impression in America and Israel that an overwhelming majority of American Jews supported that appeal, the Committee joined with six other organizations to condemn any encroachment on the civil liberties of Jews or non-Jews. Stating that their reluctance to interfere was overshadowed by the "threat of coercion," they asked Eshkol to resist the religious extremists:

> Out of their deep commitment to the principle of freedom of religion for all, Jewish organizations have played an active and significant role in the national and international promotion of human rights. As recently as January 28th the UN Sub-Commission on the Prevention of Discrimination and Protection of Minorities adopted a Draft Declaration on

the Elimination of All Forms of Religious Intolerance with the vigorous support of all American Jewish organizations.

We cannot allow the actions of one segment of American Jewry to convey the impression that the Jewish community is prepared to endorse positions directly contrary to the spirit of that declaration.

We reject the attempt of the extremist religious elements to polarize the American Jewish community into two opposing groups, religious and secularist, and their claim that they and they alone represent the Jewish religious community. The truth is that in the American Jewish community there are several recognized and acknowledged Jewish religious constituencies. The overwhelming majority of Jews, whatever their religious commitment, support the basic Jewish position of separation of Church and State and freedom of religious belief, practice and instruction for all. We abhor any attempt by governmental authority, in the United States, in Israel, in the Soviet Union, or anywhere else in the world, to interfere with the expression of religion in any of its aspects.

The statement again raised the question of interference in Israel's affairs—the appeal by the American Orthodox community to the Israeli prime minister was certainly an example of this—but for the most part the Israelis welcomed the message much more than they deplored the meddling.

IV

An organization dedicated to the protection of the security of Jews throughout the world could not ignore the problems Israelis had to contend with, even if they had their own government to look after their interests. The Committee's case rested on American self-interest and the realities of power politics, as well as on Jewish sentiment and moral principles. With the decline in British influence, only the United States was in a position to resist possible Soviet penetration into the Middle East if unrest continued there. Since Israel openly aligned itself with the West—a fact setting Israel still further apart from those Arab elements which equated the West with colonialism—the Jewish state was America's most reliable ally in the area. Thus, the Committee argued, American concern with maintaining the peace dovetailed with Israel's security needs. And when, for example, American oil interests dictated a pro-Arab policy for what were called reasons of national security, the Committee could legitimately counter this position, with the backing of the national press and labor groups.

The pro-Israel Truman administration regarded the AJC leaders as "honest brokers" in American-Israel negotiations. During the Arab-Israeli war that followed Israel's declaration of independence, they worked for a general truce with both American and Israeli representatives. Sometimes alone, sometimes with Israeli and American authorities, AJC studied solutions to the problems of Israel's military security, the Arab refugees, the Christian holy places, and the regional development of natural resources. On countless occasions Jacob Blaustein went to Washington to urge de jure recognition of Israel and her admittance into the United Nations, as well as financial assistance to the new state. His successes convinced Israeli officials of the benefits of maintaining strong contacts with the Committee.

Middle East tensions did not abate after 1948. Arab intransigence over the recognition of Israel barred an effective peace settlement, and the new state was harassed by an Arab boycott, a shipping blockade, and frequent commando raids prompting Israeli reprisals. In 1950 a Tripartite Declaration by England, France, and the United States pledged to guarantee Israel's boundaries and to maintain a balance of armaments between Israel and the Arabs, but there were few concrete suggestions for reducing friction. With the ascendancy of Gamal Abdel Nasser in Egypt came new crises: insistence that Britain evacute the Suez,

Egypt's refusal to join the Baghdad Pact, an Egyptian arms pact with Communist Czechoslovakia, and the presence of former Nazi scientists and military experts in Egypt. Soon the Arab-Israeli deadlock was magnified into an impasse between East and West.

John Foster Dulles, secretary of state in the Eisenhower administration, whose studied impartiality toward the contending parties in the Middle East contrasted sharply with the Truman administrations's friendliness toward Israel, was far more tolerant of Arab moves than were America's Western allies. (France, especially, resented Nasser's encouragement of Arab nationalism in the French possessions in North Africa.) Nor would Dulles admit that Nasser's deals for Communist arms, which upset the 1950 balance, dictated the need to supply Israel with additional weapons.

AJC, convinced that the Communist arms deals made for the concurrence of American and Israeli political objectives, approached Dulles directly in December 1955. The Committee had publicly endorsed his August 1954 statement outlining steps for achieving peace in the Middle East, among them the resettlement of refugees, security guarantees to eliminate "the pall of fear that hangs over the Arab and Israel people alike," and agreements on boundaries. Now, however, Irving M. Engel privately explained to Dulles that the arms issue required a different approach. Israel should be permitted to purchase defensive weapons from the United States, Engel insisted, and even more important, the United States should offer unconditional security pacts to both sides before tackling the problems of refugees or boundaries. Rejection of such a pact by either side would reveal its aggressive purposes. If both sides accepted, they could not refuse to negotiate the divisive issues, and those negotiations could be pressed without fear of aggression. Israel drew scant comfort, Engel pointed out, from the knowledge that the Western powers would consider what to do only after Israel was attacked. Appealing to Dulles's strong religious principles, Engel urged the security pacts as the first step toward realizing the dream of the brother-hood of man.

Engel's brief for security pacts was in line with established American postwar policy. By regional agreements such as NATO and SEATO, as well as by treaties with individual countries, the United States was committed in varying degrees to the security of more than forty nations. And throughout the world America had supplemented such alliances with military aid for self-defense. Dulles admitted that the argument was cogent and that Israel could not in fact continue to exist as a viable state in a condition of constant preparedness for war. But he insisted that the time was not ripe for security pacts. Unless the other issues were resolved, he declared, Egypt might acquire a substantial quantity of arms and become "unreasonable and unmanage-able." Dulles also was seriously weighing Egypt's demand for a portion of the Negev, which would give her land contact with Jordan; but when Engel objected, he agreed that perhaps transit rights would suffice.

Although Dulles was less than encouraging, the Committee cautioned Israel to avoid precipitate action—such as raids into Syrian territory—which, despite justifiable provocation, might alienate the State Department and the American public. Still hoping for American military aid, Israel demonstrated her good intentions by submitting to the State Department a program for a peaceful settlement that made various concessions to the Arab states: to Jordan, free access to the port of Haifa; to Egypt and Jordan, transit rights through the Negev; compensation to the Arab refugees; compliance with the Johnston regional plan on the use of the Jordan River. However, Israel adamantly refused to yield Negev land to link Egypt with Jordan, which, in Ambassa-dor Eban's words, would mean a corridor connecting one desert with a second desert by a road through a third desert.

AJC's hope for forceful leadership by the State Department did not materialize. American policy in the early months of 1956 was unclear and indecisive. Dulles urged Israel to put her faith in the 1950 Tripartite Declaration and the United Nations rather than in arms; on the other hand, the United States announced that it had no objections to British or French arms shipments to Israel. America's about-face refusal of financial help to Nasser for the Aswan Dam resulted in Egypt's nationalization of the Suez Canal Company, a serious blow to America's allies. But even when Nasser pressed for the organization of an Arab union which would have as one of its goals the elimination of Israel, Dulles was not moved by Jewish fears.

Engel met with the secretary of state again a few days after Nasser's seizure of the Suez Canal and reminded him of history's lesson:

> In the course of the past twenty-five years, the democratic countries should have learned that threats of this kind by a dictator are not empty gestures. It is indicative of the contempt they have for the democracies that they do not hesitate to "call their shots," having confidence that the democracies, through fear or divided counsel will do nothing to stop them.

Engel submitted a list of recommendations, of which the most important were (1) an assurance to Israel that her existence as a state was part of American policy; (2) settlement of the canal issue, guaranteeing freedom of navigation to all ships; and (3) defensive arms to Israel. Dulles, however, believed that Nasser's latest moves reduced the danger to Israel, because Egypt could not risk giving England and France a pretext to intervene in the region. Besides, he argued, if Nasser did bomb Israel, the defensive weapons Engel requested would be useless. Nor did Dulles agree to remedial action on two specifically American issues long of concern to AJC, which Engel raised: Arab discrimination against American Jews in civilian and military employ in Arab countries (in direct violation of treaties between those nations and the United States) and anti-Jewish propaganda by

Arab diplomats accredited to the United States.

Although the propriety of the Committee's pro-Israel positions—taken within the broader context of American self-interest—was above reproach, Israel's invasion of the Sinai Peninsula posed a serious question for American Jews. Israel's action was particularly embarrassing because it came a day after Israel's Ambassador Eban had personally assured Dulles that his government planned no such move. AJC leaders immediately impressed on Eban the grave public relations issue facing American Jews and urged Israel to mend quickly the rift with the United States. Eban, who insisted he had not been informed about the surprise attack initiated by Israeli military intelligence, hoped that American pique would subside when the United States considered the matter more carefully. He was certain that the United States, uncomfortably allied with Russia against France and England as well as against Israel, was becoming increasingly suspicious of Nasser's objectives.

The Committee decided that its position in the community and its obligations to its chapters required a statement. Public opinion generally condemned Israel for the military action, supported the American response in the UN, and wanted no involvement in the Middle East. After the UN General Assembly called for a cease-fire, the Committee sent an open letter to Dulles. Explaining Israel's aggression as the result of incessant Arab provocation, the letter aimed for more than an exoneration of the Jewish state. It emphasized the constructive possibilities inherent in the United Nation's resolution, which expressed a hope for a permanent peace. A cease-fire was not enough, the Committee maintained, for restoring the status quo would only lead to further outbreaks. It called on the United States to propose, through the United Nations, that the Arab states and Israel be required to enter negotiations for a durable peace, with the resultant treaties guaranteed by the United States and other world powers. Refusal to negotiate, the Committee suggested, should be adjudged incompatible with the UN Charter and punishable by sanctions.

The AJC letter was well received by the public, and newspapers throughout the country editorialized against a return to the status quo ante. When the fighting stopped, the Committee worked to convince Israel to renounce any expansionist aims and, at the same time, to prevent the United Nations, prompted by American initiative, from imposing sanctions upon Israel. The hope for a lasting peace, however, failed. American prestige rose in the Arab world, but the United States did not lend its influence to a constructive settlement. The Eisenhower Doctrine, enunciated in January 1957, only promised American protection against Communist aggression in the Middle East and could, in fact, serve to strengthen the Arab states vis-à-vis Israel. American relations with England and France cooled; Nasser's position remained firm despite his military defeats; the overwhelming victory of the Republicans in the November election weakened American Jewish influence with regard to the situation in Israel.

The Sinai episode revealed a new maturity in AJC's public stance. Reflecting the pluralism of mid-century American society, as well as the confidence of American Jewry, the Committee had gained enormously in self-assurance. Arguing from the vantage point of *American* interests, it did not hesitate to make clear its support of Israel. A subtle realization permeated Committee thinking on the legitimacy of contesting government policy—the realization that what was enunciated as "the national interest" was hammered out by contending forces, none necessarily any more infallible than the Committee itself. AJC no longer viewed minority groups as outside this decision-making process. Nor did it any longer feel that minority groups were limited in their support of specific causes—such as the removal of immigration restrictions and the efforts to prevent the rise of Hitler—to appeals to humanitarianism, requests for favors, or threats of a bloc vote. The Committee was now convinced that a minority could believe, and seek to convince the general public, that its goals were in fact more advantageous to the country than other alternatives.

A concrete opportunity to defend the basic tenets of pluralism came in 1960, when Congress was considering the Mutual Security Act. Senators Paul Douglas, Kenneth Keating, and twenty-eight others sponsored an amendment which would give the president the authority to withhold aid from nations obstructing free navigation of international waterways. Nasser's ban against Israel's use of the Suez Canal was the obvious target. Senator J. William Fulbright, chairman of the Foreign Relations Committee, opposed the amendment, charging that its sponsors were acting on behalf of "a pressure group in the United States which seeks to inject the Arab-Israeli dispute into domestic politics." "In recent years," he said, "we have seen the rise of organizations dedicated apparently not to America, but to foreign states and groups. The conduct of a foreign policy for America has been seriously compromised by this development."

More upset by the way Fulbright attacked the amendment than by his pro-Arab sympathies, the Committee felt impelled to uphold the right of voluntary organizations to express themselves on foreign policy. All sorts of groups, AJC pointed out, fulfilled the obligation of American citizenship by appraising current issues from the standpoint of what they considered the country's best interests and expressed their approval or opposition. For a senator to challenge the propriety of such behavior was really to challenge the very essence of the American political process.

When Irving M. Engel saw Fulbright a few months later, he aired AJC's concerns about the senator's views. The senator's remarks, Engel explained, implied that all the pro-Israel positions enunciated at various times by Congress, the major political parties, and Presidents Truman and Eisenhower were not based on principle or the desire to advance the national interest, but resulted solely from political pressure. Engel reminded Fulbright that many Americans who supported Israel were beyond the reach of such pressures. In any case, he pointed out, pressure groups influencing foreign and domestic issues had existed throughout America's history, and they had been acknowledged as a legitimate aspect of the democratic process even when James Madison discussed the role of factions in *The Federalist.*

Fulbright may not have been convinced. The Committee, however, finally articulated the position that had governed its Israel stand since 1948: organizing American support for Israel was eminently compatible with loyalty to America.

V

The establishment of Israel, while solving the problem of Jewish resettlement in the immediate postwar years, created new problems. In retaliation for Israel's victory in the 1948 fighting, several Arab states victimized the Jews living within their borders. Iraq passed a law equating Zionism with treason; Syria arrested six hundred Jews and even seized some Jewish residents of neighboring Lebanon; Egypt arrested several hundred Jews and sequestered Jewish property.

To meet the needs of the Jews under Arab rule, "the forgotten million," the American Jewish Committee broadened its foreign affairs program in 1949. When the shah of Iran came to New York at the end of 1949, Jacob Blaustein interceded with him for postponement of an order directing the expulsion of Iraqi Jews from Iran. In 1951, at the request of the Committee, the State Department secured modification of an Iraqi law cutting off emigration to Israel. In line with its policy of quiet cooperation with non-Jewish groups and individuals to establish favorable ties abroad, in 1957 AJC sent Socialist leader Norman Thomas on a trip to the Middle East, where he succeeded in opening up contacts on the highest government levels. However, the Committee's goal of full rights and security for Jews in Arab lands, including the right to emigrate freely, was never realized.

The major stumbling block was American reluctance to put pressure on the Arab governments. Officially committed to the existence of the State of Israel, the United States, particularly during the Eisenhower years, was loath to vex the Arabs still further and risk widening Soviet influence in the Middle East. The government preferred to remain silent, even regarding Arab discrimination against *American* Jews, such as travel barriers, exclusion of Jewish civilians and servicemen, and restrictions and boycotts against firms controlled or staffed by Jews. Reasoning that the achievement of peace would also resolve all other outstanding issues, the State Department refused to treat the problems of Middle Eastern Jews apart from the larger Arab-Israeli impasse. On more than one occasion American officials cited Israel's treatment of the Arab refugees or the 1956 Sinai war to explain, if not to justify, the situations brought to their attention by Committee representatives, and AJC's spirited defense of Israel's position could not sway the American policy-makers.

After the Sinai campaign Egypt stepped up the drive against its Jewish population. Within seven months some twenty thousand Jews (40 percent of the Jewish population) were forced to leave the country. AJC made the facts known to the State Department and asked for American and United Nations protests against these violations of the UN Charter and the Declaration of Human Rights. The Committee also proposed that the United States accept a number of refugees under a provision of the McCarran-Walter Immigration and Nationality Act. That clause permitted the granting of temporary visas to otherwise ineligible aliens, in emergencies and at the discretion of the attorney general, upon recommendation by the secretary of state. (It made possible the entry of thousands of Hungarian refugees forced to flee their country after the 1956 anti-Russian uprising.)

The request by the Committee and other American Jewish groups that the country do for Jewish refugees from Arab countries what had been done for the Hungarian refugees was rejected by the State and Justice Departments, as well as by the White House. The official explanation was that the administration had acted on the Hungarian matter while Congress was not in session and that "the extension of the parole provisions . . . to national or racial groups other than Hungarians must await the action of Congress on the pending [refugee] legislation." At best this was a misleading explanation; the parole provision was continued for the Hungarians when Congress was in session, and no bill was introduced in Congress to provide for Egyptian Jews. When James Marshall, on behalf of the Committee, challenged the double standard in an interview with Assistant Secretary of State William Rountree, he was given more candid reasons:

> Mr. Rountree, among other things, said that it was presumed that, in undertaking military action against Egypt, Israel, Britain and France drew up a check list of the consequences of such action which they might not like. He said that any list of consequences must have included such matters as the Suez Canal, the seizure of British and other assets in Egypt and the effect on the Jews of Egypt. . . . Mr. Rountree said that he did not see how a distinction could be made between the Egyptian refugees and the Arab refugees which would be understood by the people of the world. How did we think the Asiatic nations would react to such an attempted distinction?

VI

Involvement in Israel's affairs through cultural ties was a later development and one not regarded as "ideological imperialism" by either side.

After the Committee had demonstrated that American Jews shared neither the political loyalty of the Israelis nor many of their ideas about Diaspora Jewry, AJC turned to a positive area: the affinity between Israelis and their fellow Jews. In 1962 the

Committee established an office in Israel, where its primary function was to bring to the Israelis background information and interpretative data about the Diaspora and to emphasize the ties of history, religion, and humanity which transcended political boundaries. The purpose was threefold: to arrest the narrow parochialism of the younger generation of Israelis; to guard against a possible "de-Judaization" of Israel; and to build up the cultural reserves within the state to withstand the forces of Levantinization.

To advance these aims the Committee began publishing the bimonthly Hebrew-language magazine *Ammoth* (Evaluations), which was modeled after *Commentary* and spanned many fields of interest. *Ammoth* was aimed at the well-informed Israeli whom it sought to alert, without partisan indoctrination, to the broad range of social problems affecting him as a Jew and a human being, rather than as an Israeli citizen alone. The first issue, for example, contained an article on the Eichmann trial by the noted scholar Gershom Scholem, another on the atomic age by Hans J. Morgenthau, and a short story by Bernard Malamud. Editor Shlomo Grodzensky explained:

> We aim for a magazine of a Jewish framework and not an Israeli one; we don't seek any ideology but rather a more basic value, namely, whatever Jews do, whatever they are interested in, wherever they are found in whatever part of the world should become part and parcel of our own interest, no matter whether it is good or bad. A writer such as the American, Bernard Malamud, whose story is published herein, is presented because it is in the interest of Jews and not because his background is Jewish. The article by Hans J. Morgenthau which deals with political problems in this atomic era is of concern to human beings of our time and, therefore, we publish it here.

Ammoth was very well received by the Israelis, particularly since it steered clear of party ideologies. The Committee, in conjunction with the Hebrew University, also initiated a research project on the attitudes of Israeli youth toward Diaspora Jewry. Although the emphasis was still predominantly on what the Diaspora could offer Israel, this was no longer the only concern. By 1966 a prominent American Jewish Committee member visiting Israel could declare that Israel had to be made relevant to the younger generation of American Jewry.

Part Two

Foreword to Part 2

The founders of the American Jewish Committee would scarcely have recognized their organization as it emerged in the postwar years. No longer an agency dedicated exclusively to safeguarding the political and religious rights of Jews, AJC's purely defense and fire-fighting activities were now subordinated to positive and sustained social action. Reflecting the modern temper, which saw little value in a laissez-faire concept of minimum government, AJC took on aspects of the twentieth-century welfare state. Indeed, there were parallels between the Committee's postwar program and American postwar commitments: at home, an active government role in the promotion of social welfare; abroad, involvement commensurate with the realities of world power.

On the domestic scene the Committee's social-action program steered the organization into new fields, many as yet unexplored. In 1947 the agency embarked on a civil rights program aimed at achieving equality for all Americans in education, housing, employment, public accommodations, and related areas. Simultaneously, AJC concentrated on activating key groups to advance the aims of a democratic, pluralistic society. A notable example was its work with Christian educators and publishers to encourage the objective examination of Sunday school textbooks and lesson plans. These studies resulted in the elimination of many prejudicial references to Jews and other minorities. Committee professionals also worked with labor unions to help them combat racial and religious prejudices and educate workers to the evils of discrimination. The Committee backed experiments in intercultural education undertaken by various educational institutions. And finally, the Committee sponsored a broad, multidisciplinary examination of anti-Semitism and prejudice that resulted in the widely acclaimed five-volume *Studies in Prejudice.* The findings contributed much to an understanding of the dynamics of prejudice and laid the basis for extensive research in the field.

The range of activity illustrated the major priorities of the American Jewish Committee, as formulated by its new executive vice-president, John Slawson: to prevent more than to cure, to ferret out the root causes of social problems, to apply the teachings and methods of science to the field of human relations. The ambitious goals were expressed in the very name of AJC's impressive new headquarters, the Institute of Human Relations. Dr. Slawson has been criticized for overextending the role of a Jewish organization and for exaggerating the importance of the social sciences. But his determination in the face of opposition and apathy, and his ability to attract an exceptionally capable staff, established the Committee as a pioneering agency dedicated to a better understanding of individual and group relationships within a larger society.

The Committee's interests reflected currents in postwar America. There was an increased acceptance of pluralism and respect for group differences. Many religious and civic organizations, encouraged by the general prosperity, joined the struggle to win legal, political, and social equality for all Americans; with organized anti-Semitism on the wane, Jewish organizations, too, could turn their attention to other issues. The Survey Committee's long-range programs of preventive action outlined in the turbulent 1930s could now, in a more tranquil time, be put to the test.

The Committee's new endeavors were fully in keeping with its basic tenet that Jewish survival was most secure within the framework of a democracy, of which Jews must be full and integrated citizens. Jewish responsibility in maintaining a healthy democracy usually had to be ignored in times of crisis; now, however, the Committee acknowledged an obligation to help assure a pluralistic society, where mutual respect, understanding, and appreciation of differences governed intergroup relations, and where bigotry, discrimination, and political extremism (of both the Right and the Left) were looked upon as aberrations.

New divisions and departments were established to deal with special-interest groups, community services, research, and Jewish education; budgets and staff climbed. Budget figures were no longer an index to the Jewish condition. In 1939, when the fight against organized anti-Semitism was at its peak, Committee expenses totaled $700,000; in the late 1940s, when organized anti-Semitism was at a level far below that of the 1930s, the Committee's budget had risen to over $2 million. At the height of the Survey Committee's activity AJC employed over one hundred people; by 1946 the number had doubled. The organization sought out skilled professionals and spent an ever-increasing percentage of its budget on salaries.

The expansion of the postwar agency rendered the policy-making process correspondingly more complex. The executive committee, once the fount of decisions and execution, had already given way in importance to the smaller administrative and steering committees. By the early 1960s there were approximately five hundred members on the executive board. It met only twice a year, once in New York in conjunction with the general annual meeting and once in a major city in the West or South. With some sessions open to guests, one of its purposes was to introduce the Committee and its activities to different sections of the United States. The programs of executive meetings—addresses, panel presentations, and community reports—were structured around dominant themes: Jewish-Christian relationships, civil rights and race relations, the radical Right. Too large a group to initiate policy, the executive board passed on resolutions submitted to it by the smaller lay boards.

The major locus of lay power was the board of governors (successor to the administrative board) which included the officers and sixty elected members. Appointed by and responsible to the board were lay committees which dealt with the different areas of interest to the Committee: foreign affairs, domestic affairs, interreligious affairs, and so on. The professionals in charge of the various departments worked side by side with their corresponding lay committees. Policy now was the result of the interchange and merging of ideas between expert and layman. Usually the professional would raise an issue or suggest a program for the lay committee's consideration. The extent to which the laymen did more than approve those suggestions depended on the degree of their commitment and expertise.

The preponderance of lawyers among the Committee's active members seemed to increase involvement, for the legal minds preferred to steep themselves in the issues prior to passing judgment. Lay participation rested also on factors as diverse as the personality of the professionals and the success of the department head's efforts to "educate" his committee. Since programing could be effective only to the degree that communal leaders were partners to it, the Committee grew increasingly sensitive over the years to the problems of cultivating a corps of leaders and the interplay between professional and layman.

Once the programs were accepted in principle, their implementation was routine. More dramatic were some aspects of the Committee's defense work because of the acute and immediate dangers involved. An outbreak of armed hostilities in the Middle East, a Jewish purge in the Soviet Union, a Bricker Amendment designed to control executive treaty-making powers —these called for immediate responses geared to the gravity of the crises. But there were also the hate groups preaching anti-Semitism, which were a source of anxiety and posed periodic threats to curb immigration or to breach the separation of church and state. In this work the Committee added a new concept. Effective defense, it was reasoned, needed the strength derived from the inner resources of the Jewish community—self-respect as a group and pride in its rich cultural tradition. Integration did not permit self-segregation or ethnocentricism, but neither did it aim at assimilation. A positive Jewish identity was the mark of the adjusted individual, who neither flaunted nor fled from his Jewishness. For the first time, AJC undertook to deal with the threats for Jewish survival inherent in the political and social emancipation of the modern era.

The urgency of the problem of Jewish survival could be gauged by the postwar statistics. One-third of world Jewry had been annihilated; one-half of the remainder lived in the United States. Of the latter, about three-fourths were native-born Americans who were fast assimilating into the general culture. Principally an urban group, they spread out to suburbia during the postwar years, removing themselves further from the communal life of the old Jewish neighborhood.

Yet there were factors at work that favored a revival of Jewish identification. The majority of American Jews were third-generation Americans, grandchildren of the vast East European immigration. As the well-known historian of immigration Marcus Hansen had noted, what their fathers wanted to forget, the sons wanted to remember. Moreover, group identification in America was increasingly a matter of religion rather than ethnic origin; people were seen as Protestants, Catholics, or Jews, rather than as Germans, Italians, or Irish. American society sanctioned and even expected a religious affiliation. And suburban Jews, emulating their Christian neighbors or hoping to insulate their children against assimilation in mixed neighborhoods, were ready, indeed eager, to identify themselves as Jews.

The membership of the postwar American Jewish Committee did not immediately reflect the liberal orientation of the organization's program or its emphasis on Jewish identity. Often, though not consistently, those who opposed an expanded social-action program also questioned the need for stimulating Jewish education. Within five years of its adoption of the chapter plan in 1944, AJC had organized thirty-eight chapters and increased its membership from less than four hundred to eighteen thousand. But it aimed for like-mindedness rather than mass support, and for making Committee opinion more articulate rather than for drawing closer to the community. Although consciously seeking to broaden its base of leadership beyond the East Coast elite, it was content to attract a limited group of members. The average member of the Committee's executive in 1950 was a man in his early sixties, affluent, respected in his business or profession, and involved more in civic than in specifically Jewish affairs. He was American-born, usually of old German stock, Reform in his synagogue affiliation, and non-Zionist. Of above-average academic training, he was a moderate or conservative on political issues and had joined the Committee primarily out of a sense of noblesse oblige. The Committee deliberately sought out Jews of East European background—but only those who had "arrived" in terms of social status and wealth; AJC remained an exclusive club. A dozen years would pass before the organization would purposely open its doors to all classes in the community in line with John Slawson's dictum of working *with* Jews rather than only *for* Jews.

Style, as much as program and philosophy, distinguished the national Jewish organizations one from the other. Moderate, judicious, deliberate, with a preference for anonymity and an aversion for the dramatic—this remained the Committee's clearly recognizable way of doing things. It made use, whenever possible, of personal connections to reach statesmen, and of opinion-molders to influence the public. It explored the social sciences and applied their teachings in concrete programs, and maintained an insistence on high intellectual performance. AJC took pride in its particular approach and resisted the growing pressure for centralized community efforts. It cooperated with both Jewish and non-Jewish agencies on specific issues where the pooling of resources promised greatest advantage; but it saw no value in mandatory mergers which ignored pragmatic considerations.*

The impact of the holocaust on the Committee's postwar foreign program was pronounced. Ever conscious of the immeasurable loss world Jewry had sustained, AJC now concentrated on safeguarding the remaining reservoirs of Jewish population in the Muslim countries, Latin America, and behind the Iron Curtain, and broadened its concept of defense to include preventive action in behalf of foreign Jewish communities. It sought to strengthen Jewish cultural institutions wherever possible, share its expertise in fighting anti-Semitism, foster interreligious cooperation, and thus build a security which could ward off threats of destruction. AJC opened offices in South America and in Europe, and issued publications in Spanish, Yiddish, and French. Most important was the need to activate the communities themselves, so that they could look to their own defenses. The Committee denied, even behind closed doors, that its aim was

---

*In 1951, at the behest of the National Community Relations Advisory Council, Professor Robert MacIver of Columbia University analyzed duplication and competition in the overall operation of Jewish organizations. His recommendations for greater centralization were vehemently opposed by the Committee. Not only did the need to preserve a pluralistic outlook within the Jewish community outweigh the harm of duplication, AJC pointed out, but the work of other organizations dovetailed with, rather than duplicated, its own. For example, the Anti-Defamation League, like the Committee, had a program for business and industry; but whereas the Committee aimed to mobilize non-Jewish businessmen to fight discrimination, ADL's aim was to raise business standards in fields having a preponderance of Jewish entrepreneurs. The American Jewish Congress also maintained a research department but, unlike the Committee, never conducted or analyzed polls on anti-Semitism. Thus while ultimate goals might be the same, the emphasis of the separate agencies reinforced their common work and at the same time suited the variegated tastes of the community. On the strength of these convictions the Committee resigned from NCRAC in 1952. Fourteen years later, when the Committee rejoined, voluntarism rather than imposed centralization was recognized by mutual agreement.

"imperialistic," though it sometimes impinged on communal autonomy in efforts to block control by Jewish Communists.

Long-range preventive action was possible only if a Jewish community was relatively stable. But such action did not always involve a specific Jewish community or a specifically Jewish program—for example, the efforts in behalf of a democratic Germany. For the small Jewish remnant in Western Europe preventive action constituted primarily cultural reconstruction. The devastation of the war, plus the fact that one could no longer look to Eastern Europe to supply rabbis, educators, and Jewish community leaders who could help perpetuate the culture and traditions of Judaism, underscored the severity of the problem. The Committee's work in this area—"spiritual lend-lease," the American Jews called it—took many forms, from participation in the restitution settlements to foreign-language publications. Through its Paris office (created in 1947) and a network of correspondents in major cities, AJC cemented its ties with foreign communal leaders and organizations. Conferences of delegates from many countries in 1946 and 1955 highlighted the Committee's efforts to achieve a free exchange of ideas and its determination to share its resources with foreign Jewry for educational and human-relations purposes.

The 1946 conference led to the organization of the United Jewish Educational and Cultural Organizations (UJECO) which, under Committee sponsorship, trained teachers and provided educational materials for the European communities. A more recent joint effort supported by the Committee, the Community Service Program, studied Jewish community life and helped strengthen Jewish institutions abroad. But although the dependence on American Jewry was unmistakable, tradition, as well as the resolve to infuse new strength into the European communities, kept the Committee from falling into a guardian-ward relationship. The average Jew in France or Belgium knew little or nothing about the Committee; it served principally as an "organization's organization." For those who looked beneath the surface, however, its imprint could be discerned, be it in the gathering and publicizing of facts on anti-Semitic European groups or the sponsorship of programs for Catholic textbook revisions. In foreign affairs, too, the Committee strongly opposed any plans for "centralism."

While long-range planning and communal autonomy were central to the Committee's work in Western Europe and in Latin America, these could not be applied to Jews behind the Iron Curtain. There a single, stark imperative guided AJC activities— to gain for those Jews the minimum rights of religious and cultural expression granted other minorities. As for the Jews in the Muslim lands of North Africa and the Middle East, only short-range action was possible to meet the recurrent political emergencies.

As it had done since its inception, the Committee continued to support the full integration of Jews into their countries of residence. Now, however, AJC emphasized that integration did not mean assimilation. Convinced that optimum Jewish security depended on a democratic pluralistic society, it advocated cooperation with non-Jewish liberal and democratic elements wherever possible. Pragmatically, AJC would have been content with security alone, even under a Perónist dictatorship or Kremlin authoritarianism. Necessity also tempered the aim of integration, for survival often dictated that Jews seek refuge in other lands. Thus the Committee argued for liberal emigration and immigration policies throughout the postwar period, and where Israel was the only viable alternative to hardship or persecution, the Committee supported the right of Jews to settle there. Misgivings about Zionism slowly evaporated, and as the years went by AJC laid less and less stress on its own non-Zionist character, assuming a commitment to the survival of Israel at least as great as that of its Zionist counterparts.

The Committee's dream of a strong United Nations, which would guarantee individual freedom and security throughout the world, faded as the cold war fixed the pattern of international relations. Realistically, therefore, the Committee plotted its course around American diplomacy in the age of containment. Indeed, America's postwar stance held certain advantages. Power bred responsibilities which could not be evaded; the United States saw itself as the bulwark of the free world, the active defender of democracy everywhere. An international-minded America was likely to be more sensitive to the problems of foreign Jewries. Even more important, if Jewish interests were identified with democracy, anticommunism, and the West, they were logically aligned with American interests and could call forth American sympathy, if not intervention.* There was no longer any need to invoke the concept of "humanitarian diplomacy." For many years the Committee had propounded the tenet that anti-Semitism was antidemocratic; now the equation was enlarged: anti-Semitism equals antidemocracy equals protototalitarianism (or procommunism) equals anti-Americanism. Finally, since the United States sought to maintain and strengthen the unity of the free world, it might also be expected to encourage voluntary organizations working with counterparts abroad toward similar goals.

On the other hand, the East-West antagonism generated certain grim problems. As long as the cold war lasted, the Soviet Union was hardly open to pleas by the United States in behalf of the 2.5 to 3 million Russian Jews, even if the United States undertook such action. Nor would the United States risk further complication of the two-power standoff by championing the cause of the Jews against their Russian oppressors. The situation of the Jews in Asia and North Africa involved other considerations. In competing with Moscow for the allegiance of the Third World,

---

*Proskauer reminded Assistant Secretary of State Spruille Braden in 1945: "Mr. Justice Jackson, prosecutor for the United States, is proving at the Nuremberg war-guilt trial . . . that the pogroms in Germany before the war were inseparably linked to Germany's preparation for war against the democracies. If the world had intervened in time against Germany's policy of unbridled racism at home, it might well have been spared the agonies of war."

America was reluctant to appear as the inheritor of European imperialism. Jews in those countries were usually closely linked with European culture; if France and England bowed out and the United States refused to support the preservation of the status quo, the Jews could easily become the scapegoats of the emergent national states. And if the United States did champion persecuted Jews, their suffering was likely to be compounded by anti-American bias. Finally, if the United States felt impelled to choose an anti-Communist course even at the expense of democracy, all hope for individual freedom and security would be lost.

After the war the State Department encouraged voluntary organizations and interest groups to express their views on all aspects of American foreign policy, and frequently department officials met with representatives of such groups in formal conferences. The American Jewish Committee made its views known principally through its representative in Washington; on crucial matters it sent prominent lay officers and professionals who now spoke out frankly and confidently. Depending on the issue, AJC usually supplemented private diplomacy with campaigns to arouse national and international public opinion. Success was measured in small, concrete achievements: the modification of an expulsion decree in Iran, the prevention of population dislocations in Russia, aid for the six thousand stranded Moroccan Jewish refugees.

While its thrust was basically in behalf of Jewish concerns, AJC proved its general internationalist sensibilities in its efforts to strengthen the United Nations and in its opposition to the Bricker Amendment and the Connally Reservation on American participation in the International Court of Justice. Together with other religious organizations, it supported humanitarian causes having no direct bearing on Jews—the release of Joseph Cardinal Mindszenty in Hungary, relief for the famine-stricken in India, public tribute to the Hungarian rebels in 1956. Many of its domestic efforts, such as the campaign against the McCarran-Walter immigration bill and the activities surrounding the Rosenberg trial, also showed a deep concern with European-American misunderstandings. But the underlying aim remained Jewish defense, primarily American Jewish security. Unlike the 1906 founders, whose concern for foreign Jewry stemmed from their sense of stewardship, the AJC leaders at mid-century had been schooled in the age of totalitarianism. Anti-Semitism, which could transcend national boundaries, proved the interdependence of Jewish needs throughout the world. For American Jews, aid to coreligionists abroad and other internationalist commitments had become matters of self-interest.

13

Between Left and Right

I

World War II, like World War I, was followed by a Red scare, which again required American democracy to balance national security and civil liberties. Anti-Communist hysteria gripped the nation, spawned by the cold war, the revelations of Communist espionage, and the frustrations and ambitions of many individuals and groups. Many Americans were propelled into indiscriminate witch-hunting; countless others became mute with fear.

Congress led the official search for disloyalty, potential and actual, and its zeal was matched by the lower levels of government as well as by private organizations, industry, and the professions. Smears and guilt by association, mandatory loyalty oaths, and "preventive" law became the order of the day.

The American Jewish Committee was originally drawn into the Communist issue as it bore on anti-Semitism. The lesson of the 1930s had not faded, and the Committee maintained a constant watch over manifestations of prejudice. In 1947 AJC noted a sharp decline in organized anti-Semitism, which it attributed to prosperity and to a trend toward conservatism in the government. But the anti-Communist campaign, noted an office memorandum, posed a new threat:

> For a number of years, anti-semitic activists have assiduously promoted the smear that Jews are Communists. They have found this to be the most effective line with which they were left, since the decline of organizational activity. The acceleration of the anti-Communist campaign has come as a windfall to them, and our reports indicate a steady procession of anti-semitic operators from their regular sphere of activity onto the bandwagon of the general anti-Communist movement.

Gerald L.K. Smith, Conde McGinley, and Upton Close were but a few of the hatemongers who combined attacks upon communism with smears of Jews and Jewish organizations. The Communists, for their part, aggravated the situation by labeling all who attacked them, including President Truman, as anti-Semites.

When the matter came before the AJC executive committee, in May 1947, there were sharp differences as to what the Committee's role should be. None questioned the fact that communism was a conspiratorial, totalitarian movement and that Jews were caught up in the propaganda of both sides; but a concerted anti-Communist program, it was felt, might contribute to the growing tension between the United States and the Soviet Union and would align AJC with the same illiberal forces threatening the Jews. Even activity aimed at discrediting the smear that all Jews were Communists might boomerang and strengthen that very image in the public mind. Although some members of the executive favored a more general antitotalitarian resolution, the following statement was finally adopted: "That the staff, by the accepted methods of AJC and as part of its continuous program to strengthen democracy, direct its efforts to combat the attempt of reactionary and communistic minded groups alike falsely and viciously to identify Jews and Communists." It was understood that even this relatively narrow program would be implemented with the greatest caution, lest any action be construed as a political attack upon Russia.

The executive's reluctant decision did not end the debate. Not since the 1942 negotiations with the Zionists had there been such a lack of consensus within the Committee. Now the dissension permeated the staff and the chapters, as well as the lay committees. To dissociate Jews from communism involved more than apologetic denials; it needed a vigorous campaign to expose communism as an undemocratic, subversive force and to prove that Jewish sympathies were incompatible with Communist doctrine. Such a program, it was feared, might open the Committee to a charge of "Red-baiting," which would weaken its influence in behalf of liberal causes. John Slawson, who favored an active anti-Communist position, could not get membership support for a program that would influence the general public as well as the Jewish community, and the 1947 resolution was not implemented.

Until 1950 the Committee limited itself to a modest campaign to educate the Jewish community as to the incompatibility between communism and liberalism and to inform them about Soviet anti-Semitism. The national office distributed some materials on the nature of communism to chapters and local community relations councils. For internal use, the staff compiled surveys of Jewish attitudes on communism and the degree of Communist influence in Jewish organizations. AJC's most significant venture during this period was to underwrite scholarly research on the condition of Jewry behind the Iron Curtain, which resulted in the publication of two well-documented exposures of Soviet anti-Semitism: *The Jews in the Soviet Union* (1951) and *The Jews in the Soviet Satellites* (1953).

By 1950 the turn of events had convinced the Committee of the need to broaden its educational campaign. Public confidence was shaken by the fall of China to the Communists, the espionage trials of Alger Hiss and others, the revelation that Russia, too, had the atom bomb, and the war in Korea. The widespread fear that America was being subverted from within by Communist traitors gained added credence. Senator Joseph McCarthy began his meteoric rise. Antisubversive bills and investigative probes into both governmental and nongovernmental areas occupied much of congressional attention. When Jewish names came up in the trials and investigations, and anti-Semites joined the anti-Communist riots in Peekskill, New York, in the summer of 1949, American Jews grew more concerned over the identification of Jews with communism. Congressman John Rankin brandished a list of "subversives" in the House of Representatives and re-marked: "There is not a white Gentile in the entire group." To combat the Jewish/Communist stereotype, as well as to clarify the real nature of communism, became the task of a special AJC staff committee, under the direction of Dr. S. Andhil Fineberg.

For over four years, until the wave of McCarthyism subsided, Fineberg directed a concentrated anti-Communist campaign in the Jewish community. His department distributed vast quanti-ties of articles, pamphlets, and books exposing the totalitarian nature of communism, its insidious techniques, expansionist ideology, and discriminatory treatment of minorities. It also pro-vided material for journalists and popular radio programs. AJC chapters were encouraged to arrange lectures, forums, and adult education discussions on the subject. At the same time, they were urged to register publicly their support of American policy in Korea. When chapters responded by denouncing the Stockholm Peace Petition* or by enrolling in the anti-Communist Crusade for Freedom, such actions were cited as strong evidence against the Jewish/Communist smear. The Committee's activities were spurred by two developments abroad: the 1951–1952 anti-Semitic purges in Czechoslovakia and the Soviet Union's growing support of the Arab countries. AJC's own findings on the Krem-lin's use of anti-Semitism were presented by Irving M. Engel in

---

*Circulated by Communists and their supporters in over forty countries and interpreted by the United States as a technique to block the West's plans for UN atomic control and divert attention from Communist aggression.

testimony before a House committee on Communist aggression.

The Committee work of exposing the dangers of communism was almost unique among national Jewish organizations; the Jewish Labor Committee was the only other group that embarked on such a program. An AJC resolution urging that Jewish Communist-front organizations be barred from membership in communal institutions was transmitted to the community relations councils and chapters; and the Committee collected detailed information on the "undesirable" organizations. It was instrumental in isolating the Jewish People's Fraternal Order and the Jewish Young Fraternalists in various cities. When the Social Service Employees Union was expelled from the CIO on the grounds of being Communist-dominated, a Committee-prepared dossier convinced the New York Federation of Jewish Philanthropies not to renew its contract with that union. On the matter of Communists in the employ of Jewish organizations, the Committee formulated a hard-line position, based on research into Communist aims and tactics.

Communist propaganda directed toward Jews, the Committee found, aimed to confuse them on public issues and dupe them into ignoring communism's threat to Jewish interests. Thus it was important to prevent infiltration into Jewish organizations, and AJC privately counseled local communities seeking advice not to hire a known Communist in any professional or policy-making capacity. Lest its own loyalty program breed the same evils it condemned on the national scene, AJC cautioned that the rights of employees be scrupulously observed in determining Communist affiliation.

The Committee evoked sharp criticism from Jewish liberals in 1950 when it accepted an American Legion invitation to help found an All-American Conference to Combat Communism. Although the conference enrolled many respectable groups—religious, labor, educational, industrial, fraternal—it also attracted a sizable sprinkling of reactionary elements whose vigilantism blurred any distinctions between Communists and liberals. After considerable soul-searching and despite strong opposition from many lay and staff members, AJC agreed to join the conference. Slawson outlined his recommendations for the organization's program and the conditions for the Committee's affiliation: respect for individual liberties, attacks on *all* forms of totalitarianism and subversive elements, and a positive approach to civil rights. Determined to prevent the conference from launching a witch-hunting crusade, AJC reasoned that it could not do so by refusing to join.

The Committee achieved its goal. A few weeks after its own affiliation with the Conference to Combat Communism it succeeded in barring from membership Merwin K. Hart's National Economic Council, an organization whose propaganda campaign for a "free economy" was based principally on anti-Jewish and anti-Zionist diatribes. And largely as a result of intensive Committee efforts, the conference adopted a prodemocratic, instead of a merely anti-Communist, stand.

The Committee's very presence in the Conference to Combat Communism encouraged like-minded groups, such as the Federal Council of Churches, the AFL, and the National Education Association, to hold the line against the bigots. Together, these groups were able to block the establishment of state and local vigilante units and to discourage indiscriminate attacks on organizations not listed as subversive by the Justice Department. The conference's primary activity was its sponsorship of Know Your America Week. A Committee staff member, serving as chairman of that annual program, organized a variety of prodemocracy community projects with the participation of conservative and patriotic groups. The conference was so much under the sway of Lewis Hines of the AFL and Edwin J. Lukas of AJC, one disappointed witch-hunter complained, that no "reputable" anti-Communist would speak for it. Even after the vigilante elements had been removed, the Committee continued to serve a useful purpose as watchdog at the conference.

II

The American Jewish Committee's educational campaign against communism was not, however, matched by action in behalf of civil liberties. The agency's decision in 1950 that civil liberties were its legitimate concern, even though Jews or any other religious or racial minorities were not the only ones affected, came only in reluctant response to external pressures. Opponents of the move feared it would play into the hands of anti-Semites and those who lumped liberals with "Reds." Some worried lest AJC overextend itself in an area far removed from its traditional concerns. Edward Greenbaum, for example, argued that for Jews to fight infringements on individual freedom qua Jews constituted undesirable "self-ghettoization." Nevertheless, it was clear that the Committee's goals of safeguarding civil rights, eliminating prejudice, and promoting intercultural education could not be achieved in an atmosphere which equated safety with conformity and social experimentation with radicalism. The threat to liberty jeopardized the very basis of healthy Jewish survival.

Other groups, conservative and liberal, Jewish and non-Jewish, had rallied to the cause of civil liberties, and if the Committee desired to maintain its posture of leadership, it could not afford to keep silent.

In itself the decision on civil liberties was a momentous step, for it further transformed the Committee from a defense to a social-action agency.

At the first the Committee's mandate was severely limited. The executive cautiously resolved that it act jointly with other organizations, and then only with great selectivity. Indeed, the whole issue was tied to national security needs:

> *Whereas,* present world conditions make an effective security program essential to our national safety . . . but,
> *Whereas,* a security program conducted . . . with disre-

gard of individual rights destroys the very institutions which the program should defend; and

Whereas, there is the closest relationship between civil liberties of all citizens and the protection of the civil liberties of members of particular groups,

Therefore, be it resolved that

(1) AJC recognizes that a national security program is vital to our safety.

(2) AJC along with other American organizations should take appropriate steps to insure that in the maintenance of national security, essential freedoms are not endangered and the dignity of the individual is not impaired.

Unreconciled differences within the Committee throughout the McCarthy era prevented the initiation of any large-scale action program. Lay committees and workshops at AJC annual meetings debated such civil liberties issues as loyalty oaths, the attorney general's list of subversive organizations, investigations of the teaching profession, and censorship; but rarely was a consensus reached beyond vague generalities about the need to preserve civil liberties. A project to organize local citizens' committees on individual rights to serve both as fact finders regarding abuses of freedom and as educational forces within their communities was blocked by lay timidity. AJC gave advice and assistance in response to community requests, but it took no public stand on legislation and litigation under consideration on the state and local level. There was cooperation with other liberal organizations, such as the National Civil Liberties Clearing House, but in most instances it was discreet and informal. In 1953 AJC helped establish a loose coalition of civic, religious, and labor groups to pool information of interest to these groups. Deliberately unnamed, the venture was solely advisory and entailed no organizational commitments.

In line with the 1950 resolution, the Committee sought to steer a middle course that would meet the threats to security and protect civil liberties. Out of conviction, as well as for reasons of expediency, AJC never inveighed against security legislation or loyalty investigations per se. Its stand was best articulated in its pamphlet *American Security and Freedom,* which called for a serious but rational reaction to the menace of Communist subversion. Emphasizing the judicial process, rather than the individual's claims to unlimited freedom of speech or association, the Committee hoped to assure fair procedures in administrative and congressional loyalty programs; it did not aim to eliminate such programs entirely.

Representatives of the Committee testified before various congressional groups on the abuses of investigative techniques. The Committee also promoted the idea of a nonpartisan presidential commission to evaluate the overall security program and prevent its deterioration into hysterical and arbitrary witch-hunting. The Nimitz Commission, appointed by President Truman, failed to fill that purpose, and the Committee pressed President Eisenhower and Attorney General Herbert Brownell for safeguards. In a memorandum to the administration, AJC cited procedures it found particularly objectionable:

> The right of an accused to confrontation has been denied; the right of cross-examination is rarely accorded; public charges are made under circumstances which deny to one accused the right or opportunity to properly defend himself; the grounds upon which loyalty is called into question are often insubstantial, and unrelated to the probability of subversion.
>
> Moreover, largely imitatively, private groups and individuals, acting for themselves and without governmental or other sanction, have adopted tactics that result in uncontrolled censorship; in "blacklisting" in the fields of entertainment, education and politics; and in unbridled attacks on otherwise innocent citizens in and out of public life.

The Committee's natural caution, as well as its preference for behind-the-scenes action, kept it from embarking on a public campaign to protest the erosion of civil liberties. And while AJC disliked joining forces with nonliberal elements, it did so, reluctantly, where that seemed the most effective way to ward off greater dangers. Thus it established contact with Senator McCarthy's controversial young counsel, Roy Cohn. (When AJC's French publication, *Evidences,* was accused of expressing Stalinist views, this association helped negate the charge.) The Committee's advice to the McCarthy team against a protracted investigation of Fort Monmouth may have contributed to McCarthy's ultimate decision to end that probe. These contacts, however, led the Committee to abstain when other Jewish organizations, like the American Jewish Congress, supported the move to censure the Wisconsin senator.

In the House of Representatives, the House Committee on Un-American Activities posed an equally serious challenge to due process of law. The American Jewish Committee supplied HUAC with materials stressing the incompatibility of Judaism and communism and with facts about Soviet anti-Semitism. In 1953, when the editor of *Jewish Life,* a publication not unsympathetic to communism, appeared before HUAC, he accused it of creating a situation in the United States similar to that which had led to the Nazi murder of six million Jews. AJC's president Irving M. Engel immediately wired HUAC's chairman, Representative Harold Velde, denouncing the testimony as blatant Communist propaganda which in no way reflected American Jewish thinking. To prevent the unfavorable publicity given such incidents, representatives of the Committee, the Anti-Defamation League, and the Jewish War Veterans met with Velde and his counsel, and secured their agreement to consult the files of the Jewish organizations to determine who among prospective Jewish witnesses were known Communists. The congressman seemed aware of the danger that some of his activities might be fomenting anti-Semitism.

That same summer the *American Mercury* printed an article on subversion among the clergy, and pressure on HUAC to investigate the ministry mounted. Jews and non-Jews protested sharply when Rabbis Stephen Wise and Judah Magnes were described as Reds. Velde invited the American Jewish Committee, the National Council of Churches of Christ, and the National Catholic Welfare Conference to designate representatives to confer with him:

> First, to obtain assistance in order that the work of the Committee might be carefully appraised for any suggestions which you might offer; and, second, to make available to the religious groups the knowledge and material which have been accumulated by the House Committee on Un-American Activities through the many years of its work. . . . I, of course, fully recognize that any such conference or advice would not be an official sanction or endorsement by Jewish leaders of the operations or functions of the Committee.

The Committee accepted the invitation, despite a chorus of protest from the Jewish community castigating AJC for presuming to represent Jewish religious interests and for lending its prestige to a smear group. However, AJC president Jacob Blaustein's letter of acceptance to Velde underscored the agency's criticism of HUAC:

> Our moral obligation to discuss these matters with you stems from the recognition—which we share with you—that Judaism and Christianity are among the most effective antagonists of Communism and all other forms of totalitarianism; it stems equally from the conviction that these religious forces have also been among the principal defenders of individual political freedoms. The American Jewish Committee is proud of its historic efforts in both areas: we have constantly exposed the cynicism and conspiratorial nature of Communism, and we have arrayed ourselves alongside other American groups that promote and protect civil liberties.
> It is for these reasons that, speaking for the American Jewish Committee, we welcome the opportunity, at your request, specifically to offer to the Committee suggestions of procedures which would insure that, while exposing genu-

inely disloyal activities, innocent people and groups will not be made to suffer irreparable damage to their reputations. On the other hand, as I am sure you will readily understand, we do not feel at this time that we might properly undertake an evaluation of "the knowledge and material that have been accumulated by the House Committee on Un-American Activities through the many years of its work."

Naturally, as you have forthrightly recognized, we reserve the right to take justifiable issue with any of the procedures, operations or functions of the House Committee.

Velde's guests conferred separately before meeting with him and were able to present a united front to his committee. They proposed several modifications of HUAC's procedures to protect the rights of the accused. Within a year there was a noticeable improvement in HUAC practices. Two other results were at least as important: HUAC abandoned its plans to investigate Communist infiltration among clerical groups, and it promised to broaden its definition of un-American to include groups on the Right and to investigate hate groups which might be *anti*-Communist.

In 1954 HUAC issued its *Preliminary Report on Neo-Fascist and Hate Groups,* which exposed the anti-Semitic bent of the National Renaissance party and Conde McGinley's *Common Sense.* Although the report was criticized by right-wingers like columnist Westbrook Pegler ("a hoax") and by the American Civil Liberties Union, which argued that HUAC's targets should have been accorded a hearing, AJC was satisfied. It was the first time since 1938 that a congressional committee acknowledged the dangers of the extreme Right, and AJC felt that the HUAC report would help reduce the influence of troublesome Nazi-like groups.

III

The Committee's caution on the issue of civil liberties in no way blocked an effective response when anti-Semitism was a factor in national security programs. The problem might involve Communist charges of anti-Semitism, complaints by non-Communist Jews that anti-Semitism was the motive behind loyalty probes, or the exploitation by anti-Semites of security investigations for their own purposes.

The first category worried the Committee because of the danger that the Communist charges might delude American Jews and further the identification of Jews with Communists in the public mind. The most serious challenge came with the trial of Ethel and Julius Rosenberg, subsequently convicted of spying for Russia. The Communists had studiedly ignored the trial; but after the death sentence was announced, a Committee to Secure Justice for the Rosenbergs was created; it charged, among other things, that the trial had been anti-Semitic because the jury included no Jews, while the judge and prosecutor were frightened Jews who had succumbed to anti-Red hysteria. Supporters of the Rosenbergs also pointed out that the death penalty had never before been imposed for treason during peacetime.

Local committees in support of the Rosenbergs were set up in many cities, protesters marched around the White House, and hundreds of thousands of dollars were raised for their defense. The Jewish organizations—the *Judenrat** as the Communists referred to them—swung into action. The American Jewish Committee took the lead with a memo for chapter leaders and community relations councils, explaining how the Communists sought to exploit the Rosenberg case, and with a detailed article on the matter by Dr. Fineberg, which was distributed to rabbis and editors of Jewish journals. The National Community Relations Advisory Council followed with a statement to the Jewish

---

*The Jewish councils established by the Nazis for dealing with the Jews.

press condemning the Communists for raising the false issue of anti-Semitism. By the end of 1952 the Committee noted with satisfaction that no Jewish non-Communist organization had swallowed the Communist propaganda. At first AJC hoped that the debate over the anti-Semitism charges could be kept within the Jewish community; but when the Rosenberg Committee secured the endorsement of two world-renowned scientists, Harold Urey and Albert Einstein, and the Communists expanded their campaign to other countries, the Committee publicized its memoranda and exposés more widely. In an effort to counter anti-American sentiment fomented by the Communist propaganda on the trial, the State Department made extensive use of two articles by Dr. Fineberg. Fineberg also submitted material to the HUAC investigation of the Rosenberg Committee, with the understanding that the investigation would avoid embarrassing the Jewish community.

A different situation arose over the security program at the radar laboratories in Fort Monmouth, New Jersey. Although Jews constituted a minority of the persons employed there, most of those suspended or reclassified as a result of the security checks instituted during Eisenhower's administration were Jewish. Two lawyers who represented a majority of the ousted Jews sought the intervention of the Committee and the Anti-Defamation League, claiming that anti-Semitism was at the root of the matter. The statistics alone seemed to support their contention, and Jewish community leaders in New Jersey were understandably alarmed. After examining the evidence, AJC and the ADL concluded that there was no proof to substantiate the charge of anti-Semitism. The army's reinstatement within five years of nearly all who had been suspended in some degree bore out that conclusion. But one of the lawyers for the suspended men accused the Committee and the ADL of permitting his clients to be "sacrificed on the altar of anti-Semitism."

A third problem area involved Jewish government employees accused of conspiring with the Communists. Sometimes the charge was patently ludicrous—for example, the fraudulent letter first published in the Paris *Le Figaro,* which purported to reveal how Roosevelt had designated the president of the Orthodox Jewish religious organization, Young Israel, as his personal emissary to Stalin. (The alleged appointee was, in fact, an accountant with no interest in politics.) Perhaps most significant— and very revealing of the temper of the times—was the seriousness with which the Jewish agencies treated the suggestion of a connection between Jews and the Soviet Union. Fearful that the *Figaro* letter might be blown up into another *Protocols,* the Committee denounced it and, with the other member agencies of NCRAC, secured a retraction and apology from the Hearst papers, which had reprinted the letter in the United States.

An even more serious case broke in December 1954, when Secretary of Agriculture Ezra Taft Benson dismissed as a security risk Wolf Ladejinsky, a Russian-born Jew who had worked for the department as an agricultural expert for fifteen years. The State Department had previously cleared Ladejinsky, and Benson admitted that there was no new evidence against him. To support the dismissal, a Benson aide released to the press a letter deducing Ladejinsky's disloyalty, at least in part, from his Russian Jewish background. AJC president Irving M. Engel immediately wired the secretary:

> We are mortified to learn that a government department should give currency to such irresponsible characterizations . . . and should have employed such unwarranted allegations as corroboration of the correctness of a decision taken relative to a security risk case. . . . We urge your prompt public disavowal of the use of this communication and your taking the necessary steps to prevent the recurrence of this regrettable and harmful incident.

Benson protested his admiration for Jews and denied that the letter reflected the views of his department. A few days later he met privately with a delegation led by Murray Gurfein, chairman of AJC's Domestic Affairs Committee, and Henry Schultz of the Anti-Defamation League. Benson apologized for the release of the letter, but insisted that the department had not known that Ladejinsky was Jewish at the time his case was being evaluated and refused to reopen the case, as the delegates requested. The following day, however, the White House announced Ladejinsky's appointment to the Foreign Operations Administration and his security clearance by FOA director Harold Stassen. The Committee was convinced that the release of the letter was a blunder and that anti-Semitism was not a factor in the dismissal; Ladejinsky himself agreed. Nevertheless, the Ladejinsky case pointed up the contradictory and self-defeating elements of a repressive security program.

Since the 1930s the Committee had worried about a possible collaboration of anti-Semitic forces in the United States. It therefore observed with growing apprehension the coalition of hate groups which joined to block the appointment of Anna M. Rosenberg as assistant secretary of defense in 1950. Mrs. Rosenberg had been approved without hesitancy by the Senate Armed Services Committee. But an outcry by anti-Semites like Gerald L. K. Smith and Benjamin Freedman and such vigilantes as radio commentator Fulton Lewis, J. B. Matthews (former counsel of the Dies Committee), and Senator McCarthy's staff forced the reopening of the hearings. With the blessing of Congressmen Ed Gossett, John Rankin, and Clare Hoffman, they produced witnesses to testify that Mrs. Rosenberg ("one of the most ominous and enigmatic figures in the secret . . . Jew machine," according to Smith) was a Communist.

That the Senate committee even agreed to hear these diatribes shows the hysteria that was engendered by the Alger Hiss trial and the political weight of charges of communism. The American Jewish Committee and the Anti-Defamation League immediately provided the Senate committee with data on the background and character of Mrs. Rosenberg's accusers. It is clear from the transcript of the hearings, particularly the cross-examination by Senators Estes Kefauver and Leverett Saltonstall, that the information was put to good use. Benjamin Freedman's charges against the Jewish organizations did not save the self-styled "excommunicated Jew" from emerging as an object of ridicule, and the campaign against Mrs. Rosenberg collapsed. The Jewish organizations were prepared, if necessary, to mobilize public support for the Rosenberg appointment, for they received over one thousand unsolicited letters and telegrams, including messages from Dwight Eisenhower, James Byrnes, and Robert Patterson, supporting it. Freedman interpreted the results in *Know the Truth*, a one-edition newssheet he published, in characteristic headlines: "SMEAR BUND RESCUES ANNA M. ROSENBERG, CHARACTER ASSASSINS ACT TO INSURE CONFIRMATION, ADOPT BLACKMAIL TACTICS TO WHITEWASH SENATE INVESTIGATION." But the American Jewish Committee felt that its swift response to the crisis helped avert a potential Dreyfus affair.

IV

As the Red scare spread, the public schools became a frequent target of the witch-hunters. In Denver, Pasadena, Battle Creek, and Chicago self-appointed citizens' councils attacked local schools as hotbeds of communism and railed against textbooks containing "Communist filth." College and university faculties also came under attack, and a number of professors and instructors were driven off campus by anti-Communist smears. In the Senate, Pat McCarran expressed interest in investigating subversive trends in the public schools.

The American Jewish Committee sprang to the defense of the schools and of the human relations and intercultural programs denounced by the attackers as useless "fads and frills" of progressive education. The Committee always regarded public education as a powerful force in buttressing democratic attitudes. If conformity and regimented thinking replaced free inquiry in the classroom, America's pluralistic society would be severely endangered. Furthermore, the attack on the schools was led by known anti-Semites and other reactionaries who used their campaign to corral support from respectable circles. The most influential of the antischool forces was the National Council for American Education (NCAE), whose director, Allen Zoll, was a former Christian Fronter and the organizer of the American Patriots, Inc., a group listed as subversive by the attorney general.

The NCAE and its supporters blended legitimate grievances —the mounting costs of education and the occasional abuse or misapplication of the principles of progressive education—with bigotry; and even when the charges were not convincing, fear of being labeled a Red or an atheist usually silenced the skeptics. Neither educators nor the educational and parental organizations were sufficiently skilled in public relations techniques to lead an effective resistance. In an effort to overcome those obstacles, the Committee mobilized the resources of its various departments. It released the findings of its investigative division on the backgrounds and goals of the antischool leaders to educational organizations, the press, and local communities. The *New York Times* published a number of feature articles on the leaders of the attack on the schools and the dangers of textbook censorship.

AJC established close working relations with the National Education Association and the U.S. Office of Education. These and other groups widely distributed several AJC pamphlets about the danger to the schools. The Committee also helped get the support of organized labor for the schools and convinced veterans' groups not to join in the attack. It encouraged local communities to come to the defense of their schools. It tried to educate the public about the value of progressive and intercultural education. Privately the AJC's Legal Department aided prominent academicians who were victims of the smear campaign. But the Committee hesitated to become involved with the congressional investigation of the schools, though it finally adopted as an unpublicized policy—and for the guidance of staff only—sections of a statement drawn up by the National Council of Churches of Christ, warning against the abuse of legislative probes and the danger of intellectual regimentation.

V

One objective of the school critics was to eliminate the study of the United Nations and its specialized agencies from the curriculum—an emphasis that reflected more than bigotry or hardcore isolationism. There was growing frustration in the country about the UN's failure to end the cold war between East and West and the hot war in Korea, and to prevent a nuclear arms race. The Red scare sharpened xenophobic sentiments and encouraged America's traditional preference for avoiding international commitments.

Although the great majority of the people supported United States membership in the UN, though with varying degrees of enthusiasm, opponents of internationalism grew more vocal as the East-West impasse continued. Certain elements, notably the superpatriotic organizations, feared that the UN would develop into a world government; others, convinced that international agreements on labor and health standards or human rights would encroach on United States sovereignty and foster an international socialism or new dealism, disapproved of the UN on constitutional and economic grounds; still others questioned the wisdom of relying on such an inept organization. When the hate groups jumped aboard the anti-UN bandwagon—such individuals and groups as Conde McGinley, Gerald L.K. Smith, Merwin Hart, the American Flag Committee, the Constitutional Educational League, the Minute Women, and the Liberty Belles—the attacks became more noisy and intemperate. The image of the Jew as conspiratorial internationalist was added to that of the Jew as Communist.

The Committee was concerned not only about such anti-Semitic diatribes, but at least as much by the attacks on the United Nations. Indeed, AJC's entire postwar foreign program—launched at San Francisco by Joseph Proskauer and Jacob Blaustein in 1945—was predicated on the need to win international protection for basic human freedoms. To that end the Committee had organized the Consultative Council of Jewish Organizations (which included AJC, the Alliance Israélite Universelle, and the Anglo-Jewish Association) to serve as a consultative agency to the UN Economic and Social Council.

Through the Consultative Council or in cooperation with other nongovernmental agencies in the United States, the Committee worked with the UN and the United Nations Educational, Scientific, and Cultural Organization (UNESCO) on various matters relating to human rights, refugees, migration, and race relations. In 1952 it was elected to membership in the United States National Commission for UNESCO. AJC's special concern for the drafting of an international covenant of human rights was coupled with deliberations on possible means of enforcing those rights. The Committee urged, for example, the establishment of a standing UN human rights committee, which not only states but also private individuals and groups could petition. Related to that was its unique proposal for a UN attorney general who would have the right to institute proceedings against member states violating individual human rights. The Committee was also eager for the adoption of an international covenant on genocide; it cooperated in the drafting of the Genocide Convention and worked arduously—but to no avail—to secure its ratification by the United States.

Critics of the UN attacked both the proposed covenant on human rights and the Genocide Convention, principally on the grounds that international treaties would usurp the prerogative of American legislative and law-enforcement bodies. They found a strong rallying point in the proposal introduced by Senator John Bricker in the Eighty-second Congress. His bill would have amended the Constitution to make treaties affecting internal matters inoperative without appropriate congressional legislation; it would have forbidden the enactment of treaties on matters falling within the jurisdiction of the states and subordinated to Congress the right to enter into international agreements. The proposal was seen as an expression of congressional resentment over its exclusion by Roosevelt and Truman from major policy decisions —from the destroyer-bases deal of 1940 to the decision to fight in Korea—and it won the backing of over sixty senators. The Bricker Amendment had radical implications for the constitutional balance of power between branches and levels of government. "What the Bricker amendment does is to return to the Articles of Confederation," the *New York Times* pointed out.

The American Jewish Committee deplored the "unjustified" attacks on the UN by "anti-democratic groups and individuals whose design is to undermine public confidence in all institutions of democracy and enforce a narrow social and political conformity on American life." In conjunction with other religious and educational groups, it sponsored an educational campaign to inform the public about the nature, functions, and benefits of the UN and its affiliated agencies. And since the Bricker Amendment was supported by isolationists of all stripes and posed an immediate danger to its human rights program, AJC spoke out vigorously against the amendment. It subscribed in principle to the legal arguments against the amendment advanced by the Association of the Bar of the City of New York; but its own emphasis was on America's need to maintain its moral leadership of the free world by unhampered participation in the UN.

Resolutions by the executive committee were supplemented by personal letters from Irving M. Engel and Jacob Blaustein to fifteen hundred individuals throughout the country, advising them to mobilize local sentiment against the amendment. Chapter leaders were similarly alerted, and the national office distributed a fact sheet to newspapers, radio and TV networks, unions, and civic groups.

NOT FREE TO DESIST **366**

Fearing the havoc that the isolationists might wreak, the Eisenhower administration decided on appeasement. When Secretary of State Dulles testified before the Senate Judiciary Committee in April 1953, he made it clear that the administration was ready to trade American participation in the human rights covenant and similar conventions for the Bricker Amendment. Reversing the American position, Dulles said that the United States would not become a party to treaties on human rights but would instead use "persuasion, education, and example" to attain the goals of human freedom. Dulles admitted privately to Blaustein two weeks later that his motive had been to weaken support for the Bricker Amendment, adding that he did not believe that Congress would approve the covenant or the Genocide Convention in any case.

The American Jewish Committee initially stood by its advocacy of legally binding treaties on human rights and deplored the administration's about-face:

> The United Nations human rights program is being misunderstood as a threat to American institutions. This is unfortunate, because it is untrue. Actually, it would strengthen the United States by enlarging the area of freedom throughout the world, which is a basic objective of American foreign policy. It would also be a most potent weapon against Communism. . . .
>
> The American Jewish Committee endorses the Administration's opposition to the Bricker Resolution. At the same time, we are deeply concerned over a possible reversal of American policy with respect to human rights covenants. We are convinced that such a reversal would seriously weaken our country's moral leadership in the free world. We are also convinced that properly drawn treaties can be a means of protecting the fundamental freedoms of human beings everywhere, with full preservation of our American system of government.

The Committee realized, however, that political realities called for a change in its position. Judge Philip Halpern, of the Buffalo chapter, an Eisenhower-appointed adviser to the American delegation of the UN Commission on Human Rights in 1952, reported to the AJC executive on the constitutional and pragmatic validity of Dulles's position. His influence prevented the executive committee from adopting a resolution condemning America's "moral surrender." After months of deliberation the Committee formulated a compromise position. While appreciating the difficulties of arriving at a meaningful and binding human rights covenant, AJC stated: "We . . . reject the view that they justify abandoning action by treaty." At the same time, it added:

> To achieve the realization of the principles of the Declaration and to further the adoption of Covenants, we support the U.S. Action Program and other methods designed to attain these ends. Some of these programs are already under way under the auspices of the U.N. and its Specialized Agencies. They should be extended and intensified so that the principles of the Declaration of Human Rights may be realized in the conduct of peoples.

The Dulles-inspired Action Program was subsequently approved by the UN Commission on Human Rights. Under this plan, member states would report periodically on progress toward the goals announced in the Declaration of Human Rights; the commission would study various aspects of human rights; and the UN would supply technical assistance to governments on matters related to human rights. By cooperating in this program the American Jewish Committee shifted its own emphasis, and that of the Consultative Council of Jewish Organizations, to the promotion of human rights through means other than conventions.

VI

It was no coincidence that Senator Pat McCarran—who, at a hearing on the Bricker Amendment, had observed: "I will regret probably all the days of my life . . . that . . . I voted for the United Nations"—should emerge as the chief postwar proponent of restrictions on immigration into the United States. Representative John Wood, who had introduced a bill for American withdrawal from the UN, went a step further and declared, in a speech on the floor of the House, that racist doctrines had their validity. But many nonisolationists reaffirmed the tenets of restriction which had become American policy since the Immigration Act of 1924. The limitations written into the Displaced Persons Act of 1948 made it clear that prejudice, reinforced by fears for national security, would block all efforts to break down the restrictionist barrier. And, during the McCarthy era the term *alien-subversives* was used, along with *economic competitors* and *inferior stock,* to characterize aliens. Supporters of liberal immigration laws risked being called Communists.

The American Jewish Committee, as it had for over forty years, played a leading part in the fight for a liberal immigration policy, but its reasons for doing so had changed. Most of the DPs had been resettled; the major European reservoirs of Jewish immigration had been destroyed in the holocaust. The majority of Jews behind the Iron Curtain were not free to emigrate, and Israel's doors were open to those who were. Thus the need to provide a refuge, the primary motive behind AJC's past immigration policy, was superseded by a commitment to democratic principles and the cause of international amity. While American Jews, too, were worried about an influx of newcomers indoctrinated with nazism and communism, this consideration was outweighed by their opposition to the quota system as one based on racist doctrines inimical to America's democratic principles.

In 1948 AJC presented to the Senate subcommittee on immigration a detailed statement designed to allay the mounting fear of aliens and underscore this country's traditional role as a haven for the oppressed:

> Americanism is not to be measured by conformity to law, or zeal for education, or literacy, or any of these qualities in which immigrants may excel the native-born. Americanism is the spirit behind the welcome that America has traditionally extended to people of all races, all religions, all nationalities.

In view of the existing political climate, however, the Committee did not demand that the government drop the national-origins quota system entirely. Instead, it urged modification of the law to permit carrying over unused quotas from year to year and reallocating them. This would allow the large quotas assigned to the countries of northern and western Europe, which were never filled, to be distributed among applicants of other lands, either on a first-come, first-served basis or according to special priorities determined by Congress (religious or racial refugees, relatives of United States residents, workers with desired skills, and so on). For the first time in its history the Committee also specifically called for the right of Asiatics to immigrate to the United States and become American citizens.

The Committee also expressed concern about the civil liberties aspects of immigration policy—the rights of resident aliens and exclusion and deportation procedures; but it concentrated on modification of the quota system. The McCarran-Walter omnibus immigration bill under consideration by Congress codified the entire system of immigration laws and retained the national-origins formula, which gave preferential treatment to the countries of northwestern Europe. Although minimum quotas were granted to Asian countries, the racial bias of the measure was thinly disguised in its stress on "the similarity of cultural background."

Judge Simon Rifkind, who testified against the Senate's

McCarran bill and the House's Walter bill (these were later combined) on behalf of the Committee and other major Jewish organizations, again advanced the idea of pooling quotas. (A confirmed restrictionist called Rifkind's testimony "the most eloquent and knowledgeable statement" made by the opposition.) And as a member of the Joint Conference on Alien Legislation, a nonsectarian organization representing the proimmigration forces, the Committee helped rally the liberal critics of restrictionism.

Senator Herbert Lehman, an outspoken opponent of McCarthyism and defender of immigration reform, cooperated closely with the Committee and its allied organization in drafting a model bill. It called for the pooling of quotas and the establishment of more liberal guidelines on exclusion and expulsion. In 1952 Senators Lehman and Hubert H. Humphrey cosponsored an omnibus bill incorporating these provisions. They did not expect passage of their measure, but hoped it would serve to block the McCarran-Walter bill. They were mistaken: a coalition of Democrats and Republicans approved the McCarran-Walter bill and overrode President Truman's veto in June 1952.

There were a number of reasons for this defeat. The Committee's vigorous support of Lehman's efforts was not matched by the other organizations in the Joint Conference, some of which were satisfied to press for—and win—improvements in the McCarran-Walter bill. While the Protestant groups remained aloof, the Catholics, who were particularly interested in special-refugee legislation, refused to undercut their chances by speaking out against the bill. Even the Jewish groups, which led the antirestrictionist drive, were not in complete accord; the American Jewish Congress, for example, urged the total repudiation of the national-origins formula. And in matters of administration the usual partisan jealousies arose. The Committee provided the initiative both in NCRAC and the Joint Conference and bore the brunt of the work and expenses. But it concentrated on legal analysis and failed to spark an effective educational and publicity campaign, which usually accompanied its action. (An AJC pamphlet refuting the charge that antirestrictionists were subversives did not appear until over four years after those rumors first were widely circulated.)

"The immigration fight has only begun," wrote Oscar Handlin in the July 1952 issue of *Commentary.* And indeed, the Committee intensified its drive for reform after passage of the McCarran-Walter Immigration and Nationality Act. When President Truman set up a Special Commission on Immigration and Naturalization to survey all aspects of immigration, the Committee did all it could to keep the issue alive. It offered testimony, distributed material, and provided data for other organizations and individuals. AJC now supported the more radical proposal to scrap the national-origins quota system altogether. It recommended that an administrative or joint legislative commission determine annually the number of immigrants to be admitted, with legally established minimum and maximum limits, visas to be allocated on a worldwide first-come, first-served basis. The Committee also cautioned legislators not to lose sight of the human issues in deciding on the preferred classes of immigrants and not to regard would-be immigrants merely as economic commodities. The report of the president's special commission, published under the title *Whom We Shall Welcome,* incorporated most of the liberals' proposals but called for limiting the number of immigrants admitted annually to one-sixth of one percent of the American population, as determined by the most recent census —a number below the three hundred thousand minimum preferred by the Committee.

The presidential campaign of 1952 focused on the war in Korea; but the American Jewish Committee made sure that both political parties dealt with immigration, and they provided material to the Republicans and the Democrats. The Republican platform was less outspoken than the Democratic one on the need for revising immigration laws, but the Republican candidate, General Eisenhower, asserted emphatically that "the McCarran Immigration Law must be rewritten." After the

Republican victory, the Committee tried discreetly to press the president to make good his campaign pledge. It was a difficult task, since AJC's major government contacts over the past two decades had been primarily with Democrats. In April 1953 Irving M. Engel, a liberal Democrat, approached Senator Robert Taft on the matter. Taft informed Engel that the administration had discarded any plan for revision of the national-origins formula and denied that either Eisenhower or Vice-President Richard M. Nixon had advocated such revision during the campaign. Engel then asked Rabbi Abba Hillel Silver, the Zionist leader and a close associate of the new president, to intervene with Eisenhower; but Silver refused to listen to suggestions from the organization which had walked out of the American Jewish Conference in 1943 and NCRAC in 1952.

Its political channels ineffective, the Committee turned to mobilizing enough public sentiment to force the hand of the administration. Lehman planned a new omnibus bill in 1953 and asked the Committee's help in garnering nonpartisan and interdenominational support. The Jewish groups helped draft the bill and organized an intensified educational campaign. The Committee also sought support of Catholic and Protestant leaders, who originally had preferred to emphasize emergency legislation. In 1953, however, the Catholics shifted their strategy and joined in opposing the McCarran-Walter act.

The Committee also initiated projects to build up effective umbrella organizations. The Joint Conference on Alien Legislation no longer existed, and cooperation with Jewish organizations had become more difficult ever since the Committee and the Anti-Defamation League resigned from the NCRAC. (However, a so-called Nonauspices Committee enabled the Jewish groups to consult informally on immigration.) To facilitate cooperation among all organizations—Jewish and non-Jewish, national and local—that were interested in immigration, AJC helped establish the American Immigration Conference. (In 1960 the conference merged with the National Council of Naturalization and Citizenship to become the American Immigration and Citizenship Conference.) And in 1955 the Committee organized influential individuals in a National Commission on Immigration and Citizenship in order to give prestige to the campaign. All these groups studied immigration laws, disseminated information to the public, presented testimony to Congress, and planned other appropriate action.

Despite these varied efforts it was difficult to break through the widespread public apathy. General interest in immigration faded after the 1952 election, especially when Congress adopted a series of bills making the McCarran-Walter act less stringent and broadening the category of nonquota aliens. There was little hope of abolishing the national-origins formula as long as Congressman Francis E. Walter maintained his control of the House Immigration Subcommittee, and the liberals grew weary, particularly as civil rights problems clamored for attention. The case for immigration reform, explained one AJC staff member in 1964, suffered from "tired blood."

Nevertheless, the Committee refused to give up the fight. Though it supported piecemeal reform, it continued to emphasize that such measures fell short of the desired goal. Through resolutions, statements, and publications—from a cartoon pamphlet to a reprinted speech by Senator John F. Kennedy—it worked to keep the issue alive. It continued to press for liberal planks on immigration during election years, and whenever a chance for reform arose it alerted chapters and individuals to work toward that end. There were no immediate or dramatic results; but AJC's dogged campaign in conjunction with like-minded organizations ultimately prodded the Kennedy and Johnson administrations to action. Thirteen years after the passage of the McCarran-Walter act, the Immigration Act of 1965 finally erased the racist national-origins quota system. When President Lyndon B. Johnson signed the new law he observed that it "repairs a deep and painful flaw in the fabric of American justice."

VII

Anti-Semites tried hard to capitalize on the Jewish involvement in the immigration fight. Their efforts to join forces with the restrictionists, the isolationists, the anti-UN and anti-progressive-education camps pointed up a significant change in tactics. The bigotry and anti-Semitism of the 1930s—"exposés" of Jewish conspiracies to dominate the country and the world—had been discredited by World War II and the fall of Hitler. To command an audience, anti-Semites had to work through respectable fronts and respectable public issues. Thus Allen Zoll, whose National Council for American Education spearheaded the attack on the public schools, was a Ph.D., and John Beaty, whose book *Iron Curtain over America* repeatedly slurred the Jews, was a professor of English literature at Southern Methodist University. Anti-Semites were also spending more money than before. Newsletters and pamphlets remained the chief outlets for their poison, but their skills in printing and distribution improved over the years.

True, there were still a few old-line anti-Semites like Gerald L.K. Smith, Conde McGinley, and Gerald B. Winrod; and as long as the lunatic fringe existed, the lunatic charges persisted as well: that fluoridation of the water supply was a Jewish plot; that Adolf Eichmann was a martyr; that Jews had plotted the assassination of President Kennedy. But, as the American Jewish Committee's fact-finding division reported in the early 1950s, the graver threat was posed by the "mixed-line" groups like Merwin K. Hart's National Economic Council, whose anti-Semitism was insinuated into an ultraconservative economic and political line which won significant financial support from respectable businessmen and corporations. Equally threatening were such groups as the American Friends of the Middle East, whose specific purpose predisposed them to infiltration by professional anti-Semites.

The change brought new problems for Jewish defense, but it also reflected the successes of the defense agencies. Their educational programs, interreligious activities, and projects with special-interest groups had helped create a climate in which Jew-baiting was no longer respectable. Their ability to deal with troublemakers before serious crises erupted had forced the more blatant bigots to disband or go underground. In 1945, for example, when the American Jewish Committee learned that Senator Robert Rice Reynolds of North Carolina was planning to organize an American Nationalist party which would probably fuse the important anti-Semitic elements of the country, it alerted the Scripps-Howard newspaper syndicate, which conducted its own investigation and printed a series of articles exposing this hate movement. The Committee distributed reprints of the articles, had them translated for the foreign-language press, and, with the help of the Better Business Bureau, cautioned a variety of business groups not to contribute to the new party. As a result, Reynolds dropped his plan, and a number of anti-Semites named in the articles grew more hesitant about renewing their operations.

That same year the Committee effectively discouraged attempts to revive the Christian Front street meetings. After one rabble-rousing meeting was held in the Queens section of New York City, the Committee demanded the arrest of the leaders and filed evidence leading to their conviction and imprisonment. Their arrest impeded the distribution of vast quantities of scurrilous literature, and the legal costs of the case impaired the future work of the would-be demagogues. The Committee also introduced the tactic of quarantining rabble-rousers with the "silent treatment." Convinced that irate editorials in local newspapers and picket lines of outraged Jews only gave the hatemongers the publicity they wanted, AJC urged well-meaning liberal groups to refrain from public attacks. The strategy succeeded, and even Gerald Smith complained that his audiences shrank when adverse publicity stopped. The American Nazi party leader, George Lincoln Rockwell, used "shock tactics" to end the silent treatment. His Nazi-like uniforms and salutes and his proposals that

American Jews be sent to gas chambers provoked widespread counterdemonstrations, which the media reported in detail. Many argued that by his exhortations to genocide Rockwell forfeited the right to free speech, but the Committee, officially at least, held fast to a civil libertarian position and continued to urge quarantine as the best response.

It was more difficult to deal with anti-Semites who cloaked themselves in respectability. Besides exploiting the general fear of communism and the public school and United Nations issues described earlier, they rallied to the anti-civil-rights movement and the Arab-sponsored anti-Israel campaign. Obviously, not everyone who attacked the United Nations, subscribed to Hart's newsletter, opposed the Supreme Court's decisions on desegregation, or condemned Israel's Sinai campaign was an anti-Semite; but the combination was far from unusual. (Officially, the Arabs were "anti-Zionist," not "anti-Jewish"; but Arab propagandists used the terms "Jew" and "Zionist" interchangeably and worked closely with American anti-Semitic agitators.)

To combat these forces, the Committee depended on public exposure in various forms: it made known the fact that certain groups were branded un-American by the government; it alerted community leaders to attempts by specific individuals to infiltrate respectable circles; it provided officers and stockholders of corporations with data about some of the unsavory groups they were subsidizing; and it helped gather evidence against anti-Semites who were breaking the law. Through such publications as *Anti-Semitic Activity in the United States* and *Bigotry in Action,* as well as through articles in its *American Jewish Year Book,* the Committee documented the facts about specific anti-Semites, their methods, and their activities.

The Committee also publicized the machinations of anti-Semites in Europe and their cooperation across national boundaries. In 1960 Jewish groups were alarmed by a wave of swastika-daubings and vandalism on synagogues, cemeteries, and other Jewish property in the United States and in several

European countries. Although intensive investigation failed to show the incidents to be part of any centralized plan, they confirmed the need for preparedness to meet unexpected crises and for fresh research into the motivations behind such outbreaks.

During the 1952 election campaign the Committee noted an alarming resurgence of bigotry. Until Truman announced that he would not be a candidate, his alleged partisanship to Jews was a favorite target of anti-Semites. They later shifted their attacks to Eisenhower, whose defeat of nazism and liberal Republican sponsorship made him unacceptable. Promoting the candidacy of General Douglas MacArthur, with Senator Robert Taft as their second choice, bigot groups flooded New Hampshire with literature during the primary election campaign, branding Eisenhower as a Jew, or at the very least a "dupe of international Jewry." Although Taft's organization repudiated the scurrilous pamphlets, the anti-Semitic attacks on Eisenhower persisted until the Republican national convention.

A statement prepared by the American Jewish Committee for signature by the three major faiths called on all candidates to repudiate appeals to racial, religious, and ethnic prejudices. The statement, essentially a fair campaign practices code, was endorsed by the chairmen of both the Democratic and Republican National Committees and widely distributed. Local communities were urged to set up watchdog committees to guard against violations of the code. The Committee sponsored similar statements in succeeding election years and urged their endorsement by candidates and other molders of public opinion. At the same time, AJC warned against unfounded accusations of prejudice by one candidate against another.

In the 1960 presidential campaign, the candidacy of John Kennedy made religion one of the important issues. The Committee reiterated its warnings against bigotry in elections, and, in a resolution that echoed Judge Proskauer's defense of Al Smith in 1928, it declared:

The American Jewish Committee opposes any religious test for public office. Throughout American history citizens of many racial, religious and ethnic backgrounds have held legislative, executive and judicial office with distinction, faithfully administering the laws and carrying out the will of the people. We urge that candidates for public office be considered on the basis of their individual qualifications and their individual positions on all public issues of concern to the American people.

The Committee was also disturbed by frequent references to a "Jewish vote," and when the *New York Times* in September 1960 carried a front-page story speculating on the possible impact of the "Jewish vote" on the Kennedy-Nixon contest, AJC immediately remonstrated that no Jewish bloc vote existed. Both candidates and the *Times* endorsed the Committee's position. Nevertheless, both parties continued to court the Jewish community; indeed, a Committee-sponsored study on the 1960 election showed that Jews, like other minorities, tended to vote for what they considered to be their group interests, and that Jews as a group, despite their socioeconomic advancement, remained more loyal to the Democratic party than did other ethnic groups.

In the early and middle sixties, the Committee focused a good deal of its domestic concern on the growing assertiveness of the radical Right—a composite of many different groups, including superpatriots, economic conservatives, segregationists, isolationists, and religious fundamentalists. Theirs was an "anti" program, based on what William S. White labeled sophisticated and complex "political nihilism." Unlike true conservatives, they rejected any compromise with laissez-faire capitalism and deliberately set about undermining public respect for government leadership and authority. They subscribed to a conspiracy theory of history: traitors and evildoers were leading the nation to communism and destruction.

Right-wingers had various forums: the revival rallies of the Reverend Billy Hargis and his Christian Crusade; the Americanism "schools" and seminars conducted by Dr. Fred Schwarz as part of his Christian Anti-Communist Crusade; the bookstores featuring superpatriot and anti-Semitic literature. The most active and widely known group was the John Birch Society, which in 1963 had a full-time staff of over 120 and a membership generally estimated at between fifty and a hundred thousand persons, cutting across socioeconomic classes and combining rural and fundamentalist elements with urban and business support. Birch Society members operated on the community level, infiltrating civic organizations and intimidating teachers, librarians, and public officials by threatening phone calls and letters, campaigns of censorship, and vilification.

The American Jewish Committee joined other civic and religious organizations in condemning the radical Right groups. Not only did their extremist programs threaten the growing liberalism in the nation, they also attracted anti-Semites and other bigots and provided them with a cloak of respectability. True, Birch leader Robert Welch and others publicly disavowed anti-Semitism; but most of them tolerated the support of anti-Semites and advertised and distributed anti-Semitic and racist literature.

In January 1962 the AJC executive board declared:

> We recognize the right of all citizens to be heard on any issue. But the extreme Rightists, no less than the Communists, go beyond this prerogative; they sow fear and dissension, spreading distrust of friend and neighbor. Ultra-Rightists cry "Communist" at everyone and everything they disagree with—be it support of the United Nations, economic aid to underdeveloped nations or the Supreme Court of the United States. . . .
>
> Indiscriminate name-calling and smearing of public officials, private citizens and even religious leaders are weapons long used by the Communists, past masters of the strategy of infiltration, capture and subversion. The purpose is to replace our rules of fair play and our free exchange of ideas with secrecy and subterfuge. Indeed, some of the extreme Rightists boast of it. In customary Communist style, they

NOT FREE TO DESIST **380**

pack meetings and outnumber, outshout and outlast their opponents; they create disguised front organizations to snare the innocent and trap the unwary; they are relentless in defamation and harassment. . . .

In times like these, we need conscientious citizens, eager to keep informed and ready to understand the increasingly complex affairs of our national and international situation. . . . The American people should be given the opportunity to learn from all—Republicans, Democrats, independents, liberals and conservatives. Honest debate informs, educates and invigorates us. We need knowledge and strength for the great tasks before us, dedication to the preservation of freedom and democratic processes.

At first the Committee's antiextremist program was limited to long-range educational efforts: it sought new ways to explain and define pressing international issues and to combat communism and other forms of totalitarianism; and it tried to reach rural and fundamentalist groups with its prodemocracy message. AJC decided that it would be ill advised for American Jews to wage a separate campaign. But when the National Council of Churches —a frequent target of the ultra Right—suggested joint deliberations, the Committee planned for a major conference.

Early in 1962 representatives of over one hundred leading organizations met at Greenwich, Connecticut, at a Conference on Preserving the Democratic Process. Reviewing the activities of extremist groups of both Left and Right, and their threat to the democratic tradition of open public debate and disagreement, the delegates underscored the need "to conserve the democratic processes whereby we can agree on how to disagree without disrupting the community upon which our survival as social beings depends." The conference members undertook to continue to work together, as a clearinghouse of information on extremists, and to encourage local and regional conferences to alert the public to the danger of extremism. Meanwhile, the Committee's Division of Trend Analyses intensified its own study of the methods and activities of the ultra Right.

In 1964 the radical Right groups threw their support behind the nomination of Barry Goldwater as Republican presidential candidate, and Goldwater refused to repudiate them. Many Committee leaders were convinced that their recurring nightmare about racists and bigots capturing a major American political party had become a reality. If the extremists remained in control of the Republican machinery, there was danger that antiliberalism and anti-Semitism would be permanently joined as a political force, in traditional European fashion. "The present situation," warned AJC leader David Sher, "is so grave and dangerous that our normal mode of operation has become inappropriate. So much is at stake in this decisive struggle, which may be compared with what happened in Europe a generation ago, that we must do far more than issue statements against bigotry and engage in activity directed against violations of fair play in campaigns."

However, there was little the Committee could do by way of counteraction. As a tax-exempt organization it could not engage in political activity; and in an election year even an attack on an extremist group could be labeled political if it were associated with a major political party. The Committee's usual strategy on important issues was to ally itself with other like-minded civic or religious groups. However, it was important to reach the respectable conservatives, such as the National Association of Manufacturers and the Chamber of Commerce, with whom the Committee had had relatively little contact.

The activities of the extremist groups following the Republican National Convention convinced the Committee of the need to concentrate on local, rather than national, counteraction. For it was in the local community that extremists were most effectively at work. In outlying rural areas, ultra Right groups captured the public forum through radio and TV discussion programs, speeches, and letter-writing campaigns. Citizens of the New York metropolitan area could dial a number to hear recorded rightist messages (one such message attacked Senator Jacob Javits as "a 100 percent pro-Communist"). In the Minneapolis–St. Paul region, critics of Goldwater were harassed by hate mail, crank calls, and anonymous threats.

To enable prodemocracy voices to be heard, AJC urged its chapters, particularly those in "Goldwater country," to help organize nonpartisan committees, representing prominent citizens of all political opinions, to guard the rules of democratic procedure and to assure all groups the freedom to debate and disagree without fear of intimidation. The committees served two purposes: they helped educate the communities on the nature of extremism and they monitored extremist propaganda in the rightists' literature, broadcasts, and campaign rallies. And the Committee staff prepared materials to back up community education programs.

The 1964 election campaign ended with an overwhelming victory for Lyndon B. Johnson, but extremism did not evaporate. Its persistence on the political scene doubtless encouraged American Jewry's disposition to support liberal causes. At the same time, it impelled organizations like the American Jewish Committee to remain watchful. And just as the pattern of extremism varied from community to community, so did the means chosen to combat it.

14

"You Know the Heart of a Stranger"

The civil rights movement that dominated American life in the postwar years was stimulated by factors as diverse as the New Deal's response to the Great Depression, Harlem's artistic awakening, the antiracist spirit of World War II, and the decline of colonialism in Africa and Asia. After the war, as C. Vann Woodward has written, "the downfall of the old order in race relations . . . moved into an accelerated phase, the pace and radicalism of which would justify calling it a 'Second Reconstruction.'"

Jewish identification with the cause of equal rights has long been consistent and conspicuous. Among those who signed the call for the creation of the NAACP in 1909 were Rabbis Stephen S. Wise and Emil G. Hirsch and social workers Lillian Wald and Henry Moskowitz. In the decade following World War II, when the cause of racial equality received top priority in the liberal community, Jews flocked in increasing numbers to the civil rights movement, and Jewish organizations initiated extensive programs of social action.

To the American Jewish Committee, social action meant the achievement of basic human rights through legal action, education, and community activities, to implement legislation and court decisions. It was a task requiring imagination and perseverance, and the Committee demonstrated how effectively a private institution could contribute to easing of intergroup tensions in a modern industrialized state.

I

In May 1946 the American Jewish Committee's executive debated the broad issue of social action. Should AJC stimulate its constituency to participate actively within the political forum? Should a Jewish organization take a stand on such matters as poll taxes and price controls? The questions were not purely academic; the American Jewish Congress had already plunged into a social-action program, the NCRAC had created a legislative committee to deal with such issues, and a growing number of American Jews were deeply involved in various social causes. The Committee's failure to align itself with the liberal forces could jeopardize its leadership in the community. The activists on the executive committee favored broadening the Committee's concerns. Freedom and security were indivisible, they argued, and AJC had a responsibility to work for the rights of all groups. Their opponents, however, convinced the majority that Jews were not justified in acting as a bloc with regard to social legislation. Only issues of primary concern to Jews, the executive decided, should come within the Committee's scope.

The decision was fully in line with Committee tradition. When AJC mounted a successful campaign to prohibit discrimination in places of public accommodation in 1913, it was motivated by resort hotel advertisements stating that Jews were unwelcome; the corrective legislation "was urged in the interest of the equality of all citizens before the law." In 1946, too, the first impetus for Committee action was to protect the rights of Jews. But since primary concern did not mean exclusive concern, and since issues like fair-practices legislation involved Jews along with other groups, the Committee could move into the area of racial inequality.

Strictly speaking, John Slawson went beyond the executive's mandate when, in testimony before President Truman's Committee on Civil Rights in May 1947, he stressed the need to fuse the educational and legal approaches to further the cause of civil rights. In both areas, Slawson declared, it was up to the federal government to take the initiative with laws assuring fair employment, fair education, and fair housing, and to inspire the states to follow suit. Among his suggestions for new federal legislation Slawson included outlawing the poll tax and providing safeguards against lynchings. (Before Slawson's testimony, the Committee had limited itself to the promotion of fair-employment and fair-educational practices and to litigation contesting restrictive covenants in housing.)

Two weeks before the president's committee issued its report, *To Secure These Rights,* the AJC executive committee again considered the agency's involvement in social action, in response to an invitation from the NAACP to join with prominent civic, labor, and religious groups to secure passage of an antilynching bill by the Eightieth Congress. In 1934, when the country was in the depths of an economic depression and Jewish attention was riveted on Germany, AJC had contributed money to the NAACP for the same purpose. Now the Committee was asked to do more —to rally its members in support of legislation to put an end to an evil directed primarily against another minority group.

More significant than its antilynching resolution was the executive committee's formal commitment, with no dissent from southern members, to minority causes not specifically Jewish:

> It is resolved that the Executive Committee recognizes that there is the closest relation between the protection of the civil rights of all citizens and the protection of the civil rights of the members of particular groups; that it is a proper

exercise of the powers of our Charter that the American Jewish Committee join with other groups in the protection of the civil rights of the members of all groups irrespective of race, religion, color or national origin; and that it is our general policy so to do.

The isolated precedents of the past—the Committee's amicus curiae brief in the Oregon parochial-school case and the case involving the rights of Armenians to naturalization—had blossomed into fixed policy.

The Committee plotted its social-action program cautiously. Unlike the American Jewish Congress, which had made civil rights and social action its chief domestic activity, the Committee viewed these concerns as an extension of its traditional human-relations program. Outlawing discrimination was very important and the passage of fair-employment practice laws had educational value as well, but neither necessarily made a man like his neighbor any better. The Committee stressed the need for enforcement of existing laws at least as much as the need for new ones. It involved itself in court cases very selectively, and then only after all possibility of negotiation had been exhausted. AJC never deliberately created opportunities for court action; indeed, it rarely entered a case until the litigation had reached a higher court. Amicus curiae briefs, for the most part, are less important for their legal aspect than for linking the sponsor's prestige to a specific issue. Before becoming involved, the Committee would consider what it had to offer to the specific cause, who its allies would be, and how its actions could affect Jews. Most important, the issue had to dovetail with the needs and desires of the local community concerned.

Such a selective approach had certain disadvantages: it lacked the element of daring which could inspire Negro gratitude or prompt Jewish financial contributions; and it often exposed AJC to the criticism of doing "too little and too late." On the other hand, the Committee's ad hoc involvement prevented it from becoming merely a Jewish branch of the American Civil Liberties Union. The Committee was not prepared to sacrifice its pragmatic approach for a doctrinaire devotion to civil rights, or the totality of its interests for a specific, though crucial, area of concern. Its emphasis on grass-roots involvement also somewhat limited the national office thrust but made for a more alert and active constituency in the long run.

II

After the president's Committee on Civil Rights issued its historic report in 1947, the American Jewish Committee launched a broad educational campaign to gain acceptance of the report's recommendations, preparing a wide variety of materials on the evils of racial and religious discrimination. Both nationally and through the chapters it strove for four main goals: equality of housing, employment, public accommodations, and education. Although the rights of Jews as well as Negroes were involved in each of those areas, the kind of discrimination suffered by the two groups was quite different. Jews, for example, encountered quotas limiting their admission to medical schools; blacks faced segregated or inferior education at all levels. Jews were barred from many expensive Park Avenue apartments; Negroes faced restrictions in publicly supported housing. Qualified Jews were excluded from top-level jobs in business and the professions; Negroes were prevented from acquiring training and skills which would raise them from menial employment and were paid at a rate below that of whites for any skills they had acquired. The Committee often dealt with the less blatant anti-Jewish prejudice by suasion and high-level contacts, but the overt anti-Negro prejudice required more direct legal and social action.

During this period the Committee's civil rights guideline was *fair* rather than *full* employment, housing, and education—*equal* access to jobs, without discrimination against any race or creed, for example, rather than the creation of new jobs. In the field of education, however, it quickly became clear that "fair" was not enough and that inadequate facilities were an important factor in perpetuating discriminatory policies. Thus the Committee decided to advocate federal aid to education, although it continued to give higher priority to the fair-practices goal.

In each of the four major areas, the Committee utilized several tactics simultaneously: it promoted appropriate legislation; took part in significant litigation; pressed for stronger administrative agencies; advised public officials, Jewish communities, and private organizations; and directed popular educational programs. A sample of its activities in behalf of fair employment—which included hiring, promotion, compensation, and working conditions—illustrates AJC's variegated methods. In separate states and municipalities it assigned special field workers who, alongside the local chapters, helped in the campaigns for local Fair Employment Practices Commissions (FEPC). It drafted model FEP bills and prepared supporting testimony for FEP advocates. It joined other groups in studying the effects of discrimination in employment, and it wrote pamphlets on the economic benefits of fair employment, addressed to both business and labor. In collaboration with unions, AJC publicized progress toward fair employment and advised workers of their rights under federal and local FEP statutes. When the authority of the New York and Connecticut FEP Commissions was challenged, the Committee filed amicus curiae briefs in their support. The favorable decisions by the courts in both cases meant acceptance of the fact that the burden of contesting discrimination was transferred from the aggrieved party to a state agency. In another case entered by the Committee, the Connecticut courts went further and held that the contempt-of-court sanction could be invoked to enforce the state commission's ruling.

To aid the drive for a national FEPC, the Committee testified before congressional committees, prepared fact sheets and radio materials for public dissemination, and participated in projects initiated by the National Council for a Permanent FEPC. Its

Washington office made background material available to congressmen and senators and carefully followed the progress of the proposed federal legislation. AJC also worked closely with the president's Committee on Government Contracts during the Truman and Eisenhower administrations, providing information and suggestions on how to reduce discrimination in the hiring and promotion practices of the hundreds of contractors doing business with the government.

Convinced that civil rights progress would only come through cooperative action by a wide variety of influential organizations, the Committee sought working alliances for specific goals with groups ranging from the Southern Regional Conference to the American Legion. AJC also advocated greater federal involvement in the drives for fair employment, housing, and education. It urged the creation of a strong civil rights division in the Department of Justice and legislation to establish a permanent federal commission on civil rights. Congress had done nothing to advance the cause of civil rights since 1875, and liberal forces had little immediate hope of moving beyond the limited progress made possible by President Truman's executive order on fair employment until the Senate cloture rules were revised. Although organizations like the Committee pressed both major parties on civil rights, southern filibusters blocked significant congressional action. The dramatic breakthrough came from the courts.

III

In May 1954 a unanimous Supreme Court scrapped the "separate but equal" doctrine which had given legal sanction to racial segregation in the public schools for close to sixty years. The decision in *Brown* v. *Board of Education of Topeka* declared that, even if the physical facilities provided for black children were substantially equal, segregation made for inequality and put a stamp of inferiority on the segregated child. Segregated schooling, the court ruled, therefore violated the equal-protection clause of the Fourteenth Amendment. In support of its position on the psychological damage of segregation, the court cited a study by Negro sociologist Kenneth Clark, commissioned by the American Jewish Committee as a resource paper for the 1950 White House Conference on Children and Youth. AJC's amicus brief in the *Brown* case, subscribed to by five other organizations, made the same point:

> The unchallenged finding that segregation irreparably damages the child lifts this case out of the murky realm of speculation on the issue of "equality" of facilities, into the area of certainty that segregation and equality cannot co-exist. That which is unequal in fact cannot be equal in law.

The *Brown* decision and the Supreme Court's ruling a year later that desegregation was to proceed "with all deliberate speed" met with massive resistance in the South. A resurgent Ku Klux Klan, newly organized White Citizens Councils, the National Association for the Advancement of White People, the White Brotherhood of Atlanta, and the Southern Gentlemen of Louisiana were a few of the groups that mobilized to perpetuate racial inequality. Southern governors resurrected the early nineteenth-century doctrine of interposition and looked for other pseudolegal ways to circumvent the Supreme Court's decision. An economic boycott threatened Negroes who demanded desegration; lynching—which had virtually disappeared by 1950—returned. The South grew bolder as the country turned more conservative in the wake of McCarthyism. The segregationists' attacks on the Supreme Court were echoed by those groups which objected to the court's rulings in states'-rights and national-security cases. And in the White House the president remained passive for over three years, explaining that he did not believe one could change men's hearts by law.

Herbert H. Lehman told the American Jewish Committee at

its fiftieth anniversary meeting that the same forces of repression and fear which had threatened the foundations of liberty during the McCarthy era now focused on civil rights. And he called on the Committee to meet the challenge: "[All] who know that when the rights of any individual or group of individuals are violated, the rights of all are threatened, must now mobilize their supreme efforts for the struggle. . . . All who would live in freedom and who would struggle for it must come forward now."

Lehman's appeal had immediate relevance, for AJC's civil rights program was under attack by its southern members. The rumblings had begun in 1955, when the Committee published a report on European reactions to the lynching of a Negro boy in the South. At the annual meeting in January 1956 the southern members succeeded in preventing the publicizing of a resolution on civil rights. A special meeting between several national officers and thirty leading southern members was arranged for March, to deal with the possibility of mass resignations.

The resistance of AJC's southern members to its involvement with civil rights came more from fear than conviction. True, there were some southern Jews who believed in the separation of the races; but the prime concern of the southern members was that Jewish support for civil rights would create anti-Semitism among the segregationists.

Jews in the South constituted less than one percent of the total population. Within the homogeneous white Protestant society, Morris B. Abram of Atlanta pointed out, southern Jews had long been accepted as "honorary white Protestants," and they had responded by conforming to the standard of that society. After the Supreme Court's decision, they were expected to take their stand with the "white South." Southern Jews were afraid to raise a dissenting voice, and they worried that the opinions and actions of other Jews would be ascribed to them.

The spread of the White Citizens Council movement exacerbated Jewish fears. Jews were pressed to join local councils even though a number of the councils coupled their attacks on desegregation with anti-Semitism. (In Birmingham, Alabama, there were two units of the White Citizens Council, one for anti-Semites and one for others.) Aided and abetted by bigots and rabble-rousers throughout the country, the White Citizens Councils distributed anti-Semitic literature and revived age-old anti-Jewish canards. The *Protocols of the Elders of Zion,* Beaty's *Iron Curtain over America,* and Conde McGinley's *Common Sense* were widely quoted, and desegregation was denounced as a diabolical plot engineered by Zionists, Jew/Communists, the Jewish-led NAACP, and other Zionist-Trotskyite "Mixie-crats" (race-mixers) for the "mongrelization" of the races. The Jewish southerners had reason to worry. In 1957 and 1958 bombs were planted in seven southern synagogues. In 1959 John G. Crommelin, a retired admiral, ran for mayor of Montgomery, Alabama, on an overtly anti-Semitic platform and polled 10 percent of the vote in the primary. A year later he received 13 percent of the votes in the senatorial primary.

The influence of the White Citizens Councils reached beyond the lunatic fringe. Councils drew more support from the cities than from the rural areas usually associated with the Ku Klux Klan. They worked to infiltrate union locals and made common cause with all kinds of ultraconservative groups. And as Negro citizens began to assert themselves—in the Montgomery bus boycott of 1955, for example—the White Citizens Councils grew in membership and support.

In the policy-making circles of AJC, southern Jews argued that Jewish identification with the cause of desegregation jeopardized their own positions. Such activity, they said, would also prompt southern politicans to withhold their support on matters of direct Jewish interest, such as aid to Israel. (One AJC member warned that sustained civil rights activity by Jewish organizations would result in Jews being "driven out" of the South.) A few southern stalwarts like Harry Golden of Charlotte, North Carolina, and Morris Abram insisted that AJC continue to support desegregation on moral and tactical grounds; but the majority of southerners pleaded for the Committee to move very slowly. They did not deny that the Supreme Court decision was the law of the land and that it was important to oppose the lawless fringe. But they insisted that southern moderates could find the answers if the North did not try to force immediate desegregation upon the South. Furthermore, they pointed out, since northern schools were segregated too, in fact if not in law, northerners could hardly justify their holier-than-thou attitude. The Committee's posture, the southerners argued, must be one of moderation, and its activities discreet, unpublicized, and coupled with those of many other organizations, so that civil rights would not be interpreted as primarily a Jewish cause. Southern members should be consulted on policy decisions affecting the South, they urged, and the Committee should dissociate itself from the NAACP, at least from the latter's "aggressive" campaigns.

This pressure did not deflect the Committee from its civil rights program. Although the Committee agreed to consult with the southerners on policy, it refused to repudiate its underlying commitments to full equality. At a meeting in New Orleans in 1958, Judge Proskauer, by then the Committee's elder statesman, reminded the executive board that he was born in the South and was steeped in its tradition, but that the Committee's tradition of defending human freedom ranked higher: "I would not ask the Committee to recede from its fundamental thesis that no man is free unless all men are free." President Irving M. Engel, another southerner by birth, also rejected a moral retreat:

> I do *not* share the wistful belief held by some that if only Jews and Jewish organizations would say nothing and do nothing in this situation, the trouble would somehow magically depart. . . . Whether *we* will it or not, whether *we* join it or not, an intense conflict is under way and will remain under way until it is resolved. And while it is under way Jews —North and South—are exceedingly vulnerable. . . . Out of tragic experience our generation certainly has learned one lesson and learned it well: Jews cannot buy security *or* status

for themselves in an atmosphere where injustice is tolerated, or even worse, is sanctioned. For this is the paradox: if one seeks security alone, it will never be attained. It *must* come as the by-product of a society that holds in highest esteem all human rights, all human dignity. . . . We realize all too well the powerlessness of reasonable men in many Southern communities today. We are aware that in some communities individuals who urge nothing more than compliance with the law have lost their pulpits, their jobs, their customers, their credit. We know that in some places anyone who dares to suggest a practical and reasonable approach to the problem of desegregation is likely to be overwhelmed with abuse, charged with being a dangerous leftist, or worse. . . .

The anti-Semite, due to his very nature, will attack the Jew whether he speaks or whether he is silent. . . . Even those Jews who have joined White Citizens Councils have not thereby gained immunity. . . . *No* American has the right to turn away from these issues. And no Jew *dare* remain indifferent to them. For these are the very values and ideals that have made possible our freedom and our flourishing here in America. . . . Not all of us can be fighting soldiers in the front line of every battle, but each of us can expect and require of our organizations and our leadership that they, at least, stand visibly on the side of right. As an organization we *must* be prepared to join and to work in good faith with the many responsible individuals and organizations in the North and in the South who are today in search of honorable solutions for exceedingly difficult problems. To do less would be to assume voluntarily the status of of second class citizens, to forfeit our right, because we are Jews, to speak up as Americans in behalf of principles essential to our own and our country's welfare.

Engel reminded his fellow members that, in light of their own history, Jews had perhaps a greater responsibility to the civil rights movement than did other Americans. And Morris Abram quoted Scripture to his fellow southerners: "For you know the heart of a stranger, seeing you were strangers in the land of Egypt."

Within two years after the Supreme Court's 1954 ruling a considerable number of school districts in the border states, and even in some areas farther south, had been desegregated. But by 1957 voluntary compliance with the court's order had reached its limit. Until desegregation was translated into political policy, and the administration acted to unite the pro-Supreme-Court sentiment in the country, the dissenters would successfully block further implementation. Had the Eisenhower administration been moved by the same moral imperatives as the AJC leaders, the pace of desegregation might have been dramatically increased. And if the administration had fully backed the Warren court's ruling, AJC would have had considerably fewer problems with its southern constituency.

In an unpublicized statement transmitted privately to officials in Washington in May 1956, AJC appealed to the administration to exert its leadership in behalf of desegregation:

> We believe that the people in all sections of the country can be induced to respond to this leadership.
> We fear the absence of this leadership may well create a vacuum in which irresponsible conduct will prevail. This could only serve to make eventual resolution of the issue more difficult, and the intervening period chaotic and perhaps tragic. . . .
> All influence of our country's civic, political, business and religious leaders should be exerted to aid law-abiding citizens in complying with the law, and to furnish encouragement for the attainment of desegregation "with all deliberate speed."
> As the first and most important step . . . the President should summon, at the earliest possible moment, the most influential citizens from all parts of the country and all walks of life, to confer on this problem in all its aspects.

If Congress was not prepared to strengthen and expand existing civil rights statutes, the statement concluded, then the president should take the lead by appointing a bipartisan commission to facilitate school desegregation. But neither these recommendations, nor later suggestions for a presidential conference on educational problems relating to desegregation and for a presidential conference on law and order, were acted upon. To be sure, the Eisenhower administration successfully sponsored the Civil Rights Act of 1957 and one in 1960, but to be effective these watered-down measures required a zealous interpretation of their enforcement provisions. The American Jewish Committee missed no opportunity to urge stronger administrative procedures to augment the legislation. But it was clear that the task of mobilizing public support for desegregation rested with nongovernmental agencies.

In the absence of strong political leadership, the Committee moved to tackle the problem of maintaining law and order in the South. (In the 1950s the call for law and order came from those who urged compliance with the orders of the Supreme Court as the law of the land, and had not as yet assumed racist overtones.) The major aim was to convince leaders to spearhead the drive against lawlessness and, in cooperation with like-minded religious and civic groups, to influence the power structure in their local communities. AJC established a regional office in Atlanta. It also enlisted the cooperation of influential businessmen and industrialists to help convince southern business leaders that racial conflict was a serious economic liability.

The Committee distributed fact sheets and pamphlets identifying the various hate groups in the South, and material defending the Supreme Court's decision. It shared its data on southern anti-Semites and other bigots with law-enforcement officials. (Though it preferred the silent treatment for bigots, AJC occasionally decided that exposure was better than quarantine. John Kasper, a favorite of the neo-Fascists and anti-Semites, found himself under careful surveillance by Florida and Tennessee authorities after the Committee turned the spotlight on his rabble-rousing activities.) The Committee worked closely with southern organizations in its investigations and, in cooperation with the

Southern Regional Conference, prepared a study of over five hundred instances of racial violence. AJC emphasized to newsmen, radio and TV columnists, and the general public that all these violent acts—including the synagogue bombings—were an American rather than a Negro or Jewish problem.

Since the Supreme Court rulings were the law of the land, not only the flouting of its decisions, but also the economic harassment of Negroes demanding their rights and the attacks on the NAACP for supporting those demands were all lawless acts. The Committee quietly advanced funds to help Negroes whose credit sources were choked off and to save the one integrationist, anti-Klan, anti-White Citizens Council newspaper in Mississippi. It also helped the NAACP and the Urban League resist legislative and economic pressure, and filed an amicus brief in the case of *NAACP* v. *Alabama,* when the state tried to seize the NAACP's membership lists and to intimidate it in other ways. Pressure from its southern members, however, kept AJC from joining in the litigation involving a Quaker desegregationist in Virginia. And when moderates in several states organized "save our schools" movements to resist the closing of public schools for the purpose of thwarting integration, the Committee only endorsed their efforts unofficially. (When asked if synagogues and Jewish centers should make their facilities available where public schools were closed, AJC merely advised that such facilities not be used for segregated classes.)

The maintenance of law and order was only the first step in the Committee's program. When the danger of violence subsided, local communities were encouraged to create voluntary intergroup councils which could work to restore communication between the races and establish an atmosphere of mutual trust and cooperation in which the school desegregation issue could be tackled. AJC chapters cooperated closely with such community councils and worked also with other organizations and coalition groups, particularly the Consultative Council on Desegregation, to provide information about the techniques of peaceful desegregation. These programs were particularly successful in Miami, Atlanta, and Dallas.

The following report from the Committee's Atlanta office describes some typical chapter activities:

> Perhaps our most significant, and certainly our most expensive contribution, was in the field of human relations education. . . . The Atlanta Chapter sent three Atlanta teachers to the Boston University Workshop in Human Relations. Each is a member of the faculty of one of the high schools chosen for desegregation. . . . Extensive use of the skills and insights developed at the Workshop is being made by the teachers with their respective faculties. . . .
>
> After a long and fruitful conference with [A], officer-in-charge of the Security Detail in the Detective Division [of the Atlanta police], [B] continued to feed me material which I then passed on to [A], thereby consolidating our position as an important source upon which he could rely. In recent days I have been in almost constant contact with both . . . as the anti-Semites began converging on Atlanta from all points of the compass. . . .
>
> We have had the kind of Chapter leadership particularly qualified to influence power structure thinking, and secure enough to bring its influence to bear. A substantial number have used personal and business contacts to good advantage. . . .
>
> On another level, . . . a great deal of time and effort [went] into the Junior Chamber of Commerce which became the first civic or service club related to the business community to declare publicly for open schools, an important breakthrough at the time. . . .
>
> Among those publicly listed Organizations Assisting Schools in September (OASIS) is the Atlanta Chapter, American Jewish Committee. . . . The Civic and Service Section [of OASIS] arranged discussion groups among parents in various parts of the city. Many women in the Chapter served as discussion leaders, others as hostesses in this program. In the Religious Section I served on the Resources Committee preparing material sent to the churches, the thrust of which was to assist them in preparing their own

congregants for peaceful desegregation and to exercise a constructive influence in the community at large. Out of this effort came the "Weekend of Prayer for Law and Order" observed by literally hundreds of churches, and the Laymen's Manifesto signed by 850 Protestant, Catholic and Jewish Laymen (including Chapter officers and Board members) a piece designed to compliment the earlier Ministers' Manifestoes.

IV

While focusing on the South in the aftermath of the *Brown* decision, the Committee continued to work for equality in housing, employment, and public accommodation—all of which had also been affected by the Supreme Court ruling. In the North, school segregation reflected residential patterns, and nonsegregated housing was a prerequisite for desegregated schools. After 1954 the Committee broadened its objectives to cover private housing and de facto segregation in northern schools. As its activities expanded, AJC found itself grappling with some important questions: Did the obligation to desegregate require only opening the doors to black students, or did it include a responsibility to promote integration actively? Was integration important enough as an educational and social goal to support gerrymandering in reverse (which in effect would negate the court's "color-blindness")? Did Professor James Conant's call for the intensive enrichment of inferior schools promise greater practical advantages than token integration through such devices as busing?

AJC's national office gave considerable autonomy to its chapters in handling local school problems, but in 1959 it set the following minimum goals: (1) schools should provide programs of intergroup education; (2) inferior schools must be improved to insure equal educational opportunities; (3) school districts drawn for the purpose of excluding minorities should be changed; and (4) where a school board had a reasonable choice "in accordance with acceptable criteria," school sites should be chosen to further an integrated school population. Some chapters set more ambitious goals; New York, for example, urged that integration be made a paramount criterion in school zoning.

In the next five years, against a background of growing racial tension, AJC national policy statements endorsed crash programs to aid deprived schools and continued to stress public-school integration.

V

The early 1960s marked a turning point in the civil rights movement. The sit-ins and freedom rides heralded a new militancy on the part of black youth. Both presidential candidates in the 1960 elections committed themselves to combatting segregation, and in the next few years President Kennedy and his successor, President Johnson, led a bipartisan consensus which chalked up impressive legislative accomplishments. In the South massive resistance to school desegregation crumbled, and a variety of public accommodations were desegregated. By 1965 Jim Crow was legally dead.

The American Jewish Committee welcomed the new manifestations of national leadership. It eagerly responded to White House calls to help plan and participate in conferences on civil rights, and to the programs of the Community Relations Service (the conciliation agency created by the Civil Rights Act of 1964). Encouraged by the administration's commitment to social change, the Committee made numerous suggestions for federal action to achieve equal rights. At the same time it sought to stimulate new scientific research on race relations, in order to substitute dispassionate knowledge for the "crisis" orientation of policy-makers. In 1963 AJC convened a conference of social scientists on the subject; Gunnar Myrdal, who two decades earlier had written *The American Dilemma,* the classic racial study, was one of the prominent scholars who participated.

The AJC executive board officially endorsed "appropriate" forms of direct protest to highlight the fact that gradualism was no longer an adequate technique for achieving equality. As the sit-ins by black students captured the nation's headlines, AJC underscored the urgency of conciliation, moderation, and new channels of interracial communications. When the freedom riders of 1961 were greeted with violence in Alabama and Mississippi, the Committee condemned the brutal mob action. John Slawson spoke up firmly: "There are times in our struggle to protect our civil rights when we must take chances and test the constitutionality of barriers that have neither legal nor moral basis." The Committee supported the historic August 1963 March for Jobs and Freedom: "Peaceful demonstrations are a proper and, indeed, characteristically American means of petitioning Government for the redress of grievances and for fulfilling rights guaranteed to all Americans." AJC members participated in the march with representatives of other religious and civic organizations. Although several members questioned the wisdom of such involvement, the Committee assessed the massive outpouring for the demonstration as a victory for the moderates and a successful show of support for President Kennedy's civil rights bill.

Responding to a request from Dr. Martin Luther King, Jr., in 1964 the Committee involved itself even more actively in the civil rights march from Selma to Montgomery, Alabama. Staff members helped with publicity and planning. (The helicopters guarding the march against would-be snipers were an AJC suggestion to the Justice Department.) Orin Lehman, secretary of AJC, led a delegation in the final leg of the march, and TV coverage showed the marchers under a banner inscribed FREEDOM IS EVERYBODY'S BUSINESS. Other AJC chapters participated in sympathy marches in Washington and in their own communities. In perspective, these demonstrations marked a new type of protest acceptable to society and to the Committee. Thirty years had passed since AJC refused to sanction the milder tactic of mass meetings called to expose the condition of the Jews in Nazi Germany.

The recurrent race riots which erupted in the ghettos of many northern cities in the mid-sixties caused widespread injury, destruction, and anger. The Committee, together with many other local and national groups, examined and exposed the underlying causes of the violence. The Philadelphia chapter commissioned a study of a riot-affected community; AJC published it under the title *Case Study of a Riot: The Philadelphia Story* and gave it wide distribution. It highlighted the poor housing, education and employment patterns, abrasive police-community relations, and other deep-seated problems, and recommended positive action programs for their solution.

New needs were met by the Committee with a new phase of civil rights activity. Its goal, declared Slawson, was "to graduate in our thinking from human rights to human relations." It had become more and more obvious that there would be no real equality until there were enough jobs, homes, and classrooms for all who needed them. The emphasis therefore shifted from *fair* to *full* employment, housing, and education; and in 1964 AJC joined a number of Catholic and Protestant organizations in an ambitious antipoverty program.

The Committee was convinced, however, that the integration of blacks could be achieved only by building mutual respect and understanding between the races, and by enlisting all groups —including teachers, real-estate owners, union members, and policemen—in the black community's struggle for social justice. In 1966 the Committee established a Department of Education and Urban Programming to advance the cause of human relations through city planning and community development.

Meanwhile, AJC continued its emphasis on the employment and training of minority group workers. In the summer of 1963, following the racial violence in Birmingham, President Kennedy called on a number of religious and business leaders, among them Committee members, to help promote racial equality and intergroup harmony. The Committee responded by convening a pioneering conference of over one hundred Jewish business leaders from every section of the country to discuss the recruitment, training, and upgrading of Negro workers. The participants avoided platitudinous speeches and turned their attention to the problem of integrating black and other minority-group workers into the general labor force. They agreed that business would have to make decisions to implement social goals; that locating qualified or potentially qualified Negroes required persistence and a willingness to invest time and money; that quotas and preferential treatment were undesirable, except for special training to raise qualifications; that the smooth integration of blacks into previously all-white work forces called for expert personnel leadership and sensitization of both groups of workers. Agencies like the American Jewish Committee, it was agreed, could help by providing human-relations expertise, stimulating Negro organizations to emphasize educational programs for their people, and encouraging Jewish businessmen to support interracial job-training projects.

Though the business conference was far less dramatic than the March for Jobs and Freedom which took place one month later, it had important results of its own. It touched off a series of local and regional business meetings to discuss employment opportunities for nonwhites and stimulated a number of AJC chapters into organizing businessmen's committees and equal-opportunity councils. Under the direction of a specially created Commission on Race Relations, the AJC national office and the chapters promoted training programs for minority groups and for personnel interviewers, helped find summer jobs for teen-agers, worked to establish more realistic aptitude tests for employment, and cooperated in opening up business opportunities for small businessmen.

NOT FREE TO DESIST

In some of these ventures, the Committee worked with government agencies; but in most cases its programs were ahead of the government's, and its efforts often provided guideposts for later government undertakings. The Committee worked with the labor unions to open up apprenticeships for minorities, and it joined with the Urban League and the Randolph Institute to train young blacks so they could pass the tests required of would-be apprentices. It served on the National Interreligious Advisory Committee on Project Equality, a program promoting fair-employment practices by religious groups and by firms with which they did business. After the 1965 Watts riot, the Southern California Merit Employment Conference, initiated and staffed by the Committee, arranged to have a dozen corporations (including General Motors, Douglas Aircraft, and the California Retailers Association) send employment interviewers into the area. As a result, several hundred unemployed men and women found jobs.

The net effect of all these efforts to shape social thought and resolve racial tensions cannot be accurately measured. But there is no doubt they helped open new job opportunities for many thousands of nonwhite workers.

VI

In less than twenty years the American Jewish Committee had changed from a cautious partner to a creative pioneer in the civil rights movement. Its new and far-flung commitments came about in part as a natural consequence of involvement and of new currents within the civil rights movement. But the new role also reflected a change in Committee membership. The typical Committee member of the 1960s was younger, less affluent, more liberal in politics than his 1940s counterpart. He was drawn to the organization by a serious concern with social problems rather than the notion of a Jewish noblesse oblige. The newer members worried less about whether particular issues legitimately came within the jurisdiction of a Jewish organization; for them, and thus for the Committee of the sixties, there was no question but that the amelioration of racial unrest was a responsibility of all Americans, on both ethical and practical grounds.

Although the Committee no longer considered it a duty to link all its undertakings directly to Jewish welfare, it saw in the civil rights movement specific implications for Jews. Some officers, like John Slawson and Morris Abram, argued that the ethical imperative was especially strong for Jews in light of their own history, and that Jews were in a special position to share with the Negro community the knowledge and skills developed out of their own experiences. (Slawson pointed out that the Jewish tradition of mutual aid, which created the wide network of Jewish social-work institutions, loan banks, legal assistance, and other services that played so great a part in Jewish acculturation in this country, might be a useful example for the black community.) At the same time, it was important for Jewish institutions to think through their own policies in relation to their Negro neighbors. Should Jewish community centers enroll Negro members? Should Jewish neighborhood communal institutions follow the Jewish migration to the suburbs or remain in their old locations to serve the minority groups that were now in the majority there? What was the best way to deal with Negro anti-Semitism?

In light of the long-standing Jewish involvement in civil rights causes, American Jews viewed the increase in black anti-Semitism with understandable bitterness. The problem had been of some concern to the American Jewish Committee since the early 1940s, but it became a much more serious issue in the 1960s with the growth of black nationalist movements and the challenge to moderate Negro leadership from the more radical ranks of the black community. Many explanations were advanced for Negro anti-Semitism. James Baldwin argued that the Negro expected more from Jews than from white Christians; Richard Wright pointed out that Negroes were taught in Sunday school that the

Jews were "Christ-killers"; psychologist Kenneth Clark stated that Negroes used anti-Semitism both to vent their antiwhite hostility and to identify with the dominant white Christian society. Anger at individual "slumlords" or ghetto storekeepers, resentment against white "do-gooders," the need for a scapegoat, and demands for black power were also reasons cited for anti-Jewish feelings among Negroes—and particularly among the younger, more educated and more militant blacks.

The American Jewish Committee refused to let these manifestations divert it from its civil rights goals. To quit the field, the Committee reasoned, would play into the hands of the extremists and separatists and contribute to an open struggle between blacks and whites. Chapters were advised to protest instances of black anti-Semitism but, at the same time, to discourage the panicky flight of middle-class Jews from urban areas. The Committee met with black militants in efforts to overcome hostility stemming from misunderstandings; it called upon prominent black leaders to speak out against black anti-Semitism (James Baldwin and Ossie Davis were contacted to answer an anti-Semitic diatribe in the militant black magazine *Liberator*); and it appealed to the mass media not to provide a forum for hate-mongers.

To overcome the deep suspicion and misunderstandings that increasingly separated Jews and blacks, the Committee called for honest confrontation and direct dialogue. It organized private interracial discussion groups at members' homes and arranged for rabbis to exchange pulpits with Negro ministers. It worked with various black groups, national and local, in support of numerous social-welfare goals. And to counter charges of Zionist imperialism, AJC sponsored tours to Israel for black leaders, writers, and newspaperman, so that they could report back to their own community on what they had seen.

By these actions the Committee was saying that Jews had a greater obligation to foster mutual trust than did blacks and to prove by their deeds how misguided the black anti-Semites were.

Possibly this "turn the other cheek" approach merely reflected the general guilt feelings of American liberals. (It is difficult to imagine the Committee counseling a similar approach to Father Coughlin's followers or Ku Klux Klan sympathizers.) Time will tell if this was the right course of action for easing tensions between the two groups.

15

Integration and Identity

Compared to the gross discrimination against black Americans, the disabilities suffered by American Jews in the postwar decade were not excessively burdensome. Jews were still excluded from certain residential areas, fraternities, and resorts. There were quotas limiting their admission to certain colleges and medical schools. Very few Jews had penetrated the executive level of most powerful corporations, and even fewer had gained entry into the nation's more exclusive social clubs. For all that, Jews could hardly be considered second-class citizens. Indeed, as a group they were growing more affluent and influential.

Most Jews were not very much disturbed by social discrimination. Their reaction usually was withdrawal of some sort: resignation from a club that blackballed other Jews or held functions on exclusionary premises; passive acceptance of "Establishment" barriers and a choice of careers outside them; creation of Jewish fraternities, clubs, and residential areas to match gentile facilities. (The latter—begun at least as far back as the 1890s when Nathan Straus of R.H. Macy's was turned down by a Lakewood, New Jersey, hotel and built one next door for Jews—resulted in what John Slawson termed the "separate and superior" facilities of the Jews.) Finally, the force of self-segregation, a product of religious teachings and ethnic experiences which together made the position of the Jews different from that of other minorities in the United States, weakened the very desire for total social integration. Thus from the outset the Committee had to overcome Jewish as well as non-Jewish resistance in its program against "polite" anti-Semitism.

I

Immediately after World War II, AJC focused on the problem of Jewish admission into colleges and medical schools. In a prewar survey of the admissions practices of over five hundred liberal arts colleges, 99 percent of the schools had insisted that they did not discriminate against Catholics or Jews; in reality, however, most colleges applied strict quotas, variously disguised. While Christian applicants had a 50 percent chance of admission, their Jewish counterparts had only a 5 percent chance. In medical schools the Jewish acceptance rate was one in thirteen, compared to three out of four for non-Jews.

A special conference on higher education convened by the Committee in 1946 recommended that discrimination be fought privately in confrontations with college authorities, and publicly by denunciation of quotas and an educational campaign to win popular support for admissions based on merit. The conference urged the Committee to support the extension of educational facilities through the creation of state universities; but there was no agreement on the wisdom of establishing a university under Jewish auspices. Some feared that such a step might be interpreted as yielding to the discriminatory policies of other schools; others were opposed to the separatist implications of a Jewish-sponsored institution.

The conference inspired a number of AJC chapters to fight anti-Jewish discrimination. The New York chapter was particularly active in combatting both medical school discrimination and, with the State Commission against Discrimination, discriminatory advertising by resorts and travel agencies. (Jewish resorts were not exempt: a Florida hotel advertising kosher cuisine was induced to insert the word *nonsectarian* into the copy.)

Early in the 1950s the Committee initiated action against religious discrimination in college fraternities. AJC did not question the social values which made the fraternity system a prime index of social acceptance and prestige; it did, however, challenge the implied inferiority of Jewish students by the exclusion of them solely on the grounds of their faith. A college education at its best, AJC maintained, is an exercise in democratic living; that ideal cannot be attained if fraternities indulge in such undemocratic behavior. Beyond that, college experiences shape the attitudes of America's future business and social leaders. A study comparing the views of students who belonged to restricted fraternities with those of students with no fraternity affiliation clearly indicated that the former had grown more prejudiced by their senior year, while the latter had become less so. Discrimination in fraternities also affected college admissions; as fraternities became less restrictive, so did colleges themselves.

Immediately after the war undergraduate pressures, particularly on the part of veterans, challenged the exclusionary patterns traditionally defended by alumni groups. To help break these patterns, the Committee publicized studies critical of racial and religious exclusiveness and engaged in a many-pronged public education campaign against discrimination on the campus. (An AJC-sponsored TV drama on fraternity discrimination, "The Trophy," won a number of coveted prizes.) The Committee sponsored the National Committee on Fraternities in Education, a group of prominent academicians dedicated to eliminating campus barriers. By 1960 virtually all national Greek-letter fraternities had dropped the restrictive clauses in their charters, although most continued to limit Jewish membership. Once the official barriers had been removed, AJC called for the full integration of fraternities. But many Jewish students continued to prefer their own separate and restricted fraternities, some of which introduced "Jewish content" as a rationale for perpetuating their distinctiveness. The Committee was not at all convinced that a college fraternity was an appropriate vehicle for Jewish content. The agency endorsed integration once the official barriers had been removed, but critics within and outside the ranks insisted that boundary lines had to be found between integration and total assimilation.

II

When John Slawson called AJC's executive board to launch a concerted program against social discrimination in May 1955, he acknowledged that many Jews took a negative view of integration. Citing the Committee's "Riverton" study, a sociological survey of a Jewish community in a mid-Atlantic Coast city to which they gave a fictional name, he admitted that most Jews interviewed preferred to associate with all-Jewish or predominantly Jewish groups. Yet, he pointed out, the vast majority of Riverton's Jews were oversensitive to the attitudes of non-Jews; and in seven out of ten homes anti-Semitism was a major topic of conversation. Therefore, he concluded:

> We must work with increasing intensity in the realm of Jewish attitudes with respect to the relationship of the Jew himself to the environment. And we must question the development which, unsavory though it may sound, needs to be designated as the "gilded" ghetto.
> Here we must caution against a possible misinterpretation. Associating in pursuit of religious, cultural, and even ethnic purposes is natural and fully compatible with the American pattern. However, an association which is exclusively composed of members of one religious or ethnic

group, but which is not dedicated to the specific religious or ethnic purposes common to its members, is to be questioned.

Self-segregation in secular pursuits, Slawson insisted, was a defensive posture irrelevant to the question of Jewish identity and detrimental to the cause of Jewish equality. (Oscar Handlin, a distinguished Harvard historian, went even further, asserting that if Jews were really motivated to intermingle with Christians, discriminatory barriers would quickly give way.)

Critics of self-isolation were arguing against the "triple melting pot" trend of American society: the commonplace phenomenon of Catholics, Protestants, and Jews creating separate institutions for other-than-religious purposes. Other factors, however, supported the attack on social discrimination. Notable gains were being made in civil rights, particularly on the state and municipal levels. Admission barriers in fraternities and medical schools—areas untouched by public law—were crumbling. It was no longer considered right to choose employees, students, or neighbors on the basis of race or religion. Polls conducted by the Committee from 1950 to 1954 registered increasingly favorable attitudes toward Jews. (In 1950, for example, 69 percent of the respondents said it would make no difference to them if a Jewish family moved next door; four years later that figure had risen to 88 percent.) Surveys also indicated that Christian community leaders would strongly support programs to encourage acceptance of differences within a pluralistic society. Even in the Jewish community, especially among the youth, the postwar decline in organized anti-Semitism had strengthened the feeling of security and stimulated the desire to participate in the society as full equals of non-Jewish Americans.

Slawson, though he emphasized dignity rather than rights, argued that discrimination was a unitary problem, that there was a direct connection between the "five o'clock shadow" that sent Jews and non-Jews in separate directions at the close of the working day and the opportunity for Jews to reach the top rungs of the economic ladder. Furthermore, he argued, social discrimination was a symptom of bigotry which quietly but insidiously challenged the advances made in other spheres:

> Overt anti-Semitism is becoming relatively unfashionable in America. Human relations agencies such as ours [AJC] have played a not unconsiderable role in this gratifying achievement. . . . However, this victory—and it is a victory—is largely of the surface variety. For, as we know, fashions do change. And beneath the surface of conformity, the fires of group hostility smoulder and at times burn fiercely. Social discrimination serves to perpetuate the infection of bigotry. Social discrimination implies the inferiority and undesirability of a person on the basis of the group with which he is identified, and not on the basis of his individual worth. Social discrimination, when unchallenged, silently authorizes other discriminations.

A recent study at Cornell University had disclosed that in only 20 out of 248 cities were Jews admitted into the Junior League, fashionable country and business clubs, and exclusive residential areas. In one-third of these cities Jews were barred from all three. Unless such marks of inferiority were eliminated, Slawson warned, Jews could not be certain of lasting security in the United States.

The executive board agreed to a program against social discrimination. Judge Simon Rifkind, who presided at the 1955 meeting, commented: "This meeting, at which this subject is, for the first time, broached in all its implications, may turn out to be one of historic significance, not only for the American Jewish Committee, but for the American Jewish community, and America." The program's success depended on the active involvement of the AJC chapters, for they alone could challenge specific clubs and other social institutions in their communities. At first, however, most of the chapters approached the project gingerly, if at all. Some felt that the problem was peripheral, that no basic violation of legal or human rights was involved, and that there was an implied challenge to freedom of association. Others thought that the goals could be achieved by concentrating primarily on housing and education. Still others were reluctant to alienate gentile colleagues and neighbors. And even though the Riverton study showed that Committee members were more eager for social integration than their fellow Jews, there were some who worried about the seeming connection between integration and assimilation.

For the better part of four years the chapters which participated at all limited their activities to internal discussions and to surveys of social discrimination in their communities. The result of these investigations was encouraging. Often, it was clear, restriction and social discrimination stemmed from habit or indifference rather than from bigotry. And there was growing evidence that Christians who were alerted to the problem were ready to help. The national office formulated guidelines for local action which took into account the chapters' hesitancies. It advised working in discreet, unpublicized ways: choosing a field or institution most accessible to change, recognizing the distinction between exclusion and limitation, and being satisfied with gradual change. In this area the Committee was ready to accept "benign quotas" and urged its members not to reject invitations to clubs that were issued on that basis. It also encouraged the chapters to plan long-range projects to deal with Jewish separatism and to increase civic contacts between Jews and non-Jews. Many of AJC's educational efforts were aimed at making the public conscious of social discrimination and its implications, and it was heartened when two members of the Eisenhower cabinet deplored the injustice and national waste inherent in such practices. The Committee emphasized, however, that its objective was not to impinge upon free association, but to prevent the hardening of a caste system based on religious, ethnic, or racial differences.

To further these activities the Committee commissioned historical and sociological studies of discrimination. Such noted scholars as John Higham, Thomas Brown, and Howard Brotz examined the history of anti-Jewish prejudice in the United States, anti-Irish sentiment in American history, and discrimination against Jews in England. Writer Vance Packard surveyed the attitudes of leading Gentiles toward Jews in "Alton" (the fictional name for a large northeastern city). The findings bolstered the Committee's belief in the attainability of social equality. The scholars concluded that social discrimination derived from status drives and habit rather than from religious or racial ideologies; that Jews had not always encountered social prejudice in the United States; that younger Gentiles were receptive to change; and that as assimilation proceeded and groups lost their distinctive traits, they found increasing acceptance.

The studies did not assess the role of self-segregation in preserving Jewish identity. Packard even suggested how Jews might change their image of being clannish, the objection he heard most frequently when he asked about social mingling with Jews. And when Dr. Slawson summed up the accomplishment of the first four years, he again stressed the exclusionary behavior of Jews as a factor in perpetuating discrimination: "Insofar as group survival is concerned—intermarriage and related considerations—we should recognize by now that we cannot preserve the Jewish group by walling in its members."

III

In 1959 the Committee decided to turn its attention to discrimination in executive employment. Several surveys underscored the connection between corporate practices of exclusion and social discrimination. In some communities—Detroit or Wilmington, for example—the major corporations (the automobile companies, say, or Dupont) were also the social oligarchies. To reach the top, a corporation employee had to belong to the right clubs; indeed, a *Life* magazine survey disclosed that 73 percent of the major corporations paid all or part of the club expenses of their top executives. Since the exclusionary patterns of the executive suite and the club were mutually reinforcing, a breach in one would doubtless affect the other. Tactically, it appeared wiser to focus on business, for the strictly social institutions presented the least opportunity for change. AJC members, it was also felt, would cooperate in a business program more readily, for many continued to view the social club as lowest on their scale of priorities. When America's space race with Russia began, the needs of the national economy reinforced the case against prejudice in business.

The Committee's executive suite program got under way quickly. AJC chapters in Detroit, Pittsburgh, and other cities were started on local programs to eliminate business discrimination; the national office began discussing the absence of Jews in banking with Federal Reserve Bank officials in different cities. But much-needed data were still missing, though the underrepresentation of Jews in the top echelons of major corporations was clear. A study by Cornell University of 248 cities summed up the situation:

> In the communities that the Cornell field staff visited few Jews are found on the management level of the major local industries, or on the boards of the leading banks. Jews are seldom found on the executive levels of absentee-owned industry or in transportation, communication or other utilities.

Later studies fixed Jewish representation in the upper echelons of such industries at one-half of one percent. This low level of participation could not be ascribed to lack of qualification: Jews constituted 3.5 percent of the American population, but they accounted for 8 percent of the nation's college graduates, 22 percent of the male enrollment at Ivy League schools, and 12 to 15 percent of the Merit Scholarship winners. Jews had prospered in the United States, but their success was largely in the mercantile trades and the professions. The few Jews who were to be found in the large corporations were usually in research jobs.

Though the need for managerial talent was increasing rapidly and major corporations, like U.S. Steel and General Motors, were publicly committed to nondiscriminatory hiring policies, the statistics of executive employment told a very different story. If such corporate influences continued to dominate the American economy, the underrepresentation of Jews at the policy-making levels of industry was likely to become more pronounced. Furthermore, the country would continue to waste valuable talent.

The need for more information became increasingly clear. If companies did not purposely discriminate against Jews on religious grounds in their recruitment and promotion policies, then there were obviously some more complicated and elusive factors involved. Did Jews shy away from such employment because of certain distinct tastes or proclivities? Had centuries of economic restrictions warped the Jew's adaptability in the world of corporations? Did corporate policies discriminate in different guise—the Jew doesn't look like us, he is too aggressive, he is too much the individualist to fit on the corporate team? Answers to a great many questions were needed. Research on the interaction of the Jew and the corporation—including the factors influencing career choices, recruitment policies, and promotion procedures—was essential.

A special advisory committee on executive discrimination, headed by Paul Warburg, urged the Committee to assign top priority to such research. It called specifically for studies of recruitment and placement procedures on the executive-trainee level, promotion and advancement practices, and career choices of Jewish college students. The Falk Foundation of Pittsburgh contributed close to five hundred thousand dollars for these investigations, and after numerous conferences with deans and faculty members of leading graduate schools of business administration, the program got under way. Dr. Lewis B. Ward of Harvard studied the method of hiring management trainees to determine if prejudice, conscious or unconscious, played a role in the interviews of applicants by recruiters. He found that most of the companies which hired Protestants only (usually the larger and generally more conservative firms) did not consciously discriminate on religious grounds; rather, they stressed conformity as a criterion for employment. Companies which hired a mixed group of trainees, on the other hand, tended to emphasize intellect and skill instead. Jewish students, in turn, often avoided the company with a strict Anglo-Saxon image. Therefore, Ward pointed out, companies eager to hire Jewish trainees would have to give evidence that no barriers to promotion existed.

At the University of Michigan the Committee sponsored an examination of promotion policies in a corporation which had introduced procedures deliberately designed to correlate advancement with ability. The findings disclosed that even when company policy was opposed to discrimination, promotions were often made not simply on the basis of merit, but also on the basis of the candidate's religion, residence, club affiliation, and similar factors. And the inclusion of such factors in promotion decisions were often justified as concessions to pressures from outside the firm itself—from customers, competing businesses, and the community at large. These "third-party" pressures grew more intense with every step upward in the corporate hierarchy; thus it was clear that the community's general attitude toward minority groups would be reflected in the corporate structure. (The interrelationship between community bias and promotions was confirmed in a second study, conducted at the University of California in Los Angeles.)

A Cornell University research study dispelled the myth that Jewish students preferred careers outside large companies. No correlation existed, the findings indicated, between religious background and choice of career; Jewish college seniors displayed the same range of goals as their non-Jewish peers. And a historical study of Jews in the development of American business reinforced that finding: Jewish participation in the national economy was limited by outside pressures, particularly when industrial capitalism gave way to finance capitalism, and salaried managers replaced owner-managers.

Committee-sponsored studies also refuted the assumption, widely held in business circles, that Jews were unwilling to subject themselves to the slow climb up the corporate ladder to top leadership and preferred to enter new fields or small businesses where they could get to the top rapidly. Jews who entered graduate schools of business administration and presented themselves for executive-trainee recruitment were as prepared as any other applicant to follow the corporation's ways.

In theory the Committee opposed the yardstick of conformity by which most corporations measured prospective executives. Yet its research studies indicated that the nonconformity of Jews in the business world was either a stereotyped and largely fictitious image or a reaction to gentile practices. The issue was not really acceptance of the nonconformist, but society's rejection of the Jew, who, except for ethnic origin and religion, did conform. The implicit conclusion of the studies was that if the barriers gave way the result would be a homogenized, rather than a pluralistic, business elite.

Even before all the major research was completed, the Committee undertook a program of general education on executive-suite discrimination. Newspapers and magazines touched on the subject in editorials and feature articles. Secretary of Labor Arthur Goldberg, speaking at the Committee's annual meeting in 1961, called for the correction of discriminatory practices in industry. Vance Packard's best-selling book on executive life, *The Pyramid Climbers*, drew heavily on Committee materials. The most impressive summary of the situation was E. Digby Baltzell's *The Protestant Establishment*, a sociological study sponsored by the Committee, which discussed the patterns of social and economic discrimination against Jews and other minorities in the United States, the connection of the corporation and the club, and the dangers of a discrimination-based caste system for American society.

The Committee saw its multifaceted research program only as a prelude to action, and a number of activities were under way. The Pittsburgh chapter studied the employment policies of United States Steel; the Philadelphia chapter prepared a survey of Jewish employment in the city's banks. Both had quietly called the attention of prominent non-Jewish executives in their cities to the underutilization of Jews in the higher echelons of business. These pioneer efforts were aimed at persuading the leaders of the business community to assume responsibility for necessary changes in policy and practice. Since the program depended on persuasion, implementation rested largely with the Committee's members—men whose prestigious business and communal standing made them especially suited to the task. The national office provided them with the background data and advised them on procedures of consultation. They made the essential contacts with their non-Jewish business peers. The chapters developed inventories of Jewish management personnel in companies in their communities, and these reports were made available to corporation executives before any meetings between representatives of the Committee and the firm. In each instance the success of the undertaking depended both upon how effectively the Committee presented its case and how willing the particular firm was to study the evidence of discrimination and to institute reforms.

It was a laborious process and the return often did not match the investment. Involved was not simple anti-Jewish prejudice, but a long tradition of self-insulation by the elite. The last two citadels of a white Anglo-Saxon Protestant "Establishment" determined to perpetuate its privileges were the executive suite and the social club, and this determination did not easily yield to private pressure. Only an aroused public interest and concern could stimulate effective change.

IV

In December 1963 newspapers around the country carried an American Jewish Committee news release documenting the extent of anti-Jewish discrimination in public utilities. Jews filled less than one percent of the managerial posts in the top fifty public utility companies around the country, the release revealed, and its roster of blue-chip firms that discriminated included American Telephone and Telegraph, Consolidated Edison, and Pacific Gas & Electric, among others. The news release, authorized only by the three top lay officials, aroused considerable resentment among sectors of AJC membership. Since 1955 the agreed-upon approach had been to abstain from coercive tactics in dealing with individual private clubs or corporations, and this publicity, many members argued, was a departure from that approach. The chairman of the AJC special advisory committee on business resigned in protest; lay boards and the community representatives complained that they were not consulted. Although Slawson argued that the release should be judged as a means of implementing a policy rather than as a change in policy, it was clear that the Committee had become less and less concerned with playing down its own "visibility" in connection with its executive-suite programs.

President A. M. Sonnabend justified the action on the grounds that quiet endeavors could accomplish little and that "a general atmosphere in the country today . . . seems to recognize the right of groups to speak for themselves publicly, particularly when self-interest coincides with what is generally accepted as sound public policy." Morris Abram resorted to the example of the civil rights movement: "If the use of pattern evidence to establish discrimination against Negroes is deemed appropriate, it is no less appropriate in the case of Jews even if the economic bracket is different." The release on the utilities, therefore, was another milestone for AJC. Publicity now joined persuasion as an acceptable weapon in the executive-suite program.

The Committee sent follow-up documentation of its charges to the utilities companies it had named. Most denied discrimination, but several arranged for conferences with Committee members. The chapters in the communities concerned were alerted to concentrate on immediate action. Not all the firms involved adopted effective antidiscrimination programs, but the ice had been broken. The following report from the Pennsylvania region recorded a success story in the aftermath of the newspaper publicity:

In response to Mr. Sonnabend's follow up letters, two . . . companies invited lay and professional leadership of the American Jewish Committee to meet with them to discuss the situation. . . .

In both instances, the meetings were arranged by AJC leaders of the communities, who were present at the interviews. This was extremely helpful since having someone on hand respected by and known to the company helped to make the conferences more informal and cordial. . . . Present at the meetings were the presidents of both companies, the general counsel for each, directors of personnel, and college recruitment personnel.

In the case of both companies . . . they desired only to consider with us the problem we outlined and to discuss methods of dealing with the situation. Both utilities accepted the fact that there are very few Jews involved in management level within the companies. At this point, however, there was a divergence of view by each company on what its responsibility should be. One company began the meeting by pointing out that since it does not practice discrimination, it is entirely up to minority groups to apply for positions. If members of such groups do so in greater numbers, they argued, there would undoubtedly be a growth in the number of Jewish personnel employed. This gave us an opportunity to explain . . . that utilities and other major sections of American economic life have often been considered by the Jewish community to be unwilling to hire Jewish personnel or to advance Jews on the basis of merit. It is clear that Jewish young men are not encouraged to seek positions in these companies since they see so few Jews involved. Middle echelon ranks of the company as well as college placement officials may consider that the company does not want Jewish personnel even if top leadership of the company does not believe in or practice discrimination.

We suggested, therefore, that a policy of non-discrimination is not enough; an organization must . . . make a conscious effort to overcome the negative image the Jewish community often possesses of the utility field. If the organization accepts an affirmative program as part of its responsibility, we indicated that we would have a number of specific suggestions to make that could be helpful.

In the case of the first company, management agreed that its mind was not closed to the adoption of such an affirmative program. However, we were told that it would have to consider what effect this would have, since other minorities might also ask for similar treatment; they also wondered whether other employees might feel that one group is receiving special attention. However, this company (the second as well) pointed out that it is anxious to engage engineers and other personnel who are gravitating to "glamour" industries. Quite apart from the desire not to discriminate, the company actually needs qualified personnel. In our presence, the president of this company dictated a memo to a number of key personnel of the organization calling for a meeting to consider the issues further. . . .

The second company presented a quite different situation. There was complete acceptance of our view that the company must adopt an affirmative program that would go beyond its presently announced policy of non-discrimination. We were asked to make specific suggestions. To coincide with our visit, this organization scheduled one of its meetings of supervisory personnel—about 20—to meet with us so that we could share with the group our thoughts and suggestions on equal opportunity employment. . . . This was a unique and interesting session which the company officials later informed us was very helpful to them in reinforcing the equal opportunity message they were trying to bring to middle and upper-middle echelons of the organization.

Thereafter, we met . . . with the general counsel, the director and supervisor of employment, and several college recruiters to discuss the "how" of recruiting minority group personnel. We made a number of specific suggestions including visits by company personnel to Jewish fraternities on campus, Hillel foundations, etc. We were greatly impressed with the eagerness of company officials to hear our suggestions and treat them with seriousness. Additional information, addresses and so on have been sent to this company at their request and further contact has been arranged.

The second company, Pennsylvania Power & Light, established contacts with Hillel chapters, Jewish vocational agencies, and rabbis to broaden its recruitment practices. An equally important result was the added confidence which infused the AJC membership. Once the issue was out in the open and brought more than "beautiful lip service," as one Philadelphia member commented, the local Committee people changed from lambs to "self-disciplined lions."

V

In similar fashion AJC studied the underrepresentation of Jews at the executive level of commercial banks, savings banks, and insurance companies. Meanwhile, the chapters were urged to approach a number of different industries simultaneously and to hold direct discussions, as they had done with the utilities. The national office selected certain bellwether companies as the prime targets, on the principle that if these cooperated, smaller firms in the same industries were likely to follow suit. Pushing for a more aggressive program, the Committee now advised its members to enlist the cooperation of the customers, directors, and stockholders of the corporations. By 1966 many different companies—Eastern Airlines, Bethlehem Steel, Eastman Kodak, Scott Paper—had met with Committee representatives. Under the combined pressure of publicity, the growing shortage of executive talent, and the public demands for equal opportunity, Jews gradually moved into executive ranks from which they had been barred.

The Committee also was responsible for directing the federal government's attention to discrimination in the executive suite. An executive order of 1960, reaffirmed in 1965, outlawed hiring and promotion discrimination based on race, creed, color, and national origin in firms holding government contracts. However, while contractors had to report to the government on the employment of Negroes, Orientals, American Indians, and Spanish Americans, no such reports were required concerning religious groups. In 1963 the Committee pointed out this omission to the attention of the president's Committee on Equal Opportunity Compliance, but was told that the government's push was to insure racial equality in lower-level employment. Two years later Morris Abram wrote to Vice-President Hubert Humphrey, who was responsible for coordinating contract-compliance procedures, citing AJC's research findings and asking his help. Humphrey directed contracting firms to supply data on religious as well as racial groups, to insure full compliance with the government's avowed objectives. (In this matter the Committee had to overcome its own traditional aversion to counting Jews as a separate group.) When the contract-compliance administration was transferred to the Department of Labor, Secretary of Labor Willard Wirtz conferred with AJC representatives and publicly promised to help combat religious discrimination.

When AJC completed its survey of Jewish employees in the fifty largest banks, it submitted the findings to Wirtz, who relayed them to Secretary of the Treasury Henry H. Fowler. Not long after, an executive order extended the nondiscrimination requirements for contractors to banks handling federal funds. With the advent of the Medicare program, pressure could also be put on insurance companies serving as Medicare carriers.

The American Jewish Committee extended its executive-suite campaign to the campus. Although discrimination in student admissions and in faculty hiring had been largely eliminated, there was still a glaring absence of Jewish deans and college presidents. A survey released by the Committee in 1966 pinpointed the figures: in 775 private and public nonsectarian colleges Jews accounted for 10 to 12 percent of the student body and faculty, but only one percent of the presidencies and 2.6 percent of the deanships.

The Committee's report was widely circulated, and the initial response was encouraging. Here two important factors helped: the large investment of public funds in colleges and universities, and the widespread association of higher learning with objectivity and merit. As the report summed up:

> The academic community—in effect a public trust with a cultural orientation—traditionally prides itself on maintaining standards higher and more objective than those of privately owned business with its profit motivation. . . . Colleges and universities are, in many ways, America's most essential training grounds of democratic minds. Here less than anywhere else can the nation afford to countenance practices that give lie to the creed of equal opportunity.

VI

AJC's gains were less striking with respect to social clubs. In 1962 its Domestic Affairs Committee approved a change in the traditional but ineffective "nonaggressive" approach, endorsing "timely publicity" and other pressure tactics (e.g., persuading organizations not to schedule meetings at discriminatory clubs, alerting political candidates to the fact that membership in an exclusionary club might prove a political liability, and the like). The Committee's members, however, were more reluctant to confront (let alone to appear to coerce) club officials than corporation executives. And in this area government officials could do little more than lend moral support. The civil rights struggle had awakened the public to the evil of prejudice in the economic sphere, and no reputable firm would publicly defend discrimination in industry. But there were still respectable voices defending strictly social barriers. In January 1962 the *Wall Street Journal* commented editorially on the inability of a Negro State Department official to gain entry into the Cosmos Club:

> What is overlooked here is that one of the most fundamental of all rights is the freedom to choose one's friends and social associates; this above all is no affair of the State or of society. In exercising that right people may be blindly prejudiced, snobbish, arrogant or just plain muddle-headed. Still, it is their own affair if they prefer not to associate with Protestants, Catholics, Jews, Gentiles, white people, dark people, or undistinguished journalists; or if they prefer, as some in all these groups do, to have societies exclusively limited to their fellows with whom they feel a common bond. Any injury they do, in a free country of infinite variety, is only to themselves. But when we, as the whole society, undertake to say they cannot do so, and that every member of society must conform to one rule of conduct, then our own prejudices have become blind and the injury we do is to the whole of our society.

Accordingly, the Committee moved with caution. In 1963 it decided to tackle the university clubs in several cities. That choice alone was a compromise, for such clubs, officially comprised of college graduates who achieved distinction in business or the professions, were distinctly less private than country clubs. The usual procedure was to begin with informal negotiations involving club officials, leading Gentiles, and AJC representatives. If nothing came of these, more drastic measures followed. Some of the organizations using the offending club's facilities might be persuaded to take their business elsewhere; prominent members might be encouraged to resign; the impact of adverse publicity might be discussed with club officials. Such pressure brought quicker results than did the earlier, "nonaggressive" approach. In 1960 only two university clubs welcomed Jews; by 1965 seven had accepted Jewish applicants, one was about to do so, and five were in consultation with AJC chapters on the matter.

VII

The campaign against social discrimination can be seen as an index of broader trends. Aimed against the "last barriers," it pointed up the decline of virulent forms of anti-Semitism and showed how rapidly the acculturation of the Jews had progressed. Changes in American society—the growth of the middle class, the dominance of the cities—contributed to the speed and ease of acclimatization. No longer perched on the rim of society, the Jew was both *in* and very much *of* that society. The campaign against social discrimination and its relative success also reflected the growth of the welfare state, which increasingly circumscribed the area of private prerogative.

The crumbling of the "last barriers," however, could not but weaken Jewish identity. Discrimination historically contributed to Jewish cohesiveness. The impact of the Dreyfus affair on Theodor Herzl, the untold numbers who remembered they were Jews after the rise of Hitler, the State of Israel, which owed its creation in large measure to the forces of persecution, are only a few modern examples of the phenomenon. Non-Jews who fought for the full equality of Jews assumed ever since the French Revolution that Jewish assimilation would proceed concomitantly. It was often pointed out that assimilation was a small price for a minority to pay in exchange for acceptance by the Establishment, and in actual fact, the payment could be unconscious and painless. A Jew who made the elite club and the executive suite, whose business and social contacts were overwhelmingly gentile, might well have little desire and less time for meaningful identification with the Jewish group.

In 1964 AJC convened a conference of prominent social scientists to discuss the Committee-sponsored study by Charles

Herbert Stember on changes in the attitudes of non-Jews toward Jews. Reviewing data amassed over a twenty-year period, Dr. Stember concluded that since the end of World War II there had been "a steady erosion of hostile imagery and an increasing willingness to associate with Jews." The participants analyzed the material in historical, sociological, and psychological perspective. While much of the discussion centered on the prognosis for anti-Semitism, the problem of identity was closely intertwined. If indeed Jewish-gentile relations in the United States continued on their current course, never before experienced in Jewish history, the persistence of a Jewish minority could no longer be taken for granted. Identity had become a question of choice for the Jews themselves.

John Slawson fought as hard for the preservation of Jewish identity as he did against social discrimination. Ever since his admonitions to the 1944 annual meeting he had urged the Committee to translate them into concrete projects. AJC sponsored historical studies of different aspects of Jewish life which, unlike the earlier works by Joseph Jacobs and Herman Bernstein, aimed not to discredit anti-Semitism but to enlighten Jews. Social scientists studied Jews in contemporary America—how they made a living, what Jewish rituals they observed, how they related to non-Jews. In 1945 a conference on Jewish adjustment in America began a continuing process of encouraging scholars to review and assess the functions and the future of American Jewry.

The three-hundredth anniversary of the first settlement of Jews in the United States offered the opportunity to celebrate the course of Jewish development within a democratic framework. When the American Jewish Historical Society broached its ideas for a tercentenary program in 1954, the Committee responded enthusiastically. AJC took the lead in organizing a community-wide American Jewish Tercentenary Committee under the chairmanship of its vice-president, Ralph Samuel, and provided financial and programing assistance. The Committee's own departments also worked on the tercentenary. Significantly, AJC was not content to concentrate on the "Jewish-contributions-to-America" theme. At least as important, the Committee felt, was the need to highlight the creativity of the Jews in response to their communal needs and to stimulate American Jews to think about their past and future in a free society.

Slawson justified programs for Jewish identity on several grounds. If withdrawal from the non-Jewish milieu was unhealthy, it was just as unhealthy, he claimed, to cut off one's roots, to deny one's past or origins. Jews need neither to fear their visibility nor to shy away from self-examination as a group. Thus Slawson did not share the apprehensions of the lay leaders who opposed publication of the "Riverton" study because it exposed unfavorable attitudes toward Gentiles. More important, he was convinced that Jewish identity was intrinsically worthy of preservation and that the teachings of Judaism had relevance and applicability to contemporary problems. But he insisted that these teachings could not be reduced to a watered-down humanism. Despite the steady absorption of Jews into American life, Slawson saw favorable signs for Jewish survival. Numerous polls indicated that Jewish youngsters wanted to learn about their heritage; a pluralistic society permitted the perpetuation of distinctive cultural traits; contemporary literature alone—abounding in Jewish writers and Jewish heroes—indicated how receptive the public was to the Jew qua Jew.

However, Slawson raised questions for which there were no clear answers. Most basic of all was the question of definition. Did Jewish identity mean being a member of a religious group, a religiocultural group, or one of some other hyphenated combination? To what Jewish group did a Committee member belong who observed no religion, or who married outside the faith? And where was the line of demarcation between integration and identity? Jewish experience offered few guidelines. For two thousand years both Jew and non-Jew knew the former to be a member of a separate and distinct group. Only in the century and a half following political emancipation could the Jew attempt to bridge that separation. The Committee's own research studies showed that both groups were still unsure of the optimum meeting point.

The Committee's membership considered the question at numerous workshop and round-table discussions. They agreed that the youth must be imbued with Jewish consciousness, but no one was quite clear how this could be done. Nor was everyone convinced that a Jewish identity program, particularly if it were cast within a religious framework, rightfully belonged within the Committee's purview. On the other hand, in postwar America educational blueprints could not beg the question of religious commitment. The very image projected by the Committee further beclouded the issue. In certain Jewish quarters AJC was viewed as a group of assimilationists who spoke to Christians rather than Jews. "What's Jewish about the American Jewish Committee?" was a favorite subject for organizational introspection. To be sure, AJC published *Commentary*, operated an exceptionally fine Library of Jewish Information, made available useful data about Jews in research studies and in the *American Jewish Year Book*, and helped establish several university chairs in Jewish studies. But could the organization also serve as a catalyst to spur synagogues and Jewish schools to deal effectively with Jewish identity? At the meeting of the executive board in 1966, Slawson urged the creation of an Institute of Jewish Identity, which would undertake a program of fundamental research to parallel AJC's scientifically oriented approach to anti-Semitism.

Jewish identity had never before been a concern of the American Jewish Committee. Its earlier activities were confined to defending the rights of Jews and assuring their survival. The social-action program of the postwar Committee extended that scope to issues which some members felt had little, if any, Jewish relevance. If the organization was primarily a human-relations agency, they asked, why couldn't Gentiles be admitted as members? Particularly in light of the Committee's social-discrimination campaign, wasn't it contradictory for AJC to maintain religious barriers? In June 1965 Orin Lehman, secretary of the

Committee, moved that AJC repeal the "restrictive covenant" of its own bylaws which for sixty years had confined membership to Jews who were American citizens.* Slawson admitted that to oppose such a motion would seem parochial. He insisted, however, that its adoption would alter the Committee's foreign and domestic programs and jeopardize its growing commitment to Jewish identity. The issue was resolved by changing the requirements of eligibility to "Jews, their spouses and children." The episode vividly illustrated the interaction of the two countervailing forces: integration and identity. Officially, the American Jewish Committee supported both. In fact, it had accomplished more on the side of integration, even to the point of altering the organization's original identity. The attainment of an ideal balance posed an ongoing challenge.

*Actually, it was not until 1942 that the charter or bylaws specifically stipulated that only Jews were eligible for membership.

16

Separation of Church and State

The American Jewish Committee, which usually prided itself on a pragmatic, nondoctrinaire approach, behaved in rigorous, traditionalist fashion in matters pertaining to the separation of church and state. Like most American Jews, AJC members maintained that such separation was a prerequisite for full democratic living. The roots of that position go back to the Enlightenment, when Western liberals held that organized religion blocked advances by the forces of rationalism and stood in the way of political reform and representative government.

Jews, who for almost two thousand years had suffered restrictions and persecution in the name of religion, naturally championed the separation of church and state. Paralleling their struggle for political emancipation was a movement for self-emancipation, as they strove to break the yoke of rabbinic law which, in the name of God, prevented the Jew from taking his rightful place in the modern world.

For American Jews, both separationism and secularism were spurred by the experience of Reform Judaism in the nineteenth century. Born in Germany, Reform blossomed in the free and optimistic American society. Reform theology, itself a product of the Enlightenment, readily embraced the Jeffersonian dictum erecting a wall between church and state, particularly in the face of pervasive Protestant influence in American public schools. Reform leaders distinguished sharply between Christian culture and a Christian political state; they set the precedent for Jewish opposition to the legal recognition of a dominant church. Reform Judaism also preached cosmopolitanism and denigrated Jewish parochialism of any kind in favor of an ethical message. The universalist emphasis of Reform teachings contributed to the divorce of the synagogue from nonreligious communal issues. Hospitals, charities, newspapers, even defense organizations controlled by Jews flourished independently of synagogues and rabbis. Many of the new post-1880 immigrants infused the secularist trend with new meaning. Some substituted a socialist ideal for religion, and like Reform Jews, sought to mold the Jewish tradition in universalist terms. To these Jews, Jefferson's wall was also a Jewish wall against insularity.

In the United States after World War II separation of church and state was a key issue affecting both public and nonpublic schools. Considerations unknown in the nineteenth century—the magnitude of the nation's educational needs, the implications of a welfare state, the functions of a pluralistic society—added new dimensions to the problem. While many liberals restructured their order of priorities, Jewish insistence on the sanctity of separation persisted. Minorities had never enjoyed as much security in the United States. But as a pluralistic society accepted Jewish assertiveness more readily, the Jewish minority sharpened its attack against any entering wedge, no matter how innocuous in itself, which might breach the wall of separation. The East European dream of a vibrant, positive secularism had faded; in ideals and in ritual Reform Judaism was turning back to elements of the ancient religious heritage. From the viewpoint of both security and the Jewish rebellion against religion, rigid opposition to separation might seem anachronistic. Nevertheless, the old fears remained. Democracy meant rule by the majority, or at least that majority which made its voice heard. Could a Jewish minority really escape the invidious distinctions that were bound to arise between its own faith and Catholicism or Protestantism, if religion, even on a nondenominational basis, were linked to state power?

Organizations like the American Jewish Committee might have found numerous reasons to modify their strict separationist stand. AJC's interreligious activity, as well as its education and poverty programs, often conflicted with separationism. Yet these considerations did not significantly alter the Committee's position, which reflected an emotional and ideological commitment more compelling than pragmatic reasoning.

I

The First Amendment to the Constitution contains two clauses dealing with religion, which the Supreme Court has held binding on the states as well as on Congress. One bars Congress from making laws prohibiting the "free exercise of religion"; the other bars laws respecting "an establishment of religion." The American Jewish Committee has appeared as amicus curiae in several cases involving individual rights under these guarantees. It challenged the imposition of an oath attesting to belief in God as a prerequisite for government employment or holding office in the state of Maryland (*Torcaso* v. *Watkins*); it questioned the constitutionality of Sunday laws which worked hardship on Orthodox Jews and Seventh Day Adventists (*Gallagher* v. *Crown Kosher, Sherbert* v. *Verner*); it argued that the free exercise of religion applied not only to all religious creeds but also to those who did *not* believe in God or a Supreme Being (*Washington Ethical Society* v. *District of Columbia*).

Clearly, the "free-exercise" clause cannot always be disentangled from the "establishment of religion" clause (a religious oath for holding office, for example, impinges on both). Yet the issue of separation in matters of education—the teaching of religion or the practice of religious ritual in the public schools, as well as public aid to religious institutions—can best be analyzed in light of the "establishment" clause alone. To the Committee, the "wall of separation" between church and state was particularly vital in education. Justice Wiley B. Rutledge might have been speaking for AJC when he declared in *Everson* v. *Board of Education* in 1947:

> Two great drives are constantly in motion to abridge, in the name of education, the complete division of religion and civil authority which our forefathers made. One is to introduce religious education and observances into the public schools. The other, to obtain public funds for the aid and support of various private religious schools. . . . In my opinion, both avenues were closed by the Constitution. Neither should be opened by this Court. . . . We should not be less strict to keep strong and untarnished the one side of the shield of religious freedom than we have been of the other.

The Committee's insistence on keeping the public schools free of religious teachings, observances, and symbols reflected the traditional apprehension of a minority which believed its greatest security lay in a secular democratic society. Any official religious doctrine or act, however inoffensive, presented a challenge to that security. The Committee was also convinced that a solid wall of separation was essential to the well-being of a democratic society. (This also applied to a Jewish state; second to AJC's concern when Israel spoke out on Jewish matters outside her borders was its disapproval of religious control in Israel.) While it was not possible to dissociate religious customs and forms from the mores of a society—for example, the nationwide celebration of Christmas—they had to be kept free of official state sanction. Most American Jews agreed with this strong separationist stand. Jews who wanted religious instruction for their children managed to get it outside the public schools.

After World War II the major challenges to separation came

less from Christian teachings in the schools than from attempts
to inject pansectarian forms of observance. But the Committee
stood firm in its insistence that the government and all public
institutions must refuse to recognize religion even on a nonpref-
erential basis. The *Everson* case supported that view, for the Supreme Court defined the "establishment" clause in broad terms:

> The "establishment of religion" clause of the First
> Amendment means at least this: Neither a state nor the Fed-
> eral Government can set up a church. Neither can pass laws
> which aid one religion, aid all religions, or prefer one reli-
> gion over another. Neither can force or influence a person
> to go to or to remain away from church against his will or
> force him to profess a belief or disbelief in any religion. No
> person can be punished for entertaining or professing reli-
> gious beliefs or disbeliefs, for church attendance or non-
> attendance. No tax, in any amount, large or small, can be
> levied to support any religious activities or institutions,
> whatever they may be called, or whatever form they may
> adopt to teach or practice religion. Neither a state nor the
> Federal Government can, openly or secretly, participate in
> the affairs of any religious organizations or groups and vice
> versa.

Another factor shaping the Committee's attitude was the
importance it ascribed to public education. One of the primary
purposes of the public school, AJC believed, was to nurture the
values of democratic life, including an appreciation of and respect for different religious and ethnic groups. Introducing religious forms into the classroom, the Committee held, sharpened
divisiveness and militated against the success of a meaningful
intercultural experience. Emboldened by the growing acceptance
of a pluralistic society, the Committee and other separationist
groups sought to challenge the vestiges of Protestant coloration
which had long tinged the school system and to resist new attempts to inject religion into public classrooms. The problem
had numerous facets and varied in intensity from region to re-

gion. Most common were the instances of required Bible-reading, prayers, religious holiday observance, distribution of the Gideon Bible and released-time programs. There were also school districts which permitted clergymen to give instruction in religion or used nuns as public-school teachers. In theory, all such practices were repugnant to the separationists; but decisions about which ones to counter had to be made on the basis of which were most objectionable and most widespread.

The American Jewish Committee's only prewar involvement in the church-state debate was Louis Marshall's defense of parochial schools in the *Pierce* case in 1925. When AJC launched its drive to eliminate religious teachings and practices from the public schools shortly after World War II, there was strong public resistance. The cold war, the specter of "atheistic communism," and an increase in juvenile delinquency led many Americans to insist that schools inculcate religious teachings and values. A good American, they assumed, was one who believed in God. In 1954 Congress expressed that mood by inserting the words "under God" into the pledge of allegiance. Jews who seemed to resist this trend opened themselves to charges of secularism and godlessness. In certain communities this could have meant alienation, isolation, and perhaps even overt anti-Semitism. Herbert Ehrmann reported to the Committee in 1950 that when one Jewish family in Chelsea, Massachusetts, complained about the singing of Christmas carols in the public schools, other Jewish residents were threatened. The Committee was also aware that an aggressive separationist stance might hamper its interreligious work, which depended on mutual accommodation to reduce sectarian conflict, and could be viewed as a direct challenge to the consensus among an increasing number of religious leaders.

Ever sensitive to the pressures of community relations, particularly in areas where Jews constituted a small percentage of the population, the Committee was often less militant in commenting on church-state issues than were other Jewish organizations.

In the interests of communal peace, it cautioned local agencies against always taking a purist position on church-state separation. For example, it opposed released-time programs, under which the public schools released certain children during the regular school day to attend religious classes, but accepted as the lesser evil "dismissed" time, which shortened the school day for all children, so that those enrolled for religious instruction could attend classes. In principle it opposed Bible-reading in the classroom (a divergence from Louis Marshall's personal views); but where the practice was deeply rooted and difficult to undo, it urged that the schools avoid offending the sensibilities of any particular group. It opposed the observance of sectarian holidays, including interreligious celebrations of Christmas and Hanukkah, but recommended a circumspect Jewish communal approach to this highly explosive issue.

Through statements and articles, speeches and pamphlets, AJC preached separation to the general public. Emphasizing the intent of the constitutional proscriptions, the Committee argued that religion was a private matter, totally outside the sphere of majority rule. While the role of religion was a valid component of courses in history, literature, art, and many other public-school subjects, AJC contended, religion itself was not; inculcation of religious values was the task of the home and the church, not of the classroom. AJC prepared educational materials for local communities; it consulted with school boards and officials who prepared curriculum guidelines on the teaching of moral and spiritual values. It worked hard to enlist liberal Protestants in support of church-state separation, actively encouraging the efforts of the Institute of Church and State, a group of prominent Christian educators who argued the separationist cause. But education alone was not enough, and the Committee turned to litigation, the traditional recourse of a minority group in a democracy.

II

No predictions could be made on how the courts, and ultimately the Supreme Court, would decide church-state issues. Indeed, subsequent cases pointed up the difficulties and apparent inconsistencies of the justices in grappling with this sensitive area. The decision in the *Everson* case was claimed as a victory by both separationists and antiseparationists. Justice Hugo Black had formulated limits imposed by the establishment clause on federal and state action; but the majority proceeded to rule that providing transportation for parochial school students did not constitute aid to religion. A year later, in *McCollum* v. *Board of Education*, the Court held that a released-time program in Champaign, Illinois, was unconstitutional. The ruling, however, did not make clear whether released-time classes not conducted on public-school premises were also unconstitutional.

Despite some misgivings, the Committee joined in the amicus curiae brief filed by the Jewish groups affiliated with NCRAC and the Synagogue Council of America in the *McCollum* case. The McCollums were atheists, and some AJC leaders worried that Jewish support of the case would be equated with a defense of godlessness. Also, the influential voice of Joseph Proskauer consistently warned that militant condemnation of sectarian practices might alienate other religious groups. However, the head of AJC's interreligious department, who would be most concerned over the effect of such a position, supported a strong separationist stand. Though his program for cooperation with the Institute of Church and State was thwarted by the Proskauer wing, he helped convince a number of non-Jewish groups to file briefs in the *McCollum* case.

The *McCollum* decision actually stimulated released-time programs. The plan had originated with the Protestants, but Catholics now gave it strong support; for it not only offered a way for the church to reach Catholic children attending public schools, but it also supported the Catholic emphasis on the need for religious education. Catholic and Protestant opponents of the Supreme Court's decision joined in attacking the court's "secularist" view and pressed school officials who were against released time to approve such programs.

The Committee, the American Jewish Congress, and the Anti-Defamation League filed a joint brief in *Zorach* v. *Clauson,* a case which challenged the released-time program in New York. The Committee employed a special attorney who coordinated its fact-finding efforts to prove coercion on the schools in behalf of religious instruction. Citing these pressures, the brief called attention to the divisiveness of the released-time program and showed that school authorities were involved in administering the program even though religious classes were held outside the public-school buildings. Finally, the brief reiterated Justice Black's opinion in the *McCollum* case, which condemned state sanction of a released-time program irrespective of where the religious instruction was given. Though Jewish groups went to great lengths to explain in the brief that their position did not mean hostility to religious instruction, it aroused considerable resentment in a number of Christian circles. (Cardinal Spellman's secretary of education called the position anti-Catholic, and the New York judge who originally denied the petitioners' motion characterized invalidation of released-time programs as "a step in the direction of . . . totalitarian and communistic philosophies.")

The Supreme Court upheld the New York program in 1952, finding it markedly different from that in Champaign. In a decision spelling out a view of accommodation between church and state, Justice Douglas stated for the majority that "we are a religious people whose institutions presuppose a Supreme Being." The First Amendment enjoins separation, Douglas said, but it does not require the government to be hostile to religion or to resist efforts to widen the influence of religion. In the two released-time cases, the Supreme Court reaffirmed the need for an impregnable wall between church and state and at the same time insisted that the wall was not antireligious. Like most compromises, the court's balance failed to reassure the more outspoken proponents of both separation and accommodation.

With the public schools under heavy pressure to "inculcate moral and spiritual values" in the classroom, the Committee considered how such values could be taught without a religious framework which, in its view, automatically implied a sectarian approach. In the classroom, the Committee maintained, values were taught in every aspect of the curriculum and were reflected in the conduct and character of the teacher. The Committee encouraged an experimental program based on that approach, which was developed by the Kentucky Department of Education. Involving special workshop training for students, teachers, parents, and community workers, the Kentucky plan devised ways to teach ethics as part of cultural and social development. It explained that moral and ethical values derived from both religious teachings and human experience. While the influence of religion on human behavior was fully discussed, ethical standards were not necessarily linked to the supernatural or to religious dogma. However, since the program required a very extensive effort to win support from the teachers and the community, it did not receive widespread acceptance.

It was difficult to convince the majority of Americans that opposition to religion in the schools did not mean opposition to religion itself. In 1962 the Supreme Court ruled in the case of *Engel* v. *Vitale* that a twenty-two word nonsectarian prayer composed by the New York Board of Regents for use in the schools violated the establishment clause of the First Amendment. The court tried to make clear its distinction between the separation of church and state and attacks on religion:

> It is neither sacrilegious nor anti-religious to say that each separate government in this country should stay out of the business of writing or sanctioning official prayers and leave that purely religious function to the people themselves

and to those the people chose to look to for religious guidance.

But that view, and the argument that the court in effect invigorated religion by safeguarding freedom of conscience, were clearly in the minority. There was an immediate public outcry against the decision. Statements by Protestant and Catholic church leaders, public-opinion polls, editorials, letters to the White House, and action by members of Congress and state legislatures reflected the general sentiment that the court action was anti-God, antireligion, and prosecularism.

The Committee, which had spoken out against the regents' prayer at the time of its adoption, joined with the Anti-Defamation League to contest the prayer's constitutionality. Their brief read in part:

> The Board of Regents hoped that a prayer could be devised which would be unobjectionable to all three major religious faiths and still meaningful in terms of teaching a reverence for the Creator. The danger inherent in this process is that a state agency undertook to evaluate the spiritual needs of the student population of the public schools and to establish the means to satisfy such needs. This tends to belittle creedal differences and to establish a form of "public school religion" or "least common denominator religion." Freedom of religious belief, observance and worship can remain inviolate only so long as there is no intrusion of religious authority in secular affairs or secular authority in religious affairs. Each breach of this separation of role and function tends to beget additional breaches. . . .

The hope of the Jewish groups, shared by nonreligious groups like the American Civil Liberties Union (ACLU), was that the *Engel* decision would sweep away other religious practices in the schools. Despite the wave of public resentment, they proceeded to file briefs in cases contesting Bible-reading and the recitation of the Lord's Prayer *(Abington School District* v. *Schempp;*

Murray v. *Curlett).* Commitment to the principle of separation overrode considerations which might have dictated a course of abstention. Freedom of religion was not involved, for those students who did not wish to participate in the Bible-reading and prayer exercise could be excused. Jews were increasingly concerned with Vatican II and other efforts to foster religious ecumenism. And continuing separationist activity threatened to reawaken anti-Semitism in the United States.

But what might have cowed the Jews thirty years earlier was no longer taken so seriously. When *America,* the powerful Jesuit weekly, asked: "What will have been accomplished if our Jewish friends win all the legal immunities they seek, but thereby paint themselves into a corner of social and cultural alienation?" several Jewish groups responded with justifiable anger. The Committee publicized its own pointed rejoinder to the magazine's prediction that the Jews would reap "a harvest of fear and distrust":

> We do not agree that the Supreme Court decision was antireligious; nor do we believe that it will result in the increased "secularization" of American life. But without entering into an extensive debate on the question, we would like to point out that by accusing Jews of participating in a campaign to "secularize" the country on no evidence other than their commitment to the First Amendment, and by asserting that the general population is overwhelmingly opposed to this campaign, you have made it appear that the heightened anti-Semitic feelings over which you express such friendly concern are the product of righteous outrage against Jewish vigilance on the principle of the separation of Church and State. You therefore counsel the Jewish community to forestall the threat of anti-Semitism by abandoning or compromising its commitment to the First Amendment as it has been interpreted by the Supreme Court. Jews, you say in conclusion, must decide "what bargain they are willing to strike as one of the minorities in a pluralistic society."
>
> This seems to us a very strange piece of advice indeed

to offer in the name of pluralism. We believe, and we have always been under the impression that AMERICA believed, that pluralism involves the right of every American group to express its viewpoint and press its position through the impartial judicial process which our democratic state has established for such purposes. Is this a matter for "bargaining"? Have Catholics generally regarded it as a matter for bargaining? Have Catholics been deterred from pressing their views in the legislatures and in the courts by the worry that victory might produce "a harvest of fear and distrust"? It is, of course, true that some Catholic spokesmen have argued for a prudential approach to questions on which the Catholic viewpoint is isolated and unpopular. But, by and large, Catholics have not allowed their minority status to determine their positions on what they have considered crucial issues of principle.

The Committee carefully monitored public opinion and planned an intensive educational program to head off the tensions that were anticipated if the Supreme Court upheld the separationists in the *Schempp* and *Murray* cases. Meanwhile, in a brief filed together with the Anti-Defamation League, the Committee repeated its views on religious freedom, this time with the added authority of the *Engel* decision. The Supreme Court's opinion in the 1963 cases vindicated the Committee's long-held conviction that majority rule could not apply in matters of religion. Explaining its ban on Bible-reading and prayer recitation in the schools, the court declared:

> The place of religion in our society is an exalted one, achieved through a long tradition of reliance on the home, the church and the inviolable citadel of the individual heart and mind. We have come to recognize through bitter experience that it is not within the power of government to invade that citadel, whether its purpose or effect be to aid or oppose, to advance or retard. In the relationship between man and religion, the state is firmly committed to a position of neutrality.

The *Schempp* and *Murray* decisions evoked far less bitterness than expected. When Congress held hearings in 1964 on resolutions to amend the Constitution in order to override the Supreme Court's decisions, Protestant groups joined Jews in presenting opposing testimony. The situation was still not resolved; in some school districts the court's rulings continued to be flouted. But the national Jewish agencies could rightfully claim that their persistent endeavors had helped add new safeguards for minorities to the proscriptions of the First Amendment.

III

Recent church-state controversies have centered largely on state and federal aid to religious schools. The issue involves much more than the constitutional question of "no aid" versus "accommodation." It cannot be separated from the major concerns of postwar America: the functions of a welfare state, the space race with the Soviet Union, the goal of racial equality, the drive to stamp out poverty. The acknowledged need for an improved educational system, and the government's responsibility to fill that need, drew immediate attention to the religious institutions. Enrollment in parochial schools was rising; by the 1960s it had reached six million. It is doubtful whether radical improvements in the crisis-ridden public schools would have seriously jeopardized the existence of the sectarian schools. The perennial questions of the unfairness of forcing parents of parochial-school students to bear a double financial burden for education and of the government's obligation to private institutions which educate children in the public interest and to the public's advantage remained unresolved. The bald fact is that pressure by organized religion was strong enough to prevent the enactment of any comprehensive program of aid to education which excluded parochial schools from a share in the benefits.

In weighing its stand on aid to sectarian schools, the American Jewish Committee considered both the principle of separation of church and state and the needs of education in a democratic society. Until 1965 it recognized no conflict between the two. The logic of its civil rights program and its conviction that education played a major role in fighting prejudice led AJC to endorse federal aid to education. But it insisted that such aid be limited to tax-supported, publicly controlled elementary and secondary schools. In its Statement of Views on Religion in Public Education (1955), the Committee touched on issues which have continued to plague Congress and the courts:

> In order to equalize educational opportunities throughout the nation, Federal aid could be extended to the states for tax-supported, publicly-controlled elementary and secondary schools. Extension of such aid to non-public schools, either directly or indirectly, is opposed. Likewise opposed is the use of tax funds to supply textbooks for children in non-public schools. However, lunches and medical and dental services should be available to all children at public expense, regardless of the school they attend, provided there is public supervision and control of the program.
>
> The question of free bus transportation for children attending non-public schools should be considered on its own merits in separate legislation, and should not continue to retard the extension of Federal aid.

The Jewish community, except for the Orthodox groups which maintained their own day schools, was largely in accord. Nevertheless, there were weighty arguments which challenged the Committee's view. A pluralistic society called for the encouragement of private (including religious) educational systems; state-supported secularism posed graver threats to a free society than support of religious diversity; the "triple melting pot" concept of contemporary America required Jews to identify with a religious rather than a secularist point of view. A number of professionals on the staff of the Committee were prepared to modify their position in the interest of the long-range needs of

society and the Jewish community, and to oppose further litigation. The majority of the membership, however, would permit no
breach in the church-state wall.

In 1961 President John F. Kennedy urged the enactment of
a comprehensive program of federal aid to education at all levels.
He ruled out loans and grants to private and sectarian elementary
and secondary schools but favored aid to higher education, in the
form of scholarship funds to enable talented students to attend
colleges of their choice, as well as federal loans for college housing and construction of academic facilities. To enable private
institutions to accept additional applicants, the Kennedy program called for an annual grant of $350 to be paid directly to the
college chosen by the scholarship student.

AJC statements to congressional committees considering
the administration's proposals gave unqualified endorsement to
the aims of the New Frontier with regard to public schools and
commended the president's stand on grants and loans to private
lower schools. But the Committee refused to support the higher-
education proposals. AJC knew that private and sectarian universities enrolled close to half the college and university population
and were afraid that under sharply increased pressures for admission Jewish youths might face new restrictions. It was clear, too,
that sectarian indoctrination was a far smaller danger at the college level than in the elementary school. (In fact, it was often
difficult to determine what constituted a sectarian college, for
frequently neither the history of an institution nor its sponsorship was reflected in its curriculum or faculty.) Nevertheless, the
Committee would endorse only the provision for scholarship aid
—and even this was a compromise, since certain recipients would
doubtless choose to attend a denominational institution. All
other forms of aid to private colleges were rejected. Insisting that
its position should not be interpreted as hostility to denominational schools, the organization argued on the grounds of public
policy as well as constitutionalism:

The American Jewish Committee believes . . . that this crisis in higher education must be met within the framework of sound public policy adopted over 170 years ago—namely, that the institutions of church and state shall be kept forever separate and distinct in the United States. The separation principle is not merely a "legal issue"; it is one of the cornerstones of our democratic society, no less precious or less essential than the other liberties guaranteed by the First Amendment. . . . The American Jewish Committee does not believe that the crisis in higher education demands the destruction or sacrifice of our precious heritage of separation of church and state, the basic foundation of religious freedom in the United States. . . .

The American Jewish Committee has steadfastly held to the position that public funds should be used for public education and must not be used, either directly or indirectly, to support denominational institutions. We do not believe that it is either discriminatory or unjust to ask private institutions which quite properly insist upon their freedom from governmental control, to seek private sources of funds to create and expand their facilities. Indeed, we consider it unfair and a gross violation of the principle of separation of church and state to ask the general tax-payer to foot the bill, in whole or in part, for such denominational institutions. . . .

While we believe that in the *Everson, McCollum* and *Zorach* cases, the United States Supreme Court has interpreted the Establishment Clause of the First Amendment as a bar to the use of public funds or credits to support sectarian institutions, as well as other church-related functions, we predicate our opposition in the context of the current legislative proposal on grounds of public policy rather than constitutional law.

The American Jewish Committee believes with [President James] Madison that "it is proper to take alarm at the first experiment on our liberties." . . . Thus each breach in the wall of separation between church and state becomes a precedent for further breaches until the separation principle will no longer exist.

The administration bills for federal aid to the public schools died in committee, at least partly because of Catholic insistence that they also provide aid to parochial schools. Minority-group pressure had become so widely accepted on the American scene that Catholics did not hesitate to kill the program of a Catholic president.

The 1961 struggle, which revealed the paralyzing effect of church-state controversies on educational planning, was not lost upon Kennedy's successor. Aided by an impressive Democratic majority in Congress, Lyndon Johnson pushed through a bill providing federal aid for private and public elementary and secondary schools. The religious issue was circumvented by tying federal aid to the poverty program and by invoking the "child-benefit" theory set forth in *Cochran* v. *Louisiana* and *Everson* v. *Board of Education;* the theory holds that government support is justified if the child, not the church, reaps the benefit. The new legislation enabled parochial-school students to receive textbook loans and special educational services financed with federal funds, and provided for "shared time" programs allowing parochial-school children to attend public schools for instruction in nonsectarian subjects, such as gym, mathematics, and the sciences.

If the child-benefit theory provided a legal means for meeting the nation's educational crisis without attacking the doctrine of separation, it nevertheless constituted a breach in the church-state wall. The American Jewish Committee, which had not challenged earlier laws providing auxiliary health services for parochial-school students, viewed the expansion of that concept as indirect aid to religious schools and recognized that to support Johnson's program would mean a deviation from its traditional church-state policy.

It was clear that the country as a whole was far more concerned with the problems of poverty than with the principle of separation. Opinion polls showed a dramatic increase since 1961 in the number of Americans supporting aid to parochial schools.

Organizations and individuals long opposed to such aid (including Conservative and Reform Jews) reversed themselves. "Ignorance, not the Catholic hierarchy, is the enemy," declared the liberal *New Republic.*

After much soul-searching, the Committee decided to support the Johnson program and endorsed the bill before Congress, with certain reservations: (1) federal aid should not be used by a religious institution to acquire or expand its property; (2) federal funds should not be used for religious purposes; (3) wherever practical, a public agency should supervise the expenditure of federal funds; and (4) state and federal watchdog commissions should be set up to guard against abuses. Particularly interesting in light of a later Supreme Court ruling was the Committee's specific proposal that the bill guarantee the right of taxpayers to challenge the constitutionality of loans and grants to private schools. AJC also suggested a plan for judicial review, but the attorney general and others argued that it presented too many constitutional and practical obstacles. Finally, the Committee urged Congress to define *child benefit,* since the bill encompassed far more than had been sanctioned by the *Cochran* and *Everson* cases.

AJC's stand brought considerable criticism from its own chapters and from the more militant separationists in the Jewish community. In May 1965, a few weeks after the bill was passed, the question was reviewed at the Committee's annual meeting. While the majority seemed convinced that both AJC's shift in position and the breach in the wall of separation were warranted by the crisis in education, a sizable minority disagreed. There were equally sharp divisions on such issues as shared time and bus transportation for parochial-school students. A Church-State Study Commission was created to consider the entire matter anew, but its deliberations did not end the cleavage. Most members agreed with the commission's recommendations that within the context of the Elementary and Secondary School Act, which was expressly designed to aid disadvantaged children, such types of aid as textbook loans and remedial educational services to parochial-school students not be opposed, and that opposition to bus transportation and auxiliary services *in* parochial schools be maintained. A sizable minority opposed even limited benefits to parochial schools; another minority supported a softer line.

In final analysis the issue of federal aid to education, like that of religion in the public schools, pointed up the commitment of American Jewry (a deeper commitment than that of most other minority groups) to the principle of church-state separation. How long the Jewish community and its representative agencies will cling to this commitment—particularly if present trends continue and they find themselves increasingly outside the mainstream of American liberal thought—is a matter for speculation. Much depends on the forces underlying Jewish identity and survival. If America continues to develop as a three-faith nation, Jewish security might best be served by a more moderate stance on official recognition of religious commitments. If Jewish survival depends on religion rather than ethnic factors, separationism—insofar as it reflects secularism—will have to be modified. Ultimately these factors will determine the Jewish position on church-state matters, as well as the continued influence of the nonreligious organizations which have so long regarded the separation of church and state as immutable American doctrine.

17

The Teachings of Religion

I

In 1945 the American Jewish Committee inaugurated its Inter-religious Department designed to foster mutual understanding between Jews and Christians.

A stunned American Jewry was just beginning to grasp the full meaning of Hitler's "Final Solution," which was carried out with little opposition or outcry from the Christian world. In the United States during the preceding decade there had been cler-ics, both Catholic and Protestant, among the rabble-rousers and anti-Semites. The Committee, on the threshold of an expanded social-action program, now hoped to establish working alliances with Christian groups to combat anti-Semitism and further com-mon objectives.

Interreligious cooperation did not mean a diluted inter-denominationalism to which all religious groups could subscribe. The term *interfaith* was deliberately avoided, not only because it was unacceptable to Catholics, but also because it conjured up an image of bland do-goodism. The National Conference of Christians and Jews, the Committee believed, had been handicapped from the outset by its tendency to gloss over basic religious differences. Interreligious activity, AJC decided, must assume a commitment to a specific creed on the part of all groups involved. Recognition of doctrinal differences not only did not preclude cooperation but could well enhance mutual respect.

At AJC's fiftieth annual meeting, in 1957, representatives of each of the three major faiths joined in a symposium on the differences between religious pluralism and religion in a pluralist society. While all speakers agreed that adherence to a particular creed implied a belief in its superiority, they also agreed that in a free society each faith must recognize the rights of the others to disseminate their particular message.

The goal of the Committee's interreligious program was to blunt the divisiveness keeping groups apart; religious teachings which preached hatred and made for discord were a serious stumbling block to social harmony. It was directed primarily at "professional" Christians: leaders of ministerial associations, religious and teaching orders, theological seminaries, religious-education institutions, the religious press, and church-affiliated social-action groups. In more recent years the program has been expanded to encourage informal lay dialogues in the local communities.

That the American Jewish Committee, and not the rabbinical groups, took the lead in initiating such interreligious projects is not as strange as it seems. Not only was there a close relationship between AJC's defense work and its interreligious activity, but also there had been a tradition in the United States of keeping the synagogue separate from secular communal endeavors. Since the Committee's concern was not theology but group interaction, there was no reason why the Jewish counterparts of the professional Christians in such endeavors should not be Jewish laymen. True, the Interreligious Department was always headed by a rabbi; but it was often quipped that "you don't have to be a rabbi to resent being called Christ-killer."

The turn of events in postwar America lent added justification to the Interreligious Department. The climate generated by the cold war contributed to an upsurge in religious expression and the increased influence of religious institutions. Indeed, for the individual the popular postwar definition of Americanism assumed some form of religious belief, if not affiliation. Statistics showed the growing strength of organized religion: in 1900, 36 percent of Americans reported some kind of church affiliation; that figure rose to 49 percent in 1940, 57 percent in 1950, and 63 percent in 1961. Church construction, religious-school enrollment, and church budgets all disclosed the same trend. With this growth came a deeper involvement with social issues, both foreign and domestic.

The same increases in affiliation and involvement were evident in the Jewish community, though the growth in prestige far outstripped the numerical gains. At the end of World War II, Jews constituted roughly only 3 percent of the total American population; yet Judaism was recognized as one of the three major faiths in the nation, and—on a religious level—Jews enjoyed a status equal to that of the Protestants and Catholics. Within this framework the Committee launched its efforts to enlist the churches in a unified program of social action.

Serious obstacles still blocked successful cooperation. The growth in organized religious strength was particularly marked among fundamentalist Protestant sects, which lent a conservative coloration to American Protestant theology. Whereas liberal Protestantism was generally receptive to intergroup ventures, conservatism often meant overt antipathy to both Catholics and Jews. Within the Catholic Church age-old patterns of authoritarianism and hierarchical control lessened the possibility for effective contact with individual leaders. Not until the advent of Pope John XXIII did the Catholics as a group respond enthusiastically to the idea of interreligious activity. Deep-seated conflicts over the Catholic positions on censorship, birth control, separation of church and state, and other issues also made a working rapport among Catholics, Jews, and Protestants difficult. Even if the Jews had so desired, they could no longer keep silent on those issues. They had to take sides when both Catholics and Protestants, in attempts to bolster their respective positions, insisted on hearing Jewish opinions.

When the Committee first launched its program, few Jewish religious leaders were convinced that cooperation with other faiths was desirable. Cynicism, fear, pride, and a concentration on Jewish issues—all nurtured by a long history of minority status —left most of them indifferent to the advantages of interreligious activities.

The Committee recognized that if its program was to succeed, it would have to not only convince both Christians and Jews of the value of cooperation, but also promote a better understanding of one another's beliefs, practices, and history. It was equally clear that if the impact of such cooperation was to reach beyond the leadership to the rank and file, it had to encompass not only liberal Protestants and Jews but all shades of Christian theological belief—including the fundamentalists and the Catholics—and the Orthodox Jewish community. Nor was it enough to limit dialogues or "trialogues" to nontheological issues on which all faiths could politely agree, such as the immorality of communism, the injustice of anti-Negro discrimination, and the merits of a liberal immigration policy. Such discussions might well be useful and perhaps even influential in political decisions. But they did not touch on the essential differences causing intergroup tension.

The Committee decided to work on two levels: alliances between Jews and Christians on issues peripheral to religion; and education to overcome divisive distrust and ignorance. It joined with Catholics and Protestants to condemn the Communist-sponsored Stockholm Peace Petition, to combat bigotry in election campaigns, and to denounce the arbitrary procedure of the House Committee on Un-American Activities, and it cooperated with Christian groups in appeals for food relief for India. Here its most notable achievement perhaps was convening the 1963 National Conference on Race and Religion, the first of its kind sponsored by the three faiths. It brought together over six hundred delegates on the hundredth anniversary of the Emancipation Proclamation for the purpose of mobilizing institutionalized religion in behalf of racial equality.

These activities advanced the Committee's social objectives and at the same time strengthened the image of American Jewry as an equal working partner among the major faiths. Such cooperation also enabled the Committee to secure Protestant and Catholic help in protesting Hungarian anti-Semitism, refuting charges that Israel descrated holy places, and dealing with community tensions over church-state issues or other local problems.

The Committee developed a variety of interreligious educational programs: "brotherhood kits" and materials on interfaith unity and on the meaning of Jewish traditions and practices, for the mass media and church organizations; consultative services on interreligious cooperation for rabbis and local Jewish groups, subventions to Hebrew Union College and Vanderbilt University for the training of Christian clergymen in postbiblical Jewish history and related projects. With the Anti-Defamation League, AJC also helped fund a Department of Intergroup Education under the aegis of the National Council of Churches to give Protestant schoolchildren a better understanding of other faiths.

Admittedly, the best results were achieved with liberal Protestant groups. Contacts with the Catholics were personal and informal rather than organizational, and the Committee at first employed a special consultant to interpret the Jewish position to individual Catholic priests, editors, and writers, and to establish closer relations with Catholic educational authorities. At both Catholic and Protestant colleges and teacher-training centers the Committee promoted courses, workshops, and seminars on intercultural education and intergroup relations as a means of instilling appreciation of religious diversity. Special educational efforts were also required in the Jewish community, for the Orthodox were hostile to interfaith dialogue, and some religious leaders resented AJC's encroachment on interfaith work, which they felt belonged in their jurisdiction.

An interesting Committee-sponsored project to further education through dialogue was "the Four C's conferences." For several years, beginning in 1958, Columbia University's School of Journalism hosted an annual meeting with the editors of *Commonweal, Christian Century,* and *Commentary.* Each editor brought to the informal and unpublicized sessions a panel of religious journalists and scholars who joined in a free-form discussion of the role of religion in politics, foreign policy, and church-state matters. In a short time a frank exchange of views replaced dispassionate platitudes. Besides pointing up the social responsibilities of the molders of religious opinion, the conference clearly revealed the inaccuracies in treating any one of the three faiths as a monolith.

II

Educational projects, the Committee knew, had little value if they were superimposed on bigoted attitudes. University students were far less likely to develop respect for different religions and understanding of them if they had to unlearn prejudices held since early childhood. Since AJC was convinced that a great deal of bigotry derived from prejudicial religious textbooks and Sunday school curricula, it worked hard for more than thirty years to bring about revisions of offending texts. It is here, perhaps, that AJC has made its most significant contribution to interreligious harmony.

In 1930, when the first echoes of Hitlerism began to be heard in the United States, Morris Waldman suggested that the American Jewish Committee underwrite a study to analyze the pervasiveness of anti-Jewish prejudice in Protestant pedagogical literature. Negotiations with the Federal Council of Churches fell through, but the study was undertaken by Drew Theological Seminary (officially under the auspices of what was then called the National Council of Jews and Christians, but financed by the Committee). The findings, submitted in 1934–35 by Dr. James V. Thompson, who headed the project, pointed to numerous disparaging or hostile references to Jews and Judaism in religious textbooks and teachings. The Jews of Jesus' day fared worst, the Hebrews of the biblical period somewhat better. Often it was unclear from the writings that the early Hebrews were, in fact, the ancestors of the later Jews; almost all references to Jews were limited to the New Testament era. It was conceivable that (particularly in the rural areas) a Protestant child could come away from such teachings believing that the Jews had disappeared like other ancient races. Even if he was aware of their existence, he often knew of them only in the stereotype of the Pharisees who rejected or crucified Jesus. Dr. Thompson also surveyed the attitudes of five hundred religious teachers: 12 percent said that the Jews were responsible for the death of Jesus; 68 percent believed that Jews were "underdeveloped" but had the same potential as "whites."

Thompson's findings were made known to religious leaders and publishers, and some textbooks were revised. During the late 1930s and the war years several other textbook analyses were undertaken by the three major religious groups. AJC sponsored a study of Jewish books by a committee of the Synagogue Council of America; as a result, a number of passages which offended Christian sensibilities were dropped.

One of the biggest stumbling blocks to religious amity was the way in which Christians (particularly Catholics) recounted the Jewish role in the crucifixion. Informal talks between Dr. Louis Finkelstein, president of the Jewish Theological Seminary, who acted for the Committee, and members of the Catholic hierarchy were arranged in an attempt to enlist their support in dealing with the problem; but the meetings accomplished little. When the Committee set up its Interreligious Department, renewed efforts

efforts were directed toward the Catholics. In response to requests by AJC, the general secretary of the Catholic Biblical Association asked half a dozen publishers of religious textbooks to revise passages attributing the death of Jesus to the Jews as a whole. (He himself doubted revisions could help wipe out anti-Semitism, which he attributed to a lack of Christian charity plus "odious" Jewish traits; but he admitted that "no Jew living today can be in any way responsible for what happened two thousand years ago.") In sections of the country where bishops were sympathetic to the problem, such changes were implemented.

Far more significant was a comprehensive study of Protestant texts and lesson materials, begun at the Yale Divinity School in 1952. Conducted by Bernhard Olson, it analyzed the teachings of four types of Protestant denominations: conservative, liberal, fundamentalist, and neoorthodox. Although its emphasis was on Jewish-Christian relationships, it examined all manifestations of in-group/out-group attitudes and the correlations of ethnocentricism with theological beliefs. Olson discussed the extent of Protestant preoccupation with the Jewish image, the roots (theological and other) of that image, and how the image varied according to subject material and specific denomination. His conclusions—particularly relevant to interreligious programing —indicated that conservative theology was not necessarily based on ethnocentricism, and that there was nothing in such a theology which precluded respect for and an understanding of other religious beliefs.

Even before Olson's work *(Faith and Prejudice,* Yale University Press, 1963) was published, the American Jewish Committee was expanding the study program to other fields. Since Olson's approach and his preliminary findings were favorably received by religious educators, the Committee, with the financial help of the Ittleson Foundation, initiated similar self-analyses by Catholics and Jews. At Southern Methodist University a study complementing Olson's critically examined the techniques, rather than the content, of intergroup teaching among Protestant denominations.

The Catholic project was carried out at St. Louis University, a Jesuit institution noted for earlier research and training in human relations. Like the Yale study, it found that Catholic texts generally projected a more positive attitude toward racial and ethnic groups than toward other religions and offered suggestions for eliminating distortions involving both Protestants and Jews. The study emphasized the importance of making clear that Jesus and his contemporaries were Jews and cautioned against sweeping generalizations or value judgments about the Jews of biblical times and their modern descendants. It also stressed the need to make the crucifixion story understood in theological terms of universal sin and salvation rather than in terms of a crime committed by particular individuals.

A study of Jewish textbooks was sponsored by the Committee at the Dropsie College for Hebrew and Cognate Learning. Unlike the Catholic and Protestant materials, which, the analyses disclosed, evidenced a deep preoccupation with out-groups, the Jewish texts devoted relatively little attention to non-Jews. (The "preoccupation index" was 66 to 88 percent for Protestants, 51 percent for Catholics, and 14 percent for Jews.) Reflecting a primary concern for group survival, Jewish books usually discussed Christians in ethnic terms rather than from a religious point of view and often contained more severe criticism of certain Jewish groups than of non-Jews.

Armed with the findings of the various self-analyses, the Committee sponsored numerous dialogues and conferences with religious educators and publishers to discuss the treatment of Jews in texts and lesson materials. By emphasizing religious weaknesses in the negative treatment of out-groups, the studies challenged the creators of teaching materials to assume the responsibility for changing objectionable texts, and many Christian educators willingly accepted the challenge. Dr. Olson prepared several self-evaluation manuals for Protestant educators and consulted with them on pedagogical materials. When the Pope Pius

XII Religious Education Center in Michigan planned a new series of textbooks for parochial schools, Rabbi Marc Tanenbaum, head of AJC's Interreligious Department, was appointed a consultant. And in the late 1960s, under the auspices of the Committee-sponsored Sperry Center for Intergroup Cooperation at the International University for Social Studies "Pro Deo" in Rome, studies of religious textbooks in a number of European and Latin American countries were initiated.

III

At the final session of the Second Vatican Council in 1965, the Catholic bishops voted their approval of a statement on the Jews. The declaration acknowledged the "spiritual patrimony common to Christians and Jews [which] is so great" and recommended that "a mutual knowledge and respect" be fostered through theological studies and dialogue. The statement did not include the word *deicide,* but it denied that the death of Jesus could be blamed on all Jews of New Testament days or on the Jews of today, and emphasized that the Scriptures presented the Jews as neither "rejected by God [n]or accursed." Finally, the statement declared that the church "deplore[d]" on religious grounds any display of anti-Jewish hatred or persecution.*

*The official summary of the Statement on the Jews reads as follows:

"The Council searches into the mystery of the Church and remembers the bond that spiritually ties the people of the New Testament to Abraham's stock.

"The Church acknowledges that according to God's saving design, the beginnings of her faith and her election are already found among the Patriarchs, Moses and the Prophets. She professes that all who believe in Christ—Abraham's sons, according to the faith—are included in Abraham's call. The Church cannot forget that she received the Revelation of the Old Testament through the people with whom God in His ineffable mercy concluded the ancient Covenant.

"Indeed, the Church believes that by His Cross, Christ our Peace reconciled Jews and Gentiles, making both one in Himself.

"The Church recalls that Christ, the Virgin Mary, the Apostles, as well as most of the early Disciples sprang from the Jewish people.

The American Jewish Committee commented on the document within a matter of hours:

> The Vatican Council Declaration on the Jews has been awaited with hope by men of good will everywhere. We regret keenly some of the assertions in the Declaration, especially those that might give rise to misunderstandings.
>
> Nevertheless, we view the adoption of the Declaration, especially its repudiation of the invidious charge of the collective guilt of Jews for the death of Jesus and its rejection of anti-Semitism, as an act of justice long overdue. We trust the Declaration will afford new opportunities for improved interreligious understanding and cooperation throughout the world.

"Jerusalem did not recognize the time of her visitation, nor did the Jews, for the most part, accept the Gospel; indeed, many opposed its spreading.

"Nevertheless, God holds the Jews most dear for the sake of the Fathers; His gift and call are irrevocable. In company with the Prophets and Paul the Apostle, the Church awaits that day, known to God alone, on which all peoples will address the Lord in a single voice and 'serve Him shoulder to shoulder.'

"Since the spiritual patrimony common to Christians and Jews is so great, the Council wants to foster and recommend a mutual knowledge and respect which is the fruit, above all, of Biblical and theological studies as well as of fraternal dialogues.

"Although the Jewish authorities and those who followed their lead pressed for the death of Christ, nevertheless what happened to Christ in His Passion cannot be attributed to all Jews, without distinction, then alive, nor to the Jews of today.

"Although the Church is the new people of God, the Jews should not be presented as rejected by God or accursed, as if this follows from Holy Scriptures.

"May all see to it, then, that in catechetical work or in preaching the Word of God, they do not teach anything that is inconsistent with the truth of the Gospel and with the spirit of Christ.

"Moreover the Church, which rejects every persecution against any man, mindful of the common patrimony with the Jews and moved not by political reasons but by the Gospel's spiritual love, deplores hatred, persecutions, displays of anti-Semitism directed against Jews at any time and by anyone.

"As the Church has always held and holds now, Christ underwent His Passion and death freely, because of the sins of men and out of infinite love, in order that all may reach salvation. It is, therefore, the burden of the Church's preaching to proclaim the Cross of Christ as the sign of God's all-embracing love and as the fountain from which every grace flows."

It was clear that AJC evaluated the Vatican Council declaration in terms of justice, and not as a favor granted the Jews by the church; that it felt justice had been shortchanged by what was clearly a compromise statement; and that the real test of the statement's value lay in its future implementation. For more than five years AJC had quietly labored for a radical excision of the theological roots of anti-Semitism. It believed that an official repudiation of the deicide charge was in order and that if the church was truly interested in promoting harmony and goodwill, it would make a significant and dramatic move toward greater interfaith understanding.

The issue was complicated by Arab propaganda, Jewish pride, pressures from governments, the Vatican's economic and political interests in Italy, and the liberal-conservative differences within the Catholic hierarchy. That all of these difficulties were ultimately overcome testifies to the strength of a new ideological current in the Catholic Church. In Rome that current was epitomized in the figure of John XXIII and the spirit of *aggiornamento* (modernization of the church); in the United States it accounted for the ferment among an aroused laity which was often more forward-thinking than the clergy. To update the church, to make its teachings more relevant to modern society, to strengthen its position in the Western world by proving that church doctrine was in harmony with democratic tenets—these were the aims of the progressives. After the Nazi holocaust any remnant of church-condoned anti-Semitism was unacceptable. The Vatican Council's statement on the Jews, like its declaration on religious liberty, became a symbol of progressive Catholicism. And to Jewish groups the progressive trends in the church offered the hope that religious teachings which had nurtured anti-Semitism for two thousand years would be authoritatively repudiated.

In 1947 a Committee representative participated in a conference of Catholic, Protestant, and Jewish leaders at Seelisburg, Switzerland, which called on Christians to revise their teachings about Jews. The conferees underscored the connection between Christian doctrine and anti-Semitism, but it was clear that only official action by the highest church leaders could effect truly meaningful changes. Early in the 1950s members of the Committee joined in support of the International University for Social Studies "Pro Deo" in Rome. Approved but not run by the church, the university stressed the democratic values inherent in the three major faiths and the need for intergroup communication to apply those values to social problems. However, the Committee envisaged not simply another liberal-arts institution with a faculty and student body of various religious and ethnic backgrounds. It hoped that the church would underwrite the progressive philosophy of the school as a way of achieving intergroup understanding. After John XXIII became pope, there were signs of a growing friendliness toward Jews on the part of the Vatican, including changes in liturgical phrases insulting to Jews and denunciations of religious intolerance and the past horrors of fascism. Overall progress, however, remained uneven.

The Vatican Council presented the opportunity for an official church statement on the Jews which would establish a uniform liberal policy for every diocese. In an audience with Pope John in October 1960, Jules Isaac, a French scholar and historian whose research on the Christian roots of anti-Semitism was well known and respected in church circles, proposed that one of the commissions preparing for the forthcoming Ecumenical Council deal specifically with the question of teachings concerning Jews. The pope directed Augustin Cardinal Bea, in charge of a special Secretariat for Promoting Christian Unity, to consider Isaac's proposals. "Vous êtes assuré d'avoir plus que de l'espoir" (Rest assured that you can count on more than mere hope), the cardinal wrote Isaac.

The American Jewish Committee learned from Isaac and other contacts that Bea was interested in hearing Jewish opinions. The cardinal had already received a memorandum drawn up by a group of Catholic theologians at Appeldoorn, Holland, which argued for rewriting the catechism and liturgy to improve relations with Jews. Bea told a newspaper correspondent in Rome that he thought Jules Isaac's thesis exaggerated, but that he would consider suggestions on how to deal with the charge of deicide and with teachings and liturgical passages concerning Jews.

After consultation with European and American Catholic and Jewish experts, the American Jewish Committee decided it would be best for Jews to forward materials and documentations to Bea on an informal basis. (Bea had advised that Jews *only* take up theological issues and nothing bearing on the State of Israel, which the Vatican refused to recognize.) A representative body of religious and secular organizations, such as Nahum Goldmann of the World Jewish Congress proposed, could not claim to represent all shades of Jewish opinion and would inevitably lead to friction in the Jewish community. Furthermore, AJC believed, an attempt by a representative body to negotiate on the treatment of Jews in Catholic doctrine would remove the issue from its theological plane and create the impression of a compromise between the two faiths. Any action the Vatican Council might take would have far greater impact if it stemmed from church initiative. The Committee was convinced it could be of greatest service by providing the data amassed through the textbook studies and by serving as a liaison between Jewish theologians and Catholic authorities. In a direct communication from AJC president Herbert Ehrmann to the pope in December 1960, and indirectly through its "Pro Deo" University contacts, the Committee apprised the Vatican of its willingness to cooperate.

The pope expressed sympathy with the Committee's ideas, and shortly thereafter Vatican officials informed Zachariah Shuster, head of AJC's European office, that they would welcome a detailed memorandum on the problems of Catholic-Jewish relations. AJC submitted a careful analysis, drawing heavily upon the St. Louis studies; it added recommendations for revisions, prepared with the advice of Jewish religious authorities. In July 1961 the Committee received direct encouragement from Cardinal Bea in a private meeting with Shuster and Ralph Friedman. Bea suggested a second memorandum dealing with Catholic liturgy, and the Committee representatives agreed. They expressed the hope that the Ecumenical Council would not only correct historical inaccuracies, but would also offer some positive encouragement to interreligious cooperation. The cardinal promised that there would be opportunities for further exchange of views. The Committee assigned Professor Eric Werner, authority on Jewish and Christian liturgy, to prepare an analysis of "The Image of the Jews and Judaism in Catholic Liturgy." The memorandum was approved by Catholic liturgical authorities in the U. S. and was then forwarded to Cardinal Bea. A few months later the Committee introduced Professor Abraham Heschel, the noted theological scholar on the faculty of The Jewish Theological Seminary of America, to Cardinal Bea, and the latter welcomed Heschel's offer to prepare a statement outlining possible steps toward constructive Catholic-Jewish relations. The memorandum on liturgy and Dr. Heschel's document, *On Improving Catholic-Jewish Relations* (which called for Catholic repudiation of the deicide charge and church recognition of the Jews as Jews, and not as potential converts) reached Bea's secretariat before it prepared its draft statement on the church and the Jews.

Meanwhile, the general public was becoming more aware of the need to redefine Christian-Jewish attitudes. The Committee's French periodical, *Evidences,* published a widely discussed symposium on Christian teachings about Jews. More significantly, the capture and trial of Adolf Eichmann raised directly the troublesome questions of Christian complicity in the holocaust. In December 1961 the Protestant World Council of Churches forcefully condemned anti-Semitism and stated categorically that the Jewish people of today could not be held responsible for the crucifixion.

Opposition from two sources—the Arab states and the conservative prelates of the Roman curia—succeeded in shelving the

Jewish issue during the first session of the Ecumenical Council in the fall of 1962. They capitalized on a move by Nahum Goldmann, who, despite known opposition from the Vatican and a great many Jewish leaders, announced the appointment by the World Jewish Congress of an Israeli as unofficial Jewish representative to the council. As a result, the Vatican's friendliness toward the Jews cooled noticeably; anti-Semitic propaganda increased behind the scenes. Bea and his secretariat still labored for a meaningful statement on the Jews, but the cardinal warned that other church leaders would need more persuasion than ever. He suggested that the Committee might be called upon to seek the support of the ranking Catholic prelates in the United States and Latin America.

One positive result did emerge from the first session: Bea and his staff actively canvassed the leaders of the American delegation to the council, whose views on the Jewish question were as yet unknown, and succeeded in eliciting expressions of support. Richard Cardinal Cushing, who announced upon his arrival in Rome that "this is the occasion for Catholics, Protestants, and Jews to better know each other," urged his American colleagues to do everything they could to achieve Bea's plan, declaring: "If it is necessary that I go to the council in a yarmulke in order to support Bea's plan in favor of the Jews, I shall be glad to do so." The other American cardinals also spoke out, though with varying degrees of enthusiasm, demonstrating, as Daniel Callahan wrote, that the American clerics were "hardly as conservative or reactionary as many Americans and Europeans take them to be." However, American support did not necessarily mean any initiative on the Jewish issue.

Bea appeared more optimistic when he arrived in the United States for a lecture at Harvard in the spring of 1963. Publicly he stressed the need for fraternal unity; privately he told members of the American Jewish Committee that progress was being made, that the pope agreed with him on the Jewish matter. At AJC headquarters in New York, Bea conferred with six prominent rabbis, who represented the three branches of Judaism. He told them that his secretariat was concentrating on the deicide charge, the recognition of Jews qua Jews, and the historical roots of Christianity in the Hebrew Bible. Again he was frank in his optimism. Two months later Pope John died.

The elevation of Cardinal Montini as Pope Paul VI, in June 1963, changed neither Bea's determination to present a strong statement to the council nor the conservative opposition to his program. Two weeks after the second session opened, a front-page story in the *New York Times* summarized the statement to be proposed. According to the account, the document which would be part of a schema on ecumenism, would reject the idea that Jews, rather than humanity, were to blame for the death of Jesus; it would condemn hatred and persecution of Jews; and it would acknowledge the Jewish roots of the church. The Committee was afraid that the story might touch off indiscreet reactions or pressures by Jewish groups, but its fear was unwarranted. A few days later Bea gave the awaited signal: Jewish organizations ought to express to the church leaders their support of the declaration. Through its New York, Paris, and Latin American offices, AJC urged Jewish leaders throughout the world to cable Bea and others of their concern and approval.

When the declaration was submitted to the Vatican Council on November 8, 1963, its exact contents were not made public, but a summary released by the church confirmed the earlier *Times* report. The charge of deicide, as well as any scriptural sanction for anti-Semitism, was explicitly rejected. Despite the warm approval shown at the council for the declaration, however, and the favorable reaction it evoked in Jewish and liberal Catholic circles, the opposition proved superior in political maneuvering. An intensified campaign by the Arab states under the leadership of Egypt's President Nasser, the intransigence of many conservative Italian bishops, and Italian political and economic tensions converged to create pressures which successfully blocked a vote on the chapters relating to the Jews and to religious liberty. The progressive forces were caught unprepared. The American bishops, a potentially powerful group that favored both chapters, had made no effort to act as an articulate, organized faction or to seek out the pope directly, as their opponents had. The progressives and their sympathizers learned from the second session that sympathy was not enough and that theological considerations were only one of the many factors which would determine the final outcome.

Acting on Catholic advice, as well as on its own experience in political maneuvering, the Committee changed its tactics in 1964. The success of the statement on the Jews depended on the liberal prelates' intervention with the pope and on pressure from non-Catholic and nonreligious forces to offset that from the Arabs and the conservative Italian politicians and businessmen. AJC therefore shifted from fact-gathering to persuasion to convincing the liberal clergy of the need to act. The politicking of the opposition continued unabated, and reports from Rome after the second session told of plans to change the context of the statement, to weaken Bea's power over the decree, and to water down the actual contents.

Until 1964 the center of activity and initiative had been AJC's European office. Now the New York headquarters became at least an equal partner in planning strategy. The problem was not to elicit support, but to sensitize the liberal prelates to Jewish apprehensions about the declaration and to the need for strong initiative to overcome the opposition. Jacob Blaustein established close contact with Archbishop Lawrence Shehan of Baltimore. Joseph Proskauer persuaded his old friend Francis Cardinal Spellman to endorse the Vatican Council statement publicly. Cardinal Spellman agreed to appear at the Committee's annual meeting; in a widely circulated speech he forthrightly rejected the notion that religious doctrine in any way condoned anti-Semitism. Other high-ranking Catholic prelates—Cushing of Boston, Krol of Philadelphia, Wright of Pittsburgh, Dearden of Detroit, Tracy of Louisiana—also spoke out.

Cushing planned to go even further: he told John Slawson and Marc Tanenbaum that he was drafting a statement to be signed by several of his colleagues and sent to the pope. Joseph Cardinal Ritter of St. Louis planned to aid Cushing's efforts. Cushing also discussed the matter with conservative Cardinal Cicognani in Rome, who assured him that both issues of concern to the Americans would be acted upon.

Committee delegates voiced their concern directly to Pope Paul VI in a private audience in May 1964. The pontiff had been briefed on AJC's work in behalf of religious freedom, and he was particularly impressed by Mrs. Leonard M. Sperry's endowment of a center for intergroup education at "Pro Deo" University. He expressed his sympathy with the sufferings of the Jews and his hope that ethnic differences would never serve as a reason for abridging human rights. When pressed on the specific issue of the deicide charge, which Committee spokesman indicated was the heart of any statement on the Jews, the pope would only say that he had read Spellman's speech and that "Cardinal Spellman spoke my sentiments." It was the pope's first commitment on the subject, and the Committee, with Vatican permission, gave it wide publicity.

Despite the encouraging signs, however, word came from Rome that the draft on the Jews had been set in a new and less forceful framework, and that the word *deicide* had been deleted. Cardinal Bea visited the United States once more, this time apparently to mobilize sufficient support from American prelates to effect a revision from the floor at the coming council session. When word came that the conservatives would again forestall action on both the declaration on religious liberty and the statement on the Jews, the earlier optimism faded. American Catholic leaders acknowledged a new urgency to press the liberal cause. As Cardinal Cushing stated: "The voice of the Church on religious liberty and our relations to the Jewish people is being awaited in universities, in national and international organizations, in Christian and non-Christian communities, in the press and elsewhere and it is being awaited with urgent expectancy."

Clearly, the American prelates had much at stake. They remembered that the church's views on religious liberty had been more than an academic issue during the presidential campaign of 1960. If they failed to champion the statement on religious liberty as well as the declaration on the Jews, (particularly after their weak showing at the second session), they would lose face not only with their own laity, but also with American Protestants and Jews. As the representatives of a faith which flourished in a pluralistic democracy, they were the logical choice to contest the conservative elements at the council. Their actions could influence the prestige of the American Catholic hierarchy and the church in the United States for years to come.

The Committee learned that Cardinals Spellman, Cushing, Meyer, and Ritter all urged the pope to restore the clause dealing with the deicide charge. Archbishop Lucey of San Antonio suggested that if the council failed to act, the American bishops might adopt a statement of their own. Besides intensifying its contacts with the American leaders, the Committee also sought help from other quarters. A delegation to South America met with five churchmen and stressed the importance of the matter. In Europe, Shuster enlisted the aid of Vittorino Veronese, an Italian businessman and former director general of UNESCO who was also a friend of Pope Paul. Morris Abram and John Slawson called on Archbishop Iakovos, head of the Greek Orthodox Church in North and South America, who promised to convey a good word to Patriarch Athenagoras.

Knowing that Arab diplomats had impressed the Vatican with their governments' opposition to liberal formulas concerning Jews, the Committee also approached the Johnson administration. The United States had no accredited representative to the Vatican, but since other secular governments were already involved, an informal opinion might legitimately be relayed. Secretary of State Dean Rusk was sympathetic, as was the American ambassador to Italy; Speaker John McCormack raised the question directly with President Johnson. It was the summer before a national election, and the issue was obviously a delicate one which could offend Catholics, Protestants, Jews, and Arabs. The president refused to send a personal envoy to Pope Paul, but his "concern" was unofficially transmitted to the Vatican.

Whether Committee intervention in fact strengthened the draft under preparation is not known; the new version, which was made public by the New York *Herald-Tribune* in September 1964, fell far short of AJC's expectations. It lacked a forthright condemnation of the deicide charge, and it included a conversion appeal which implied that acceptance of the Jews was contingent on their entry into the church. A wave of resentment swept the Jewish community and increased opposition to Jewish involvement with the Ecumenical Council. Even when the council was first planned, there were those who questioned the motives of the church in relation to the Jews and insisted that Jews had no role in the Catholic deliberations. The inaction of the council's first and second sessions and the weakened 1964 draft of the statement on the Jews swelled the chorus of Jewish criticism, particularly among religious leaders, against Jewish organizations which persisted in their "undignified" pressure on the Catholic hierarchy.

Opposition to the statement by the council, which, ironically, joined rabbis to conservative Catholic clerics, did not sidetrack the Committee from its purpose. It publicly denounced the missionary tone of the new draft and made its disappointment clear to the prominent American churchmen. On September 14, in a frank conversation with the pope, Professor Heschel and Zachariah Shuster spelled out the Jewish objections to the revised statement—which were in no way allayed by the pope's rejoinder. The declaration, the pope said, was a religious document addressed to Catholics, and he found nothing offensive in it. He added that Jews could not dispute the right of the church to voice its hopes concerning conversion, and that too much advice from the outside might cause the council to remove the issue from the agenda entirely. Although increasingly sensitive to charges of

Jewish pressure, the Committee was still convinced that a vigorously worded statement by the council, without proselytizing
implications, would be extremely valuable. In October, in an
attempt to establish unity within the Jewish community, AJC
joined with thirteen other Jewish organizations in a "Statement
to the Jewish Community":

> Throughout our history we Jews have been the bearers
> of a distinctive religious commitment. No matter how great
> the pressures, no sacrifice has been too great for us to main-
> tain our unique religious character.
>
> A concern with the common destiny of all men is deeply
> rooted in our spiritual heritage. We, therefore, note with
> satisfaction the development of increasingly harmonious re-
> lationships among the great faiths that have engendered
> common positions and actions on vital humanitarian issues.
> The ever increasing contact between peoples in the modern
> world has created new dimensions in human relations which
> Jews have welcomed and in which they have fully par-
> ticipated. Yet today, no less than in the past, the Jew remains
> steadfast in his historic commitment, determined to preserve
> his faith and heritage.
>
> The Ecumenical Council currently meeting in Rome is
> a convocation of the religious leadership of the Catholic
> church, concerned with the problems of Christian unity and
> the definition of Catholic religious doctrine. It would, there-
> fore, be improper for the Jewish community which is not a
> part of Christianity or its ecumenical movement to offer
> suggestions concerning religious doctrine to this Council.
> However, it is our hope, that this Council will further har-
> monious relationships among the religions of the world to
> seek solutions to the problems of mankind.
>
> All men of good will are encouraged by the concern of
> this Council with the fact that certain teachings of the church
> have been used at times as a source of antisemitism. It is to
> be hoped that the final determination of the Council will
> contribute to the effective elimination of antisemitism and all
> sources of bigotry and prejudice and will lead to better un-
> derstanding amongst all peoples.

If the pope could not understand why Jewish sensibilities were aroused, he did respect the demand for revision which echoed in the Vatican Council's halls. The American prelates, in particular, had grown bolder, and their dramatic thrusts belied their reputation for conservatism and docility. They argued forcefully for the inclusion of the deicide passage, for a strong condemnation of anti-Semitism, and for a change in the statement appealing for conversion. The liberals succeeded in sending the statement back for major revisions; it emerged even stronger than that of 1963. The conservatives were able to forestall a vote on the statement on religious liberty, but that move strengthened the Americans' determination to gain approval for the declaration on the Jews. On November 20, 1964, the latter was adopted by an overwhelming vote of 1,770 to 185.

Shuster's private report from Rome emphasized the important role of the American prelates:

> We owe enormous gratitude to the U.S. bishops for their valiant stand during the entire third session on all major issues and particularly on the declarations concerning religious liberty and on the Jews. It is impossible to exaggerate their sense of devotion, their relentless energy and their going to the limit in their efforts to obtain the adoption of these declarations.

According to Shuster's account, the American bishops left Rome a wiser, more sophisticated, and more liberally committed group:

> They were rather disappointed over the maneuvers to frustrate the adoption of the declaration on religious liberty; at the same time they were elated by the fact that these maneuvers have mobilized them into action, and that they had given an example to the entire church of the militancy of the progressive wing; (one of the Americans declared at a press conference that "Collegiality started right now," which was an indication of the self-assertion by the bishops against Vatican authorities); they showed deep satisfaction over the adoption of the declaration on Jews.

The battle was still not won. According to council procedure, the draft might yet be revised radically before it came up for a final vote. And the near-unanimity suggested by the November vote was largely deceiving. Immediately after the close of the third session the opponents of the Jewish declaration—the Arabs, the conservative bishops of the curia, and other groups which, for political reasons, aligned themselves with the traditionalists within the church—planned their strongest counter-attack.

The Arabs, pressing their cause through ecclesiastical and political channels, warned the pope and the Vatican Secretariat of State of the dangers inherent in a pro-Jewish (which they equated with a pro-Israel) stance, and urged Western governments seeking favorable trade relations with Arab countries to influence their local hierarchies against the statement. The conservatives prepared a report for the prelates of the different countries, marshaling theological and political arguments for shelving the statement. After they noted the "power" of the American Jewish Committee in pressing for the statement's adoption, the apostolic delegate to the United States was advised to curtail contacts between American bishops and Jewish leaders.

All the opposition forces recognized the American hierarchy as their chief stumbling block. In a tone reminiscent of classical anti-Semitic propaganda, they depicted the declaration as a product of Jewish political motives and Jewish influences in the United States and argued that these influences were behind the position of the American clerics. Under this barrage, the pope admitted that he did not fully agree with the formulation of the declaration. When four American cardinals petitioned the pope to expedite passage of the statement without changes, he replied that he might be forced to introduce certain modifications and asked the Americans to follow a policy of silence regarding the matter. The papal secretary of state, Cardinal Cicognani, preferred that the Vatican Council not even deliberate on the matter; he reassured the Arabs that the Vatican had no intention of recognizing Israel.

AJC's apprehension mounted in 1965 when word came from Rome that the statement had been turned over to a special ad hoc committee headed by a conservative. Other reports indicated that conservatives might be willing to trade their support of the declaration on religious liberty for a watered-down declaration on the Jews, and that the latter statement might not even be brought before the council's fourth and final session. Pope Paul gave public evidence of his shift to the conservative side when he discoursed in a Lenten sermon on "the clash between Jesus and the Jewish people—the people predestined to await the Messiah but who just at the right moment did not recognize him, fought him and slandered him, and finally killed him." Sources at the Vatican confirmed that this particular passage was not an unintended slip, but a deliberate trial balloon.

The Committee publicly expressed its disappointment over this and other published accounts of opposition to the statement. But it could not reveal its knowledge of the opposition's behind-the-scenes machinations without lending credence to the charge that the Jews were pressuring the church and perhaps giving the conservatives a pretext for shelving the statement. It was important, however, that the progressives not be lulled into a false sense of security.

At the end of April 1965 the *New York Times* broke the story of the conservative and Arab pressures on the pope and the Vatican's support of a weaker statement. A few days later, at the dedication of a new "Pro Deo" University building in Rome, Judge Proskauer reminded his audience, which included several cardinals, of the explicit need to deny the deicide charge. But not until June, when reports came through that the pope had withdrawn the statement on the Jews from the council's agenda, were the progressives fully aroused. Shehan of Baltimore, now a cardinal, forwarded to the pope two petitions signed by over twenty American Catholic leaders. Although denials from the Vatican confused the picture, newspapers in different parts of the world continued to publish similar stories. These reports provided an opportunity for the Committee to talk to key religious leaders and to urge editorial support for the statement in Catholic periodicals. In a more important move, representatives of the Committee elicited the cooperation of the Protestant World Council of Churches, which, during the annual congress of German Protestant churches, expressed its concern about the fate of the declaration. The attendant publicity had the desired effect: Cardinal Cicognani was impressed with the importance of the issue, and the statement was restored to the agenda.

A new spurt of Committee activity resulted from a conversation between Rabbi Tanenbaum and a prominent Italian bishop late in August. The bishop reported that the pope still insisted the declaration could not pass in its 1964 form, and he urged that counter pressure be mobilized to offset the conservative and Arab opposition. Again the Committee sought out its progressive friends.

When the Vatican Council reconvened in mid-September, the uncompromising position of the progressives, together with the direct intervention of the pope, saved the statement on religious liberty. The new and weakened text of the declaration on the Jews became known at the end of September. All reference to deicide had been deleted, and the church no longer "condemned" anti-Semitism. It was obviously a compromise statement intended to pacify liberals without alienating the opposition. Many liberals even insisted that the new draft was superior to the old. Time had worked to help the opposition, for the zeal of the reformers could not be sustained indefinitely. The Committee continued to press for stronger revisions up until final promulgation by the pope, but to no avail. Had there never been an earlier version, the declaration as adopted would have been hailed with greater satisfaction.

The full significance of the declaration, the American Jewish Committee believed, was still unknown. The text was only a beginning. If it could help point the way to a new era of interreligious harmony, all the efforts that had been expended would prove justified. An encouraging development was the promulgation of guidelines on Catholic-Jewish relations by a special commission established by the American bishops. Aimed at implementing the directive and spirit of the Vatican Council's statement, the guidelines warmly endorsed interreligious cooperation on both clerical and lay levels, and specifically disavowed conversion as the purpose of interfaith encounter. They further recommended the revision of school texts and prayer books which depicted Jews and Judaism in negative terms, and they called for "a frank and honest treatment of the history of Christian anti-Semitism." In forthright terms, the bishops pointed up the particular relevance of the Vatican declaration to the American hierarchy:

> The Church in America is faced with a historic opportunity to advance the cause of Catholic-Jewish harmony throughout the world—an opportunity to continue the leadership taken in that direction by our American bishops during the great debate on the Statement at the Council. In the United States lives the largest Jewish community in the world. In the United States, a land that has welcomed immigrants and refugees from persecution, the Church has committed herself without reserve to the American ideal of equal opportunity and justice for all. In such a setting the Church in America today is providentially situated to distinguish itself in pursuit of the purposes of the Council's Statement.

18

To Light a Candle

"One can help light a candle rather than curse the darkness." With these words paraphrasing an old proverb, an official of the American High Commission concluded an address on the obstacles to building a democratic postwar Germany. "To light a candle" aptly summarizes the policy of the American Jewish Committee with respect to Germany after World War II. Unlike many in the Jewish community, the Committee refused to dismiss Germany as unregenerate or demand her quarantine outside the pale of civilization. The Committee had not supported the short-lived Morgenthau Plan, which sought to reduce Germany to a pastoral economy, maintaining that "it was neither feasible nor desirable to create a slum country in the heart of Europe." It was more realistic, AJC contended, to work for a democratic Germany which would resume her place among the nations and make restitution to the surviving Jewish remnant. Those goals were better served by constructive cooperation than by ostracism.

I

The resurgence of German anti-Semitism immediately after the war prompted AJC's initial concern. Anti-Jewish hatred did not disappear with the defeat of the German armies or the near-total extermination of the once populous and affluent German Jewish community. AJC observers who toured the defeated country, as well as American occupation authorities, noted that anti-Semitism was still a palpable presence. A survey conducted by the Information Control Division in 1947 disclosed that:

> At the time of this study about four in ten people in the Zone (39%) can be said to be very seriously disposed to exhibit racial prejudice. Another fifth of the population (22%) easily go along with the more extreme positions and cannot be expected to counter any expressions of anti-Semitism. Thus about six in ten (61%) of the Germans are deeply imbued with racist feeling.

Convinced that a nation's attitude toward Jews was a barometer of its democratic spirit, the Committee was certain that German prejudice could only be combatted through a program of general reeducation.

There were only some twenty thousand Jews left in Germany. The persistence of anti-Semitic feeling exacerbated the plight of the DPs and infected the American occupation troops, but those were problems of comparatively short duration. The Committee was more concerned with an anti-Semitic Germany as the focus for the spread of bigotry throughout Europe. A peace treaty which might have secured Jewish rights under international protection—a goal toward which the Committee expended much effort—never materialized. Attempts at "denazification" and democratization in the American zone had little effect. Indeed, the very idea of reeducation, as the Committee noted, was suspect to the Germans as an occupation-sponsored imposition. Nor were the Germans prepared to acknowledge their responsibility for Hitler's genocide policy. According to the report of the Information Control Division:

> [For] every German who felt moral revulsion over the fact of the unprecedented exterminations, there were perhaps many more who rejected them, on grounds of expedience, as a great "mistake" which had resulted in great political harm to Germany. Such statements not only revealed a completely inadequate moral reaction, but indicated the prevalence of the belief that the world's "jews" [*sic*] . . . had played a substantial part in bringing about war against Nazi Germany and in the subsequent defeat of Germany.

Most distressing of all was the shift in American policy toward Germany. Originally, the occupation authorities followed a harsh approach—weeding out the war criminals, forbidding fraternization, reducing the German standard of living, keeping industrial productivity down. But the Western Allies were confronted by Russia's refusal to honor its commitment to treat Germany as one economic unit and to supply the western zones with foodstuffs from the eastern sector. The only alternative to continued American and British financial support lay in revitalizing West Germany's industrial production, thus enabling the country to purchase its own food. Since Russia treated Germany as a coveted prize in the East-West competition, the country became the West's first line of defense against the expansion of communism. Only a thriving, industrialized Germany, it was reasoned, could spur the recovery of the continent and keep Western Europe out of Soviet clutches. Meanwhile, Russia was slowing down the denazification program in its sector and wooing Nazis and nationalists to its brand of totalitarianism.

To encourage the country's economic comeback the Western Allies restored greater political and economic power to the West Germans. The new policy was announced by Secretary of State James F. Byrnes less than a year and a half after V-E Day

and was amplified in July 1947 in a directive from the joint chiefs
of staff. The new approach also recognized the cultural needs of
the Germans, while placing less emphasis on denazification. (The
Americans had by then put the denazification program in German hands.) In 1949, following the Russian blockade of Berlin,
the German Federal Republic was established, an Allied High
Commission replaced the military authorities, and Germany became a partner in the European aid program. The High Commission for Germany (HICOG) strengthened the political and
economic institutions of the country and took steps to end the
occupation. Meanwhile, the Communist challenge in Korea intensified Allied determination to rearm West Germany. France
resisted the longest, but in 1955, ten years after V-E Day, a
sovereign and rearmed West Germany was admitted into NATO.

II

To the American Jewish Committee the sequence of events was
a graphic illustration of Geroge Orwell's antiutopian tracts. If the
United States insisted on treating Germany as an ally, with scant
regard to the antidemocratic forces within that country, the results could be dangerous. By lending aid and comfort to neo-
Nazis in Germany and elsewhere (who could cite U.S. actions as
vindications of Hitler's own anti-Russian bias), America would
tarnish her image as the defender of democracy; that in turn
would weaken the efforts of American Jews to aid Jews abroad.
As Americans, the leaders of the Committee did not challenge
the need to rebuild Germany; as Jews, they feared the resurrec-
tion of an unreformed state in which anti-Semitism had been part
of the national culture since the Protestant Reformation.

In October 1947 AJC pledged its full resources in support
of a government-sponsored program for German reeducation.
The Committee had already submitted recommendations for
combatting anti-Semitism to the occupation authorities, and as a

result of its urging, General Lucius D. Clay appointed Dr. Herman Wells, president of Indiana University, as a special adviser on reeducation. AJC also cooperated with American officials in preparing articles and other materials for publication in Germany. However, it quickly became apparent that the military government was proceeding on an ad hoc basis and that there was no underlying plan guiding its work. The Committee suggested the creation of an advisory council, or brain trust, in Washington to examine the War Department's failure in denazification and to coordinate reeducation methods, but the suggestion was not followed up. As military expediency increasingly overshadowed reeducation, the Committee warned that "the economic regeneration of Germany must not be permitted to override the necessity of denazification." In private conversations with the secretary of state and with President Truman, AJC argued both the unreliability of a totalitarian ally and the potential threat to Western democratic unity and world peace inherent in an ultranationalistic Germany. Supporting right-wing industrialists while neglecting the need for a democratic rank and file, the Committee warned, was a poor design for the containment of Russia. The Committee grew more apprehensive as it noted the return of industrialists with Nazi records to positions of control; the influx of Nazis into the lower echelons of government, the teaching profession, and publishing; the proliferation of neo-Nazi groups; and the continued use of Nazi textbooks in German schools. AJC hoped that the government would reassert its insistence on a democratic Germany and actively supported a 1950 Senate resolution calling for the creation of a presidential commission to provide a master plan to deal with the problem.

Lack of long-range American planning for German reeducation was matched by uncertainty in the Committee on how to proceed. The American authorities encouraged the cooperation of voluntary groups, but by 1948 only two agencies—the National Conference of Christians and Jews and the International Relief and Rescue Committee—had formulated programs for advancing democracy in Germany. Since the Committee was quite certain that German reeducation could only be meaningful if the Germans themselves planned and implemented it, it was hard to see what AJC's role should be. The first task was to ferret out local elements to assume responsibility for reeducation; and to be ready with ideas, materials, and facilities to guide those elements and smooth their way. But where were those elements to be found? Was the search for democrats automatically limited to labor and socialist circles? Would the program be weakened if it were tied to the less popular leftist political forces? AJC visitors to Germany conferred with sympathetic leaders of the Social Democratic party, and for a while the organization considered active cooperation with German labor. In light of American foreign policy, however, the favored group of both the American and German governments was conservative business—which weakened still further the appeal of the Left.

At the beginning, therefore, AJC limited its support of native German forces to the Lessing Association, a group headed by local German authorities and dedicated to fighting intolerance, and to a lecture tour by the dramatist and novelist Fritz von Unruh. For Germans coming to the United States under a program for exchange visitors, the Committee staff conducted seminars on the objectives and techniques of human-relations work. At AJC's suggestion, Washington also included instruction on human relations in the training program for visiting German labor leaders. But these efforts were admittedly thin. Nor did the Committee-sponsored deliberations of a small group of social scientists experienced in German affairs yield better results. John Slawson candidly told the AJC's Foreign Affairs Committee, in April 1951: "Unless we can formulate a bold and basic position which we can convey to our government, we should quit dabbling altogether in German problems."

A second factor which accounted for Committee floundering was the consensus that a Jewish organization should not tackle the problem alone. Both the cause of democracy in Germany and the security of German Jews might suffer, AJC reasoned, if it were known that Jews were sponsoring the projects in democracy, particularly in cooperation with the Left. Nor were American Jews eager to stand alone against American public opinion, which generally greeted the reinstatement of Nazis to positions of power and the commutation of sentences for war criminals with apathy.

The Committee's argument that a nationalistic, undemocratic Germany would menace world peace made little headway against the American military position. Most Americans believed that the United States had no alternative to rebuilding a strong anti-Russian Germany, even if reeducation suffered. The Committee's members sympathized with the need to contain Russia, and the agency was not prepared to challenge American policy in public debate, both for reasons of principle and for fear of alienating the government. AJC was also concerned that an emphasis on the dangers of anti-Semitism would be interpreted as Jewish vindictiveness. Therefore it initially resolved that any major policy recommendations should be made with the endorsement of a broad segment of nonsectarian public opinion. In 1948 the Committee invited a number of prominent educators to formulate plans for German democratization. Through the NCRAC it organized the Citizens' Council for a Democratic Germany to unite liberal individuals and organizations (including labor unions and Americans for Democratic Action) for the purpose of promoting programs of reeducation. Even AJC's own specially appointed committee on Germany was not exclusively Jewish. But all these efforts simply underlined the fact that liberal opinion in the United States was confused by the seeming contradiction between the need to resist Russia and the need to democratize Germany.

III

In the face of these obstacles it would have been easier for the Committee to write Germany off its agenda. The influence of American public opinion in Germany was waning rapidly, and the resurgence of neonazism led a great many liberal groups to despair of ever seeing a democratic Germany. AJC also knew that its efforts to provide constructive aid to the new Germany could isolate it from the American Jewish community. (At the end of 1950 the American Jewish Congress criticized the World Medical Association for voting to admit the organized doctors of Germany, and a few months later the Jewish Community Council of Detroit rejected Walter Reuther's invitation to welcome Mayor Ernst Reuter of Berlin.) But the Committee resolved to challenge the holding of group stereotypes for Germans, yet resisting them for Jews.

Assured of the sympathy of U.S. High Commissioner John J. McCloy and certain German leaders, the Committee drew up an independent statement of policy which was made public in May 1951. The statement minced no words about the dangers of an unregenerate Germany, but simultaneously rejected the quarantine position. Calling upon the United States and its allies to intensify programs of reeducation, it also suggested actions that the German Federal Republic might undertake to convince the Western world that it was sincere in its democratic intentions. Positive reaction to the statement by the State Department, liberal German circles, and even the Yiddish press exceeded the Committee's expectations. AJC was convinced that the statement also contributed to Adenauer's decision to declare his government's readiness to negotiate Jewish claims against Germany.

The statement by AJC did not indicate what it planned as its role, but in 1950 and 1951, in consultation with the State Department, German leaders, and HICOG officials, the Committee formulated the following proposals: (1) the unification of the democratic forces in Germany into a permanent national agency for the defense and development of human rights and the improvement of group relations; (2) the convocation of a German National Conference on Human Rights and Group Relations, sponsored by Germans, to launch the national agency; (3) AJC-sponsored visits to the United States by German leaders in the field of group relations; and (4) an educational program to promote in Germany an appreciation of Judaism and Jewish contributions to civilization.

The first two proposals, which were particularly ambitious, had great potential significance as a counterpoise to reactionary and racist circles. They were endorsed by McCloy, who since the beginning of his term as high commissioner had emphasized the need for democratic reform, and they evoked serious interest from the president of the German Federal Republic and the state secretary on foreign affairs. To help implement those proposals HICOG invited Committee staff member Edwin Lukas to Germany in 1952. Lukas, who fittingly dubbed the project "Operation Candle," encountered serious obstacles. He found an appalling indifference among German youth to any democratic movement, a bitter cleavage among German political groups, and a paucity of liberals who might promote the venture. Despite McCloy's sympathy, Lukas discovered, the lower-level HICOG personnel were not enthusiastic about the project. One official asked him how it was possible "to cultivate the hatred by Germans of Communists and communism, while you develop among them an understanding and a decent respect for the rest of humanity." But since the need to encourage voluntary liberal groups grew even more urgent as HICOG prepared to terminate the occupation, Lukas persisted. He organized a small committee of Germans to serve as the nucleus for a national agency. HICOG pledged between sixty and a hundred thousand dollars for the agency's first annual budget, and at Lukas's suggestion it promised to turn over to that agency many of the educational functions begun by the occupation. Despite these arrangements, the project failed to get off the ground. A reduction in HICOG's staff forced it to withdraw its cooperation from the venture, and the German leaders themselves were not sufficiently motivated even to convene the first assembly.

Thus by the mid-1950s all cooperative, constructive approaches to Germany had seemingly failed. Democratic values could not be imposed from the top down, and there was no prodemocratic base strong enough to justify hopes for a new German spirit. Those who preached reform had no more impact on the new, prosperous, self-reliant Germany than those who had preached quarantine. Clearly, it was not enough for the American government merely to indicate support for the ambitious programs of voluntary agencies. Germany would not be convinced of the project's importance unless it was an American official priority. True, the German government observed all the correct forms, and even outlawed the overt neo-Nazi Socialist Reich party. But its leadership was content to denounce anti-Semitism rather than take positive action to promote respect for religious differences. The renewed outbreaks of anti-Semitism in the 1950s—the numerous physical attacks on Jews, dissemination of hate literature, and frequent vandalism of Jewish property—indicated that bigotry was still very widespread throughout Germany. Restitution payments helped salve the conscience of some Germans; but others looked upon them more as a punishment imposed on a defeated nation than as a moral claim to be met. And West Germany's cooperation with the State of Israel, while politically expedient for both countries, did not affect German attitudes toward Jews.

IV

Despite the failure of "Operation Candle," the American Jewish Committee continued to concern itself deeply with conditions in Germany. Even after West Germany gained independence and emerged as the most prosperous country in Europe, anti-Semitism remained a problem. Analysts discarded the earlier hypotheses correlating prejudice with economic insecurity and explained that, at least in part, anti-Semitism was nurtured by the materialistic atmosphere surrounding Germany's "economic miracle." Public opinion had not changed noticeably since the 1947 study by the Information Control Division; a similar survey in 1958 revealed that 39 percent of the Germans were "definitely anti-Semitic" and 29 percent "conditionally anti-Semitic."

Ever since AJC published in 1950 *The New Threat from Germany*, by Arthur Mayer, chairman of its committee on Germany, the Committee carefully studied all evidence of a Nazi resurgence, as well as recurrent manifestations of anti-Semitism in West Germany. The relationship between the two was obvious, for the right-wing groups were the self-appointed successors to Hitler's "New Order." Even if they did not openly use the tactics of a Goebbels or a Streicher, their ideology remained consistently antidemocratic and encouraged anti-Semitic eruptions. The Committee gathered data on the new German ultranationalist parties and published the information in three pamphlets documenting the parties' methods, programs, supporters, and influences. The pamphlet also noted the cooperation of German rightists with neo-Nazi groups in other lands and pointed out how little was being done to counteract them. Though this material was submitted to American and German authorities, the growth of neo-Nazism was not stemmed.

In 1958 the Committee became alarmed by a sharp increase in West German anti-Semitic activity, including verbal attacks and social boycotts, a new wave of cemetery and synagogue desecrations, and intensified anti-Semitic propaganda from Arab and East European sources. Widely disseminated hate literature minimized the Nazi atrocities and suggested that the mass murders were a Jewish fabrication. In an effort to arouse official concern, the Committee directed inquiries on the matter to the West German president, Theodore Heuss, Chancellor Konrad Adenauer, and Dr. Erich Ollenhauer, chairman of the Social

Democratic party, but none saw any reason for alarm. All three denied that anti-Semitism infected the German people as a whole, and they urged confidence in the majority of their countrymen. During a BBC-TV interview in February 1959 Chancellor Adenauer asserted categorically that "anti-Semitism was a characteristic of national socialism; both together have disappeared," and blamed the anti-Semitic outbreaks on Communist agents. Disturbed by the superficial response of the German politicians, AJC tried for but could get not get any greater reassurance from the American State Department. The department acknowledged the seriousness of the anti-Semitic incidents, but noted that democracy was still a relatively new form of political organization in Germany.

From the numerous discussions and inquiries instigated by the Committee in 1959 a basic consensus emerged: the political leadership in West Germany and the majority of the information media were committed to democratic principles and active resistance to anti-Semitism, but the German public was by and large indifferent. Most analysts saw little hope for the generation which had reached maturity under Hitler. The only chance for constructive gains, they posited, lay in the education of the youth.

When John Slawson and Zachariah Shuster visited Germany in the summer of 1959 to examine the problem in consultation with educators and sociologists, they delved more deeply into the possibilities of inculcating democratic values among the young. The most promising vehicle for such a program, several forward-looking educators told AJC visitors, was the classroom. Courses in political and social studies, thus far neglected by the German high schools, were suggested specifically, since they might offer instruction in civic morality, the citizen's relationships with his government in a democracy, and the social responsibilities of the citizen. Another shortcoming of the curriculum, the Germans readily admitted, was the omission of contemporary history— particularly an objective study of the Third Reich. German youth's appalling ignorance about the Hitler era had been dramatically revealed shortly before, in April, by a German television reporter who interviewed fourteen- to seventeen-year-old students in twelve schools. Asked what they knew about Hitler and the Nazi era, 90 percent responded with such answers as: "Hitler revived Germany." "He did away with unemployment and built the Autobahn." "He was a man with a moustache." Most seemed totally ignorant of Nazi anti-Semitism, and the highest estimate offered of the number of Jews killed by Nazis was thirty thousand. Another survey conducted informally by one school principal showed that the pro-Nazi prejudices of the parents had rubbed off on the children. In addition, school textbooks either repressed or minimized Nazi crimes, and teachers and school supervisors frequently demonstrated a pro-Nazi bias.

Slawson and Shuster did find some bright spots, however, in the generally gloomy picture. The state of Hesse had instructed all high-school history classes to pay full attention to the post-1918 period, and similar decrees were expected in other states. Encouraged by these findings, the Committee decided to try again to help advance the development of democracy in West Germany through an intensified *German* program of political education.

V

The Bad Godesburg Conference in October 1959 was an opportunity for the Committee to present its ideas to sympathetic Germans and Americans. Sponsored by the American Council for Germany and the Atlantic Bridge (a nonpartisan German group dedicated to fostering German-American understanding), the conference was called to discuss the major problems confronting the Western democracies, particularly the East-West conflict over Berlin. The Committee sought out the American initiators of the conference—John McCloy, Professors Harry Gideonse, James Conant, George Shuster—and convinced them to include on the agenda the subject of democratic education. Irving M. Engel, honorary president of AJC, was a delegate to the conference. Like so many Jews, he admitted that though he was intellectually convinced of the need to cooperate with the democratic forces within Germany, he had emotional resistance to visiting that country. He went only because of the potential benefits of the Committee's undertaking. Engel addressed the conference on two occasions, stressing the need to cement not only the economic and military links of the Western democracies, but the ideological and cultural as well. He suggested extensive intellectual exchange programs between America and Germany. His audience of Germans and Americans prominent in government, business, and education reacted enthusiastically. A small group of educators met separately to discuss the weaknesses of the German educational system. They admitted to the shortcomings of their schools and seemed particularly impressed by the seriousness with which men like McCloy and Conant treated the subject.

After the conference Engel and Zachariah Shuster were received privately by Chancellor Adenauer. The American Jewish Committee was hoping that the German government, at least in its pronouncements, would officially endorse a prodemocratic educational movement. The school programs could be strengthened a good deal if German voluntary organizations and the political leadership agreed to coordinate their educational efforts. But the Chancellor would not commit himself. He spoke in friendly terms about Israel, German Jews, and the advances still to be made in education, and he agreed that voluntary organizations in America and Germany could play a useful role in a prodemocracy endeavor. He hoped, he added, that Germans would turn their attention to spiritual problems when their economic well-being was assured.

The Bad Godesburg Conference brought a fruitful exchange of ideas and a meeting of minds on a number of important issues. But its sessions were devoid of any sense of urgency. The calm

had no basis in fact, for scarcely three months later vandals dese-
crated a synagogue in Cologne, daubing it with Nazi symbols and
slogans—an episode that touched off an epidemic of swastika-
smearings throughout Germany and other parts of the world. By
the spring of 1960 over a thousand anti-Semitic incidents had
been recorded.

AJC reacted to the German outbreaks with a strongly
worded message to the German ambassador to the United States,
Wilhelm Grewe, documenting the manifestations of anti-Semitism in Germany during the preceding two years and naming the
groups which were contributing to the rise of neonazism. The
Committee demanded an effective investigation, the prosecution
of those responsible for the new outrages, the reinstitution of
denazification procedures, the removal of former Nazis from official positions, and the outlawing of neo-Nazi parties and foreign
fascist groups. It also stressed the need for the rapid development of a democratic educational program by the West German
federal and state governments.

Ambassador Grewe promised that more would be done
through the schools to enlighten the youth, but he denied that
the manifestations of neonazism had a bearing on the course of
German democracy. The official German white paper on the
subject attributed the anti-Semitic outbreaks to juvenile delinquency and Communist instigation, an explanation which the
Committee called a "dangerous over-simplification." Although
AJC was criticized for adopting a hard line toward the Adenauer
government, the organization did not reduce its pressure. Jacob
Blaustein, in a private meeting with Adenauer in June 1960,
urged the chancellor not to take lightly AJC's concern about a
possible resurgence of neonazism and anti-Semitism, and emphasized that an effective system of democratic education was the
responsibility of the West German federal government.

The Committee continued its examination and exposure of
neo-Nazi currents in Germany during the 1960s. The major
thrust of its German program, however, remained education for

democracy. With financial support from the Ford Foundation and the New World Foundation, AJC arranged for a team of German educators to visit the United States in the fall of 1960 under the sponsorship of the Institute of International Education. The teachers conferred with American educators and observed classes in social studies and teacher training. By the end of 1966 twelve such teams had been brought to the United States, and the German government and two German foundations were lending financial support. (Jacob Blaustein's effort to raise money for the project from leading German industrialists like Krupp was a determined and novel attempt to ally big business with political democracy. Unfortunately, the effort failed.) The participants were selected by Dr. Max Horkheimer, the Committee's consultant in Germany, and head of the Institute for Social Research at the University of Frankfurt. He also coordinated the activities of the returning teams, who, using new curricula, techniques, and textbooks, worked together to stimulate interest in the democratization of the German schools. The follow-up program with the returning teachers—or "multipliers," as they thought of themselves—later came under the wing of a separate Bureau of Studies of the Sociology of Political Education.

The results were gratifying but modest. John Slawson reported after a trip to Germany and Austria in 1966 that the school atmosphere and teacher behavior still reflected authoritarian traditions. Teachers exhibited no great eagerness for educational reform, and the general public was apathetic about educational issues. Even more discouraging was the annual report of the German minister of the interior, which documented a rise in anti-Semitic and totalitarian activities. To the American Jewish Committee in 1966, the future of democracy and human rights in Germany was at best uncertain. All the organization could do to help was to expand its efforts to "teach the teachers." History alone would decide whether the Germans could develop an identity free of aggressive nationalism.

19

Behind the Iron Curtain

I

Until Hitler's armies were crushed the American Jewish Committee paid scant attention to the problem of Jewish security in the Soviet Union. In the 1920s special commissioned reports and other information reaching Jewish organizations gave evidence of a new anti-Semitism taking shape under communism. Russia was the only country in the world which had officially outlawed anti-Semitism and imposed punishments for crimes against Jews. At the same time, government restrictions on religious life were aimed at the complete stifling of Judaism.

The obstacles to religious survival in the Soviet Union were dramatically detailed by Rabbi Menahem Mendel Schneersohn and Rabbi Gourary, leaders of the Lubavitcher sect of the Hasidic movement, in a meeting with Cyrus Adler and several members of the AJC executive in the winter of 1929. The rabbis had come to the United States to seek diplomatic aid from the government and financial help from the Jewish community. Rabbi Gourary warned AJC that the situation for religious Jews in Russia was "hopeless"—indeed, as threatening as in the days of the czars. The Committee, though sympathetic, was wary of taking independent action. It discussed the matter with other Jewish organizations and joined in a resolution with the Synagogue Council of

America, but ultimately decided that political pressure would be to no avail.

Four years later, when Rabbi Gourary again appealed to the Committee, Adler found a way to register Jewish concern with the State Department. In the wake of the Roosevelt-Litvinov conversations on American diplomatic recognition of the Soviet Union, the Committee presented a petition, signed by representatives of the three major faiths, calling attention to Russia's suppression of religious liberty. (Maxim Litvinov, USSR commissar for foreign affairs, had assured Roosevelt that the right to religious instruction was guaranteed to all Soviet citizens.) The petition apparently had no effect, and American concern for Soviet Jewry was soon overshadowed by the mounting Nazi threat. At any rate, apprehensions about the totalitarian aspects of the Soviet regime were somewhat allayed by Russia's entry into the League of Nations in 1934 and its Popular Front strategy: alliance with the Western democracies against the Axis nations.

When the Soviet Union became a fighting ally against Hitler, Jews, like most other Americans, admired Soviet heroism and contributed generously to Russian relief. AJC sent a message to Ambassador Andrei Gromyko on the third anniversary of the Nazi invasion of Russia, but adopted no special resolution applauding the Russian war effort. A friendly Russia was vital to Jewish postwar security, but, as Morris Waldman explained, the Committee could not forget the "long history of Soviet hostility to religion in general and to the practice of Judaism in particular."

American Jewry knew little of the government-sanctioned anti-Semitism which erupted in many parts of the Soviet Union during the war years, and Russian Jews, understandably enough, also chose to ignore it after the great victory which saved them from Nazi extermination. Moreover, in 1947 the Soviet Union supported the partition of Palestine and in May 1948 hastened to recognize the newly created Jewish State of Israel. But Soviet Jewry's hopes for a secure future were as illusory as the expectation that the wartime alliance with England and the United States would modify Russia's long-range aims regarding the West.

II

From 1948 to 1953 all the peculiar ingredients of Soviet anti-Semitism—the endemic totalitarianism of the regime, Stalin's paranoia, the cold war, and the centuries-old tradition of popular anti-Semitism in Russia—came together with disastrous repercussions. Jews were removed from virtually all positions of authority. Yiddish schools, theaters, newspapers, and publishing houses were shut down. Jews were publicly excoriated for their so-called cosmopolitanism and their alleged Zionist sympathies. And just before Stalin's death the infamous "doctors' plot" accusation was made, in which a group of prominent physicians, most of them Jewish, were accused of conspiring to murder Soviet leaders. The doctors were ultimately exonerated, but the animus remained. Official anti-Semitism also surfaced in most of the Soviet satellites, endangering the cultural and spiritual existence of the remnants of East European Jewry.

Even before the Stalin-inspired persecution of Soviet Jews reached its peak, the American Jewish Committee undertook to expose anti-Semitism behind the Iron Curtain. At the outset AJC's primary goal was to discredit communism among American Jews. Braving charges of Red-baiting and warmongering, the Committee not only publicized analyses of the conspiratorial and totalitarian nature of the Communist ideology, but also amassed voluminous evidence on the disabilities suffered by Soviet Jews. The Committee's intensive research campaign coincided with the last, so-called black years of the Stalin regime. The two major Committee-sponsored studies, *Jews in the Soviet Union,* by Solomon Schwarz (1951) and *Jews in the Soviet Satellites,* by Peter Meyer et al. (1953) made revelations which were first denied by the Communists and subsequently admitted in the de-Stalinization orgy of 1956.

AJC interpreted Soviet anti-Semitism not merely as conventional Jew-hatred, but as an important facet of the Soviet challenge to democracy, a means to seduce totalitarian forces throughout the world into joining an anti-American bloc. Thus, the Committee linked its own campaign to the ideological thrust of American foreign policy. "Our effort," Jacob Blaustein declared, "has been directed at making it clear that Communist anti-Semitism is a common threat to all free men."

The Committee utilized its research findings for several purposes: to alert the United States and the UN to the Soviet treatment of minorities; to educate American and European Jewish communities about communism and the Communists in their midst; and to arouse public opinion with the hope of cutting Russia off from its allies and the neutral nations. Toward these ends, Irving M. Engel testified on the history of postwar Soviet anti-Semitism before the House Committee on Communist Aggression; AJC gave financial support to anti-Communist Jewish groups and newspapers in Europe; the Committee's French-language publication *Evidences* carried articles by French intellectuals denouncing Soviet anti-Semitism; and data on the Soviet treatment of Jews were provided to the State Department for presentation to the UN.

AJC was convinced that the plight of Soviet Jewry would be ameliorated only if there was a worldwide moral revulsion against Soviet anti-Semitism. Even a totalitarian country, the Committee believed, was sensitive to world opinion, and AJC set about mobilizing that opinion in support of the Soviet Jews. For its efforts, the Committee became the target of Soviet propaganda attacks and was charged by the Russians with complicity in alleged Jewish plots of espionage, sabotage, and counterrevoloution. In 1953, at the height of the Stalinist persecutions, one Soviet literary magazine described the Committee and the JDC: "The ringleaders of Joint are also the leaders of the American Jewish Committee. They belong to the richest families in the United States . . . the Rockefellers, the Kuhn, Loeb & Co., the Warburgs, Lehmans, and Fords rule the roost. . . ."

The Committee's campaign to expose the Soviet persecutions was not hampered by the agonizing deliberations over the advisability of action which had marked its programs with respect to Germany in the 1930s. The Hitler experience had convinced American Jews that counteraction could not aggravate the situation, and might even help. True, the Soviet Union never enacted racist legislation or openly preached genocide; but if not checked, the cultural, religious, and economic repression of Soviet Jewry could mean the ultimate extinction of Judaism.

There were other reasons why the Committee launched its campaign without waiting for calls of help from Soviet Jews. Russian Jews had no organizations similar to the German Centralverein which claimed the right to speak on their behalf. And the Americans were not afraid of jeopardizing their own position, as they were in the 1930s, as long as their aims coincided with American policy toward the Soviet Union, and certainly as long as the Soviets attacked Protestants and Catholics as well as Jews. Finally, there was the grim lesson of the thirties to remind American Jews that anti-Semitism was an exportable commodity. Thus when two Russian Jews criticized Jewish sponsorship of a public rally against Soviet anti-Semitism in 1965, AJC President Morris Abram joined four other American Jewish leaders to declare: "As Jews we share natural bonds with other Jews, and we will continue to insist upon the right to protest on their behalf if their voices be muffled. Our allegations are not made lightly and we are prepared to air the evidence of our grievances to the entire community."

III

The death of Joseph Stalin, though followed by Soviet repudiation of the "doctors' plot" charges, aroused no bright hopes among American Jewish leaders. They interpreted the gesture as mere tokenism stemming from the power struggle in the Soviet hierarchy, and adopted a wait-and-see attitude toward the new Soviet regime. In October 1953 the AJC executive committee announced, on the basis of information from reliable sources, that the Soviet Union and the satellites were "covertly continuing their ruthless persecution of all minorities and religions."

But even though the Committee doubted that the Soviet government would have a change of heart on the treatment of the Jews, it stood ready to take advantage of any situation promising a degree of amelioration. The summit meetings of big-power foreign ministers in 1954 and 1955, and particularly the Big Four conference in Geneva in July 1955, attended by Eisenhower, Eden, Bulganin, and Faure, appeared to offer just such an opportunity. The Committee suggested that the Soviet Union might prove its peaceful intentions by concrete actions with respect to its own Jewish citizens, including amnesty and release of prisoners arrested because of religious activities; reunification of families through emigration; official action to permit reestablishment of Jewish religious and cultural life; and government measures against anti-Semitism. These demands, the Committee pointed out, would require no radical about-face by the Soviet government; nor did they call for special privileges for the Jews, since the Soviet constitution guaranteed the cultural rights of all ethnic groups and there was legislation on the books outlawing racial incitement and discrimination.

The glow of the "Geneva spirit" led AJC to ponder whether this was not an opportune time to raise these issues directly with the Soviet government, either by contacting Soviet officials in the United States or by sending a Committee delegation to the Soviet Union. The ultimate decision not to do so was taken after consultation with the State Department. Although American officials did not oppose the project directly, they warned against too much optimism with regard to Soviet concessions and pointed out that the Russians could reap a considerable propaganda advantage from a Committee visit. When the foreign ministers failed to reach concrete agreements on an East-West détente, the department was even more discouraging. Assistant Secretary of State Livingston T. Merchant told AJC representatives Stroock and Engel, in January 1956, that the Russians were no longer interested in Western contacts and goodwill: "Specifically with regard to their relationship with Jewry, they seem to have made up their minds in an even more drastic manner: their openly hostile position towards Israel clearly indicates that they pay no heed whatsoever to Jewish sensibilities and interests and are not prepared to make concessions in any related direction."

During the decade following Stalin's death, the Committee kept watch on the conditions of Soviet Jewry, analyzing official Russian statements and sifting reports of American visitors and Jewish emigrés who managed to find their way out of Eastern Europe. AJC learned that the physical persecution of Stalin's last years had been replaced by a calculated policy of forced assimilation designed to extinguish the Jews as a separate group. In the early Leninist period after the Russian Revolution, assimilation was encouraged by granting Jews full economic and social equality and the same cultural rights as other nationalities. The new regime, however, made use of social, economic, and cultural persecution to erode the last traces of Jewish identity. Besides suppressing Jewish culture, the Soviets also discriminated against Jews in education, employment, and government service, singled them out as special targets in official attacks on "economic crimes," and alleged that they maintained "international ties" with Jews in other countries. Although some vestiges of religious life were permitted, synagogue leaders were often removed from office and jailed, and even the baking of matzot for Passover was banned in the early 1960s. Such official discrimination encouraged and reinforced the folk anti-Semitism always rampant in Russia and left Soviet Jewry with a deep sense of hopelessness regarding their future. At the same time, it aroused a strong desire for Jewish identity in many who might otherwise have been willing to assimilate and a deep pride in the State of Israel. Just as fallacious as Soviet denials of anti-Semitism were the official explanations that Jews were not interested in living as Jews.

Although the American Jewish Committee had always predicated Jewish well-being on political democracy, the AJC leaders were prepared to trim their ideal to fit the realities. They asked for Soviet Jewry no more than equal citizenship rights within the totalitarian framework, and the right of emigration for individuals wishing to leave. AJC considered Israel's hope of a mass exodus totally unrealistic, particularly while the Soviet Union kept the exits closed. The Committee was also convinced that most Russian Jews would not leave even if they could. More important, the Committee insisted that "to negate the Diaspora" undermined the security of the Jews in their countries of residence. Freedom to flee persecution was essential, but so was the right to live in the land of one's birth or choice without being persecuted. In behalf of Soviet Jewry, the Committee elected to pursue both goals.

AJC's principal weapons in this campaign were its informal contacts with the United States government and the weight of public opinion. The State Department ruled that the problem was an internal one for the Soviet Union and hence out of bounds to normal diplomacy; but it agreed that U.S. representatives in Moscow might raise the matter informally at an opportune moment. American officials also encouraged the Committee to seek out private individuals, American and European, who might intercede with Soviet officials in behalf of Russian Jewry. Thus when such prominent Americans as Eleanor Roosevelt and Adlai Stevenson or British and French socialist leaders inquired, in the course of private meetings with Russian officials, about anti-Jewish discrimination, the Committee hoped their probing would prove useful. When Nikita Khrushchev visited the United States in 1959, AJC prevailed on President Eisenhower and other officials to raise with him the question of Soviet Jewry. Eisenhower's successor, President Kennedy, took particular notice of the plight of the Russian Jews, and approved direct representations by

American officials to the Soviet Union. No action was taken, however, because of Kennedy's assassination.

One direct Committee initiative may have helped avert a potential disaster for Soviet Jewry. In December 1958 the Committee received reliable reports that Soviet officials were considering a proposal—to be introduced at the next congress of the Communist party—for the renewed resettlement of Soviet Jews in the so-called Autonomous Region of Birobidzhan. (Earlier efforts to create a Jewish settlement in that remote Asiatic region had failed miserably.) From one point of view the move was in line with the Committee's arguments: if Soviet Jews were indeed to receive due recognition as a nationality, the assignment of territory to them was entirely logical. But AJC knew that few Soviet Jews would voluntarily agree to move to the Chinese border and that some form of compulsion would be necessary for the resettlement to take place. Such a forced dislocation, the Committee feared, might pave the way for other anti-Jewish measures and even for the total extinction of Jews as a group. Nor was it a good sign that approval of the project came from Arab sources, which viewed the Jewish settlement in Birobidzhan as a blow against Israel.

The Committee succeeded in getting an appointment with Deputy Premier Anastas Mikoyan, then on a visit to the United States. It was the first time in the more than forty-year existence of the U.S.S.R. that representatives of a Jewish organization met with a top Soviet official to discuss the situation of Soviet Jewry. The Committee delegation, consisting of Herbert Lehman, Irving M. Engel, Jacob Blaustein, and Ralph Friedman, conferred with Mikoyan for almost two hours. They argued against the Birobidzhan Plan, pointing out its original failure, its lack of appeal, and the injustice of compulsory transfers of population, and reminded Mikoyan that Khrushchev had condemned Stalin publicly for such transfers. Mikoyan reacted indignantly: there was no intention to send the Jews anywhere; the Committee was paying undue attention to unfounded rumors. He also denied categorically the charges of official Soviet discrimination against Jews. Not only was anti-Semitism nonexistent in the Soviet Union, he maintained, but Jews in fact were eager to give up their cultural distinctiveness.

The Committee prevailed upon Mikoyan to deny publicly the Birobidzhan project. The congress of the Communist party, convening a few days later, did not consider the Birobidzhan proposal, and European diplomatic circles reported that it had been removed from the agenda at Mikoyan's last-minute suggestion.

The Committee kept alive the hope of establishing direct contacts with high Soviet officials, but it would take no such step without the approval of the State Department. Meanwhile, AJC continued to expose the facts of Soviet anti-Jewish discrimination in pamphlets and articles, special fact sheets, and resolutions of the membership and the executive.

The Committee did not ignore the persecution of other groups in the Soviet Union, but it emphasized the special disabilities of the Jews, over and above the general antireligious orientation of the Soviet government. The distinction was documented in a memorandum of fact that AJC leaders left with Mikoyan after their meeting, as well as in an open cable to Khrushchev in 1962, cosponsored by leaders of the major faiths in the United States. Similar evidence was cited in a memorandum submitted through the Consultative Council of Jewish Organizations to the UN Subcommission on Discrimination and Minorities, and in a special booklet circulated unofficially to the subcommission during its investigation of the swastika-daubings in many countries in 1959. For two years the Committee worked quietly with the Synagogue Council of America in an effort to win for Soviet Jews parity with other religious groups, a goal that could not be realized. Soviet policy toward the Jews, as one knowledgeable analyst wrote, combined inconsistency with irrationality:

In sum, Soviet policy places the Jews in an inextricable
vise. They are allowed neither to assimilate, nor live a full
Jewish life, nor to emigrate (as many would wish) to Israel
or any other place where they might live freely as Jews. The
policy stems, in turn, from doctrinal contradictions abetted
by traditional anti-Jewish sentiments. On the one hand, the
authorities want the Jews to assimilate; on the other hand,
they irrationally fear the full penetration of Soviet life which
assimilation implies. So the Jews are formally recognized as
a nationality, as a religious group, as equal citizens—but are
at the same time deprived of their national and religious
rights as a group, and of full equality as individuals. . . .
Soviet policy as a whole, then, amounts to spiritual strangulation—the deprivation of Soviet Jewry's natural right to
know the Jewish past and to participate in the Jewish present.
And without a past and a present, the future is precarious
indeed.

The condition of the Jews in the East European satellite
countries was hardly better. In Poland, Hungary, and Rumania,
after 1956, Jews were caught between the millstones of communism and nationalism, each using anti-Semitism for its own purposes. As economic and social dislocation spread, emigration
seemed the only solution.

The Committee found itself in a deep dilemma, particularly
when Poland and Rumania actively endorsed emigration. A mass
exodus could undermine the security of Jews throughout the
world and contribute to the extinction of Jewish life in Eastern
Europe. And since Israel was the only available haven, such a
mass emigration would vindicate the Zionist philosophy of the
ingathering of the exiles and repudiate the Diaspora-centered
beliefs of the non-Zionists. In practical terms, too, vast transfers
of population foreshadowed grave problems of relief and
rehabilitation. On the other hand, such government-sponsored
emigration might be the one opportunity for tens of thousands
of Jews to build a secure future. Time was of the essence, for
Soviet pressures could force the satellite governments to shut
their doors.

Once again, the Committee tempered its traditional stand in light of the practical realities. It had always insisted on the right of individuals to migrate freely; now AJC also accepted emigration as the most feasible solution where group dislocation was particularly acute. It helped convince the Polish government to admit JDC and ORT* representatives to provide for the relief needs of the prospective emigrants (particularly the repatriates from Russia), and it pressed for the reunification of thousands of Rumanian Jews with their families in Israel. It reactivated a special committee on migrations, and, with other Jewish organizations, searched for possible havens other than Israel. At the same time, Polish and Rumanian officials in the United States were sounded out regarding their governments' readiness to encourage emigration. Officially, the Committee would always champion the right of Jews to enjoy security in any corner of the world; realistically, it labored in the late 1950s to ease the way for those who could and would flee the Communist bloc.

IV

At the end of 1963 the Committee took stock of the Soviet situation and came to the conclusion that only strong expressions of public opinion might yet move the regime to repudiate official anti-Jewish discrimination and prevent anti-Semitic excesses by local administrators. AJC sought increased pressure on the Soviet government from every source possible: private diplomacy with key Communist figures; public demonstrations; statements by prominent intellectual and religious figures, especially known advocates of peaceful coexistence (Bertrand Russell's letter to Khrushchev was considered particularly valuable); opinions voiced through the United Nations. In its expanded drive the Committee reached out for the widest possible support, purposely ignoring the divisive issues of Zionism, mass emigration, or the cold war. The lay boards of AJC underscored the humanitarian aspect:

*Organization for Rehabilitation and Training.

Having witnessed in our generation the annihilation of nearly one-third of the Jews of the world, we feel we must arouse mankind to the plight of nearly three million Jews— about one-quarter of the present world's Jewish population —who are threatened with the destruction of their cultural and religious identity.

By thus appealing to the world's conscience, the AJC does not seek to encourage international hostility towards the Soviet Union. We ask only that the Soviet Union uphold its own constitution and laws, and treat its Jewish population on the basis of equality with all other groups.

To help mobilize public opinion, the Committee actively worked for the creation, in 1964, of the American Jewish Conference on Soviet Jewry, a clearinghouse of two dozen organizations which has served to express the united Jewish community's condemnation of Soviet practices, arouse the sympathies of non-Jews for Soviet Jewry's plight, and present a single, resolute case to the American government. At the same time, AJC continued its own efforts to enlist the cooperation of both prominent individuals and the public at large. AJC campaigned for the adoption of platform planks by the major political parties and for congressional resolutions condemning Soviet anti-Semitism. It provided background material for the United States Information Agency aimed at arousing popular opinion abroad, and AJC's Paris office contributed its resources to an intensified campaign in Western Europe. When Committee President Morris Abram, a U.S. representative to the UN Commission on Human Rights, exposed the Nazi-like anti-Semitism contained in *Judaism without Embellishment*, an official Soviet tract published by the Ukrainian Academy of Sciences, worldwide protests by liberals, neutralists, and Communists eventually forced Soviet authorities to recall the book.

But even if, as the American State Department asserted, the public-opinion campaign put the Soviet Union on the defensive and prevented intensified discrimination, the drive had obvious limitations. Sustaining popular indignation was extremely difficult; and public opinion without diplomatic pressure was unlikely to bring about significant changes in Soviet policy. There also remained the important need to strengthen Soviet Jewish leadership and buttress the psychological resources of Russian Jewry— clearly a task to be approached with utmost discretion.

Leaders of the Committee and the American Jewish Conference on Soviet Jewry hoped for the American government's adopting the position that one of the requisites for a meaningful relaxation of East-West tensions was an amelioration of Soviet anti-Semitism. The State Department assured American Jewish leaders of its sympathy, but refused to make the issue one of official diplomatic discussion. It was sufficient, the department indicated, that the Soviet Union knew the sentiments of President Johnson and Secretary of State Rusk, as expressed in messages to Jewish groups. In its testimony in support of a Senate resolution condemning Soviet discrimination, the Committee appealed for "humanitarian diplomacy," but the State Department did not feel called upon to comment on that long-outmoded theme. Given American Jewry's deep commitment to the basic tenets of America's postwar foreign policy, Jewish organizations would hardly attempt to force the administration's hand, as the Committee had done with respect to abrogation in 1911. One American official admitted that louder protests against Germany in the 1930s might have helped save Jews, but he cautioned the Jewish community not to equate the Russian and Nazi situations. In the State Department's view the public-opinion drive, despite its limitations, was the safest and wisest approach. The department suggested that special attention be paid the countries of Latin America, Asia, and Africa. Explaining that he was not the most popular person in the world nor was the United States the most popular country, Dean Rusk added that cooperation from East Europeans could be particularly helpful.

American officials agreed, however, that the mobilization of world opinion was but a first step. The United States' ambassador to Moscow, Foy Kohler, was genuinely sympathetic to the plight of the Jews, but noted that only the evolution of Soviet society would bring a change. In the interim, Kohler—echoing the fear that continues to haunt American Jews—agreed that persistent discrimination could force the death of the Russian Jewish community.

20

Communities in Transition

I

The Arab nationalist movement in North Africa had been gathering momentum since the 1930s, but it startled the Western world in the mid-1950s with its seemingly sudden success. Encouraged by the newly emergent states of Africa and Asia, which had thrown off colonialist control, and particularly by the independent Muslim countries, the North African nationalists effectively capitalized on France's postwar weakness and the disintegration of the French empire in Southeast Asia. France recognized Tunisia's right to independence in 1954 (fully achieved in 1957) and relinquished control over Morocco in 1956. Zachariah Shuster, at AJC's Paris office, summed up these developments in a report to the agency's Foreign Affairs Committee in January 1956: "Two years ago, the Jewish world paid no attention to North Africa—today we have a real Jewish problem on our hands there."

Involved was the future of some 80,000 Tunisian Jews (not including 20,000 who were French nationals) and 220,000 Moroccan Jews. (Independence for Algeria, the only one of the three North African territories which was an integral part of

France, was still a dim prospect in 1954.) The presence of Jews in Tunisia and Morocco antedated the Arab invasions of those countries. Under Muslim rule they had been set apart culturally, socially, and politically for centuries; in Tunisia, Jews were considered nationals of the country, but in Morocco, a less developed, theocratic state, they were protégés of the sultan, with inferior status fixed by Koranic law.

Although the masses were still wretchedly poor, French rule offered new economic, cultural, and educational opportunities to which many Jews responded. Identifying with the European powers and assisted by Western Jews, particularly the Alliance Israélite Universelle, many forged ahead socially and economically, often outstripping their Arab countrymen. Since North African Jewry equated the French with emancipation and the Arabs with subjugation, they were not likely to join the nationalists in their struggle for independence from France.

The future, however, lay clearly with the nationalists. The question then was whether North African Jews could be assured of security in independent, predominantly Arab states. The deeply rooted Muslim tradition, which political legislation alone could not undo, sanctioned perpetual inferiority for nonbelievers. In the past that tradition had expressed itself in outbursts of fanaticism and physical violence by the uneducated masses. Governments unschooled in administration, challenged by internal dissension, and striving to create new political and social institutions could hardly be relied upon as bulwarks of protection. Independence also jeopardized the economic position achieved by the French-acculturated Jews. Not only lower-echelon bureaucrats and those whose businesses were tied to French interests would be dislocated by the ouster of the colonial regime. The new governments would inevitably seek to bolster the development of an Arab middle class by displacing the former bourgeoisie. Minorities would doubtless suffer cultural disabilities as well, for nationalist fervor had not yet achieved a stability which could tolerate a plurality of cultures.

Other factors complicated the Jewish position in North Africa. Nationalist leaders questioned the loyalty of the Jews, who had been recipients of French favors and were steeped in Western culture. At the same time, the new states were being vigorously wooed by the Arab League, which sought to convince the North African lands that their Jewish populations must be regarded as traitorous Zionists.

Their experience in Libya helped fan Jewish alarm. Granted independence by the UN in 1952, Libya started out with a democratic constitution guaranteeing the rights of the native Jews. (The American Jewish Committee helped formulate those safeguards.) The majority of Libya's Jews, fearing chaos and persecution, had departed before independence; subsequent events justified their fears. Libya succumbed to the domination of the Arab League and combined a violent anti-Israel posture with government-inspired discrimination against its few thousand remaining Jews.

Emigration was an imperfect solution. Israel was the only available sanctuary, and even there North African Jews, particularly those from the hinterland, could not escape the cultural and social shock of being plunged into a modern society. There were other obstacles. Israel's capacity to absorb a North African mass immigration was limited. Moreover, the North African governments did not encourage a mass exodus of their Jewish populations, for they were unwilling to lose valuable economic assets or to support a significant buildup of manpower in Israel. Despite the conflicting pressures, however, thousands of North African Jews decided on emigration as soon as the French government granted autonomy to Tunisia.

The American Jewish Committee was cautious in its approach to a complex situation. The ideal solution, according to its integrationist policy, was the creation of new democratic states with whose goals the Jews could identify fully and which would grant them full equality and freedom to maintain their own religious and cultural institutions. Under such conditions, the North

African states could prove the possibility of fruitful coexistence of modern Arabs and Jews and help achieve lasting peace between Israel and her Arab neighbors.

Furthering such a solution represented an exciting challenge, but the Committee could not afford to gamble with human lives. The Committee appraised the day-to-day developments in North Africa, the desires of the native Jewish communities, the international policies of France and the United States, and the objectives of the Arab nationalists. It was kept informed by on-the-spot reports from staff members abroad, direct communications from community leaders, conferences with French, American, and Arab officials, exchanges of information with Israelis and with European Jewish organizations (primarily the Alliance), and special visits to North Africa in 1954 and 1957 by prominent AJC laymen. After repeated evaluations the Committee adopted a two-pronged approach: it supported North African Jewry's right to remain in the new states as equal citizens with independent religious and cultural institutions *and* their right to emigrate freely with their possessions.

Though the very enunciation of the second choice obviously implied some doubt about the possibility of achieving full integration, AJC demanded that Jewish religious institutions in the independent North African states share equally in state aid and that the Jews be permitted to maintain their own schools. In Morocco, where Jews were not permitted to become Moroccan nationals, AJC also asked for minority rights and for Jewish representation on all government bodies. Where the Western democratic tradition had not been experienced, the Committee reasoned, it made little sense to argue the finer points of separation of church and state, the democratizing influence of public schools, and the dangers of political groupings along ethnic lines.

II

Until Morocco and Tunisia achieved complete independence, the French government was central to Committee strategy. In discussions with French officials in the United States, Paris, and North Africa, as well as in conferences with the State Department, AJC indicated what it considered French responsibilities. It was up to France, the Committee insisted, to see to it that during the transition period the area remained free of violence, specifically, free of anti-Jewish outbreaks. Since France valued the North African Jews for their pro-French sentiments and considered them a link between the local French population and the Arabs, the French government frowned on emigration. Internal stability, the Committee pointed out, would reduce the pressure for emigration, as would negotiated minority guarantees. Memoranda outlining the demands of the North African Jewish communities, which paralleled the Committee's minority rights formula, were submitted both in Paris and in Washington. AJC could not publicly voice its convictions that French withdrawal would endanger the Jews, but, eager to avert another Libya, it did express the hope that France would retain some supervision over the guarantees to be granted to the minorities. However, both the U.S. State Department and French ambassador to the United States Georges Bonnet questioned the feasibility of such supervision. The Committee also urged France to increase her economic aid to North Africa, in order to contribute to the physical well-being and the political stability of the area. And it argued that it was in the French interest to keep North Africa in the Western orbit.

A primary focus of Committee strategy was the nationalist leadership. As soon as France agreed to grant autonomy to Tunisia, Zachariah Shuster conferred with Arab leaders there and discussed Jewish security with Prime Minister Tahar Ben Ammar and two cabinet members. In the envisioned democratic, secular state, they assured him, there would be equality for all citizens, regardless of race or religion; and Arab League politics would not predominate in the country's development. When Shuster returned to Paris he heard the same principles affirmed by nationalist leader Habib Bourguiba.

The situation in Morocco presented other complications. More backward than Tunisia, Morocco seethed with religious fanaticism; the independence party, Istiqlal, had a decidedly religious character. In 1954 France promised large-scale reforms; but since she had not yet decided on a definite course of action, Morocco's political future was uncertain. There was much popular unrest, and an Arab mob in Petitjean massacred seven Jews. Shuster conferred with several Istiqlal leaders in Paris and America, together with a JDC official and a representative of the Moroccan Jewish community. The Jews warned that anti-Semitic violence would not further the nationalist cause, and they urged the Moroccans to announce publicly the type of independent state they envisioned. Again, the nationalist response was friendly and assuring.

The initial contacts set the pattern for further meetings with the Arabs, both before and after Tunisia and Morocco achieved independence. On the occasion of the Committee's forty-ninth annual meeting, Prime Minister Si Bekkai of Morocco made a statement repeating promises already given by the nationalist parties and by the sultan himself:

> Independent Morocco will remain faithful to her traditions based on non-discrimination, whether racial or religious. Moroccan Jews will enjoy the same rights and same duties as their fellow Moroccans of the Moslem faith. They will attain the same responsibilities which are inherent in the rights of all Moroccan citizens.

When Committee leaders met with Bourguiba, by then prime minister of Tunisia, in December 1956, he expressed full agreement with AJC on the principles of equality of citizenship, religious freedom, free emigration, and independent communal institutions. He also asserted that Tunisia made a clear distinction between its own Jewish population and Israelis.

Such assurances, which it equated with moderate and pro-Western leadership, encouraged the Committee to stand firm on its basic formula. Aware that support of the moderates would prevent the success of the extremist elements (extremism in turn would strengthen those Jewish organizations which preached emigration), the Committee could do little to influence the course of diplomacy. AJC was in no position to pressure the French for meaningful assistance which might undercut the extremists; and it could not sway the American government to exert such pressure. Nor was the Committee prepared to transform the North African Jews into superpatriots, to convince them that their future lay exclusively with the nationalist cause, or to renounce its insistence on the right of emigration. Vague promises of financial aid from public and private sources in the West carried little weight in an area wooed by powerful contending blocs. And it was unlikely that public opinion, even if it could be aroused, could play a significant role.

The Committee counted on American government support of its demands. It privately argued with officials that French withdrawal would create a political vacuum in North Africa which communism would hasten to fill; that American economic and strategic interests would be jeopardized if North Africa turned against the West; that Arab League propaganda, which was in fact anti-West, was flooding the area; and that forced emigration of North African Jews to Israel would complicate the Middle East situation. The State Department listened sympathetically and agreed. It shared information with the Committee and encouraged AJC to continue its own diplomatic efforts. Admitting uncertainty over the trend of events, particularly in Morocco, Assistant Secretary George V. Allen even went so far as to question the realism of the Committee's integrationist formula. But the department would not be pushed. The desire to keep French goodwill and a reluctance to appear in colonial guise before the

Third World undergirded America's disinclination to intervene. Since there was no evidence of blatant Communist aggression in the area, the United States could not be persuaded to pick up the pieces of the French empire, as she had done in Southeast Asia.

III

The American Jewish Committee was the only major American Jewish organization which approached the North African problem with the primary goal of achieving freedom and equality through integration. Unlike other groups, it chose to combat the dangers that could result in mass emigration rather than to counsel retreat. The Committee was confident that if its formula was implemented, emigration would virtually cease. North African Jewry did not want to leave the countries where its roots were so deep. In the first flush of religious exultation over the creation of a Jewish state, twenty-five thousand had left for Israel. But even those propelled by nationalist sentiment grew disillusioned when they learned of the difficulties that North Africans faced in Israel.

Opponents of the Committee's approach were less optimistic about the future of North African Jewry. Seared by the Nazi era, their impulse was to save Jewish lives before time ran out. Supporters of the Committee's position replied that alarmism alienated the French and Arabs, while it siphoned off funds which could be used to strengthen the communal institutions of North African Jewry. But honest differences of opinion within the Jewish community were compounded by organizational competition in fund raising. Moderation yielded smaller sums than dramatic calls to rescue, and organizations advocating the evacuation of North Africa held a decided advantage. Amid mutual recriminations, those favoring integration were accused of being concerned primarily with communal stability elsewhere, while those arguing for emigration were charged with a willingness to sacrifice North African security for the sake of Zionist ideology or their organization's financial advantage. Both sides quieted down in 1955 when it became clear that unrest in Morocco and Tunisia was not usually directed against the Jews, and that in any case Israel could not absorb a mass North African immigration. Zionist and Israeli spokesmen cautioned against panic, for North Africa did not yet constitute an area of crisis. For its part, the Committee admitted more candidly the need to prepare for such eventuality.

Though the situation seemed to cry out for interorganizational unity, the rivalry for prestige and power continued unabated. Shuster reported that after his first interview with Tunisian leaders, the World Jewish Congress moved to wrest leadership from the Committee. Shuster suggested as a counterthrust a special delegation to the region (which the B'nai B'rith also contemplated), a move that heightened the resentment of World Jewish Congress partisans and other critics against what they considered AJC's uninvited interference.

In July 1955 the Jewish community leaders of Morocco and Tunisia, fearful that differences in approach and opinion might endanger their position with the local authorities, proposed coordination of all organizational activity in their behalf. Despite the Committee's long-standing aversion to joint ventures, it agreed, calculating that only the World Jewish Congress stood to lose. Because the World Jewish Congress considered itself the sole legitimate voice of world Jewry, acceptance of the proposal would damage its claims to monopoly; refusal, however, would expose its thrust for power and alienate Jewish opinion throughout the world.

At the start of the deliberations for a coordinating body, which were to be handled by the Alliance Israélite Universelle, the Committee refrained from public activity with regard to North Africa. Less inhibited about offending the Alliance (which resented intervention in its province), the World Jewish Congress hedged in its reply and intensified its own efforts. The

Committee watched with growing alarm as the Congress sought to build up its influence in North Africa. Even more harmful, the Committee felt, were contradictory statements by Congress officials—one insisting that Jewish security depended on the continued presence of the French, another expounding the coincidence of Jewish and nationalist aims.

When the World Jewish Congress officially reversed its pro-French position, in late August, the Committee concluded that its objective was to undermine the native Jewish communal organizations and impose its own control over the area in cooperation with the Muslims. During negotiations between a French commission and Moroccan nationalist representatives, an uninvited Congress delegation went so far as to attack Moroccan Jewish leaders publicly for opposing Moroccan independence. "Rarely was there in Jewish life such an ugly spectacle as this," the Committee's Paris office reported. The official Jewish representatives attempted to reassure the Muslims, while insisting that the nationalists recognize the numerous problems of the Jewish community.

No one at the time pointed out the interesting turnabout: the Zionists were calling for Jewish allegiance to a Diaspora national movement, and the non-Zionists (some would even say assimilationists) were resisting unqualified identification with the cause of the majority. Even more confusing, at the same time that Zionist organizations publicly stressed the urgent need for emigration, World Jewish Congress president Nahum Goldmann predicted, in conversations with AJC's Irving M. Engel and Simon Rifkind, that for the next two years at least, Moroccan Jewry faced no serious threat. He offered his own plans for collaboration on North Africa, as well as a proposal for a new world Jewish body, both unacceptable to the Committee.

IV

The climate in Tunisia after independence was not hospitable to minorities. To be sure, the constitution which recognized Islam as the national religion and Arabic as the official language also guaranteed the freedom of all religions. And, in fact, Jews did enjoy equal political rights. Until 1961 the Bourguiba government maintained a decidedly pro-Western outlook and spurned full cooperation with the Arab League. But fervid nationalism permitted no significant social or cultural deviation from the majority. National bonds transcended religious ties, Bourguiba explained to an American Jewish Committee delegation in 1957. For that reason, his government had intervened with Muslim Egypt in behalf of Tunisian Jews in Egypt. And for the same reason he expected undivided allegiance from Tunisian Jewry; Zionism was unacceptable. "Do not have your body in Tunisia and your heart elsewhere," he specifically warned the Jews.

In actuality much more than Zionism was involved. There were Jewish schools and welfare agencies supported by and for Jews, branches of foreign Jewish organizations which distributed relief to Jews, Jewish community councils—thus far subsidized by the government—which represented Jews qua Jews. Nationalist zeal saw such institutions as symbolizing separatism and foreignism, and regarded them as obstacles to the building of a strong nation. If the Jewish institutions were not to be abolished altogether, the only solution seemed to be to open them up to the entire population either through nationalization or "integration."

Irving M. Engel, who headed the 1957 AJC delegation to Tunisia, tried to enlighten Bourguiba about the values of pluralism. Representatives of the Federation of Jewish Communities in Tunisia specifically requested such intervention because they thought the Americans' plea would carry greater weight than their own. They desired integration, they assured the Committee delegates, but only full freedom to retain their Jewish cultural identity could allay fears of forced assimilation. (Unfortunately, the Jewish member of the Tunisian cabinet, André Barouch, believed that separate Jewish organizational life was diametrically opposed to the integration process.)

At the meeting Engel quietly disputed the Bourguiba's assumption that a separate religious-cultural identification conflicted with national loyalty. "In the eyes of American democratic society," Engel said, "there is no such conflict. A man is a better American citizen for being a better Jew, and a better Jew for being a better American citizen." Bourguiba was not convinced and made it clear that his government would withhold subsidies to Jewish community organizations which included non-Tunisian nationals. He did promise that a reorganized body of Tunisian Jews of proven nationalist sentiment would be permitted to carry on religious, cultural, and welfare activities, and that foreign Jewish organizations would be permitted to aid the community financially. But he rejected a Committee offer to supply an expert who would devise a system beneficial to both Tunisia and the Tunisian Jews.

The AJC delegates also met with U.S. Ambassador G. Lewis Jones and quickly learned that they could expect no support from American officials. Jones explained that the Tunisian government kept an unofficial blacklist of those who had not actively participated in the nationalist movement, and that the Jews had not cooperated sufficiently in that cause. He suggested that the Tunisian Jewish community might demonstrate a change in attitude by extending its welfare services—or at least 25 percent of them—to Muslims. The fact that American Jewish charities would then be funding Muslim relief, and that this was quite contrary to the usual practice of Christian and Jewish relief organizations operating in other countries, did not seem to disturb him. The AJC delegation could only leave the matter to the Tunisian Federation of Jewish Communities, which continued trying to convince the government of Tunisian Jewry's patriotism.

A year later, when members of the AJC Foreign Affairs Committee met with a Tunisian delegate to the UN, the Committee conceded that officials of Jewish community councils should be Tunisian nationals. It pleaded, however, that the contemplated reform of the community structure permit the Jews to continue their traditional relief and welfare activities, in addition to their specifically religious tasks. If foreign Jewish institutions should lose their independence in any merger in a national system, AJC argued, the ensuing "leveling down" of educational and welfare services would ultimately prove detrimental to the country at large. Nevertheless, in 1958 and 1959 the Tunisian government restricted official Jewish functions to religious matters, confiscated a Jewish cemetery in Tunis, and placed ever-increasing obstacles in the way of foreign Jewish organizations. The government "will not permit them [the Jews] to live in a closed circle of their own," declared Tunisia's minister of justice. When the Committee reviewed the situation for the State Department, the director of the department's North African Bureau suggested that the Jews make "token gifts" to the Muslim population.

As these developments unfolded Tunisian Jews, although still more favored than the Jewries of neighboring countries, grew less and less hopeful about their future in independent Tunisia, particularly as their particular economic problems (beyond those facing the country at large) added to their hardships. Many Tunisian Jews experienced discrimination in employment; and when the new state tightened its regulation of the economy, the Jews, many of whom were small entrepreneurs, were especially hard hit. During the Franco-Tunisian clash over Bizerte in 1961, Jews were attacked for their alleged pro-French sympathy. That episode, which pushed Tunisia closer to the Arab League and further from the West, dimmed any remaining hope that Tunisia would become the model of Muslim-Jewish harmony. Some fifteen to twenty-five thousand Jews left Tunisia in the twelve months ending July 1962, and the exodus continued; in the next three years an estimated fifty to sixty thousand persons departed, and more would have left had they been permitted to take their belongings with them. By the end of 1965, less than twelve thousand Jews remained in Tunisia.

V

Moroccan Jews faced the same economic and communal problems as the Jews in Tunisia. Their position, in fact, was decidedly worse: their security and rights did not rest on a constitutional base, but only on the personal promises of the sultan and his ministers. Since Morocco was less westernized than Tunisia, the weakness of its middle class and the pervasiveness of its religious tradition offered less hope for the establishment of a democratic state. Internal political dissension also increased the intolerance of the nationalists toward non-Muslims. Further, Morocco cooperated closely with the Arab League, whose propaganda deliberately blurred the distinction between Jews and Zionists. The government's intense anti-Israel stand included a rigid ban on emigration to Israel; since Israel was the only haven available to them, Moroccan Jews were trapped. These factors ultimately forced the Committee to reconsider its efforts to secure the integration of the Moroccan Jewish community into the life of the independent state, and, like other Jewish organizations, AJC shifted its focus to emigration.

From 1954 until June 1956—when the Moroccan government ordered the immediate dissolution of Kadimah, an organization sponsored by the Jewish Agency to expedite the transfer of Jews to Israel—about forty thousand Moroccan Jews left the country. When the ban on emigration was instituted, two thousand prospective emigrants had assembled at a camp awaiting departure. They and six thousand others processed for emigration had already liquidated all their possessions. With the dissolution of the camp, these Jews had no future to look forward to and no past to which they could return.

When AJC representatives hastened to Washington to plead

for American intervention in the matter, they found little encouragement. The Arab states had already communicated their views to the State Department, expressing Morocco's reluctance to lose a valuable element of its population and protesting the deliberate stimulation of emigration from North Africa by Israel and by American Jews. The State Department made it clear that while the United States might intervene in behalf of the stranded Jews on humanitarian grounds, it would not jeopardize national interests by supporting emigration in general. State Department spokesmen doubted that Morocco would permit even individual (as opposed to group) emigration to Israel; and since no other country would welcome the poor and illiterate Moroccan Jews, they agreed that the future looked black. American intercession in Rabat finally induced the sultan to authorize the emigration of the camp inmates, whose number had risen to over six thousand. But to the leaders of the Committee it appeared as if another Iron Curtain had sealed off a sizable segment of Jewry. AJC refrained from public condemnation of Morocco lest it aggravate the situation, and its continued pressure on American officials to uphold the right of individual emigration as well as its search for havens other than Israel had little effect.

In 1957 the Committee delegation to North Africa learned of the mounting restrictions on the departure of individual Moroccan Jews. "The Jewish community," AJC noted, "feels that it is a prisoner in Morocco." The delegation discussed the emigration ban with Prime Minister Si Bekkai, emphasizing its harmful psychological effects. The delegation insisted on the recognition of emigration as a basic human right and argued that such recognition would eliminate clandestine emigration, if not the very desire to emigrate. To this the prime minister replied that the "human right of movement must be balanced and limited by the interests of the state."

At subsequent interviews with the Moroccan ambassador in the United States and the Moroccan foreign minister, the Committee similarly argued for lifting the ban. AJC privately questioned the wisdom of the illegal emigration organized by the Zionists; publicly, however, it consistently maintained that Moroccan restrictions were responsible. As the situation deteriorated, the movement of Jews within the country was curtailed; illegal searches and arbitrary arrests by a special police division prevented their escape; they were victimized by profiteers who sold them invalid permits or gave empty promises of safe conduct across the borders. The American embassy protested its helplessness, pointing out that Morocco's growing inclination toward the Arab League made it difficult enough to insure the maintenance of American air bases there. There was scant comfort in the knowledge that Morocco's harder line toward Jews reflected Arab League influence rather than Moroccan convictions.

The situation came to a head in 1961. First, an African summit conference in Casablanca, attended by Egypt's President Nasser, touched off a wave of anti-Semitic police brutality. Then shortly after the conference a ship carrying forty-two illegal emigrants from Morocco sank in the Mediterranean. The tragedy evoked a spate of anti-Zionist and anti-Jewish articles in the Moroccan press, as well as police crackdowns on suspected distributors of a pamphlet calling on Moroccan Jews to emigrate to Israel. Criticism of Morocco mounted in various parts of the world. The Committee representative in Washington again urged the State Department to indicate its support of emigration. The Committee also consulted on the preparation of a memorandum to the king of Morocco and joined with other Jewish organizations to raise the Moroccan human rights issue with the UN. In an interchange with the Moroccan ambassador, Irving M. Engel bluntly rejected the charge that Zionist propaganda was to blame for the rise in emigration and for Morocco's anti-Jewish actions.

To indicate to the Moroccan government the widespread public interest in the Jewish situation, AJC prevailed on two prominent Protestants, Drs. Eugene Carson Blake and Harold E. Fey, to visit the country in June 1961. The mission received little cooperation from American and Moroccan officials, but Dr. Fey's moving article in the *Christian Century* helped bring the Jewish plight to the attention of American churchgoers.

A few months later the ban on emigration was lifted, and thousands of middle- and upper-class Jews left the country. Shuster described the activity at the port of Casablanca at a Committee meeting: "Usually the boat comes in after midnight, very quietly. And immediately after midnight, dozens of young boys disperse through the city, to pick up people who are all ready to go, and bring them in small taxis or in station wagons. The emigrants are quickly put on the boat, and it leaves before sunrise. That is what happens every few days."

By the end of 1965 only seventy thousand Jews remained in Morocco. One reporter summed up the mood of this remnant: "They were not working for the future because they did not believe in a future. The springs of hope had been poisoned for them."

VI

The situation in Algeria, where seven years of bloody strife preceded independence, posed a different problem. France refused to consider independence; her stiff resistance bred an ever more extreme and violent rebel leadership. Both sides expected unequivocal support from the Jews, who were trapped in a cruel dilemma. A community of about 140,000, they had identified with the French since 1830, enjoyed French citizenship since the Crémieux decree of 1870, and prospered under France's rule. Independence promised no advantages, particularly if it brought intolerant nationalism and Arab fanaticism.

In the deepening political crisis, the French authorities pressed Algerian Jewry—most of whom sided with the French— for a show of support. A negative response could lead to military repression and heightened anti-Semitism in both France and Algeria. But an open alliance with the French had its pitfalls too.

Algeria's *colons* had a long tradition of anti-Semitism; they did nothing to defend the Jews against rebel attacks when the war began. A pro-French stand invited further violence on the part of the Muslims and could seal the death warrant for Algerian Jewry if the French were ultimately defeated. The rebel leadership (Front of National Liberation, FLN) pressed even harder than the French, demanding an open and collective pledge of loyalty from the Jewish community and underscoring their demands with physical intimidation. The Jews had lived in Algeria for two thousand years, the nationalists argued, and no acquired citizenship could alter the fact that they "belonged to the land."

The political uncertainties lasted until 1962; meanwhile, there was little any organization abroad could do. Algerian Jews were afraid that outside intervention might worsen their situation. The Jewish community stated publicly that no Jewish organization could deliver a collective pledge of political support and stressed the Jews' desire for friendly relations with both sides.

Obviously, AJC's formula for Morocco and Tunisia was irrelevant here. It therefore limited itself to discreet representations to French and FLN officials. With the French, Irving M. Engel discussed the problem of colonial anti-Semitism and pleaded for government protection against popular violence. With the FLN, the Committee sought, through a variety of influential intermediaries—including leaders of American labor unions and even President Bourguiba of Tunisia—to show the justification of the Algerian Jewish community's unaligned position and to bring to an end the intimidation of the Jews. When two employees of the Jewish Agency were kidnapped, representatives of the Committee dealt directly with a member of the FLN in a rescue attempt.

In 1961, when negotiations for a final settlement between France and the rebels were under way, Engel, Irving Kane, president of the Conference of Jewish Federations, and Label Katz, president of B'nai B'rith, met privately with Abdel Kader Chanderli of the FLN. Emphasizing their purely private role, they set forth the basic rights they hoped would be granted to Algerian Jews in the settlement. Chanderli said little to allay the Jewish leaders' fears regarding an independent Algeria. He did not agree that Algerian Jewry enjoyed the same status as Europeans in Algeria; if they elected to retain French citizenship, he warned, they would incur resentment. Chanderli denied that the Algerian Muslims were anti-Jewish and charged that Jews who professed support of universal rights had not favored such rights for Algerian Muslims. He denounced Israel's support of France and indicated that an independent Algeria would not recognize the right of emigration.

Although the Evian Agreement of 1962 guaranteed the rights of Algerian Jews on a par with Europeans, most Jews did not wait to see how these rights would be honored. In 1962, as the final and most bitter battle raged between the nationalists and the French, the Jewish exodus was in full swing. Schools and welfare organizations shut their doors, synagogues were closed, and Torah scrolls shipped to France and Israel. By October fewer than ten thousand Jews remained in Algeria.

Regarding themselves as Frenchmen, most Algerian Jews sought refuge in France, not in Israel. Their immediate needs strained the resources of both public and private welfare agencies. To help relieve that strain, the Committee prevailed on the American Embassy in Paris to release surplus military equipment for distribution by the Joint Distribution Committee. Equally important was the need for quick absorption of the North Africans—traditional in outlook, Sephardic in rite—into the more secular Ashkenazic communities of France. Working through Community Service Program, the Committee helped prepare and distribute special program aids and techniques to assist French organizations and community leaders in the integrating of the old and the new. The reservoir of North African Jewry had dried up, and France was now the fourth largest Jewish center in the world.

21

Missionary Diplomacy

The American Jewish Committee's Latin American program differed significantly from its other foreign commitments. Launched officially in 1948 with the establishment of an office in Buenos Aires, the program came into being not in response to any crisis, but to lend support to the activities of the communities concerned. In broadest terms it was a foray into "missionary diplomacy"*—a combination of noblesse oblige and a conviction that AJC was an appropriate model for the Jewish communities in Latin America. A 1948 Committee report explained the Latin America program as the "result of a feeling . . . that the American

---

*The term *missionary diplomacy*, with all its implications, is borrowed from Professor Arthur Link's description of Woodrow Wilson's foreign policy. On Wilson and Secretary of State Bryan, Link has written: "[They] were both . . . confident that they comprehended the peace and well-being of other countries better than the leaders of those countries themselves. This urge to do good, to render disinterested service, was so compelling that it motivated interference in the internal affairs of other nations on such a scale as the United States had not heretofore attempted. . . . Many other factors were involved . . . but . . . paramount in their motivation was the ambition to do justly, to advance the cause of international peace, and to give to other peoples the blessings of democracy and Christianity." Arthur S. Link, *Woodrow Wilson and the Progressive Era* (New York, 1954), pp. 81–82.

Jewish Committee has a mission to accomplish within, and on behalf of, the Jewish communities scattered throughout the Southern countries of the [hemisphere]."

I

To be sure, there were more immediate reasons for the Committee's initial interest in Central and South America. During the 1930s and the war years, considerable Nazi infiltration made the area a major center of pro-German propaganda. Such anti-Semitic inroads, the Committee feared, could jeopardize the position of Jews in the hemisphere, at the very time when the area was gaining importance as a possible haven for refugees from nazism. There was also concern over the differences in treatment of native-born and naturalized American Jews by certain Latin American governments, which could conceivably begin to discriminate against American Jews on racial lines.

Through reports from local correspondents and special surveys conducted by staff members, the Committee tried to assess Jewish prospects in Latin America. It discussed the interrelated problems of Jewish defense and immigration with South American officials, the State Department, and other Jewish organizations. If the pro-Nazi forces gained in influence, the Latin American countries might close their doors to European Jews, and large numbers of as yet unassimilated new immigrants could become ready targets for the anti-Semites.

Latin American Jewish communities appeared ill equipped to meet the challenges of these contingencies. "The [Latin American] communities have very little conception of organization," wrote Morris Waldman early in 1937. "The communities need to be effectually organized for constructive community services as well as for an ordinary management of their public relations. . . . There is an opportunity for us, by stimulation, advice and perhaps some financial assistance, to help build up healthy Jewish communities in these countries that would serve as the strongest bulwark against anti-Jewish agitation."

World War II diverted the Committee from undertakings designed to strengthen the internal resources of the Latin American Jewish communities. Its initial efforts were centered on a campaign to combat Nazi propaganda with press and radio materials stressing prodemocracy themes, and on financial support to such groups as the Mexican Committee against Racism. The Committee preferred to remain in the background, encouraging local citizens to take on these tasks. But it could not leave to the inexperienced communities the effective implementation of the program, which involved contacts with cooperative press and radio channels in the United States and in South America.

The thrust of the program was to unite Jews and non-Jews in the fight against the common danger of nazism. The American government encouraged the venture, which meshed with its good-neighbor policy and efforts to forge hemispheric solidarity. The official blessing of the State Department brought many advantages; Washington's cooperation in persuading South American countries to admit certain refugees was particularly important. And when Waldman was about to visit Latin America, it was the State Department that advised him to impress upon the United States ambassadors that anti-Semitism was an index of anti-Americanism.

After the war, Latin America took on a new importance. It was now the home of some six hundred thousand Jews—almost twice the number remaining in Western Europe—and a major world Jewish center. The time was ripe, the Committee decided, for Latin American Jews to learn to create the kind of healthy communal life which would guarantee their security and survival.

II

How successful the Committee would be in its Latin American program depended on the needs of the individual Jewish communities, their position in the larger society, and their receptivity to projects of defense, integration, and identity. When AJC first embarked on its Latin American program in 1946, it had only begun to explore those factors. During the first decade the Committee perhaps learned more than it was able to teach. The primary focus was the Argentine community of 350,000, the largest in South America. After an initial period of establishing contacts and garnering support, the Committee's Buenos Aires office was opened under the direction of Maximo Yagupsky. Yagupsky, who grew up in a Baron de Hirsch agricultural colony in Argentina, had been given intensive training in AJC's national office.

Committee reports and studies on the Latin American scene in the decade corresponding roughly with Juan Perón's rule (1945–55) consistently reinforced the conviction that its tutelage was needed. The Jewish community of Argentina, the studies pointed up, was insecure, isolated from the general population, and unrealistic in evaluating its position. External factors explained much of the insecurity and isolation. The country was under the rule of a dictator who, though not unfriendly to the Jews, could change their fortunes at will. The ruling class was dominated by a military and landed aristocracy which excluded Jews, and the latter's middle-class occupations sharply set them apart from the farmers and industrial workers as well. A strong and reactionary Catholic Church maintained a decisive influence on education and popular prejudices. The Nazi legacy of anti-Semitism was now fed by Arab agitation. And the Jews, the Committee concluded, were prevented from properly coping with the situation by their own unreal, stultifying attitudes.

Most Argentine Jews had an East European background, and nearly half of them had immigrated between the two wars. Their community goals were closer to the shtetl pattern of voluntary isolation from the larger community than to integration with the surrounding culture. They were more secularist than religious. A small minority identified with communism. The majority were strongly Zionist and felt close to such groups as the World Jewish Congress. Ideologically, they considered themselves transients en route to Israel; in reality, however, they had no plans to leave Argentina. They wanted a Jewish education for their children but did little about it. Though comparatively affluent, they neither established significant local Jewish institutions (although they contributed heavily to Zionist and foreign Jewish causes) nor created a class of professional Jewish leaders. Their source of cultural creativity—East European Jewry—had dried up, leaving them without intellectual inspiration. In sum, by historical accident and conditioning, as well as by choice, the Jews of Argentina were not realizing their full potential, either as Argentinians or as Jews.

In its determination to set Argentine Jewry on new paths, the Committee faced serious obstacles. There was suspicion and antipathy in much of Latin America toward any group associated with the "Colossus of the North," "Yankee imperialism," and "big-stick diplomacy." Even if the Jewish community did not itself have many anti-American prejudices, it was wary of ties with American groups that might evoke disfavor on the part of non-Jewish nationalists. Nor were the Committee's Jewish credentials very acceptable to the Argentine Jews, who had been conditioned on this matter by the World Jewish Congress. Organizational bickering aside, many Argentine Jews wondered why a self-respecting community should become the "sphere of influence" of a foreign organization, especially one with which it seemed to have so little in common. And even if the Committee could overcome its negative image, the question of relevance remained. How pertinent was integration to an immigrant community caught between a ruling class dominated by the church and the military, and a mass population it viewed as culturally inferior? How meaningful was a public relations program geared to the

United States, stressing contacts with government officials and intellectual circles, in a society where the government was often shaky and lacked popular support, and intellectual influence was blunted by widespread illiteracy? Were defense activities tailored to the United States experience applicable, or even necessary, in a country where anti-Semitism had been relatively unknown before Hitler?

Before a program for Argentine Jewry could be implemented, Yagupsky had to sell the community on the American Jewish Committee and its values. When news of his impending arrival spread, the World Jewish Congress warned its adherents of the "danger"; leftist groups conjured up a threat of "American Jewish reaction"; and Orthodox leaders predicted an onslaught on traditional synagogue forms and practices. Nevertheless, Yagupsky spread his message. Gradually, in meetings with individuals and small groups, he succeeded in convincing a number of prominent communal leaders that their community's well-being demanded the Committee's presence. By stressing the Committee's activities with respect to Palestine, he was able to counteract the charges of anti-Zionism and assimilationism spread by the DAIA,* the central organization representing Jewish communal groups in Argentina, which was an affiliate of the World Jewish Congress. In less than two years Yagupsky was able to report:

> In Argentina, the principal center of Latin American Jewry, we have fostered the creation of a nucleus of financially strong and intellectually capable leaders. These banded together into an organization called the Argentine Jewish Organization . . . with a program similar to that of the American Jewish Committee, anxious for our cooperation and advice. These leaders control a synagogal community, they control a good part of the Jewish education of the country and various philanthropic organizations. As a symbol of friendship, they sent two representatives to our London Conference of Jewish Organizations. . . . We have organized

*Delegacion de Asociaciones Israelitas Argentinas.

a registry of leaders and organizations to which we periodically send direct information and pamphlets in Spanish and with which we maintain a permanent correspondence. Our office is a center of Jewish information for leaders and organizations of Argentina; it is also a center for visits of all sorts of people who come from Argentina to the United States.

Since the Argentine Jewish Organization asked for the Committee's assistance, AJC could justify setting up its Buenos Aires office as a response to Argentine overtures. The Argentine Jewish Organization became the Instituto Judio Argentino de Cultura e Informacíon in mid-1948. Like its parent organization in the United States, the Instituto was run by a small group of affluent businessmen and professionals imbued with a sense of communal responsibility, who preferred the "like-minded" to the "mass" approach to membership. In function, the lines of demarcation between the Instituto and the Committee's office were not clearly fixed; often the Committee acted in the name of the Instituto. As the Instituto became more firmly entrenched and more apt to resent a steward-ward relationship, the Committee was going to have to decide whether it preferred "visibility" or be content to missionize from the sidelines.

III

The activities of both the Instituto and the Committee's office in Buenos Aires were conditioned by the fact that Argentina was ruled by a dictator. The Perón government was not anti-Semitic, but Jewish organizations in Argentina could not safely champion political democracy. Though the Committee lent discreet aid to the Pan-American Association for Freedom and Democracy, it refrained from overtly antagonizing the totalitarian regime. Conformity was the more prudent course, but this too raised problems for the Jewish community. A strong pro-Perón stance could alienate liberal opinion, the natural ally of minority interests. Also, as the years went on the Argentine Jews themselves began to lack confidence in democracy, pleading for protection and favors instead of asserting their right, as would have been the case in the pre-Perón era.

When Perón's administration clamped down on private institutions, the Instituto felt the increasing pressure. In 1950 Yagupsky reported that the police, wary of the Instituto's publications, were keeping the organization under surveillance. The secretary was questioned about the membership; Yagupsky himself was being watched and followed. He corresponded with New York in Yiddish (to make the censor's task more difficult), and he mailed confidential reports from neighboring countries. In 1953, when an anti-Perón campaign was countered with political terror, the Instituto was forced to suspend its activities temporarily. Its president, Simon Mirelman, the only prominent Jew affiliated with a major Jewish organization who had not publicly declared his support of Perón, was imprisoned. Despite the Committee's stigma as a foreign organization, Yagupsky's intervention with individual officials apparently effected Mirelman's release two months later.

Since the Jews of Argentina had their own organizations to represent their interests to the government, AJC's contacts with Argentine officials were nonpolitical. The Americans did alert their own government's representatives to the Committee's work in Latin America—which, it was hoped, would enhance the goodwill of the United States; but as long as Jews were not singled out for special disabilities or persecution, the Committee did not ask for diplomatic intercession.

The Perón regime flouted civil liberties, discriminated against Jewish applicants for immigration, and tolerated the support of openly anti-Semitic groups. But the dictator's attitude toward the Argentine Jewish community was benevolent, obviating the need for intensive defense activities and permitting the Committee and the Instituto to concentrate on enhancing the

Jewish image in the eyes of both Jews and non-Jews. The Committee hoped to strengthen the Jewish community by increasing the larger community's knowledge of Jewish cultural traditions and values. A greater appreciation of Jewish values by non-Jews would bolster the self-confidence of Jews and encourage them to participate more fully in the larger society.

The Instituto established press contacts, distributing a daily newsletter to hundreds of periodicals outside of Buenos Aires and preparing religious news items for newspaper use. (An article describing Passover and the seder ritual appeared in *La Prensa* in 1949 and was acknowledged to be the first of its kind.) The Instituto also ran a radio program on matters of Jewish concern, which was broadcast throughout South America. In 1953, in cooperation with the Committee, the Instituto began publication of a Spanish quarterly, *Comentario,* patterned after *Commentary* and the French-language *Evidences.* Like its U.S. model, the magazine proved highly successful in winning friends and increasing understanding of Jewish issues. Before *Comentario,* non-Jews in Latin America had never published in Jewish periodicals.

The Committee recognized that Latin America was not ripe for a human-relations program tied to the general values of cultural pluralism and only indirectly concerned with Jewish interests. The Instituto made clear its support of the UN's human rights programs, but its educational thrust with non-Jewish audiences concentrated on Jews qua Jews. Thus instead of championing the separation of church and society, the Instituto published a textbook on the Jewish religion for use in elementary schools. It also promoted exhibits of Jewish books and art, concerts of Jewish music, books on Argentine Jewish heroes, and other programs underscoring the role of the Jews in the history and culture of the country. After World War II, AJC eschewed the "Jewish contributions to civilization" approach in the United States. But the relatively young minority group working to gain recognition as Argentinians still found it useful. Too often Jews in Argentina were looked upon as aliens. "We have many subjects of your country living here," an Argentinian provincial official told the Israeli ambassador.

The Instituto made good use of personal contacts. In its very first year it organized a committee of rabbis and its own representatives to keep in touch with Catholic leaders. A special Argentine-Israeli cultural exchange program was created to promote understanding of the State of Israel; the Instituto also made it possible for several influential clergymen to visit Israel. (At least one such pilgrim, an anti-Semitic bishop, was converted into a well-disposed sympathizer.)

The importance of interfaith cooperation was borne out when rumors spread among the Catholic masses that the Jews had instigated the Perón regime's oppressive measures against the church. Expressions of support and sympathy for the church's plight by many prominent Jewish leaders helped dispel the rumors and cement ties between the two religious groups. When Yagupsky accompanied Rabbi Guillermo Schlesinger of Buenos Aires on a visit to Cardinal Caggiano's secretary—no meaningless gesture in light of police surveillance of Yagupsky—the church official was touched. He assured his visitors that "when the Perón regime falls, the Jews need not be apprehensive since the church will not allow the Jewish community to be mistreated." And indeed, after Perón's downfall, increased church participation in political affairs made these earlier ties even more valuable.

The expanding programs of education and interfaith contacts during the Perón era proved that American methods could be adapted to Argentina. Relationships established by the Committee and the Instituto helped forestall the distribution of the *Protocols of the Elders of Zion,* Henry Ford's *The International Jew,* and other anti-Semitic books, films, and pamphlets. Over the years the Latin American Jews, too, became increasingly convinced of the efficacy of the Committee's approach. One AJC action in Chile, in 1954, reinforced their confidence. Dr. Simon Segal, head of the AJC Foreign Affairs Department, recounted the story:

A general national convention was scheduled in Chile to deal with the problem of Communism. The convention was called by the Conservative Catholic Party and representatives of all other parties were invited. The Jewish community was greatly disturbed because it foresaw that the convention will assume anti-Semitic aspects since the organizers repeatedly made the Jews responsible for Communism in Latin America. It was also taken for granted that the convention will come out against immigration into Chile which really meant to the leaders Jewish immigration. Our representative was called in to meet with the convention leaders. They gave him a hearing. He presented our two books, *Jews in the Soviet Union* and *Jews in the Satellite Countries,* our various statements opposing Communism and a great deal of other materials. The result was that there was no resolution against immigration and that the resolution against Communism did not make the association between Jews and Communists. Our representative reports that it is significant, that in Latin America religious Catholic leaders as well as political leaders for the first time heard that the Jews are opposed to Communism.

IV

The Committee and the Instituto were particularly successful in keeping Latin American Jewry informed about Jewish affairs. Besides *Comentario,* a Yiddish newsletter, *Yedies,* was distributed to all Jewish periodicals; *Informative del AJC,* a bulletin of Committee activities and views, contained editorials which were frequently reprinted in the Jewish press; a comprehensive survey of the Jewish communities of Latin America, prepared by Jacob Shatzky, was published in Spanish and Yiddish. As the Instituto gradually expanded its publishing program, it provided Spanish translations of Committee-sponsored books and pamphlets on anti-Semitism, nazism, neonazism.

While the Instituto and the Committee stressed the community's identity as *Argentinian Jews,* they never engaged in frontal attacks on Zionists and took considerable pains to demonstrate AJC's pro-Israel position. The Committee's campaign to win friends for Israel among Catholics, and its direct cooperation with the Jewish state on such matters as the Blaustein–Ben-Gurion understanding, did much to dispel the old anti-Zionist image. The World Jewish Congress continued to attack the Committee as well as the Instituto, but the prominence enjoyed by certain members of the Instituto (Simon Mirelman was also president of the Argentine United Jewish Appeal; Dr. Mario Schteingart was president of the B'nai B'rith) helped blunt that opposition.

Since the Instituto attempted to reinforce, rather than to replace, existing Jewish organizations in Argentina, it maintained contact with all major religious and social groups. Meanwhile, the Committee was initiating cooperative programs for Latin American Jewry with other American Jewish organizations, including a social-work study, sponsored by the National Council of Jewish Women, and a residency training program in New York hospitals for Latin American Jewish physicians, sponsored jointly with the Federation of Jewish Philanthropies. The Committee also supported a project for the training of Latin American rabbis and teachers in New York, and even considered publishing a Conservative prayer book in Spanish. It is doubtful whether the Committee could have mustered lay acceptance for any domestic activities along these lines. In a sense, it was easier to formulate blueprints for foreign communities than for the American scene, for the emphasis and nuances of such programs were left largely to the professional staff and were not subjected to the same scrutiny by chapters and lay committees as were the domestic programs.

V

By the end of the Perón era, solid foundations had been laid for the Instituto's public relations and Jewish identity programs. The cost to the Committee was modest; besides Yagupsky's salary, the major expense was the publication of *Comentario*. In the next decade, despite political upheavals and recurring economic problems, the programs became more varied and sophisticated. More and more AJC projects and tactics found their way to Argentina. Research on problems of concern to Latin American Jewry and seminars and lectures on human relations became important Instituto activities. In a remarkably short time the Instituto was adapting to its purposes much of the basic methodology of the parent organization throughout the Slawson era.

With repeated successes, the Committee's early doubts about its ability to influence community life outside the United States dissipated. Using Argentina as its model, AJC expanded its program in Latin America. In 1957 the Instituto Brasileiro-Judáico de Cultura e Divulgação was established; shortly afterward the Committee opened offices in Rio de Janeiro, São Paulo, and Mexico City.

Two official missions by AJC laymen helped to augment Committee influence in Latin America. The first, in 1958, was led by President Irving M. Engel and Honorary President Jacob Blaustein; the second, in 1964, by President Morris Abram. As with earlier visits by AJC leaders to Europe and North Africa, the purpose was to explore at first hand the needs of the Jewish communities and to establish favorable contacts with foreign leaders and American government officials. Neither staff reports nor written messages could substitute for personal contact in conveying a spirit of friendship and concern. The American visitors were warmly received by the Jewish communities, including Zionists, and got favorable publicity in the Jewish and non-Jewish press. The Committee delegations coupled explanations of the agency's purposes and philosophy with offers of assistance to their fellow Jews. Abraham Monk, successor to Yagupsky, wrote of the 1958 mission: "[One] of the main results of the AJC's visit was to stir up a high degree of awareness of American Jewish life and to start seeking in its patterns some solutions for local problems. Up to now, such solutions were exclusively sought in the former trends of Eastern European Jewish life and in the Israeli structure." And an Israeli consul summed up popular reaction to the 1964 visit: "If Morris Abram wants to run for President of Argentina, the job is his."

In recent years the Committee and the Institutos have sought to expand their interreligious activity, balancing, as in the United States, a desire for cooperation and a determination to resist excessive religious control in educational and social matters. Meaningful cooperation, however, rested upon recognition of the right of minority faiths to disseminate their teachings freely, and such recognition was rare. The traditional conservatism of the Latin American hierarchy was reinforced by the political power of the church; and there was no pluralistic democratic society to propel it toward liberalism.

Jewish leaders undertook to establish working alliances with the more progressive prelates. Their achievements, though modest, were radically new for Latin America: Christian-Jewish brotherhoods were organized in Argentina, Brazil and Uruguay; three-faith radio and television programs were inaugurated; Argentina's Cardinal Caggiano made an official visit to a synagogue; the Brazilian Instituto's *Comentário* (published in Portuguese) reported on a study of catechismal teachings about Jews. A more ambitious undertaking was the effort in the early 1960s to win the support of the four cardinals in Argentina and Brazil for the Vatican Council's proposed declaration on the Jews. Approached by the Institutos as well as by the visiting Committee delegation, the prelates declared their agreement with the document's principles. But implementation of the spirit of the Ecumenical Council posed a far more serious challenge. In Argentina, despite the restiveness of the younger priests, the church was not ready to accept a rapprochement between Catholicism and other religions. Interreligious work remained, in the words of progressive-minded Father Carlos Cucchetti, "a pioneering mission."

The Committee leaders who went to Latin America in 1958 and 1964 also gave much attention to the problem of Jewish identity, noting the lack of trained leadership and educational materials. Of special concern was the pronounced generation gap and the tendency of Jewish youth to reject the segregationist approach of their parents. Without a grounding in Jewish culture and values, these young people were apt to reject also their very identity as Jews.

The Institutos and the Committee responded in various ways—an expanded publication program, including works on Judaism and Jewish education as well as on anti-Semitism and totalitarianism; traveling exhibits on Jewish themes; the donation of libraries to Christian-Jewish brotherhoods and to the chairs of Hebrew civilization at the Universities of Rio de Janeiro and São Paulo; a documentation center serving as archives and reference library at the Sociedad Hebraica in Buenos Aires. A School of Community Leadership was established in Buenos Aires, offering to community workers and lay leaders courses in Jewish education, social work, and community organization. And a series of sociological surveys that probed the attitudes of Jewish university students and young married couples toward Jews and non-Jews provided realistic guideposts for planning for the communities' needs. They also served to bind AJC closer to its Latin American counterparts, for the same problems of assimilation, intermarriage, and alienated youth faced the Jewries of both continents.

The needs of the youth and of the scattered Jewish communities outside the major cities were central to the recommendations of the 1964 delegation. In December of that year, the Committee's executive board allocated special funds for a Community Service Program to be developed by the Latin American offices in cooperation with the Institutos. It was to be patterned on the European Community Service Program but shaped to the needs of Latin America. Special guides were prepared for community leaders on a wide range of subjects, religious and cultural. Lectures, conferences on identity and Jewish education, and leadership seminars were organized in response to requests by communities for guidance and information. In 1965 the Committee invited representatives of other American Jewish organizations concerned with South American Jewry to consult on the problem of Jewish identity. John Slawson suggested that the groups develop a "culture corps" of rabbis and teachers who would visit Latin America and spark a variety of cultural programs. While the Committee sought new ways to cope with the problems of Jewish identity in Latin America, its achievements continued to enhance its prestige. Far more significantly, it imbued Latin American Jewry with an increasing concern for achieving a meaningful Jewish life.

VI

Identity was only half of the Committee prescription for a healthy Jewish existence. Integration, the second part of the Committee formula, lagged far behind in Latin America and could not be achieved as long as the majority society maintained its barriers and the minority group lacked the desire to tear them down. The situation in Argentina pointed up the difficulty, if not the impossibility, of Jewish integration in a nondemocratic, monolithic country.

For a time Perón's downfall raised hopes for the development of democracy. Leaders of the Instituto, the first Jewish group to be received by the provisional president, General Pedro Aramburu, reiterated their loyalty to democratic principles. The natural affinity of Jews for democracy, they asserted, had not been destroyed by "Perónization." In New York the Committee agreed that the time had come to work actively with liberal groups for a viable democratic and pluralistic society. But despite the key contacts established in political circles, and the appointment of individual Jews to important political office under Aramburu's successor, Arturo Frondizi (1958–1962), the Committee was forced to recognize that prospects for integration in Argentina were dim.

Between 1958 and 1962 there were thirty-five attempted coups in Argentina. The Perónist tradition remained alive, particularly in labor circles; and recurrent economic crises, which demanded government regulation, underscored the vulnerability of the middle class. The church and the military were still the major political forces; neither stood for liberalism, social mobility, or pluralism. The Jews were afraid to commit themselves politically or socially. An unstable government could easily be toppled, and there was always the danger that Jews would be a scapegoat. Most important of all, after Perón's ouster, anti-Semitism grew alarmingly, convincing the Jews that even a democratically elected government did not necessarily make for a democratic society.

Anti-Semitism in Argentina during the 1950s and 1960s came from two sources, Nazi and Arab. Often it was a combination of the two. Nazi agents, enjoying the friendship of the government, had successfully penetrated the country just before and during the war. Subsidies from the German Embassy to Argentine periodicals helped give their propaganda wide circulation. Until 1945 Buenos Aires served as a major spy center for the Germans; after the war Argentina became the haven for a significant number of former Nazi officers, most notably Adolf Eichmann. Perón disavowed anti-Semitism, but his government made good use of the Nazis in civilian and military capacities. Their publications and hatemongering continued and slowly influenced right-wing nationalist circles.

The Arabs in Argentina, about equal in number to the Jews, had lived in harmony with the Jews until the creation of the State of Israel and Arab League propaganda drove the two groups apart. Anti-Semitism, cloaked as anti-Zionism, became the link between Arab and Nazi. Isolated incidents in the late 1950s showed that anti-Semites abroad—the Ku Klux Klan, Einar Aberg of Sweden, and others—were contributing to the agitation. Nor did Argentina escape the "swastika epidemic" which erupted in Germany and spread throughout the world in 1959 and 1960.

Though the Nazis and Arabs were better equipped to win public support, the Jews fought back. At the time of the Suez crisis, for example, the Instituto made extensive use of the mass media and Committee-prepared material to counteract the increased sympathy for Nasser and the Arabs. When the Arabs sent a delegation of labor leaders to Egypt, the Instituto persuaded two of the delegates to visit Israel also and report on progress there.

By 1960 combatting anti-Semitism in Latin America had changed from a long-range objective to an immediate need. After the swastika outbreaks, the Instituto and the Committee publicized the AJC memorandum on the subject to Ambassador Grewe of Germany and sought condemnation of racial and religious bigotry from both private groups and the Argentine congress. An officer of the Instituto participated in a TV discussion on neonazism and, as a result, was invited by the Bonn government to visit Germany and study the efforts to stamp out anti-Semitism there.

The swastika episodes had barely died down in May 1960, when three Israeli agents kidnapped Adolf Eichmann from a Buenos Aires suburb. The Jewish community leaders were seized by panic. Would public opinion, aroused by this violation of Argentina's sovereignty, turn against Israel and the Jews? Indeed, the Nazi-Arab coalition had long emphasized that the divided loyalties of the Jews would lead them to side with Israel.

The Committee and Instituto, in cooperation with other Jewish groups, went into action emphasizing the magnitude of Eichmann's crimes against humanity. Meanwhile, Yagupsky labored behind the scenes to bring Israeli and Argentine officials together so that there could be an eventual resolution of the dispute. The Eichmann case affected the Jews of Argentina long after the rupture between the two countries had been healed. Anti-Semites retaliated for the Nazi's trial and sentence with frequent attacks on Jews, synagogues, and Jewish-owned businesses. For those whose memories of Nazi Germany were still alive, the cries of "Death to the Jews" could not be dismissed lightly.

The most prominent of the anti-Semitic groups was Tacuara, a Nazi-like nationalist organization of upper-class youths, which averaged about ten attacks on Jews a month over a period of three years. In June 1962 a Jewish student, Graciela Sirota, was kidnapped and a swastika carved on her chest. A similar attack on another Jewish student a few days later was followed by a shutdown of Jewish businesses in protest against police unwillingness to find the criminals. There was also an exchange of gunfire between the police and a Jewish self-defense group. Minister of the Interior Carlos Androgue issued a forceful statement—prepared in consultation with the Instituto—pledging government actions to curb anti-Semitic excesses. But the police did little. One reporter described the traumatic impact of those events on the Jewish community:

> The psychological implications of the events were much stronger than any political or practical aspect of the question. It is difficult to describe in detail the feelings of the members of the community, which had just celebrated the hundredth anniversary of its existence. Among the elements which constituted that feeling were rage, bitterness, physical fear, disappointment, surprise, and also combativeness. The Sirota case, as well as several other events that followed later, was a tremendous shock, particularly to those Argentinian Jews born in the country and sometimes sons of native parents, for many of whom this was the first occasion on which they were compelled to meditate and ponder on their destiny as Jews and as individuals.

In the following year, emigration to Israel reached new heights.

The issue was of course, much broader than Tacuara. Other contributing factors were the Arab League, the anti-Semitism of Catholic Church members, army maneuvering for political leverage, resentment against the profiteering middle class, and the impotence of the civilian government. No private organization could hope to tackle the root political and economic causes; but the Committee and Instituto did all they possibly could to ameliorate the condition of the Jews. The Instituto pressed the Argentine government to punish those who incited bigotry and to investigate the activities of Arab agents. The Nazi-like character of the anti-Semites was emphasized in countless materials supplied to the mass media by the Instituto and various cooperating liberal organizations. Sociological studies of anti-Semitism were sponsored at the University of Buenos Aires, among them Professor Gino Germani's analysis, "Ideological Anti-Semitism and Traditional Anti-Semitism." And the 1964 AJC delegation to Argentina recommended that the Instituto establish its own fact-finding unit to keep track of anti-Semitic activities.

While encouraging the Instituto to undertake greater responsibilities in its own defense, the Committee pursued a parallel, but distinct, line of activity. The crisis was too great, the AJC believed, to leave the matter entirely to Latin American Jews. Undeterred by the skepticism and criticism of both its Argentinian followers and rivals, the Committee publicized and denounced the anti-Semitic developments. From 1961 on, it reported periodically to the State Department and asked for American intercession through diplomatic representatives and military attachés. AJC leaders appealed to Argentine diplomats in the United States and discussed anti-Semitism when it entertained official visitors from Argentina at the New York headquarters. In 1964 the Committee delegation, under police escort while in Buenos Aires, told officials how seriously outsiders viewed the situation. Shortly after it departed, Argentina revoked the visa of Hussein Triki, the chief Arab League propagandist who had been working with Nazis and neo-Nazis ever since World War II.

The church's position on anti-Semitic developments, particularly its failure to restrain those who overtly supported right-wing activities, was also of direct concern to the Committee. Father Julio Meinvielle, the spiritual mentor of Tacuara, was the best-known example. In his widely read book, *The Jew in the Mystery of History,* Meinvielle recounted the canard of the conspiracy of the Jews, "the messengers and imps of Satan," to rule the world. The Committee asked its influential Catholic friends to intercede directly with the Vatican. Shuster of the AJC Paris office subsequently reported that Cardinal Bea had declared indignantly that Meinvielle's book contained passages which were "impossible from a Catholic point of view." Eventually Father Meinvielle was forbidden to publish anything for six months or to say Mass for two months.

Unlike American Jewry, the Jews of Argentina could not argue that the nationalist, military, and clerical anti-Semitism they were experiencing was "un-Argentinian." Those interceding with Argentine officials could emphasize that the Arab propagandists were foreign agents, and they could also inform United States officials that nationalist anti-Semitism was closely linked to anti-Americanism. But until the tradition of a strong civilian, democratic, and secular government took root, anti-Semitism would recur.

After twenty years the Committee's "missionary diplomacy" continued. Each success inspired new ventures. For the Institutos, the Committee continued to serve as pump-primer in ideas and material resources. For the isolated communities outside the big cities, the Committee expanded its own operations through its Community Service Program. It became increasingly unlikely that AJC would phase out its Latin American activities. Organizational pride alone would permit no retreat, for B'nai B'rith had created a rival program, and the World Jewish Congress was charging the Committee with "colonialism." Most important, the experience of two decades taught AJC that the Latin American communities were not so very different from those in the United States. Intercommunity bonds could only strengthen the Jews in their response to common challenges.

22

Prologue to the Next Sixty

The American Jewish Committee marked its sixtieth anniversary in 1966. With a membership of over forty thousand and an operating budget of $4.5 million, the organization bore little surface resemblance to the small circle of *Hofjuden* of 1906, or even to the "Jewish 400" of the early 1940s. AJC now thought of itself primarily as a human-relations agency, and not as a defense agency. John Slawson liked to call it a movement—an organization which, in addition to intergroup and worldwide defense activity, represented a particular philosophy of modern Jewish living.

The Committee's longevity can be explained largely in terms of its broadened horizons. When its executive committee resolved, in 1947, that the rights of other groups constituted a legitimate concern for a Jewish agency, it guaranteed an unlimited life-span for the Committee. The resolution had postulated the indivisibility of an open society and declared that the freedom of any individual or group to realize its potential was bound up with the freedoms of all. Accordingly, the defense of American Jews fused with the continuing need to guard the traditional promise of freedom which America held out to all citizens.

The Committee's activities in behalf of civil rights and its concern with urban problems demonstrated that a welfare state did not obviate the need for private organizations. The latter were freer to experiment, research past experiences, and test out new theories. The intergroup skills of the American Jewish Committee were particularly significant. In Slawson's words: "As the Government assigns more and more of its resources to improving the well-being of the people, the private agency is given the opportunity and responsibilities for conserving and enriching the human factor in what might otherwise become a mechanistic and impersonal process."

In strictly logical terms, therefore, there was a role for the Committee quite apart from the American Jewish community. But in recent years the Committee has focused ever more strongly on the internal strength of American Jewry. The stimulus for a program of Jewish identity underwent several changes during the postwar era. Originally viewed as a tool of self-defense in the struggle for equality, it later became a mental-hygiene aid to help the individual Jew function as an integrated individual in an integrated society. Most recently, thanks to the efforts of John Slawson particularly, the Committee has emphasized the intrinsic richness of the Jewish tradition and its embodiment of a code of behavior which has lost none of its relevancy for modern society.

The attitudes of American Jews helped push the Committee into formulating an intensive identity program. An image study commissioned by the Committee in 1962 revealed that communal-minded Jews believed that assimilation was perhaps the major crisis confronting the community and that the American Jewish Committee was, in the eyes of the community, more assimilationist than survivalist. Stung by these findings, the Committee has committed itself to the preservation of the Jewish group in the United States. The program has necessarily remained open-ended; its goal is to anticipate and provide for the long-range needs of the community. This does not imply the revival of the early patrician concept of steward and ward in relation to the Jewish masses, but rather a determination to work with and not for the community. In broader perspective, a strong Jewish identity will test how well subgroups in a pluralist society can cultivate differences in the face of counter pressures for conformity.

Even if the Committee were assured of a continuing raison d'être through programs of urban affairs or Jewish identity, it could not surrender its narrower defense activities. The Six-Day War of 1967, for instance, which lies outside the scope of this study, affected the security of Jews from Algeria to Argentina. Even in the United States the war had serious reverberations in theological circles and in the black community. And though the self-interests of entrenched organizations lend a measure of credibility to the quip that "if anti-Semitism didn't exist, the Jewish defense organizations would have to invent it," the dangers of bigotry remain a reality.

The prognosis for anti-Semitism in the United States was the subject of a conference convened by the Committee in 1964. Unlike a similar conference twenty years earlier, the participants approached the phenomenon of prejudice through studies of social forces rather than personality factors. An analysis by sociologist Charles Herbert Stember of public-opinion polls reaching back to 1937 pointed to what one AJC staff member called "the case of the vanishing anti-Semitism." Stember's conclusions were most optimistic. His data revealed that hostility against the Jews had steadily eroded, despite the tensions generated by McCarthyism and the cold war, Jewish involvement with the State of Israel, and increased competition for social status. "Stember finds that discrimination as well as prejudice have dwindled to the point where they no longer reinforce each other and that 'in both feeling and behavior' toward this minority, the American public has undergone such a profound change since the Second World War that it is 'unlikely to be reversed by anything short of a catastrophic crisis,' " one conferee summarized.

Several other participants at the conference were prepared to bury American anti-Semitism. But those steeped in Jewish history were less sanguine. How accurate were attitudes gleaned from polls, they asked, particularly if accepted fashion frowned upon prejudicial views? Was anti-Semitism only the result of juxtapositions of social forces—or did it have an independent existence?

Quite possibly the conventional forms of prejudice and anti-Semitism—the kind fought by Louis Marshall in the 1920s and the Survey Committee in the 1930s—had lost their momentum. The traditional source for such infection was to be found among the militant antiliberals of the Right. Perhaps, as the optimists in 1964 suggested, worry about the Right had lost most of its validity. But if anti-Semitism continues to rise within black and New Left groups, the future may vindicate the pessimists and prove that the Right has no monopoly on Jew-hatred.

In the early 1960s the leaders of the American Jewish Committee began to worry over the vitality and growth potential of the organization. The Committee, in fact, had virtually stopped growing. The number of enrolled members in 1956 was 26,400; four years later the figure stood at 27,800. At that rate, the organization could not hope to sustain in money or in manpower a dynamic program. And numbers did not tell the whole story. President A. M. Sonnabend, reporting to the AJC executive board in 1961, pointed to two weaknesses in the quality of the Committee's membership: it did not reflect the broad spectrum of interests within the Jewish community, and it lacked younger men who could constitute the reservoirs of vigorous leadership.

When the chapter movement was launched in 1944, its orientation was "like-mindedness." The goal was to seek out members who thought and behaved like the traditional Committee man and to preserve the elitist quality of the organization by shunning the masses. To members and nonmembers alike, the image of AJC fifteen years later was one of a closed club or a family circle. Essentially, the archetype was still of World War II vintage. The Committee had not kept pace with the rapid Americanization of the "new" Jewish immigrants, the postwar redistribution of wealth within the Jewish community, or the developments within the Conservative and Orthodox synagogue movements.

What began as private soul-searching was broadened—in true Committee fashion—into an objective study of the Committee's image by Social Research, Inc. Nonmembers influential in local Jewish affairs were questioned about the Committee and its activities, and an analysis was made of their responses. The findings revealed that even within that hand-picked group the Committee was only fairly well known. Its general image was that of a defense agency fighting discrimination and striving for Jewish integration (interpreted by many respondents to mean assimilation). It was seen as operating primarily through personal and behind-the-scenes influence, with scant regard for other Jewish organizations. Its members were described as wealthy, conservative, German Jewish in background, socially exclusive, well connected in the larger community, and cautious in their Jewishness. Most respondents agreed that the Committee had made significant intellectual contributions to both the Jewish and non-Jewish communities; but they did not feel it spoke specifically to Jews. It was generally viewed as a top-heavy national organization which selected its membership very carefully, whose local chapters existed primarily to finance the agency. Whether the traits attributed to the Committee were admired or disparaged depended on the individual respondent. What elicited the most uniform praise was the organization's intellectual quality. (The historian who examines the findings can only wonder how many of the respondents were raised in homes where the American Jewish Committee axiomatically meant the "assimilationist *Yahudim*" who fought Louis Brandeis, Stephen Wise, and the Zionist cause.)

Whatever the genesis of the image, if the Committee wanted to broaden its base it faced a serious public relations challenge. The image study bore out the executive board's own observations and pointed up other problems in communicating with the community. Few people, it appeared, knew anything about the Committee's foreign affairs program and its pioneering efforts to safeguard Jewish identity. The vitality, dedication, and sense of urgency about its goals, which the Committee was eager to nurture in a reinvigorated membership, could not develop without an understanding of those goals.

Part of the problem, according to Slawson and others, derived from the fact that the Committee did not approach the community directly, through fund raising, but received its funds through allocations from local Jewish federations, and the Joint Defense Appeal (JDA), then the fund-raising arm of the Committee and the Anti-Defamation League. The Joint Defense Appeal, which concentrated on the domestic educational and defense programs of both agencies, served to reinforce the Committee's image as a defense agency on a par with the ADL, while it ignored both the Committee's foreign and Jewish communal programs. In addition, restrictions on separate fund raising imposed by the JDA agreement obstructed the expansion of activities other than domestic defense. At the end of 1962, following lengthy and often acrimonious negotiations with the ADL over a new agreement, the Committee terminated the JDA contract. The move was more than financially significant. It forced the Committee to embark on intensive fund-raising campaigns of its own and underscored the need for more dues-paying members. Thus the twin goals of manpower and money fused and provided both the opportunity and challenge to "sell" the organization to the public.

Taking its cue from the image study, as well as from its immediate needs, the Committee labored to present a new image. Slawson pushed vigorously for an end to exclusiveness and deliberate invisibility. The Public Relations Department launched a local and national publicity campaign to familiarize the Jewish community with the work of AJC and the active involvement of young chapter members. A national Membership

Department, created in 1964, sought out elements in the community which heretofore had generally ignored—or had been ignored by—the Committee: Zionists, labor, East Europeans, and the Conservative and Orthodox. AJC consciously worked to build up its Jewishness. It talked more about identity and Jewish education. And it changed its "loner" status within the Jewish community by cooperating more readily with other agencies.

The money came in and so did the members. By 1966 the membership figure stood at 41,200. Concomitantly, the Committee "type" was gradually changing. Compared to his 1950 counterpart, the average active member in the late 1960s was younger, less wealthy, more liberal in his politics, and not necessarily Reform in religious conviction. He came to the Committee out of a deep interest in national and world affairs, rather than for reasons of noblesse oblige. Like his predecessor, his civic affiliations were more pronounced than his organizational Jewish ties. But he was committed to Israel without fear of being accused of dual allegiance, and he showed a marked concern about Jewish identity for himself and his children.

Numbers alone could not guarantee the vitality of the organization. During the 1960s, the Committee embarked on various programs designed to develop lay leadership, increase lay involvement in activities previously neglected or left solely to the professionals, and equip members with practical skills in handling local community relations problems. Envisioned was a new relationship between the professional staff and the membership, with the latter trained to share in implementing policy. Leadership training was also part of the effort to build up the importance of the chapters in relation to the national office, and the Committee planned changes in its structure to spread the opportunities for the experience of leadership. Increasingly, the local communities were the site of "the action"—whether it involved calming urban confrontations, planning interreligious dialogues, or challenging executive-suite discrimination. Besides nurturing those already enrolled, the Committee tried to seek out "natural leaders," men and women interested in communal affairs and of a caliber sufficiently high to influence others. The influence of the national organization ultimately depended on its grass-roots strength. Inactive chapters, or those whose voices were not heard in national councils, could not attract the dynamic members the Committee hoped for.

Cutting a new figure posed a number of new questions. Could the Committee project the strong Jewish image it sought if it continued to concentrate on human rights for all groups and to work primarily within the non-Jewish community? How could the Committee strike a balance between mass and class? Was it possible to preserve its distinctive style if it repudiated its elitist makeup and competed in the marketplace with mass organizations? If the Committee gave up its traditional role as the elite among American Jews (Slawson called it replacing blue bloods with red bloods) wouldn't this mean sacrificing the variety inherent in pluralism for the homogeneity of democratization? True, the Committee distinctly rejected the role of a mass organization; but how large was "mass"? And wouldn't any restriction in size lend credence to the charge of exclusiveness?

From the point of view of American social history, the evolution in the Committee's makeup is as instructive as the evolution in its activities. It reflects the maturation of an immigrant group with new interests and new material resources. It reveals the pressures of a democratic society, forcing self-appointed stewards to abandon individual action for organization and forcing organizations, in turn, to heed more than to lead the constituencies they represented.

As the United States approaches its two hundredth anniversary, scores of new books doubtless will be written about the development of an American civilization. Ethnic groups and their institutions, long neglected by historians, tell much about that development. The story of the American Jewish Committee during its first sixty years is but one case in point. It testifies to the clashes and adjustments, influences and pressures, mutual enrichment and absorption inherent in the confrontation between minority and majority. For although the Committee was grounded philosophically in talmudic precepts of communal responsibility and patterned directly on European Jewish models, its ideals flourished because they were nurtured in an American matrix. To fight bigotry and to defend human freedoms, to uphold rational order, due process of law, and individual merit were in the self-interest of the group. But they were also the national ideals stamped by the Enlightenment upon eighteenth-century America. Even the Committee's foreign interests—to protect the rights of Jews abroad, to find havens of refuge for the persecuted—affirmed the nation's role as the trustee and exemplar of liberty for the entire world. The American Jewish Committee not only derived strength from American ideals, it helped sustain them. As reformer, critic, pressure group, or gadfly, the organization never ceased to remind the nation of its responsibilities to the cause of freedom. At the same time the Committee labored unceasingly to extend freedom's boundaries. They, who had staked their faith on the promise of America and had shared in the country's benefits, became America's champions.

Notes

This study is based primarily on the voluminous correspondence and memoranda in the archives and records department of the American Jewish Committee. To list each paper separately in standard footnote form would encumber the narrative and lengthen the book. Instead, references are given only to the manuscript files from which the relevant papers were drawn. Material from other primary sources as well as secondary works are itemized in groupings which correspond to the divisions within each chapter. The abbreviations in these Notes follow exactly the headings of the Committee's files.

CHAPTER 1

Introduction & I

S.M. Dubnow, *History of the Jews in Russia and Poland,* trans. from the Russian by I. Friedlaender, 3 vols. (Philadelphia, 1916–20), III, chs. 31, 33–36.

Nathan Schachner, *The Price of Liberty* (New York, 1948), ch. 1.

Naomi W. Cohen, *A Dual Heritage* (Philadelphia, 1969), chs. 4, 7.

Clifton J. Childs, *The German Americans in Politics, 1914–1917* (Madison, Wisc., 1939), p. 3.

Robert H. Bremner, *American Philanthropy* (Chicago, 1960), pp. 10, 13, 28, 45, 50, 72, 111–12.

On the different Jewish organizations, see articles in the *Jewish Encyclopedia* and the *Universal Jewish Encyclopedia;* Z. Szajkowski, "The Alliance Israélite Universelle in the United States, 1860–1949," *Publications of the American Jewish Historical Society (PAJHS),* XXXIX (June 1950).
American Jewish Year Book (AJYB), VIII (1906–07), pp. 115, 117.
Charles Reznikoff, ed., *Louis Marshall: Champion of Liberty,* 2 vols. (Philadelphia, 1957), I, pp. 18–25.
Cyrus Adler, *I Have Considered the Days* (Philadelphia, 1945), pp. 245–46.
Jacob H. Schiff Papers (Jewish Theological Seminary), Box 21: Schiff to I. Zangwill, Jan. 7, 1910.
Cyrus Adler in *American Hebrew,* Jan. 5, 1906.

II & III

Minutes of the conference on organization, Feb. 3 and 4, 1906.
Jewish Morning Journal, Feb. 9, 1906.
Schachner, *Price of Liberty,* pp. 12–18.
The profile of the delegates was based on information culled from biographies, biographical dictionaries, encyclopedias, communal histories, and *AJYB.*

IV

Minutes of the second meeting for organization, May 19, 1906.
Schachner, *Price of Liberty,* pp. 18–25.

V

Schachner, *Price of Liberty,* pp. 25–28.
Minutes of the meetings of the committee of 15, July 1, Oct. 7, 1906; of a subcommittee, Oct. 14, 1906; of general committee, Nov. 11, 1906.
New York Herald and *New York Daily Tribune* for Nov. 12, 1906.
Yonathan Shapiro, "Leadership of the American Zionist Organization, 1897–1930" (unpublished doctoral dissertation, Columbia University, 1964), p. 3.

The fifty charter members of the American Jewish Committee were Cyrus Adler (Washington, D.C.); M. Anfaenger (Denver); Nathan Barnet (Paterson, N.J.); Nathan Bijur (New York); Henry M. Butzel (Detroit); Joseph H. Cohen (New York); Moses H. Cone (Greensboro, N.C.); Harry Cutler (Providence); L.N. Dembitz (Louisville); Harry Friedenwald (Baltimore); Daniel Guggenheim (New York); Ambrose Guiterman (St. Paul); Emil G. Hirsch (Chicago); Jacob H. Hollander (Baltimore); B. Horwich (Chicago); Godfrey M. Hyams (Providence); Leon Kamaiky (New York); Isaac H. Kempner (Galveston); Adolf Kraus (Chicago); Edward Lauterbach (New York); B.L. Levinthal (Philadelphia); E.W. Lewin-Epstein (New York); Adolph Lewisohn (New York); David H. Lieberman (New York); Morris Loeb (New York); Julian W. Mack (Chicago); J.L. Magnes (New York); Martin A. Marks (Cleveland); Louis Marshall (New York); Elias Michael (St. Louis); Isidore Newman (New Orleans); David Philipson (Cincinnati); M. Rosenbaum (Philadelphia); Simon W. Rosendale (Albany); Julius Rosenwald (Chicago); Victor Rosewater (Omaha); Jacob H. Schiff (New York); Max Senior (Cincinnati); Sigmund Sichel (Portland); Max C. Sloss (San Francisco); Isador Sobel (Erie, Pa.); Joseph Stolz (Chicago); Oscar S. Straus (New York); Ferdinand Strauss (Boston); Cyrus L. Sulzberger (New York); Mayer Sulzberger (Philadelphia); J. Trieber (Little Rock); J. Voorsanger (San Francisco); A. Leo Weil (Pittsburgh); and Simon Wolf (Washington, D.C.).

CHAPTER 2

I

Information on finances and structural changes was culled from the bylaws and annual reports of the American Jewish Committee which appear in *AJYB*.
Archives: folders—Cyrus Sulzberger; Anti-Jewish Manifestations/Army and Navy Register; Chronological File—1931 news releases; financial pledges for 1908-9.
Adler Papers: chronological folders—Oct. 1907, Dec. 1919, Jan., Nov. 1920, Feb.–Mar. 1927, Nov. 1928, Dec. 1933.
Marshall Papers: folder-P/Minority Rights.
Waldman Papers: Nov. 1931.
Transcript of the Annual Meeting, Nov. 8, 1908.
The Day, Nov. 8, 1925.
Proceedings at dinner of the American Jewish Committee, May 7, 1929.
Reznikoff, *Marshall*, I, p. 35.
Minutes of Executive Committee, Nov. 8, 1913, Aug. 31, 1914, Jan. 12, 1919, Oct. 17, 1926.
Arthur A. Goren, "The New York Kehillah: 1908–1922" (unpublish-

ed doctoral dissertation, Columbia University, 1966), pp. 19–77, 391.

II

Archives: folder—Cyrus Sulzberger; Chronological File—June 1916.
Adler Papers: chronological folders—Apr. 1907, May 1908, Nov. 1909, June 1910, Apr. 1911, Oct. 1912, Aug.–Sept. 1915, Aug. 1916, July 1920, Feb. 1925, Oct. 1929, Nov. 1932.
Proceedings at dinner of the American Jewish Committee, May 7, 1929.
The Day, June 26, 1925.
Jewish Guardian, Dec. 21, 1928.
Forward, Oct. 20, 1923.
Interview with Harry Schneiderman, Nov. 17, 1966; with Lewis L. Strauss, Jan. 24, 1967.
Minutes of Executive Committee, Nov. 25, 1906, Nov. 9, 1907, Jan. 1, 1909, Oct. 13, 1912.
Morton Rosenstock, *Louis Marshall: Defender of Jewish Rights* (Detroit, 1965), pp. 26–27, 69.
Harry Schneiderman, "AJC: The Early Years," *Committee Reporter,* XVII (Mar., May, Oct., Dec., 1960).
Cohen, *A Dual Heritage,* p. 130.
AJYB, XXXV (1933–34), pp. 145–56; XLII (1940–41), pp. 23–144.

III

Adler Papers: chronological folders—June 1908, Mar. 1911, June–July 1912, Feb. 1914, June–July 1916.
Archives: folders—Politics, Politics/Jewish Vote; Chronological File—Nov. 1927.
M. Sulzberger Papers: Nov. 1908.
Reznikoff, *Marshall,* I, pp. 55–56, 89–90; II, pp. 809–13.
William Allen White, *Autobiography* (New York, 1946), p. 401.
Rosenstock, *Marshall,* pp. 91–92.
Cohen, *A Dual Heritage,* pp. 175–76, 218–21.
Minutes of Executive Committee, May 12, 1912, Nov. 8, 1913, Nov. 15, 1924, Mar. 14, 1926.
AJYB, XII (1910–11), pp. 352–53; XXVI (1924–25), pp. 637–39; XXVIII (1926–27), p. 472.

IV

Adler Papers: chronological folders—Dec. 1906, Oct. 1907, Sept. 1908, Jan., Mar.–Apr. 1911, Mar., Dec. 1916, June 1917, Jan. 1918, Oct. 1926, Dec. 1927, July 1928.

AJYB, XVI (1914–15), p. 383; XIX (1917–18), p. 409; XXII (1920–21), p. 425; XXV (1923–24), pp. 379–80; XXXI (1929–30), pp. 359–60.

Minutes of Executive Committee, Oct. 6, 1907, Dec. 28, 1909, Feb. 20, 1910, Nov. 11, 1911, Oct. 13, 1912, Aug. 13, 1913, Nov. 8, 1913, Nov. 9, 1913, Jan. 18, 1914, Oct. 15, 1916, Jan. 9, Feb. 13, Nov. 13, Dec. 11, 1921, Feb. 12, 1922, Feb. 8, 1925, Oct. 17, 1926, June 16, 1929.

V

AD/ANN 44–60: Attitude of B'nai B'rith and Union of American Hebrew Congregations on Founding of AJC.

Adler Papers: chronological folders—Apr. 1908, Jan.–Feb. 1910, Sept.–Oct. 1915, Feb. 1920.

Minutes of Executive Committee, Nov. 25, 1906, Jan. 27, Apr. 21, Oct. 6, 1907, Oct. 8, 1908, Apr. 20, Aug. 13, Nov. 18, 1913, July 21, 1915, Apr. 15, May 16, 1917, Mar. 14, 1920, Apr. 14, 1929.

CHAPTER 3

Introduction & I

Adler Papers: chronological folders—Feb. 1913. Nissim Behar, director of the National Liberal Immigration League, counted over eighty organizations which stood for restriction (Adler Papers: Mar. 24, 1911).

Marion T. Bennett, *American Immigration Policies* (Washington, D.C., 1963), pp. 31, 332, 334.

Maldwyn A. Jones, *American Immigration* (Chicago, 1960), pp. 216–70.

John Higham, *Strangers in the Land* (Atheneum paperback. New York, 1963), chs. 3, 4, 6.

Barbara M. Solomon, *Ancestors and Immigrants* (Wiley paperback. New York, 1965), chs. 4–7.

Oscar Handlin, *Immigration as a Factor in American History* (Englewood Cliffs, N.J., 1959), pp. 185–86.

II

Minutes of Executive Committee, Jan. 27, 1907.
M. Sulzberger Papers: Jan.–Feb. 1907.
Adler Papers: chronological folders—Dec. 1906–Feb. 1907.
Bennett, *American Immigration Policies*, p. 25.
Higham, *Strangers in the Land*, pp. 124, 127–30.
Cohen, *A Dual Heritage*, pp. 152–53.

III

M. Sulzberger Papers: Jan., Sept., Nov. 1909, Jan. 1910, Mar. 1911.
Adler Papers: chronological folders—Feb. 1907, Feb.–May, Sept. 1908,
Apr.–May, Aug.–Dec. 1909, Jan.–Mar., May 1910, Jan.–Apr. 1911.
Minutes of Executive Committee, Mar. 10, Apr. 21, Oct. 6, Nov. 9, 1907,
May 10, 1908, Aug. 25, Dec. 28, 1909, Feb. 20, May 29, Sept. 26, Nov.
12, 1910, Feb. 19, Mar. 19, Apr. 23, Nov. 11, 1911.
AJYB, X (1908–9), p. 245; XII (1910–11), pp. 19–98, 344–49; XIII
(1911–12), pp. 299–305.
Cyrus Adler, *Jacob H. Schiff: His Life and Letters*, 2 vols. (Garden City, New
York, 1929), II, pp. 94–114.
Reznikoff, *Marshall*, I, p. 83.
Cohen, *A Dual Heritage*, pp. 139 ff., 153–57.
Archives: Chronological File—Feb., Apr. 1910.

IV

M. Sulzberger Papers: Mar. 1912.
Marshall Papers: folder—C/Immigration.
Adler Papers: chronological folders—Jan.–July, Oct., Dec., 1912, Jan.–
Feb. 1913.
Minutes of Executive Committee, May 12, Oct. 13, 1912, Jan. 1, Apr. 20,
1913.
AJYB, XIV (1912–13), pp. 294–95; XV (1913–14), pp. 455–57; XVI
(1914–15), pp. 392–97.
Higham, *Strangers in the Land*, pp. 189–93, 202–3.
Schachner, *Price of Liberty*, p. 52.
Cyrus L. Sulzberger, "Is Immigration a Menace?" Address delivered at
the 39th National Conference of Charities and Corrections, June 12,
1912.

Chapter 4

This chapter is a revised version of the author's article "The Abrogation of the Russo-American Treaty of 1832," *Jewish Social Studies*, XXV (Jan. 1963), pp. 3–41. Full documentation appears there.

The added items on John Slawson are from Israel-Palestine/American Citizenship and AD/ANN 44–60.

Chapter 5

Introduction & I

Joseph Rappaport, "Jewish Immigrants and World War I" (unpublished doctoral dissertation, Columbia University, 1951), p. 184.

Adler Papers: chronological folders—Jan., Mar.–Apr., June–Sept. 1913.

Marshall Papers: folders—P/Minority Rights, C/Rumania.

Archives: Chronological File—Nov. 1912.

Minutes of Executive Committee, Oct. 6, 1907, Jan. 1, Nov. 13, 1909, Feb. 9, 1911, Jan. 1, Apr. 20, Aug. 13, Nov. 8, 1913, Jan. 8, 1914.

Reznikoff, *Marshall*, II, pp. 501–5.

AJYB, XII (1910–11), pp. 351–52; XV (1913–14), pp. 188–206, 239–41; XVI (1914–15), pp. 382–88; XVII (1915–16), pp. 369–70.

Cyrus Adler and Aaron M. Margalith, *With Firmness in the Right* (New York, 1946), pp. 134–38.

II

Ismar Elbogen, *A Century of Jewish Life*, trans. by Moses Hadas (Philadelphia, 1945), pp. 453–69.

Adler Papers: chronological folders—May 1916.

Marshall Papers: folders—P/Minority Rights, C/Palestine.

Jacob H. Schiff Papers (American Jewish Archives): H. Schneiderman to Schiff, May 3, 1916.

Minutes of Executive Committee, Aug. 13, 1913, Jan. 18, Aug. 31, Nov. 7, 1914, Apr. 9, 1916.

Archives: Chronological File—Sept.–Oct. 1914.

AJYB, XVII (1915–16), pp. 359–69; XVIII (1916–17), pp. 305–10; XIX (1917–18), pp. 451–58; XX (1918–19), pp. 374–75.

A.S. Yahuda, *The Defense of Palestinian Jewry during the First World War* (Hebrew. Jerusalem, 1952).

III

Rappaport "Jewish Immigrants and World War I," pp. 78, 124, 378–83. On Schiff's conflicting sentiments with respect to the belligerents, see Adler, *Schiff*, II, pp. 178–93.
Adler Papers: chronological folders—Nov. 1914, June 1915, June–July, 1916.
Marshall Papers: folder—P/Minority Rights.
Archives: folder—Jacob H. Schiff.
Minutes of Executive Committee, Aug. 31, Nov, 7, 1914, Mar. 7, May 9, Sept. 20, 1915.
AJYB, XVII (1915–16), p. 376.
Cohen, *A Dual Heritage*, pp. 172, 235–37, 241, 243–45.
Reznikoff, *Marshall*, II, pp. 510–13, 903.

IV

Minutes of Executive Committee, Aug. 31, 1914, Jan. 9, Feb. 13, Mar. 7, May 9, June 30, July 13, 21, 28, Aug. 11, Sept. 20, Oct. 10, Nov. 13, 1915, Mar. 12, Apr. 9, May 13, Oct. 15, 1916.
Adler Papers: chronological folders—June–July, Sept.–Oct., Dec. 1915, Mar., May–Aug., 1916.
Marshall Papers: folders—C/AJCongress.
Archives: folders—AJCongress, Jacob H. Schiff; Chronological File—1915–16.
New York Times, June 5, 1916.
Hebrew Standard, June 25, 1915.
American Hebrew, Mar. 24, 1916.
Jacob H. Schiff Papers (American Jewish Archives): Schiff to L. Brandeis, Feb. 29, 1916; F. Frankfurter to L. Marshall, June 23, 1916.
AJYB, XVIII (1916–17), pp. 310–23, 324–51, 354; XIX (1917–18), pp. 440–51.
Goren, "New York Kehillah," pp. 397–412.
Shapiro, "Leadership of the American Zionist Organization," pp. 190–230.
Oscar I. Janowsky, *The Jews and Minority Rights* (New York, 1933), pp. 161–90.
American Jewish Congress, *To the Jews of America* (New York, 1915).

V

Adler Papers: chronological folders—Mar., May 1917. The Committee hoped for the appointment of a Jew as an American consul to some Russian city.

Marshall Papers: folder—P/Minority Rights/Russia.

Minutes of Executive Committee, May 16, 1917, Nov. 19, 1918.

AJYB, XX (1918–19), pp. 370–73.

Cohen, *A Dual Heritage*, pp. 254–55.

VI

Minutes of Executive Committee, Apr. 15, May 16, Nov. 10, Dec. 9, 1917.

Adler Papers: chronological folders—June–July, Sept., 1917.

Marshall Papers: folder—P/Minority Rights/Russia.

Reznikoff, *Marshall*, II, pp. 971–74.

Cohen, *A Dual Heritage*, p. 254.

AJYB, XX (1918–19), p. 391; XXI (1919–20), pp. 627–48.

Chapter 6

Introduction & I

Max J. Kohler, "Jewish Rights at International Congresses," *AJYB*, XIX (1917–18), pp. 106–60.

Report of Proceedings of the American Jewish Congress, Philadelphia, Pa., December 1918.

Minutes of Executive Committee, May 12, 1912, Aug. 13, Nov. 8, 1913, Jan. 18, 1914, Mar. 12, 1916, Feb. 2, Apr. 7, 10, 1918.

AJYB, XVIII (1916–17), pp. 321–22.

Adler Papers: chronological folders—May 1909, Nov. 1910, Feb. Apr., Oct. 1912, May, July, Oct., 1913, June, Sept.–Oct. 1915, June 1916, May 1918.

M. Sulzberger Papers: Nov. 1910, Jan. 1918.

Moses Rischin, "The American Jewish Committee and Zionism," *Herzl Year Book*, V (1963).

Naomi W. Cohen, "The *Maccabaean's* Message: A Study in American Zionism until World War I," *Jewish Social Studies*, XVIII (July 1956).
Frank E. Manuel, *The Realities of American-Palestine Relations* (Washington, D.C., 1949), ch. 3, p. 157.
Cohen, *A Dual Heritage*, pp. 66–67, 87–90, 139–44.
Dos Yiddishe Folk, Aug. 13, 1915.
Reznikoff, *Marshall*, I, pp. 351–53; II, pp. 566, 585–96, 704–25.
Marshall Papers: folder—C/Palestine.

II

Report of Proceedings of the American Jewish Congress, December 1918.
Archives: folders—Jacob H. Schiff, Cyrus L. Sulzberger.
Adler Papers: chronological folders—June 1915, Apr. 1916, Dec. 1917, Apr., June 1918, Mar. 1919.
Marshall Papers: folders—C/AJCongress, P/Minority Rights/Poland.
Minutes of Executive Committee, Feb. 3, May 13, 1916, Nov. 10, 1917, Jan. 13, Sept. 24, Oct. 20, Nov. 9, Dec. 9, 1918, Jan. 12, 1919.
Reznikoff, *Marshall*, II, pp. 531, 536, 538, 551–52, 566, 585–99, 714.

III

Proceedings of Adjourned Session of American Jewish Congress, Philadelphia, Pa., May 30, 31, 1920, pp. 82–112.
Cyrus Adler, Diary.
Adler Papers: chronological folders—Apr. 1917, Jan.–Mar. 1919.
Marshall Papers: folders—Peace Conference, P/Minority Rights.
Janowsky, *Jews and Minority Rights*, pp. 333–41.
American Hebrew, Mar. 24, 1916.
Jewish Comment, June 8, 1917.
Jewish Chronicle, July 18, 1919.
Reznikoff, *Marshall*, II, pp. 556–68.

IV

Adler, Diary.
Adler Papers: chronological folders—June–Aug. 1919.
Marshall Papers: folders—Peace Conference, P/Minority Rights/Russia.
Cohen, *A Dual Heritage*, pp. 268–70.
The Reminiscences of Boris A. Bakhmeteff (Oral History Research Office, Columbia University), pp. 430 ff.

V

Marshall Papers: folders—Peace Conference, P/Minority Rights.
Reznikoff, *Marshall,* II, pp. 676–701.
AJYB, XXVIII (1926–27), p. 437.

Chapter 7

Introduction & I

Norman Cohn, *Warrant for Genocide* (New York, 1967), pp. 156–64.
Reznikoff, *Marshall,* I, pp. 204, 328, 333.
Robert K. Murray, *Red Scare: A Study of National Hysteria, 1919–1920* (McGraw-Hill paperback. New York, 1964).
William E. Leuchtenburg, *The Perils of Prosperity* (Chicago, 1958), ch. 4.
E. Digby Baltzell, *The Protestant Establishment* (Vintage Books. New York, 1966), ch. 9.
Higham, *Strangers in the Land,* pp. 268–70, 279–81.
Stanley Coben, "A Study of Nativism," *Political Science Quarterly,* LXXIX (March 1964).
Adler Papers: chronological folders—June 1918–Feb. 1919, June, Aug., Sept., Dec. 1919, Jan.–Mar., Oct.–Dec. 1920, Jan.–Feb. 1921, Mar. 1922.
Marshall Papers: folders—P/Minority Rights/Russia, C/Politics.
Minutes of Executive Committee: Dec. 19, 1918, Feb. 16, 1919, Mar. 14, 1920.
Anti-Semitism Files: *Protocols,* Ford.
Archives: folders—Brasol, *Protocols.*
Reminiscences of Bakhmeteff, pp. 430–34.
Transcript of Annual Meeting, Nov. 14, 1920 (remarks by Adolf Kraus).
Bolshevik Propaganda. Hearings before a subcommittee of the Committee on the Judiciary, U.S. Senate, 65th Congress, 3rd Session (and thereafter) pursuant to Senate Resolutions 439 and 469, Feb. 11, 1919, to Mar. 10, 1919 (Washington, D.C., 1919), pp. 112–16, 120, 132, 135, 140, 141–43, 206–7, 269, 321, 378–81, 383–415.
Rosenstock, *Marshall,* pp. 116, 120–24.
Norman Bentwich, *For Zion's Sake: A Biography of Judah L. Magnes* (Philadelphia, 1954), pp. 105–10.
Norman Hapgood, "The Inside Story of Henry Ford's Jew Mania," *Hearst's International,* XLI–XLII (June–Nov. 1922).

New York Tribune, Oct. 25, 29, 1918; *New York Times,* Dec. 12, 1918, Feb. 15, 1919.

II

Adler Papers: chronological folders—Feb. 1919, June–Dec. 1920, Oct. 1921, May 1925.

AJYB, XXIII (1921–22), pp. 313–17, 367–77.

Hapgood, "The Inside Story."

Rosenstock, *Marshall,* pp. 128–35, 149–57, 164–75.

Higham, *Strangers in the Land,* pp. 282–84.

Norman Cohn, "The Myth of the Jewish World-Conspiracy," *Commentary,* XLI (June 1966).

Reznikoff, *Marshall,* I, pp. 330–38, 354–55, 367, 374, 380.

Archives: folders—Ford, Schiff, Brown.

Jacob H. Schiff Papers (American Jewish Archives): Schiff to H. Schneiderman, June 28, 1920.

Transcript of Annual Meeting, Nov. 14, 1920.

Minutes of Executive Committee, June 23, Oct. 10, Nov. 13, 1920.

Marshall Papers: C/Anti-Semitism, Miscellaneous Typescripts, C/Ford, C/Ford/Retraction.

Herman Bernstein, *The History of a Lie* (New York, 1921).

———, *The Truth about "The Protocols of Zion"* (New York, 1935).

John S. Curtiss, *An Appraisal of the Protocols of Zion* (New York, 1942).

III

Reznikoff, *Marshall,* I, pp. 390–94, 426.

Higham, *Strangers in the Land,* pp. 285–99.

David M. Chalmers, *Hooded Americanism* (Quadrangle paperback. Chicago, 1968), ch. 4.

Minutes of Executive Committee, Sept. 28, Dec. 10, 1922, Mar. 12, May 27, Nov. 17, 1923, Feb. 10, Oct. 5, Nov. 15, 1924.

AJYB, XXVI (1924–25), pp. 639–42.

Anti-Semitism Files: Ku Klux Klan.

Archives: Chronological File—Nov.–Dec. 1922; *Texas American,* Feb. 23, 1923.

Brief for American Jewish Committee, Louis Marshall, amicus curiae, *Pierce* v. *Society of the Sisters,* Supreme Court of the United States, October Term 1924.

IV

Higham, *Strangers in the Land*, pp. 267–70, 309.
Robert A. Divine, *American Immigration Policy, 1924–1952* (New Haven, 1957), pp. 14, 18, 49–51.
Rosenstock, *Marshall*, pp. 217–23.
Reznikoff, *Marshall*, I, pp. 159–241 *passim;* II, p. 746.
Bennett, *American Immigration Policies*, p. 49.
Mark Wischnitzer, *To Dwell in Safety* (Philadelphia, 1949), pp. 155–56.
Minutes of Executive Committee, Nov. 17, 1923.
AJYB, XXII (1920–21), pp. 411 ff.; XXIII (1921–22), p. 354; XXIV (1922–23), p. 344; XXV (1923–24), p. 376; XXVI (1924–25), p. 644; XXVII (1925–26), p. 422; XXVIII (1926–27), pp. 439–68; XXIX (1927–28), p. 395; XXX (1928–1929), p. 272; XXXI (1929–30), pp. 339–46.
Adler Papers: chronological folders—Feb.–Sept. 1920, Mar.–May 1921, Aug. 1922, Dec. 1924–Feb. 1925.

V

Rosenstock, *Marshall*, pp. 241–55.
Ralph P. Boas, "Jew-Baiting in America," *Atlantic Monthly*, CXXVII (May 1921).
Heywood Broun and George Britt, *Christians Only* (New York, 1931).
Bruno Lasker, ed., *Jewish Experience in America* (New York, 1930), p. 69.
Baltzell, *Protestant Establishment*, ch. 9.
Philip M. Brown, "Zionism and Anti-Semitism," *North American Review*, CCX (Nov. 1919), p. 662.
Marshall Papers: folders—C/Discrimination.
AJYB, XXXI (1929–30), pp. 21–22, 347–52.
Adler Papers: chronological folders—July 14, 1920.
Minutes of Executive Committee, Apr. 12, May 17, Oct. 18, 1925.
Proceedings at dinner of the American Jewish Committee, May 7, 1929.

VI

Max Gottschalk and Abraham G. Duker, *Jews in the Post-War World* (New York, 1945), pp. 51–58.
Reznikoff, *Marshall*, II, pp. 628–33, 647–74, 753.
Morris D. Waldman, *Nor by Power* (New York, 1953), p. 41.
Annual reports of AJC in *AJYB*, XXIII (1921–22), XXVI (1924–25),

XXVII (1925–26), XXVIII (1926–27), XXIX (1927–28), XXX (1928–29), XXXI (1929–30), XXXII (1930–31).
Adler Papers: chronological folders—June 1927, July 1928.
Marshall Papers: folders—P/Minority Rights (and subcategories Poland, Rumania, Russia), Peace Conference, C/Poland, C/American Jewish Congress, C/Immigration.
Felix Warburg Papers (American Jewish Archives): A. Margolin to Warburg, May 17, 1928.
Archives: folder—Germany.
Jewish Tribune, May 20, 1927.
Minutes of Executive Committee, Dec. 11, 1921, Jan. 14, Feb. 12, 1922, Feb. 8, 1925, May 1, 1927, Apr. 1, 1928.

VII

Marshall Papers: folders—P/Minority Rights, C/Ford/Retraction, C/Discrimination.
Archives: Chronological File—Aug. 1924, Feb. 1928, July 1929; folders —JTA (1926–27). (The bulk of Landau's report is missing from the files.)
Adler Papers: chronological folders—Nov. 1920, Apr.–May 1921, Oct.–Nov. 1923, Oct. 1927; topical folders—Germany, Nov. 1931.
Minutes of Executive Committee, Nov. 11, 1922, Nov. 17, 1923, Oct. 18, 1925, Oct. 17, Dec. 12, 1926, Mar. 20, Nov. 12, 1927.
Reznikoff, *Marshall,* I, pp. 380–88.
Waldman, *Nor by Power,* pp. 40 ff.
New York Times, Dec. 20, 1922.
AJYB, XXV (1923–24), p. 385; XXVII (1925–26), p. 458.
George J. Mintzer and Newman Levy, *The International Anti-Semitic Conspiracy* (New York, 1946), pp. 5–8.

VIII

Reznikoff, *Marshall,* II, pp. 725–41, 745–90.
Chaim Weizmann, *Trial and Error,* 2 vols. (Philadelphia, 1949), II, pp. 308–14.
Shapiro, "Leadership of the American Zionist Organization," ch. 6.
Adler, *I Have Considered the Days,* pp. 387–93.
AJYB, XXVII (1925–26), pp. 470–72; XXVIII (1926–27), p. 512; XXXI (1929–30), pp. 382–85; XXXII (1930–31) pp. 58–63.
Memorandum: The Jewish Agency and the Non-Zionists, June 14, 1944.

Adler Papers: chronological folders—Jan.–Feb. 1921, Sept. 1929; topical folders—Palestine I.
Archives: folders—Palestine Disturbances (1929); Chronological File—Nov. 29, 1929.
Minutes of Executive Committee, Sept. 15, 1929.

Chapter 8

Introduction & I

Archives: folders—Germany (and subcategories), JTA, Waldman; Chronological File—July 1929, Jan. 1936.
Adler Papers: chronological folders—Sept.–Oct. 1929, Mar., June 1932, Mar. 1933; topical folders—Germany.
Warburg Papers: C. Adler to Warburg, Apr. 1, 1931.
Minutes of Executive Committee, Apr. 14, Nov. 9, Dec. 8, 1929, Jan. 12, Dec. 14, 1930, Jan. 11, Feb. 15, Mar. 22, 1931, Mar. 13, Apr. 10, 1932.
Special Conference of the American Jewish Committee, Nov. 9, 1930.
AJYB, XXXII (1930–31), pp. 93–99; XXXV (1933–34), pp. 22–25.
Waldman, *Nor by Power*, pp. 39–41, 465.
New York World-Telegram, Mar. 10, 1932.
Herbert A. Strauss, "Jewish Defense against Antisemitism and National Socialism in the Last Years of the Weimar Republic" (summary of Arnold Paucker, *Der Juedische Abwehrkampf gegen Antisemitismus und Nationalsozialismus in den letzten Jahren der Weimarer Republik*, Hamburg, 1968).

II

Léon Poliakov, *Harvest of Hate* (Syracuse, 1954), ch. 1.
Waldman Papers: Apr.–June 1933, Aug. 1934, Oct. 1935, Aug. 1938.
State Department Files (National Archives), file 862.4016: 691, 398, 941, 1190, 1192, 1203, 1260, 1268; file 611.6212/9.
Archives: folders—Germany/Boycott, Waldman, Fagen, AJCongress; Chronological File—May 1933, May, July–Aug. 1934.
Warburg Papers: J. Proskauer to Warburg, May 15, 1933.
Adler Papers: chronological folders—July, Oct.–Nov. 1933, May, Aug.–Sept. 1934; topical folders—Laski, Philadelphia, Germany.
Germany / 1931–33; / Boycott; / Nazism / Jewish Agencies / AJC-AJCongress.
U.S. Bureau of the Census, *Historical Statistics of the United States, Colonial*

Times to 1957 (Washington, D.C., 1960), p. 564. I am indebted to Professor Elliot Zupnick for his aid in weighing the economic implications of Waldman's suggestions.

Minutes of Executive Committee, Mar. 19, 1933, Feb. 28, 1935.

Minutes of Committee on Policy, May 15, 1933.

AJYB, XXXV (1933–34), pp. 28–31, 54–55; XXXVI (1934–35), pp. 428, 430–31.

Ambassador Dodd's Diary, ed. by William E. Dodd, Jr. and Martha Dodd (New York, 1941), pp. 10, 100, 106–7, 134, 145, 248–49.

Waldman, *Nor by Power*, pp. 49–51.

New York World-Telegram, Sept. 26, 1933, Feb. 5, 1935; *New York Post*, July 6, 1934; *New York Herald-Tribune*, Sept. 2, 1934; *Commonweal*, June 29, 1934.

Schachner, *Price of Liberty*, p. 117.

Stephen S. Wise, *Challenging Years* (New York, 1949), pp. 219, 224, 238, 260–61.

M. Gottlieb, "The First of April Boycott and the Reaction of the American Jewish Community," *American Jewish Historical Quarterly*, LVII (June 1968), pp. 516–56.

III

State Department Files/862.4016: 398, 399, 776, 941.

Waldman Papers: Feb., Apr.–May 1933, May 1934, Mar. 1935.

Adler Papers: chronological folders—June 1934; topical folders—Italy. Germany/Boycott/England.

Archives: folders—Laski; Chronological File—May 1933.

Warburg Papers: Ralph Easley to W. Wiseman, Apr. 4, 1933; to M. Waldman, Dec. 8, 1933; Warburg to C. Adler, Jan. 25, 1935.

Minutes of Executive Committee, Apr. 9, 1933, Dec. 15, 18, 1934.

New York Sun, Mar. 17, 1933.

AJYB, XXXVII (1935–36), pp. 161–62.

IV

Selig Adler, *The Isolationist Impulse* (Collier paperback. New York, 1961), ch. 11.

Manfred Jonas, *Isolationism in America, 1935–1941* (Ithaca, 1966), ch. 5.

Arnold A. Offner, *American Appeasement* (Cambridge, Mass., 1969), pp. 59–61, 68, 80–83.

State Department Files/862.4016: Mar. 1933 passim for public protests;

80, 115, 116, 283A, 323, 324, 370, 412, 482, 499, 536, 680, 681, 691, 1121, 1260, 1495, 1523, 1598; 611.6212/9; 862.015311/23, 26; 862.-00/2958.

Adler Papers: chronological folders—Jan.–July 1933, Apr. 1934, June 1935; topical folders—Germany.

Waldman Papers: Dec. 1932, Apr.–Aug., Dec. 1933, Mar. 1935.

Political Philosophies/Hitlerisms.

Germany/1931–33.

Archives: folders—Becker, Weil, AJCongress, League; Chronological File—June 1933, Jan., Aug., Dec. 1934; Administrative File: Survey Committee (minutes).

Warburg Papers: C. Adler to Warburg, Apr. 26, 1934; Warburg to W. Dodd, May 20, June 14, 1935; M. Waldman to G. Messersmith, May 3, 1937.

Ambassador Dodd's Diary, pp. 5, 9, 36–37, 86–89, 100, 157.

Minutes of Executive Committee, May 9, June 5, 1933, Jan. 21, Feb. 22, 1934.

Minutes of Committee on Policy, May 15, 1933.

AJC, *The Jews in Nazi Germany* (New York, 1933), pp. 59–63.

New York Times, Mar. 24, 1933.

AJYB, XXXV (1933–34), pp. 48–50; XXXVI (1934–35), pp. 434–37; XXXVIII (1936–37), pp. 617–23.

V

Adler Papers: chronological folders—Mar. 1934; topical folders—Laski.

Waldman Papers: Oct. 1933, Jan. 1947.

Warburg Papers: J. McDonald to O. d'Avigdor Goldsmid, Nov. 17, 1934.

Ambassador Dodd's Diary, pp. 78–79, 145–56, 188.

Waldman, *Nor by Power,* pp. 52–55.

AJYB, XXXV (1933–34), pp. 74–101; XXXVI (1934–35), pp. 89–119, 243–46, 440–43.

VI

Adler Papers: chronological folders—Apr.–July 1933, Jan. 1934; topical folders—Germany, Laski.

Archives: folders—Butler, Olympics, Waldman/European trips.

Waldman Papers: Apr.–May 1933, Oct. 1935.

Minutes of Executive Committee (title sometimes varies), Apr. 9, 19, Nov. 1, Dec. 9, 28, 1933, Jan. 21, Sept. 13, 1934, Oct. 1, 1935.

Ambassador Dodd's Diary, pp. 9–10.
AJYB, XXXVI (1934–35), pp. 441–47; XXXVIII (1936–37), pp. 181–87, 627–28.
New York Times, Nov. 27, 1935.

VII

Adler Papers: chronological folders—June 1932, Nov. 1934, Mar. 1935; topical folders—Germany, Laski, Waldman.
Waldman Papers: Feb.–June 1933, Oct. 1935, June, Nov.–Dec. 1937, Jan., May 1938.
Archives: folders—JCIO, Wallach, Waldman, Waldman/European trips, Leo Simon, Paris Bureau, Catholic-Jewish Relations/H.E. Pamphlet, Catholic-Jewish Relations/Pro Deo; Chronological File—Feb. 1934, Nov. 1936, Dec. 1937.
Warburg Papers: M. Waldman to B. Kahn, Sept. 8, 1930; Warburg to Lord Melchett, Mar. 15, 1935; M. Waldman to S. Stroock, June 12, 1935, Jan. 25, May 4, 1937; to Warburg, June 9, July 21, 1937; to N. Laski, Oct. 27, 1936; H. Schneiderman to Warburg, May 6, 1936; G. Messersmith to M. Waldman, Jan. 12, 1937.
Interview with Lewis L. Strauss, Jan. 24, 1967; with Sidney Wallach, Mar. 17, 1967.
Waldman, *Nor by Power,* ch. 9.
Jewish Chronicle, June 25, 1937.
Minutes of Executive Committee, Mar. 13, Apr. 10, 1932, June 16, 1937.
AJYB, XXXVI (1934–35), pp. 414, 464–71; XXXVII (1935–36), pp. 411–13.

VIII

Archives: folders—Waldman, Wallach; Chronological File—May 1936; news release [Aug. 1936]; Administrative File: Survey Committee (minutes).
Mintzer and Levy, *International Anti-Semitic Conspiracy,* pp. 9–13, 20–22, 27.
Waldman Papers: Aug. 1933, Mar. 1935, Jan. 1936.
Keith Sward, *The Legend of Henry Ford* (New York, 1948), pp. 452–60.
Sol M. Stroock, "German Persecution before the League" (radio address, Aug. 6, 1936).
Minutes of Executive Committee, Apr. 1, 1936, Mar. 23, 1937.
AJYB, XXXVII (1935–36), pp. 176–77, 416–17; XXXVIII (1936–37), pp.

596, 612–13; XXXIX (1937–38), pp. 801–5; XL (1938–39), p. 594. At this time the Committee published *The Truth about "The Protocols of Zion,"* a revised edition of Herman Bernstein's exposé of the *Protocols.*
Oscar I. Janowsky and Melvin M. Fagen, *International Aspects of German Racial Policies* (New York, 1937).

IX

Waldman Papers: June, Nov.–Dec. 1937, Dec. 1938.
Archives: folders—Waldman, Wallach; Administrative File: Survey Committee (minutes).
Warburg Papers: A. Richards to M. Waldman, July 13, Aug. 3, 1937; G. Backer, July 23, 1937; M. Waldman to Warburg, July 22, 1937; to E. Greenbaum et al., July 21, 1937.
Waldman, *Nor by Power,* pp. 67–70.
Robert E. Osgood, *Ideals and Self-Interest in America's Foreign Relations* (University of Chicago paperback. Chicago, 1964), pp. 365, 411–13.

X

Adler Papers: topical folders—Germany.
Warburg Papers: H. Lehman to Warburg, July 14, 1936. Warburg was cochairman of the Council for German Jewry, an Anglo-American group established in 1936 which coordinated the collection of huge sums of money for the vocational training and resettlement of German Jewish youth. Warburg's correspondence with Herbert Samuel, Osmond d'Avigdor Goldsmid, and Neville Laski from 1935 until his death bears upon numerous aspects of the refugee situation. See also entries under Council for German Jews.
Germany/1931–33; *Germany/1933–45.
Political Philosophies/Hitlerisms.
State Department Files/862.4016: 586, 680, 1115.
Waldman Papers: Apr., June, Oct. 1933, Oct. 1935.
Minutes of Executive Committee: Apr. 19, May 9, June 5, Nov. 1, 1933, Jan. 21, Feb. 22, Apr. 17, 1934.
Minutes of Committee on Policy, Sept. 1, 1933.
Minutes of Committee on Aid to German Children, Jan. 3, 1934.
Archives: Administrative File: May 1938; Chronological File—Mar. 1934.
Franklin D. Roosevelt Papers (Hyde Park): File OF 133: Roosevelt to H. Lehman, Nov. 13, 1935, July 2, 1936; to Wm. Green, Dec. 8, 1933; Wm.

Green to Roosevelt, Sept. 22, 1933; H. Lehman to Roosevelt, Nov. 1, 1935; J. McDonald to F. Warburg, Oct. 10, 29, 1935; file 198: from secretary of state, June 17, 1936.
AJYB, XXXVI (1934–35), pp. 437–40; XXXVII (1935–36), pp. 427–30; XXXVIII (1936–37), p. 628; XXXIX (1937–38), pp. 269, 824–25.
David S. Wyman, *Paper Walls, America and the Refugee Crisis, 1938–41* (Amherst, 1968), ch. 1.

XI

Archives: folders—Waldman; Chronological File—1937; news release Nov. 1938.
Waldman Papers: Sept., Nov. 1938.
New York Times, Nov. 16, 1938.
Adler Papers: topical folders—Stroock, Germany.
Arthur D. Morse, *While Six Million Died* (New York, 1968), pp. 203–4.
Wyman, *Paper Walls*, ch. 3.
Roosevelt Papers: File 198: B. Cohen to M. Le Hand, Nov. 10, 1938; from S. Welles, Oct. 10, 1938; File 198A: items for 1938; File PSF Italy-Phillips: Roosevelt to W. Phillips, Sept. 15, 1938; File OF 3186: Roosevelt to I. Lehman, Mar. 30, 1938; I. Lehman to Roosevelt, Mar. 28, 1938, H. Lehman to Roosevelt, Mar. 31, 1938, memorandum—Apr. 11, 1938; File 3186—Roosevelt to M. Taylor, Nov. 23, 1938, to H. Ickes, Aug. 13, 1940.
Lewis L. Strauss, *Men and Decisions* (Garden City, New York, 1962), pp. 110–13; letter from Strauss to author, Feb. 3, 1967.

XII

Archives: folders—Palestine, Waldman, Paris Bureau; Chronological File—July 1937.
Waldman Papers: Aug. 1933, Nov. 1937, Nov.–Dec. 1938, Mar., July 1939, Mar. 1940.
Adler Papers: chronological folders—May 1935; topical folders—Germany.
Israel-Palestine/1938, 1939;/Conferences—1938, 1939.
Warburg Papers: C. Adler to Warburg, Aug. 24, Nov. 20, Dec. 24, 1936; Warburg to O. d'Avigdor Goldsmid, May 13, June 17, Sept. 28, 1937; to C. Weizmann, July 17, 1937; to S. S. Wise, Sept. 1937; to I. Lehman, July 20, 1937; H. Lehman to Warburg, Aug. 12, 1937.
AJYB, XXXIII (1931–32), pp. 368–69; XXXIX (1937–38), pp. 819–20;

XL (1938–39), pp. 105–9, 586–87, 591, 625–28; XLI (1939–40), pp. 200–5.

J.C. Hurewitz, *The Struggle for Palestine* (New York, 1950), pp. 94–102.

Samuel Halperin, *The Political World of American Zionism* (Detroit, 1961), pp. 118–21.

Adler, *I Have Considered the Days*, pp. 425–26.

Proceedings, Thirty-first Annual Meeting of AJC, Jan. 13, 1938, pp. 25–63.

M.J. Karpf, *American Non-Zionists and Palestine Partition*, 1938.

_____, *Partition of Palestine and Its Consequences*, 1938.

Cyrus Adler, *Observations on the Report of the Palestine Royal Commission*, 1938.

The Jewish Agency and the Non-Zionists, 1944.

Chapter 9

Introduction

Adler Papers: chronological folders—Sept. 1929, Apr. 1930, Jan. 1931, Mar. 1932.

Archives: folders—Unity, Palestine, Bressler.

I

Archives: folders—Luedecke, Germany-1932, JTA-1931, Rosenberg, Wallach, Proskauer; Administrative File: Survey Committee (minutes, memoranda, correspondence); Polls: 1933.

Waldman Papers: June, Aug., Oct. 1933, June 1934.

Adler Papers: topical folders—Philadelphia, Germany, Waldman, G/Miscellaneous.

Interview with Lewis L. Strauss, Jan. 24, 1967; with Sidney Wallach, Mar. 17, 1967.

*Germany/1933–45.

Minutes of Executive Committee, Apr. 1, Oct. 19, 1936, Jan. 9, 1937.

Edward S. Greenbaum, *A Lawyer's Job* (New York, 1967), pp. 120–24.

AJYB, XXXVI (1934–35), p. 462.

Ludwig Lore, "Nazi Politics in America," *The Nation*, Nov. 29, 1933.

II

Archives: folders—Anti-Jewish Manifestations, Anti-Jewish Manifestations/Johnson, Laski; Administrative File: Survey Committee; Chronological File—May 1938, Dec. 1939.
Charles Herbert Stember et al., *Jews in the Mind of America* (New York, 1966), pp. 53–55, 60–61, 65, 69, 79–82, 116, 118, 121–24, 144–50.
Interview with Richard Rothschild, Sept. 27, 1967; two memoranda on the six-point plan in Mr. Rothschild's possession.
Adler Papers: chronological folders—June 1934; topical folders—Laski. Immigration/Refugees/1938–44.

III

Archives: Administrative File: Survey Committee, Education Department; Chronological File—Outline of Talks [1937], Dec. 1939.
Minutes of Executive Committee, Dec. 5, 1934.
Adler Papers: chronological folders—May, July 1933, Jan. 1934; topical folders—Waldman.
Germany/1931–33.

IV

Morton Keller, "Jews and the Character of American Life since 1930," in Stember et al., *Jews in the Mind of America,* pp. 259–71.
Donald S. Strong, *Organized Anti-Semitism in America* (Washington, D.C., 1941), pp. 122–23, 144–46, 150–51, 160, 167, 172–75.
In 1939 the Federal Council of the Churches of Christ thought 150 to be a conservative estimate of the number of existing anti-Semitic organizations. FCCC, *Information Service,* June 10, 1939. The AJC estimate appears in a memorandum from David Danzig to Dessie Kushell, Dec. 13, 1950.
Lore, "Nazi Politics in America."
"Nazi Propaganda in the United States," *American Hebrew,* Oct. 13, 1933 et seq.
Mintzer and Levy, *International Anti-Semitic Conspiracy,* pp. 43–44.
Waldman Papers: June 1933, Nov. 1934, Feb.–Mar. 1935, Aug. 1938, Jan. 1940; file on Dies; undated memorandum, A.L. Bernheim to A. Stroock.
Archives: folders—Edmondson; Administrative File: Survey Committee (minutes, reports), Legal and Investigative; Chronological File—June 1935, June 1936, Feb. 1937.

Adler Papers: chronological folders—July 1933, Apr., June 1934; topical folders—Laski, Pennsylvania.
Warburg Papers: H. Schneiderman to members, Executive Committee, Apr. 3, 1936.
Minutes of Executive Committee, Sept. 13, 1934, Feb. 28, 1935, June 2, 1939.
Minutes of Committee on Policy, Sept. 1, Oct. 18, 1933.
New York Herald-Tribune, Mar. 22, 1934.
Anti-Semitism Files: Ford, Edmondson.
AJYB, XL (1938–39), p. 121.
Arthur M. Schlesinger, Jr., *Politics of Upheaval* (Boston, 1960), pp. 84–85.

V

Warburg Papers: H. Schneiderman to A. Emanuel, Apr. 27, 1936.
Archives: folders—Anti-Semitic Manifestations/Johnson, Laski, Catholic-Jewish Relations, Catholic-Jewish Relations/Pro Deo, Easley; Administrative File: Survey Committee (minutes); Chronological File—Sept.–Nov. 1936, Feb. 1937.
Adler Papers: chronological folders—Apr. 1927, Nov. 1928, Mar. 1930, Apr. 1933, May 1934; topical folders—Philadelphia, Russian Refugees.
Waldman Papers: Dec. 1935.
Political Philosophies / Communism, 1935–39; / Communism / Jewish Stereotype.
Minutes of Executive Committee, Oct. 17, 1926, May 1, 1927, Dec. 8, 1929, Jan. 12, Feb. 9, Mar. 16, 1930, Jan. 21, May 14, 1934.
A Public Statement on Communism and Jews by AJC, B'nai B'rith, Jewish Labor Committee, 1935.
New York Evening Journal, Sept. 25, 1936; *The Day,* Oct. 22, 1935.
Mintzer and Levy, *International Anti-Semitic Conspiracy,* p. 46.
Strong, *Organized Anti-Semitism,* p. 147.
Schlesinger, *Politics of Upheaval,* pp. 84–95.

VI

American Hebrew, Nov. 27, 1936.
Strong, *Organized Anti-Semitism,* ch. 5.
Charles J. Tull, *Father Coughlin and the New Deal* (Syracuse, 1965), esp. ch. 6.
"Father Coughlin: Priest and Politician," *Propaganda Analysis,* II-9 (June 7, 1939).

James Wechsler, "The Coughlin Terror," *The Nation,* July 22, 1939.
Waldman Papers: May 1934, Mar., May 1935, Aug. 1938, May 1939, Mar. 1940; two files on Coughlin.
Fact-Finding Dept: undated memo [1940].
Archives: Administrative File: Legal and Investigative.
Mintzer and Levy, *International Anti-Semitic Conspiracy,* pp. 47–51, 57.
Anti-Semitism Files: Coughlin.
Minutes of Executive Committee, June 2, 1939.
General Jewish Council, *Father Coughlin, His "Facts" and Arguments* (New York, 1939).

VII

Adler Papers: chronological folders—Mar.–Apr. 1932, Nov.–Dec. 1933, July–Aug., Oct. 1934, May 1935; topical folders—Germany, General Jewish Council, Stroock, Waldman, American Jewish Congress.
Archives: folders—IOBB, Germany/Conference with AJCongress, Proskauer, Anti-Semitic Manifestations/Army and Navy Register, American Jewish Congress, Wise, World Jewish Congress; Chronological File—Sept. 1934, May 1937, June 1938; Administrative File: Survey Committee (minutes, correspondence).
Warburg Papers: C. Adler to AJCongress, Jan. 14, 1935; to Warburg, Aug. 25, 1936; E. Bernays to M. Waldman, Jan. 2, 1935.
Waldman Papers: July, Aug., Oct., Dec., 1933, July 1938.
Germany/1931–33;/AJC-AJCongress;/Nazism/Jewish Agencies/AJC-AJCongress.
General Jewish Council/1938–43;/Fund Raising.
World Jewish Congress.
Minutes of Executive Committee, Oct. 30, 1932, Jan. 8, Feb. 12, 1933, Sept. 13, Oct. 30, Dec. 5, 1934, Feb. 28, 1935, May 11, 1936.
AJYB, XXXVII (1935–36), pp. 434–40; XXXVIII (1936–37), pp. 207–11; XL (1938–39), pp. 138–39.
AJC, *The Proposed World Jewish Congress* (New York, 1935).
———, *But the Proposed World Jewish Congress Will Not Represent* [New York, 1936].
Time, June 20, 1938.
The Day, Mar. 5, 1935.
World Jewish Congress, *Unity in Dispersion* (New York, 1948), part 1.
Louis Lipsky, "The Lost Cause of Unity," *Congress Bulletin,* Nov. 29, 1940.

Chapter 10

Introduction & I

AJYB, XLII (1940–41), p. 643.
Archives: Administrative File: Program and Policies, Survey Committee (reports, correspondence); Chronological File—Dec. 1931.
Waldman Papers: Oct., Dec. 1939, June, Dec. 1940; undated memorandum on Lindbergh speech.
Political Philosophies/Nazism 1941–42.
War & Peace/1934–42.
Anti-Semitism Files: America First Committee.
Richard C. Rothschild, "Are American Jews Falling into the Nazi Trap?" *Contemporary Jewish Record*, III (Jan.–Feb. 1940).
S. A. Fineberg, *Overcoming Anti-Semitism* (New York, 1943).
————, "Strategy of Error," *Contemporary Jewish Record*, VIII (Feb. 1945).
Philadelphia Anti-Defamation Council and the American Jewish Committee, *To Bigotry No Sanction*, rev. ed. (Philadelphia, 1941), pp. 36–37.
"Cincinnatus," *War! War! War!* third ed., pp. 3–4.
Wayne S. Cole, *America First* (Madison, 1953), chs. 7, 8.

II

Archives: Administrative File: Survey Committee (reports), Programs and Policies, Public Relations, Reorganization; Chronological File—Mar. 1942, Dec. 1943, Dec. 1945.
Waldman Papers: Feb. 1944; undated memo on Nazi "Divide and Rule" propaganda.
War & Peace/Civilian Defense, 1941–42.
AD/D & D/Public Relations, 1945.
Minutes of Executive Committee, Nov. 6, 1945.
Minutes of Administrative Committee, Nov. 4, 1942, Jan. 19, Feb. 15, Mar. 14, June 13, 1944, Mar. 13, 1945.
Committee Reporter, Mar. Apr., May, June, July, Oct. 1944.
AJC, *Conference on Research in the Field of Anti-Semitism* (New York, 1944).
Samuel Rosenman, ed., *The Public Papers and Addresses of Franklin D. Roosevelt*, 13 vols. (New York, 1942–50), XI, p. 39.

III

Archives: Administrative File: Programs and Policies.
Waldman Papers: Apr.–June, Aug.–Sept. 1940; undated memorandum on Senator Lundeen.
AD/D & D/Community Service Dept./Reports 1941–46; Community Service Unit.
Minutes of Administrative Committee, Feb. 15, 1944.
AJYB, XLVI (1944–45), pp. 134–45; XLVII (1945–46), pp. 271, 680.

IV

AJYB, XVII (1915–16), pp. 360–63; XXXVIII (1936–37), p. 636; XLIV (1942–43), pp. 53–60, 467.
Waldman, *Nor by Power*, p. 238.
Joseph M. Proskauer, *A Segment of My Times* (New York, 1950), chs. 5–7, 14.
Joint Emergency Committee: Proskauer to Lazaron.

V

Roosevelt Papers: file 3186: B. Long to Roosevelt, Sept. 18, 1940; J. McDonald to Roosevelt, Oct. 8, 1940.
Germany/Nazism/Jewish Agencies;/Nazism/Atrocities.
Joint Emergency Committee.
Program for the Rescue of Jews from Nazi-Occupied Europe, submitted to the Bermuda Refugee Conference by the Joint Emergency Committee for European Jewish Affairs, Apr. 14, 1943.
Hungary/1944.
U.S. Government/War Refugee Board.
War & Peace/World War II/Peace Organizations.
Waldman Papers: memorandum on talk with Stettinius and Pehle [1944]; memorandum on Waldman's and Landau's talk with Travers [1944].
Interview with Simon Segal, Apr. 12, 1967.
Jewish Morning Journal, July 12, 1942.
Raul Hilberg, *The Destruction of European Jewry* (Chicago, 1961), pp. 671, 720–21.
Wischnitzer, *To Dwell in Safety*, pp. 245–54.
Morse, *While Six Million Died*, chs. 5, 17, 18, 20, 21.
Eugene Duschinsky, "Hungary," in *The Jews in the Soviet Satellites* (Syracuse, 1953), pp. 387–90.

AJYB, XLV (1943–44), pp. 357–62.
Maurice R. Davie, *Refugees in America* (New York, 1947), pp. 12–13.

VI

Waldman Papers: Mar. 1940; Apr.–June, July, Sept., Nov.–Dec. 1942;
files: Zionism/Non-Zionism, Weizmann-Stroock Negotiations.
Minutes of Administrative Committee, Mar. 15, 1940.
AD/ANN: June 1943.
Zionism/Zionist–Non-Zionist Conferences, 1942–43;/Weizmann visit.
Archives: folders—Zionist–Non-Zionist Conference; Chronological File
—Oct. 1942.
Waldman, *Nor by Power,* chs. 19–21, p. 252.
Thirty-sixth Annual Meeting, Jan. 31, 1943, pp. 4–48; Thirty-seventh
Annual Meeting, Jan. 30, 1944, pp. 50–59.
Congress Weekly, Feb. 5, 19, 1943.
AJYB, XLV (1943–44), pp. 608–10, 638–45.
Halperin, *Political World of American Zionism,* pp. 121–28.

VII

Meeting of the Executive Committee (transcript), Oct. 24, 1943, pp. 5–35, 165–66.
Minutes of Administrative Committee, Jan. 12, Oct. 30, Nov. 9, 1943.
Archives: Chronological File—Oct. 1942, Feb. 1943.
Waldman Papers: Feb.–Mar., June–July, Oct. 1943.
Waldman, *Nor by Power,* chs. 22, 23.
American Jewish Conference/AJC;/Committee Withdrawal;/Committee Withdrawal/Public Opinion Analysis.
Proskauer, memorandum Dec. 1943.
Halperin, *Political World of American Zionism,* pp. 129–36.
Schachner, *Price of Liberty,* pp. 147–51.
The Autobiography of Nahum Goldmann: Sixty Years of Jewish Life, trans. by H. Sebba (New York, 1969), pp. 222–23.

VIII

AJYB, XLVI (1944–45), pp. 583–87.
Thirty-seventh Annual Meeting, Jan. 30, 1944, pp. 2–104, 165–70.
Minutes of Administrative Committee, Feb. 13, 1945.
Archives: Administrative File: Programs and Policies.
Interview with Alan M. Stroock, Oct. 24, 1967.

AJC, *Forty-third Annual Report*, 1949, p. 87.

Time, May 20, 1966.

An early negative critique of *Commentary* appeared in Milton Steinberg's *A Believing Jew* (New York, 1951), ch. 9.

Chapter 11

Introduction & I

War & Peace/1945;/World War II/Liberated Countries;/Peace Studies. West Germany/Emigration-Immigration/DPs.

Gottschalk, Max.

FAD/Activities, 1943–52;/Reports and Highlights;/Overseas Committee: Minutes, Dec. 1, 1942, Apr. 4, May 23, 1944; Plan for Activities of the Overseas Committee [1942];/Africa, North/Crémieux Decree/Abrogation.

Archives: folders—JTA (1942).

Waldman Papers: Nov. 1942.

North Africa/Anti-Semitism/Crémieux Decree/Revocation.

Algeria/Jews/Cremieux.

Hannah Arendt, "Why the Crémieux Decree Was Abrogated," *Contemporary Jewish Record*, VI (April 1943).

AJYB, XLIII (1941–42), pp. 720–21, 736–51; XLV (1943–44), pp. 647–48, 668–77; XLVI (1944–45), pp. 560–61, 572; XLVII (1945–46), p. 716.

II

AJYB, XLII (1940–41), p. 650; XLV (1943–44), pp. 647, 672; XLVI (1944–45), pp. 572–73.

FAD/Plan for Activities of the Overseas Committee [1942]; Minutes of Sub-Committee of Human Rights, Feb. 2, 1945; San Francisco Conference.

War & Peace/World War II/Peace Organizations; UN-San Francisco Conference.

Gottschalk, Max.

U.S. Government/State Department.

JSX/Blaustein/Speeches

AJC, *To the Counsellors of Peace*, March 1945.

———, *A World Charter for Human Rights* [1945].

———, *Human Rights in the Peace Treaties*, April 1946, pp. 1–9.

Hersh Lauterpacht, *An International Bill of the Rights of Man* (New York, 1945).

Morris D. Waldman, "Beyond National Self-determination," *Contemporary Jewish Record,* VII (June 1944).

In Dec. 1944 AJC published its own Declaration of Human Rights, which earned the endorsement of 1,326 prominent Americans. It read (*Committee Reporter,* Jan. 1945):

"With the inevitable end of Hitler, the struggle begins, not of tank and plane, but of heart and soul and brain to forge a world in which humanity may live in peace.

"This new world must be based on the recognition that the individual human being is the cornerstone of our culture and our civilization. All that we cherish must rest on the dignity and inviolability of the person, of his sacred right to live and to develop under God, in whose image he was created.

"With this creed as our foundation, we declare:

"1. That an International Bill of Human Rights must be promulgated to guarantee for every man, woman and child, of every race and creed and in every country, the fundamental rights of life, liberty and the pursuit of happiness.

"2. No plea of sovereignty shall ever again be allowed to permit any nation to deprive those within its borders of these fundamental rights on the claim that these are matters of internal concern.

"3. Hitlerism has demonstrated that bigotry and persecution by a barbarous nation throws upon the peace-loving nations the burden of relief and redress. Therefore it is a matter of international concern to stamp out infractions of basic human rights.

"4. To those who have suffered under the Hitler regime because of race or creed or national origin, there shall be given fair redress.

"5. To those who have been driven from the land of their birth there shall be given the opportunity to return, unaffected in their rights by the Nazi despotism.

"6. To those who wander the earth unable or unwilling to return to scenes of unforgettable horror shall be given aid and comfort to find new homes and begin new lives in other parts of the world. This must be made possible by international agreement.

"Thus, anew, may we justify the ways of God to man. Thus we may take a vital step forward on the long road at the end of which civilization seeks to create a world based upon the common fatherhood of God and the common brotherhood of man."

Jerold Auerbach, "Human Rights at San Francisco," *American Jewish Archives,* XVI (Apr. 1964), pp. 59–68.

Oscar I. Janowsky, "The Human Rights Issue at the San Francisco Conference," *Menorah Journal,* XXXIV (Spring 1946), pp. 29–55.

Proskauer suggested several ways in which the bill of rights might be implemented when he testified before the UN Commission on Human Rights. *Committee Reporter,* June 1946. See also the recommendations of the Consultative Council of Jewish Organizations (made up of AJC, Anglo-Jewish Association, Alliance Israélite Universelle). *Implementation of an International Covenant of Human Rights* (New York, 1949).

III

J.L. Flaiszer, "The Jewish Case at the 1946 Peace Conference" (typescript).

War & Peace/Paris Peace Conference 1946;/AJC Peace Studies;/Peace Organizations.

Waldman Papers: Sept. 1946.

Statements Submitted to the Paris Conference by the World Jewish Congress, American Jewish Conference, American Jewish Committee, Board of Deputies of British Jews, Anglo-Jewish Association, Conseil Représentatif des Juifs de France, Alliance Israélite Universelle, South African Jewish Board of Deputies, Paris, Aug. 20, 1946.

Jewish Morning Journal, Apr. 26, 1945.

AJYB, XLIX (1947–48), pp. 562–72.

IV

FAD/Restitution—summaries by E. Hevesi and M. Hoffenstein;/AJC Documents, 1945–65;/J. Blaustein and U.S. Government, 1963–65.

War & Peace/World War II/Reparations.

West Germany/AJC/U.S. Government.

Blaustein, Jacob.

To the Counsellors of Peace, pp. 2–3.

Jacob Blaustein, "A Chapter in Partnership" (address), Dec. 9, 1965.

————, "A Dramatic Era in History" (address), May 15, 1966.

New York Times, Sept. 28, 1951.

Autobiography of Nahum Goldmann, ch. 22.

V

FAD/Nazi Trials/AJC/Statute of Limitations;/Restitution/AJC Documents, 1945–65.
War & Peace/World War II/Trials.
Germany/Nazism/Jewish Agencies;/Nazism/War Criminals.
To the Counsellors of Peace, pp. 101–8.
Morse, *While Six Million Died,* ch. 21.
Vertical Files: Germany/War Criminals/AJC.
Cordell Hull, *The Memoirs of Cordell Hull,* 2 vols. (New York, 1948), II, pp. 1289–91.

VI

Germany/1945, 1946.
West Germany/Emigration-Immigration/Adviser of Jewish Affairs;/Emigration-Immigration/DPs/AJC-UNRRA;/Emigration-Immigration/Jewish Agencies.
Immigration/DPs/Jewish Organizations.
Blaustein, Jacob.
Minutes of Administrative Committee, Oct. 9, 1945.
New York Times, Sept. 4, 1946.
Committee Reporter, Apr., May, 1946.
Zachariah Shuster, "Must the Jews Quit Europe?," *Commentary,* I (Dec. 1945).
Meeting on AJC history, Apr. 28, 1967.

VII

Germany/1946.
Immigration/AJC;/DPs/U.S.;/DPs/U.S./AJC.
West Germany/Emigration-Immigration/DPs.
U.S. Government/State Department.
Blaustein, Jacob.
FAD/Minutes of Immigration Subcommittee, Nov. 25, Dec. 17, 1946, Sept. 30, 1947;/National Citizens Committee on DPs;/1948 DP legislation;/Immigration-1948;/DP Report 1948.
Waldman Papers: Sept. 1943.
Vertical Files: DPs/U.S.;DPs/U.S./AJC; Immigration/U.S./AJC 1940–51.
Statement of Hon. Herbert H. Lehman before the Subcommittee on Immigration and

Naturalization, House of Representatives, July 2, 1947, pp. 5–6.
To the Counsellors of Peace, p. 47.
Minutes of Administrative Committee, Dec. 4, 1945, Oct. 2, 1946, Mar. 2, Apr. 6, 1948.
Minutes of Steering Committee, Oct. 6, 1945, Sept. 26, 1949.
AJC, *Fortieth Annual Report,* 1946, p. 97.
Committee Reporter, Oct.–Dec. 1946, Feb.–Mar., May, Aug., Nov. 1947, July–Aug. 1948.
Life, Sept. 23, 1946.
New York Times, Dec. 23, 1945.
Divine, *American Immigration Policy,* chs. 6, 7.

Chapter 12

I

On Jan. 20, 1944, Wallace Murray reported to Hull, Stettinius, and Long that Morris Waldman "has repeatedly emphasized the grave fear of his committee and like-minded Jewish citizens of this country that unless a stop can be put to the nationalist agitation of the Zionists, it is to be feared that a greatly increased anti-Semitic movement in this country will arise after the war." Box 200, Breckinridge Long Papers, Library of Congress. Courtesy of Mr. Arthur D. Morse.

Israel/1943, 1944, 1945, 1946, 1948.
Israel-Palestine/AJC; /U.S., 1945–48; /Federalization Plan/Anglo-American Committee of Inquiry/AJC;/Partition/AJC;/Anglo-American Committee of Inquiry;/Immigration/Refugees;/UN;/Anglo-Jewish Association;/American Jews;/Partition/Public Relations;/Partition/Christian Groups;/AJC/Lovett-Proskauer correspondence;/Ihud;/Trusteeship;/UN-U.S.
Blaustein, Jacob.
Proskauer, Joseph.
Anglo-Jewish Association.
War & Peace: Jewish problems at Yalta, Mar. 21, 1955;/UN–San Francisco Conference;/Paris Peace Conference, 1946.
Immigration/DPs/Jewish Organizations.
U.S. Government/State Department, 1944, 1945.
FAD: Minutes of Palestine Subcommittee, Nov. 20, 1946.
Waldman Papers: Jan., June 1944.
Minutes of Executive Committee, May 9, 1944, Nov. 6, 1945, May 4–5,

Sept. 15, 1946, May 10–11, Oct. 10–11, 1947, May 1–2, 1948.
Minutes of Administrative Committee, June 5, Oct. 9, 1945, Dec. 3, 1946, Nov. 4, 1947, Mar. 2, 24, 1948.
Minutes of Steering Committee, July 10, Aug. 22, Sept. 21, Nov. 3, 1944, Sept. 14, 1946, Apr. 9, May 7, 1947, Mar. 17, 1948.
Interview with Alan M. Stroock, Oct. 25, 1967.
The Reminiscences of Joseph M. Proskauer (Oral History Research Office, Columbia University), pp. 13–15.
Proskauer, *A Segment of My Times*, pp. 242–45.
Autobiography of Goldmann, ch. 20.
Harry S. Truman, *Memoirs: Years of Trial and Hope* (Signet edition. New York, 1965), pp. 159, 185–99. In a letter to Jacob Blaustein, Feb. 12, 1949, Truman commented on his action with respect to Palestine:

"I became thoroughly disgusted with some of the high pressure groups during the difficult times through which we had to go from 1946 to date, and it was in spite of the obstructive effort of some of them that the program was finally carried through. It is now up to the new State to make good on its own and I am of the opinion that it will. The United Nations Commission is well on the way of establishing an armistice on which a negotiated peace can be obtained. That has been my program from the beginning, when I first suggested that one hundred thousand Jews from Displaced Persons Camps in Germany be allowed to enter Palestine. There has never been a change of attitude on my part, although a great many people have charged me with everything from rape to murder on this program."

FAD: Restitution/J. Blaustein and U.S. Government. Cf. Jonathan Daniels, *The Man from Independence* (Philadelphia, 1950), pp. 317–30.
To the Counsellors of Peace, pp. 72–79.
In Peace and Dignity. Testimony of the American Jewish Committee before the Anglo-American Committee of Inquiry on Palestine (New York, 1946).
AJC, *Toward Peace and Equity* (New York, 1946), pp. 123–25, 131–36.
————, *Statement Submitted to the United Nations Committee of Inquiry into Palestine*, May 31, 1947, p. 10.
————, *Proposed American Action in the Security Council Relative to Palestine*, Feb. 5, 1948.
Thirty-seventh Annual Report, 1943, pp. 112–23; *Thirty-ninth Annual Report*, 1945, pp. 55–56; *Fortieth Annual Report*, 1946, pp. 73–78, 94–96; *Forty-first Annual Report*, 1947, pp. 109–23; *Forty-second Annual Report*, 1948, pp. 23–27, 100–2.
Committee Reporter, Apr., May 1948.

New York Times, Aug. 20, 1946, Mar. 21, 26, 1948.
New York Herald-Tribune, Jan, 21, 1948.
Palestine Post, June 6, 1947.
Louis Shub, "Palestine in the United Nations and the U.S.," *AJYB,* L (1948–49), pp. 236–67.

II

Minutes of Executive Committee, Oct. 16–17, 1948, May 7–8, Oct. 22–23, 1949, Oct. 13–14, 1951.
Minutes of Administrative Committee, Mar. 8, June 7, 1949.
Minutes of Steering Committee, Feb. 13, 1950.
Israel/Visits/Blaustein;/American Jews/AJC;/Diaspora.
Zionism/Jewish Nationalism;/Ben-Gurion–Blaustein Statements.
Archives: folder—Israel/Blaustein.
Vertical Files: Israel/American Jews.
Reminiscences of Proskauer, pp. 60, 120.
New York Times, Dec. 29, 30, 1960.
AJC, *Forty-second Annual Report,* 1948, pp. 8–9.
———, *In Vigilant Brotherhood* (New York, 1964), pp. 64–70.
The Committee's charges against the American Council for Judaism appear in *Nature and Consequences of the Public Relations Activities of the American Council for Judaism* (New York, 1957).
Lucy S. Dawidowicz, "United States, Israel, and the Middle East," *AJYB,* LXIII (1962), p. 285.

III

Israel/Visits/Blaustein.
FAD: Israel/Religion 1964.
Irving M. Engel, "Israel through American Eyes" (address), May 1949.

IV

Alexander De Conde, *A History of American Foreign Policy* (New York, 1963), pp. 745–57. On anti-Israel sentiment in America, see, for example, H.S. Coffin, "Perils to America in the New Jewish State," *Christianity and Crisis,* Feb. 21, 1949.
Meeting of the Executive Committee (transcript), Oct. 22, 1949, pp. 4–5, 10–11.
FAD: Restitution—1952; Interviews.

Middle East/Holy Places;/Arab Refugees;/Conferences/IR;/Arab-Israeli Conflicts/AJC;/Nov.–Dec. 1956, Jan.–May 1957 (the Committee sent a second message to Dulles on Jan. 17, 1957).

U.S. Government/State Department/Dulles.

Vertical Files: Near East/Arab Refugees/AJC; Israel/American Jews/AJC.

AJC, *The Assault on American Citizenship* (New York, 1956). In July 1956 the Committee published *Steps to Middle East Peace* which outlined recommendations for short-term and long-term policies in the area against a background of American objectives.

Minutes of Administrative Board, Nov. 1, 1955, Nov. 13, Dec. 4, 1956.

Minutes of Steering Committee, Feb. 25, 1957.

John Foster Dulles, *The Middle East.* Address before the Council on Foreign Relations, Aug. 26, 1955 (Washington, D.C., 1955).

Herman Finer, *Dulles over Suez* (Chicago, 1964), ch. 17, p. 14.

Return to the Status Quo Ante? Editorial Comment on Israel's Case in the United States Press (New York, [1957]).

Committee Reporter, Sept. 1956.

Israel/American Jews/AJC.

AJC, *In Vigilant Brotherhood*, pp. 30, 35–48.

Fulbright, J.W.

AJYB, LXII (1961), p. 190.

V

Minutes of Executive Committee, Jan. 22, 1949, Jan. 21, 1950, May 5–6, 1951.

Minutes of Administrative Committee, Jan. 3, 1950, June 5, 1951; of Administrative Board, June 7, 1957.

Minutes of FAC, Jan. 5, 1948, July 7, 1949, June 18, Nov. 27, 1956, Jan. 7, Mar. 13, 1957.

AJC, *Report of the Forty-fourth Annual Meeting*, 1951, pp. 49, 116–17.

————, *Proceedings of the Fiftieth Anniversary Observance* (New York, 1958), pp. 232–33.

Middle East/Visits 1957;/Arab-Israeli Conflicts/AJC/Meetings.

Iran/1950.

Iraq/U.S. Government;/General (Rees, E.).

Blaustein, Jacob.

Syria/1949–57.

Egypt/1956–57; Egypt/U.S.;/Emigration-Immigration/U.S./AJC;/Emigration-Immigration/U.S./Jewish Agencies.

U.S. Government/State Department.
North Africa/U.S./AJC/Meetings/Government Officials.
AD/C Mig.
AJC, *The Plight of the Jews in Egypt* (New York, 1957).
———, *In Vigilant Brotherhood*, pp. 44–47. The Committee strongly fought Arab discrimination against American Jews during the years 1956–62.
AJYB, LIX (1958), pp. 98–104.

VI

FAD: Israel/Publications—Ammoth;/Publications—Ammoth/Founding.
Vertical Files: Israel/American Jews/AJC.
AJC, *This Is Our Home* (Pamphlet series. New York, 1950–56).
Jerusalem Post, Mar. 25, 1965, July 8, 1966.
Interview with Nathan Weisman, Dec. 15, 1967.

Foreword to Part II

Eric F. Goldman, *The Crucial Decade—And After* (Vintage Books. New York, 1960).
Will Herberg, *Protestant-Catholic-Jew* (New York, 1955).
AD/PRO/CA/Membership.
AD/ORG, 1943.
AD/ANN 1936–61;/Statements, 1947–57.
Program statements of various departments, submitted to D. Kushell, Dec. 1950 (unsorted departmental files); Statement of Principles Affecting AJC Program in the Area of Civic Action, Aug. 29, 1949 (UDF).
C.K. Simon to I.M. Engel, Feb. 7, 1955; S. Hirsh to J. Slawson, Apr. 13, 1964 (files of Selma Hirsh).
John Slawson, "The American Jewish Committee Today" (address), May 4, 1946.
———, "Current Concerns of the American Jewish Committee" (address), May 9, 1954.
———, *Trends in the American Jewish Community* (New York, 1960).
———, *Integration and Identity* (New York, 1960).
Interview with John Slawson, Jan. 3, 1968; with Nathan Weisman, Dec. 15, 1967; with Selma Hirsh, Jan. 22, 1971.

Jewish Community Relations Work Today, The American Jewish Committee's Views on the MacIver Report (New York, 1952).

AJC, *Statement of Withdrawal from the National Community Relations Advisory Council,* Sept. 22, 1952.

Minutes of the Board of Governors, June 7, 1966.

Meeting on AJC history, Apr. 28, 1967.

Budget Dept: Comparative statements of income and expenses, 1943–1959.

Additional material in this foreword, other than that treated at greater length in separate chapters, has been culled from the annual reports of the AJC, the minutes of the FAC, and statements in the files FA/Activities and P/Foreign Affairs/Paris Office. Proskauer's letter is in Argentina/Anti-Semitism.

Chapter 13

I

Earl Latham, *The Communist Controversy in Washington from the New Deal to McCarthy* (Cambridge, Mass., 1966), part 4.

Donald J. Kemper, *Decade of Fear: Senator Hennings and Civil Liberties* (Columbia, Mo., 1965), ix–x, pp. 74–92.

Alan Barth, *The Loyalty of Free Men* (New York, 1951), ch. 5.

Eleanor Bontecou, *The Federal Loyalty-Security Program* (New York, 1953), chs. 4, 6, 7.

Political Philosophies/Communism, Aug.–Dec. 1951;/Communism/Jews;/Communism/AJC Program;/Communism/Ad Hoc Committee.

UDF: memoranda on anti-Communist program, 1948–53.

AACCC/Participants;/Participants/AJC.

AD/D & D/PRO-AS/AAC.

Committee Reporter, Sept. 1950.

Minutes of Executive Committee, May 10–11, 1947, Apr. 29–30, Oct. 14–15, 1950, May 8–9, 1954.

Minutes of DAC, Mar. 16, 1948, May 23, June 27, Aug. 16, 23, 1950, June 24, 1954.

Minutes of Administrative Committee, Mar. 8, 1949, Feb. 6, 1951.

Congressional Record, 81st Congress, 2nd Session, p. 13725 (Aug. 29, 1950).

AJYB, LII (1951), pp. 62–64; LIV (1953), pp. 345–49; LV (1954), pp. 287–95.

James Rorty and Winifred Raushenbush, "The Lessons of the Peekskill Riots," *Commentary*, X (Oct. 1950), pp. 309–23.

Treatment of the Jews by the Soviet. Seventh Interim Report of Hearings before the Select Committee on Communist Aggression, House of Representatives, 83rd Congress, 2nd Session (Washington, D.C., 1954), pp. 1–13.

The two most widely distributed pamphlets were *The Hands of Esau* (New York, 1951) and Irwin Ross, *The Communists: Friends or Foes of Civil Liberties* (New York, 1950).

II

Minutes of Executive Committee, Apr. 29–30, 1950, May 2–3, 1953, May 8–9, 1954, Oct. 22–23, 1955.

Minutes of DAC, Oct. 10, 1950, Dec. 16, 1952, Mar. 17, 1953, Jan. 26, Feb. 23, Mar. 23, May 18, June 24, 1954.

Minutes of Administrative Committee, June 1, 1954.

UDF: staff memoranda on civil liberties, 1949–54.

Civil Liberties/AJC/PRO;/Liaison Groups.

Budget, 1952, 1953: statements of Legal Affairs Department.

AD/D & D/Legal/Reports—Leskes: 1953–55.

U.S. Government/Legislation/Internal Security Act;/Loyalty and Security Program/President's Conference;/Loyalty and Security Program/McCarthyism;/Congress/House Committee on Un-American Activities.

Meeting on AJC history, Apr. 28, 1967 (remarks of Edwin J. Lukas).

Political Philosophies/Communism, 1949–54;/Communism/Jews.

Maurice J. Goldbloom, *American Security and Freedom* (New York, 1954).

Commission on Government Security. Hearings before a Subcommittee on Reorganization of the Committee on Government Operations. U.S. Senate, 84th Congress, 1st Session (Washington, D.C., 1955), pp. 457–61.

Congress Weekly, Dec. 7, 1953.

J.B. Matthews, "Reds and Our Churches," *American Mercury*, LXXVII (July 1953), pp. 3–13.

U.S. House of Representatives, Committee on Un-American Activities, *Preliminary Report on Neo-Fascist and Hate Groups* (Washington, D.C., 1954).

Committee Reporter, Nov.–Dec. 1953, p. 3; *Committee Reporter News-Letter*, Summer 1953, p. 1.

III

UDF: reports from Fineberg to Slawson, June 2, 1952, Jan. 21, 1953.
Political Philosophies/Communism/Jews;/Communism/Committees—
Staff/Reports;/Communism/AJC Program.
S.A. Fineberg, *The Rosenberg Case: Fact and Fiction* (New York, 1953).
U.S. Government/Congress/House Committee on Un-American Activities;/Loyalty and Security/Ladejinsky Case.
NJ/Communal Issues/Loyalty/Fort Monmouth Investigation.
Minutes of Executive Committee, May 5–6, 1951.
Minutes of DAC, Apr. 3, 1951.
Minutes of Administrative Committee, Jan. 9, 1951.
AD/ANN, 1944–60.
Kemper, *Decade of Fear*, pp. 94–95, 99.
Arnold Forster and Benjamin R. Epstein, *The Trouble-Makers* (New York, 1952), ch. 2, p. 103.
Nomination of Anna M. Rosenberg to be Assistant Secretary of Defense, Hearings before the Committee on Armed Services, U.S. Senate, 81st Congress, 2nd Session, Part 2 (Washington, D.C., 1950), pp. 145–201, 335–71.
Joseph and Stewart Alsop, in *New York Herald-Tribune*, Dec. 17, 1950.
Know the Truth (Freedman's paper), Jan. 2, 1951.

IV

Minutes of DAC, Feb. 6, 1951, June 3, Dec. 16, 1952, Mar. 17, 1953.
Minutes of Administrative Committee, June 5, 1951, Jan. 3, 1952.
Minutes of Executive Committee, Oct. 25–26, 1952.
Education/Attacks/AJC Policy.
AJC, "The Current Attacks on Public Education—A Fact Sheet," Mar. 1, 1951.
———, *Report of the Forty-sixth Annual Meeting*, 1953, pp. 30–33; *Report of the Forty-fifth Annual Meeting*, 1952, pp. 28–31.

V

Alexander Uhl, *The Assault on the UN* (Washington, D.C., 1953).
Gordon D. Hall, *The Hate Campaign against the U.N.* (Boston, 1952).
Blaustein testified before a Senate subcommittee on the need to ratify the genocide convention. Jacob Blaustein, *The Eyes of the World Are upon Us* (New York, 1950).
Consultative Council of Jewish Organizations, *A United Nations Attorney-*

General or High Commissioner for Human Rights (New York, 1950).
Committee Reporter, Nov.–Dec. 1952.
AJC, *Report of the Forty-fourth Annual Meeting,* 1951, pp. 51–54, 76, 115;
Report of the Forty-sixth Annual Meeting, 1953, pp. 127–28.
New York Times, Jan. 7, 1954.
U.N./AJC;/Information and Education/Attacks;/Information and Education/Counterattacks/AJC.
International Affairs/Bricker Proposal/AJC.
Vertical Files: U.S. Treaties/Bricker/AJC.
Treaties and Executive Agreements. Hearings before a Subcommittee of the Committee on the Judiciary, U.S. Senate, 83rd Congress, 1st Session on S.J. Res. 1 and S.J. Res. 43 (Washington, D.C., 1953), pp. 825, 886, 898.
FAD/Committees/International Organizations/Agenda.
International Programs/U.N. 51–62.
Minutes of Executive Committee, Oct. 14–15, 1950, Oct. 25–26, 1952, May 3, Oct. 25, 1953, May 8–9, 1954.
Minutes of DAC, Oct. 10, 1950, Dec. 16, 1952, Nov. 17, 1953.
Minutes of Administrative Committee, June 6, 1950, June 19, 1952, Apr. 7, Dec. 1, 1953.

VI

Treaties and Executive Agreements. Hearings before a Subcommittee of the Committee on the Judiciary, U.S. Senate, 82nd Congress, 2nd Session on S.J. Res. 130 (Washington, D.C., 1952), p. 145.
Hall, *The Hate Campaign against the U.N.,* p. 29.
Bennett, *American Immigration Policies,* ch. 13, pp. 153–69, 311.
Divine, *American Immigration Policy,* pp. 146, 157–58, ch. 9.
UDF: S. Liskofsky to Staff Policy Committee, Nov. 16, 1948; Americanizing Our Immigration Laws, Testimony of the American Jewish Committee before the Immigration Subcommittee of the Senate Judiciary Committee, Sept. 1948 (published in pamphlet form in 1949); Summary Analysis of Proposed Omnibus Immigration Bill Submitted by Judge Simon H. Rifkind, Mar. 22, 1951.
Immigration, 1951, 1952, 1953, 1955, 1957;/AJC;/AJC/Committee/Minutes;/Legislation;/Legislation/Immigration and Naturalization Act/Amendatory Bills/Lehman Omnibus Bill;/Legislation/Immigration and Naturalization Act/Amendatory Bills/McCarran-Walter;/Conference of Jewish Organizations;/U.S. Policy;/U.S. Policy/AJC.
AJYB, LVII (1956), p. 179.
JSX/Immigration 66.

U.S. President's Commission on Immigration and Naturalization, *Whom We Shall Welcome* (Washington, D.C., 1952). The Committee published and circulated a short summary of that report.
New York Times, Oct. 18, 21, 22, 1952.
Allan Nevins, *Herbert H. Lehman and His Era* (New York, 1963), ch. 17, pp. 355–61.
The numerous resolutions and statements appear in the proceedings of the annual meetings and the meetings of the Executive and Administrative Committees (later = Boards).
AJC, *The Fence* (New York, 1956).
John F. Kennedy, *Let the Lady Hold Up Her Head* (New York, 1957).
The pamphlet to refute the charge of subversion was *American Immigration Policy,* published by the American Immigration Conference in 1957.
FAD 64/Immigration/Legislation/AJC Policy; 63–65/Immigration/AJC Chapter Activity.
New York Herald-Tribune, Oct. 4, 1965.

VII

Minutes of DAC, Apr. 3, 1951, Mar. 26, 1952, Feb. 17, June 8, 1953, Feb. 23, Apr. 20, June 22, 1954, Mar. 15, June 21, Nov. 15, 1955. (The issue of Arab diplomats in the U.S. who indulged in smears against Jews was informally brought to the attention of the State Department.) Dec. 20, 1955, June 19, 1956, Jan. 12, Feb. 17, May 18, Sept. 7, 1960, Feb. 15, Sept. 28, Nov. 20, Dec. 19, 1961, Feb. 20, Apr. 2, 1962, Nov. 19, 1963, May 19, July 21, Oct. 20, 1964; minutes of subcommittee of DAC, Sept. 23, 1964; summary of round table, Apr. 28, 1961; joint meeting of DAC and the Civil Rights and Civil Liberties Committee, June 29, 1960.
Minutes of Administrative Committee, Oct. 1, 1952; of Administrative Board, Mar. 1, Oct. 4, 1960, Mar. 7, Oct. 3, 1961, Jan. 9, Mar. 6, 1962; of Board of Governors, Oct. 6, 1964.
Minutes of Executive Committee, Oct. 23–24, 1954; of Executive Board, May 11–13, 1956, Oct. 28–30, 1960, Jan. 19–21, 1962; Informal Summary of Executive Board Meeting, Dec. 4–6, 1964.
Department of Trend Analyses: E. Stern to Mrs. M. Ascoli, Sept. 3, 1953.
AJYB, LIV (1953), pp. 90–91; LV (1954), pp. 73–74; LIX (1958), p. 105; LXII (1961), pp. 127–28; LXIII (1962), p. 196; LXVI (1965), pp. 201, 202–8.
Publications by the American Jewish Committee on anti-Semitism: *Bigot Seeks Buildup: The "News" Techniques of George Lincoln Rockwell* (New York, 1962); *Anti-Semitic Activity in the United States* (New York, 1954); *Bigotry in*

Action (Three editions. New York, 1958, 1961, 1963); *As the U.N. Probes Prejudice* (New York, 1960); *Current Anti-Semitic Activities Abroad* (New York, 1963); *Why the Swastika?* (New York, 1962); S.A. Fineberg, *Deflating the Professional Bigot* (New York, 1967).

Committee Reporter, Dec. 1954, July, Sept., 1956, D. Danzig in May 1960; *Committee Reporter News-Letter*, Sept.–Oct., 1952.

New York Times, Sept. 1, 3, 4, 1960.

Proskauer, *A Segment of My Times*, ch. 6.

Ralph Lord Roy, *Apostles of Discord* (Boston, 1953), ch. 2.

Lucy S. Dawidowicz and Leon J. Goldstein, *Politics in a Pluralist Democracy* (New York, 1963).

AD/D & D/Legal 43–60.

New York World-Telegram, July 16–21, 1945.

AD/ANN 44–60.

AD/PRO 49–38.

Capsule biographies of anti-Semitic agitators were distributed to select lists of communal leaders. (*Timely Biographies*, New York, 1948.) Zoll's organization was exposed during the fight over the public schools. AJC succeeded in having the tax-exempt status of Judge George W. Armstrong's foundation revoked. Ostensibly a foundation for religious and charitable purposes, it served as a distribution center for anti-Semitic material.

Politics/Bigotry and Prejudice/AJC;/Bigotry and Prejudice/Dissident Political Movements;/Bigotry and Prejudice/Anti-Semitic Activity;/Bloc Voting/AJC Statements.

For detailed analyses by AJC of right-wing groups see files under PRO/ AD/Extremism/Radical Right. See essays in Daniel Bell, ed., *The Radical Right* (Vintage Books. New York, 1962).

PRO/AD/Extremism/Anti-Semitism;/AD 61–62/Extremism/Radical Right/Conference on Preserving the Democratic Process;/AD 64/Extremism/Presidential Election Campaign.

BDS/Extremism;/Extremism/AJC;/Extremism/Bigotry in Election Campaigns;/Extremism/Bigotry in Election Campaign Committee.

CAD/Extremism/Area Directors Meeting.

Among the materials distributed by AJC were a question-and-answer pamphlet, *What Is Extremism?* and articles: Alan F. Westin, "The John Birch Society," *Commentary*, XXXII (Aug. 1961), pp. 93–104, and David Danzig, "Rightists, Racists and Separatists: A White Bloc in the Making?" *Commentary*, XXXVIII (August 1964), pp. 28–32.

Chapter 14

I

Charles F. Kellogg, *NAACP*, vol. 1, 1909–20 (Baltimore, 1967), pp. 298–99.

Harvey Wish, ed., *The Negro since Emancipation* (Englewood Cliffs, N.J., 1964), p. 6.

C. Vann Woodward, *The Strange Career of Jim Crow* (Oxford-Galaxy. New York, 1966), pp. 118–35.

War & Peace/1946.

Minutes of Executive Committee, Dec. 5, 1934, May 4–5, 1946, Oct. 11–12, 1947.

AJYB, XVI (1914–15), p. 398; XXVIII (1926–27), pp. 467–68, 472–74.

AJC, *Forty-first Annual Report*, 1947, p. 37.

UDF: memoranda on civil rights program, 1947–50; testimony and report to president's Committee on Civil Rights, 1947.

AD/D & D/Legal/Program.

Civil Rights/AJC/Chapters.

U.S. President's Committee on Civil Rights, *To Secure These Rights* (Washington, D.C., 1947).

II

Civil Rights, 1950– ;/AJC/Reports;/AJC/Committee/Reports;/AJC;/AJC/Chapter Reports;/Fed. Commission;/Legislation/Hearings/AJC Statements.

AD/D & D/Civil Rights 1949–54;/Civil Rights/Reports.

AD/D & D/Legal, 1943–60;/Legal/Program.

UDF: activities on civil rights in employment, 1947–48.

Civil Liberties/AJC/Program.

Integration/AJC.

Minutes of DAC, Mar. 16, Apr. 20, 1948, Feb. 28, Mar. 28, 1950.

Engel, Irving M., Testimony.

Committee Reporter, Nov. 1946.

Milton Konvitz, *A Century of Civil Rights*, with a Study of *State Law against Discrimination* by Theodore Leskes (Columbia paperback. New York, 1967), pp. 196, 203–15.

AJC, *Report of the Forty-fourth Annual Meeting*, 1951, p. 41.

Brief of amici curiae in *Commission on Civil Rights of the State of Connecticut v. International Brotherhood of Electrical Workers;* Brief of American Jewish

Committee and Anti-Defamation League of B'nai B'rith as amici curiae in the case of *Draper* v. *Clark Dairy;* Brief of the American Jewish Committee (New York chapter) and the Anti-Defamation League of B'nai B'rith (New York regional office) as amici curiae, *Ivory* v. *Edwards.*

III

Brief on behalf of American Civil Liberties Union, American Ethical Union, American Jewish Committee, Anti-Defamation League of B'nai B'rith, Japanese American Citizens League, and Unitarian Fellowship for Social Justice, *Brown* v. *Board of Education of Topeka.*
Integration, 1953–61;/AJC;/Supreme Court Decision/AJC;/AJC/ Southern Leaders;/AJC-ADL;/AJC/Conference on Educational Problems/South/AJC.
U.S. Government/White House Conference on Children.
Hate Groups/South.
Minutes of DAC, Apr. 19, 1955, June 19, Oct. 13, 1956, Jan. 16, Apr. 12, 1957, Mar. 19, Apr. 25, Nov. 17, 1958, Jan. 21, Feb. 18, Oct. 30, 1959, May 18, 1960.
Minutes of Administrative Board, Oct. 1, 1957, Mar. 4, April 1, 1958.
Minutes of Executive Board, May 11–13, 1956, Oct. 24–26, 1958, Oct. 30–Nov. 1, 1959; Transcript of Executive Board Meeting, May 13, 1956.
Civil Rights/Legislation/Hearings/AJC Statements;/Legislation/Act of 1957/Hearings;/Legislation/Act of 1960/Hearings.
Interview with Edwin J. Lukas, Dec. 18, 1967.
Woodward, *Strange Career of Jim Crow,* pp. 138–39, 150–68.
Kemper, *Decade of Fear,* ch. 7.
Milton Konvitz, *Expanding Liberties* (New York, 1966), pp. 61–66, 245–55.
The Supreme Court did not permit the Committee to file its brief on the NAACP case. Because of its stand on that case, some southern Jews contemplated withholding funds from the Joint Defense Appeal of the Committee, Anti-Defamation League, and B'nai B'rith.
Alexander Bickel, *Politics and the Warren Court* (New York, 1965), pp. 14–15, 50–59, 87.
AJC Program Activities, Nov.–Dec. 1955, Mar.–June 1956.
Work in Progress, Jan. 15, 1957.
Proceedings of the Fiftieth Anniversary Observance of the American Jewish Committee, Apr. 10–14, 1957 (New York, 1958), pp. 13–21.
Report of the AJC for 1956, p. 32.
AJC, *Proceedings of the Fifty-first Annual Meeting,* 1958, p. 31.
AJYB, LVI (1955), pp. 223–25; LVII (1956), pp. 182–84; LVIII (1957),

pp. 142–44; LIX (1958), pp. 105–8; LX (1959), pp. 44–50; LXI (1960), p. 45; LXII (1961), p. 110.
Mississippi/Communal Issues/Race/Till Case.
Georgia/Atlanta/Communal Issues/Integration.
Texas/Dallas/Communal Issues/Integration.
"Recent Attacks upon the Supreme Court: A Statement by Members of the Bar," reprinted from *American Bar Association Journal*, Dec. 1956.

IV

CRS-L/Housing/AJC Policy 1959–62.
AD/D & D/Civil Rights 1949–54.
Integration/North;/AJC.
Minutes of DAC, Sept. 18, 1957, Apr. 25, 1958, Jan. 21, 1959, Feb. 15, Dec. 19, 1961, Apr. 2, 1962, May 19, 1964, Apr. 19, 1966.
Minutes of Administrative Board, Mar. 3, 1959, Mar. 6, Apr. 3, 1962; of Board of Governors, June 2, 1964.
Minutes of Executive Board, Oct. 26–27, 1957, Nov. 1–3, 1963.

V

Woodward, *Strange Career of Jim Crow*, pp. 168–91.
Bickel, *Politics and the Warren Court*, pp. 57–59.
CRS-L/Civil Rights 1959–62.
CRS-R/Fleischman; /Race Relations/Alabama/Selma-Montgomery March/AJC;/Race Relations/AJC.
Minutes of DAC, Feb. 15, 1961, Feb. 18, 1964, Feb. 16, June 16, Dec. 14, 1965; of joint meetings DAC and Committee on Civil Rights and Civil Liberties, Apr. 22, 1960.
Minutes of Administrative Board, Apr. 4, Oct. 3, 1961, June 18, 1963, Jan. 7, 1964; of Board of Governors, Apr. 6, Oct. 2, Dec. 7, 1965.
Proceedings of Executive Board Meeting, Nov. 1, 1963.
Minutes of Executive Board, Nov. 1–3, 1963, Oct. 28–30, 1966.
Minutes of Committee on Race Relations, July 24, Sept. 10, 1963, Mar. 10, 1964.
Summary Report of New York Retailers Meeting, Oct. 29, 1963.
PRO/AD/Race Relations and Civil Rights;/AD/Civil Rights.
PRO/AS/LCBC;/AS/Budget;/AS/Race Relations.
JSX/Civil Rights;/Civil Rights Legislation/National Citizens Committee;/Integration.

CAD/Race Relations;/Race Relations/Special Washington Conference;/Race and Religion/Myrdal Conference.
BDS/Race Relations/Special Washington Conference.
MEC/Race Relations/Conference.
Integration/AJC-ADL.
Public Accommodations/Freedom Riders.
Poverty/AJC.
AJC, Policies and Programs on Race Relations and Urban Affairs, May 1967.
Leonora E. Berson, *Case Study of a Riot: The Philadelphia Story* (New York, 1966).

VI

Minutes of Executive Board, Nov. 1–3, 1963, Oct. 28–30, 1966.
Minutes of DAC, Nov. 17, 1958, Feb. 19, Mar. 20, Apr. 24, 1963, Apr. 20, 1965; summary of DAC-sponsored round table, May 16, 1963.
Minutes of Board of Governors, Feb. 1, 1966.
CAD/Race Relations/Special Washington Conference;/Race Relations/Negro-Jewish.
Race Relations/Negroes/Jewish-Negro Relations;/AJC (and subcategories);/Negro-Jewish Tensions/AJC/Meeting with Negro Leaders.
JSX/Civil Rights;/Integration/South.
PRO/AS/Race Relations/Negro-Jewish; /AS/Round Tables/Negro-Jewish Relations; AS/LCBC.
PRO/AD/Race Relations and Civil Rights, Negro-Jewish.
MEC/St. Comm./Background and Mailings.
AJC, Policies and Programs on Race Relations and Urban Affairs, May 1967.
Interview with Nathan Weisman, Dec. 15, 1967.
A.G. Wolfe, Negro Anti-Semitism: A Survey, Mar. 15, 1966.
John Slawson, "Mutual Aid and the Negro," *Commentary*, XLI (April 1966).

Chapter 15

I

John Higham, "Social Discrimination against Jews in America, 1830–1930," *PAJHS*, XLVII (Sept. 1957), p. 15.

John Slawson, "An Examination of Some Basic Assumptions Underlying Jewish Community Relations Programs," *Journal of Jewish Communal Services*, XXXVI (Dec. 1959), p. 118.

————, *Social Discrimination: The Last Barrier* (New York, 1955), pp. 4–5, 12–13.

UDF: Conference on higher education for Jews—statement, 1947.

Minutes of Administrative Committee, June 10, Nov. 6, 1946, Nov. 6, 1952.

Minutes of DAC, Oct. 8, 1952, Mar. 15, 1955, Oct. 13, 1956.

Civil Rights/1953–60;/Program.

Social Discrimination/AJC.

National Committee on Fraternities in Education.

Alfred McClung Lee, *Fraternities without Brotherhood* (Boston, 1955), esp. pp. xii, 77–101.

AJC Program Activities, Sept.–Oct. 1955.

New York/Communal Issues/Education/Admission-Medical Schools.

Dan W. Dodson, "Religious Prejudice in Colleges," *American Mercury*, LXIII (July 1946).

Frank Kingdon, "Discrimination in Medical Colleges," *American Mercury*, LXI (Oct. 1945).

II

Social Discrimination/AJC;/AJC/Annual Meetings;/AJC/DAC;/AJC/Exec. Board;/AJC/Chapters.

Civil Rights/1950–63;/Legislation/AJC.

Slawson, *Social Discrimination.*

John Slawson, *The Unequal Treatment of Equals* (New York, 1960).

Minutes of DAC, June 21, Oct. 22, 1955, May 12, Dec. 19, 1956, Apr. 2, Dec. 18, 1957, Jan. 15, Mar. 19, 1958.

Minutes of Executive Board, May 7–8, 1955, Oct. 30–Nov. 1, 1959; transcript of May 7–8, 1955, meetings, p. 117.

Higham, "Social Discrimination."

Thomas N. Brown, "Social Discrimination against the Irish in the United States," Nov. 1958.

J & J/Images/Studies/Alton. Much of Vance Packard's material was incorporated into his book *The Status Seekers* (New York, 1959), chs. 13, 16, 19; see also Packard, "The Hidden Persuaders," in *Committee Reporter*, Oct. 1958.

Marshall Sklare and Marc Vosk, *The Riverton Study* (New York, 1957), pp. 32–47.

III

Business/Executive Employment/AJC;/Executive Employment/AJC/ Chapters;/Executive Employment/AJC/Analysis & Proposals.
Business & Industry/Executive Employment;/Executive Employment/ AJC;/AJC (and subcategories).
JSX/Executive Employment.
Minutes of Administrative Board, Dec. 2, 1958, May 6, 1959, June 6, 1961.
Minutes of DAC, Apr. 17, 1959.
Slawson, *Unequal Treatment of Equals,* pp. 16–17.
Interview with Lawrence Bloomgarden, Mar. 18, 1968.
Draft of AJC pamphlet, "Fighting Discrimination in the Executive Suite," Aug. 11, 1967, pp. 6–8, 10, 15–33, 37–38.
Work in Progress, June 5, 1961.
CRS-D/Business & Industry/Executive Suite.
New York Times, Nov. 8, 1960, May 1, 1961.
John P. Dean, "Patterns of Socialization and Association between Jews and Non-Jews," *Jewish Social Studies,* XVII (July 1955), p. 249.
Lewis B. Ward, "The Ethnics of Executive Selection," *Harvard Business Review,* XLIII (Mar.–Apr. 1965).
Discrimination without Prejudice: A Study of Promotion Practices in Industry (University of Michigan, 1964).
Moses Rischin, "Study of Big Business and Anti-Semitism," 1961.

IV

Vertical Files: Discrimination/Employment/Executive (Public Utilities).
Minutes of Administrative Board, Jan. 7, Feb. 4, 1964.
AJC, *Patterns of Exclusion from the Executive Suite: The Public Utilities Industry* (New York, 1963).
CRS-D/Business & Industry/Public Utilities.
CAD/Employment/Executive.
DOM/AS/Executive Suite & Social Discrimination.

V

Minutes of DAC, Mar. 20, 1963, Apr. 19, 1966.
Minutes of Board of Governors, Nov. 10, 1964, Mar. 2, 1965.
Business & Industry/AJC.

Social Discrimination/AJC.
DOM/AS/Executive Suite & Social Discrimination.
PRO/AS/Executive Suite.
CRS-D/Business & Industry/Letter to Secretary of Labor Wirtz;/Business & Industry/Humphrey-Abram correspondence.
New York Times, Nov. 14, 1965, Mar. 20, 1966.
"Fighting Discrimination in the Executive Suite" (draft), pp. 34–63.
AJC, *Jews in College and University Administration* (New York, 1966).

VI

Social Discrimination/AJC/DAC.
Minutes of DAC, Nov. 20, 1962. The DAC shelved the suggestion to seek the revocation of the food and liquor licenses of exclusionary clubs.
Ibid., Feb. 19, 1963.
Business & Industry/AJC/Committee.
CRS-D/Social Discrimination.
DOM/AS/Executive Suite & Social Discrimination.
John Slawson and Lawrence Bloomgarden. *The Unequal Treatment of Equals,* rev. ed. (New York, 1965), pp. 20–21.
Wall Street Journal, Jan. 15, 1962.

VII

UDF: Conference on Jewish adjustment, 1945.
Report of the Conference on Group Life in America, Arden House, November 1956 (New York, 1957).
American Jewish Tercentenary;/AJC.
John Slawson, *Integration and Identity* (New York, 1960).
———, *The Realities of Jewish Integration* (New York, 1963).
Minutes of Board of Governors, June 22, 1965, Feb. 1, 1966.
Minutes of Executive Board, Oct. 28–30, 1966.
Proceedings of the Sixtieth Anniversary Meeting, May 12–15, 1966, pp. 158–59, 177–80.
S. Hirsh to John Slawson, Mar. 31, 1964 (files of S. Hirsh).
J & J/Attitudes/Studies/Riverton (and subcategories).
Stember et al., *Jews in the Mind of America,* pp. 3–28.
Marshall Sklare, "The Trouble With 'Our Crowd,' " *Commentary,* XLV (Jan. 1968), p. 60.
JSX/P/Membership & Dues.
"The Image, Role and Potential of the American Jewish Committee,"

prepared by Social Research, Inc., Mar. 1963, pp. 171–73.

Benjamin B. Ringer, *The Edge of Friendliness, The Lakeville Studies,* vol. 2 (New York, 1967), chs. 7, 8, 9, 13.

Chapter 16

I

Brief of American Jewish Committee, Anti-Defamation League of B'nai B'rith, and Unitarian Fellowship for Social Justice, amici curiae, *Torcaso* v. *Watkins,* Supreme Court of the U.S., October Term 1960.

Brief of American Jewish Committee and Anti-Defamation League of B'nai B'rith, amici curiae, *Gallagher* v. *Crown Kosher Supermarket,* Supreme Court of the U.S., October Term 1960.

Brief of American Jewish Committee, Anti-Defamation League of B'nai B'rith, and American Civil Liberties Union, amici curiae, *Sherbert* v. *Verner,* Supreme Court of the U.S. October Term 1962.

Brief for American Jewish Committee, amicus curiae, *Washington Ethical Society* v. *District of Columbia,* U.S. Court of Appeals for the District of Columbia Circuit, 1957.

UDF: memoranda on religion in the public schools, 1947–50.

Everson v. *Board of Education,* 330 U.S., 15–16, 63.

Nathan Schachner, "Church, State and Education," *AJYB,* XLIX (1947–48), pp. 1–48.

Minutes of Steering Committee, May 17, 1950.

Minutes of Executive Committee, May 10–11, 1947, Apr. 29, 1950; of Executive Board, Oct. 12–14, 1956.

Minutes of DAC, July 13, 1949, Apr. 25, May 23, Nov. 2, 1950, Dec. 21, 1954.

Minutes of Administrative Committee, Dec. 3, 1946, June 3, 1947, Apr. 6, 1948, Jan. 4, June 7, 1949, June 6, Dec. 5, 1950, Nov. 19, 1951, Jan. 5, 1954.

Civil Rights/AJC/Committee Reports.

Church-State/AJC;/AJC/Statement of Views;/Conferences.

AD/D & D/I & I/Program.

IR/AJC.

AJC Program Activities, May, July–Aug., Sept.–Oct., Nov.–Dec. 1955, Jan., July–Aug. 1956, July–Aug. 1957, Jan.–Feb., Mar.–Apr., May–June, Sept.–Oct. 1958, Jan.–Apr. 1959.

AJC, *Religion in Public Education* (Three editions. New York, 1955, 1957, 1964).

————, *Church, State and the Public Schools* (New York, 1963).

Reznikoff, Marshall, II, pp. 967–70.

Philip Jacobson, "Should the Ayes Always Have It?," *Christian Century,* Oct. 22, 1958.

"The Jew in American Society," *Commonweal,* Sept. 28, 1962.

II

Everson v. Board of Education, 330 U.S. 1; *McCollum v. Board of Education,* 333 U.S. 203.

Brief of Amici Curiae and Motion, Synagogue Council of America and NCRAC, *McCollum v. Board of Education,* Supreme Court of the U.S., October Term 1947.

AD/D & D/I & I/Program.

Illinois/Communal Issues/Religion & Schools/McCollum v. Board of Education.

Zorach v. Clauson, 343 U.S. 306, 313–14.

Brief for Appellants, *Zorach v. Clauson,* Supreme Court of U.S., October Term 1961.

N.Y./Communal Issues/Religion and Schools/Released Time/Zorach v. Clauson.

Church-State/AJC.

J. Mansir Tydings, "Kentucky Pioneers," *Religious Education,* July–Aug. 1956.

Engel v. Vitale, 370 U.S. 421, 435.

Brief of American Jewish Committee and Anti-Defamation League of B'nai B'rith as amici curiae, *Engel v. Vitale,* Supreme Court of the U.S., October Term 1961.

N.Y./Communal Issues/Religion and Schools/Prayer;/Communal Issues/Religion and Schools/Prayer/Engel v. Vitale (and subcategories).

Public Reaction to the *Engel v. Vitale* Decision, Sept. 11, 1962 (AJC research memo).

America, Sept. 1, 8, 1962.

Theodore Leskes, "Religious Dimensions of Church-State Relations" (lecture), July 9, 1962.

New York Times, Sept. 2, 1962.

DOM/AS/Church-State.

Abington Township v. Schempp, Murray v. Curlett, 374 U.S. 203, 226.

Brief of American Jewish Committee and Anti-Defamation League of B'nai B'rith as amici curiae, *Murray v. Curlett, Abington v. Schempp,* Supreme Court of the U.S., October Term 1962.

CRS-D/Church-State/Prayer Decision/Schempp-Murray; /Church-State/Prayer Amendment/Congressional Hearings.

CAD/School Prayer and Bible Reading;/School Prayer and Bible Reading/Becker Amendment.

Bible Reading after the *Schempp-Murray* Decision, Dec. 1963 (AJC research memo).

Minutes of Administrative Committee, Jan. 4, June 7, 1949, Nov. 2, 1950, Mar. 6, Nov. 19, 1951; of Administrative Board, Oct. 2, 1962, June 18, 1963.

Henry J. Abraham, *Freedom and the Court* (New York, 1967), ch. 6.

Konvitz, *Expanding Liberties*, ch. 1.

III

Ed/Federal Aid;/Federal Aid/AJC;/Federal Aid/AJC/Statements;/Federal Aid/Religious Affiliations/Schools/NCWC.

CRS-D 65/Church-State/Federal Aid to Education (and subcategories;/Church-State/Church-State Study Committee.

CRS-L/Church-State/Federal Aid to Education/AJC Statement;/Church-State/Federal Aid to Sectarian Colleges and Universities;/Church-State/Federal Aid to Education/AJC.

JSX 65 Ed./Federal Aid/AJC.

DOM/AS/Church-State;/Church-State/Schools;/Church-State Study Committee;/Church-State/Annual Meeting.

PRO/AS 61–65/Ed./Federal Aid to Education; 61–67/Ed./Federal Aid/AJC Policy.

CAD/Ed. (1965);/Shared Time.

Statement by Morris B. Abram . . . on H.R. 2362, Elementary and Secondary Education Act of 1965, Feb. 3, 1965.

Lucy Dawidowicz, "Changing Public Opinion on Church-State Questions" (research memo, May 7, 1963).

———,"Church and State," *AJYB*, LXVII (1966), pp. 133–41.

Milton Himmelfarb, "Church and State: How High a Wall?," *Commentary*, XLII (July 1966).

Will Herberg, "The Sectarian Conflict over Church and State," *Commentary*, XIV (Nov. 1952).

Philip Jacobson, "Church-State Issues," *AJYB*, LXIII (1962), pp. 175–81.

Minutes of Administrative Board, Mar. 7, Apr. 4, 1961, Nov. 12, 1963; of Board of Governors, Feb. 2, Apr. 6, 1965.

Minutes of DAC, Feb. 6, 1951, June 22, 1954, Feb. 15, Mar. 15, Mar. 30, 1961, Sept. 27, 1962, Jan. 19, June 16, 1965, Mar. 15, Apr. 19, 1966. Abraham, *Freedom and the Court*, pp. 225–41.

Chapter 17

I

IR/AJC;/AJC/Statements;/4 C's Conference/Proceedings;/4 C's Conference /Reports.
AD/D & D/I & I 44–62;/I & I/Program;/I & I/Reports.
CAD/IR 58–64;/1963-NCRR/Reports and Suggestions.
Interview with Judith H. Banki, May 10, 1968.
AJC Program Activities, May–June 1958.
Minutes of Administrative Committee, Jan. 4, Feb. 17, June 7, 1949.
Minutes of DAC, June 15, 1948, Jan. 18, June 17, 1949, Mar. 28, 1950.
AJC, *Report of the Forty-fifth Annual Meeting*, 1952, pp. 32, 43; *Report of the Forty-sixth Annual Meeting*, 1953, p. 34; *Report of the Forty-seventh Annual Meeting*, p. 47; *Proceedings of the Fiftieth Anniversary Observance*, pp. 70–93.
David Danzig, "The New Status of Religious Groups," *Journal of Intergroup Relations*, II (Winter 1960–61).

II

Archives: folders—Religious Textbooks.
Minutes of Executive Committee, Oct. 12, 1930, Feb. 5, May 10, Oct. 25, 1931, May 22, 1932.
Minutes of Board of Governors, June 22, 1965.
J.V. Thompson et al., "A Study of Jew-Christian Relationships as Found in Official Church School Materials" (mimeographed, 3 vols., 1934).
————, "A Study of Official Protestant School Materials for Children, Young People and Adults, as Related to Inter-Racial Inter-Cultural Attitudes" (mimeographed, 2 vols., 1934–35).
Intergroup Education/Texts/Catholic;/Texts/AJC;/Religious Textbooks/Texts/Catholic;/Texts/Program;/Religious Texts/Catholic/St. Louis (and subcategories);/Religion/Texts.
IAD/Yale Project/Report on Findings.
Bernhard E. Olson, *Faith and Prejudice* (New Haven, 1963).
Vertical Files: Religious Education/Textbooks, Catholic/AJC;/Text-

books, Protestant /AJC;/Textbooks/AJC.
Work in Progress, Sept., Nov. 1960, June 1961, Jan., Apr., June, Oct. 1962, Jan. 1963.
Articles on religious textbooks in *Contemporary Jewish Record* of Oct. 1941, Feb. 1943, and in *Religious Education*, Mar.–Apr. 1960.
Interview with Judith H. Banki, May 10, 1968.

III

AJC prepared a privately circulated memorandum on Vatican II called *The Second Vatican Council's Declaration on the Jews* (Nov. 1965). A preliminary draft, which provides more detailed information but goes up only to the summer of 1964, is "The Vatican Decree on Jews and Judaism and the American Jewish Committee" (Aug. 28, 1964).
Interview with John Slawson, Jan. 3, 1968.
Judith Hershcopf, "The Church and the Jews: The Struggle at Vatican Council II," *AJYB*, LXVI (1965), pp. 99–136; LXVII (1966), pp. 45–77.
JSX-IR/Ecumenical Council (and subcategories);/Catholic-Jew/Papal Audience.
PEI-PUBS/Ecumenical Council/Abstracts.
PRO/AD/Ecumenical Council.
IAD/Ecumenical Council (and subcategories).
IR/Pro Deo, 1959–61;/Ecumenical (and subfolders).
Vertical Files: Catholic-Jewish Relations/Vatican Council II;/Vatican Council II/AJC. For instances of growing Catholic-Jewish cooperation after Vatican Council II, see Vertical Files: Catholic-Jewish Relations/US/AJC, and Minutes of Board of Governors, Feb. 1, Oct. 4, 1966.
Daniel Callahan, *The Mind of the Catholic Layman* (New York, 1963), quotation on p. 145.
Michael Serafian, *The Pilgrim* (New York, 1964).
Joseph Roddy, "How the Jews Changed Catholic Thinking," *Look*, Jan. 25, 1966.
Richard Cardinal Cushing, "The Second Vatican Council, Its Meaning for Mankind" (address delivered under auspices of the National Conference of Christians and Jews), Feb. 20, 1964.
Secretariat for Catholic-Jewish Relations, *Guidelines for Catholic-Jewish Relations* [Washington, D.C., 1967].
F.E. Cartus, "Vatican II and the Jews," *Commentary*, XXXIX (Jan. 1965).
———, "The Vatican Council Ends," *Harper's*, CCXXXI (Sept. 1965).
E.C. Bianchi, "A Talk with Cardinal Bea," *America*, Aug. 11, 1962.

Chapter 18

I & II

Germany/1947;/1952;/Re-Education;/AJC Reports.
Germany-West/AJC; AJC/Reports; /Human Relations/Operation Candle/AJC; /Re-Education/C Reports; /AJC/Visits; /Re-Education/ U.S. Government;/Re-Education/U.S. Government/AJC.
UDF: memoranda on democratic education in Germany, 1947–48.
JSX/U.S. Department of State.
Engel, Irving M./Speeches.
Administrative Committee, 48–49/Mailings.
New York Times, Feb. 7, 1950.
Minutes of Executive Committee of FAC, Apr. 26, 1948, Apr. 23, 1951.
Minutes of FAC, Apr. 23, May 28, 1947, Mar. 10, May 7, 1948.
Harold Zink, *The United States in Germany, 1944–1955* (Princeton, 1957), pp. 92–100.
John W. Spanier, *American Foreign Policy since World War II*, second ed. (New York, 1962), pp. 52–56.

III

Germany/1952;/1955–56;/AJC/Statements.
Germany-West/AJC;/AJC/State Department; /Re-Education;/Human Relations/Operation Candle; /Re-Education/U.S. Government; /Re-Education/U.S. Government/AJC; /AJC/U.S. Government/State Department;/Neo-Nazism/U.S./AJC.
Minutes of Ad Hoc Subcommittee on German Activities, Oct. 31, 1951.
Minutes of Staff Meeting on HICOG's German Program, Dec. 3, 1951.
Minutes of FAC, Oct. 8, 1951.
AJC, *Neo-Nazi Strength and Strategy in West Germany* (New York, 1953), p. 12.
T.H. Tetens, *The New Germany and the Old Nazis* (New York, 1961), esp. chs. 11, 17.

IV

AJC, *The Recent Growth of Neo-Nazism in Europe* (New York, 1951).
———, *Neo-Nazi and Nationalist Movements in West Germany* (New York, 1952).

————, *Neo-Nazi Strength and Strategy.*
————, *As the U.N. Probes Prejudice,* pp. 7–12.
Tetens, *The New Germany,* pp. 75, 151, ch. 18.
Minutes of FAC, Jan. 19, 1955, Oct. 13, 1956, Jan. 7, 1959.
Minutes of Executive Board, May 11–13, 1956, Oct. 28–30, 1960.
Proceedings of the Fiftieth Anniversary Observance, pp. 227–28.
U.S. Government/State Department.
Germany-West/Government Officials/Adenauer/AJC;/Neo-Nazism/
U.S./AJC; /AJC/Visits; /Re-Education/AJC; /Re-Education/Meeting; /
Re-Education/Bad Godesburg/AJC.
Engel, Irving M./Documents.
In 1955, as a result of negotiations stimulated by AJC, the American
Council on Germany and the Ford Foundation commissioned German
journalist Hans Wallenberg to investigate and report the progress
of democratic institutions in Germany. Germany-West/AJC-ADL
Memo.

V

Germany-West/Re-Education/AJC–Institute of International Education;/Re-Education/Educators' Visits;/Neo-Nazism/AJC/Reports/Paris Office;/Neo-Nazism/AJC/Resolutions;/AJC Visits (Blaustein);/Neo-Nazism/AJC/Meetings/German Ambassador.
FAD 59–62/Germany/Education; 64–65/Germany/Education;/Germany/AJC Program/Industry:Blaustein-Beitz;/Restitution/AJC Documents 1945–65; current: Fact Sheet 1967.
Engel, Irving M./Speeches.
"Neo-Nazism Twenty Years after Hitler," *Reports on the Foreign Scene,* Aug. 1965.
Minutes of FAC, Feb. 3, 1960, Feb. 16, Apr. 28, 1961, May 17, 1963, Sept. 16, 1965.
JSX/Foreign Countries/Germany West;/Foreign Countries/Germany West [Education];/Germany West;/Germany West/Education;/Slawson/Trip to Germany and Austria.
Vertical Files: Germany/Education/AJC.
AJC, *The Year's Activities 1964–65,* pp. 25–26.

Chapter 19

I

Minutes of Executive Committee, Sept. 24, 1918, Dec. 11, 1921, Oct. 17, 1926, Nov. 9, Dec. 8, 1929, Jan. 12, Feb. 9, Mar. 16, 24, 1930.
Archives: folders—Russia/Rabbis, Russia/Refugees, Russia/Religious Persecution, Russia/Margolin.
Adler Papers: chronological folders—Apr. 1923, Nov. 1928, Mar. 1930, Jan. 1932, June 1934; topical folders—Philadelphia, Russian Refugees.
Russia/1941–44;/Biro-Bidjan; Russian Delegates in U.S., 1943.
Solomon M. Schwarz, *The Jews in the Soviet Union* (Syracuse, 1951), part 2, chs. 1–6.
Salo W. Baron, *The Russian Jew under Tsars and Soviets* (New York, 1964), chs. 11–16.

II

UDF: B. Fabian, "The Problem of Eastern European Jewry," Dec. 18, 1948.
Soviet and Satellites/AJC Releases;/Anti-Semitism/Counteraction.
PRO/FA/Round Table; Paris Office/Program, 1953.
Engel, Irving M./Testimony.
U.S. Government/State Department/Satellite Project.
Vertical Files: Russia/Anti-Semitism/AJC.
Minutes of FAC, Jan. 20, 1953.
Minutes of Administrative Committee, Mar. 8, Apr. 5, 1949, Dec. 2, 1952, Jan. 6, Mar. 3, 1953.
Minutes of Executive Committee, May 7–8, 1949, May 2–3, 1953.
FAD/Soviet/Anti-Semitism/AJC Program.
AJYB, LI (1950), pp. 336–40; LV (1954), pp. 272–80.
AJC, *The Plight of the Jews in Eastern Europe* (New York, 1959), pp. 3, 10–11, 14, 15.
———, "Jewish Life in the Soviet Sphere," *Foreign Scene*, I (June 1949).
———, *Now They Admit It* (New York, 1956).
Baron, *The Russian Jew under Tsars and Soviets*, ch. 16.
Schwarz, *The Jews in the Soviet Union*, part 2, ch. 7.
"The New Red Anti-Semitism," (Beacon-*Commentary* Study. 1953).
A. Skerpan, "Aspects of Soviet Antisemitism," (AJC reprint from *Antioch Review*, Fall 1952).
Interview with Jerry Goodman, Oct. 30, 1968.

III

Vertical Files: Russia/Anti-Semitism/AJC; Europe, East/Anti-Semitism/ AJC.
Soviet and Satellites/AJC Action.
Soviet/Mikoyan Visit/Reports;/Jews/Annual Meeting;/AJC/Trips and Visits; /Jews/AJC; /Anti-Semitism/AJC (and subfolders); /Anti-Semitism;/Anti-Semitism/U.S.
FAD/Soviet/Anti-Semitism/U.S. Government;/Soviet/Anti-Semitism/ U.S. Government/AJC;/Soviet/Anti-Semitism;/Soviet/Visits;/Soviet/ Anti-Semitism/AJC Program.
U.S. Government/State Department.
JSX/Soviet/Anti-Semitism.
PRO/FAD/R.
Lehman, Herbert.
Engel, Irving M./Government Officials/Meeting Reports.
Minutes of Executive Committee, Oct. 25, 1953.
Minutes of Administrative Board, Mar. 3, May 5, 1959, Jan. 8, Nov. 12, 1963.
Minutes of FAC, Nov. 21, 1955, Jan. 11, Nov. 27, 1956, Jan. 29, Mar. 13, May 28, Sept. 24, Oct. 26, Dec. 4, 1957, Jan. 28, Apr. 25, Oct. 8, Dec. 1, 1958, Jan. 7, Feb. 10, Mar. 2, June 8, 1959, Feb. 3, Apr. 22, Dec. 11, 1960; transcript, Nov. 1, 1963.
Baron, *The Russian Jew under Tsars and Soviets,* p. 349.
AJC, *As the U.N. Probes Prejudice,* pp. 17–18.
———, *Current Anti-Semitic Activities Abroad* (New York, 1963), p. 34.
———, *Plight of the Jews in Eastern Europe,* passim.
———, *Proceedings of the Fifty-second Annual Meeting,* 1959, pp. 46–48.

IV

FAD/Soviet/Anti-Semitism/Program-AJC;/Soviet/Anti-Semitism/U.S. Government/AJC;/Soviet/Anti-Semitism/American Jewish Conference on Soviet Jewry-Organization.
JSX/Soviet/Government Officials;/65-Soviet Jews;/Soviet Union/Jews/ 66–67;/Soviet Union/66–67.
Interview with Jerry Goodman, Oct. 30, 1968.
Vertical Files: Russia/Anti-Semitism/AJC;/Anti-Semitism/American Jewish Conference on Soviet Jewry.
Minutes of Executive Board, Nov. 1–3, 1963.
Minutes of Administrative Board, Nov. 12, Dec. 3, 1963, Mar. 3, 1964;

of Board of Governors, June 2, 1964, Feb. 2, June 22, 1965.
Minutes of FAC, Sept. 23, 1963, May 2, 1964, Sept. 16, 1965; transcripts
—Sept. 23, Nov. 1, 1963.
Jerry Goodman, "American Response to Soviet Anti-Jewish Policies,"
AJYB, LXVI (1965), pp. 312–19.

Chapter 20

I & II

A.N. Chouraqui, *Between East and West*, trans. by M. Bernet (Philadelphia,
1968), esp. chs. 12, 13, 15.
AJC, *What of Their Future? The Half-Million Jews of North Africa* (New York,
1955).
UDF: The Jews of Europe and North Africa, July–Nov. 1950.
Vertical Files: Russia/Anti-Semitism/AJC (Shuster address—1953).
North Africa/Morocco-Tunisia/AJC (and subcategories);/U.S./AJC/
Meetings-Government Officials;/Jewish Communities/Coordination-
Jewish Organizations.
Morocco/1954.
Libya/Reports, 1950–51;/AJC.
U.S. Government/State Department.
Engel, Irving M./Government Officials/Meeting Reports.
Minutes of FAC, Apr. 23, 1951, Jan. 19, 1955, Jan. 5, 11, 27–28, 1956.

III

Chouraqui, *Between East and West*, ch. 16.
Hal Lehrman, "North Africa's Dilemmas for American Jewry," *Commen-
tary*, XIX (March 1955).
AJYB, LVII (1956), pp. 461–62.
Goldmann, Nahum.
Morocco/1955;/Jews;/Jews/Emigration.
North Africa/Morocco-Tunisia/AJC(and subcategories);/U.S./AJC/
Meetings;/U.S./AJC/Reports;/Jewish Communities;/Jewish Commu-
nities/Coordination-Jewish Organizations.
Committee Reporter, July 1956.
AJC Program Activities, July–Aug. 1955, Sept.–Dec. 1956.
Minutes of FAC, Jan. 11, Oct. 13, Nov. 27, 1956, Jan. 7, 1957.

IV

Minutes of FAC, May 12, 1956, Sept. 24, Oct. 26, 1957, Apr. 25, Oct. 8, 1958, Feb. 28, 1962.
Accounts of Tunisia in annual volumes of *AJYB*, 1957–1966.
North Africa/Morocco-Tunisia/AJC/Delegation 1957; /Morocco-Tunisia / AJC / Delegation / Reports; / U.S. / AJC / Meetings; / U.S. / AJC / Meetings/Government Officials.
Tunisia/1958–59.
U.S. Government/State Department.
Engel, Irving M./Government Officials/Meeting Reports.

V

Accounts of Morocco in annual volumes of *AJYB*, 1957–1966.
Minutes of FAC, June 18, 1956, Sept. 24, Oct. 26, 1957, Jan. 28, Apr. 25, 1958, May 4, June 8, Dec. 21, 1959, Feb. 16, 1961, Feb. 28, May 3, 1962.
Morocco/1957–62;/Jews/Emigration;/Fey-Blake Mission, 1961.
PRO/FA, 1962.
North Africa/U.S./AJC/Meetings;/U.S./AJC/Meetings/Government Officials; /Morocco-Tunisia/AJC (and subcategories); /Jewish Communities.
U.S. Government/State Department.
"Morocco," *Reports on the Foreign Scene*, April 1961.

VI

Algeria, 1957–61;/Jew;/Jewish Agencies;/Jewish Agencies/Community Federation.
North Africa/Jewish Communities; /U.S./AJC/Meetings; /Morocco-Tunisia/AJC/Delegation 1957.
France/AJC/Visits.
PRO/Europe/Offices Abroad, 1962.
FAD/Algeria, 61–65;/Algeria 61–63/Reports; 67/Europe/Community Service; 65–66/Europe/Community Service Reports; 61–64/France/-Refugees/North Africa; "French Jewry Today—The Impact of North African Immigration."
"Algeria," *Reports on the Foreign Scene*, July 1962.
Minutes of FAC, Feb. 28, May 3, 1962, May 17, 1963.
AJYB, LX (1959), pp. 277–78; LXIV (1963), pp. 403–11.

Chapter 21

I

Latin America/AJC 1942–49.

Waldman, *Nor by Power*, chs. 15–16.

Waldman Papers: Nov. 1940, Feb. 1941.

FAD: Minutes of Overseas Committee, Jan. 9, Feb. 26, Dec. 1, 1942, Apr. 4, 24, June 19, 1944, Jan. 13, Mar. 31, 1945; Plan for Activities of the Overseas Committee [1942]; Report on Overseas Activities, Sept. 24, 1942; Report of Overseas Committee on South American Problem, Sept. 1942; Foreign Affairs Activities, Report, Oct. 10, 1944; Overseas Activities of the AJC 1906–1943.

Archives: Chronological File—Mar., Sept. 1940, Sept. 1941.

Minutes of Administrative Committee, Oct. 21, 1942.

AJYB, XLIV (1942–43), pp. 469, 482; XLVIII (1946–47), pp. 599–600.

U.S. Government/State Department.

II, III & IV

John Slawson, *The AJC, What It Is, What It Does* (New York, 1965), p. 14.

Waldman Papers: comments on Hochstein's memo [1949].

Argentina/U.S./Embassy;/Anti-Semitism.

Latin America/AJC, 1942–49, 1950–62;/AJC/Reports;/AJC Office/BA (Yagupsky), 1946–55.

Minutes of FAC, Dec. 10, 1946, Sept. 30, 1947, June 6, 1950, Jan. 27–28, 1956.

FAD/Israel/TA Office (Yagupsky)—1966.

Simon Segal, "Prospects for Jewry in Latin America," transcript of 45th Annual Meeting, Jan. 27, 1952.

I.L. Horowitz, "The Jewish Community of Buenos Aires," *Jewish Journal of Sociology*, IV (Dec. 1962), pp. 147–71. (Horowitz published a very similar article under the same title in *Jewish Social Studies*, XXIV [Oct. 1962]).

The Committee was told that its educational work with respect to the UN helped to bring about ratification of the Genocide Convention in 1956 by Argentina, Chile, and Uruguay, FAD 64/LA/AJC Program (background information, 1948–1964).

V

Interview with Hanna F. Desser, June 19, 1969.
Minutes of Administrative Board, May 7, 1957; of Board of Governors, Mar. 2, 1965.
Minutes of FAC, Apr. 27, 1951, Oct. 8, 1958.
The American Jewish Committee in Latin America (New York, 1965).
AJC, *Mission to Our Neighbors* (New York, 1958).
Latin America/AJC Visit-1958/Reports;/AJC Visit-1958;/AJC Office/BA (Yagupsky), 1956, 1960.
FAD/Program Items; 62/AJC Office/BA;/LA/AJC Delegation 64/U.S.-Washington, D.C.;64/LA/AJC Program (and Reports); 65/LA/AJC Community Service.
FAD, "A Report on Developments in the Argentine Catholic Church since the Ecumenical Council," Feb. 1966; "The Community Service Program in Latin America," Aug. 1968; Report on the American Jewish Committee Delegation to Latin America, Aug. 2–22, 1964.
JSX/LA/AJC Delegation.
Horowitz, "Jewish Community of Buenos Aires," p. 150.

VI

Argentina/1958–60;/Anti-Semitism;/Anti-Semitism/Tacuara;/U.S.
Latin America/AJC 1950–62;/AJC/Reports;/AJC Office/BA (Yagupsky) —1956.
FAD/Argentina/Anti-Semitism (and subcategories, 1962–1966); 64/LA/AJC Program/Reports;/Program Items.
JSX 63–64/Argentina/Neo-Nazism.
Vertical Files: Latin America/Argentina/Anti-Semitism;/Argentina/Anti-Semitism/AJC.
James R. Scobie, *Argentina: A City and a Nation* (New York, 1964), ch. 9.
Eichmann/AJC;/Argentine-Israeli Tensions/AJC.
Transcript of Meeting of Executive Board, Jan. 19–21, 1962, pp. 286–87.
FAD, Report of the American Jewish Committee Delegation to Latin America, Aug. 2–22, 1964.
Phil Baum (for Commission on International Affairs, American Jewish Congress), "Argentina: A Jewish Community in Jeopardy," Oct. 5, 1962.
Julio Adin, "Nationalism and Neo-Nazism in Argentina," *In the Dispersion,* V–VI (Spring 1966), pp. 139–60.
Natan Lerner, "A Note on Argentine Jewry Today," *Jewish Journal of Sociology,* VI (July 1964), pp. 77–78.

Moshe Pearlman, *The Capture and Trial of Adolf Eichmann* (New York, 1963), ch. 6.
Minutes of FAC, Jan. 27–28, 1956, May 8, Oct. 26, 1957, Sept. 28, 1960, Apr. 28, 1961, Feb. 28, Oct. 31, 1962, May 17, 1963, May 2, 1964.
Minutes of Board of Governors, Dec. 7, 1965, Feb. 1, 1966.
FAD 65/LA/B'nai B'rith-ADL 1965.

Chapter 22

John Slawson, "Problems and Guidelines." Address at the 58th Annual Meeting, May 20, 1965; address by John Slawson at National Executive Board Meeting, Dec. 4, 1964; address by John Slawson at JDA Southwest Regional Meeting, Feb. 3, 1961; remarks by John Slawson at 56th Annual Meeting, 1963; address by John Slawson at 57th Annual Meeting, May 1, 1964.

————, "The Crucial Problem of Our Time," Remarks at . . . the General Assembly of the Council of Jewish Federation and Welfare Funds, Nov. 17, 1962.

————, *Toward a Community Program for Jewish Identity* (New York, 1967).
CAD 63–64/Constituency/Image Study Reports /Constituency/Image Study Reports/Implementation.
JSX/CA/Constituency and Leadership/National Growth Committee.
CAD/Membership and Dues/Statistics.
DOM/Membership and Constituency.
*Leadership Training
JDA/Breakup/Contract Negotiations.
Interviews with Nathan Weisman, Dec. 15, 1967, Jan. 17, 1969.
Remarks by Professor Arthur Mann at conference on oral history, AJC, June 4, 1968.
Selma Hirsh to John Slawson, Mar. 31, Apr. 2, 1964 (files of Selma Hirsh).
Minutes of Executive Board, Oct. 30–Nov. 1, 1959, Jan. 21–22, Oct. 28–29, 1961, Nov. 9–11, 1962, Dec. 4–6, 1964; Oct. 28–30, 1966.
Minutes of Administrative Board, Mar. 7, Apr. 4, 1961, Jan. 9, June 5, Aug. 16, 1962; Minutes of Board of Governors, Oct. 6, 1964, Mar. 7, 1967.
Stember et al., *Jews in the Mind of America,* introduction and essays by Higham, Keller, and Halpern.

*Compiled by Carol Kahn

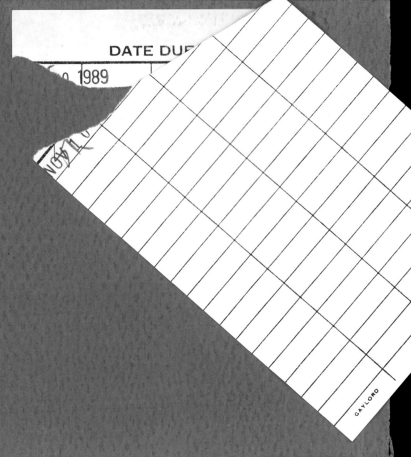